SECOND EDITION

KILMAN DISTILLER

PSYCHOPATHOLOGY The Science

derstanding Deviance

JAMES D. PAGE   TEMPLE UNIVERSITY

ALDINE PUBLISHING COMPANY   CHICAGO

ABOUT THE AUTHOR

James D. Page is Professor of Psychology at Temple
University, and for many years was Director of Clinical
Training at Temple. He received his B.A., M.S., and Ph.D. at
Columbia University. An eminent scholar and researcher,
Professor Page has written numerous articles published in
major psychology journals. He is author of such successful
books as *Modern Society and Mental Disease*, *Abnormal
Psychology*, and *Approaches to Psychopathology*.

First published 1975 by
Aldine Publishing Company
529 South Wabash Avenue
Chicago, Illinois 60605

ISBN   0–202–26079–8   clothbound edition
Library of Congress Catalog Number   74–18217
Printed in the United States of America

Preface

The increasing interest of college students in courses on psychopathology or abnormal psychology is related to the expansion of the subject matter to include the study, treatment, and prevention of problems associated with alcoholism, drug abuse, suicide, and sexual dysfunction and deviation. The addition of these highly prevalent sources of human distress to the more traditional topics of neurosis, psychosis and personality disorders in children has made the science of psychopathology more relevant.

In this second edition I have attempted to provide fuller coverage of this broadening perspective. Two separate chapters are devoted to alcoholism and drug abuse. New and enlarged chapters have been written on suicidal behavior and sexual deviations. The material on therapy has been expanded; more attention has been given to changing trends in theoretical approaches, the increasing use of group and family therapy, the shift from hospital to community care of disturbed persons, and the increasing utilization of nonprofessional mental health workers. Changes have been made in all other chapters to update clinical and research data.

Interestingly, the broadening of the field of psychopathology has served to highlight the common features of deviant behavior and at the same time to emphasize the continuity and overlap of normal and deviant behavior. A common characteristic of the diverse forms of psychopathology is that they all represent deviations from the expected and accepted social norm. Applicable descriptive terms include *deficient, inappropriate, atypical, irrational,* and *maladaptive.*

More significantly, all of the recognized forms of behavior pathology involve relatively uncontrollable disturbances or inadequacies in psychosocial functioning that result in subjective distress, interpersonal discord, and societal concern. The key word is *patho,* the ancient Greek word for psychic suffering. The differentiation of pathological from normal behavior and the assessment of the severity of psychopathology rest basically on the evaluation made by society and the individual of the perceived detrimental effect of any particular behavior. Depending on its appraised purpose or attending consequence, the same behavior may be evaluated as normal or pathological.

This approach to evaluation is consistent with my general premise that the so-called "symptoms" of psychopathology represent extreme variations of normal behavior. The principles and processes involved in perception, thinking, emotional expression, and problem-solving are the same in normal and disturbed persons. The quality of the end result varies, but this too is relative. The determinants of abnormal behavior are as complex and varied as the determinants of normal behavior. Both are the products of the cumulative interaction of the individual's particular genetic potentialities, his constitutional make-up, his sociocultural and physical environment, and his personal life experiences. Behavior change, for better or worse, may occur at any time as the result of significant modification in the net interactive effect of these variables. The fact that disturbed persons resemble the general population in more ways than they resemble one another is further evidence of the continuity and overlap of normal and abnormal behavior. The varied codeterminants of behavior and behavior change favor a multidisciplinary approach.

My emphasis on a cross-cultural orientation is more than a reflection of personal interest. This approach provides a check on the validity of suggested concepts and interpretations. Societies may differ in their tolerance for specific kinds of behavior but there appears to be general agreement that the criteria for differentiating deviant from normal behavior are universal. The varied terms coined to identify behavior pathology (*spirit possession, madness, lunacy, berserk*) all imply the presence of uncontrolled, irrational, detrimental behavior. The observation of similar behavior patterns in disturbed persons throughout the world adds weight to the interpretation that so-called clinical syndromes represent characteristic ways in which human beings react to intolerable stress situations. Finally, the omnipresence of psychopathology suggests that the contributory causes are related to universal human problems rather than to stresses confined to a particular era or place. The inevitable occurrence of marked individual differences in adaptive resources guarantees that in all societies there will be some individuals who are highly vulnerable to the frustrations, challenges, and disappointments of human existence.

At the head of my list of acknowledgements I should like to indicate my indebtedness to the long list of theorists, clinicians, and researchers whose contributions constitute the substance of this book. The reactions of my students have influenced the selection and organization of material. In the preparation of the second edition I have taken advantage of the wealth of talent available at Temple University for spur-of-the-moment consultations; colleagues who made constructive suggestions include Ruth Clifford, Jay Efran, James Framo, John Gordon, Herbert Hamsher, John McBrearty, and Herbert Rappaport. Barbara Hardy did an excellent job of copyediting. The readability of the book has been greatly improved by the many contributions of Nanci Connors and Alexander J. Morin, who were also mainly responsible for the format and illustrations. I enjoyed working with them on publication details. Finally, I want to express my appreciation to each of the many secretaries who helped at different times with the typing of the manuscript.

JAMES D. PAGE

Contents

Preface   v

1. The Nature of Abnormal Behavior   2
2. The Classification of Psychosocial Problems   22
3. Criteria of Psychopathology   48
4. Abnormal Behavior in Historical Perspective   74
5. Psychological Theories and Therapies   105
6. Biological Factors   140
7. Sociocultural Theories   160
8. Schizophrenic Reactions   181
9. Origins of Schizophrenic Behavior   209
10. Affective Disorders   230
11. Neurotic Reactions   252
12. Personality Disorders   289
13. Alcoholism   310
14. Drug Use and Abuse   329
15. Psychopathology and Sex   352
16. Sexual Variations and Deviations   367
17. Physical Disorders with Associated Psychosocial Disturbances   396
18. Disordered Behavior in Children   416
19. Suicidal Behavior   441
20. Social Deviance and Community Mental Health   469

Glossary   481
Photo Credits   497
Name Index   499
Subject Index   505

PSYCHOPATHOLOGY

1 · The Nature of Abnormal Behavior

A Rake's Progress, Bethlehem Hospital, William Hogarth

Psychopathology* shares with other behavior sciences a basic interest in understanding why human beings behave as they do. The main difference is expressed by the word element *patho*, from the Greek term for suffering. Psychopathology is specifically concerned with the study of persons who engage in behavior that is a source of undue distress, detriment, or threat to the individual, his family, and his society. Such behavior may range in severity from mild, transient disturbances to extreme withdrawal or violence. The individual may be tormented by feelings of inferiority, fear, guilt, melancholy, confusion of identity, and other inner conflicts. Escape or refuge from the difficulties of life may be sought in amnesia, compulsive rituals, a more satisfying world of fantasy, or the use of alcohol and drugs. The destructive emotions of anger and resentment may be internalized, turned against the self, and expressed in physical disabilities, feelings of depression, or suicidal behavior. Or these destructive emotions may be externalized and directed against others in the form of paranoid suspicion, aggressive acts, or antisocial behavior.

Other terms commonly used to identify the subject matter of psychopathology are *abnormal, deviant, maladaptive,* and *disordered* behavior. A good case can be made for the use of each of these terms. Psychopathological behavior is in fact atypical, deviates from the expected norm, is less adaptive and more disorganized. However, the use of these terms is best restricted (as in this text) to situations where behavior pathology also involves subjective distress or social concern. Distress and social concern are the critical factors that motivate the individual to seek treatment or leads the family or society to insist that remedial action be taken. As a rule, little attention is given to nonconforming and nonadaptive behavior so long as it is not perceived as significantly offensive, harmful, or distressing to the individual or others.

THE UNIVERSALITY OF PSYCHOPATHOLOGICAL BEHAVIOR

The scientific study of psychopathology is a recent development, but its subject matter has fascinated and disturbed man throughout his history. Innumerable terms have been used from ancient to modern times to identify objectionable deviant behavior; some of the more familiar are *madness, possession* (by evil spirits), *insanity, lunacy, mental illness,* and *personality disorder.*

There is a dual significance in the fact that every known language includes at least one word that specifically refers to seemingly irrational disturbances in psychosocial functioning. First, it establishes the universality and timelessness of aberrant human reactions. Second, the invention and use of special terms to denote abnormal behavior indicate that people everywhere have long

---

* This term and other technical and possibly unfamiliar terms are briefly defined in the glossary that follows the last page of text of this book.

THE SUFFERING OF THE PSYCHOLOGICALLY DISTURBED: THREE CASES

The importance of distress in confirming a diagnosis of behavior pathology is best illustrated by the case records of obviously disturbed persons.

The Case of Tom

Tom, a bright fifteen-year-old boy, was referred to a clinical psychologist because he was failing in his schoolwork. Subsequent information supplied by the school counselor and the boy's parents indicated a more serious personality problem. His teachers reported that they were unable to make contact with him. He would passively listen to what they had to say, but there was never any response to indicate that their message was getting through. His classmates called him "dummy." His one friend was suspected of being a homosexual who was taking advantage of Tom's docility. Tom was the second child in an upper middle class home. His father was a successful businessman who had given up any attempt to understand his "odd-ball" son. His pride and joy was his first-born daughter, an outgoing, highly popular girl and an excellent student. The mother was a self-effacing, unhappy woman with personal problems of her own. At home, Tom spent most of his time locked in his room. He was still afraid of the dark and kept a small light on while sleeping. When he was ten years old, he was found lying naked on his front lawn on a cross he had made by nailing two boards together. On another occasion, when his parents invited several friends to help celebrate his birthday, Tom disappeared shortly after the start of the party and didn't return until late that night.

The Case of Mrs. Jones

Mrs. Jones, a forty-five-year-old woman, became depressed following a hysterectomy (an operation removing her ovaries and reproductive organs). Although she had made an excellent recovery from two earlier attacks of melancholy, she was convinced that this time there was no hope for her. She talked vaguely of ending her life since her husband no longer loved her, her only daughter had left home, and she had made a mess of everything. A recurring theme was that no one would miss her when she died. She refused to see a doctor because she had been given a series of electroshock treatments during her last attack and was afraid she would receive the same treatment again. She slept poorly, had no appetite, and was too exhausted to do anything during the day. A picture of despair, she would only talk about her physical complaints and the hopelessness of her condition. Her husband was exasperated with her refusal to see a doctor, bored with her endless complaints, and spent as little time as possible with her.

The Case of Lee

Lee, a twenty-one-year-old college student, requested an immediate appointment at the Psychological Clinic to discuss a personal problem. When seen later that day, he stated that he was afraid he was losing control of himself. He was afraid something terrible was going to happen to him. For no apparent reason he would periodically break out in a cold sweat and feel weak and jittery. On some occasions he would experience difficulty in breathing and a pain in his chest. During the night he had terrifying nightmares in which he was usually the victim of an attack and on the verge of being killed. He was worried about his mediocre grades, which would make it difficult for him to get into graduate school. He was afraid of getting too closely involved with girls. On several occasions he had canceled dates at the last minute because of gastric pains and a tightening sensation around the shoulders. On two occasions when he had intercourse with girls, he became so worried that he might have picked up a venereal disease that he persuaded a doctor to give him a penicillin injection.

been aware of certain distinctive features of psychopathology that differentiate it from crime, immoral conduct, and other types of deviance from group norms. The familiarity of the general public with the distinguishing characteristics of psychopathology is evidenced by the fact that the diagnosis of madness, however it may be labeled, is initially made by the victim himself or by his family and close associates.

The specific characteristics differentiating psychopathological behavior from other forms of deviant behavior and from normal behavior will be considered in greater detail later on. A common feature of most of the different names applied to psychologically disturbed individuals in diverse cultures and at different times is the implication that these persons have little voluntary control over their behavior, at least in some areas of life in which most people react quite differently. In former centuries it was assumed that evil spirits or lunar influences were responsible for the unpredictable reactions of "possessed" victims. More recently abnormal behavior has been interpreted as the involuntary byproduct of a disease, as the expression of unconscious impulses, or as faulty habit patterns. In any case, the relatively uncontrolled nature of pathological behavior has been repeatedly and consistently observed; it is the explanations for it that have changed. The various names of madness also agree in conveying the idea that the behavior they designate is defective, unexpected, irrational, inappropriate, disruptive, and detrimental. A further implication is that persons who exhibit this sort of behavior are troubled and troublesome.

A distinction must be made between basic features of pathological behavior that are essentially constant in all societies and incidental, culture-dependent aspects that are variable. Basically, psychosocial disorders in all societies are characterized by disturbances in volition, thinking, feeling, communication, and conduct that interfere with effective and satisfying personal and social adjustment. A person with significant defects in these critical psychosocial func-

tions would in all probability be considered abnormal in any society. But the outward form or surface symptoms of such disturbances and the interpretations provided for them vary from culture to culture.

In much the same way that people acquire the expressive styles and beliefs of their own societies, they also learn how possessed or mentally disturbed persons are expected to behave. Thus a depressed, suicidal person in a primitive society may imagine he has a moth sickness that compels him to jump into the community campfire. A similarly afflicted person in a highly moralistic society may seek death through drowning, in order to be cleansed of his sins. In an unusual manifestation of madness in ancient times, known as lycanthropy, the afflicted person imagined himself to be a wild beast (usually a wolf), in human form, and acted accordingly. The underlying condition is still with us under the new label of *depersonalization*. Since it is no longer fashionable to believe that people can transform themselves into animals, the expressed symptoms have changed. Today, a person suffering from depersonalization is more apt to report a hazy sense of loss of identity or a distortion of body image. The body may seem altered in some way, may be felt to be changing into something undesirable, or may be experienced as if it belonged to another person.

Other seemingly exotic examples of psychopathology noted in former times and in primitive societies also turn out, on closer examination, to be essentially equivalent to the more "rational" symptoms observed in present-day mental patients (Yap, 1951; Arieti and Meth, 1959). There is obviously no basic difference between the illiterate person who claims his thoughts are being read and controlled by the "evil eye" and his more sophisticated contemporary who claims his mind is controlled by an electronic computer. Nor is there any real difference between the African tribesman who believes he is being watched and followed by a giant leopard and the deluded New Yorker who imagines he is being watched and followed by the FBI. The mentally dis-

THE UNIVERSALITY OF PSYCHOPATHOLOGY: A JAPANESE EXAMPLE

An example of the universality of the basic characteristics of psychopathology is provided by the great Japanese classic *The Tale of Genji*. This eleventh-century novel by Murasaki Shikibu contains a description of what appears to be a psychotic reaction in a lady of the court (Page, 1962). At the time of her entrance into the story, she is in her thirties. Her illness started several years before, and her behavior has been getting progressively more peculiar, uncontrolled, and unpredictable. In keeping with the high standards of neatness and cleanliness of the court ladies, she has previously been tidy and well groomed. Now her hair is in a hopeless tangle. Although there are many servants in the household, she allows no one to come near her, and her room has become filthy and disordered. Periodically she behaves violently. At other times she weeps quietly by herself, imagining (without cause) that her husband is speaking ill of her father. For days she lies motionless on her bed in a state of complete exhaustion. At times she seems barely conscious of what is going on around her. In accord with the modern concept of ambivalence, she is described as perverse: her frenzy drives her to play the most unaccountable and offensive tricks on the very people she most wishes to please.

For some time she has refused to permit her husband to make love to her, and has been unable to manage the household. The husband concludes that her illness is permanent, and going from bad to worse. He therefore feels justified in bringing a younger woman into the home as mistress and homemaker. On one occasion, finding his wife lucid for a moment, the husband takes advantage of the opportunity to explain to her in a calm, reassuring manner that her illness has made it necessary to have another woman in the house, but that he will always provide for her, look after her, and treat her kindly. The wife seems to understand and accept the situation, as a good Japanese wife should.

That evening, when the husband dresses for his visit to the other woman, she helps him with his coat. But as he is about to put on his riding cloak, she suddenly leaps up, seizes a large charcoal brazier, and empties it over his head. The servants who witness the scene are terrified that the husband will "not understand"; if he thinks she is in possession of her senses and has deliberately covered him with burning coals, he may leave her. The husband, however, realizes that she cannot be held responsible, though he is angered by the look of complete unconcern with which she surveys the havoc

turbed person in our own society who senses that he is losing self-control and asks to be hospitalized before he commits some horrible crime is exhibiting essentially the same behavior as the Ojibwa Indian who believes he is possessed by a cannibalistic monster called *windigo*, and in terror commits suicide or asks to be killed before he starts eating his family and friends, whom he perceives as beginning to resemble edible animals (Wallace, 1966). The modern housewife who in a moment of desperate confusion impulsively kills her children to punish her husband or to protect them from future misfortunes is a psychological cousin of Medea of the Greek myth.

CHANGING CONCEPTS OF ABNORMAL BEHAVIOR

Supernatural Explanations

Until the eighteenth century, aberrant behavior was generally attributed to some form of supernatural intervention. Most proposed explanations assumed that the affected individual was a victim of evil spirits, sorcery, soul loss, astrological influences, or some other outside force. At she has just created. But he controls himself and, acting much as a contemporary husband would do in a similar situation, sends for professional help. Priests are called in to exorcise the madwoman, who by this time is cursing and raving. After being pulled about and cudgeled by the priests for some time, she becomes somewhat quieter; but the next day she is still distracted and resumes her raving. Fearful that she may again attempt to disfigure him, the husband stays out of her way for the next several days.

Reflecting the popular belief of that period, the author of *Genji* casually says the woman is "possessed." But two more plausible explanations are also offered. The husband, "who knew her as she ought to be, could realize that her present savagery and malice were merely the result of her illness, but a stranger would be terrified and disgusted." And anticipating by some eight hundred years Freud's (1949) comparison of psychosis with the acting out of a dream with all its absurdities, delusions, and illusions, the author has the husband explain to his wife that her distorted mental state is due to the fact that she has abandoned herself unresistingly to wild dreams and imaginings.

Lady Murasaki composing the Tale of Genji. *A print (1720) by the Japanese artist, Okomura Masanobu.*

times it was believed that madness was an expression of divine punishment inflicted on sinners and wicked persons who had made a pact with the devil.

The biblical account of Jesus expelling the devils from a possessed man provides an example of earlier views on mental disorders, demonology and exorcism. Casting out the devils involved a risk that they might enter the bodies of bystanders. Jesus avoided this danger by sending the devils into a herd of swine, which promptly rushed to the sea and were drowned. The possessed man was described as living among the tombs, crying day and night, and cutting himself with stones. He had often in the past been bound by fetters and chains, which he had broken into pieces. When asked his name, he replied, "My name is Legion, for we are many."

Although short on scientific validity, supernatural interpretations of madness were based on actual observations of disordered behavior. As such, they provide significant insights into the universal characteristics of behavior pathology. The concept of demonic possession is consistent with current thinking that severely disturbed mental patients do not have adequate control over their behavior and hence

Christ casting out devils. A fifteenth century woodcut by an anonymous Dutch artist.

should not be held strictly accountable for their actions. The evil spirits of the past have been internalized and renamed hate, envy, hostility, aggression, and sex. Divine punishment has been replaced by the tyranny of the superego as the explanation for guilt and depressive states

Popular interest in supernatural explanations of behavior has not diminished by their loss of scientific respectability. Astrology is big business. Books and motion pictures dealing with devils and exorcism have a ready market. A major reason for the strong and timeless appeal of supernatural concepts is that they free the individual of personal responsibiliy for his actions. Belief in witches, devils, and the stars also eliminates the need for complicated answers and rigorous proofs in response to difficult questions.

The Concept of Mental Disease

The idea that behavioral disturbances are due to some underlying brain or biochemical defect was initially introduced about 400 B.C. by the comparatively enlightened physicians of ancient Greece, who disagreed with the then popular belief that madness was caused by divine or demonic intervention. Largely as a result of the influence of Greek physicians who migrated to other countries, the mental disease concept was for a time accepted in Rome and other Mediterranean countries. Following the decline of Greco-Roman civilization, however, physical explanations of abnormal behavior were again replaced by supernatural beliefs. Advances in medicine during the nineteenth century rekindled interest in the extension of the notion of illness to include "diseases" of the mind as well as of the body.

The concept of mental illness was first applied to those severely disturbed patients who were characterized by confusion, disorientation, profound apathy, hallucinations, hyperactivity and acute excitement, rigidity of posture, and stuporous depressive states. Since these "symptoms" superficially resembled the delirious reactions of patients with high fevers and the behavior of intoxicated or drugged persons, it seemed reasonable to assume that psychotic patients were suffering from some as yet undetermined lesions of the brain, metabolic disturbances, or other organic defects. From this premise it followed that research efforts should be directed toward the identification of specific physical causes and the development of medical cures. An early biochemical formulation of the mental disease concept was reported by Thudichum in 1884:

Many forms of insanity are unquestionably the external manifestations of the effects upon the brain substance of poisons fermented within the body, just as mental aberrations accompanying chronic alcoholic intoxication are the accumulated effects of a relatively simple poison fermented out of the body. These poisons we shall, I have no doubt, be able to isolate after we know the normal chemistry to its uttermost detail. And then will come in their turn the crowning discoveries of the antidotes to the poisons and to the fermenting causes and processes which produce them.

During the late nineteenth and early twentieth centuries, Emil Kraepelin, a German psychiatrist, gained strong support for the mental illness concept by developing a widely accepted nomenclature and classification system based on the medical model of independent diseases. According to Kraepelin (1907), mental disorders were disease entities analogous to physical diseases. More specifically, he held that the diseases of the mind, like the diseases of the body, could be subdivided into separate types, each of which had its specific organic cause, was distinguished by a specific pattern of symptoms, and followed a characteristic course with a predictable outcome. Since the disease was considered the critical factor, Kraepelin's approach stressed the importance of isolating and identifying the symptoms that were associated with each disease. Precise diagnosis and detailed classification were considered the first critical steps in determining the specific organic cause for each disorder. In accordance with the traditional medical model of infectious diseases, it was assumed

that once the underlying neurological or biochemical cause had been discovered and corrected, the symptoms would disappear. Little attention was given to possible psychosocial determinants, personal frustrations and conflicts, or the psychological meaning of symptoms. This narrowly defined disease model was especially favored by psychiatrists working with hospitalized psychotic patients.

The concept of illness was gradually extended to include neuroses, antisocial behavior, alcoholism, childhood maladjustments, marital problems, and other mild forms of deviant behavior. For these more benign disorders, some psychological agent —intrapsychic conflict, sexual repression, fixation, emotional trauma, unresolved guilt —was usually considered the underlying cause. The rationale, however, remained the same. It was presumed that these milder disturbances in behavior represented surface manifestations of some specific, internal source of "psychic infection," which had to be identified and eliminated. The conversion of mental disorders to the medical model was facilitated by the use of such familiar terms as patient, diagnosis, therapy, cure, and mental hospital. The mental illness concept reached its peak of popularity and acceptance during the early decades of the present century. In more recent years the premises and implications of this "sickness" model have been challenged by psychiatrists, psychologists, and sociologists. Thomas Szasz (1961), a psychiatrist, has referred to the mental illness concept as a myth that has outlived its usefulness.

Criticisms of the mental illness concept. A major practical criticism centers about the sterility of the disease model. A half century of intensive research has failed to substantiate the basic assumption that disturbances in behavior are directly caused by neurophysiological pathogenic agents. The disease approach has been successful only for certain disorders, marked by gross neurological or physical defects, which were formerly mistakenly diagnosed as mental disorders because of the concomitant presence of impairments in psychological func-

Thomas S. Szasz, an American psychiatrist, who has been a persistent critic of the medical model of mental illness and of the associated medical and legal implications of the involuntary hospitalization, enforced treatment, and deprivation of rights of mental patients.

tioning. An outstanding example is *general paresis,* a neurological disorder associated with mental disturbances, which has been found to be due to diffuse brain damage caused by syphilis. The search for specific psychological defects responsible for particular forms of mild mental disorders has also been unproductive. It is now generally recognized that the causes of disturbances in behavior—severe or mild—are multiple and varied.

A second major criticism of the mental disease concept is that it has promoted a pessimistic attitude regarding treatment and prognosis. Interest in experimentation was dampened by acceptance of the premise that there was little purpose in therapy until the underlying causes were first determined. This negative attitude was reinforced by the disappointing results obtained when drastic empirical procedures were tried, including brain surgery and shock techniques. The development of modern psychoactive drugs has greatly facilitated the care and management of patients, but no claim is made that these drugs are specific cures. The role of tranquilizing and energizing drugs is comparable to that of aspirin in providing temporary relief of symptoms.

A third general criticism has to do with the impact of the mental illness model on the patient's perception of himself, the image conveyed to the public, and the attending consequences. At the time it was initially introduced, the concept of mental illness served the useful purpose of encouraging public acceptance of the idea that the psychologically disturbed were sick individuals in need of treatment rather than witches, sinners, or malingerers. The extension of the medical umbrella to cover mental disorders, however, has been only partly effective in transferring to the mentally ill the sympathetic attitudes traditionally expressed toward the physically ill. The prefix "mental" has led to a number of unfavorable inferences and practices. Classifying a person as "mentally ill" has come to serve as justification for subjecting him to isolation, involuntary incarceration, brain surgery, and various unpleasant forms of physical and psychological treatment (Sarbin, 1969). Persons labeled "mentally ill" tend to be feared, avoided, rejected, sometimes pitied but nearly always degraded. The process that converts a person into a mental patient carries with it the potentiality for self-devaluation. To be labeled and considered a mental patient or even a

Visual and verbal images of mental illness, from newspapers and magazines, reflecting the stereotyped labels applied to deviant behavior.

former mental patient does little to boost one's self-esteem or social acceptance (Phillips, 1963).

According to Thomas Scheff (1966a), the social deviant's acceptance of the label "mental patient" may lead to his acting out a culturally defined role. Questions asked by doctors while the patient is being examined often provide useful cues as to how he is expected to behave. The patient who learns and plays his designated role well, as defined by the cultural stereotype, is rewarded by receiving special sickness benefits. Those who deviate from the expected role may be denied these benefits. Those who protest too vigorously against being considered sick or confined to a hospital are often regarded as acutely disturbed and are isolated or sedated until they learn to conform. Scheff maintains that once a person

has been publicly labeled a mental patient, he often meets discrimination when he tries to reestablish himself within the community following his recovery. A kind of vicious circle is established: the more the social deviant enters into the role of the mentally ill, the more he is defined by others as mentally ill, and the more he is defined by others as mentally ill, the more he enters into the role, and so on. An important feature of Scheff's hypothesis is that deviant behavior is often transitory. The labeling of such behavior as mental illness by society and the acceptance of this verdict by the patient have the effect of stabilizing and fixing him in his deviant role.

Emerging Concepts

Loss of confidence in the validity and utility

of the mental disease concept has led to a critical rethinking of the nature of abnormal behavior. Issues of causation and treatment in particular are being viewed from a broader perspective. The current trend is to deemphasize medical terms and approaches and to attach greater importance to psychological, sociological, educational, and legal concepts. The use of the term "mental disease" has to a large extent been dropped. Agreement has not yet been reached on a new term. Some widely used interim designations include "mental disturbances," "behavior disorders," and "psychosocial problems." Szasz (1961) has proposed that mental disorders should be redefined as *problems in living,* which involve deviations from accepted moral, social, ethical, and legal norms. Scheff (1966b) and others favor the concept of *residual deviance* or *residual rule-breaking.* According to this viewpoint, mental disorders are more appropriately defined as residual forms of rule-breaking for which society has no explicit label. Residual deviance (mental disorder) is what is left after all other forms of violation of norms such as crime, immorality, perversion, drunkenness, and bad manners, have been excluded. Erik Erikson (1968) has contributed the concept of *identity crisis* to describe mental disturbances occurring mainly in young persons. Theodore Sarbin (1969) has suggested that the mentally disturbed should be viewed as persons who have failed to establish acceptable social identities or roles.

Multiple interacting causes. Studies of specific biological, psychological, and sociocultural factors are still being conducted. However, the current objective is limited to an assessment of the relative importance of specific factors as contributory agents. The hope of someday discovering a single cause for each disorder has been abandoned. Most authorities today agree that while the determinants of abnormal behavior may differ from those of normal behavior, they are no less complex and varied. Standard textbooks on theories of normal personality development (Hall and Lindzey, 1970) and on

theories of psychopathology (Millon, 1973) cover basically the same material. The broad generalization that the personality and behavior of the normal individual reflect his total life history, as shaped by the cumulative interaction of his genetic inheritance, his physical and social environments, and his personal experiences, is equally applicable to the personality and behavior of persons described as mentally disturbed.

The key words are "individual," "cumulative interaction," and "total life history." As the product of a distinctive combination of interactive determinants, every individual—and this includes identical twins—differs in certain respects from every other person. The uniqueness of each individual is responsible for the infinite variations in personality traits and reaction patterns noted in normal and abnormal persons. But as Kluckhohn and Murray (1961) have noted, every man is in certain respects like all other men, and in certain respects every man is more like some other men than others. Similarities observed among individuals are presumably due to the presence of common or equivalent determinants.

Students of behavior agree that the effects of nature and nurture are so tightly meshed and interdependent as to be practically inseparable. Biological factors influence the individual's selection of his environment and the use he makes of it. Environmental factors influence the development of the individual's genetic potentialities, so that some are realized and others are not. Because of inherent differences in mental capacities and temperament, children reared in the same home will differ markedly in learning, exploratory activities, acquired attitudes, and reaction to shared experiences. Given a particular set of genes, an infant may develop one of several potential personalities depending on the culture in which he is reared, his socioeconomic opportunities, the personalities of his parents, their style of child rearing, and his personal life experiences. The interaction of multiple determinants limits, but does not rule out, the importance of specific variables. Other factors being constant, the odds in favor of normal behavior are greatly increased if a child inherits sound genes rather than defective ones; is reared in a stable home by loving parents rather than in a disrupted home by rejecting parents; and is rarely rather than frequently subjected to extreme stress. "Other factors," however, are seldom constant in real life. Depending on the interactive significance of other variables, the potential contribution of specific "good" or "bad" determinants may be accentuated, suppressed, distorted, or even reversed. The promises of heredity can be canceled by the environment and vice versa.

My major purpose in emphasizing the terms *cumulative interaction* and *total life history* is to correct two popular misconceptions regarding the causes of mental disorders. Among the general public there is a common tendency to attribute mental illness to some recent traumatic experience such as a disappointing love affair, a death in the family, business reverses, or whatever. However, traumatic situations that are followed by overt symptoms of disturbance are more appropriately interpreted as precipitating factors that release or trigger reactions in predisposed individuals whose adaptive resources have been progressively depleted over many years.

The second misconception, encouraged by many theories of psychopathology, is that early childhood experiences are of crucial significance in the development of behavior disorders. It is true that the roots of behavior pathology are often established during the early formative years. But whether the final outcome is a healthy or twisted personality is determined in great measure by the presence of favorable or unfavorable influences during the adolescence and adulthood. Attempts to relate specific early child-rearing practices to adult personality have been unsuccessful (Orlansky, 1949; Sewell, 1952). There is no evidence that any isolated childhood experience, such as strictness of toilet training, is the cause of mental disorder during adulthood. A more valid explanation is that the method

of toilet training and other specific childhood events reflect—for good or ill—the pattern of mothering and the family climate to which the child is exposed day after day and year after year until he leaves home (Schaefer and Bayley, 1960). And even then the child with a history of adverse childhood training may, through his choice of a marital partner, re-create in his own family the same pathogenic environment he left behind. There is also the possibility that in revolting against the way he was reared, the individual may go to the opposite extreme and create a different but equally pathogenic environment in his own home.

Another factor that contributes to the belief in the importance of the early formative years is the continuing influence of genetic defects. Genetic defects that cause faulty personality development during childhood continue to exert their harmful effect throughout the life of the individual. However, once more it should be noted that personality development is a continuous process, ever responsive to current and future influences. At any point during adolescence and adulthood, significant experiences may modify personality organization and functioning for better or for worse. No one is destined to become a mental patient because of his heredity or childhood experiences. Conversely, a good genetic endowment or a favorable childhood may increase one's resistance to adverse influences in later life, but it does not guarantee immunity against the development of a mental disorder.

The normal-abnormal continuum. In contrast to earlier approaches that accentuated the differences between normal and abnormal behavior, the present trend is to restore the psychologically disturbed to the human fold by accentuating the unbroken continuity of behavior. The personality traits and reactions of mental patients may thus be viewed as more extreme, more inappropriate, and more maladaptive manifestations of traits and reactions observed in "normal" persons. What distinguishes the disturbed individual is a set of personality attributes, shaped by his total developmental history, which are not adequate to enable him to cope effectively with the pressures and problems of life. The adaptive resources of some individuals are so limited that they "break" under the ordinary difficulties of everyday life. For others, an extremely severe stress may be required to precipitate impaired functioning. More often than not it is difficult to pinpoint the precipitating factor. Some seemingly minor or incidental experience may serve as the last straw for a person already overburdened with an accumulation of problems or faulty habits of adjustment, resulting in psychological collapse.

The notion of a continuum provides a simpler and far more cogent explanation for "symptoms" than the indefensible hypothesis that they represent the surface expression of some underlying disease. In addition, the conclusion that abnormal behavior is an extreme manifestation of characteristic human behavior accounts for the occurrence of essentially similar patterns of maladaptive reactions in all societies and in the same society over time. More specifically, most so-called mental symptoms represent extreme variations of the ways in which human beings characteristically behave when overwhelmed by the stresses

Table 1.1. Common Defense Mechanisms.

Defense mechanism	Characteristics
Repression	Exclusion from consciousness of memories, impulses, and ideas that would evoke anxiety, fear, guilt, or shame if the individual were aware of them. Repressed desires and thoughts are not permanently lost or forgotten. They are pushed back to the outer, darker fringes of consciousness, where their continued but unacknowledged presence may contribute to vague feelings of anxiety and be revealed in dreams and other situations when vigilance is reduced. Repression may range in severity from the selective forgetting of unpleasant appointments to the "loss" of large segments of childhood memories. Repressed hostile feelings may be expressed in psychosomatic symptoms.
Compensation	Exaggerated efforts to attain success or distinction in one's area of inferiority or in some other field. A common defense against feelings of inadequacy, failure, or personal defects, either real or imagined.
Rationalization	Invention of "good" reasons to discount failures or to justify actions that might otherwise be damaging to one's self-esteem. Thus disappointments may be softened by "sour grape" rationalization: personal defects and misfortunes may be converted into blessings in disguise ("sweet lemon" rationalization).
Projection	Attributing blame for one's weaknesses, mistakes, and misdeeds to others as a means of safeguarding self-esteem and avoiding self-censure. Parents may project blame for their marital unhappiness on their children; students tempted to cheat on exams may project their guilt on others and claim they got better grades because they cheated. Paranoid delusions of persecution are usually based on projection, with imaginary enemies blamed for personal failure.
Reaction formation	Defending one's self against undesired personal qualities or temptations by self-deception, believing and acting as if one did not have the qualities or were repelled by what actually tempts him. Thus a

and disappointments of life. Typical human reactions to stress, which under certain conditions are referred to as symptoms, include confusion and indecision; impairment in learning, memory, thinking, and judgment; incoherent communication; emotional overreaction with concomitant somatic symptoms; self-blame and self-attack; hostile-aggressive behavior directed against others; and withdrawal-surrender-escape reactions. Another common reaction to stress that is shared by normal and disturbed persons is the unconscious utilization of one or more of the defense mechanisms described in Table 1.1. Both

groups find these defenses useful in preserving self-esteem, averting further disorganization, or restoring some sort of order and equilibrium. The main differences between normal stress reactions and "abnormal symptoms" is that the latter are more persistent, less appropriate as responses to the person's experiences, less controlled, more severe, more incapacitating, and more disturbing to the individual and his society.

New therapy concepts. The ineffectiveness of techniques designed to locate and resolve intrapsychic conflicts dating back to early childhood has led to a shift in strategy.

Defense mechanism	Characteristics
	mother who unconsciously rejects her child may be overly affectionate and protective; extreme modesty may constitute a protective reaction against repressed erotic desires. Self-appointed censors of public morals may be reflecting their own strong but repressed temptation to engage in the activities they overtly condemn.
Denial	Unconscious, selective perceptual blindness to unpleasant facts that protects the individual from the necessity of facing intolerable thoughts, wishes, deeds, and situations. Older people may not see the obvious signs of their deterioration. Denial of reality is the basis of many delusions.
Regression	Retreat from current difficulties by reversion to immature or infantile modes of gratification and behavior. First-born children often react to the presence of a new baby by reverting to infantile speech or to bedwetting.
Displacement	Transference of emotional feelings from one person or object to another, "safer" person or object. Thus hostile feelings aroused by a spouse may be redirected and discharged against a family pet.
Identification	Related to imitation and role copying but more thorough-going than either, since the individual who identifies with significant others adopts their attitudes, values, and behavior as his own. Usually the individual identifies with the desirable attributes of others, but he may also identify with their undesirable characteristics—aggressiveness, for example. An important factor in personality development.
Introjection	A special form of identification in which the attitudes, values, and behavior of another person are internalized. Feelings associated with this other person are now directed toward the self or experienced as part of the self. Mainly associated with depressive states following the death of a loved one, a form of incorporation in which the survivor feels the dead weight of the introjected person within himself.

Newer forms of psychotherapy focus on the here-and-now problems confronting the individual. Particular attention is given to identifying current personal, interpersonal, and environmental factors that support and maintain maladaptive behavior. The goals have been scaled down. Psychotherapy is no longer regarded as a magic tool for creating happy, successful personalities. The more realistic objective of modern therapy is to modify those aspects of behavior that interfere with reasonable standards of personal functioning. The attainment of this objective may involve the elimination of specific symptoms, a change of attitude, the development of increased self-direction and responsibility, the acquisition of social skills, and so on. In other words, the present thrust is toward extending the individual's contol of his behavior and the choices available to him. An important feature of the new approaches is that increased demands are made on the patient to be an active partner in the therapeutic process. Psychotherapy is viewed as a learning or problem-solving experience in which therapist and client, working together in an atmosphere of understanding and trust, objectively examine the client's current difficulties and "mistakes" and consider alternative courses that are consistent with his potentialities and the realities of his situation. Final decisions, however, rest with the client, who sooner or later must assume responsibility for living his own life.

Another important change has been the freeing of therapy from the confines of the traditional one-to-one relationship in which doctor and patient are restricted to their respective formal roles. This has been achieved through greater use of family and group therapy. Both approaches provide a more natural setting for the spontaneous expression of feelings, the communication of information, immediate feedback, and trying out new behavior. The groups may be structured to permit sharing experiences and interacting with persons of the same or opposite sex and with similar or different problems. Participants usually focus on their most immediate problems, and use may be made of public disclosure, direct confrontation, physical contact, and marathon sessions.

Changes in care of the disturbed. Other recent changes have been more directly concerned with improving facilities and procedures for coping with the magnitude of the mental health problem. The extent of the need for services is indicated in Table 1.2. During 1971 more than four million persons in the United States received treatment in some kind of psychiatric facility. This number represents 2 percent of the total population. The figures do not include patients seen in private practice, unrecorded cases, and nontreated persons with problems of equal severity. If all psychologically disturbed persons were included, the prevalence rate for the year would be close to 5 percent. Of those receiving treatment in a psychiatric facility, 42 percent were inpatients and the remaining 58 percent were seen in outpatient or day care centers.

A major advance in the care of disturbed patients has been the discovery of drugs that are highly effective in alleviating distress and controlling behavior that is disturbing to others. Drug medication has made it possible for many patients to carry on their usual activities and to be accepted by their families and communities. The availability of these new drugs has similarly facilitated the early discharge of hospitalized patients.

Starting in 1963, the federal government, with the cooperation of local and state agencies, has been endeavoring to extend and improve the delivery of psychiatric services to low income and non-urban people through the establishment of community mental health centers. Several hundred such centers are currently in operation, offering inpatient and outpatient care, day and night emergency services, partial hospitalization, and day care. Many centers also provide aftercare for patients discharged from mental hospitals, treatment for drug addicts, and special programs for the mentally retarded. Plans call for setting up about two thousand community centers, each serving an area of about 100,000 people.

Nineteen percent of all patients receiving treatment in some kind of psychiatric facility during 1971 were seen in community mental health centers.

The search for alternatives to hospitalization has led to the development in general hospitals of psychiatric wards for short-term treatment. This kind of service accounted for 13 percent of the patients treated in 1971. Other procedures also reducing admissions to mental hospitals include greater use of home treatment and family therapy. More attention is being given to the rehabilitation of discharged patients by providing living accommodations for them in what are called *halfway houses,* which serve as transitional facilities between the mental hospital and full return to the community.

The needs for manpower resulting from the expansion of services have been met in part by training nonprofessionals as mental health workers. This procedure has worked out well. Trained nonprofessionals, who live in the same community as clients or have similar backgrounds, have been found to be more understanding of the real problems confronting their clients than professionals, and seem to be equally effective as therapists. These findings are consistent with other observations that favor peer group therapy, as for example the treatment of alcoholics by rehabilitated alcoholics.

Professional personnel. As long as mental disorders were considered a kind of sickness, a strong case could be made for the need for physicians to exercise control over the treatment of patients in office practice, psychiatric clinics, and mental hospitals. The medical specialty of psychiatry still

Table 1.2. The Use of Psychiatric Facilities in the United States (Patient Care Episodes* by Type of Facility, 1971).

	Number	Percent
All facilities, all episodes	4,190,913	100.0
Inpatient episodes	1,755,816	41.9
State & county mental hospitals	745,259	17.9
Private mental hospitals	97,963	2.3
Veterans' Administration hospitals	176,800	4.2
General hospital psychiatric services	542,642	12.9
Residential treatment centers for emotionally disturbed children	28,637	0.7
Community mental health centers	130,088	3.1
Other multiservice facilities	34,427	0.8
Outpatient episodes	2,316,754	55.3
Community mental health centers	622,906	14.9
Other outpatient services	1,693,848	40.4
Day care episodes	118,343	2.8
Community mental health centers	43,653	1.0
Other day care services	74,690	1.8

* Episode refers to the number of residents in inpatient facilities at the beginning of the year or the total number of persons on the rolls of outpatient facilities, plus the total additions to these facilities during the year.

SOURCE: Department of Health, Education, and Welfare, Survey and Reports Section, Statistical Note 92, August 1973.

PROFESSIONALS ACTIVE IN THE MENTAL HEALTH FIELD

All of the social and biological sciences, as well as the humanities, are involved with one or another of the multiple facets of psychopathology (Page, 1966). Pastoral counseling is an important activity of the clergy of all faiths. The legal profession is directly concerned with laws regulating the admission of patients to mental hospitals, the determination of mental incompetence, and the establishment of criteria for a defense of insanity. The medical sciences are directly involved in the neurological aspects of deviant behavior, psychopharmacology, and genetic research. In a 1969 survey conducted by the National Institute of Mental Health, it was noted that 29 percent of sociologists and 15 percent of anthropologists in institutions of higher education reported mental health as one of their professional specialties. The closest ties of psychopathology are with the professions of psychiatry, psychoanalysis, clinical psychology, and psychiatric social work.

Psychiatry is the medical specialty devoted to the diagnosis, treatment, and study of mental disorders. To qualify as a psychiatrist, a person must complete the usual requirements for an M.D. degree and then take postgraduate training in psychiatry. In the treatment of mental patients, psychia-

trists rely mainly on therapeutic interview techniques. As licensed physicians they may administer drugs and apply various biophysical therapies.

Psychoanalysis is a particular school of thought and a special form of therapy. Psychoanalysts accept the Freudian or neo-Freudian interpretation of mental disorders and adhere to certain formal treatment procedures that stress the recall and interpretation of significant early childhood experiences, with emphasis on repressed, unconscious material. Specific psychoanalytic procedures include the establishment of a transference relationship between patient and analyst, free association, and dream analysis. Any professionally qualified person in the field of mental health who has undergone psychoanalysis himself and who is a graduate of a recognized psychoanalytic training institute may call himself a psychoanalyst. However, most psychoanalytic training institutes in this country accept only physicians as trainees. As a result, psychoanaylsis is essentially a subdivision of psychiatry. About 10 percent of all psychiatrists in the United States describe themselves as psychoanalysts. Most of them are located in large cities.

Clinical psychology is a specialty within the general field of psychology, devoted to the diagnosis, treatment, and study of personality disorders. Qualifying training includes the completion of a doctoral degree

remains the dominant profession in the mental health field. The emergence of psychological and sociological concepts as substitutes for the medical model, however, has markedly increased the involvement of other disciplines and professions. Clinical psychology especially has made giant strides in recent years toward attaining an independent status equal to that of psychiatry. George Albee (1969) and others have suggested that the time has come for psychology to divorce itself from medicine and develop its own concepts, treatment centers, and techniques. As replacements for the tra-

ditional clinics and hospitals, he favors the establishment of special schools and social centers where educational and training procedures would be employed to build up the individual's strengths and assets. An advantage claimed by Albee for such centers is that they would relieve the shortage of professional personnel in the mental health field, since they could be staffed by college graduates who had received some special training.

In defense of the medical point of view, Roy Grinker (1969) has pointed out that there is considerable advantage in retaining in psychology and one or more years of internship. Clinical psychologists may use any psychological treatment procedures they are qualified by training to administer. A currently favored approach is the application of learning theory principles to behavior modification.

Most *psychiatric social workers* have graduate degrees in social work. Their duties include interviewing patients and relatives, follow-up home visits, and supervision in the community of patients discharged from mental institutions. In recent years psychiatric social workers have become increasingly involved in family therapy and marital counseling.

Members of all four professions work in mental hospitals, community clinics, universities, and related social agencies. All may engage in private practice, but a much higher proportion of psychoanalysts and psychiatrists devote full time to office practice. Particularly in hospital and clinic settings psychiatrists, clinical psychologists, and psychiatric social workers may function as a team, with each contributing the special skills of his profession. Traditionally the psychiatrist has assumed major responsibility for treatment, the clinical psychologist for psychodiagnosis and research, and the psychiatric social worker for taking case histories and counseling the relatives of patients. The more recent trend has been in the direction of overlapping roles. Clinical

psychologists and psychiatric social workers are becoming more active in therapy and psychiatrists are becoming more involved in research.

The extent to which the four professions are active in the mental health field varies in different parts of the country. A survey of the total population of professional personnel working in a Chicago metropolitan community found that 25 percent were psychiatrists, 16 percent were psychoanalysts, 33 percent were clinical psychologists, and 26 percent were psychiatric social workers (Spray, 1968). Considerable variation was noted with respect to the major activities of the four groups. Eighty-five percent of the psychoanalysts listed therapy as their major activity as compared to 70 percent of the psychiatrists, 21 percent of the clinical psychologists, and 20 percent of the psychiatric social workers. Twenty-two percent of clinical psychologists listed teaching and research as their major activities as compared to 11 percent of psychiatric social workers, 9 percent of psychiatrists, and 5 percent of psychoanalysts. The balance of the time was spent in counseling, casework, diagnosis, administration, and supervision.

Other professionals actively involved in working with psychologically disturbed children and adults include school psychologists, school counselors, vocational counselors, psychiatric nurses, occupational therapists, and recreational therapists.

the traditional diagnostic categories, since so much information is available on their causes, courses of development, therapies, and so on. He regards much of the current controversy as a problem in semantics and believes that a closer collaborative effort between medicine and other disciplines is preferable to parceling out territories to various professional groups. Grinker observes that psychology, with its emphasis on learning principles, has made and can continue to make an important contribution, but he thinks this can best be done within the present medical framework. If psychologists

were to withdraw from psychiatric institutions and establish their own therapy centers, their own language, their own therapeutic techniques, Grinker suggests that psychologists would isolate themselves from the mainstream of psychiatry to their own and everyone else's loss.

But the controversy about models, concepts, and terminology is not an exercise in semantics. The familiar rhyme, "Sticks and stones may break my bones but names will never hurt me," is not true. The derogatory names usually applied to psychologically disturbed individuals can and do hurt, and should be abandoned. Popular misconceptions regarding the danger to be expected from mental patients and regarding their incurability should be corrected. If behavior disturbances were regarded as problems in living, as indeed they are, they would assume a less unfavorable image in the public mind, and this improved image itself would have therapeutic value. On the other hand, care should be taken not to throw out the baby along with the bath water. The routine hospitalization of mental patients has not been successful but short-term hospitalization is highly to be recommended for the emergency care of acutely disturbed, assaultive, and suicidal people. The discrediting of the sickness model has not diminished either the effectiveness or the desirability of modern drugs for the control and amelioration of psychotic symptoms. The future calls for bold innovations and increased involvement of all the behavioral and social sciences, medicine included, in furthering our understanding of problems in living and in developing more effective therapeutic and preventive measures.

SUMMARY

The field of psychopathology, as defined in this book, covers a broad spectrum of deviant and inappropriate behavior that causes distress to the individual, his family, and society. These maladaptive reactions include mild personality deficits, psychosomatic complaints, neurotic reactions, alcoholism, drug abuse, sex problems, suicide, and psychotic disturbances. At various times these and related forms of abnormal behavior have been referred to as madness, demonic possession, mental disease, personality disorders, residual deviance, and problems in living. The outward expression of disordered behavior and the explanations offered for it may vary from culture to culture but the basic features are timeless and much the same the world over. The essential sameness of behavior pathology in all cultures is due to the fact that "mental symptoms" represent extreme variations of the ways in which human beings characteristically behave when they are overwhelmed by the stresses of life. Symptoms differ from "normal" stress reactions in being more persistent, less appropriate, more severe, less controlled, and more disturbing to the individual and his society. Abnormal and normal behavior represent different positions along a continuum. The determinants of abnormal behavior differ qualitatively from the determinants of normal behavior but are no less complex and varied.

Until the eighteenth century madness was generally attributed to supernatural influences. The disease concept of mental disorders was popular during the late nineteenth and early twentieth centuries. The numerous criticisms of this medical approach have stimulated interest in broader concepts by which mental disorders are viewed as psychosocial problems in living or special examples of norm violation. Recent interpretations have been accompanied by a radical shift in therapeutic approaches. Modern psychotherapy focuses on reeducation and social rehabilitation rather than on uncovering and resolving intrapsychic conflicts. Learning principles are utilized in the alleviation of current personality problems and the strengthening of psychological assets.

References

Albee, G. W. "Emerging Concepts of Mental Illness and Models of Treatment: The Psychological Point of View." *American Journal of Psychiatry* 125 (1969): 870-76.

Arieti, S., and Meth, J. M. "Rare, Unclassifiable, Exotic Psychotic Syndromes." In *American Handbook of Psychiatry*, ed. S. Arieti, vol. 1, pp. 546-63. New York: Basic Books, 1959.

Erikson, E. H. *Identity: Youth and Crisis.* New York: Norton, 1968.

Freud, S. *An Outline of Psychoanalysis.* New York: Norton, 1949.

Grinker, R. R. "Emerging Concepts of Mental Illness and Models of Treatment: The Medical Point of View." *American Journal of Psychiatry* 125 (1969): 865-69.

Hall, C. S., and Lindzey, G. *Theories of Personality.* (2nd ed.) New York: Wiley, 1970.

Kluckhohn, C., and Murray, H. A. "Personality Formation: The Determinants." In *Personality in Nature, Society, and Culture,* ed. Kluckhohn and Murray, pp. 53-67. New York: Knopf, 1961

Kraepelin, E. *Clinical Psychiatry.* New York: Macmillan, 1907.

Linton, R. *Culture and Mental Disorders.* Springfield, Ill.: Charles C Thomas, 1956.

Millon, T. *Theories of Psychopathology and Personality* (2nd ed.) Philadelphia: Saunders, 1973.

National Institute of Mental Health. *Sociologists and Anthropologists.* Public Health Service publication no. 1884. Washington, D.C.: U.S. Government Printing Office, 1969.

Orlansky, H. "Infant Care and Personality." *Psychological Bulletin* 46 (1949): 1-48.

Page, J. D. "Description of a Psychotic Reaction in Eleventh-Century Japan." *American Journal of Psychiatry* 119 (1962): 271-72.

———. *Approaches to Psychopathology.* New York: Columbia University Press, 1966.

Phillips, D. L. "Rejection as a Consequence of Seeking Help for Mental Disorders." *American Socological Review* 28 (1963): 963-72.

Sarbin, T. R. "The Scientific Status of the Mental Illness Metaphor." In *Changing Perspectives in Mental Illness,* ed. S. C. Plog and R. B. Edgarton. New York: Holt, Rinehart & Winston, 1969.

Schaefer, E. R., and Bayley, N. "Consistency of Maternal Behavior from Infancy to Preadolescence." *Journal of Abnormal Psychology* 61 (1960): 1-6.

Scheff, T. J. *Being Mentally Ill.* Chicago: Aldine, 1966(a).

———. "A Sociological Theory of Mental Disorders." In *Approaches to Psychopathology,* ed. J. Page. New York: Columbia University Press, 1966(b).

Sewell, W. H. "Infant Training and the Personality of the Child." *American Journal of Sociology* 58 (1952): 150-57.

Shikibu, M. *The Tale of Genji,* trans. Arthur Waley. New York: Random House, 1960.

Spray, S. L. "Mental Health Professions and the Division of Labor in a Metropolitan Community." *Psychiatry* 31 (1968): 51-60.

Szasz, T. S. *The Myth of Mental Illness.* New York: Harper & Row, 1961.

Thudichum, J. W. L. *A Treatise on the Chemical Constitution of the Brain.* London: Balliere, Tindall & Cox, 1884.

Wallace, F. C. "Anthropology and Psychopathology." In *Approaches to Psychopathology,* ed. J. Page, pp. 30-59. New York: Columbia University Press, 1966.

Yap, P. M. "Mental Diseases Peculiar to Certain Cultures." *Journal of Mental Science* 97 (1951): 313-27.

2 · The Classification of Psychosocial Problems

The Four Humors, from a medieval drawing

Sanguine   Choleric   Phlegmatic   Melancholic

The influence of the disease concept on the classification of abnormal behavior is apparent in the choice of diagnostic labels, such as *schizophrenia, neurasthenia, involutional melancholia,* and *hypochondriasis.* The idea of grouping mental disorders into categories and subtypes cannot be entirely blamed on the adoption of the medical model, however. Man is an inveterate classifier. Confronted by the confusing differences among individuals, human beings commonly seek to simplify the situation by arranging them in neat but obviously artificial categories: good and bad; tall, medium, and short; bright, average, and stupid. The myriad manifestations of abnormal behavior are similarly placed in arbitrary categories: simpleminded, crazy, nervous, or simply peculiar. The more sophisticated prefer to use such terms as retarded, psychotic, neurotic, and disturbed. The utility of these terms is limited by the fact that they are too broad and ambiguous to be meaningful when they are applied to specific individuals.

One of the earliest attempts at classifying mental disorders is reported in the writings of Hippocrates (460-357 b.c.). Hippocrates recognized three principal mental diseases: mania (uncontrolled excitement), melancholia (varied forms of psychoses), and phrenesis, or frenzy. The latter apparently referred to acute delirium reactions marked by fever and excitement. He also described cases that would now be classified as phobias, hypochondriasis, and obsessive-compulsive reactions. In the intervening twenty-three centuries, hundreds of other diagnostic labels have been coined. The naming game has not been limited to Western societies. Primitive people have also invented descriptive terms to differentiate various types of madness. The Iban people

of Sarawak recognize nineteen different forms (Schmidt, 1964).

Modern psychiatry still favors the classification of mental disorders into major categories and subcategories. Emil Kraepelin (1856-1929), a German psychiatrist, is credited with establishing the first widely used psychiatric classification. Kraepelin's original contribution consisted of the concepts of *dementia praecox* (later renamed schizophrenia) and *manic-depressive psychosis.* His detailed descriptions of the symptom patterns associated with these two major psychoses and their subtypes still constitute the nucleus of current psychiatric classification. The wide acceptance and continued use of Kraepelin's ideas have had the advantage of promoting a uniform nomenclature—at the high cost of perpetuating outdated terms and concepts.

Periodically, makeshift attempts have been made to improve the classifications. To a large extent the psychopathologists of each country have gone their own ways in making additions and revisions. As a consequence, the classification systems in current use vary from country to country, and in some countries from hospital to hospital (Stengel, 1959). The diagnosis applied to a particular patient thus depends more on his place of residence than on his mental condition. The official French classification for example, includes several diagnostic labels that are not used elsewhere: acute confused state, chronic systematized delirium, mental disequilibrium. Technically there are no schizophrenic patients in France, since the official classification system does not include schizophrenia as a diagnostic category. Even in countries where the same labels are used, they are often interpreted differently. In the United States the diagnosis of schizophrenia

Emil Kraepelin (1865-1926), a German psychiatrist noted for his pioneer work in the clinical description, differentiation, and classification of mental disorders. He believed in the concept of separate mental disorders, each of which was assumed to have a biological or organic cause.

is applied to a wide variety of mental patients, many of whom would be classified in England as suffering from a psychotic depressive reaction. The results of a cross-national study indicate that one-third of all persons admitted to mental hospitals in England and Wales are diagnosed as suffering from some type of affective psychosis, as compared with 11 percent in the United States (Kramer, 1969). Conversely, about twice as many patients are classified as schizophrenics in the United States as in England.

Comprehensive reviews of the purposes, advantages, and shortcomings of psychiatric classification have been reported by Katz, Cole, and Barton (1965) and Zubin (1967). Karl Menninger (1963) has contributed an excellent historical perspective. Some repeatedly noted but as yet unresolved problems are these:

1. Who should be classified as a mental patient and why? A commonly used operational definition is that a person is a mental patient if he seeks or is referred for treatment for some disturbance or impairment in behavior that causes distress, disability, discomfort, or concern to the individual or his society. The objection to this definition is

that it is too broad. Frequently reported complaints by self-referred patients include feelings of depression, loss of control of thoughts, suicidal impulses, sexual problems, loneliness, courtship and marital problems, and failure of the patient to meet his own expectations. A person may be referred for treatment by a member of his family, a friend, or some public official, on the grounds that he is a danger to himself or others, is unable to care for himself, or is unwilling or unable to conform to expected social standards. More specific symptoms may include threats, excessive belligerence, conduct embarrassing or irritating to family or friends, excessive drinking, refusal to speak or eat, underachievement, immaturity of behavior, and social incompetence. Law-enforcement agents may refer lawbreakers for treatment when it is suspected that they are not criminally responsible for their actions or are unable to assist in their own defense because of mental disorders (Gruenberg, 1965). To be meaningful and useful, a classification system should have some rational, unifying base. The reasons for psychiatric referral are too varied to justify including all of them under the common heading of mental disorders.

2. How many categories of abnormal behavior should there be, and which should be included? The need for classifying the diverse manifestations of abnormal behavior in some orderly way is universally acknowledged. Disagreement exists as to choice of method, number of classes and subtypes, and the criteria that should be used for their selection. The root of controversies associated with these issues is that the "symptoms" of mental patients do not fit neatly into clearly defined, discrete categories. Each patient to some extent exhibits a unique combination of traits and reactions. Any classification restricted to a manageable number of categories is of necessity artificial. The traditional and still most widely accepted procedure has been to rely on insights derived from clinical observations in identifying recurring combinations of symptoms that appear to occur together as a cluster or syndrome. However, the variations in symptom constellation noted among mental patients merge and overlap to such an extent that decisions as to the number and kinds of diagnostic categories selected are necessarily arbitrary and subject to constant revision.

The classification systems in current use in various countries consist of eight to twelve major categories, most of which include subdivisions that provide for more specific diagnosis. Thus a particular patient's behavior may be classified as psychotic and diagnosed more precisely as a schizophrenic, manic, or depressive reaction. This traditional approach to classification has been consistently used by the American Psychiatric Association, whose members have been mainly responsible for the development of a uniform nomenclature system in the United States. The 1968 revision, which is described in the following section, is the most recent of a long series of essentially similar revisions dating back to 1917. General acceptance of the APA nomenclature system for diagnosis, preparation of statistical reports, and teaching purposes has given it official status in this country. The APA system and similar classifications adopted in other countries have served the important function of providing a convenient and reasonably effective method for organizing and recording the data of psychopathology. When applied and interpreted in a consistent fashion, the standard diagnostic labels provide a useful language for communicating technical information, though they have a number of shortcomings: (a) the recognized categories and subtypes have ill-defined, overlapping boundaries; (b) the inference that the separate categories constitute separate kinds of disorders is highly questionable; (c) the built-in rule of one diagnosis per patient ignores the wide range of significant differences among similarly diagnosed persons; and (d) the exclusive preoccupation with "symptoms" fails to take account of the patient's assets and strengths, which are as important to the total clinical picture as his defects.

1968 APA CLASSIFICATION (DSM-II)*

Recognizing the essential sameness of psychological disturbances in all countries, the World Health Organization has for some time been promoting a standard international nomenclature for diagnosis and classification. In 1968 the American Psychiatric Association officially adopted, with minor modifications, the Eighth Revision of the International Classification of Diseases. The ten major categories and the principal subtypes—which are described in greater detail in subsequent chapters—are listed and briefly described in Table 2.1.

The APA classification adheres closely to the medical model of disease. The first six categories (mental retardation, organic brain syndrome, psychosis, neurosis, psychophysiological disorders, and personality disorders) are considered to represent separate forms of mental illness. It is acknowledged that the remaining four categories may be

* The initials refer to *Diagnostic and Statistical Manual*, 2nd edition.

THE CLASSIFICATION OF PSYCHOSOCIAL PROBLEMS

interpreted as isolated reactions or situational maladjustments rather than clearly defined disorders. But the emphasis remains on the presence of symptoms. In principle, the symptoms constitute the main basis for choice of diagnosis. The diagnostic process consists in comparing the individual patient's behavior (as determined by clinical

Table 2.1. 1968 APA Classification of Mental Disorders (DSM-II).

Classification	Symptoms	Subcategories*
Mental retardation	Subnormal intellectual functioning, usually originating at birth or during early childhood; impairment of learning ability and social adjustment or maturation	Various, from borderline to profound; also differentiated with reference to associated physical condition

Organic brain syndrome (resulting from impairment of brain tissue function from whatever cause)	Impairment of orientation, memory, judgment, comprehension, learning ability, etc.; instability and shallowness of affect	Nonpsychotic organic brain syndrome
		Organic brain syndrome accompanied by psychotic symptoms:
		  senile dementia
		  alcoholic psychosis
		  cerebral arteriosclerosis
		  general paresis

Psychosis	Gross impairment of psychological functioning resulting in inability to meet ordinary demands of life; severe perceptual distortions (hallucinations, delusions); profound alterations in mood: marked impairment of thought and memory	Schizophrenia (disturbances in thinking, social withdrawal, bizarre behavior) Affective psychosis (extreme depression or elation that so dominates the mental life of the patient that he loses contact with his environment in either small or great degree) Paranoid states (delusions, usually persecutory or grandiose)

Neurosis	Anxiety, either directly felt and expressed or controlled by conversion, displacement, or other psychological mechanism; no gross distortion or misrepresentation of external reality; no gross personality disorganization	Various, including:
		  anxiety neurosis
		  phobias
		  hysteria
		  obsessive-compulsive neurosis
		  depressive neurosis
		  neurasthenia
		  depersonalization
		  hypochondria

* See the glossary for brief definitions of technical terms.

examination, psychological tests, and case-history data) with the symptom descriptions accompanying the categories. In actual practice, however, subjective considerations and the examiner's training background influence the choice of diagnosis.

Agreement among examining clinicians is fostered by their general acceptance of cer-

Classification	Symptoms	Subcategories
Psychophysiological (psychosomatic) disorders	Various physical symptoms caused by emotional factors; usually limited to symptoms involving a single organ system that is under control of autonomic nervous system	Mainly skin, musculoskeletal, respiratory, cardiovascular, gastrointestinal, and genito-urinary disorders of psychogenic origin
Personality disorders	Deeply ingrained behavior patterns related to patient's basic personality structure; generally recognizable by time of adolescence or earlier	Various, including: personality disorders sexual deviations alcoholism drug addiction or dependence
Special symptoms	Usually limited to a single specific symptom, which varies from patient to patient	Various, including: speech disorders specific learning problems tics and other psychomotor disorders sleep disorders feeding disorders eneuresis encopresis cephalalgia
Transient situational disturbances	Acute but temporary reactions to overwhelming environmental stress, with no apparent underlying mental disorder; symptoms vary in severity	Many, classified according to patient's developmental stage (adjustment reactions of infancy, childhood, adolescence, adult life, old age)
Behavior disorders of childhood and adolescence	Behavior disorders more transient and fluid than psychoses, neuroses, and personality disorders, but more stable, internalized, and resistant to treatment than transient situational disturbances	Various, including: hyperkinetic reaction withdrawing reaction overanxious reaction runaway reaction unsocialized aggressive reaction group delinquent reaction
Conditions without manifest psychiatric disorder and nonspecific conditions	Problems of sufficient severity to warrant examination and treatment although patients are psychiatrically normal	Various, including: social maladjustment marital maladjustment occupational maladjustment dyssocial behavior

tain rules. For example, when a patient exhibits a variety of symptoms that cut across two or more categories, the rule is to assign the diagnostic label that is associated with the more severe disorder. Thus a depressed or fearful patient who also presents hallucinations and delusions is diagnosed as psychotic rather than neurotic. Another rule is that the diagnosis of organic brain syndrome takes precedence over other possible diagnoses if there is any evidence of brain damage. The age of the patient is an important determining factor. A special category is reserved for children. Alcoholism in young people or incipient alcoholism at any age is classified as a personality disorder; chronic alcoholism in persons past middle age is usually categorized as chronic brain syndrome. The diagnosis of schizophrenia is preferred to affective disorder for a psychosis occurring during adolescence.

The choice of diagnostic category is also influenced by the duration of symptoms. Severe as well as mild reactions to known stressful experiences are classified as transient situational disturbances if they terminate in a few hours or days. If prolonged, the same reactions are assigned some other diagnostic label that seems to fit the persisting symptoms.

Evaluation

A serious limitation of the APA classification is that it fails to define what is a mental disorder or to spell out criteria for assigning a person to any particular category. After it has been decided that a person is suffering from some mental disorder, the descriptions of symptoms of the various disorders included in the APA manual provide a frame of reference for arriving at a specific diagnosis; but the manual is silent on the critical questions of how and on what basis the initial decision is made. The presence of symptoms may be a dependable indicator of certain physical diseases, since some physical symptoms (such as the presence of cancer cells or blood in the urine) are noted only in sick persons, but there are no absolute or fixed symptoms of mental disorders.

Any and all of the traits or reactions indentified as symptoms in the APA classification are also present in the general population. Whether a particular trait or reaction is considered normal or abnormal is determined by its attending consequences and society's evaluation of it. For example, if two fully clothed persons jump off a high bridge into ice-cold water within seconds of each other, the first may be described as suicidally depressed and the second as a hero.

Some so-called mental symptoms differ mainly in degree from similar personality traits commonly noted in the general population. Among alleged symptoms that actually represent intensified "normal" personality traits are extreme suspiciousness, heightened irritability, excessive dependency, and emotional instability. As previously indicated, other so-called mental symptoms differ from "normal" reactions to overwhelming stress mainly in severity, duration, and appropriateness. A strong case could be made for interpreting the "disorders" included in the APA classification as various ways in which human beings often react to stress. This explanation is readily applicable to manic excitement, depressive-surrender reactions, alcoholism, runaway behavior in children, and the emotional over-responsiveness of neurotics. In addition, schizophrenia could be considered a massive social withdrawal reaction and paranoia a form of projection marked by heightened defensiveness and belligerence, all of which are exhibited at one time or another by just about everyone.

A second major criticism is the misleading implication that the ten listed categories constitute separate and distinct disorders. The clearly defined symptomatic distinctions made between categories in manuals and textbooks do not hold up when applied to actual patients. Symptoms that are considered key characteristics of a particular disorder are often absent in patients diagnosed as suffering from that disorder, but may be present in patients placed in some other category. This overlapping of symptoms across clinically defined categories has been documented in a statistical study conducted by Zigler and Phillips (1961). Some representative findings are summarized in Table 2.2. The investigators concluded that "although some relationships exist between symptoms and diagnoses, the magnitude of these relationships is generally so small that membership in a particular diagnostic group conveys only minimal information about the symptomatology for the patient."

For classification purposes, it may be expedient to include in the same diagnostic category individuals who share certain traits or behavior styles; but it is a mistake to assume that persons assigned to a particular category constitute a homogeneous group. Similarly diagnosed persons are known to differ markedly in their personality assets and liabilities, the constellation and severity of their symptoms, their prospects for recovery, and their responsiveness to specific therapies. Nor is it safe to assume that patients who exhibit similar symptoms

share similar developmental histories, inasmuch as the same syndromes may result from varying combinations of causes. Failure to take account of the heterogeneity of patients to whom the same diagnostic label has been applied has been a major obstacle in research efforts aimed at identifying the causes of particular disorders and devising specific treatments for them.

Finally, the APA classification lacks cohesiveness. There is no consistent, unifying rationale. Mental deficiency, for example, is totally unrelated to the other disorders. Some disorders are differentiated on the basis of their presumed cause, others on the basis of the age of the patient or the social setting associated with the behavior disturbance.

The most cogent argument for continued use of the traditional diagnostic categories included in the APA classification is that some orderly medium for the systematic

Table 2.2. The Overlap of Symptoms Observed Across Diagnostic Categories (Percentages of Individuals Manifesting Each Symptom).

Symptom	Total sample (N = 793)	Manic-depressive behavior (N = 75)	Psycho-neurotic behavior (N = 152)	Character disorder (N = 279)	Schizo-phrenic behavior (N = 287)
Depression	38%	64%	58%	31%	28%
Suspiciousness	35	25	16	17	65
Hallucinations	19	11	4	12	35
Suicidal ideas	15	29	23	15	8
Withdrawal	14	4	12	7	25
Assaultiveness	12	5	6	18	5
Self-depreciation	12	16	16	8	13
Maniacal outbursts	9	11	6	7	12
Bizarre ideas	9	11	1	2	20
Apathy	8	8	8	4	11
Euphoria	5	17	2	2	5
Mood swings	5	9	5	4	4

Adapted from E. Zigler and L. Phillips, "Psychiatric Diagnoses and Symptomatology," *Journal of Abnormal and Social Psychology*, 63 (1961): 69–75.

organization of the data of psychopathology is essential for teaching and administrative purposes and for meaningful communication among professional workers. Alternative proposals, which we shall consider later, are still being explored. Until some better system is devised, tested, and widely accepted, there is no real choice. On the plus side, retention of the traditional nomenclature has the following advantages:

1. Official acceptance of the 1968 revision by the American Psychiatric Association guarantees that, barring some dramatic change, it will continue for several years to be the nationally accepted reference for the preparation of local, state, and national statistical reports on mental disorders in the United States.
2. The 1968 revision is very similar to the recommended international classification, and its use therefore facilitates cross-cultural comparative studies.
3. The research literature of past and current studies is based on the use of the traditional APA nomenclature. Much of this material could be discarded without any great loss, but some is highly informative and valuable.
4. The traditional diagnostic labels have considerable empirical usefulness in identifying the nature and extent of psychosocial malfunctioning and in differentiating severe, moderate, mild, and transient disturbances. For example, a diagnosis of paranoid state conveys a great deal of information about the patient's behavior, however blurred the category may be for other purposes.

In view of these advantages, we are justified in using the 1968 APA revision. On the other hand, there is no need to accept this classification uncritically and in toto. By the simple expedient of redefining concepts and terms it is possible to correct some of the more obvious errors of the APA classification. In line with this compromise solution, the term "mental disorder" is used in this book to refer to defects in psychosocial functioning that differ mainly in degree and duration from similar disturbances in functioning that are commonly noted in normal individuals. The traditional diagnostic terms will be used simply as convenient labels for describing certain kinds of reaction patterns or clusters of traits that tend to occur together. In other words, only the symptom information customarily associated with the traditional diagnostic categories will be retained. Thus the designation "schizophrenia" merely indicates the general behavior pattern exhibited by a patient. This is quite different from referring to an individual as a schizophrenic, or implying that he is the victim of a specific disorder called schizophrenia. When I designate a person as schizophrenic, I mean that he is out of touch with and seemingly indifferent to his social environment, is more or less exclusively absorbed with his inner private world, and exhibits any of a variety of related symptoms. With these reservations and modifications in mind, we can now proceed to a general description of the traditional diagnostic categories as listed in the 1968 APA classification.

TRADITIONAL DIAGNOSTIC CATEGORIES

Mental Retardation

Older labels for the condition we now call *mental retardation* include mental deficiency and feeblemindedness. Diagnosis is based on intelligence testing and social history data that indicate subnormal intellectual functioning from infancy or early childhood, with impairment of learning or social maturation or both. The degree of retardation may be indicated by such terms as borderline, mild, moderate, severe, and profound. In addition, patients may be classified with respect to associated or known cause. The main clinical subcategories include retardation following infection, intoxication, trauma, or some other physical agent, and retardation associated with disorders of metabolism, gross brain disease, diseases and conditions due to unknown prenatal influence, chromosomal abnormality, premature birth, or psychosocial or environmental deprivation. Mental retardation has strong historical ties with clinical psychology and psychiatry, but in recent years medicine and education have become increasingly involved in this field.

Organic Brain Syndrome

Organic brain syndrome is a broad category that includes all mental disorders, exclusive of mental retardation, that are caused by or associated with diffuse impairment of brain tissue function from any cause. The basic common syndrome consists of mild to severe impairment of orientation, memory, comprehension, learning ability, and judgment, plus instability and shallowness of feelings. This constellation of symptoms is directly attributable to impairment of brain tissue functioning. In addition to the core syndrome, patients with brain disorders may also exhibit a variety of psychotic, neurotic, or other behavioral symptoms. These associated or superimposed symptoms may be precipitated by the organic brain disorder, but they are more directly related to the patient's inherent personality, emotional conflicts, home situation, and other psychosocial factors.

A distinction is made between acute and chronic brain disorders and between psychotic and nonpsychotic disorders. The term "acute" is applied to reversible or temporary disorders, such as the symptoms associated with alcoholic intoxication. When the brain has been permanently damaged, the condition is referred to as chronic. Patients with acute or chronic brain damage are classified as psychotic if their psychosocial functioning is so grossly impaired that they are unable to meet the ordinary demands of life. The principal psychoses associated with organic brain syndrome are senile dementia, psychosis with cerebral arteriosclerosis, alcoholic psychosis, and psychosis with epilepsy.

Senile dementia is a diagnosis applied to elderly persons, usually over sixty-five years old, who manifest some evidence of organic brain syndrome. The symptoms include impairment of memory for recent events, self-centeredness, disorientation, difficulty in assimilating new experiences, and childish emotionality. Deterioration may be minimal or may progress to a vegetative existence. Psychosis with *cerebral arteriosclerosis* is a chronic disorder distinguished by blockage of the cerebral arteries. Characteristic symptoms include mental confusion, impairment in learning and memory, poor judgment, and emotional instability. The category of psychosis with *epilepsy* is restricted to epileptic seizures of unknown or genetic origin, in which the psychotic component consists of clouding of consciousness before or after a convulsive attack. At such times the patient may be extremely confused, experience hallucinations, be terrified, or engage in acts of violence.

The diagnosis of nonpsychotic organic brain syndrome is applied to brain-damaged patients exhibiting only the core syndrome, or the core syndrome plus other relatively mild behavioral disturbances.

Psychosis

The label of *psychosis* is essentially restricted to the most severe behavior disorders that occur in adults and children. A differentiation has historically been made between organic psychoses, associated with observable or presumed brain damage, and functional psychoses, in which there is no clear evidence of gross organic pathology. Organic psychoses are classified as organic brain syndrome. When no specific mention is made of organic involvement, the term "psychosis" refers to so-called *functional* disorders. The general assumption is that functional disorders are mainly due to the interaction of predisposing genetic defects and adverse life experiences. The specific symptoms associated with psychotic behavior vary considerably from patient to patient and may overlap with similar symptoms observed in patients assigned to other diagnostic categories.

A distinctive feature of psychotic behavior is that it is relatively independent of voluntary control or external reality. The psychotic individual may be troubled by unwanted thoughts or emotions that are inappropriate to his current life, or he may report sensations and perceptions that either have no factual external basis or that represent a gross misinterpretation of actual events. A second distinctive feature consists of varying degrees of personality disintegration with consequent impairment in personal and social functioning. As a rule, the behavior of psychotic individuals is so defective and disorganized that they require care or supervision. Most psychotic patients are unable to relate effectively to other persons, to support themselves, or to manage their affairs with reasonable competence. When the patient's behavior endangers his life or presents an intolerable threat or severe distress to the community, voluntary or compulsory commitment to a mental hospital is usually recommended. Otherwise, treatment in the home, a general hospital, or an outpatient clinic is currently favored.

The psychotic person finds it difficult or impossible to differentiate between fantasies and actual experiences. Wishes tend to be confused with facts; imagined dangers, slights, and misdeeds are accepted as real, and real ones are grossly exaggerated or misinterpreted. Whereas normal people attempt to adapt their behavior to the expectations and demands of the physical and social environment, the psychotic's reactions are dominated by inner dictates. In the context of his private, inner orientations, a psychotic individual's overt behavior may be meaningful and logical; but to an outsider, unaware of what is going on in the patient's mind, the ideas, feelings, and actions he expresses may well seem irrational and frightening in their apparent lack of control and in their unpredictability. It is difficult even for a close friend to understand why a formerly quiet,

polite student should one day stand up in class, accuse the professor of reading his mind and stealing his ideas, and later barricade himself in his room and threaten to kill anyone who tries to enter.

The disintegration of personality and distortion of reality characteristic of psychoses are strikingly apparent in *delusions* and *hallucinations*. Delusions are persistent false beliefs, out of keeping with the individual's cultural background, which he uncritically accepts as true. Thus a patient may mistakenly but firmly believe that people are talking about him and spreading lies about him, that he has unusual powers, that his body has been changed in some mysterious way, or that he has committed some unmentionable sin. Hallucinations consist of sensory perceptions experienced while awake in the absence of pertinent external stimuli. In contrast to an illusion, which represents an erroneous perception of a real sensory impression—mistaking a twisted branch for a snake, for instance—a hallucination is a cerebral or mental phenomenon that is produced independently of the sense organs. In the words of Jean Esquirol, who initially described the psychological nature of hallucinations in 1817: "A person is said to labor under a hallucination . . . who has a thorough conviction of the perception of a sensation, when no external object, suited to excite this sensation, has impressed the senses." Most hallucinations are auditory: the patient "hears" voices. Second in order of frequency are visions. Gustatory, olfactory, and kinesthetic hallucinations are relatively uncommon and difficult to differentiate from illusions.

The reaction of patients to hallucinations is variable. When the content of the experience is pleasant or is interpreted as a favorable message from God, the patient may be amused or elated. As a rule, however, hallucinations are perceived as warnings, threats, and accusations that evoke alarm, anger, and fear. The voices may be fought against or automatically obeyed. Hallucinations are independent of the sense organ's ability to function as well as of

*Self-portrait (1888) by
the Belgian artist James
Ensor of terrifying
hallucinatory
experiences.
Hallucinations in
mental patients usually
consist of accusatory,
deriding, and
threatening voices that
the tormented victim
is powerless to turn off.*

external stimuli. Blind patients may "see" visions and deaf patients may "hear" voices if at some time in the past their vision or hearing has been normal. The "voices" are widely interpreted as representing the externalized projection of the patient's own thoughts. In effect, the patient is covertly talking to himself. (McGuigen [1966] has demonstrated that the onset of auditory hallucinations is preceded by an increase in covert oral behavior, as measured by a recording instrument attached to the larynx.) Delusions and hallucinations are not exclusively limited to psychotic persons. Other types of mental patients, and normal persons as well, may also hold onto false beliefs and experience hallucinations. What distinguishes psychotic behavior is not the presence or absence of delusions and hallucinations per se, but rather the extent to which they dominate and distort the person's perceptions, feelings, and actions.

Psychotic reactions are subdivided into three major categories: *schizophrenia, af-fective disorders*, and *paranoid states*. Schizophrenia is distinguished by disturbances in thinking and social withdrawal. The affective psychoses include extreme mood swings that usually terminate in good recovery after a few weeks or months. During the acute phase patients may be excited, elated, and hyperactive, or depressed, sad, and underactive. In contrast to other psychotic reactions that are accompanied by a general disorganization of personality and gross impairment in general functioning, paranoia and paranoid states consist mainly of a persecutory or grandiose delusional system in an otherwise relatively intact personality. The patient's functioning is unaffected in areas outside his delusional system.

Neurosis

The terms *psychoneurosis* and *neurosis* are used interchangeably. Neurotic behavior is distinguished from psychotic behavior by the relative absence of significant personality disorganization and the absence of gross impairment in reality testing and in social functioning. Persons described as neurotic may repress or attempt to ignore unpleasant facts, but they do not distort or falsify external reality to the extent of experiencing delusions and hallucinations. Neurotic reactions are a source of acute personal distress and they frequently interfere with the individual's capacity for enjoyment and achievement, but they do not interfere unduly with his ability to carry on his work and other routine activities. Treatment, if any, is usually conducted in outpatient clinics and therapists' offices. As a rule, the neurotic takes the initiative in seeking therapy.

The chief characteristic of neurosis is anxiety, which is often mixed with guilt feelings. A favored theory is that neurotic anxiety is an expression of unconscious inner conflicts. The anxiety may be directly expressed in the form of an overwhelming feeling of apprehension with concomitant rapid heartbeat, difficulty in breathing, and related physical symptoms associated with acute emotional disturbances. Other neurotic reactions include

Table 2.3. Psychoses and Neuroses Compared.

Psychoses	Neuroses
Marked loss of voluntary control over thoughts, emotions, and impulses. A psychosis may be compared to the automatic turning on of a master switch that takes over and regulates the individual's perceptions, feelings, and actions.	Some impairment of volition, but the individual is aware of the threatened loss of self-control. With effort, he can usually moderate the loss or resume control.
Impaired capacity for differentiating between reality and subjective experiences. Fantasies are accepted as events. Reality may be altered by the substitution of subjective experiences (delusions and hallucinations).	The individual can discriminate between reality and subjective experiences, but personal factors may unduly influence and distort perception of external stimuli and events. The individual may try to ignore reality, but he does not substitute subjective experiences for it.
The patient accepts his condition. He may not realize or may deny there is anything wrong with him or his behavior. He lives his psychosis.	The neurotic is aware of the presence of symptoms, and in most instances tries to control them and seeks outside help.
Marked personality disorganization. Capacity for effective and appropriate social functioning is particularly impaired. Hospitalization or supervised home care is usually required.	Functioning capacity may be lowered but personality remains relatively intact, so that the individual may continue to function relatively effectively with respect to his regular occupational, home, social, and community affairs. Interpersonal relations may be disturbing but are not destroyed.

amnesia, irrational fears, dual personality, chronic fatigue, obsessive thoughts, compulsive rituals, depressed feelings, and hysterical conversion symptoms. These varied reactions are thought to represent indirect manifestations of or defenses against basic anxiety. Some of the main criteria used to differentiate neuroses from psychoses are summarized in Table 2.3.

Psychophysiological Disorders

Psychophysiological disorders, more popularly called psychosomatic disorders, are caused by emotional factors and are characterized by physical symptoms involving a single organ system, usually one that is under the control of the autonomic nervous system, such as the respiratory, cardiovascular, and gastrointestinal systems. Emotional factors appear to be especially significant in such disorders as hypertension, peptic ulcer, asthma, anorexia (loss of appetite), menstrual difficulties, migraine, and dermatitis. Since these disorders may also have physical causes, it is important to rule out any possible physical cause before assuming their psychological origin.

Personality Disorders

Personality disorders include a variety of deeply ingrained maladaptive patterns of behavior that appear to be directly related to the basic personality makeup of the individual. Subjective anxiety is minimal. This designation is somewhat confusing, since all psychological disturbances may be described as personality disorders; an alternate label that is often applied is *character disorders*. A further source of possible confusion is the fact that one of the four subtypes listed in the APA classification is also referred to as "personality disorders." This subcategory consists mainly of individuals who in personality structure resemble psychotics or neurotics—people with paranoid personalities, explosive personalities, hysterical personalities, and passive-aggressive personalities—but are not now either psychotic or neurotic. The three other subcategories are sexual deviations, alcoholism, and drug dependence.

Special Symptoms

The category of special symptoms is restricted to patients whose psychopathology is manifested by a single specific symptom, such as reading disability, insomnia, stuttering, and anorexia nervosa (loss of appetite accompanied by emaciation). Common fear reactions present in otherwise normal persons—fears of dogs, snakes, spiders, riding in airplanes, and so on—are more appropriately included in this category than regarded as neurotic phobias.

Transient Situational Disturbances

This category is reserved for acute reactions to overwhelming stress that occur in individuals without any apparent underlying mental disorder. The reaction may be mild or severe. Symptomatic manifestations may be similar to those associated with neurosis, psychosis, or other disorders. The critical factor is that the disturbance is a *transient* reaction to a specific stress. If the symptoms persist after the stress is removed, another diagnosis is indicated. Panic reactions to terrifying experiences and grief over the death of a loved one would be included under this heading. Other examples include the jealousy reactions of children to the birth of a sibling, depressive reactions following school failure, anxiety related to separation (by death or distance) from people on whom one is dependent, fear reactions associated with military combat, and feelings of rejection and worthlessness associated with forced retirement in elderly persons.

Behavior Disorders of Childhood and Adolescence

Behavior disturbances in children which resemble those seen in adults are assigned the same diagnostic labels as those applied to adults. The use of subcategories, such as childhood schizophrenia, takes care of age-related variations in symptomatology. The category of "Behavior Disorders of Childhood and Adolescence" is intended for behavior that does not fit any of the adult categories or that is mainly observed in children and adolescents. Six main subtypes are described in DSM-II.

1. Hyperkinetic reaction, marked by overactivity, restlessness, distractibility, and short attention span.
2. Withdrawal reaction, characterized by shyness, timidity, seclusiveness, detachment, and sensitivity.
3. Overanxious reaction, distinguished by chronic anxiety, excessive and unrealistic fears, nightmares, gross lack of self-confidence, inhibition, and immaturity.
4. Runaway reaction, diagnosed when a child stays away from home for a day or more, usually because he feels rejected.
5. Unsocialized aggressive reaction, characterized by disobedience, quarrelsomeness, physical or verbal aggressiveness, destructiveness, stealing, lying, and hostile teasing of other children.
6. Group delinquent reaction, in which the individual has acquired the values and behavior pattern of a delinquent peer group; this behavior may include stealing, truancy, staying out late, and sexual delinquency.

Conditions without Manifest Psychiatric Disorder

This category is reserved for basically normal persons who present problems of varying severity that are more appropriately described as maladjustments than as diagnosable mental disorders. Examples include marital problems, occupational maladjustments, and difficulties associated with adapting to an unfamiliar culture or conflicts arising from divided loyalties to two cultures. This category may also be used for individuals—for example, racketeers and prostitutes—who engage in *dyssocial* *behavior* but are not classifiable as antisocial personalities.

PREVALENCE AND INCIDENCE OF PSYCHOSOCIAL DISORDERS

Statistics on the occurrence of mental disorders are usually expressed in terms of expectancy, prevalence, and incidence rates. Expectancy figures represent actuarial predictions of the probability that a person may be expected to develop a mental disorder at some time during his life. Prevalence rates indicate the total number of mentally disturbed persons per unit of population as of a particular time. Incidence rates indicate the number of new cases occurring during the year per 100,000 of the general population.

With the exception of field studies, which usually include both treated and untreated cases, most statistical reports are limited to treated cases. The magnitude of expectancy, prevalence, and incidence rates is a function of the criteria employed (Dohrenwend and Dohrenwend, 1965). If only grossly incapacitating or definitely harmful reactions that persist for several months were counted, about 10 percent of the population might be expected to develop a severe mental disorder (exclusive of senile deterioration) sometime during their lives. A rough estimate is that on any particular day about 2 percent of the total population show moderate to severe disturbances in psychosocial functioning (the prevalence rate). Another 1 percent develop a serious problem during the year (the incidence rate). If transient difficulties that last only a few days and mild disturbances were included, the lifetime expectancy, current prevalence rate, and incidence rate would have to be multiplied by at least four.

Data with respect to the relative incidence of particular disorders vary with the type of treatment facility examined. Comparative figures on outpatients and hospitalized patients are reported in Table 2.4. For persons attending outpatient clinics, the most common diagnosis is neurosis. Next in order of frequency are schizophrenia, transient situational reactions, and personality disorders. Together these four disorders account for over 60 percent of all admissions to outpatient services. Each of the other listed diagnoses (alcohol disorders, behavior disorders in children and adolescents, affective psychosis, other organic brain syndromes, drug disorders, and mental retardation) is responsible only for 3 to 5 percent of outpatient admissions. The figures for diagnostic categories among persons attending community mental health centers are very similar to those noted for clinic outpatients.

The distribution of patients admitted to state and county mental hospitals is quite different. In the United States every other person admitted to a public mental hospital is labeled as either a schizophrenic or an alcoholic; each of these two categories accounts for about 25 percent of all hospital admissions. The diagnosis of "other organic brain syndromes," which is mainly applied to elderly persons, covers 11 percent of admissions. About one out of ten persons admitted is diagnosed as suffering from neurosis. The proportional representation of affective psychosis, drug-related disorders, and mental retardation is about the same among inpatients and outpatients; each of these diagnostic categories accounts for 3 to 4 percent of hospital admissions.

RELIABILITY OF DIAGNOSIS

The usual procedure in evaluating the reliability of diagnosis is to ascertain the degree of agreement between two or more clini-

Table 2.4. The Incidence of Disorders by Diagnosis and by Treatment Facility (Admissions to Outpatient Psychiatric Services and to State and County Mental Hospitals, 1969).

| | Percent of total admissions | |
| | Outpatient psychiatric services N = 881,000 | State and county mental hospitals N = 368,000 |
Diagnosis		
Neuroses	19	9
Schizophrenia	17	27
Transient situational reactions	15	—
Personality disorders	11	7
Alcoholic disorders	5	26
Childhood behavior disorders	5	—
Conditions without manifest psychiatric disorders	5	—
Affective psychoses	3	4
Other organic brain syndromes	3	11
Drug disorders	2	3
Mental retardation	3	3
All other disorders	12	10

SOURCE: National Institute of Mental Health, Survey and Reports Section, Statistical Notes 26-50, September 1971.

cians classifying the same patient. Most of the older studies stress the low reliability of psychiatric diagnosis. However, Beck (1962) and others have noted that these earlier investigations were poorly controlled. Methodological errors in earlier studies included a small number of cases, the selection of nonrepresentative patient populations, marked differences in experience and training among judges, lack of uniform information about patients, and long time intervals between first and second diagnoses. When attempts have been made to correct for these errors, reliability figures have been more encouraging. Summary findings based on later studies (Schmidt and Fonda, 1956; Norris, 1959; Kreitman et al., 1961; and Sandifer et al., 1964) indicate 80-90 percent agreement among judges for organic brain syndrome, 75-85 percent agreement for psychoses, and 55-70 percent agreement for neuroses. For all mental patients reported on two separate occasions to a central psychiatric register, Babigan (1965) noted 79 percent agreement between initial and subsequent diagnoses by different examiners. These reliability figures for the major categories are quite impressive, particularly when the vagueness of the categories, the subjectivity of the evaluative process, and the contaminating effect of examiner bias are taken into account (Matarazzo, 1965). With respect to more specific diagnosis, interexaminer agreement of about 70 percent has been reported in several studies of schizophrenia. Reliability studies indicate low diagnostic consistency for other types of psychoses and neuroses.

The process by which different examiners arrive at the same diagnosis is not clearly understood. Clinicians typically explain their agreement by noting that diagnosis is made on the basis of the symptomatic picture presented by the patient. This explanation is not very convincing, since experienced clinicians are well aware that many symptoms are associated with more than one diagnosis. A more cogent explanation is that examiners tend to make unconscious interpretations of the social significance of particular symptoms or combinations of symptoms. When symptoms are associated with serious impairment in functioning, a diagnosis of psychosis is made. Patients with similar symptoms who exhibit mild impairment are assigned some more benign diagnosis, such as neurosis or personality disorder. Experimental evidence relating psychiatric diagnosis to level of social competence has been reported by Phillips, Broverman, and Zigler (1966).

Since psychiatric diagnoses influence the clinical conception of the nature of the disorder, the choice of treatment, and the prognosis, it is reassuring to know that the labels assigned to patients have some measure of reliability. Positive findings of diagnostic consistency among examiners, however, should not be regarded as proof of the existence of separate major categories. Interjudge agreement in diagnosis is contingent on the judges' learning and adhering to a predetermined set of differentiating criteria. By accepting and following a standard set of guidelines, a number of examiners can easily agree 80 or more percent of the time when they place people in discrete categories even on the basis of traits that are obviously not discrete at all, but arbitrary points on a continuum—tall, medium, short, for example, or bright, average, and dull.

THE "SEPARATE DISORDER" CONTROVERSY

The great majority of psychopathologists today agree that—with the possible exception of certain psychoses—most so-called mental disorders are disorders in name only. The conventional psychiatric labels serve to identify and differentiate behavior patterns that essentially differ in intensity, appropriateness, and severity of distress from similar behavior observed in "normal" persons. This broad use of the term "disorder" applies to maladaptive personality types, paranoid states, alcoholism, drug abuse, suicidal behavior, antisocial behavior, sex deviations, and most behavior problems noted in children and adolescents. The controversy regarding the concept of specific and separate disorders is more or less confined to two questions. Is there a clear difference between psychosis and neurosis? Are schizophrenia and manic depressive psychosis two separate and distinct disorders?

The neurosis vs. psychosis issue boils down to neurosis vs. schizophrenia. There may be significant differences between neurotic and psychotic depressions, but the overlap in symptoms makes it difficult to defend the hypothesis that the two are separate disorders. Clinical and research data with respect to the relation of neurosis to schizophrenia have been reviewed by Rosenthal (1970). His findings may be interpreted as supporting either the notion of separate disorders or of variations in degree. Most persons initially diagnosed as suffering from a neurosis retain this diagnosis throughout their patient status. If their condition worsens over time, the change in diagnosis is from mild to severe neurosis. On the other hand, some individuals initially show neurotic symptoms and then move on to psychotic symptoms. Others, described as cases of *pseudoneurotic schizophrenia*, exhibit a mixture of symptoms. Studies of the developmental histories of schizophrenic patients indicate that many show earlier signs of heightened anxiety, obsessive compulsive traits, and other neurotic symptoms. Genetic investigations of the families of schizophrenic patients have consistently revealed a high incidence of neurosis and of antisocial behavior among their siblings and children.

Studies of the effect of external stress on the incidence of neurosis and psychosis provide more consistent evidence in favor of the separate disorder concept. On examining the incidence of psychiatric disorders among military personnel over a period of many years, Glass (1957) found that the severity of external stress had a direct effect on the incidence of neurotic behavior, but no demonstrable impact on the incidence of psychosis. The incidence of neurotic behavior in the armed forces is higher in wartime than during peace. It rises when combat stress is high and drops when battle stress is reduced. Victorious units have a lower incidence of neurotic reactions than defeated or demoralized units. On the other hand, the incidence rate of psychotic behavior among members of the armed forces is about the same year after year and is unaffected by war, peace, the severity of combat stress, defeats, or victories. Data on civilian populations also indicate that severe stresses increase the incidence of neurotic behavior but have no significant effect on the relative occurrence of psychotic behavior (Reid, 1961). These findings suggest that psychotic reactions are mainly determined by constitutional factors whereas neurotic reactions are more influenced by current stress situations. Consistent with these differences, the traditional approach has been to favor drugs, shock techniques, and other biological forms of therapy for psychosis, and psychotherapy for neurosis.

With respect to the relation of schizophrenia to manic depressive psychosis, Rosenthal (1970) concluded from his survey of the literature that the two disorders, in their more typical manifestations, are genetically distinct. The usual rule is for children to develop the same psychosis as their parents. Children of manic depressive parents, if they should become psychotic, occasionally develop schizophrenia, but schizophrenic parents rarely have manic depressive children. Studies of psychosis in identical twins indicate that when one is a clear-cut schizophrenic, the other is never a clear-cut manic depressive. The clinical features of the two disorders in their typical form are different. Schizophrenia is primarily characterized by thought disturbances; manic depressive psychosis is mainly a disorder of mood, affect, and activity level. Their course and outcome are also different. Manic depressive attacks are usually of short duration;

Karl A. Menninger, a prominent and highly influential leader in American psychiatry and the mental health movement for many years. His advocacy of the unitary concept of mental disorders (1963) is one of his more recent contributions.

they may recur, but in between attacks, the person shows no obvious signs of psychopathology. Schizophrenia is more a permanent life style marked by periodic variations in the intensity of symptoms. Finally, the two disorders respond differently to the same treatment. Electroshock and antidepressant drugs are highly effective in the treatment of psychotic depressions, while neither of these treatments are effective with schizophrenics. Lithium salts are very effective in controlling manic excitement, but they have little value in calming disturbed schizophrenics. These sharp differences, however, only hold for typical and clear-cut cases. In less typical cases, the boundary lines are blurred. A substantial number of patients, usually diagnosed as "schizo-affective," show a mixture of schizophrenic and manic depressive symptoms.

Unitary Concept

Karl Menninger (1963), an American psychoanalyst, has been an outspoken critic of the concept of separate and distinct psychiatric categories. He advocates a unitary concept in which health and disease are viewed as opposite ends of a continuum. The normal end of the continuum is represented by health, happiness, success, and achievement. At the disease end, there is misery, failure, and delirium. Mental health is not static; it fluctuates along the scale in accordance with the stresses the individual experiences and his adaptive resources. Successive stages can be marked off on the continuum to indicate the relative severity of mental illness as reflected in degree of disorganization, lack of control, personal discomfort, and social maladjustment. Menninger interprets symptoms as emergency devices that the individual uses to help restore his equilibrium when it is threatened. At first, relatively mild devices are employed. If these succeed, they may continue for as long as they are needed and then disappear. If these mild regulatory devices fail, however, the individual may be forced to resort to more drastic devices at an increased cost in impaired functioning and inner suffering.

The progressive stages or levels of dysfunction described by Menninger are summarized in Figure 2.1. Normal coping devices that usually are of short duration or have negligible adverse effects include crying, boasting, daydreaming, retreat into sleep, and moderate use of alcohol. If the stress persists and the individual is unable to work out a better solution, first-level dysfunction symptoms may appear—worry, somatic complaints, impotence, and so on. Depending on his adaptive resources and life circumstances, the individual may move upward toward health or step down further.

Symptoms at the second level of dysfunction represent more desperate emergency reactions, and the devices employed to cope with them are those traditionally labeled as neurosis or character disorder.

Movement from this level may also be up or down. If it's down, the next step is a breakdown of control and the emergence of aggressive-hostile behavior. The fourth level of dysfunction represents an admission of defeat that is associated with futile protests, inward withdrawal, despondency, confusion, and general disorganization. Even the "psychotic" level may be transitory, a temporary retreat from life. There is still a good possibility that treatment and the natural recuperative processes of the organism will restore equilibrium and put the patient back on the road to health. The fifth stage is the end of the line, and

Mental health
● Normal coping devices:
  crying, working, sleeping, boasting, use of alcoholic beverages, daydreaming.

● First level of dysfunction:
  worry, instability, inhibition, minor somatic symptoms, mild sexual dysfunction.

● Second level of dysfunction:
  fainting, phobias, intoxication, compulsions, self-mutilation, perverse sexual behavior, inadequate personality, use of addictive drugs.

● Third level of dysfunction:
  breakdown in control of aggressive impulses leading to chronic or episodic acts of violence.

● Fourth level of dysfunction:
  pervasive feelings of despondency and hopelessness; erratic disorganized excitement; bizarre behavior, mutism, posturing, incoherent speech; paranoid delusional themes; confused delirious states.

● Fifth level of dysfunction:
  gross deterioration, suicide, continuous wild excitement leading to death from exhaustion.

Mental illness

Figure 2.1. Menninger's Unitary Concept of Mental Disorders. Symptoms are here interpreted as emergency coping reactions to stress rather than as manifestations of specific diseases. The severity of symptoms is related to and fluctuates with the severity of mental disequilibrium.

there is little hope of return.

It is apparent that Menninger has no quarrel with the concept of mental illness. He accepts the occurrence of the traditional, clinically observed syndromes. His main contention is that these syndromes, along with other manifest symptoms, should be regarded as variations in the level or degree of dysfunction rather than as separate disorders.

The underlying premise that the same individual may at various times exhibit "neurotic" or "psychotic" symptoms has significant implications. For example, it might be argued that if the various reaction patterns of mentally disordered persons represent makeshift adjustments to life problems, there can be no sound justification for research directed toward the discovery of disorder-specific causes and disorder-specific therapies. Instead, research efforts might more profitably be concentrated on general causes applicable to all types of abnormal behavior and on broad-spectrum therapies. But the issue isn't that simple. There remains the troublesome problem of explaining why some patients stop at the first or second level of dysfunction while others drop down to level four or five. And why do some patients show good recovery while others remain at the same levels for long periods or progressively decline? One possible explanation is that differences in genetic endowment and life experiences contribute to individual differences in adaptive resources. In other words, the causes, and possibly the required treatment, for higher level (psychotic) dysfunctions differ from those for lower level dysfunctions.

Statistically Identified Syndromes

Starting in 1933 with the pioneer studies of T. V. Moore, researchers have attempted to develop more objective and precise classification systems based on statistical evidence rather than clinical impressions. The procedure is known as the "factorial" approach. The first step consists in collecting pertinent observational, interview, or test information on a large, heterogeneous population of mental patients. These data are then analyzed with the aid of appropriate statistical techniques to locate related traits or "factors" that occur together as a cluster and that are relatively independent of other symptom clusters or syndromes. The factorial approach has been employed in distinguishing the main syndromes noted in behavior problems in children (Dreger et al., 1964), in neuroses (O'Connor, 1953), and in psychoses (Wittenborn, 1964).

The series of studies on the syndromes of psychoses reported by Lorr, Klett, and McNair (1963) provides a good example of the method. These investigators developed a special scale (Inpatient Multidimensional Psychiatric Scale) consisting of seventy-five behavioral items. Using the scale as a guide, the examiner interviews the patient and then rates all items. His findings are converted to standard scores that indicate the patient's relative standing with respect to each of the basic syndromes identified. The ten major syndromes defined by Lorr and his associates are described in Table 2.5. These syndromes were initially established by studies of patients in the United States. Similar psychotic syndromes have been reported in studies of hospitalized patients in Japan and five European countries (Lorr and Klett, 1969). In a more recent study, Lorr, Klett, and Cave (1967) reduce the ten psychotic syndromes listed in Table 2.5 to five higher order constructs. These are hypothesized to represent disorganized hyperactivity, schizophrenic disorganization, paranoid process, hostile paranoia, and anxious depression.

As is apparent, the syndromes isolated by statistical techniques correspond fairly well with recognized clinical syndromes. The agreement is not surprising, since the traditional diagnostic categories are based on the observed recurrence of certain clusters of symptoms. There are, however, some critical differences. In contrast to the traditional reliance on subjective clinical

Table 2.5. Ten Major Syndromes of Psychosis.

Syndrome	Characteristics
Excitement	Lack of restraint, excessive speed in speech and action, elevated mood, overactivity, dominance over others
Hostile belligerence	Irritability, suspiciousness, bitterness, contempt and criticism of others
Paranoid projection	Patient believes that people talk about, conspire against, and persecute him; he feels controlled by external forces
Grandiose expansiveness	Attitude of superiority; patient hears voices praising him, believes he has unusual powers
Perceptual distortion	Patient hears voices, sees visions, believes familiar things have changed
Anxious intropunitiveness	Patient is critical of himself, apprehensive, depressed, suicidal; expresses feelings of guilt and sinfulness
Retardation and apathy	Slowed speech and movements, lack of goals; patient is uncommunicative, forgetful
Disorientation	Patient does not know where he is, how old he is, the season of the year
Motor disturbances	Patient assumes peculiar postures, talks to himself, grins or giggles inappropriately
Conceptual disorganization	Patient gives irrelevant or incoherent answers to questions, repeats words or fixed phrases, drifts away from the subject under discussion

Adapted from M. Lorr, C. J. Klett, and D. M. McNair, *The Syndromes of Psychosis* (New York: Macmillan, 1963).

impressions, the factorial approach involves the recording and measurement of designated traits. The greater objectivity of the latter procedure makes for greater interexaminer reliability. The traditional classification system requires the examiner to assign a patient to a single diagnostic category—either he's schizophrenic or he isn't—and no provision is made for obvious qualitative or quantitative differences among patients assigned to the same category. The factorial approach assumes that each syndrome represents a dimension of personality and that every individual exhibits all of the syndromes in varying degrees.

A major criticism of this statistical approach is that the specific syndrome identified is a function of the input data. When investigators study similar populations but ask different questions of their subjects, the reported syndromes vary in number and in kind. For example, Phillips and Rabinovitch (1958) reported three major syndromes that could be interpreted as avoidance of others, self-depreciation and turning against others. On the basis of the response of patients to a structured clinical interview, Burdock and Hardesty (1968) identified ten basic trait clusters that differ somewhat from the Lorr list: (1) anger-hostility, (2) conceptual dysfunction, (3) fear-worry, (4) incongruous behavior, (5) incongruous ideation, (6) lethargy-dejection, (7) perceptual dysfunction, (8) physical complaints, (9) self-depreciation, and (10) sexual problems. So far the factorial approach has been limited to research studies. Further work is needed to determine which and how many factors are relevant for classification purposes.

An important advantage of the factorial approach is that it avoids futile controversy as to whether a neurosis is a mild form of a psychosis or whether a person in developing a psychosis first goes through an intermediate neurotic stage. If we accept H. J. Eysenck's (1961) findings, which indicate that neuroticism and psychoticism are independent factors, the diagnostic issue is not whether a person is neurotic or psychotic but whether he scores higher on the neuroticism dimension than on the psychoticism dimension. If a person shows a relative predominance of neurotic reactions and later his neurosis becomes more severe, he will still be classified as neurotic. On the other hand, a marked increase in psychotic behavior with a diminution of neurotic behavior would necessitate a change of classification from neurosis to psychosis. Theoretically, a person may show an equal amount of neuroticism and psychoticism, and in such cases there is a tendency to favor a diagnosis of psychosis.

Individual Case Study

A third alternative is to recognize the uniqueness of each individual and to concentrate on the study of single cases. The rationale is that more can be learned about the nature, causes, treatment, and prevention of personality disturbances through the intensive study of individual patients than through the study of groups, since the heterogeneity of groups tends to confuse one's observations. Adolf Meyer (1866-1950), founder of the psychobiological school of psychiatry, was an early advocate of this approach. Meyer viewed psychological disturbances as maladaptive habit patterns acquired by the individual as the natural result of his particular physical, social, and psychological life history (Lief, 1948; Muncie, 1959). In the past the individual approach has been mainly utilized in case studies and autobiographical reports by former patients. More recently, well-controlled experimental studies have been conducted on single cases (Krasner and Ullmann, 1965; Davidson and Costello, 1969).

The utility of the method is best illustrated by the contributions of Freud. Most of his theories represent generalizations derived from insights gained in the comprehensive study of individual patients. The single-case method has been found particularly effective in developing and demonstrating procedures for behavior modification (Ullmann and Krasner, 1965). Procedures worked out in individual cases

THE SINGLE CASE: FREUD AND SCHREBER

Daniel Schreber's autobiographical memoirs give us an excellent illustration of the potentialities of the single-case method. This classical case study, which was originally reported in 1903, provided the basis for Freud's views on the role of latent homosexuality in paranoia. The Schreber case also offers strong support for the unitary concept of mental symptomatology. (Niederland, 1974).

Schreber served for many years as judge of the county court in Leipzig. At the time of his first admission to a psychiatric clinic, at the age of forty-two, his outstanding symptom was severe hypochondriasis. He was discharged after six months and resumed his judicial duties. Then at the age of fifty-one he had a relapse and was hospitalized for nine years during which time he wrote his memoirs. The second illness started off as an anxiety neurosis. This was followed by hypochondriacal delusions and suicidal depression. Later he exhibited catatonic stupor, maniacal excitement, compulsive bellowing, negativism, obsessive-compulsive behavior, and massive delusions. He believed that he was gradually being transformed into a female. At various times he could have been diagnosed on the basis of his changing symptoms as suffering from schizophrenia, chronic mania, involutional melancholia, paranoia, obsessional neurosis, and transvestism.

Despite his severe symptoms, his capacity for clear and logical reasoning remained unimpaired. His superior intelligence enabled him to examine his madness and offer reasonable explanations for his strange behavior. Unfortunately, we have no record of his adjustment in his community following his discharge from the hospital.

have been shown to be readily applicable to other patients with similar problems.

SUMMARY

The principal objection to the use of the term "mental disorders" is the misleading implication that the disorders represent separate and distinct "diseases," each of which has its own unique cause, symptomatic manifestations, and specific treatment. This objection may be circumvented by substituting the broader dictionary definition of disorder (dysfunction, disturbance, disruption) for the restricted and questionable medical connotation of disease. The dictionary definition, which emphasizes the perceived effects of disordered behavior, is the one that has been adopted for this book.

Within this context, there are many advantages in retaining the traditional "diagnostic" disorders of psychiatry as descriptive labels. These labels, referring to frequently noted behavior patterns, provide a convenient medium for classifying and imposing a semblance of order on the confusing data of psychopathology. In addition, there is some factual basis for the claim that the traditional diagnostic labels constitute a convenient shorthand for communicating useful information about the nature of psychosocial impairment, the severity of personality disintegration, the probable prognosis, and the recommended mode of treatment.

However, the artificiality of the arbitrarily defined categories, plus the fact that persons assigned the same diagnosis often have little in common, limits the accuracy and usefulness of the information communicated. Clinical inferences associated with a designated disorder frequently do not apply to individual cases. When the rules for identifying particular "disorders" are clearly defined and uniformly interpreted, examiners show a reasonable level of agreement in the diagnosis and differentiation of mental retardation, organic brain syndromes, psychosis, and neurosis. For specific subtypes and milder reactions, interexaminer reliability is low.

What have been traditionally referred to as separate disorders represent extremely maladaptive and disturbing expressions of patterns of behavior commonly observed in normal individuals under stress. The major varieties of patterns observed in mental patients are more appropriately regarded as examples of personality types or behavior styles than as discrete forms of mental disorder.

The statistical method of factor analysis provides a more objective technique for identifying these recurring syndromes than the traditional diagnostic procedure based on clinical impressions. The factor approach sidesteps the "disorder" controversy and in addition provides a more comprehensive profile of the individual on the basis of his relative rating on each syndrome. The unitary concept of behavior disturbances, advocated by Menninger, has particular significance in the controversy about whether severe disturbances are discrete entities or may be located on a continuous spectrum of behavior from what is regarded as normal to what is regarded as abnormal.

References

American Psychiatric Association. *Diagnostic and Statistical Manual of Mental Disorders.* Washington, D.C., 1968.

Babigan, H. W. "Diagnostic Consistency and Change in a Follow-up Study of 1,215 Patients." *American Journal of Psychiatry* 121 (1965): 895-901.

Beck, A. T. "Reliability of Psychiatric Diagnoses: 1. A Critique of Systematic Studies." *American Journal of Psychiatry* 119 (1962): 210-16.

Burdock, E. I., and Hardesty, A. S. "Psychological Test for Psychopathology." *Journal of Abnormal Psychology* 73, no 1 (1968): 62-69.

Davidson, P.O., and Costello, C. G. *Experimental Studies of Single Cases.* New York: Van Nostrand Reinhold, 1969.

Dohrenwend, B. P., and Dohrenwend, B. S. "The Problem of Validity in Field Studies of Psychological Disorder." *Journal of Abnormal Psychology* 70 (1965): 52-69.

Dreger, R. M., et al. "Behavioral Classification Project." *Journal of Consulting Psychology* 28 (1964): 1-13.

Esquirol, J. E. D. *Mental Maladies: A Treatise on Insanity,* trans. E. K. Hunt. Philadelphia: Lee & Blanchard, 1845.

Eysenck, H. J. "Classification and the Problems of Diagnosis." In *Handbook of Abnormal Psychology,* ed. H. J. Eysenck. New York: Basic Books, 1961.

Gardner, E. A. "The Role of the Classification System in Outpatient Psychiatry." In *Classification in Psychiatry and Psychopathology,* ed. M. M. Katz, J. O. Cole, and W. E. Barton, Public Health Service publication no. 1584. Washington, D.C.: U.S. Government Printing Office, 1968.

Glass, A. J. "Observations upon the Epidemiology of Mental Illness in Troops During Warfare." In *Symposium on Preventive and Social Psychiatry,* sponsored by Walter Reed Army Institute of Research and National Research Council. Washington, D. C.: U.S. Government Printing Office, 1957.

Gruenberg, E. M. "Epidemiology and Medical Care." In *Classification in Psychiatry and Psychopathology,* ed. Katz, Cole, and Barton, pp. 76-98.

Katz, M. M.; Cole, J. O.; and Barton, W. E., eds. *Classification in Psychiatry and Psychopathology,* Public Health Service publication no. 1584. Washington, D.C.: U.S. Government Printing Office, 1965.

Kramer, M. "Cross-National Study of Diagnosis of the Mental Disorders: Origin of the Problem." *American Journal of Psychiatry* (supplement) 125, no. 10 (1969): 1-11.

Krasner, L., and Ullmann, L. P. *Research in Behavior Modification.* New York: Holt, Rinehart & Winston, 1965.

Kreitman, N.; Sainsbury, P.; Morrissey, J.; Towers, J.; and Scrivener, J. "The Reliability of Psychiatric Assessment: An Analysis." *Journal of Mental Science* 107 (1961): 887-908.

Lief, A., ed. *The Common-Sense Psychiatry of Adolf Meyer.* New York: McGraw-Hill, 1948.

Lorr, M., and Klett, C. J. "Cross-Cultural Comparison of Psychotic Syndromes." *Journal of Abnormal Psychology* 74, no. 4 (1969): 531-43.

——, ——, and Cave, R. "Higher-Level Psychotic Syndromes." *Journal of Abnormal Psychology* 72, no. 1 (1967): 74-77.

——, ——, and McNair, D. M. *The Syndromes of Psychosis.* New York: Macmillan, 1963.

McGuigen, F. J. "Covert Oral Behavior and Auditory Hallucinations." *Psychophysiology* 3 (1966): 73-80.

Matarazzo, J. D. "The Interview." In *Handbook of Clinical Psychology*, ed. B. B. Wolman, pp. 403-50. New York: McGraw-Hill, 1965.

Menninger, K.; Mayman, M.; and Pruyser, P. *The Vital Balance.* New York: Viking Press, 1963.

Moore, T. V. "The Essential Psychoses and Their Fundamental Syndromes." *Studies in Psychology and Psychiatry* 3 (1933): 1-128.

Muncie, W. "The Psychobiological Approach." In *American Handbook of Psychiatry*, ed S. Arieti, pp. 1317-32. New York: Basic Books, 1959.

Niederland, W. G. *The Scheber Case.* New York: Quadrangle/New York Times Book Co., 1974.

Norris, V. *Mental Illness in London.* London: Chapman & Hall, 1959.

O'Connor, J. P. "A Statistical Test of Psychoneurotic Syndromes." *Journal of Abnormal and Social Psychology* 48 (1953): 581-84.

Phillips, L.; Broverman, I. K.; and Zigler, E. "Social Competence and Psychiatric Diagnosis." *Journal of Abnormal Psychology* 71 (1966): 209-14.

——— and Rabinovitch, M. S. "Social Role and Patterns of Symptomatic Behaviors." *Journal of Abnormal and Social Psychology* 57 (1958): 181-86.

Reid, D. D. "Precipitating Proximal Factors in the Occurrence of Mental Disorder: Epidemiological Evidence." *Milbank Memorial Fund Quarterly* 2 (1961): 229-45.

Rosenthal, D. *Genetic Theory and Abnormal Behavior.* New York: McGraw-Hill, 1970.

Sandifer, M. G., Jr.; Pettus, C.; and Quade, D. "A Study of Psychiatric Diagnosis." *Journal of Nervous and Mental Disease* 139 (1964): 350-56.

Schmidt, H. O., and Fonda, C. P. "The Reliability of Psychiatric Diagnosis." *Journal of Abnormal and Social Psychology* 52 (1956): 262-67.

Schmidt, K. E. "Folk Psychiatry in Sarawak." In *Magic, Faith, and Healing*, ed. A. Kiev. New York: Free Press, Macmillan, 1964.

Schreber, D. P. *Memoirs of My Nervous Illness* (1903), ed. and trans. J. Macalpine and R. A. Hunter. London: Dawson & Sons, 1955.

Stengel, E. "Classification of Mental Disorders." *Bulletin of the World Health Organization* 21 (1959): 601-63.

Ullmann, L. P., and Krasner, L. *Case Studies in Behavior Modification.* New York: Holt, Rinehart & Winston, 1965.

Wittenborn, J. R. "Psychotic Dimensions in Male and Female Hospital Patients: Principal Components Analysis." *Journal of Nervous and Mental Disease* 138 (1964): 460-67.

Zigler, E., and Phillips, L. "Psychiatric Diagnoses and Symptomatology." *Journal of Abnormal and Social Psychology* 63 (1961): 69-75.

Zubin, J. "Classification of the Behavior Disorders." *Annual Review of Psychology* 18 (1967): 378-406.

3 · Criteria of Psychopathology

Credulity, Superstition and Fanaticism. A Medley,
William Hogarth

In daily life, evaluations and decisions are constantly being made, and with reasonable accuracy, as to the relative normality or abnormality of our own behavior and others'. On what basis are these decisions made? Is it possible to isolate and identify the key criteria? Do the rules vary from culture to culture, or are they universal? The complexity of the problem precludes simple or final answers. Psychopathological behavior is more easily recognized than defined. In ordinary life the recognition of disordered functioning is greatly simplified by the fact that the evaluation is a global and continuous process that takes into consideration the previous personality of the individual, the appropriateness of his behavior in its total context, and the net effect of the behavior on the individual and others. These important modifying factors are not readily incorporated in specifically defined criteria. The more precisely the criteria are defined, the more exceptions there are likely to be. On the other hand, the more broadly the criteria are defined, the less useful they are.

Any criteria that are proposed must take account of certain known facts. Since the onset of behavior that suggests psychopathology is usually detected initially by the individual himself and his family and associates, one basic requirement is that the signs be readily observable by the average person. Second, the continuity of normal and abnormal behavior requires that the criteria be applicable to all degrees of disordered functioning, from slips of the tongue and "freezing" on examinations, which are periodically observed in normal persons, to the most severe forms of psychotic disturbance. Finally, the criteria must be culture-free. As we saw earlier, the outward forms of abnormal behavior are in great measure shaped by the models and learning experiences of the cultures in which they occur, but the essential features remain the same in all cultures.

The incidental nature of cultural differences in symptoms has been highlighted in studies reported by Tooth (1950), Carothers (1953), and others, which show that the Westernization of non-Western peoples is accompanied by a corresponding shift in symptomatology. As preliterate people become more sophisticated, the supernatural content of their delusions is gradually replaced by more "modern" symptoms, such as complaints of control by electricity, hypochondriacal reactions, and paranoid trends (Lambo, 1955). A distinction must also be made between the recognition of abnormality and the tolerance of it, since some societies are more tolerant of certain forms of disruptive behavior than others. Cultures differ markedly in their interpretations of the causes of abnormal behavior, in their attitudes, and in the treatment of people in whom it occurs. However, a person classified as mentally disturbed in one society would in all probability be regarded as abnormal in all societies. Even when a person's delusions are generally consistent with the beliefs of his society, the disorganized quality of other facets of his life establishes his abnormality. A concise summary of the cross-cultural aspects of abnormality is presented by Ralph Linton (1956, p. 62):

All societies provide examples of psychotics, neurotics, and hysterics, who are recognized as such by members of that society. The symptomatologies associated with these abnormal states differ from society to society in ways which strongly suggest that they are shaped by cultural influences. The methods employed by different societies in dealing with individuals of these different types, including the social utilization of certain forms of psychotic abnormality, also differ. However, it seems certain that abnormality of this sort is absolute. . . . Individuals having the constitutional defects responsible for such abnormalities would be abnormal in any society. At most, particular cultural factors may lead to the manifestation or suppression of symptoms at various levels of defect intensity.

SOME BROAD CRITERIA

The Presence of Symptoms

As we noted earlier, the existence of a mental disorder cannot be defined or inferred from symptoms alone, since there are no fixed and absolute symptoms of mental disorder. Any and all of the ideas, feelings, and reactions noted in mental patients are also observed in more moderate, better controlled, and more socially acceptable form in normal individuals and in patients who have been declared "cured." It is only after a trait or reaction has been critically examined and evaluated as abnormal that it can be considered a symptom. Under different circumstances and in different settings, the same reaction would be regarded as normal. Anxiety, suspiciousness, depressed moods, feelings of hostility, and guilt reactions are experienced by the mentally sound as well as the unsound. The same may be said for more favorable traits —affection, altruism, joy, friendliness.

Normal people as well as mentally disturbed persons distort reality to suit their needs, cling to obviously false beliefs, and are troubled by conflicts. The more bizarre feelings and actions of the psychotic are experienced by normal individuals in their dreams and fantasies. Anyone who has had difficulty shaking off the effects of a terrifying nightmare or who has drifted off into a hazy, confused, dreamlike state while running a high fever has a pretty good idea of what it means to be psychotic. The prejudices of normal people resemble the delusions of the mentally disturbed in that they are irrational and often false subjective beliefs that cannot be readily corrected by factual evidence or appeals to reason.

Almost any symptom may be a normal or even a laudable act if it is adequate and appropriate in time, place, and manner of expression, and if its effects are beneficial to the individual and his society. Apprehension is a normal reaction to danger, grief is a normal reaction to a tragic personal experience, and anger is a normal reaction to injustice. For a person to kill a stranger when "ordered" to do so by an imaginary voice is certainly a sign of abnormality, but there are many situations (self-defense, soldiers in combat) in which society sanctions the killing of strangers. For a layman to claim communication with God suggests psychopathology, but some degree of literal or figurative communication with God is expected of religious leaders in most societies. Instead of being symptomatic of a neurosis, guilt is an asset when it serves to motivate good moral conduct. Fear may also have positive value. In studies made of persons exposed to stress situations, it has been found that anticipatory fear acts as a safeguard against more pathological reactions (Janis, 1966), and the defensive function of anticipatory fear has been substantiated in animal studies (Martin and Hall, 1941).

The importance of evaluating the appropriateness and consequences of specific traits also applies to seemingly normal behavior. Orderliness for the sake of order approaches symptomatic compulsive behavior. The mother who "lives for her children" may be suspected of neurotic manipulation rather than nobility of character, if the objective of her self-sacrifice is the permanent enslavement of her children.

Deviation from the Norm

The vague criterion of norm deviation poses two problems: defining the norm, and distinguishing between favorable and un-

*Joan of Arc listening
to her angels, by
M. P. Lagarde*

favorable deviations. A popular but not very enlightening interpretation of what is normal is based on the statistical model, which arbitrarily defines as normal the usual, most commonly noted, or typical reactions of any large majority of the population. All unusual or atypical reactions, whether good, bad, or indifferent, are considered abnormal. This criterion has the merit of including most people within the normal fold and of recognizing the relativity of normality and abnormality. However, exclusive dependence on the frequency of any form of behavior, independent of its value, is a major limitation. On the basis of the statistical criterion, the essence of normality would be simply what

is most common. Behavior that is better than average would paradoxically have to be described as abnormal. As a rule, the reactions of the majority satisfy minimal standards of sound behavior; but on occasion the majority may panic, participate in mob violence, or be misled into sanctioning concentration camps and other atrocities.

Another important drawback of the statistical criterion is that it is culture-bound. With respect to mental health, it does not matter much whether behavior that is common in one culture is seldom observed in another or the same culture in a later generation. What is important is the relative effectiveness of behavior in satisfying human needs and in contributing to the psychobiosocial well-being and enhancement of the individual and his society. As far as these objectives are concerned, the statistical criterion is useful in delimiting *average normal* behavior—the way most of the people behave most of the time. Normal functioning that is better than average is more appropriately designated as *ideal normal* than as abnormal. The term "abnormal" is best restricted to defective, disordered functioning.

Defining deviation from the norm on the basis of the *relative unexpectedness* of behavior is a refinement of the statistical model. The reactions of the mentally disturbed are admittedly more unexpected and unpredictable than those of normal individuals. On the other hand, many unexpected reactions either have no bearing on mental health or are indicative more of ideal normal than of abnormal behavior. Outstanding acts of kindness or flashes of brilliance in average students may be unexpected, but they are entirely normal. Furthermore, not all unexpected detrimental reactions are abnormal in the pathological sense. As we saw in Chapter 1, in our discussion of Scheff's (1966) concept of residual deviance, the field of behavior pathology is restricted to residual norm violations for which society provides no explicit label. Undesirable deviations from the norm, whether expected or not, are not usually included under the heading of mental disorders if some more specific designation is pertinent, such as criminal behavior, sexual perversion, or sinfulness.

The *social conformity* criterion of normality is subject to the general criticism that carbon-copy behavior is a poor measure of normality. Conversely, originality and individuality are not defensible criteria of abnormality. Most societies encourage their members to acquire and accept the prevailing behavior patterns and value systems. Conformity is desired because it contributes to the solidarity of the group, promotes harmony in interpersonal relations, and provides stability and continuity to the culture. On the other hand, most societies allow for individual variations and

changes over time, implicitly recognizing that rigid conformity is neither satisfying to individual self-esteem nor beneficial to society. To be just like everyone else is to be a nonentity, a ditto mark, a nameless face in the crowd.

Conformity is an adaptive device, not a goal. It is essentially instrumental behavior, helpful in satisfying social needs (Walker and Heyns, 1962). A person may conform to a group's behavior patterns in order to gain or retain membership in the group, but his real goal is to be accepted and approved as a distinct person. The usual solution is a compromise. The individual conforms sufficiently to maintain membership in the group while simultaneously developing and preserving a separate personal identity. Society accepts the conformist, but it recognizes and rewards the individual whose favorable distinctive actions set him apart from and ahead of everyone else. In short, leaders are more honored than followers. Experimental studies have shown that outstanding leaders are characterized by independence of thought and action and steadfast adherence to their own convictions and perceptions despite apparent disagreement with the group (Crutchfield, 1955).

With respect to mental health, the reasons for conformity or nonconformity are more significant than the degree. The mentality disturbed do not indulge in nonconforming behavior because they reject the cultural model or wish to be different. Many desperately want to be more like other people; but because of their faulty perception of the social norm and their relative inability to control their thoughts and actions, they are unable to do so. Nonconforming behavior among normal persons is usually a matter of voluntary choice. The nonconforming behavior of hippies differs from that of the mentally disturbed in its deliberate flaunting of conventionally accepted behavior. The high degree of social conformity observed in some mentally disturbed persons is often a defense against insecurity. In addition to enabling one to avoid the stresses of decision-making, conformity reduces personal responsibility for one's actions. For the timid and ill at ease, conformity provides protective camouflage.

SOME SPECIFIC CRITERIA

A number of attempts have been made to identify more precisely the salient characteristics of abnormal and normal behavior. While differing in their choices of critical factors, most authorities agree in favoring multiple criteria, each conceived as a continuum ranging from normal behavior at one end through borderline reactions to abnormal behavior at the other end. A second point of agreement, particularly represented by the contributions of Jahoda, Shoben, Kluckhohn, and Linton, has been the selection of traits observable in many different cultures. According to Marie Jahoda (1958), the mentally disturbed differ from normal persons in being relatively deficient in these key characteristics: (1) awareness, acceptance, and correctness of self-concept; (2) continued growth and self-actualization; (3) integration and unity of personality; (4) autonomy and self-reliance; (5) perception of reality and social sensitivity; and (6) mastery of the environment and adequacy in meeting the demands of life. Deficiencies in these traits are assumed to indicate abnormality.

Edward Shoben (1957) maintains that behavior is normal to the extent that it reflects man's unique capacity for symbolization and social involvement. Among the distinctive human potentialities correlated with normal behavior, Shoben lists aptitude for capitalizing on past experience, self-control, ability to envision ideals, social reliability, and capacity to act independently in relation to others and at the same time to acknowledge one's need for others. Clyde Kluckhohn's position (as reported by Leighton, Clausen, and Wilson, 1957), is that all cultures define as mentally ill those persons who are inaccessible to communication, whose behavior is drastically at variance with cultural norms, and who do not have adequate control over their aggressive impulses. The inability of the mentally disturbed person to transmit, receive, and decode messages involving thoughts and feelings has also been noted by Ruesch and Bateson (1951). For Linton (1956, p. 63), "the tests of absolute normalcy are the individual's ability to apprehend reality as understood by his society, to act in terms of this reality, and to be effectively shaped by his society during his developmental period."

Normal behavior includes, then, (1) effective psychological functioning (competence in self-evaluation, reality-testing, learning, meeting demands of life), (2) appropriate social functioning (social sensitivity, dependability, actions in accord with cultural norms), and (3) self-control and integration of personality. The effect of normal and abnormal functioning on the individual and his society adds two additional differentiating criteria. Normal behavior is (4) personally satisfying and (5) socially acceptable, whereas abnormal behavior is a source of discomfort or distress to the individual and his family and associates.

BASIC CRITERIA

Although the extensive theoretical, clinical, and experimental literature on psychopathology is primarily concerned with the causes, diagnosis, and treatment of mental disorders, it is also a rich source of information on the distinguishing characteristics of mental patients. The main conclusion that may be derived from this heterogeneous material is that some criteria are more valid than others; but all five of the criteria listed in Figure 3.1, as well as other, less well-defined ones, are involved in evaluating mental health. To complicate matters, a person may be rated as normal with respect to one or more of these criteria and abnormal in regard to others. The final decision entails a balancing of positive and negative components. This is an ever-present problem, since all mental patients retain some areas of normal functioning.

A final qualifying point is that the cri-teria for mental disorders are more stringent than those for abnormal behavior. Momentary and infrequent abnormal acts that have no significant detrimental effects on the person or his society are usually not considered signs of mental disorder. This

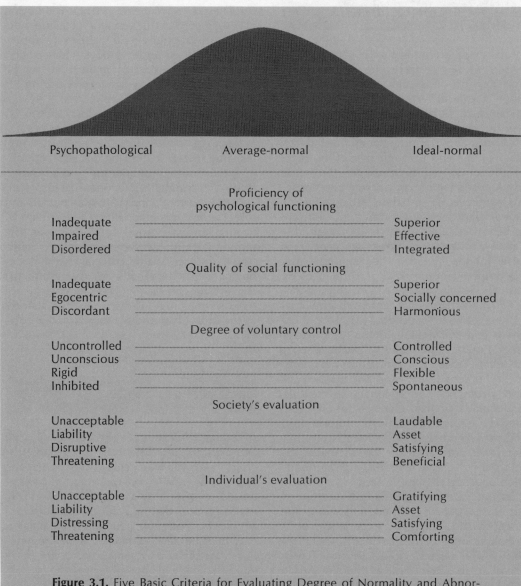

	Psychopathological	Average-normal	Ideal-normal

Proficiency of psychological functioning

Inadequate		Superior
Impaired		Effective
Disordered		Integrated

Quality of social functioning

Inadequate		Superior
Egocentric		Socially concerned
Discordant		Harmonious

Degree of voluntary control

Uncontrolled		Controlled
Unconscious		Conscious
Rigid		Flexible
Inhibited		Spontaneous

Society's evaluation

Unacceptable		Laudable
Liability		Asset
Disruptive		Satisfying
Threatening		Beneficial

Individual's evaluation

Unacceptable		Gratifying
Liability		Asset
Distressing		Satisfying
Threatening		Comforting

Figure 3.1. Five Basic Criteria for Evaluating Degree of Normality and Abnormality.

differentiation is consistent with the continuum concept, which holds that mental disorders represent extreme manifestations of abnormal reactions that are also noted in normal individuals.

Defective Psychological Functioning

Clinical and experimental data confirm that that the severity of psychological deficit and psychopathology are positively related. The mental functions most impaired tend to be the more distinctively human abilities: attention, perception, reasoning, reality-testing, judgment, learning, memory, communication, and creativity. In brain-damaged persons there is often a permanent loss of these capacities. In psychologically disturbed persons the capacity is retained but its use is impaired or distorted. Thus a person may have the capacity to think, but not to think logically. The impairment may often be reduced by increasing the patient's motivation.

Experimental studies (summarized by Lang and Buss, 1965) indicate that defective functioning often appears to be due to the disruptive effects of intrusive stimuli. This condition, referred to as *overinclusion*, is marked by an apparent inability to screen out mental acts, emotions, impulses, ideas, and external stimuli that interfere with performance. Overinclusion has been attributed to a lowering of vigilance or to impairment in the voluntary control of behavior. The latter explanation has the advantage of also accounting for the over-exclusion of associations and stimuli observed in depressed patients.

Defective Social Functioning

The essentials of this criterion, as suggested by Scheff, Kluckhohn, and Linton, consist of the relative inability of the individual (1) to apprehend and be effectively shaped by the cultural model and (2) to refrain from engaging in actions that are drastically at variance with the cultural norm. The term "inability" serves to exclude criminal, immoral, and other presumably voluntary forms of social deviation. The focus on local culture serves to discount intercultural variations in customs, values, and interpersonal relationships.

In effect, the acknowledgment of the culture as the frame of reference is a restatement of the principle that the relative normality or abnormality of a specific behavior can be evaluated only in terms of its situational effectiveness and appropriateness. In cultures similar to ours, which emphasize the importance of harmonious social relationships and individual responsibility, the major signs of defective social functioning include inadequate control of aggressive impulses, excessive distrust and suspicion of others, incoherent communication, irresponsibility, self-destructive tendencies, and psychological incapacity for self-care and autonomous behavior.

A more pervasive defect is related to what Alfred Adler (1939) referred to as a lack of *social interest*. In developing his basic theory, that much of human behavior may be explained on the basis of striving for superiority to compensate for universal feelings of inferiority, Adler was confronted with the problem of differentiating between the compensatory style of life of neurotics and that of normal individuals. He concluded that the strivings for superiority of normal individuals are tempered by a genuine interest in the feelings and welfare of others. The life style of the neurotic, on the other hand, is egocentric. His goal is to achieve a personal sense of superiority, whether real or imaginary, without regard to the feelings of his associates or the interests of society. The egocentrism of the disturbed person is not like that of the show-off. In most instances the disturbed individual avoids attracting attention to himself, and his egocentrism is more precisely described as a narrowing of interest to himself. This self-centeredness may include other members of the family who are perceived as extensions of himself. Although the disturbed person may be aware of and interact with his social environment, he is usually so preoccupied with his circumscribed world that he has

Alfred Adler (1870-1937), founder of Individual Psychology. A basic Adlerian concept is that strivings for superiority to compensate for universal feelings of inferiority, when combined with social concern, favor mental health. Egocentric strivings devoid of concern for the welfare of others lead to neurosis and unhappiness.

little interest in other people, except insofar as their behavior has some direct personal significance to him.

A dramatic example of this self-centeredness has been reported by Wilmer (1958, p. 4). A hospitalized psychiatric patient witnessed the sudden and rather violent death of a fellow inmate. "It's been a long day for John Allen," he remarked to the attending physician as they both looked upon the body. "Is that his name?" inquired the doctor. "No," replied the patient. *"I'm* John Allen." The marked lack of social feeling that is characteristic of autistic children practically from birth suggests that their inability to establish close emotional ties with others may be at least partly biological in origin. In most adult patients, however, limited emotional involvement with others and great preoccupation with themselves appear to be acquired defenses against repeated disappointments encountered in earlier social experiences.

Loss of Self-Control

Impairment of conscious self-control is the most critical single criterion of psychopathology. The unexpectedness, inappro-

priateness, irrationality, and defective quality of abnormal behavior is due to the fact that it is uncontrolled. Public awareness of this loss of control is reflected in such popular descriptive terms as "out of one's mind," "running amok," "going berserk," and "having a nervous breakdown." The most convincing evidence is provided by the disturbed person himself. Try as he will, the neurotic cannot rid himself of his fears and compulsions, even when he realizes they are senseless. A major source of the psychotic's anguish is the realization that he has no control over his feelings and impulses and is powerless to turn off the threatening voices and disturbing thoughts that assail him. The invention of enemies, who for some unknown reason are controlling his sensations and actions, represents an attempt to make sense of the inexplicable. As a precaution against the threat of loss of control, the psychotic person may drastically curtail his activities, strengthen his inhibitions, and become rigid in thought and action. These defensive measures involve a renunciation of freedom and of control.

The overcontrolled person has little freedom of choice; his actions are prescribed as well as circumscribed. Loss of self-control is particularly evident in serious mental disorders, but it is also characteristic of minor disturbances in adults and children: temper tantrums, enuresis (bed-wetting), poor concentration, restlessness, impulsivity, and stammering.

All theories of psychopathology since ancient times have in one way or another acknowledged the obvious impairment of voluntary control accompanying mental disorders. One of the earliest tests of madness, reported by Homer, was based on this observation. When the members of the conscription committee for the Trojan wars called on Ulysses, they found the reluctant warrior plowing the beach and sowing it with salt. To find out whether Ulysses was really mad or only feigning madness, they placed his son Telemachus in the path of the plow. To avoid killing his infant son, Ulysses changed the direction of the plow, and in so doing demonstrated that he was in command of his faculties and his actions, and hence was only pretending to be mad.

The theory of demonology recognized the helplessness of the disturbed person by assigning responsibility for his disordered behavior to evil spirits who somehow had gained possession of him. The concepts of bewitchment and lunacy similarly attributed the control of behavior to external sources. With the rejection of supernatural explanations, the origin of disordered behavior has been localized within the individual; but the relative loss of voluntary control in mental disorders is still recognized. A significant corollary of the disease concept of psychopathology was the assumption that the mentally ill person had no more control over his disordered behavior than the physically ill patient had over his physical symptoms. The lack of responsibility of the mentally disturbed person for his behavior is the keystone of legal tests of insanity. Criminal culpability is based on the premise that the individual is capable of rational choice, and of his own free will chooses to engage in offenses he knows are wrong.

The *tension theory* developed by Pierre Janet (1943), a French psychiatrist, provides an ingenious explanation for the loss of functions observed in neurotics. Janet's basic premise was that a certain level of psychic energy is essential for the integration of the various parts of the mind. If the tension level is reduced below a critical point, certain functions become dissociated from the mainstream of consciousness. These emancipated functions, which are no longer subject to volition, may be temporarily lost or may continue to operate independently. As a rule, a relatively small segment of the mind becomes dissociated, and the symptomatic manifestation consists mainly of amnesia, inability to speak or to move some part of the body, irrational fear, a recurring tic or spasm, or some other relatively specific dysfunction. Occasionally a massive dissociation, amounting to a division of the personality, occurs. In this case the two separated personalities may alternate, so that the individual may have access only to memories and functions that are part of the personality in charge at the time.

Janet held that the energy level is mainly determined by individual heredity. Factors that may deplete the energy supply include debilitating physical disease, excessive fatigue, and emotional shock. The significance of loss of control in schizophrenics was emphasized by Eugen Bleuler (1950), who maintained that the primary symptoms in this group of disorders consist of a looseness of the associative links in thinking, ambivalence, and the dominance of behavior by fantasies.

The issue of conscious control of behavior pervades psychoanalytic theory and treatment. According to Freud (1949), mental disorders occur when the ego or conscious portion of the personality, which is charged with the triple responsibility of holding in check repressed impulses (from the id), heeding the prohibitions of the superego, and adapting to the demands of reality, loses mastery of the situation. Mental symptoms represent the involuntary acting out of unconscious impulses and

Karen Horney (1885-1952), a German-born American psychoanalyst who differed with Freud by attaching greater importance to interpersonal and cultural factors and by recognizing the shaping influence of life experiences beyond early childhood. In her interpretation of neurosis she stressed the rigidity of neurotics and their one-track approach to conflicts and problems.

emergency defenses against a more serious breakdown in functioning. The essence of neurotic behavior, as defined by Lawrence Kubie (1958), is that it is rigidly channeled by forces that determine the automatic repetition of certain acts, irrespective of their appropriateness or any other consideration. One of the major aims of psychoanalytic therapy is to restore and extend ego control by uncovering the unconscious and thereby increasing the conscious portion of the personality that is more accessible to voluntary control.

The restricted flexibility of neurotic behavior, emphasized by Karen Horney, calls attention to another facet of the impairment of self-control. For Horney (1945), the core of neurosis is a conflict born of incompatible and irreconcilable attitudes toward other persons. The basic conflict interferes with adaptive, appropriate behavior by imposing a rigid one-track response. The origin of the conflict is traced to adverse parent-child relationships that make the child feel helpless, insecure, and anxious. Adverse factors may include parental inconsistencies, overdomination, indifference, lack of reliable warmth, unkept promises, and so on. In attempting to cope with a social word that is perceived as un-

predictable and potentially hostile, the child has three choices. He may *(a)* move toward people and attempt to obtain a feeling of security and belonging by being submissive and dependent; *(b)* move against people and fight his way through life; or *(c)* move away from people and build a world of his own, in which books, nature, and dreams take the place of social interaction.

If early childhood experiences are not too destructive or if the damage produced is offset by more favorable experiences during adolescence, the child learns to combine and integrate all three approaches so that they complement one another. The normal individual is thus free to move toward, against, or away from people, and can alter his reaction to fit the situation. The neurotic, on the other hand, has no choice. He is a prisoner of the particular pattern of responses established during early childhood. Whether these responses are appropriate or not, there is only one move he can make. In all situations, he can either comply, fight, or remain aloof. If he tries to step outside of the rigid mold, he is overwhelmed by anxiety. Illustrative of the neurotic's dilemma is the person who needs and wants friends, but who is unable to relate to others or can relate to them only in an aggressive or hostile manner.

The concept of man as a self-knowing and self-regulating organism responding to stimuli and making decisions on the basis of rational, deliberate choice is more an ideal than real. However, it is precisely because it is an ideal, a model of the way men wish to behave, that conscious voluntary control is a sound criterion of optimal normal behavior. Control of one's thoughts, feelings, impulses, and behavior is a prerequisite for peace of mind, self-confidence, and spontaneity of reactions. Problem-solving and successful adaptation depend in great measure on one's capacity to shift deliberately from one course of action to another, to experiment, and to alter objectives at will. Unless a person has command of himself, he cannot afford the exhilarating but risky experience of letting himself go, exploring the unknown, and reaching for the stars. Disciplined self-direction is required for responsibility, dependability, and accountability in meeting one's social obligations. Without self-control, no one could postpone the immediate gratification of desires for more satisfying delayed rewards.

Society's Evaluation

The presence and severity of defective or uncontrolled psychosocial functioning may be directly observed or inferred from the individual's behavior, his own descriptions of himself, interview information, and the case histories prepared by others who have seen him. With the aid of standardized tests (such as the Wechsler Adult Intelligence Scale, the Rorschach Inkblot Test, the Thematic Apperception Test, and the Minnesota Multiphasic Personality Inventory), the amount of impairment or the deviation of specific functions from the norm may be expressed in quantitative terms. These and other sources of data provide the raw material for evaluating behavior, but the actual decision as to the presence of psychopathology is made by the individual himself and by the society of which he is a member.

The evaluating process centers about three basic questions: Do the available data indicate an impairment or disorder of psychosocial functioning? Is the dysfunction so severe that it significantly disrupts the individual's social and personal adjustment? Can the disturbance in behavior be accounted for on the basis of some "natural" explanation, such as physical illness, ignorance, intoxication, or a recent traumatic experience? A clear verdict of psychopathology requires affirmative answers to the first two questions and a negative answer to the third. When differences of opinion exist between society and the individual, greater weight is given to society's evaluation if the behavior is considered likely to have a detrimental effect on the group; but if the behavior has a greater effect on personal adjustment than on the welfare of the group, greater importance is attached to the individual's own evaluation.

The role of society as the arbiter of normal and abnormal behavior is shared by three groups: (a) the family and close friends of the individual; (b) neighbors, associates, and other persons having direct contact with him; and (c) professionally trained persons recognized by the society as experts or authorized evaluators. In our society formal diagnosis is chiefly the responsibility of psychiatrists and clinical psychologists. Other specialists who may be involved in diagnosis include psychiatric social workers and counseling psychologists. Although court officials are not directly concerned with diagnosis, they are charged with the task of interpreting and enforcing laws pertaining to criminal responsibility, compulsory hospitalization when it is in the public interest, and safeguarding the person and property of the mentally incompetent.

Relatives, friends, and professional experts may differ in the relative emphasis they place on various criteria. Certain criteria may be more heavily weighted in some cultures than in others. In general, however, there appears to be substantial agreement within and between cultures with respect to two main points. Behavior is evaluated as pathological (1) if psychosocial functioning is so impaired and disordered that the individual is unable to cope with the ordinary problems of human life and (2) if aggressive impulses are uncontrolled and uncontrollable.

In extreme instances, behavior disorder may be so marked that the individual is incapable of caring for himself or maintaining even minimal contact with his social environment. Milder degrees of impairment may be characterized by undue dependency, ineffectualness, substandard productivity, and social inadequacy. In interpreting these deficiencies, the critical factor is the relative *inability* of the individual to care for himself because of involuntary psychosocial defects. Deliberate substandard performance and behavior disorders due to physical disease, drugs, and age are excluded. Uncontrolled aggression is not tolerated in any society, since unprovoked and unpredictable attacks endanger the welfare and safety of the group. To a lesser degree, society is also intolerant of persons whose erratic and impulsive behavior is a source of annoyance or apprehension.

To these two basic criteria may be added a third that has special significance for the family group. This has to do with the acute emotional distress exhibited by most patients. Members of the family may deny or overlook disordered functioning in a loved one, but their compassion for the all too apparent suffering of the bewildered, tormented, or depressed person may convince them that he is mentally ill and in urgent need of treatment. Therapists also attach considerable significance to the severity of the inner distress of the individual in their evaluation of abnormal behavior.

At the family and community level, there is often a reluctance to interpret deviant behavior as evidence of mental disorder. A person who by professional psychiatric standards would be classified as mentally disturbed may be described by his peer group as "strange," "odd," "high-strung," or "different." Unless he engages in some drastic actions the unequivocal decision that he is in fact mentally ill may be evaded for months or even years. Mild deviations are often discounted by associates on the grounds that "everyone has some peculiarities" or "there are all kinds of people in the world" (Cummings and Cummings, 1957). Sporadic disturbances in functioning and mood changes may be attributed to the fact that the person is upset, tired, or not feeling well. Consistent with the concept of residual deviance, serious or persistent maladaptive reactions may be explained as due to poor health, overwork, loss of sleep, drinking, or change of life (Yarrow et al., 1955). Whenever possible, an attempt is made to account for disorganized behavior as a natural, normal reaction to a specific situation or traumatic experience. Only as a last resort is the label of mental disorder applied to behavior that is perceived by the peer group as irrational and inappropriate.

In evaluating normal behavior, there is essential agreement by family, community, and specialist that to satisfy *minimum* requirements of mental health, the individual should be about as able as other members of his peer group to take care of himself, to cope with everyday problems, and to get along with his social group. If he is an asset to his community, a comfort and joy to his family, and a social benefactor, so much the better.

The Personal Distress Factor

A final and indispensable criterion for evaluating the relative normality of behavior is the subjective feeling of the individual. Particularly in mild disorders, when no obvious psychological deficits are discernible and social adjustment is adequate, inner torment may be the main indicator of psychopathology. The anguish of the mentally disturbed is often a blend of anxiety, dread, guilt, dejection, rage, and hate. The individual may be bewildered, seething with resentment, or full of self-pity. The net effect is that he is miserably and hopelessly unhappy—so much so that relief may be sought in death.

Emotional distress and unhappiness are, of course, also noted in normal individuals. What distinguishes the mentally disturbed person is the seeming inappropriateness of his anguish. Relatives, friends, and even the person himself are unable to offer any reasonable explanation for the presence, duration, and severity of the emotional disturbance. The normal person who has good cause to be frightened, depressed or angry may be no less disturbed and unhappy; but the appropriateness of his reaction, which usually gains him the understanding and support of associates, somehow makes his distress more bearable.

The mental patient's emotional reaction is incongruous because, while he adjusts his behavior to fit his personal standards like everyone else, his standards differ in degree or in kind from those of society. A simple example is the student with high academic aspirations who is unhappy and plagued with feelings of inferiority whenever he receives a B grade. His roommate may be delighted with C grades but regards himself as a failure if he is not elected president of the class. Unrealistic values acquired during childhood may result in acute guilt feelings for transgressions that society overlooks or forgives, and which the individual may intellectually realize are trivial or no longer reasonable. His nervous system is less accommodating, however; it neither forgets nor forgives.

The imbalance between behavior and self-concept in persons with mental disorders has been confirmed in several experimental studies (Wylie, 1961), in which it has been noted that neurotics report a greater discrepancy than normal individuals between their actual selves and their ideal selves. These findings suggest the possibility that a narrowing of the gap between the patient's descriptions of his actual and his ideal self may be a good indication of the effectiveness of therapy: the smaller the discrepancy following therapy, the greater

the improvement (Rogers, 1951).

CRITERIA IN SUMMARY

As is apparent from our discussion of specific criteria, the concepts of normality and abnormality are closely associated with basic human values. This relationship has been explored in a series of articles compiled by Nunokawa (1965). With the universality of psychopathology in mind, I have focused on those criteria that reflect more or less universally accepted human values. Thus it is reasonable to assume that all societies prefer their members to be capable of self-control rather than uncontrolled, to be psychologically competent rather than incompetent, to be rational rather than irrational, to be assets rather than liabilities or threats to the community, and to be contented rather than miserably unhappy.

With respect to the psychopathological implications of these values, three modifying factors must be considered. The first is related to the familiar concept of residual deviance. As a rule, deviation from accepted cultural standards is not regarded as a sign of psychopathology if some other explanation can be made for it: physical illness, a natural reaction following a traumatic experience, intoxication, fatigue, sinfulness, criminality, bad temper, stupidity. Second, an allowance has to be made for minor local variations in the spelling out of common values. Societies may agree in principle that behavior is abnormal if it constitutes an intolerable threat to the well-being of the group but differ in evaluating the kinds of behavior that are regarded as threats and in specifying what represents an intolerable threat. Similarly, standards of adequate psychosocial functioning may be higher in one society than in another.

The third factor is the relativity of normality and abnormality. If we look at the pattern of differences among individuals in any population with regard to such easily measured physical traits as height or weight, we can portray it in the form of the familiar bell-shaped curve shown in Figure 3.1. A relatively small proportion of the total population will be found at the extremes of the curve, and most people will be found in the middle ranges of the distribution. We may reasonably infer that if accurate scales were available for measuring the five criteria of mental disorder we have discussed, the same would be the case; only a few people would have composite scores that would place them at the pathological or the ideal-normal ends of the curve, and the great majority of the population would be described as "average-normal."

The unbroken continuity of scores has a direct bearing on the meaningfulness of estimates regarding the prevalence of mental disorders. Depending on the arbitrarily selected cutoff point that differentiates psychopathological from average-normal behavior, the proportion of the total population classified as mentally disturbed may range from less that 1 percent to 25 percent. The use of different procedures and standards in establishing cutoff points provides the simplest explanation for the wide discrepancies reported in field studies of the relative prevalence of psychological disorders in different communities (Dohrenwend and Dohrenwend, 1965).

Subject to these modifying factors, behavior may be defined as abnormal to the extent that it is not subject to voluntary control, is characterized by inadequate, inappropriate, and maladaptive psychosocial functioning, and is evaluated by the individual and his society as a liability or a source of intolerable distress or threat. Conversely, behavior may be defined as normal (average through ideal) to the degree that it is subject to voluntary control, represents the optimal development and expression of higher order psychosocial functions, and is considered to contribute to the satisfaction and enhancement of the individual and the society to which he belongs.

MOTIVATION PATTERN AND PSYCHOPATHOLOGY

Although not directly related to criteria for differentiating normal from abnormal behavior, a significant difference between normal and abnormal persons is their approach to life. By and large, normal individuals have a positive orientation. Even if they have not been successful in achieving their past goals, they retain hope for the future. Frustrations and conflicts are regarded as problems to be resolved and challenges to be met. Normal individuals are task-oriented. They strive toward achievement, rewards, and happiness. The motivational pattern of the disturbed person, on the other hand, is often essentially negative. His main concern is to defend himself against possible failure, guilt, and rejection. Frustrations and conflicts are perceived as crises, leading to despair, resignation, and further defensive measures. Basic needs for achievement and recognition are expressed in unrealistic and grandiose goals. These may serve as compensations for low self-esteem, but the disturbed person makes no real or sustained effort to translate his ambitions into achievements. Constantly preoccupied with protecting himself from possible failures and disappointments, he faces a gloomy, unrewarding future.

PSYCHOPATHOLOGY AND CULTURAL RELATIVISM

Wide individual variations in personality and behavior characterize the populations of all societies. However, the socialization process, whereby cultural values are inculcated in the young, may accentuate or inhibit the manifestation of latent human potentialities and thereby impart distinctive qualities to the behavior of people in different groups. These differences in cultural indoctrination account for tribal and national characteristics and for the "strange" ways of foreigners. An interesting contribution of anthropological research has been the observation that in primitive and relatively isolated societies the socialization process occasionally encourages the development and casual acceptance of behavior patterns that resemble reactions considered symptomatic of mental disorder in other societies.

This observation was for a time erroneously interpreted as supporting the doctrine of *cultural relativism*; that is, the idea that behavior regarded as pathological in one society may be normal in another. Although the writings of Ruth Benedict (1934) are frequently cited as the principal source of evidence supporting the concept of cultural relativism, it should be noted that Dr. Benedict repudiated this interpretation of her data (in a private communication to Wegrocki, 1939). Far from wishing to prove the cultural relativism of psychopathology, she was actually seeking to demonstrate how cultural influences selectively promote or inhibit the development and overt expression of latent human potentialities. Through describing people who were well-adjusted in terms of their own society but who exhibited behavior patterns that would be considered mental symptoms in our society, she wanted to show that "interculturally adequate functioning and fixed symptoms could not be equated."

It is now generally recognized that the concept of relativism was based on the illogical premise that if *A* resembles *B*, then *A* must be the same as *B*. There is a world of difference between the disordered, inappropriate, and detrimental reactions of mentally disturbed persons in this country and the seemingly similar but adequately controlled and socially approved reactions observed in some other societies. The senseless mutilation of victims by a demented person in our culture cannot be equated with the headhunting or scalping

practices of some tribes. The taking of a head or scalp in cultures that formerly sanctioned such activities was incidental to the basic objective, which in most instances was to kill a recognized enemy of one's tribe. The anatomical souvenir was both a proof and a memento of the warrior's skill and bravery in combat, a gory equivalent of the souvenirs of battle brought home by soldiers everywhere. A headhunter in New Guinea who started collecting the heads of members of his own village (an act that would be comparable to homicide in our society) would be promptly executed by his fellows as irresponsible and dangerous.

An American housewife who believed that any neighbor who entered her kitchen did so for the sole purpose of poisoning her food would qualify as a pathologically suspicious person; but a Dobuan housewife who thought the same thing would be considered prudent and normal, and for a good reason. From infancy the Dobuans are taught to believe that anyone who has not shared the milk of their mother is a potential enemy and, given a chance, will do them harm (Fortune, 1932). This is not a delusion; it is a fact of Dobuan life that must be faced. Neighbors and even husbands and wives do try their hand at casting spells and practicing black magic on one another. To be unaware of or to ignore this reality would suggest some impairment in perception and judgment. But even here the rule of appropriateness holds. A Dobuan may covet his neighbor's yams, but the only "normal" way he may get them is to use black magic on them, so that they will tunnel their way underground and pop up in his garden.

The trance states of a shaman or medicine man in a preliterate society may superficially resemble the trance states of mentally disordered persons in our society, but there is the important difference of voluntary control. The trance state of the disturbed person is involuntary and independent of self-control. The trance state of the shaman, like that of a spiritualistic medium

A shaman with a patient. Confidence in the therapist, his powers and his procedures, is a critical factor in treatment.

in our society, is part of his professional act. The shaman decides when he will go into a trance and when he will come out of it. A hysterical personality may be a prerequisite for going into a genuine trance, but the ability to do so on demand and only on appropriate occasions indicate normal functioning.

The shaman's purpose in going into a trance is to communicate with the spirit world. Fraud would be suspected if he didn't make a convincing show of sending his spirit out of his body. No words of wisdom or guidance are expected from the deranged person, but the shaman, if he wishes to keep his job and prestige, is expected to bring back messages that will satisfy his clients, whose requests are usually concerned with the prediction of future events and the curing of illness. To do this with seemingly reasonable efficacy, he must have his wits about him. Far from being out of touch with his environment, confused and dazed—as is true of the disturbed person subject to trance states—he must be astute, alert, and a step or two ahead of his clients. From her analysis of

field studies of shamanism among the Alaskan Eskimos on St. Lawrence Island, Jane Murphy (1964, p. 77) concluded:

For a shaman to become a successful healer he had often to display an exceptional ability in emotional control and in taking responsibility. Despite the frenzy reached in a seance and the seizures of possession, the performance as a whole is a highly styled drama, the impact of which is largely related to its control by the key director—the shaman. In addition, the full-fledged shaman who is capable of dealing with the crises of illness and death and of offering psychological support to groups of individuals taken into his spiritual custody displays qualities that can hardly be separated from those of leadership, responsibility, and power.

How a person who is classified as deranged in one society would fare in another depends on many things. One important factor is the relative tolerance of the second culture toward the particular form of disorder. It is quite possible that some cultures would accept obvious pathology more than others, but none of them would regard the person as normal. The essence of

MEGALOMANIA OR COMMON SENSE? THE CASE OF THE KWAKIUTL POTLATCH

The necessity of evaluating the nature and consequences of an act before passing judgment on its psychiatric significance is well illustrated by the former potlatch custom of the Kwakiutl Indians on Vancouver Island. According to Ruth Benedict, the behavior of the host at these affairs, if accepted at face value, would resemble the ravings of megalomaniac paranoid persons in our society. Actually, the potlatch was an institution that conformed to all the listed criteria of normality.

In brief, the potlatch consisted of a meeting of chiefs of neighboring tribes. On these occasions the host made grandiose claims for his tribe, insulted his invited guests, and tried his best to humiliate them by giving away and destroying blankets, canoes, oil, incised copper tablets, and other valuable objects. The guests' honor required them to reciprocate even more lavishly at a later date. On the surface, the boasting, the insulting behavior, and the destruction of property might appear pathological; but it was all a prearranged show in which each participant acted out his role according to recognized rules. The designated role of the host was to build up the prestige of his tribe by belittling rivals through the conspicuous

destruction of wealth. The prescribed role of the guests was to suffer through the ordeal in silence and await their turn to play the part of the bragging, insulting, property-destroying host. The boasts and taunts were limited to previously agreed-upon areas and were conventional and stereotyped.

The potlatch was the Kwakiutl's substitute for war (Codere, 1950); verbal insults took the place of arrows, and goods were destroyed instead of human beings. The tribe whose chief disposed of the greatest amount of property was the winner. But this would have been a Pyrrhic victory if the winner were impoverished. To avoid this calamity, which would have had psychopathological overtones, the chief was permitted to give away and destroy only the property that the tribe had collected over a period of months and put aside for this specific purpose. In other words, an expendable portion of the wealth of the tribe was budgeted for a spectacular advertising program designed to gain prestige. In many respects, the potlatch was similar to the war of words that is being fought today in the United Nations and reinforced by the competition among rival nations to see which can launch the biggest and most expensive satellites. (The dangers were also similar, for in spite of the rules, it was not unknown for a chief to bankrupt himself.)

Distribution of blankets by Kwakiutl Indians during a potlatch ceremony.

The normality of the potlatch is further illustrated by the rules that governed similar activities within the tribe. A commoner who wished to gain or maintain prestige could call in his friends and neighbors and build up his ego by a great show of giving away his belongings. However, the friends were honor-bound to repay the host by returning more than they had received from him within a year or suffer loss of face. Meanwhile, someone else was likely to make him the not entirely willing recipient of similar gifts, which he in turn was required to return with interest. The situation could become very complicated and very expensive, but if a man could manage to exercise sufficient control over the gift-giving, he could achieve enormous prestige. Somewhat analogous practices of self-aggrandizement through conspicuous consumption and conspicuous waste in our society have been described by Thorstein Veblen (1934). "Keeping ahead of the Joneses" is a more subtle variant of the potlatch.

psychopathology, as Linton noted (1956), lies in the person's inability to function adequately and appropriately in the context of reality as reality is defined and understood in his society. Since the ways in which reality can be defined are limited, this defect would accompany the patient and be apparent anywhere. A paranoid person who went to a society where suspiciousness was an accepted trait would be quickly spotted as "peculiar" because he would be suspicious about the wrong things at the wrong times in the wrong way. In other words, he would be unable to follow the ancient rule, "When in Rome, do as the Romans do."

In discussing the attitudes of primitive peoples toward the mentally disturbed, Linton acknowledges that disturbed persons are sometimes regarded with awe and treated well. But the relatively favorable status of the psychotic is due more to fear than to anything else. The superstitious belief that the psychotic is possessed by evil spirits tends to make people wary of incurring the hostility and wrath of these spirits. There is no society where the genuine psychotic is liked, admired, or given high social status. In order to gain prestige and acquire power, a leader must be capable of appraising situations in realistic terms and of exploiting situations to his advantage. This is an ability the psychotic does not have. When the patient is violent, so that the nuisance of caring for him is greater than the fear of evil spirits, it is not uncommon for primitive societies to kill him and seek comfort in the rationalization that his "soul" had already gone away, and it was only the body that was making trouble.

LEGAL CRITERIA OF MENTAL DISORDERS, INSANITY, AND INCOMPETENCE

Legal standards of abnormal behavior are influenced by but independent of other criteria. The law is specifically concerned with establishing rules and procedures for (1) the hospitalization of the mentally deranged, (2) the determination of insanity in criminal cases, and (3) defining and determining mental incompetence.

Voluntary and Involuntary Hospitalization

The law distinguishes between involuntary and voluntary admission to mental hospitals. In the United States, each state has its own statutory criteria for hospital admission. Most other countries have national regulations. Involuntary hospitalization, which deprives the patient of his freedom against his will, is based on the police power of government to take actions that it considers necessary to safeguard the public welfare. Most of the older statutes specifically limited the state's power to the commitment to hospitals of persons who were dangerous to themselves or others. More recent legislation permits the involuntary hospitalization of anyone who needs care or treatment but lacks sufficient capacity to make a responsible decision. Thus a person may be hospitalized without his consent to prevent harm to other persons or to property, to relieve his family of responsibility for his care, and to provide asylum if he is regarded as a social misfit.

Involuntary hospitalization has two main objectives: to protect the individual and society and to provide treatment. Since committed patients are deprived of their freedom, the courts and legislatures in the United States have recently become sensitive to issues concerned with the civil liberties of the mentally ill. Some important decisions have recently been handed down by courts. In the case of *Lake* v. *Cameron* (1966), a federal circuit court ruled that before an indigent person can be committed involuntarily to a mental hospital, the state must explore alternatives less drastic than full-time hospitalization. In the case of *Rouse* v. *Cameron* (1967), a federal court ruled that a mental patient must either be given adequate treatment or be released.

In 1969 California adopted a statute that distinguishes three classes of persons who may be involuntarily hospitalized: those who are gravely disordered and whose care can be entrusted to a conservor, those who are imminently suicidal, and those who are imminently dangerous to others. The imminently suicidal person can be confined for two successive fourteen-day periods; at the end of that time, he must be released even if he is still suicidal. A person considered imminently dangerous by virtue of the fact that he has actually inflicted physical harm on another can be confined against his will, after a hearing, for ninety days. If during the initial ninety-day confinement he has threatened, attempted to harm, or actually inflicted physical harm on another, he may be confined for an additional ninety days.

The actual procedure for involuntary hospitalization varies from country to country and from state to state within the U.S. In most instances, the first step is taken by a member of the family, who arranges for a psychiatric examination of the patient. If the physician's examination indicates sufficient grounds for hospitalization, a formal application is filed with the proper authorities. The next steps are likely to include serving the patient with a legal notice, a prehearing examination, and court commitment. Most states make provision for trial by jury to determine cause for hospitalization, but this procedure is usually waived in uncontested civil cases. Involuntary hospitalization is usually for an indeterminate period, with the time release left to the discretion of hospital authorities. All states recognize the right of the patient to correspond with attorneys and pertinent public officials and to seek a writ of habeas corpus as a means of securing his discharge.

Alternatively, patients may apply directly for hospital treatment. The procedures are essentially similar to those for admission to a general hospital for a physical disorder. In many European countries over 80 percent of hospitalized patients have sought admission voluntarily. The major advantage of voluntary admission is that the patient may secure his release on short notice by written application. If the voluntarily admitted patient poses a definite threat to himself or others, however, the hospital may arrange for his involuntary detention.

Insanity

Insanity is a legal concept that has no medical or psychological counterpart. Strictly defined, the term "insanity" refers only to such gross mental impairment that a person cannot distinguish right from wrong, and therefore cannot be held responsible for his acts. The concept of insanity has been introduced to cover exceptions to the basic rationale of criminal law, which assumes that all adult persons are capable of free and rational choice. It follows that

WHO IS INSANE? THE LEGAL TESTS

M'Naghten rules.

The M'Naghten rules were formulated in England following the trial and acquittal of Daniel M'Naghten in 1843 on a charge of murder. M'Naghten, who believed that he was being persecuted by the Tory party, had intended to kill the Prime Minister, Sir Robert Pell. In error he shot and killed the Prime Minister's private secretary. He was found not guilty on grounds of insanity. Stimulated by interest in this case, the House of Lords asked the judges of England a series of questions related to the law of insanity and crime. Their answers to two of these questions, which were specifically concerned with what jurors should be told when insanity is offered as a defense by a person charged with the commission of a crime, have come to be known as the M'Naghten rules (Whitlock, 1963, p. 20). In part the judges stated:

Jurors ought to be told in all cases that every man is to be presumed to be sane, and to be possess a sufficient degree of reason to be responsible for his crimes, until the contrary be proven to their satisfaction; and that to establish a defense on the ground of insanity, it must be clearly proved that, at the time of committing the act, the party accused was labouring under such a defect of reason, from disease of the mind, as not to know the nature and quality of the act he was doing or, if he did know it, that he did not know he was doing what was wrong.

Alone or in combination with other tests of criminal responsibility, the M'Naghten rules are applied in most states in this country. In essence the critical issue is whether the defendant had the capacity to know right from wrong with respect to the specific act with which he is charged. The principal limitation is that the rules pertain only to impairment of cognitive or intellectual functions, whereas insanity affects the will, the emotions, and the whole personality of the patient. Because of a mental disease a person may commit a crime even though he knows the act is wrong and forbidden by law. The law's answer to this objection is that the purpose of the rules is not to exclude all mentally disabled persons from criminal culpability, but only those who are incapable of making rational choices, for whom punishment would serve no useful purpose. Other criticisms and sources of controversy involve the ambiguity of such terms as "wrong" and "know." Do the rules apply to moral or legal wrongs or both? Should knowledge of the nature and quality of one's act be limited to intellectual awareness, or should it include what clinicians refer to as "emotional" insight?

Irresistible impulse test.

The purpose of the irresistible impulse test is to exclude from criminal responsibility persons who know the difference between right and wrong but who are driven to commit a criminal act by an irresistible impulse resulting from a mental condition. An obvious difficulty is the problem of distinguishing between irresistible and unresisted impulses. A second source of possible disagreement is the status of impulsive criminal acts committed during moments of rage, jealousy, or some other overriding passion. The irresistible impulse criterion has the advantage of acknowledging the impaired self-control of the mental patient. When used in conjunction with the M'Naghten rules, it allows for defects in volitional as well as cognitive abilities. The irresistible impulse test has been accepted in about fifteen states, but it is nowhere relied on as the sole criterion. Where it is accepted, it is always used in combination with the M'Naghten rules or some other criterion of criminal responsibility.

if a person willfully engages in illegal offenses with criminal intent, he is responsible for his actions and liable to punishment. The law further assumes that punishment is warranted as a means of deterring the individual and others from

The New Hampshire and Durham tests.

As early as 1871 the New Hampshire Supreme Court rejected the M'Naghten rules and offered a new rule: that a defendant is not guilty if the crime of which he is accused is the product or result of a mental disease. Eighty-three years later the "product rule" of New Hampshire was accepted with minor modifications by the United States Court of Appeals for the District of Columbia. In the case of *Durham* v. *United States* (1954) this court held that "an accused is not criminally responsible if his unlawful act was the product of mental disease or mental defect." A later amplification of the ruling includes a statement to the effect that an act is the product of a disease if it would not have occurred except for the disease or defect.

From the point of view of the psychiatrist and clinical psychologist, the advantage of the Durham rule is that it permits him to report his findings in his own language rather than in the cramped expressions of legal terminology (Watson, 1959). Specifically, the psychiatrist is asked to supply psychiatric data and his opinion on three questions: (1) Has the defendant a mental illness? (2) Is the alleged criminal act a product of the mental illness? (3) How did the mental illness cause the defendant to commit the alleged crime? Questions of guilt and criminal responsibility are for the jury to decide.

Critics of the Durham test have commented on the ambiguity of the key terms "mental disease" and "product." The former is a relative and changing concept. A psychiatrist's labeling of a defendant as having a mental disease does not make it so. It is more reasonable to consider the commission of a crime as an integral component than as an isolated product of a mental disorder. Roche (1958) has suggested that the "product" question is a legal rather than a psychiatric issue, and should be answered by a jury.

Model Penal Code.

The Durham rule was adopted by the Court of Appeals of the District of Columbia in 1954. The same court, in 1972, unanimously set aside the Durham rule and replaced it with the criterion of insanity described in the Model Penal Code of the American Law Institute. This rule, which has been adopted in essence by the other federal circuit courts of appeals, states: "A person is not responsible for criminal conduct if at the time of such conduct as a result of mental disease or defect he lacks substantial capacity to appreciate the wrongfulness of his conduct or to conform his conduct to the requirements of the law." The change from the Durham rule to the Model Penal Code was based on a court decision involving a man named Brawner, who had been convicted of second degree murder. The new rule is therefore also referred to as *the Brawner decision*.

The reasons for the rejection of the Durham rule have been discussed by Judge Bazelon (1974), the man who wrote the opinion on the Durham case. In essence, the Durham rule gave the psychiatrist too much authority in deciding whether the unlawful act committed by the accused was a product of a mental disease. Under the new rule, the psychiatrist may still testify as to the existence or absence of a mental disease, but he will be required to provide additional information, subject to cross-examination, with respect to the causal relationship between such a disease and the defendant's capacity to appreciate the wrongfulness of his conduct and to control his behavior. On the basis of evidence submitted by the defense and the prosecution, the jury decides criminal responsibility.

committing crimes. The applicability of these legal premises to the mentally deranged has long been questioned. For many centuries madness was regarded as an extenuating factor in criminal cases. It was not until 1843, however, that a definite set of criteria for evaluating insanity, known as the M'Naghten rules, was established.

The determination of insanity is a judicial function. Psychiatrists and psychologists may be called as expert witnesses to state their opinions regarding the mental status of the defendant, but the decision rests with the court. When a defendant is adjudged criminally irresponsible on the grounds of insanity, he may be committed to a mental hospital, referred for treatment, or discharged; he is not imprisoned. The mitigating features of insanity are applicable only in those cases to which the criteria apply. The fact that a criminal is clearly suffering from a mental illness does not exonerate him from criminal responsibility. With respect to the M'Naghten rules, for example, a mentally ill person is considered legally responsible if at the time of committing a crime he knew the nature and the quality of his offense and knew that what he was doing was wrong. The position of the law in such cases is that the presence of a mental disorder that began after the commission of the crime is irrelevant. The purpose of the M'Naghten rules is to exclude from criminal culpability only those people who, because of mental illness, are incapable of distinguishing right from wrong.

Mental Incompetence

The legal concept of *incompetence* comes under civil law. Here the problem is not to determine criminal responsibility, but simply to protect the person and property of the mentally incompetent and at the same time safeguard the interests of his relatives and society. Incompetence is not dependent on the presence or absence of a mental disorder or hospitalization. A person requiring hospitalization for a mental disorder can still be considered legally competent to handle his affairs. Conversely, a person adjudged incompetent by a court may or may not be diagnosed as suffering from some mental disorder. The legal criterion of incompetence is directly concerned with the individual's inability to manage his person and property with ordinary prudence. The inability may be due to mental or physical disability, senility, or spendthrift tendencies. A person adjudged incompetent is deprived of his civil rights and has a legal status comparable to that of a minor. In the case of mental patients, incompetence proceedings may be merged with hospitalization or treated separately.

As a rule, incompetence proceedings are initiated by a relative or friend, who files a petition with the appropriate court. This is followed by a court hearing. Several states provide for a jury trial. If the court finds the defendant incompetent, a guardian is usually appointed to look after him and his property. Contracts and public transactions entered into by a person adjudged incompetent are invalid. Incompetence is often a critical feature of litigation over the validity of wills.

PSYCHOPATHOLOGY AND CRIMINAL BEHAVIOR

Strictly defined, a crime consists of the violation, by an act of commission or omission, and with criminal intent, of recognized laws of society for which punishment is prescribed by law. This restriction automatically excludes all manifestations of psychopathology that do not involve specified legal offenses. The total crime rate for mentally deranged persons is no higher than that for the general population (Rappeport and Lassen, 1965, 1966). When the deranged do commit criminal acts, a distinction is made between culpable offenses and crimes for which the individual is not held criminally responsible by reason of insanity.

The criteria established for defining abnormal behavior provide a convenient set of guidelines for differentiating criminal behavior from antisocial forms of psychopathology. A person is considered criminal rather than insane if he commits an offense punishable by law and shows no significant impairment in higher order psychological functioning or in his ability to exercise voluntary control over his actions. Society usually considers such behavior criminal if the evidence suggests that the offender was in possession of his mental faculties and willfully engaged in some antisocial act for personal gain. As might be expected, it is sometimes difficult to make a clear distinction between criminal and psychopathological behavior. There is often an element of doubt in cases involving impulsive antisocial acts, "purposeless" crimes, and crimes that are so clumsily performed as to invite apprehension. The boundary lines are particularly hazy when offenses represent violations of the moral rather than the legal code.

These doubtful cases, along with other ill-defined antisocial acts, are included under the heading of *sociopathy*. This is admittedly a category of expediency, but it has the merit of recognizing and identifying borderline reactions. The *sociopath* is one whose actions cause society to suffer; the principal victims of his self-centeredness, irresponsibility, and exploitation are his family, friends, and associates. The sociopath does not accept the moral or ethical rules of his society and feels no guilt or remorse for his antisocial actions. This pattern of immediate self-gratification in disregard of the distress caused others, starts early in childhood and persists throughout adulthood. A fuller discussion of the sociopathic personality is in Chapter 12.

SUMMARY

No act, feeling, or thought is, of itself, normal or abnormal. Behavior that deviates from the usual, the expected, or the conventional may be abnormal, superior, or qualitatively equivalent to the norm. Before a meaningful decision can be made as to the relative normality or abnormality of a specific trait or reaction, it is essential to consider the appropriateness of the behavior, to assess the degree of impairment in functioning, and to evaluate the consequences of the behavior for the individual and his society. To take account of infinite variations in appropriateness, effectiveness, and value, we may regard extreme abnormal and "ideal" normal behavior as opposite ends of a continuum. In most instances, specific examples of behavior would be rated in the middle ranges and designated as "average normal."

Key criteria for differentiating abnormal from normal behavior have to do with (1) the relative proficiency of higher order psychological functioning, (2) the relative appropriateness of social behavior, (3) the degree of voluntary control, (4) the degree to which the behavior is perceived and evaluated by society as desirable and beneficial or as unacceptable and detrimental, and (5) the degree to which the behavior is perceived by the individual as satisfying or distressing. Each criterion is considered a separate continuum. The decision as to the relative normality or abnormality of observed behavior depends on a composite evaluation.

In principle, the proposed criteria are applicable in all societies. Some cultures may be more tolerant than others of specific forms of deviant behavior, but no society would regard as normal a person whose behavior was so impaired, disordered, and uncontrolled that he constituted a liability, a threat, or a source of undue distress to himself and his social group. Since there are no fixed or absolute mental symptoms, no psychiatric significance should be attached to the observation that patterns associated with mental disorders in one culture may be casually accepted in another.

Criminal behavior is any act for which punishment is prescribed by law and which is committed with criminal intent. Since most forms of abnormal behavior do not involve legal violations, a clear distinction can usually be made between psychopathological and criminal behavior. In doubtful cases, the criteria described for differentiating normal from abnormal behavior are also helpful in differentiating abnormal from criminal behavior. Unless there is evidence of some significant impairment in self-control or higher order mental functioning, the commission of an illegal offense is considered a criminal act.

The legal concept of insanity is focused on the issue of criminal responsibility. However, the proposed rules of insanity are quite similar to the criteria described for defining abnormal behavior. For example, the M'Naghten rules are mainly concerned with impairment in higher order psychological functions. The key point is whether the defendant was aware of the nature and quality of his act and could distinguish right from wrong at the time of committing the crime. The Model Penal Code and the "irresistible impulse," New Hampshire, and Durham rules all imply a loss of voluntary control as a criterion for the determination of insanity.

References

Adler, A. Social Interest. New York: Putnam, 1939.

Bazelon, D. L. "Psychiatrists and the Adversary Process." Scientific American 230 (1974): 18-23.

Benedict, R. Patterns of Culture. Boston: Houghton Mifflin, 1934.

Bleuler, E. Dementia Praecox or the Group of Schizophrenics. New York: International Universities Press, 1950.

Carothers, J. C. The African Mind in Health and Disease, monograph 17. Geneva: World Health Organization, 1953.

Codere, H. Fighting with Property. American Ethnological Society monograph 18. New York: J. J. Augustin, 1950.

Crutchfield, R. S. "Conformity and Character." American Psychologist 10 (1955): 191-98.

Cummings, E., and Cummings, J. Closed Ranks: An Experiment in Mental Health Education. Cambridge: Harvard University Press, 1957.

Dohrenwend, B. P., and Dohrenwend, B. S. "The Problem of Validity in Field Studies of Psychological Disorder." Journal of Abnormal Psychology 70 (1965): 52-69.

Fortune, R. F. Sorcerers of Dobu. New York: Sutton, 1932.

Freud, S. An Outline of Psychoanalysis. New York: Norton, 1949.

Horney, K. Our Inner Conflicts. New York: Norton, 1945.

Jahoda, M. Current Concepts of Positive Mental Health. New York: Basic Books, 1958.

Janet, P. The Major Symptoms of Hysteria. New York: Macmillan, 1943.

Janis, I. L. Contours of Fear: Psychological Studies of War, Disaster, Illness, and Experimentally Induced Stress. New York: Wiley, 1966.

Kubie, L. S. "Neurotic Process as a Focus of Physiological and Psychoanalytic Research." Journal of Mental Science 104 (1958): 518-34.

Lambo, T. A. "The Role of Cultural Factors in Paranoid Psychosis Among Yomeba Tribe." Journal of Mental Science 101 (1955): 239-66.

Lang, P. J., and Buss, A. H. "Psychological Deficit in Schizophrenia: 11. Interference and Activation." Journal of Abnormal Psychology 10 (1965): 77-106.

Leighton, A. H.; Clausen, J. A.; and Wilson, R. N. "Some Issues Reexamined." In Explorations in Social Psychiatry, ed. A. H. Leighton et al., p. 104. New York: Basic Books, 1957.

Lindman, F. T., and McIntyre, D. M., Jr. "The Mentally Disabled and the Law." Reports of the American Bar Foundation on the Rights of the Mentally Ill. Chicago: University of Chicago Press, 1961.

Linton, R. Culture and Mental Disorders. Springfield, Ill.: Charles C Thomas, 1956.

Martin, R. F., and Hall, C. S. "Emotional Behavior in the Rat. V. The Incidence of Behavior Derangements Resulting from Air-Blast Stimulation in Emotional and Non-Emotional Strains of Rats." Journal of Comparative Psychology 32 (1941): 191-204.

Murphy, J. M. "Social Change and Mental Health." In Causes of Mental Disorder: A Review of Epidemiological Knowledge, pp. 280-340. New York: Milbank Memorial Fund, 1959.

———. "Cross-Cultural Studies in the Prevalence of Psychiatric Disorders." World Mental Health 14 (1962): 53-65.

————. "Psychotherapeutic Aspects of Shamanism on St. Lawrence Island, Alaska." In *Magic, Faith, and Healing,* ed. A. Kiev, pp. 53-83. New York: Free Press, Macmillan, 1964.

Nunokawa, W. D. *Human Values and Abnormal Behavior.* Chicago: Scott, Foresman, 1965.

Rappeport, J. R., and Lassen, G. "Dangerousness: Arrest Rate Comparisons of Discharged Patients and the General Population." *American Journal of Psychiatry* 121 (1965): 776-83.

———— and ————. "The Dangerousness of Female Patients: A Comparison of the Discharge Rate of Discharged Psychiatric Patients and the General Population." *American Journal of Psychiatry* 123 (1966): 413-19.

Roche, P. Q. *The Criminal Mind.* New York: Farrar, Straus & Cudahy, 1958.

Rogers, C. R. *Client-Centered Therapy.* Boston: Houghton Mifflin, 1951.

Ruesch, J., and Bateson, G. *Communication: The Social Matrix of Psychiatry.* New York: Norton, 1951.

Scheff, T. J. "A Sociological Theory of Mental Disorders." In *Approaches to Psychopathology,* ed. J. Page. New York: Columbia University Press, 1966.

Shoben, E. J. "Toward a Concept of the Normal Personality." *American Psychologist* 12 (1957): 183-89.

Tooth, G. C. *Studies in Mental Illness in the Gold Coast.* London: Her Majesty's Stationery Office, 1950.

Veblen, T. *The Theory of the Leisure Class.* New York: Modern Library, 1934.

Walker, E. L., and Heyns, R. W. *An Anatomy for Conformity.* Englewood Cliffs, N.J.: Prentice-Hall, 1962.

Watson, A. S. "Durham Plus Five Years: Development of the Law of Criminal Responsibility in the District of Columbia." *American Journal of Psychiatry* 116 (1959): 289-97.

Wegrocki, H. J. "A Critique of Cultural and Statistical Concepts of Abnormality." *Journal of Abnormal and Social Psychology* 34 (1939): 166-78.

Whitlock, F. A. *Criminal Responsibility and Mental Illness.* London: Butterworth, 1963.

Wilmer, H. A. *Social Psychiatry in Action: A Therapeutic Community.* Springfield, Ill.: Charles C Thomas, 1958.

Wylie, R. C. *The Self Concept.* Lincoln: University of Nebraska Press, 1961.

Yap, P. M. "Mental Diseases Peculiar to Certain Cultures: A Survey of Comparative Psychiatry." *Journal of Mental Science* 97 (1951): 313-27.

Yarrow, M. R.; Schwartz, C. G.; Murphy, H. S.; and Deasy, L. C. "The Psychological Meaning of Mental Illness in the Family." *Journal of Social Issues* 11 (1955): 12-24.

4 · Abnormal Behavior in Historical Perspective

Nebuchadnezzar, William Blake

From prehistoric times groups of people have been confronted with the problem of what to do with deviant members whose disorganized, relatively uncontrolled behavior constituted a liability, a threat, or a source of intolerable distress. The words used to describe these troubled and troublesome individuals, the interpretations proposed to explain their strange behavior, and the actions taken in behalf of or against them make a fascinating chapter in man's endless struggle against superstitious beliefs and inhumane practices. The usual zigzag pattern of human progress is clearly evident in the history of psychopathology. Periods of advance have been followed by periods of stagnation and regression. Time and again similar concepts have emerged, faded, and been rediscovered. Some of the recurring ideas are best dismissed as repeated errors. Others represent significant, enduring insights into behavior pathology.

ABNORMAL BEHAVIOR IN TRIBAL AND ANCIENT SOCIETIES

Spirit Possession

The invention of a spirit world provided prehistoric and nonliterate man with a simple explanation for all unusual or perplexing phenomena. Realizing his relative powerlessness, early man attributed favorable events to the actions of good spirits and unfavorable occurrences to intervention by evil spirits. This universally applicable concept of causation was ideally suited to explain hallucinations, delusions, and other irrational and seemingly uncontrollable reactions associated with madness. The obvious explanation was that a spirit had somehow entered the body of the victim and gained possession of his senses, speech, and actions. In various places at various times over thousands of years spirits have been identified as demons, furies, imps, incubi, and devils. The discovery of partially healed pierced skulls dating back to the Stone Age has led to the intriguing speculation that Paleolithic man not only accepted the notion of spirit possession but worked out an ingenious cure: chipping a hole in the head of "possessed" persons to facilitate the departure of the evil spirits (Selling, 1943).

Toward the end of the first half of the twentieth century, modern man also briefly experimented with drilling holes in the skulls of mental patients. The latter-day rationale, however, was that cutting the neural pathways connecting prefrontal lobes with the older centers of the brain that regulate emotions might alleviate the emotional distress of mental patients. Modern man no longer believes in spirit possession, but old superstitions fade slowly. When a friend ceases to be his familiar self and starts to act strangely, we still ask, "What's got into him?"

Nonliterate Societies

Five main theories of disease causation have been noted among nonliterative societies (Clements, 1932). In addition to possession by spirits, disease was thought to be caused by loss of soul, breach of taboo, sorcery, and object intrusion. The soul-loss theory is based on the assumption

Pre-Columbian trephined (pierced) skulls from Peru. The idea that these holes were punched in the skulls of deviant persons to let out entrapped evil spirits is an "educated" inference; there is no proof.

that a person's soul wanders about at night while he is asleep, and may leave the body when he sneezes or is suddenly frightened. The capture of the detached soul by the ever-present evil spirits causes illness. This theory may be related to the clinical observation that many mental patients are confused, out of touch with their environment, or complain of loss of identity. Jane Murphy (1964) has described two forms of treatment that are practiced by the shamans of an Eskimo village on St. Lawrence Island. The shaman first sends out his spirit-familiar to search for and release the captured soul. If this fails, the shaman may conduct a ceremony to change the name of the patient, thus giving him a new soul.

"Moth sickness" among the Navajo Indians provides an interesting example of taboo violation as the reputed cause of disordered behavior (Kaplan and Johnson, 1964). If a man violates the incest taboo with his sister, it is thought that a moth will thereupon crawl inside his head and exert pressure between his eyes, which will cause him to be attracted to flames, like the moth, until finally he is driven to jump into the fire. Sorcery assumes that disease results from the enmity of other persons, who work their evil will by means of witchcraft, black magic, voodoo, and the evil eye. Treatment consists of magical countermeasures: secret rituals, potions, effigies, and so on. Finally, disease has been thought to be caused by foreign objects in the patient's body. To cure the disease, the medicine man has to remove the objects by sucking them out or administering emetics.

Such theories and therapies are less scientific than those in our own society, but there are basic similarities between them. The theory of taboo violation is related to current views on the role of guilt. The suspiciousness and hostility often observed in mental patients fit in nicely with a belief in sorcery. Spirit possession and lost-soul theories seem curiously applicable to the pervasive anxiety and feelings of helplessness commonly observed in mental patients. The object-intrusion hypothesis is analogous to the theory of organic pathol-

THE SHAMAN AS PSYCHOTHERAPIST: A CASE FROM GHANA

The prestige of the shaman is in some respects greater than that of his modern counterpart. In primitive societies the medicine man may function as physician, priest, magician, moral arbiter, and judge. These varied roles are illustrated in the following account (Field, 1955, p. 820) of psychotherapeutic practices in rural Ghana. Witchcraft is here accepted as the basic cause of disturbance. Bewitched patients, most of whom would be classified as neurotic or depressed in our society, attend special shrines in the forest.

The practitioner conducts the first hearing of any case ceremonially before his shrine. The accompanying ritual need not concern us here, except in its function of enhancing prestige, strengthening suggestion, and fortifying reassurance. He then most thoroughly investigates the family history and the stresses to which the suppliant is subjected. He ferrets out the envies, spites, rivalries, marital troubles, kinship disputes, and temperamental clashes. Ruthlessly he lays bare everyone's secrets. Astonishing tales of guilt and misdemeanor often emerge. Then he sums up the situation as he sees it and as the suppliants have now to see it. He announces who should confess and apologize to whom. He admonishes, he advises, he knocks heads together. He cleanses, he reassures. Sometimes he keeps a suppliant for a long stay of treatment in his forest compound, giving food and a change of scenery. Between him and the suppliant springs up a striking transference which he handles with masterly skills, referring his own influence over the suppliant to the deity of the shrine, to whose permanent protection he is now commended.

ogy. The clinical observations that treatment is more successful when patient and therapist agree on the causes of illness and when both have confidence in the effectiveness of the procedures employed are equally applicable in primitive and Western societies. The common practice among tribal people of extending treatment to the entire family has recently been adopted by modern psychiatry. Extended group therapy is helpful in reducing the isolation and rejection of the patient and in facilitating his reacceptance by his group. Other points of similarity include the use of suggestion, persuasion, and confession.

Ancient Times

The popular belief in ancient Egypt, Israel, Greece, and Rome was that madness was caused by spirits sent by some god or goddess. A distinction was made between persons whose benign behavior suggested possession by good spirits and those who were violent and destructive, who were believed to be possessed by evil spirits. The early books of the Bible stressed the idea that madness was a divine punishment: "The Lord shall smite thee with madness." Two of the four kinds of madness described by Plato (429-347 B.C.) in *Phaedrus* implied possession by good spirits. These were prophetic madness, as illustrated by the ecstatic state of Apollo's oracle at Delphi, and poetic madness, in which the muses provided inspiration for creativity. The other two types were erotic madness and ritual madness, induced by orgiastic religious rites. The assumption of divine causation had the advantage of reducing or eliminating personal responsibility.

Plato recommended that if a mad person engaged in antisocial behavior, he should not be punished, but should undergo purification rites. His family should pay damages and assume responsibility for keeping him from wandering about the city. Plato's views on the etiology of mental disorders were clouded with mysticism. He recognized the contribution of psychological and intrapsychic factors to irrational behavior, but at the same time accepted supernatural explanations.

The more enlightened Hippocratic physicians of ancient Greece rejected the popular belief in spirit possession (Chadwick and Mann, 1950). Hippocrates (460-357 B.C.) maintained that an unhealthy brain was the "seat of madness and delirium, of the fears and frights that assail us, often by night, sometimes even by day: there lies the cause of insomnia and sleep-walking, of thoughts that will not come, forgotten duties and eccentricities." The unhealthy state of the brain was thought to be related to an imbalance in the body "humors," probably hereditary. The recognized bodily fluids or humors consisted of blood, yellow bile, phlegm, and black bile. An excess of blood was considered a favorable factor, leading to a "sanguine" temperament—a cheerful, hopeful attitude. A predominance of yellow bile was associated with choleric or irascible behavior. Too much phlegm resulted in sluggishness and apathy. Melancholy was thought to be caused by an excess of black bile. A favored treatment for mental disorders was the administration of hellebore, a plant with purgative properties that is related to the buttercup family.

The Hippocratic concept of humors, and particularly the belief that melancholia resulted from an excess of black bile, persisted for many centuries. The specific treatment, logical enough if one accepts the premise, consisted in bleeding the patient as a means of eliminating the excess bile. The darkness of the blood provided a measure and proof of the presence of black bile. Bloodletting was approved and practiced by recognized medical authorities well into the nineteenth century. The seeming effectiveness of profuse bleeding in quieting disturbed patients was partly a matter of suggestion—doctor and patient believed

the dramatic procedure would work, and it did—and partly the physical shock and exhaustion resulting from loss of blood.

Hippocrates considered *hysteria* a physical disorder limited to women. The classical symptoms of this disorder—paralysis of an arm or leg or loss of voice—were assumed to be due to the lodging of the uterus in various parts of the body during the course of its restless wanderings. The recommended remedy of marriage and pregnancy suggests that the ancient Greeks associated the illness with sexual frustration. Two thousand years later, Freud suggested a similar interpretation. Since "hysteria" is derived from the Greek word for uterus, this diagnosis was applied only to female patients. This practice continued up until the late nineteenth century, despite repeated clinical observations that hysterical symptoms also occurred in men.

The rational approach to mental illness seeded in Greece was transplanted to ancient Rome by Greek physicians. One of the more enlightened psychiatrists in Rome during the first century B.C. was Asclepiades, who differentiated chronic from acute diseases and related mental disorders to emotional disturbances. He objected to bloodletting and mechanical restraints and advocated the use of baths, music therapy, and occupational therapy. Cicero (106-43 B.C.) also stressed the significance of emotional disturbances. Interestingly, the strongest of the four passions or perturbations described by Cicero was *libido*, or violent desire. He maintained that in cases of "furor" the breakdown in intellectual capacity made the person legally irresponsible for his actions. Under Roman law, the mentally ill were deprived of their freedom of action, and guardians were appointed to look after their business affairs.

Case reports of mental patients by Plutarch and Aretaeus during the first century A.D. leave no doubt that the major psychological forms of human afflictions were the same then as they are now. Anticipating later discoveries, Aretaeus noted that mania and melancholia were different phases of the same disorder and that cer-

Bloodletting in the grand manner. In the poem accompanying this 17th century print, the lady speaks, "Courage, Sir, you have begun, and I'll be brave; tighten the bandage, puncture with confidence, make a good opening. Ah, that gush of blood surprises you? How phlebotomy purifies the spirits and cleanses the blood of great putrefaction." Abraham Bosse, "La Saigrée."

tain mental diseases appeared to be extreme manifestations of the preexisting personality makeup of the patient. Galen (130-200 A.D.), the last of the great Roman physicians, attributed mental disorders to disharmony between the rational, irrational, and lustful parts of the soul; that is, to faulty personality integration. His major contribution consisted in collecting and coordinating the medical knowledge of his time. This information was forgotten during the succeeding centuries and subsequently had to be rediscovered (Zilboorg and Henry, 1941; Mora, 1967).

THE MIDDLE AGES

The concept of mental disorder as a result of natural causes and the humane treatment introduced by the ancient Greeks and Romans were for a time preserved in the Arab world. The first asylums and mental hospitals were built in Baghdad, Damascus, and other Near Eastern cities as early as the eighth or ninth century. Medieval Europe slipped back to belief in demonic possession. Since demonology fell within the province of the church, the clergy assumed responsibility for treatment. Up

Mass execution of the citizens of Haarlem as disciples of the Devil, under the Duke of Alba, in 1573

until about the thirteenth century, the official position of the church was that the insane were innocent victims of the devil. During this period many of the mentally disturbed found refuge in convents and monasteries. Some of the milder techniques used by the priests for driving out demons included prayer, exorcism, sprinkling with holy water, and visits to shrines. If these methods failed, a deranged person might be fed vile concoctions or flogged, in the expectation that the devils within him would tire of so unsatisfactory a host and move out.

Witchcraft

Never far removed from the concept of possession by demons was the suspicion that possessed persons were actually witches in league with the devil. Many alleged witches were in fact heretics who continued to worship pagan deities and engage in pagan rites. Beginning about the fourteenth century, demonology, witchcraft, and mental disease were linked together. It was mainly women who were accused of witchcraft, since it was commonly believed that the insatiable lust of women led them to invite possession by the devil and do his bidding, to the harm of men (Robbins, 1959).

Church and state united in a campaign against witches. Inquisitors were appointed to hunt down and bring to justice the traitorous witches, who, forsaking their allegiance to God, had joined the forces of Satan. This tragic decision may have been partly dictated by the need for scapegoats to blame for the uncertainties and tensions of a society plagued by epidemics and torn by the political, religious, and social dissensions that marked the disintegration of the feudal system. In 1487 two monks, Johann Sprenger and Heinrich Krämer, published the *Malleus maleficarum* ("A

Hammer for Witches"), which served as a handbook for the detection, indictment, trial, and punishment of witches (Summers, 1951). The mentally deranged, and especially those who claimed special powers or whose feelings of guilt led them to confess freely to all sorts of wrongdoing, were natural targets.

During this reign of horror, which lasted for two centuries and briefly touched this country (in the Salem witch trials), thousands of confused, disturbed, or merely disliked persons were convicted of witchcraft and burned (Lea, 1939). In Massachusetts there were no burnings; all the witches of Salem were hanged, except one (a man), who was pressed to death by stones. About fifty times as many women as men were condemned. During the sixteenth century Johann Weyer, a German physician, and Reginald Scot, an English justice of the peace, attempted to expose the fallacy of confusing mental illness with witchcraft. It was not until 1738, however, that England repealed the Witchcraft Acts, and not before 1782 was the last European witch decapitated in Switzerland. A witch was killed in Mexico as recently as the nineteenth century, and in many parts of the world the belief in witches has still not completely died out.

Mass Hysteria

The episodes of so-called mass hysteria that swept through Europe from the thirteenth to the eighteenth centuries are more appropriately described as examples of mass suggestibility or group contagion than as manifestations of mental illness. These events were usually set off when one person started to sing, dance, bark, or throw a fit, and others followed suit. As people copied and reinforced one another's behavior, the process could be kept up for several hours or even days, or it could be quickly terminated by the simple expedient of separating the participants.

The dancing mania constituted one of the more standardized forms of mass hysteria that occurred during the Middle Ages

(Sigerist, 1943). In Germany and most of Europe this was expressed in the dance of St. Vitus. The selection of a saint as the patron avoided the taint of demonic possession. The participants formed circles, hand in hand, and continued dancing for hours in wild delirium until at length they fell to the ground in a state of exhaustion. During the dancing they acted as if possessed. They appeared to have lost all control of their senses, and neither saw nor heard what was going on around them. They were haunted by visions of spirits whose names they shrieked out. Some reported afterward that they felt they had been immersed in a stream of blood, which obliged them to leap as high as they could. Frequently the dance terminated in convulsions when the dancers saw the heavens open and the Saviour enthroned with the Virgin Mary. At other times, they fell to the ground and groaned as if in the agonies of death.

In Apulia in southeast Italy, the dance took on a local form called *tarantism*. The urge to dance was believed to have been caused by the bite of a ground spider, the tarantula. Usually the dancers were happy, uninhibited, and shouted with joy. Occasionally the reaction was less cheerful, and following the spider bite, some people wept for days on end and experienced great misery. Tarantism was geographically limited; in other parts of Italy, the spider bite had no effect.

Hunter and Macalpine (1963) cite an example of an "epidemic of hysterics" that occurred in 1787 in a cotton factory. A girl put a mouse inside the blouse of another girl who had a great dread of mice. The second girl immediately started to have a fit, which continued for twenty-four hours. On the following day three more girls were seized in the same manner, on the third day six more, and on the fourth day another fourteen—twenty-four in all. It was thought that some disease had been introduced in a bag of cotton. Symptoms included anxiety, strangulation, tearing of hair, and dashing the head against the walls. A doctor was called. He promptly cured all the patients by administering electric shocks from a portable electric machine. No new cases occurred after the community was assured that the complaint was merely nervous and easily cured.

More recent examples of mass hysteria include the widespread panic reactions of listeners to Orson Welles's radio dramatization of H. G. Wells's *The War of the Worlds* in 1938 (Cantril, 1947) and the episode of the phantom anesthetist of Mattoon (Johnson, 1945). In the town of Mattoon, Illinois, a woman reported to the police that a prowler had crept up to her open window and sprayed her and her daughter with a sweet-smelling gas, causing nausea and partial paralysis of the legs. The local newspaper published the story, and a large number of people then developed similar symptoms.

THE SIXTEENTH TO EIGHTEENTH CENTURIES

The gradual decline in belief in demons and witchcraft reopened the age-old questions of the causes of aberrant behavior and the ways in which the mentally ill should be treated. During this period there was a revival of interest in theories of humoral imbalance, for which the prescribed treatment was bloodletting. Increased attention was also given to two other beliefs with a long history: the therapeutic use of shock and the effect of the stars and moon on behavior. Popular interest in astrology was exploited by Mesmer in his development of a new therapeutic technique, which today is recognized as hypnosis. The attitude of the public toward the mentally deranged continued to be extremely unfavorable. Although they were no longer burned as witches the psychologically disturbed were neglected, feared, abused, and rejected. The presence of an "insane" person in the family was regarded as a disgrace and was kept a closely

guarded secret. The more fortunate of these disturbed persons were kept at home, where more often than not they were locked up in attics, barns, and cellars. The homeless, if harmless, were treated as pariahs. Ill fed, poorly clad, ridiculed, and driven from place to place, they led the lives of unwanted dogs. If they seemed to pose a threat to others, they were jailed or shut up in lunatic asylums.

Shock Therapy

The history of psychiatry is spotted with the periodic discovery of the use of shock as a way to restore sanity (Zilboorg and Henry, 1941). Under the guise of therapy, mental patients in the past have been lowered into snake pits, tossed from high cliffs into the sea, beaten over the head, had hot irons applied to their heads to straighten out their thinking, and spun in whirling contraptions until they lost consciousness. During the seventeenth century Van Helmont of the Netherlands advocated extinguishing madness by ducking the patient's head under water until his "upper parts" were drowned, after which he was, if possible, revived. The famous English neurologist Thomas Willis (1621–1677) treated a "furious" maid by ordering that she be carried out of the house in the middle of the night and put in a boat. There her clothes were pulled off and she was tied with a rope and dunked in the river to the brink of death (Hunter and Macalpine, 1963).

In the 1930s more "scientific" shock therapies were introduced. Insulin was used to produce a deep coma; drugs and electric shock were used to produce convulsions. No valid scientific explanation for these primitive measures has ever been offered. The temporary improvement occasionally noted following shock treatment may be due to the mobilization of resources against a real threat to existence, just as stuporous patients may be temporarily restored to normal functioning by forcing them to breathe an asphyxiating gas mixture containing an excess of carbon dioxide for a

The circulating swing, 1818, was supposed to bring the depressive back to sound reasoning.

few moments. When psychotic persons acquire some acute physical illness, their mental symptoms are often temporarily improved. A threat to life apparently takes precedence over psychological problems.

Lunacy

The popular term *lunacy* is a legacy of the superstitious belief that the moon was somehow associated with madness. For a time, institutions for the mentally disturbed were officially called lunatic asylums. The supporting evidence for the lunacy theory was the repeatedly confirmed observation that mental disturbances tend to be intensified on nights when the moon is full. Two down-to-earth explanations for this lunar effect are that (1) mental patients may act out their expected role and (2) the increased illumination on full-moon nights keeps the patients awake and active.

Mesmerism and Hypnosis

Although his theories and practices bordered on quackery, Franz A. Mesmer (1734–1815) may be credited with stimulating scientific interest in the importance of psychological factors in the etiology and treatment of mental disorders. A student of theology, astrology, and medicine, this Austrian physician mixed his learning to develop a dramatic technique that became known as *mesmerism*. His basic theory was that an invisible magnetic fluid emanating from the stars influenced the health of human beings. An imbalance of this fluid in the body caused illness. The imbalance could be corrected by the touch of a magnetic wand. Later Mesmer became convinced that his hands had healing power because the magic fluid also flowed from his own body in the form of "animal magnetism." Following some initial success in Vienna, he was accused of being a charla-

Moonstruck ("lunatic") women dancing in a town square, from a 17th century French engraving.

tan by his medical colleagues and forced to leave the city.

In 1778 he went to Paris, where his showmanship won him a brilliant but short career. In the words of Zilboorg and Henry (1941, p. 343), "He magnetized people in private and in public, singly and en masse, bringing them into what was called a *crisis*, that is to say a variety of singular attacks of laughing, crying, convulsive contortions, unconsciousness, and clairvoyance." People flocked to his treatment salon, where they gathered around a *baquet*, a troughlike structure from which protruded iron rods that could be applied to various parts of the body. At the critical moment Mesmer, dressed in flowing robes and with magic wand in hand, would appear and direct the treatment. The impressive ritual, the touching and stroking of the patient's body to reestablish the balance of the magnetic influence, and the confidence of the patient in the efficacy of the treatment were undoubt-

edly effective in temporarily improving many neurotic symptoms.

But the spectacular, theatrical aspects of mesmerism also made it a passing fad. In 1784 a comedy that poked fun at Mesmer was successfully presented in Paris. In the same year a committee of distinguished scientists appointed by the Academy of Science to investigate magnetism turned in an unfavorable report. The committee concluded that the key to the phenomenon was imagination. The claimed effects of magnetism could be produced by imagination alone; magnetism without the critical ingredients of faith and imagination produced nothing. The committee further reported that the repeated excitement of the imagination to induce crisis was harmful and that the spectacle of public magnetic treatments might lead observers to imitate the crisis behavior noted in others. Mesmer's flourishing practice dwindled and he retired to private life.

There is some doubt whether Mesmer was an outright fraud who attempted to exploit the gullible, or a sincere person who accidentally stumbled on a powerful therapeutic technique that was too complex for him to grasp. His idea of animal magnetism is similar to the present-day concept of rapport and the intangible effect of the personality of the therapist on the patient. Mesmerism, which was renamed hypnosis by James Braid in 1843, has turned out to be the phoenix of medicine and psychopathology. Repeatedly buried by criticism, it keeps on rising again. From about 1840 to 1850 mesmerism was used to induce an anesthetic trance state for the performance of painless surgical operations by Elliotson in England and Esdaille in India. The opposition of more conservative physicians, together with the development of gases for inducing anesthesia, soon discouraged this practice; but the anesthetic effects of hypnosis are currently being used in dentistry and obstetrics.

The use of hypnosis as a curative agent for neuroses, earlier recognized by Elliotson and others, was richly documented by A. A. Liébault (1823-1904) and H. Bernheim (1837-1919) in France. Liébault and Bernheim established that the curative effect of hypnosis was based on the power of suggestions given to the patient while he was in a sleeplike state. After World War I another French doctor, Émile Coué (1924), discovered the curative effects of conscious autosuggestion. Treatment consisted of the repetition twenty times each morning and night of the magic formula: "Day by day in every way I am getting better and better."

In addition to demonstrating the effectiveness of suggestion in the removal of symptoms, the early studies of hypnosis provided strong support for the theory that psychological factors were responsible for the physical symptoms of hysteria. A significant late-nineteenth-century observation made at Jean Charcot's famous neurological clinic at the Salpêtrière in Paris was that the whole range of bodily symptoms associated with hysteria (paralysis, deafness, anesthesia, fits) could be readily produced and eliminated by the simple expedient of verbal suggestions given to the hypnotized subject. The ease with which the symptoms could be manipulated by the examiner ruled out neurophysiological explanations. One of Charcot's more significant discoveries was that when a hysterical patient reported a paralysis or anesthesia of the hand or leg, the extent of the loss of function was defined by the part of the hand covered by a glove or the part of the leg extending from the knee downward. In short, the symptoms were demarcated by the popularly recognized limits of the body rather than by the anatomical distribution of nerves.

However, Charcot (1825-1893) erred in concluding that hypnosis is related to hysteria and that only persons with hysterical tendencies are hypnotizable. The alternative view of Liébault and Bernheim, that hypnosis is simply a condition of increased suggestibility and that most willing and cooperative persons can be hypnotized, has prevailed.

Custodial Asylums

Special institutions for the custody of mental patients were established in several countries before the fifteenth century. However, Spain is credited with building the first hospital in Europe specifically for the care of the mentally ill, in 1409 in Valencia. Spanish priests also built the first mental hospital on the American continent in Mexico in 1556. In 1547 Henry VIII gave the Hospital of St. Mary of Bethlehem to the city of London to serve as an asylum for lunatics. Bethlehem, popularly pronounced "Bedlam," soon deteriorated from a hospital to a zoo where the insane were brutally treated and exposed to the public for a fee. The term "bedlam" is derived from the confused scenes associated with this institution. It was a favorite amusement in old London to visit the place to watch the antics of the madmen. This practice was not abolished until the late eighteenth century.

*Jean Charcot
lecturing at the
Salpêtrière clinic in
Paris.*

In other European countries, where custodial institutions for the insane began to appear during the seventeenth and eighteenth centuries, the mentally ill fared no better. The incarceration of lunatics was essentially a police action designed to protect society. The welfare and treatment of the inmates was of no importance. The attitude of the keepers of the early public asylums was that the insane were senseless, dangerous brutes who could be kept under control only by chains and the generous application of whips. Treatment was anchored in the use of force and the curative value of discipline and fear. Royalty was not exempted. When King George III had one of his recurring attacks of mania, his attendants had no compunction about knocking him down and tying him up.

In colonial America conditions were possibly worse (Deutsch, 1946). In 1751 Benjamin Franklin drew up a petition recommending that a hospital be built to care for the increasing number of "persons distempered in mind and deprived of their rational faculties: who were a source of terror to their neighbors, wasted their substance to

the injury of themselves and their families, and were exploited by the wicked." A few years later some rooms were reserved for mental patients in the cellar of the Pennsylvania Hospital. It was not until 1773 that the first mental hospital in this country was constructed, in Williamsburg, Virginia. As in Europe, the mentally ill in colonial America were chained to their cell walls, bled, purged, beaten, and whirled.

HUMANE REFORMS

Toward the end of the eighteenth century, enlightened leaders, including A. Muller in Germany and V. Chiarugi in Italy, protested against brutal restraints and demanded more humane care for the deranged. In France the champion of humane reforms was Philippe Pinel (1745-1826). Although he is best known as the man who freed the insane from their chains, Pinel can justifiably be given the higher title of father of modern psychiatry. His *Treatise on Insanity*, published in 1801, established him as one of the great pioneers. His contributions included:

1. Introduction of the concept that a mental hospital should be a place of treatment rather than for custodial care. Pinel held that most forms of mental disease were transitory. Under favorable conditions they ran their course and were self-corrective. While recognizing that the passage of time was the main healing agent, he believed that recovery could be facilitated through good physical care, an adequate diet, and the establishment of a therapeutic hospital environment marked by kindliness and optimal liberty for each patient consistent with safety.

2. Rejection of the then popular practices of bloodletting, excessive administration of drugs, and reliance on punitive measures. He wrote: "To detain maniacs in constant seclusion, and load them with chains, to leave them defenseless to the brutality of underlings, on the pretense of danger to be dreaded from their ex-travagances: in a word, to rule them with a rod of iron, is a system of superintendence more distinguished for its convenience than for its humanity or its success."

3. Introduction of a scientific approach to the study of mental disorders. He maintained that a detailed case record should be kept on each patient. The record should include the historical development of the disorder from its onset, a register of new facts and changes as they occurred, and a follow-up of the eventual outcome. The numerous case histories reported in his book illustrate the unchanging nature of behavior pathology. His detailed case records led him to conclude that there was no direct connection between the specific character of the symptoms and the nature of the presumed cause. Consistent with his scientific approach, Pinel maintained that before any claim could be made for the effectiveness of any treatment procedure, one should first know the outcome of the disorder when left to the

Pinel ordering the unshackling of female mental patients at the Salpêtrière, about 1795, from a painting by Robert T. Fleury.

Madhouse scene from an engraving by the 19th century German artist Wilhelm Kaulbach.

unassisted efforts of nature; that is, spontaneous recovery, no change, or deterioration.

4. Development of a simple classification system consisting of five major forms of mental disorders: melancholia, mania without delusions, mania with delusions, dementia or the loss of the thinking faculty, and idiocy.

5. Recognition of the importance of emotional and psychogenic factors in the etiology of most mental disorders. He thought that attacks of mania were generally no more than irascible emotions prolonged beyond their ordinary limits.

The reform movement in England was spearheaded by the Quakers, who, under the leadership of William Tuke, opened the York Retreat in 1796 to provide a mild system of treatment based on understanding, affection, liberty, and comfort. Progress was slow, however, particularly in large public asylums. The use of chains was gradually discouraged, but patients were still restrained by leather straps and straitjackets. In 1840 R. G. Hill reported a three-year experiment in total nonrestraint in a small English asylum. The results were spectacular. All recent cases were discharged as recovered; inmates were orderly, quiet, and clean in their personal habits; and no suicides or serious accidents occurred. However, opposition to the system, particularly by the attendants, was so great that Hill was forced to resign his appointment.

It remained for John Conolly (1784-1866) to demonstrate that Hill's technique of abolishing mechanical restraint could be successfully applied in a large public asylum. The elimination of all restraint was only one part of Conolly's system. His chief concern was to create what in recent years has been called a *therapeutic community* conducive to the prompt recovery of the patient. This included the selection and training of kind, cheerful, and conscientious attendants, individualized treatment, and the replacement of fear with hope.

Although the humane movement of the mid-nineteenth century was limited to a few hospitals, it was highly effective. For all admissions to selected hospitals in England and Massachusetts during the period

1830-1850, the recovery or improvement rate at discharge was about 60 percent (Hunter and Macalpine, 1963; Bockoven, 1956). For patients admitted within a year of the onset of their illness, the recovery or improvement rate was 70 percent. Even more impressive, most recovered or improved patients remained well the rest of their lives. In a follow-up study conducted by Park on over a thousand patients hospitalized between 1833 and 1846, information gathered thirty-six to sixty years after hospitalization showed that 54 percent had remained well or were in reasonably good mental health when they died (Bockoven, 1956). These results compare very favorably with those of the best mental health programs of today. These early optimistic figures were apparently influenced by favorable patient response to the personal interest in their welfare shown by the hospital staff and to the spirit of enthusiasm and confidence with which the new techniques were used.

The effectiveness of these intangible, subjective factors in relieving symptoms and modifying behavior is now well recognized. Medicine provides numerous similar examples of the direct relationship of the therapeutic effectiveness of new drugs and the physician's confidence in the treatment, which somehow is communicated to the patient. Commenting on this phenomenon, Sir William Osler facetiously advised that new drugs should be used when they first come out, before they cease to be effective. The high recovery rate reported by mid-nineteenth-century hospital administrators who were deeply concerned with the welfare of their patients may be attributed to what has been recently described as the *Hawthorne effect*. While investigating the effects of physical changes in the environment of factory workers at the Hawthorne plant of the Western Electric Company, a group of industrial psychologists discovered that the production of workers was influenced mainly by management's interest in trying to improve working conditions (Roethlisberger, 1941). The critical factor was not the nature of the physical

change but the more complex issue of worker morale. Innovations such as increasing the amount of illumination, lengthening rest periods, and serving special lunches were found to increase the production of experimental groups. At the same time, control groups who were aware of the ongoing experiment but whose own work conditions were not changed showed an almost equal improvement in production.

The favorable results attained in the few model hospitals of the mid-nineteenth century were neither typical of the period nor predictive of the immediate future. As more and bigger mental hospitals were built during the late nineteenth and early twentieth centuries, treatment became more impersonal and less effective. The earlier spirit of optimism was gradually replaced by a pessimistic attitude toward the curability of psychoses. The popular view that psychoses were diseases analogous to physical disorders for which no medical cure had yet been discovered, discouraged therapeutic efforts and kept discharges to a minimum. A more hopeful attitude toward the treatment of severe mental disorders did not appear again until after the close of World War II.

THE "MENTAL DISEASE" ERA: 1850-1950

Custodial Hospitals

During the century when psychoses were viewed as diseases, Western society regarded the wholesale commitment of mental patients to locked institutions located in rural areas as an ideal solution that protected society and at the same time was in the patient's best interests. The medical concept of disease cannot be blamed for the dismal conditions of the custodial mental hospitals of the late nineteenth century and the first half of the twentieth century; but the assumption that the treatment of psychoses was futile until the underlying

A patient in the Somerset County Madhouse Pa. having his dungeon cleaned out. Feb? 15. 1869.   *E. Haskell.*

physical causes were discovered did not help much.

As late as 1950 most mental hospitals were crowded and often unhygienic. As a rule, food was inadequate, monotonous, and unappetizing, and dietary deficiencies were common. There were little or no provisions for stimulating the patients' interests or occupying their time. As long as patients remained docile and sat quietly week after week, doing absolutely nothing, they were left alone. But if they became restless and obstreperous, they were immediately sedated, immobilized in straitjackets, or isolated in padded cells. A common technique for quieting disturbed patients consisted of wrapping them in wet sheets till they resembled Egyptian mummies. Too often the medical staff consisted of underpaid physicians who were untrained in psychiatry and were responsible for so many patients that their activities were limited to treating incidental physical illnesses and keeping up with administrative details.

The prevailing attitude toward the patients was one of wary apprehension. Patients were confined in locked wards with barred windows. When let out for an occasional airing or a trip to the auditorium to see a movie, they were herded under guard. Fear of what patients might do was carried to such extremes that they were denied the use of forks and knives, so that all meals had to be eaten with spoons. It was considered too risky to trust a patient with matches, pens, lighters, or belts. In short, patients were perceived as dangerous and "crazy," and they behaved accordingly.

During the first half of the twentieth century, hospital regimes were based on the sincerely believed but untested premise that mental patients were totally incompetent. Attendants supervised every move; patients were told when to go to bed, what clothes to wear, and when and where to smoke. Attendants were selected for their size and strength, since their job was to maintain order and discipline, prevent destructive or suicidal behavior, and enforce security measures. They were not expected to have any understanding of behavior disorders, to accept patients as fellow human beings in distress, or to be interested in them as individuals. Care of a sort was provided, but no one actually cared much for the individual patient. This impersonal atmosphere tended to create a silent society in which no one communicated with anyone else; the names of doctors, nurses, and attendants were often unknown to those in

The fractious patient in spread eagle form receiving medical treatment of Douch bath in the Penn.ᵃ Hospital for the Insane, July 4th. 1868.
E. Haskell.

their charge, meals were eaten in silence, and patients who shared the same ward month after month remained strangers to one another.

This approach had limited therapeutic value. However well-meaning, the dull, repressive, dependency-encouraging program tended to fix or accentuate mental disorders and make them in fact incurable. The good patient was the robot who passively adapted to the program without protest and did what he was told with no show of initiative or independence. A patient who reacted against the forced confinement, arbitrary rules, and tedious idleness was labeled as troublesome and assigned to a "disturbed" ward. If such a transfer upset the patient even more, as they usually did, he was subjected to massive sedation, physical restraint, and the "quiet room." Docile patients characterized by social withdrawal were given every opportunity to retreat completely into a dream world, to become slovenly in their personal habits, to spend their days staring blankly into space, and to regress to a simple vegetative state. The social apathy encouraged by this type of regime was strikingly illustrated during World War II by the reaction to air raids of chronic pa-

tients in English mental hospitals (Hemphill, 1941). The blaring of sirens, the continuous gunfire, and the explosion of bombs in the vicinity of mental hospitals had no more impact on the patients than watching a motion picture. Having left the world of reality, they had no interest in what was happening on the outside.

Several writers have suggested that the bleak and impersonal environment of custodial hospitals may be mainly responsible for converting acute transitory reactions to chronic incurable conditions (Goffman, 1961; Kantor and Gelineau, 1965; Ullmann, 1967). The term *social breakdown syndrome* has been applied by Ernest Gruenberg (1967) and others to the dependency, apathy, withdrawal, and lack of responsibility fostered by institutionalization. The development of social breakdown appears to be directly related to the duration of hospital stay. Once chronicity has been established, the possibility of rehabilitation and release to the community is very slim. Various studies (summarized by Paul, 1969) indicate that after two years of continued hospitalization in a traditional mental institution, the probability of release and prolonged stay in the community runs only to about 6 percent.

Drastic Physical Treatment

The discouraging state of mental hospitals during the first half of the present century is largely past history. The better mental hospitals of today more closely resemble general hospitals. The emphasis is on intensive treatment, social rehabilitation, and early discharge. A major reason for dwelling on past conditions is that only by seeing clearly how desperate the situation really was can we understand the wide acceptance of insulin shock therapy, electroconvulsive therapy, and brain surgery during the 1930s and 1940s. In retrospect, these drastic measures may seem reminiscent of the punitive "curative" methods used in bygone centuries; but in their day, they were widely used and highly regarded (Kolinowsky and Hoch, 1952; Freedman et al., 1967).

The first of the treatments by biological ordeal, introduced by Sakel in 1933, consisted of massive injections of *insulin*. By reducing the sugar content of the blood and thereby interfering with the normal metabolic processes in the brain, insulin therapy produced a deep coma marked by diffuse motor, sensory, and autonomic disturbances. The severity of the neurobiochemical changes brought considerable risk to the life of the patient, so the method required good hospital facilities and excellent medical and nursing staffs. No sound rationale for the method was ever presented. The treatment rested on the hope that the massive neurobiochemical upheaval might miraculously straighten out whatever was wrong with the patient. Although some success was reported with certain types of schizophrenic patients, most of the recoveries turned out to be temporary (Staudt and Zubin, 1957). The final verdict appears to be that insulin shock was moderately helpful in shortening the hospital stay of selected patients who would eventually have been discharged as improved even if they had received no treatment.

In 1934 Meduna advanced the theory that a biological antagonism existed between schizophrenia and convulsions, and that there were therapeutic possibilities in subjecting schizophrenic patients to a series of convulsions. As a means of inducing convulsions, he recommended injecting patients with *metrazol*. One technical objection to the method was that it was difficult to control the severity of the convulsion. If too little of the drug was given, there was no convulsion; if too much, the violence of the patient's movements caused bone fractures and other injuries. A second disadvantage was that the patients objected strenuously to the treatment because of the acute fear they experienced in the brief interval between the injection and the loss of consciousness that accompanied the onset of the convulsion. The use of metrazol was therefore discontinued after Cerletti and Bini demonstrated in 1938 that better controlled convulsions, marked by immediate loss of consciousness, could be more conveniently induced by passing an electric current of 100 volts or so for a fraction of a second across electrodes placed on the sides of the forehead. Electroshock sharply reduces the amount of oxygen in the brain, as insulin therapy does, but for a different reason. Insulin reduces the amount of glucose available for oxidation; the high brain activity during electroshock depletes the available supply of oxygen and glucose.

Contrary to Meduna's original hypothesis, electroconvulsive shock therapy has been found to be ineffective with schizophrenics but useful in the treatment of the depressive reactions. However, the procedure creates understandable resistance in patients. Unfavorable complications associated with electroshock include transient memory impairment and a low but real risk of fractures of the vertebrae, dislocation of the jaw, and respiratory arrest. A variety of psychological, psychoanalytic, and neurological theories have been advanced, but no convincing rationale for the use of electroconvulsive therapy (ECT) has yet emerged (Miller, 1967).

The most drastic of the extreme physical therapies, initiated by pioneer studies reported by Moniz in 1936 and Freeman and

An illustration of the bleak, custodial type of institution of the past, which promoted progressive deterioration and the social breakdown syndrome.

A group therapy session of Norwich (Conn.) State Hospital for the Mentally Ill takes place in a home-like atmosphere within the institution. Here two women work on handicrafts while others participate in a group therapy session. The Mini-Unit is a program to humanize treatment.

Watts in 1942, consisted of various surgical procedures designed to slice, puncture, mash, or remove certain areas of the prefrontal lobes of the brain. As a rule, this radical surgical approach was restricted to severely disturbed and unmanageable patients who failed to respond to insulin or electroshock therapy. The underlying theory was that severing the nerve fibers connecting the frontal lobe with the thalamus (considered to be the control center of the emotions) would help relieve emotional unrest. In some instances, the operation did have the effect of transforming restless and destructive patients into relaxed and more easily managed ones. But all treated patients were left with permanent brain damage. Most received no benefit from the operation, and some were reduced to lethargic, insensitive, deteriorated shells of human beings. Psychosurgery has been discontinued for mental patients, but serendipity saved it from being a total loss: the procedure has been found effective in reducing intractable pain in cases of incurable cancer.

MENTAL HOSPITALS TODAY AND TOMORROW

Mental hospitals today serve two quite distinct purposes. One is to provide intensive short-term care and treatment for acute or new cases. The other is to provide care for chronic cases.

New Admissions

Modern mental hospitals endeavor to create a therapeutic environment for recently admitted patients. Extensive use is made of psychoactive drugs, individual and group therapy, and social activities, to restore normal functioning and to prevent withdrawal, dependency, and the social breakdown syndrome. Patients are treated as responsible human beings and are given considerable freedom. Admission wards are open and comfortably furnished. Voluntary admission, a procedure similar to admission to general medical hospitals, is encouraged and has several advantages. It avoids the traumatic experience associated with compulsory commitment and the resentment often aroused when a person is "put away" against his will. The duration of hospital stay of legally committed patients is essentially at the discretion of hospital authorities, whereas, the voluntarily admitted patient may request his release whenever he wishes. Requests for release are honored except in those comparatively few instances when there is good reason to believe that release might unduly endanger the welfare of the patient or of society.

The aim of modern mental hospitals is to discharge patients as soon as possible. Fifty percent of all admissions to state and county mental hospitals in the United States during 1971 were released after a hospital stay of forty-one days or less. Seventy-five percent were released within three months and close to 90 percent by the end of six months (National Institute of Mental Health, 1973). Some patients relapse and are readmitted, but the great majority can and do remain in the community when adequate provisions are made for continued treatment in outpatient clinics and other facilities.

The policy of quick release avoids the risk of the social breakdown syndrome and chronicity. However, there are serious objections to even a brief stay in a mental hospital. As long as society retains negative attitudes of fear, distrust, and avoidance toward the psychologically disturbed, the explicit and permanent labeling of a person as a former inmate of a mental hospital may adversely affect his self-image, his acceptance by family and associates, and his chances of responsible employment.

In recent years, there has been increasing pressure to develop alternatives to admission to mental hospitals. Considerable progress has been made in expanding psychiatric services in general medical hospitals, outpatient clinics, and community mental health centers. Nationwide figures compiled by the National Institute of Mental Health show that during the period between 1966 and 1971 the use of inpatient care increased about 10 percent while the use of outpatient care increased over 100 percent. Facilities showing the greatest increase are indicated in Figure 4.1 (over).

It is interesting to note that despite the tremendous increase in the use of outpatient services, the total number of admissions to state and county mental hospitals has also shown an annual increase. The first sign of the leveling off of admissions occurred in the period between 1971 and 1972 (Figure 4.2.). Many states are currently trying to decrease admissions by adopting more rigorous screening procedures—for example, by requiring applicants to be first examined and treated at community centers, outpatient clinics, or general hospitals. The failures of these first-line treatment centers may be admitted to a mental hospital as a last resort.

The present policy of discouraging hospital admissions and of promptly releasing those admitted makes it difficult to evaluate the effectiveness of hospital treatment. For answers to this question it is necessary to turn to older studies. In a review of this literature by Gerald Paul (1969), the most consistently noted findings were: (1) the longer a person remained in a mental hospital, the poorer were his chances of release; (2) the prognosis was poor for patients whose chief method of adjustment before hospitalization was withdrawal from social interaction; (3) the discharge rate was higher for married patients than for single, divorced, or widowed patients; and (4) educational level and socioeconomic status were positively correlated with favorable outcome.

Data reported by Bockoven and Soloman (1954) are representative of the therapeutic effectiveness of the better mental hospitals during the 1950s. The population studied consisted of one hundred actively psychotic patients admitted to the Boston Psychiatric Hospital. The average length of hospital stay was seventy-five days. By the end of this period, 70 percent were returned to the community and the remainder were transferred to mental hospitals for continued care. One year after discharge, 72 percent were in the community and 20 percent were in other mental hospitals; the remainder had either died or moved out of the state. At the end of five years, seventy-six of the original hundred patients were living in the community, twelve were in mental hospitals, and twelve had either died or left the state. Those in the community were not necessarily completely cured, but their level of social functioning was adequate to permit them to get along. These favorable results were obtained without the aid of modern drugs, which were just beginning to come into use at the time the study was undertaken.

Chronic Patients

Chronic patients constitute approximately two-thirds of the resident hospital population. Most of these are long-term residents who have been continuously hospitalized for five or more years, and some have spent the major portion of their lives in mental hospitals. Heroic attempts to rehabilitate these "hard core" chronic cases have so far had meager success. *Vocational retraining* has been found to be moderately successful in improving work skills, but experimental groups do not differ from nontrained control groups with respect to rehospitalization or personal and social adjustment (Paul, 1969). *Milieu therapy,* which is characterized by increased social interaction, encouragement of informal communication between staff and patients, and group activities directed toward "normal" functioning, has been shown to be effective in decreasing bizarre behavior and improving social reactions. Several studies (Ellsworth, 1964; Sanders et al., 1967) have reported high discharge rates for chronic patients exposed to milieu or intensive resocialization programs. Most discharged

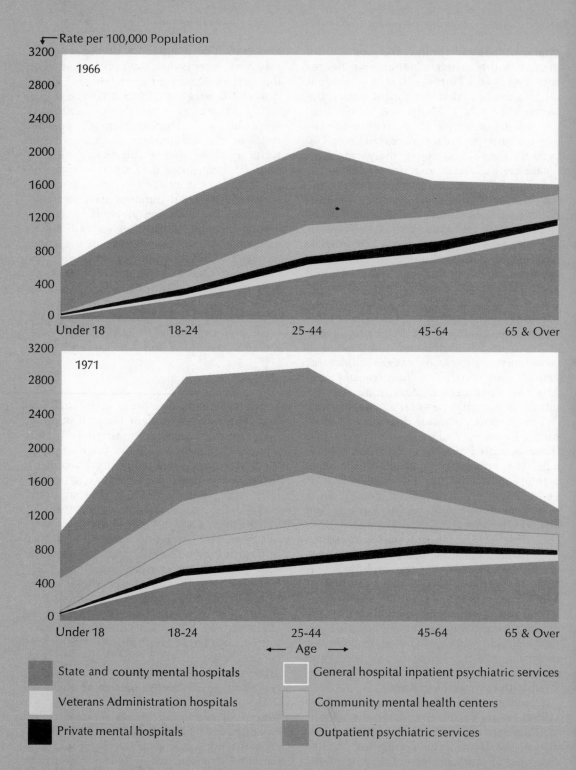

Figure 4.1. The Increasing Use of Outpatient Care (Number of Patient Care Episodes per 100,000 Population by Type of Facility and by Age, 1966 and 1971).

patients, however, fail to adjust in the community and have to be rehospitalized. When correction is made for rehospitalization, the net release figures are only slightly higher for experimental than nontrained groups, if they differ at all (Paul, 1969).

A promising new approach is the establishment of what Teodoro Ayllon has called *token economy wards* for chronic hospitalized patients. This procedure involves the application of basic principles of social learning and motivation in a rigidly controlled environment. The principle of positive reinforcement is used to increase the frequency of desired behavior. Aides, nurses, and other ward personnel are instructed to maintain close observation of the patients. Whenever a patient makes a "good" response (making his bed, interacting well with others, being on time for meals), a staff member immediately reinforces the favorable action by giving the patient one or more tokens—special cards or poker chips that serve as money on the ward. Each day the patient must earn enough tokens to pay for his meals, bed, and extras such as the privilege of living in better quarters, special snacks, reading material, and choice of clothing.

The reinforcement program is tailored to the individual so that all may earn enough tokens to provide for the essentials with little effort. Improvement in behavior results in a higher rate of reinforcement. If the patient makes no favorable responses or fights the system and thus fails to earn the required tokens, he may have to skip a meal or sleep on a cot rather than a comfortable bed. Apart from some periodic mild deprivation, the use of coercive or preventive measures to eliminate eccentric or symptomatic behavior is avoided on ethical and moral grounds. It is assumed that simply ignoring (not reinforcing) undesirable behavior will result in the decrease of such behavior and its eventual elimination. In view of the extent of control exercised by the environment in token economy programs, special attention is paid to safeguarding patients' rights. Pa-

tients are given the opportunity to transfer to another ward whenever they wish (Ayllon and Azrin, 1968).

Token economy programs have been found to be highly effective in furthering self-maintenance, increasing social responsiveness, and decreasing bizarre behavior. So far the major goal of such programs has been to improve personal and social behavior within the hospital. There are some indications that the programs may contribute to increased discharge rates. However, the continued application of reinforcement principles in the community may be necessary to preserve and extend the improvements begun within the hospital. One way this can be done is to establish special "halfway houses" in the community, where patients live and work together in a controlled environment.

The Decreasing Hospital Population

A significant recent change on the psychiatric scene has been the dramatic reduction in the resident population of state and county mental hospitals (Figure 4.2). From 1961 to 1972 the resident hospital population in the United States dropped from 527,000 to 276,000, a decrease of 48 percent. The greatest decrease has been in the older population (forty-five years of age and over). The policy of releasing practically all new admissions within a few months has indirectly contributed to the decrease by limiting the number of annual additions to the resident population. The two main direct causes of the decrease have been death and the release to the community of chronic patients who are no longer actively disturbed. A large number of those released have been elderly men and women who have been transferred to nursing homes for the aged. Younger chronic patients, in varying stages of remission, have been released to the care of their families or community agencies. Many released patients have been placed in boarding homes and special hotels operated by social welfare agencies. Some of the less disabled

ABNORMAL BEHAVIOR IN HISTORICAL PERSPECTIVE

are employed, most are on public welfare or social security.

The high cost of providing prolonged hospital care is the chief practical reason for the current policy of emptying out the mental hospitals. There are also legal, sociopolitical, and psychiatric considerations that center on the principle that per-

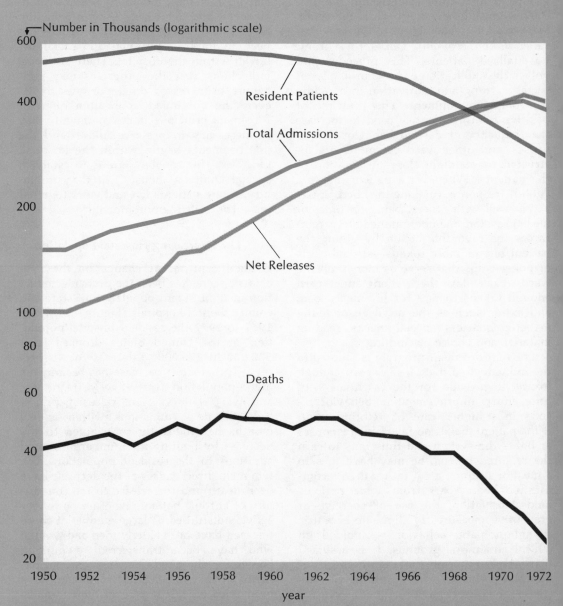

Figure 4.2. Trend Changes in Mental Hospital Population (Number of Resident Patients, Total Admissions, Net Releases, and Deaths, State and County Mental Hospitals, 1950-1972).

SOURCE: National Institute of Mental Health. "Provisional Patient Movement and Administrative Data State and County Mental Health Hospital Inpatient Services." Survey and Reports Section, Statistical Note 77, March 1973.

sons should not be confined to institutions unless they are dangerous to themselves or others. This is a sound principle, but then society has a following obligation to provide adequate services in the community for the psychologically handicapped and mentally disabled. Treatment alone is not enough. Particularly for chronic patients without families, means or appropriate skills, society must assume greater responsibility for providing adequate housing, financial aid, employment, recreational opportunities, and legal assistance.

The weak link in hospital treatment is failure to provide adequate follow-up care and treatment for discharged patients. Chronic patients in particular need continued community support to prevent relapse and rehospitalization. Prerelease training programs designed to help families to cope effectively with discharged patients is one possible solution. Supplementary measures include day centers, outpatient clinics, and sheltered workshops. For patients who have no families to go to, an alternative possibility is the establishment of special homes in the community where small groups of patients may create a mutually supportive "family group" of their own.

A NEW LOOK AT HOSPITALIZATION AND THE CHRONIC PATIENT

While critical of the rationale and therapeutic effectiveness of mental hospitals, Braginsky, Braginsky, and Ring (1969) question whether hospital practices are entirely to blame for "creating" chronic patients. Their view is that many patients choose continued hospitalization as a career. Braginsky and his associates do not deny or minimize the fact that hospitalized patients have genuine problems. What they object to is the prevalent belief that chronic patients suffer from some disintegrative disease that results in the profound impairment of virtually all their psychological functions.

Particularly for patients whose mental condition is sufficiently benign to permit them to live in open wards, hospitalization provides a perpetual vacation from the cares and responsibilities of the outside world. The accommodations at a public mental hospital are not so luxurious as at a first-class resort, but the advantages, facilities, and mode of living are similar. The permanent resident in a good modern mental hospital literally has it made. Food, shelter, clothing, medical and dental care, and other necessities are provided without charge. The patient has unlimited leisure to do as he pleases. Furthermore, he is encouraged as part of his treatment to listen to music, watch movies and television, read, swim, bowl, shoot pool, take long walks, cultivate hobbies, attend classes in arts and crafts, go to parties within the institution and so on. All that is expected of him in return is that he accept the label of mental patient and act the part well enough to avoid being discharged. By learning and playing the hospital game well, patients may in great measure control the length of their stay, the extent of their privileges, and the time and conditions of their discharge (if they wish to be discharged) and readmission.

Braginsky and his associates may have exaggerated the situation a bit in viewing the patient-hospital relationship "as a function of a hedonistic calculus where the hospital is seen as a potential pleasure dome and the patient as an architect of his own personal Shangri-La" (p. 132), but they have bolstered their hypothesis with a series of confirmatory studies. According to their findings, chronic patients are by no means as disoriented, helpless, and ineffectual as they are usually considered. When it serves their purposes, they are capable of pursuing and attaining rational goals. Observational and experimental data indicate that chronic patients on open wards are manipulative and resourceful individuals who are able to satisfy their primary motivations with surprising frequency and ease. When taking tests or being interviewed, schizophrenics, who have been traditionally described as out of touch with reality and devoid of insight, can and do regulate the impression they make on the hospital staff so the staff will act in accordance with their goals. Patients who want to leave the hospital present self-descriptions that play down their psychopathology. On the other hand, those who prefer to remain in the hospital skillfully describe themselves as "too sick" to be discharged, but not so disturbed that they will be exiled to the closed wards.

The particular motivations of patients determine the kinds of information they learn about the hospital's facilities and personnel. If their primary objective is to enjoy a long hospital stay, they systematically go about structuring their activities to permit maximum freedom within the institution while making sure they will not be considered eligible for release. Possible threats to their preferred style of life are averted by ingratiating behavior or the selective avoidance of those staff members who might limit their actions. Some patients are masters of the art of being invisible. Those who plan a long stay in the hospital soon arrange matters so they can lead the kind of life they formerly were able to enjoy only on weekends or on vacation. In short, madness has its methods. Many chronic patients realize they have a good thing going and take full advantage of it.

The exploitation of mental hospitals by some patients is, of course, not restricted to American ingenuity. I remember a conversation I had some years ago with an administrator of the mental hospital program in France, who was concerned with the possible abuse of recently enacted laws that liberalized hospital admission procedures. It seems there was an astonishing increase in the number of Parisians who applied for voluntary, short-term admission during the vacation season to mental hospitals located near coastal resort areas.

Whether one believes that hospitals cre-ate chronic patients or that patients elect to remain long-term hospital guests, the results are the same. Chronic patients accumulate in mental hospitals, and the longer they stay, the poorer is their chance of return to the community. Braginsky and his associates acknowledge that mental hospitals serve a useful purpose in providing a temporary refuge from intolerable life problems. However, they believe that the hypocrisy and degradation associated with acceptance of the patient role is too high a price to pay for some relief from societal pressures. As an alternative, they advocate the establishment of retreat communities, somewhat analogous to the monasteries and convents of the Middle Ages, where troubled persons can go to enjoy a respite from daily life and find renewal. The retreats would consist of publicly supported small communities. Facilities would be similar to those available at vacation resorts. There would be no necessity to have or maintain symptoms to satisfy residence requirements; length of stay would be determined by the needs and wishes of the individual and the availability of space. It is assumed that most would want to return home after a brief stay. Persons who decided to remain as permanent residents could participate in running the establishment.

Braginsky and his associates have deliberately overstated their case for emphasis. It is true that all large mental hospitals have a substantial number of fairly well-adjusted patients for whom the hospital provides a convenient and relatively comfortable retreat. In most instances the staff tacitly goes along with their wishes, because the patients serve useful functions as assistants to attendants and ward workers. Other "recovered" patients are kept on because previous release has resulted in their prompt readmission. For most patients, however, hospitalization offers little reward. Recently admitted acutely disturbed patients are obviously unhappy. Their goals are relief from their symptoms and early discharge. The chronic patients in the locked back wards, who constitute the great majority of the resident population, derive little pleasure from their drab, restricted environment. For these long-term cases, small nursing homes may provide a better solution than hospitalization.

A simple safeguard against encouraging newly admitted persons to become chronic patients might be to limit any patient's stay in a mental hospital to three months. If at the end of this period a patient still required psychiatric attention, some alternative form of community care could be provided. The proved effectiveness of modern drugs in moderating symptoms has virtually eliminated the need for prolonged hospitalization.

PSYCHOTHERAPEUTIC DRUGS

The fortuitous discovery of psychopharmaceutical drugs, starting about 1952 has revolutionized the care of mental patients. The drugs have no curative power but they are highly effective in relieving symptoms during the natural course of the disorder. Psychotherapeutic drugs are classified on the basis of their use or effect; the four major types are *antipsychotic, antimanic, antidepressant,* and *antianxiety*. The generic and trade names of a few representative drugs of each type are listed in Table 4.1. Recent books by Hollister (1973) and Honigsfeld and Howard (1973) provide detailed information about the available drugs, their suggested areas of application, and their side effects.

Table 4.1. Some Representative Psychotherapeutic Drugs.

Type or Use	Generic name	Trade name
Antipsychotic	Chlorpromazine	Thorazine
	Fluphenazine	Prolixin
	Haloperidol	Haldol
	Thioridazine	Mellaril
Antimanic	Lithium	Eskalith
		Litonate
Antidepressant	Imipramine	Tofranil
	Phenelzine	Nardil
	Amitriptyline	Elavil
Antianxiety	Azacyclonol	Frenquel
	Hydroxyzine	Atarax
	Diazepam	Valium
	Meprobamate	Equanil
	Chlordiazepoxide	Librium

Antipsychotic drugs are also known as "tranquilizers," because many of them produce a marked state of relaxation without inducing sleep. Such drugs are particularly effective in controlling hyperactivity, autistic behavior, disturbances in thinking, impulsiveness, and combativeness. They also have a moderating effect on hallucinations, paranoid delusions, and peculiar mannerisms. As a result, patients on medication show less bizarre behavior and are in better contact with their social environment. Hospitalized patients can be allowed greater freedom and self-direction than was possible before. As soon as their more disruptive symptoms are brought under chemical control they can be discharged and referred for further treatment in the community. Whether a discharged patient can get along in the community or has to be hospitalized often depends on his cooperativeness and dependability in taking his medication. This difficulty has recently been partly solved by the development of drugs that have a long-lasting effect; a single injection of a drug called *Prolixin,* for example, controls symptoms for a period of two weeks, and only at the end of this period is it necessary for the patient to return to the clinic for another injection.

There are wide individual differences in drug reactions, so the choice of drug and dosage level must be adapted to the particular patient. After the optimum dosage has been determined, the standard policy is to reduce the dosage to minimize possible side effects. Common side effects include muscular rigidity, a stiff shuffling gait, tremor, and a fixed facial expression. Other reactions may include blurred vision, dizziness, and skin rashes.

The specific antimanic drug is *lithium carbonate,* which produces a prompt reduction of the symptoms associated with manic states. In a few days the euphoric mood, hyperactivity, flight of ideas, and voluble speech are brought under control. A characteristic of manic patients is that they tend to have recurring episodes of either mania or depression. Experimental studies are currently being conducted to see if these recurring attacks can be prevented by keeping the patient under constant medication with lithium. This continued treatment requires careful medical monitoring.

The antidepressant drugs provide a substitute for electroconvulsant shock in the treatment of both retarded and agitated depressions. Patients with persistent irrational fears and those who experience unexplained panic attacks also tend to react favorably to antidepressant drugs. Antianxiety drugs are used mainly with patients suffering from neurosis. They are also recommended for use with alcoholics to ease tension and in the treatment of sleep problems.

SUMMARY

The various theories of psychopathology proposed by primitive, ancient, and modern man represent attempts to explain dysfunctions in accordance with prevailing beliefs and knowledge. Early hypotheses were about evenly divided between theories of external causation (spirit intervention, disease, sorcery, demonic possession, lunacy, bewitchment) and theories of internal or personal causation (loss of soul, breach of taboo, object intrusion, brain disease). In general, treatment procedures were related to the assumed cause.

Another variable in treatment has been the periodic confusion of madness with badness. When possession by spirits was considered an accident over which the victim had no control, treatment was sympathetic and gentle. When collusion with evil spirits or witchcraft was inferred, harsher measures were used. Human suggestibility provides the simplest explanation for the periodic outbreaks of mass hysteria. Suggestion was also largely responsible for the dramatic effects and cures produced by Mesmer during the latter part of the eighteenth century.

Special institutions for the care of the mentally ill were established in Arabic countries as early as 800 A.D. A few small hospitals were started in several European countries during the fifteenth and sixteenth centuries. These early hospitals usually provided no more than custodial care. During the seventeenth and eighteenth centuries, when the mentally ill were degraded to the status of wild animals, mistreatment was the rule. Humane reforms were introduced toward the end of the eighteenth century. The revival of interest in the Hippocratic idea that mental disorders were the products of organic pathology helped reduce the stigma associated with mental illness. The application of the medical model of disease to behavior disorders influenced the rapid expansion of mental hospital facilities in this country during the first half of the twentieth century. Acceptance of the disease model favored experimentation with drastic shock techniques during the 1930s and 1940s, but an important contributory factor was the desperate need to provide some kind of active treatment.

The present trend is to avoid admitting patients to special mental institutions whenever possible, and to treat them instead in general hospitals and other community facilities. A major criticism of the former practice of encouraging patients to enter mental hospitals is that the isolation of patients from the community and the dull, rigid hospital routine tend to encourage chronicity and the development of the social breakdown syndrome. At the same time, some chronic patients use mental hospitals as comfortable retirement centers. Modern mental hospitals emphasize intensive treatment and early discharge. Current methods of rehabilitating chronic hospitalized patients include milieu therapy and token economy programs. Both techniques have been found to be effective in improving the "normal" functioning of patients within the hospital.

The present weak link in the therapeutic chain is the frequent relapse of patients after they return to the community. The rate of rehospitalization could be reduced through the development of more effective aftercare community programs. The discovery of tranquilizing and antidepressant drugs has been a major factor in revolutionizing the care and management of mental patients.

References

Ayllon, T., and Azrin, N. *The Token Economy: A Motivational System for Therapy and Rehabilitation.* New York: Appleton-Century-Crofts, 1968.

Bockoven, J. S. "Moral Treatment in American Psychiatry." *Journal of Nervous and Mental Disease* 124 (1956): 167-94, 292-321.

———— and Soloman, H. C. "Five-Year Follow-up Study of One Hundred Patients Committed to the Boston Psychiatric Hospital." *New England Journal of Medicine* 251 (1954): 81-87.

Braginsky, B. M.; Braginsky, D. D.; and Ring, K. *Methods of Madness: The Mental Hospital as a Last Resort.* New York: Holt, Rinehart & Winston, 1969.

Cantril, H. *The Invasion from Mars.* Princeton, N.J.: Princeton University Press, 1947.

Chadwick, J., and Mann, W. N. *The Medical Works of Hippocrates,* pp. 190-91. Oxford: Blackwell Scientific Publications, 1950.

Clements, F. E. "Primitive Concepts of Disease." *University of California Publications in American Archeology and Ethnology* 32, no. 2 (1932): 185-252.

Coué, E., and Orton, J. L. *Conscious Autosuggestion.* New York: Appleton-Century-Crofts, 1924.

Deutsch, A. *The Mentally Ill in America.* New York: Columbia University Press, 1946.

Ellsworth, R. B. "The Psychiatric Aide as Rehabilitation Therapist." *Rehabilitation Counseling Bulletin* 7 (1964): 81-86.

Field, M. J. "Witchcraft as a Primitive Interpretation of Mental Disorders." *Journal of Mental Science* 101 (1955): 826-33.

Freedman, A. M.; Kaplan, H. I.; and Kaplan, H. S., eds. *Comprehensive Textbook of Psychiatry,* pp. 1251-95. Baltimore, Md.: Williams & Wilkins, 1967.

Freeman, W., and Watts, J. W. *Psychosurgery.* Springfield, Ill.: Charles C Thomas, 1942.

Goffman, E. *Asylums.* Garden City, N.Y.: Doubleday, 1961.

Gruenberg, E. M. "The Social Breakdown Syndrome: Some Origins." *American Journal of Psychiatry* 123 (1967): 12-20.

Hemphill, R. D. "The Influence of War on Mental Disease." *Journal of Mental Science* 87 (1941): 170-82.

Hollister, L. E. *Clinical Use of Psychotherapeutic Drugs*. Springfield, Ill.: Charles C Thomas, 1973.

Honigfeld, G. and Howard, A. *Psychiatric Drugs: A Desk Reference*. New York: Academic Press, 1973.

Hunter, R., and Macalpine, I. *Three Hundred Years of Psychiatry, 1535-1860*. London: Oxford University Press, 1963.

Johnson, D. M. "The Phantom Anesthetist of Mattoon: A Field Study of Mass Hysteria." *Journal of Abnormal and Social Psychology* 40 (1945): 175-86.

Kantor, D., and Gelineau, V. "Social Processes in Support of Chronic Deviance." *International Journal of Social Psychiatry* 11 (1965): 280-89.

Kaplan, B., and Johnson, D. "The Social Meaning of Navaho Psychopathology and Psychotherapy." In *Magic, Faith and Healing*, ed. A. Kiev. New York: Free Press, Macmillan, 1964.

Kolinowsky, L. B., and Hoch, P. *Shock Treatments, Psychosurgery, and Other Somatic Therapies in Psychiatry*. New York: Grune & Stratton, 1952.

Lea, H. C. *Materials Toward a History of Witchcraft*, ed. A. C. Howland, 3 vols. Philadelphia: University of Pennsylvania Press, 1939.

Miller, E. "Psychological Theories of ECT: A Review." *British Journal of Psychiatry* 113 (1967): 301-11.

Mora, G. "History of Psychiatry." In *Comprehensive Textbook of Psychiatry*, ed. A. M. Freedman and H. I. Kaplan, pp. 2-34. Baltimore: Williams & Wilkins, 1967.

Murphy, J. M. "Psychotherapeutic Aspect of Shamanism on St. Lawrence Island, Alaska." In *Magic, Faith, and Healing*, ed. A. Kiev, pp. 53-83. New York: Free Press, Macmillan, 1964.

National Institute of Mental Health. "Length of Stay of Admissions to State and County Mental Hospitals, United States 1971." Survey and Report Section, Statistical Note 74, February 1973.

Paul, G. L. "Chronic Mental Patients: Current Status—Future Directions." *Psychological Bulletin* 71 (1969): 81-94.

Pinel, P. *A Treatise on Insanity* (1801). New York: Hafner, 1962.

Robbins, R. H. *The Encyclopedia of Witchcraft and Demonology*. New York: Crown, 1959.

Roethlisberger, F. J. *Management and Morale*. Cambridge: Harvard University Press, 1941.

Sanders, R.; Smith, R. S.; and Weinman, B. S. *Chronic Psychosis and Recovery*. San Francisco: Jossey-Bass, 1967.

Selling, L. S. *Men Against Madness*. New York: Garden City Books, 1943.

Sigerist, H. E. *Civilization and Disease*. Ithaca, N.Y.: Cornell University Press, 1943.

Staudt, V., and Zubin, J. "A Biometric Evaluation of the Somatotherapies in Schizophrenia." *Psychological Bulletin* 54 (1957): 171-96.

Summers, M. *Malleus maleficarum*. London: Pushkin Press, 1951.

Ullmann, L. P. *Institution and Outcome: A Comparative Study of Psychiatric Hospitals*. New York: Pergamon Press, 1967.

Zilboorg, G., and Henry, G. W. *A History of Medical Psychology*. New York: Norton, 1941.

5 · Psychological Theories and Therapies

The Thinker, Auguste Rodin

In the realm of psychopathology, speculations regarding causation and therapeutic procedures go hand in hand. The effectiveness of therapy is greatly enhanced when the patient and therapist agree about the cause of the patient's difficulties and when both perceive the treatment as appropriate to the assumed cause. Patient-therapist accord in the interpretation and treatment of behavior helps explain the comparable therapeutic success of the witch doctor, the faith healer, the pill dispenser, the psychoanalyst, the behavior modifier, and the existential therapist.

In former times, when people believed that madness was caused by demonic possession, the obvious treatment was to get the devils out by punching holes in the patient's skull, exorcism, or other means. The logical treatment for bewitchment was countermagic to break the spell. Violation of taboos called for expiation, sacrifice, or cleansing rites. The situation today is complicated by the greater diversity of theories, but the principle remains the same. If patient and therapist believe that repressed childhood memories or early parent-child conflicts are the cause of current adult difficulties, the remedy lies in uncovering and coming to terms with the buried memories and traumatic experiences of the past, and in freeing the individual of earlier fixations. Unlearning is the answer to behavior pathology thought to be the product of earlier learning experiences. For patients who complain of the meaninglessness, futility, or emptiness of their existence, the appropriate solution is to fill the inner void with meaning and purpose.

When the patient disagrees with the explanation offered by his therapist for his condition or sees no connection between his notion of relevant treatment and that provided, the common outcome is the discontinuance of psychotherapy, treatment failure, and a change of therapist. A well-known example is the ineffectiveness of conventional psychotherapeutic approaches in the treatment of the poor. Poor, uneducated people, tend to attribute their emotional problems and symptoms to physical causes, their desperate economic circumstances, or their current life difficulties. They reject as irrelevant the therapist's concern with their early parent-child relationship, their past conditioning experiences, their lack of inner unity, or their need for greater self-actualization.

THE ROLE OF THEORIES

Theories are tentative principles offered to explain observed phenomena. A theory is, by definition, speculative and expendable. It does not have to be true to be useful. Negative findings that discount the importance of a suggested explanation serve the useful purpose of narrowing the field of inquiry to more promising alternatives. What is required of a theory is that it be relevant to the facts and capable of generating testable hypotheses.

Even good theories that are based on

empirical observations are merely promising ideas in need of supportive evidence. A common practice in scientific research is to develop a series of alternative theories that may be tested one after the other to determine which, if any, have some factual basis. The more substantiated theories are then reexamined so the researcher may determine which one provides the simplest and most economical explanation for the observed phenomenon. A partisan commitment to a particular theory has the advantage of focusing attention on specific variables and encouraging their detailed study. But care must be exercised in accepting and defending as gospel what ought to be regarded as an expendable hypothesis.

An excellent illustration of the role, value, and tentativeness of theories is provided by the contributions of Sigmund Freud, the founder of psychoanalysis. Freud's claim to fame rests on his genius as a creator of provocative theories. The originality of his insights opened new perspectives and stimulated extensive research on the interpretation of dreams, human psychosexual development, the role of the unconscious, the significance of early parent-child relations in the etiology of neuroses, psychotherapy, and a host of related topics.

Freud was strongly biased in favor of his theories and reserved to himself alone the right to add to them and revise them. As a scientist, however, he recognized the speculative nature of his ideas. In discussing his theory of human drives he stated (1922, p. 76): "I might be asked whether I am myself convinced of the views here set forth, and if so how far. My answer would be that I am neither convinced myself, nor am I seeking to arouse conviction in others. More accurately, I do not know how far I believe them." On another occasion he wrote (1935, p. 144): "Looking back, then, over the patchwork of my life's labors, I can say that I have made many beginnings and thrown out many suggestions. Something will come of them in the future. But I cannot tell myself whether it will be much or little."

MAJOR PSYCHOLOGICAL THEORIES AND ASSOCIATED THERAPIES

Most of the large and ever-increasing number of theories that trace psychopathology to psychological causes may be roughly grouped into three major categories: intrapsychic, behavioral, and humanistic. A rapidly developing fourth psychogenic category is that of family systems theory. We will summarize their principal characteristics below, and describe each of them more fully later in this chapter.

Intrapsychic theories. The most elaborate, the oldest, and the best known of the intrapsychic theories is Freudian *psychoanalysis*. Other theories that represent modifications of classical psychoanalysis, or which are patterned after the intrapsychic model, are those of Erik Erikson, Harry Stack Sullivan, Erich Fromm, and Karen Horney. Two more recent additions that overlap somewhat with the humanistic approach are Frederick Perls' *gestalt theory* and therapy and Eric Berne's *transactional analysis*.

The general premises of the intrapsychic psychoanalytic model vary somewhat from theory to theory, but the central assumption is that some inner conflict or personality disunity (usually related to early childhood experience) is the underlying cause of surface symptoms. Treatment typically focuses on a search for self-understanding, with the goal of creating increased internal harmony. Therapy may be on an individual or a group basis. In either instance, the emphasis is usually on "talking out," self-disclosure, and gaining insight.

Behavioral theories. Probably the outstanding characteristic of behavioral theories is that their major concern is with the individual's currently troublesome symptoms, and especially with those that are directly observable. The reported or observed symptoms are assumed to constitute the disorder. A second characteristic is the

THEORIES AND THERAPIES

inference that the symptoms are learned. Treatment consists in unlearning no longer serviceable (maladaptive) behavior and learning more effective substitute behavior. A wide variety of *behavior modification* techniques have been developed to eliminate specific undesired behavior. Outstanding contributors to learning theory and behavior therapy include B. F. Skinner, Joseph Wolpe, Albert Bandura, and Thomas Stampfl. The differences between the intrapsychic and the behavioral learning models are summarized in Table 5.1.

Humanistic Theories. The distinctive characteristic of these theories is their emphasis on the positive attitudes of man. Humanistic psychologists are concerned with the uniqueness and dignity of man, his growth, meaning, positive self-regard, creativity, self-actualization, autonomy, being, and authenticity. Although there is considerable overlap among them, a distinction is made between self-concept theories, the phenomenological approach, and the existential viewpoint. Alfred Adler, the founder of individual psychology, may be

INTRAPSYCHIC VERSUS BEHAVIORAL APPROACHES TO PSYCHOPATHOLOGY

	Intrapsychic Psychoanalytic Model	Behavioral Learning Model
Focus	Total personality structure and functioning. Main importance attached to the inferred inner life and feelings of the person.	Specific, current, problem behavior that is objectively observable.
Source of difficulty	Intrapsychic disturbances that usually have their origins in early childhood. Lack of personality integration.	Formerly learned responses that are currently regarded as maladaptive or undesirable.
Symptom interpretation	Incidental, surface manifestation of the real inner problem. Symptom will persist or be replaced with other symptoms as long as the underlying problem is unresolved.	There is no buried inner problem. The symptom is the disorder. All that is required is to remove specific identified "symptoms" as they occur.
Relevant diagnostic information	Inner dynamics, nature of conflicts, defenses, significant interpersonal relationships.	Personal and external factors that serve to reinforce and maintain the specific target behavior.
Goal of therapy	Reconstruction or integration of the total personality. This requires elimination of the basic cause of the problem.	Removal or moderation of the specific behavior response (or lack of response) that is perceived as the problem. This may involve either decreasing the frequency of undesired responses or increasing the frequency of more adaptive responses. The original cause is unimportant.

considered an early forerunner of the humanistic perspective. Some of the more recent leaders and advocates of this general approach are Rollo May, Carl Rogers, Abraham Maslow, Viktor Frankl, and Ronald Laing.

Family systems theory. Practically all psychogenic theories imply or specifically state that the mental health of the parents, the nature of parent-child relationships, the stability and emotional atmosphere of the home, and other family influences are major contributory factors to psychopathol-

ogy. The unique aspect of family theory is that the patient is the family rather than the individual. This point of view arose out of clinical observations that the effectiveness of treating individual members of a family was largely influenced and frequently undone by the actions of the family. Often clinical improvement in one member of the family was followed by the appearance of other symptoms in another member. In other words, the presence of symptoms in individual members appeared to be an expression of family pathology

	Intrapsychic Psychoanalytic Model	Behavioral Learning Model
Therapeutic process	Self-understanding, emotional insight.	Direct modification of specific, current problem behavior.
Methods	Self-exploration in depth. Procedures include verbal report, free association, dream analysis, interpretation, and transference.	New responses acquired through conditioning and other learning procedures. Specific methods include desensitization, emotional flooding, assertive training, aversive conditioning, and model imitation.
Other concepts and key terms	Repression, resistance, defenses, anxiety reduction, internalized hostility.	Reinforcement, relaxation, extinction, stimulus generalization, shaping.
Role of therapist	Permissive. Patient is expected to work through his difficulties. Therapist listens, observes, serves as catalyst, occasionally interprets or evaluates.	Therapist assumes control and is highly directive.
Characteristics of "suitable" patients	Well educated, middle or upper class, good verbal skills and not too seriously disturbed.	Method is more effective with some types of patients than others, but is applicable to all.
Duration of treatment	One or more years. Several visits a week preferred.	Variable, but usually limited to a few sessions.

Sigmund Freud (1856-1939), and his future wife, Martha Bernays. This photo was taken in 1885 before Freud's development of psychoanalysis.

and not of some personality defect, faulty habit pattern, or psychic conflict within the individual. If the family is the patient, the obvious corrective procedure is family therapy.

Family therapy was launched during the 1950s. Early pioneers include Ackerman, Bell, Jackson, Boszormenyi-Nagy, Framo, Satir, and Bowen. The origins, vigorous growth, and currently flourishing status of family theory and therapy are described in books by Haley (1971), Ferber et al. (1972), and Sager and Kaplan (1972).

PSYCHOANALYSIS

Freud was initially interested in under-

standing and explaining neurosis and in developing new methods of treatment. Gradually he incorporated his views on psychopathology within a more general framework that encompassed normal as well as abnormal behavior. In this broader context, neuroses were regarded as an extreme variation of normal personality development and functioning. Freud consistently acknowledged the importance of genetic and constitutional factors. A biological foundation was ascribed to many of his key concepts. His major contributions, which collectively constitute the substance of psychoanalysis, consisted of several loosely interrelated theoretical constructs on the determinism of behavior, the role of the unconscious, the libido hypothesis, the structure of personality, and human psychosexual development. These are best described in his own lucid writings (Freud, 1933, 1956). Other good references are the books by Hendrick (1939) and Holzman (1970).

The Determination Hypothesis

A fundamental tenet of psychoanalysis is that behavior is motivated. There are underlying antecedent causes and psychological explanations for the way people behave. Freud saw meaning and purpose even in such seemingly accidental occurrences as slips of the tongue, forgetting of the name of a friend, misplacing objects, and the content of dreams. To Freud, dreams represented attempts at wish fulfillment. The concept of determinism was also applied to mental symptoms. Among other possible explanations, neurotic symptoms might represent indirect forms of wish fulfillment, defenses against anxiety, and compromise solutions to conflicts.

Freud recognized two basic life drives. The first, which was by far the strongest, consisted of libido or sexual impulses, which were broadly interpreted to include a number of pleasurable activities. The second consisted of ego drives which served the organic needs of nutrition and self-preservation. In his later years (1922)

Freud added the controversial concept of a death drive to explain aggressive, destructive, and suicidal behavior.

This motivational system was supplemented by certain guiding principles. The behavior of children, sociopaths, and many neurotics was thought to be mainly dominated by the *pleasure principle*. This principle, which is the controlling factor in the sex drive, is characterized by the avoidance of pain and the seeking of pleasure through the immediate gratification of emotional needs, regardless of future consequences. In older and more mature persons, the pleasure principle comes under the control of the *reality principle*, which encourages the temporary denial of immediate pleasure in the interest of longer term gain. The reality principle is closely associated with the ego drives. Its purpose is to regulate the behavior of the individual so that his actions conform to the moral, social, and physical requirements of the external world. The death drive is guided by the *nirvana principle*. In his use of this term, Freud retained some of its Buddhist connotation of final release from disturbing desires and life problems through death.

The Role of the Unconscious

Freud believed that much behavior was motivated by unconscious forces. He distinguished three levels of consciousness: the *conscious*, the *preconscious*, and the *unconscious*. The conscious consists of events, memories, and impulses of which the individual is clearly aware at the moment. The preconscious is the storehouse of surface memories and desires of which one is not conscious at the moment, but which are readily recallable. The unconscious is a convenient abstraction for identifying thoughts, emotions, memories, and impulses that are not readily accessible to voluntary control. Their presence is indicated by the fact that they influence behavior even though the individual is not aware of their existence or nature.

The unconscious includes primitive sexual and aggressive impulses that are part of man's biological heritage. The second major source of unconscious material consists of thoughts, memories, and wishes that were once conscious but which have been repressed because they were too shocking, painful, or shameful to tolerate. Unconscious material is denied direct access to awareness because it would be disturbing to the individual. Unconscious impulses are not dormant, however. They are constantly seeking expression. Often they may slip past the censor in the disguised form of fantasies and dreams. Much of the strange behavior of the mentally disturbed is attributed to the acting out of unconscious wishes and conflicts. In contrast to the contents of consciousness, which are internally consistent and related to current events, the contents of the unconscious are timeless, independent of logic, and unconcerned with the demands of reality or the rules of society.

The Libido Hypothesis

The term *libido* is a Latin word that originally connoted sexual passion. Freud used the word in two ways: to indicate the aim and the energy strength of the sex drive. The libido hypothesis assumed that most of the energy generated by the metabolic processes of the body was transformed into sexual energy, and that the discharge of this energy followed a predetermined course. During early childhood, libido energy is mainly concentrated and discharged in the oral and anal regions. Later on, the major flow is to the genital region, with sex activity as the main outlet. If the appropriate outlet is blocked, some substitute object or channel of expression may be sought. Thus sex energy that ideally should be directed toward a heterosexual object may be displaced on a person of the same sex, resulting in homosexual urges, or displaced on an object that serves as a fetish.

Personality Structure

As an aid in describing the inner dynamics of behavior, Freud arbitrarily arranged the varied and often antagonistic drives, needs, values, attributes, and functions of the personality into three categories. Each was conceived as a separate component of the total personality. The fictional separation was personified by the now familiar names of *id, superego,* and *ego.*

The id is the agent of the unconscious. It is dedicated to the immediate gratification of sexual and aggressive impulses and the uninhibited pursuit of pleasure. It is unconcerned with the demands of reality, with morals, social values, or logic. Contradictory impulses may coexist side by side, neither influencing the other. The superego is partly conscious but mainly unconscious. It is the component of the personality that is charged with the responsibility of enforcing the morals, values, and ethics the child acquires through introjection from his parents and society. It also includes moral inclinations acquired through biological evolution. The superego serves as both conscience and ego ideal. The ego is mainly conscious but it maintains contact with the unconscious. It corresponds to the "I" that is concerned with the mundane functions of perceiving, learning, remembering, and thinking. Freud thought of the ego as an extension of the id that had been modified through interaction with the external world to serve the needs of the id and self-preservation.

Heinz Hartmann (1939) upgraded the autonomy and functions of the ego. He proposed that the newborn child possesses innate ego functions that permit him to adapt to an average expectable environment. When necessary for survival and optimal adaptation, the ego may take on the added task of modifying the environment. The position of the ego in relation to the id and the superego is that of administrative officer. Its main duties are to (1) satisfy the self-preservation and adaptation needs of the individual, (2) modulate the primitive wishes of the id so they may be expressed in a manner consistent with the requirements of the outer world, (3) enforce repression, and (4) reconcile the antagonistic strivings of the id and superego.

In the discharge of its many duties, the ego often becomes the battleground for conflicts between the demands of the id and the restrictions of society and between the strivings of the id and the prohibitions of the superego. Failure on the part of the ego to perform its diverse functions adequately leads to anxiety and the emergence of neurotic defenses. As Greenson has noted (1959, p. 1402), all neurotic phenomena "are the result of an insufficiency of the ego's normal function of control. . . . Symptoms are either manifestations of involuntary discharges or rigidities which indicate inappropriate and unrealistic controls."

The conflict in neurosis is usually between the ego and the id, but the superego may also participate. When allied with the id against the ego, the superego may contribute to depressions, obsessive-compulsive reactions, and some forms of masochism. According to psychoanalytic doctrine, a psychosis represents a complete breakdown of ego control and defenses and the free and direct expression of id impulses and unconscious material.

The Psychodynamic Hypothesis

The psychodynamic hypothesis is concerned with the interpretation of behavior. It attempts to answer such questions as "What makes Sammy run?" Why are some persons obsessed with a need to be loved? Why do people drink to excess, become depressed, develop specific neurotic symptoms? According to psychoanalytic theory, the answers to these and related questions are to be found in a person's childhood experiences. Parent-child relationships and the pressures and disappointments of early life influence not only the child's immediate response but his adult behavior as well. Feelings of rejection during childhood may lead to cravings for affection or retaliatory acts of violence in adulthood. Unresolved dependency needs may result in dependence on alcohol and drugs. Adult preoccupation with power, money or status may be related to early feelings of insecurity. Social withdrawal and distrust may represent a defense against the risk of repetition of earlier disappointments and betrayal. Oedipal fixations foreshadow sex problems in later years.

Usually the individual is not consciously aware of the extent to which his adult behavior is determined by his childhood experience. If he should engage in irrational behavior, he is unable to explain or refrain from repeating it, even though he may realize its irrationality. For example: A medical school graduate for three years avoided passing the state board examination, the last hurdle in becoming a licensed physician. The first time around he took and failed the examination. This did not bother him unduly since it was his first attempt and several of his classmates also failed. He obtained an internship, which did not require that he be licensed, and spent the next year preparing for a second try—but he "forgot" the date and remembered it only the next day. The following year he remembered the date but overslept.

At this point he decided he needed help and started psychoanalytic therapy. During his analysis he discovered the reason for his irrational behavior. From early childhood, his father had repeatedly stated that he lived only to see his son become a doctor. In terms of psychodynamic theory, the message as originally perceived by the child and stored in his unconscious was awesome and magical. The father's life was in his son's hands. The moment the son became a doctor, the father would die, killed by the son's action.

Psychosexual Development

According to psychoanalytic theory, human psychosexual development follows a biologically predetermined sequence. The area of concentration of libido energy and its appropriate form of expression shift in each successive stage. Each stage is marked by certain personality traits. The main phases are:

Oral stage. From birth to about eighteen months, sex energy is concentrated in the region of the mouth. This is the period of dependency, receiving, and oral incorporation. Later on, biting or oral aggressive behavior becomes dominant. Some residual manifestations of the oral phase in adults are smoking, drinking, and kissing. Oral character traits include optimism or pessimism, trust or distrust, and placidness or aggressiveness. Fixation at and subsequent regression to the oral phase are associated with the psychoses and with certain forms of alcoholism.

Anal stage. From about eighteen months to three years, the erogenous zones consist of the anus, rectum, and bladder. Expulsion and retention are the main sources of pleasure. During this period the child who is not toilet-trained may come into conflict with his parents. Anal character traits include orderliness, punctuality, stubbornness, irresponsibility, overgenerosity, stinginess, and submissiveness. Fixation and regression at this level are associated with obsessive-compulsion reactions and certain types of character disorders.

Phallic stage. Between the ages of three and six years, the sex organs become the erogenous zones. Pleasurable sensations obtained from touching and feeling may lead to masturbation. The object of the libido is now shifted from the bodily self to the parent of the opposite sex. The boy's desire for his mother and feelings of hostile rivalry toward his father are referred to as the *Oedipus complex.* The girl's desire for her father and feelings of hostile rivalry toward her mother are called the *Electra complex.* Fixation and regression at this level are associated with the neuroses.

Latency stage. From about six to twelve years, interest in sex is secondary to interest in intellectual and physical activities. This is also a period of increased aggressiveness, represented by fighting, particularly in boys. The child spends an increasing amount of time outside the home with friends of the same sex. Codes of behavior become more structured. Fixation and regression at this level are associated with certain character disorders.

Erik Erikson, a psychoanalyst identified with ego psychology. His account of the stages of psychosexual growth stresses the importance of basic trust during infancy and the ego identity struggles of adolescence.

Genital stage. With the onset of puberty at about the age of twelve, interest in sex is revived. During puberty it is mainly expressed in a return of earlier phases. The intensification of both sex and aggressive drives during adolescence leads to romantic infatuations, radical idealism, rebelliousness against authority, and a search for personal identity. Heterosexual maturity, the final stage of psychosexual development, is usually not attained until early adulthood.

Normal, healthy individuals proceed smoothly from one phase to the next. As adults they have stable, satisfying heterosexual interests and attachments. The person potentially subject to a mental disorder remains fixated or arrested at a childhood level of development. Fixation may be due to either inadequate or excessive gratification. It is assumed that adjustment difficulties in adult life lead to regression to the individual's point of fixation. The earlier the fixation and subsequent level of regression, the more severe the disorder. The fixation constitutes the nucleus of the difficulty, and the adult disorder is built around this core.

ERIK ERIKSON'S DEVELOPMENTAL SEQUENCE

Freud's theory of psychosexual development has been criticized on the grounds that it places undue emphasis on the early childhood period, is too narrowly confined to the biological aspects of sex, and fails to take adequate account of the psychosocial aspects of human development. Erikson (1963), an American psychoanalyst, has attempted to improve the Freudian model by outlining a broader eight-stage sequence of psychosocial development. Each of the stages, described in Table 5.1, is assumed to be distinguished by a specific conflict and associated with specific traits. Succeeding stages are dependent on the solution and integration of earlier ones.

The two contributions of Erikson that have gained widest acceptance are his concept of basic trust during infancy and his analysis of identity crises during adolescence. Optimum identity is marked by a sense of psychosocial wellbeing, a feeling of being at home in one's body, a sense of knowing where one is going, and inner confidence of anticipated recognition from significant others (Erikson, 1968). The neurotic is confused and uncertain about these things.

Psychoanalytic Treatment

Analytic therapy is intensive, long-term, and expensive. Four to five treatment sessions per week for a period of two or more years are required for a complete analysis. Somewhat oversimplified, analytic treatment has two intermediate objectives. One is to retrace the patient's psychosexual development with the aim of locating the source of his problem and freeing him from early childhood fixations and distortions. The second is to help him uncover, understand, and come to terms with troublesome unconscious material so that repression is no longer necessary. Utilizing insights thus gained, the analyst then works toward the reconstruction of a sounder personality, one that is capable of coping more effectively with life problems and of deriving satisfaction from normal heterosexual activities. In other words, the goal is to strengthen the ego at the expense of the id by making the unconscious conscious.

Psychoanalysts maintain that if current symptoms are eliminated by direct or short-term techniques that fail to penetrate to the underlying causes, they will soon be followed by other substitute symptoms.

The four main analytic techniques are *free association, dream analysis, interpretation,* and *transference.* Free association and dream analysis are used to tap the unconscious. In free association the patient reclines on a couch and reports whatever words, thoughts, or feelings happen to come to mind, no matter how trivial or personal they may seem. This procedure facilitates the expression of repressed memories and impulses, which are constantly seeking discharge. Freud referred to dreams as "the royal road to the unconscious." During sleep, when ego vigilance is reduced, repressed ideas and impulses are expressed in slightly disguised form in dreams. Free associations elicited by the manifest content of a dream lead to its latent content or real meaning. These procedures are not as simple as they may seem. The patient resists the recall of painful or guilt-laden memories. Helping the patient to overcome his resistance is an important part of the analyst's task.

The role of the analyst has been de-

Table 5.1. Erikson's Eight Stages of Psychosocial Development.

Stages	Basic conflict	Associated basic virtues
Oral-sensory	Basic trust vs. mistrust	Hope
Muscular-anal	Autonomy vs. doubt	Will power
Locomotor-genital	Initiative vs. guilt	Purpose
Latency	Industry vs. inferiority	Competence
Puberty/adolescence	Identity vs. role confusion	Fidelity
Young adulthood	Intimacy vs. isolation	Love
Adulthood	Generativity vs. stagnation	Care
Maturity	Ego integrity vs. despair	Wisdom

Adapted from Erik Erikson, *Childhood and Society* (New York: Norton, 1963).

scribed as one of compassionate neutrality. He listens, occasionally suggests a possible interpretation, is understanding and considerate. At the same time he takes care not to permit his own personality to intrude upon the patient. One of his main functions is to serve as a transference object. Transference is a special relationship that develops between the patient and his analyst. In expressing and reliving his past, the patient transfers to the analyst the affection, resentment, hostility, and guilt he formerly felt toward his parents and other significant figures. Transference brings the neurosis into the open, where it can be examined and analyzed. The displaced, inappropriate, and often intense reactions of the patient toward his analyst are referred to as a *transference neurosis*. The interpretation of this neurosis helps the patient gain insight into his problems and to realize that his childish feelings and reactions are no longer appropriate or rational in the context of his adult life. The resolution of the transference neurosis is an important part of the cure. Freed of childhood fixations and the necessity of expending large amounts of energy to maintain repression, the patient can move on to normal interrelationships and more productive activities.

An Evaluation of Classical Psychoanalysis

The theories of classical psychoanalysis have been repeatedly attacked, not only by outsiders but by dissenters within the psychoanalytic group. The main targets have been Freud's views on sex, the unconscious, and the critical importance of early childhood experiences in determining behavior. Sex, even when broadly interpreted to encompass affection and love, is only one of several basic human needs. The appropriateness of assigning sexual significance to the early stages of infantile development has been frequently challenged. Cross-cultural studies have failed to confirm the universality of the Oedipus complex. Studies designed to test psychoana-

lytically derived hypotheses regarding early parent-child relations have resulted in inconclusive findings (Medinnus, 1967). In a sense, these findings do not contradict psychoanalytic theory, since Freud hedged his bets to provide for opposite effects. However, his heads-I-win-tails-you-lose strategem is a major weakness, since it makes his theories untestable.

The major criticism of psychoanalysis as a form of treatment is that it is no more effective than shorter, more economical, and less esoteric procedures that are more widely applicable (Eysenck, 1965). The classical techniques of free association, dream analysis, and transference require that the patient be relatively healthy, highly motivated, and adept in expressing and interpreting his thoughts and feelings. Despite these criticisms, classical psychoanalysis remains the favored approach of many psychiatrists and clinical psychologists. Most psychoanalysts who question the validity of some Freudian theories nevertheless continue to use the classical method of treatment.

OTHER INTRAPSYCHIC THEORIES

Harry Stack Sullivan

Harry Stack Sullivan (1892-1949) was particularly interested in understanding schizophrenia, which he regarded as a grave disorder in living rather than a disease entity. He believed the disorder occurred chiefly in persons "fixed" at the early adolescent level of personality, where sexual problems of intimacy with others are pressing issues (Mullahy, 1967). In his concern with schizophrenia, Sullivan (1953) differed from most psychoanalytic theorists, whose hypotheses were derived mainly from the study of neurotic patients. He recognized two basic motives: satisfying the biological needs of the organism for food, water, sleep, and sex, and pursuit of the psycho-

Harry Stack Sullivan (1892-1949), an American psychiatrist, was an early advocate of the importance of interpersonal relations in the etiology and treatment of mental disorders. He is also known for his theories regarding the development of a self-concept and his division of the self into the "good me," the "bad me," and the denied "not me."

logical need for security. The latter includes the need for status recognition and the need for intimacy with others.

Satisfaction of these needs requires interaction with others from birth to death. During his early years, the child is mainly dependent on his mother for survival. The good mother, who responds to the infant's signs of need with tenderness, promotes the development of confidence in interpersonal situations and a sense of security. The mother who responds to the child's signals of need with anxiety communicates her emotional disturbance to the infant. The repeated occurrence of anxiety in interpersonal contacts inside and outside the home favors a self-system or personality marked by feelings of insecurity. If the individual is reasonably successful in fulfilling his biological and psychological needs with a minimum of anxiety, his confidence in himself is increased along with his self-esteem. Excessive anxiety, combined with low self-esteem and a feeling of insecurity in interpersonal situations, leads to personality disintegration and mental illness.

Attitudes toward the self, which constitute the core of the self-system, mainly reflect the appraisals made of an individual by his parents, peers, teachers, and associates. A distinction is made between the "good me," the "bad me," and the "not me." Those aspects of personality that elicit approval from significant others are considered part of the "good me"; those that lead to disapproval and anxiety are part of the "bad me"; and those that evoke rejection, shame, and loathing may become part of the "not me." Since the overt manifestation of "not me" and "bad me" behavior patterns would result in massive anxiety and loss of self-esteem, they tend to be repressed or dissociated.

These self-system referents are learned and subject to modification as the individual matures and progresses through what Sullivan described as the stages of infancy, childhood, juvenile era, preadolescence, and adolescence. The first two stages cover the first five years of life, when the child's conception of himself is essentially determined by the pattern of mothering and intrafamilial experiences he encounters. During the juvenile period, from five to eight, the child's range of experiences is extended to include interactions with peers and teachers. These new learning experiences may reinforce or alter the child's previously acquired perception of himself and his behavior patterns. The preadolescent period, covering the years from eight to twelve, is marked by the need for a close relationship with one or more peers of the same sex. A major change at this age is a transition from egocentrism to collaboration and nonsexual love. The establishment of a close relationship with one or more peers, plus the sharing of interests and feelings, helps the preadolescent to see the world as others see it. His self-appraisals may be clarified or modified.

The period of adolescence is marked by a gradual shift from dependence to independence. Decisions involving vocational choice and moral standards may be associated with significant changes in the self-system and in self-esteem. With the development of the gonads, interpersonal relations become complicated by the sex urge. The need for intimacy with a person of the opposite sex may conflict with the need for security if attempts to establish a heterosexual relationship meet with rejection or disdain.

Mental disorders, according to Sullivan, result from distorted perceptions of the self and others, which in turn are associated with the repressed or dissociated "not me." If the anxiety resulting from a threatened loss of control is checked by substitutive techniques, such as obsessive-compulsive rituals, the outcome is a neurosis. If substitutive techniques fail and the dissociated impulses emerge into conscious awareness, the outcome is panic and the emergence of psychotic symptoms. The focus of therapy is on the self-system of the individual and the defenses he has developed to cope with his insecurities. The role of the therapist is that of a participant observer. A major objective of therapy is to correct the individual's distorted perception of himself and others in the direction of greater "consensual validation." Personality reconstruction is considered desirable but not essential. A more limited but still acceptable goal is for the patient to recognize the sources of his anxiety and

to learn more adaptive patterns of personal interaction.

Sullivan was more interested in therapy than in developing a systematic theory. The strength of his approach was also its weakness: he confined himself to a limited range of observable data. The dynamics of intrapsychic processes were largely neglected.

Karen Horney

Karen Horney's position represents a moderate modification of classical psychoanalysis. She rejected Freud's biologically oriented view that the basic conflict in psychoneuroses is between man's inherent sexual and aggressive drives and the repressing forces of society. According to Horney (1939, 1945), psychoneuroses are generated by disturbances in human relationships and are influenced by cultural factors. Although acknowledging the prime significance of early childhood experiences in molding the neurotic personality, she also recognized the importance of conflicts in later life. The child early acquires feelings of isolation and insecurity as a result of exposure to such adverse environmental influences as absence of affection, parental domination, and overprotection. He develops a basic anxiety that causes him to dread the environment as a whole, and he builds up defenses to protect himself from his anxiety. In attempting to get along in a potentially hostile world, the child represses his own hostile impulses and may (a) move toward people and obtain security and a sense of belonging by being submissive and dependent, (b) move against people and aggressively fight them on his way in the world, or (c) move away from people and live in an isolated private world. Normal people combine and integrate these three attitudes and thus achieve a balanced, unified personality.

For reasons Horney does not explain, the neurotic has a rigid personality and is unable to achieve this unity, with the consequence that these contradictory attitudes remain irreconcilable. Horney maintained that it is this conflict between contradictory and incompatible attitudes that constitutes the basic core of neuroses. The important point is not the presence of a conflict but the nature of the conflict. Normal people frequently have conflicts, but these are concerned with an actual and voluntary choice between two desirable possibilities; for example, whether to marry or go to graduate school. The neurotic is driven by equally compelling forces in opposite directions, and he has no choice in the matter. Thus a student may be torn between a desire for friends and a dislike of people. The neurotic is also characterized by a discrepancy between his potentialities and his accomplishments.

The aim of therapy is to resolve inner conflicts by changing those conditions within the personality which have brought them into being. The standard psychoanalytic techniques are used to help the patient become aware of his conflicts and their effect on his personality.

Erich Fromm

Erich Fromm has been mainly concerned with the impact of modern society on personality development and psychopathology. Acting through the agency of the family, society imposes a "social character" on the individual. Fromm describes five basic character types: receptive, exploitive, hoarding, marketing, and productive. Each of them occurs in all societies, but in various periods of history the social climate may favor the development of one or another of these character types. Modern society, according to Fromm, tends to produce a standard, uniform personality that can be readily sold and exchanged in the marketplace. Typical traits associated with the marketing character are opportunism, inconsistency, suppression of individual qualities, and lack of genuineness in human relationships. The need to think, act, and feel like everyone else thwarts man's need for individual identity and expression and interferes with meaningful relationships with other persons and with nature. Neuroses and antisocial behavior represent attempts to escape from a "sick" conformity-imposing society that alienates man's basic needs and creates overwhelming feelings of loneliness.

With respect to treatment, Fromm relies on the usual psychoanalytic techniques. His writings have attracted more popular than scientific interest. His vision of utopia is a communitarian humanistic society made up of productive, creative individuals.

Berne and Transactional Analysis

Eric Berne (1961, 1972) focused on the individual's discordant transactions with others as the source of behavior pathology. One of his basic theoretical premises was that everyone has three ego states: at different times and on different occasions he is the Parent, the Adult, or the Child. When acting the Parent role, he acts, thinks and feels as one of his parents did when he was little. The Parent is moralistic, controlling and critical; he is also nurturing and sympathetic. The Adult is objective, realistic and adaptive. The Child feels, acts and responds as might be expected of a two to five year old; in this state, the individual is spontaneous, emotional, fun-loving, and he may also be dependent and at times rebellious.

Since everyone has these three ego states, interpersonal encounters may be complicated. Transactions are described as favorable when they are complementary—for example, when a husband acts as a Parent in his relations with his wife and she responds appropriately as a Child. Transactions are described as unfavorable or crossed when the response is unexpected and inappropriate. In the example cited, difficulties will arise if the wife's response is Adult to Parent.

Transactions may have ulterior purposes, which Berne described in *Games People Play* (1964). These games are not played for fun. The player exploits some weakness in another person to get him to participate in some activity. After the "mark" (victim) is hooked, the player "pulls a

Eric Berne (1910-1970), the originator of transactional analysis. Key tenets include the importance of interpersonal relations (games people play), the interactions of parent-adult-child ego states, and subjective evaluations of the self and others.

switch" which ends the game with a "payoff." The concealment of motives and misdirection is illustrated by the game *NIGYSOB*. A wife transmits covert messages to her husband that she would be relieved if he would let her alone and that he is free to have extramarital sex affairs. The husband proceeds to do so, seemingly with the tacit consent of his wife. For a time, she appears to ignore his obvious infidelity, but after she has accumulated sufficient evidence, she angrily confronts him with her proof and the payoff line, "Now I've Got You, You Son of a Bitch."

Another basic concept of transactional analysis has to do with the individual's appraisal of self and others. The psychological position of the mentally healthy is expressed by the evaluative statement, "I'm O.K. with myself and you're O.K. with me." The characteristic position of paranoids is, "I'm O.K., You're not O.K." and that of depressed persons is, "I'm not O.K., You're O.K." Schizophrenics typically perceive self and others as "not O.K."

Transactional analysis is usually conducted with small groups. Members meet once a week; the length of treatment varies, but a year or more is recommended. The group provides a natural setting for transactions between persons. Feedback from the therapist and the group contributes to the increased self-awareness and insight of the members. The emphasis is on intellectual self-understanding rather than emotional catharsis.

A standard procedure is for the therapist and client to agree beforehand on a contract. The purpose of the contract is to state explicitly the goal of the current phase of the treatment. The immediate goal is usually the alleviation of a particular symptom or correction of some undesired behavior. When this has been achieved, the therapist and client may agree on another contract covering another complaint.

An important advantage of transactional analysis is that its concepts are easily confirmed. Clients readily see themselves interacting with others on the basis of their Child, Adult, and Parent state and playing the games Berne has described. The contract arrangement gives structure and direction to therapy. The emphasis on intellectual understanding may be considered a plus or a minus factor.

Perls and Gestalt Therapy

The term *gestalt* refers to an organized configuration. Gestalt therapy, as developed by Frederick Perls (1969) stresses the importance of helping the patient become an integrated and whole person. The theory is a mixture of psychoanalytic and existential concepts. Its main premise is that patients suffering from neuroses and personality disorders are unaware of or unwilling to accept undesirable or painful parts of their personality. The aim of therapy is to help the patient expand his self-awareness and to complete the "unfinished business" of digesting and assimilating previously ignored or denied parts of the self. Through reclaiming and integrating the fragmented parts, the individual becomes a whole person. He also becomes a more self-reliant, competent, and authentic person.

The procedures of gestalt therapy have been described by Levitsky and Perls (1970). Therapy is conducted in a group setting but on an individual basis; the members take turns sitting on the "hot seat," reserved for the patient who chooses to work on his problem. Gestalt therapists acknowledge the importance of past experiences in blocking awareness; however, they concentrate on *now* awareness. "The

ERIC BERNE: GAMES PEOPLE PLAY

- Let's You and Him Fight
  A woman sets up a competition between two men, and while they are fighting, she goes off with a third.

- Blemish
  A player is not comfortable with a stranger until he finds some weakness or defect in him, in order to avoid responsibility for his own blemishes.

- Why Don't You—But
  A person solicits help from another, but knocks down all suggestions, in order to prove that others, not the player, are inadequate.

- Uproar
  Two persons, accused and defendant, start a fight in order to avoid intimacy.

- Cops and Robbers
  A game played by losers; a player gets a payoff by acting chagrined when caught although he plans to get caught.

- Kick Me
  A player provokes a situation in which another person puts him down to prove that "I'm not O.K."

- See What You Made Me Do
  A player responds to an irritating interruption by dropping something or making a mistake; the punch line gets rid of the intruder. A modification is projecting blame by saying "You got me into this."

- Wooden Leg
  Handicaps are used as excuses for failure or for avoidance of responsibility for actions.

- Stupid
  Others are manipulated into calling the player stupid or acting toward him as if he were which gives the player an excuse to do little or nothing.

idea of the now, of the immediate moment, of the content and structure of the present experience is one of the most potent, most pregnant, and most elusive principles of gestalt therapy."

Communication between patient and therapist and other members of the group is in the present tense. The patient is told to talk directly to the listener rather than at him. The use of "I" language is encouraged to promote a sense of personal responsibility and involvement with one's feelings and body. If the patient says, "My voice sounds like it is crying" he is asked to try saying, "I am crying." The tendency of neurotics to avoid unpleasant experiences (and thereby evade confronting problems) is dealt with by asking the patient to stay with any unpleasant thought or feeling that may occur, to elaborate on the *what* and the *how* of his now feelings.

Gestalt therapy makes extensive use of role playing, but with a novel twist. It is assumed that all persons and things that are encountered in fantasies and dreams represent parts of the self. Awareness of these parts of self is encouraged by having the patient imagine and play out all the significant roles that are present in his fantasies and dreams. For example, if he relates a dream in which he is riding a horse and is being pursued by a man on a motorcycle, he is asked to play the horse and the motorcycle as well as the two persons in his dream.

The emphasis of gestalt therapy on the here and now, its existential concern with awareness, growth, and autonomy, and its flexibility of procedures have contributed to the increasing popularity of this approach to behavior disturbance.

BEHAVIORAL LEARNING THEORIES

Learning is a difficult term to define. The occurrence of learning is inferred from the presence of some new activity, a change in behavior, or an increased probability that a given stimulus will elicit a particular response. However, as Hilgard and Bower note (1966, p. 2), learning is only one of several possible explanations for behavior change. "Learning is the process by which an activity originates or is changed through reacting to an encountered situation, provided that the characteristics of the change in activity cannot be explained on the basis of native response tendencies, maturation, or temporary states of the organism (e.g., fatigue, drugs, etc.)."

In addition, the prevalent assumption that learning is mainly concerned with the manipulation of stimuli and responses tends to disregard the fact that learning is a function of the total organism. How a person will react to current stimuli and what he will learn from exposure to certain experiences will depend on his genetic potentialities, his prior developmental history, the state of the organism at the time, and a host of other modifying variables. Commenting on the latter point, Mowrer writes (1965, p. 245): "Stimuli never produce or cause behavioral responses in the manner implied by S-R connectionism or reflexology. A stimulus S may suggest a particular response R. But the fact that S is present does not at all mean that the subject is obliged or 'forced' to make a particular R—or, indeed, any R at all."

Classical Conditioning

Classical conditioning is also known as Pavlovian conditioning, after its discoverer, I. P. Pavlov (1849-1936). In his early work, Pavlov (1927) demonstrated how "irrational" behavior (a dog salivating at the sound of a bell, for example) can be learned. He trained a dog to stand in a loose harness in a quiet room where there was a minimum of distracting stimuli. A bell was sounded, and a few seconds later food was presented to the animal. On the early trials, the sounding of the bell did not elicit salivation, but the food did. After

Ivan P. Pavlov (1849-1936), Russian physiologist and psychologist, shown in his laboratory. In addition to his discovery of classical or respondent conditioning, Pavlov is known for his pioneer work in the production of "experimental neurosis" in dogs.

a number of trials in which the sounding of the bell was paired with the presentation of food, the sound of the bell alone elicited salivation. When the bell was repeatedly sounded without being immediately followed by the presentation of food, salivation gradually decreased and finally stopped. This process is called *experimental extinction.*

In Pavlov's experiments the food presented to the dog constituted an *unconditioned stimulus;* the sound of the bell was a *conditioned stimulus.* Salivation associated with the presentation of food was an *unconditioned response;* salivation in response to the conditioned stimulus of the bell was a *conditioned response.* Once a conditioned stimulus has been established, similar but different stimuli—for example, a sound other than that produced by the bell—may elicit the conditioned response. This phenomenon is referred to as *stimulus generalization.* Selective *discrimination* of

and response to a particular signal is established by pairing the unconditioned stimulus (food) only with the specific signal. Discrimination training leads to the extinction of the response to generalized but inappropriate stimuli.

Classical conditioning offers a possible explanation for the acquisition of irrational fears and other disruptive emotional responses. In 1920 Watson and Rayner experimentally demonstrated the conditioning of a fear reaction in an eleven-month-old child named Albert. Previous observations had shown that Albert had no fear of a white rat but was readily frightened by unexpected loud noises. The white rat (conditioned stimulus) was presented to Albert, and just as his hand touched the animal, a steel bar was struck with a hammer behind his head (unconditioned stimulus). Albert reacted to the sound with a violent startle, fell forward, and buried his face in the mattress. A repetition of the

B. F. Skinner, a leading American psychologist. His research and writings have been highly influential in establishing the importance of operant conditioning principles in learning and in the application of these principles to educational problems, personality development, psychopathology, behavior modification, and other fields.

paired stimuli elicited a similar reaction with whimpering. A week later the white rat was presented without any accompanying sound. Albert quickly started to reach for the rat, but when the rat nosed his hand, Albert quickly jerked his hand away. He was then exposed to five more paired presentations of the rat with the noise. When the rat was next presented, Albert started to cry and crawl away as rapidly as he could. At the following and final session, it was observed that Albert's conditioned fear had spread or become generalized to include a variety of furry objects: a rabbit, a dog, a fur coat, and a Santa Claus mask.

Operant Conditioning

Operant conditioning is most closely associated with the contributions of B. F. Skinner (1938, 1957). Ferster and Perrot (1968) have provided a convenient summary of its basic principles and technical terms. One important difference between classical and operant conditioning is that the order of the response is reversed. In classical conditioning the subject is presented with a stimulus, which elicits a re-

sponse. In operant conditioning, the experimenter waits until the subject makes a desired response or some approximation of it, and then reinforces the behavior by a suitable reward.

For example, if the experimenter wants to get a noncommunicative mental patient to talk, he may sit with him and speak casually or engage in some sort of activity that will encourage conversation. Whenever the patient says something, the experimenter shows interest and responds in a friendly manner, thus reinforcing the act of speaking in the patient with the aim of increasing the frequency of his speech. If the patient says nothing, the experimenter may initially reinforce any mouth movement by offering the patient a cigarette or some chewing gum. After mouth movements have been reinforced until they are readily elicited, the patient may be required to make a vocal sound before his behavior is rewarded. During later trials, intelligible speech may be required before the patient is given a reinforcer. This step-by-step process is referred to as *successive approximation* or *shaping*. The rate of learning is usually improved if reinforcement is intermittent rather than continuous.

Operant conditioning may be used in the

acquisition or modification of almost any behavior that is within the repertoire and capabilities of an organism. This gives it an important advantage over classical conditioning, which is largely limited to simple reflex or emotional behavior. Operant conditioning may also be used to deal with undesired behavior, which may be decreased or eliminated by the omission of reinforcement, or *negative reinforcement*. Negative reinforcement may consist of the denial of a desired or expected object or response, or the administration of shock or some other aversive stimulus.

A standard technique for decreasing the occurrence of temper tantrums in children is to ignore the child completely when he engages in such behavior. Teodoro Ayllon (1963) has described an interesting example of the use of food deprivation as a negative reinforcement for food stealing by an obese mental patient. Whenever the woman approached a table other than the one reserved for her or took an excessive amount of food from the dining-room counter, nurses immediately removed her from the room and she missed the meal. In two weeks she stopped stealing food.

A somewhat paradoxical learning technique that may be considered a special form of negative reinforcement is called *satiation*. The procedure has long been used by owners of candy stores, who have learned from experience that if they encourage new employees to eat all the candy they want, most employees soon become literally "fed up" with candy and rarely want any. The satiation technique has been effective in helping people to stop smoking (Resnick, 1968). Subjects were required to double or triple their former consumption of cigarettes for a week. A follow-up inquiry conducted four months later showed that the satiated subjects had reduced the number of cigarettes smoked per day more than 50 percent. Twenty-five of the forty satiated subjects, or about 60 percent, had stopped smoking. In contrast, the smoking rate for most members of a control group remained unchanged, and only four of the twenty control subjects

had stopped smoking by the end of the four-month follow-up period.

Two other techniques closely related to satiation are *negative practice* and *implosive therapy*. Negative practice consists in deliberately repeating over and over again some undesirable motor habit (Dunlap, 1932; Yates, 1958). The technique has been found fairly effective in eliminating tics, spasms, stammering, and other motor habits. One possible explanation is that the repeated voluntary performance of a habit brings it under voluntary control. In operant terms, the endless repetition may be considered aversive training.

Implosive therapy has been described by Stampfl and Levis (1967), who recommend its use in the treatment of a wide variety of psychopathological problems. It is based on the hypothesis that past conditioning causes certain objects and situations to elicit anxiety. Patients are asked to imagine or verbalize these anxiety-producing stimuli, to dwell on them at length and repeatedly. By reinstating or symbolically reproducing them in the therapeutic situation where the usual reinforcement does not occur, the anxiety response is extinguished. As in all operant procedures, it is irrelevant whether the patient understands or accepts the significance of the cues. All that is necessary to eliminate the anxiety is to represent the conditioned cues in the absence of primary reinforcement. In effect, the therapist forces the patient to flood himself with anxiety-provoking cues that he would normally attempt to avoid. The repeated nonreinforced exposure leads to the extinction of the anxiety.

Modeling Behavior

Albert Bandura (1962, 1969) has emphasized the use of *modeling* procedures in the acquisition of new behavior and the modification of established behavior. Modeling consists of imitating the behavior of another person, and thus is essentially a form of social learning. For modeling behavior to occur, the individual must have the necessary skills to imitate the model and

Albert Bandura, an American psychologist noted for his studies of aggression and the use of models as a medium for imitative learning and behavior modification.

be motivated to do so. When backed up by positive reinforcement, imitation is an efficient technique for learning the social roles that are expected of a person in various situations.

The social value of acquired performances and roles will, of course, depend on the model. Thus, a child exposed to undesirable models may learn to be aggressive, fearful, suspicious, hypochondriacal, exploitative, or antisocial. In the absence of appropriate models, he may fail to acquire the varied skills and roles required for effective functioning. The absence of competence in varied roles may contribute to the rigidity and nonadaptiveness that is characteristic of psychopathological behavior.

Learning Theory and Behavior Disorders

The idea that behavior disorders consist primarily of maladaptive attitudes and reaction patterns resulting from errors or deficiencies in learning is not new. J. B. Watson—the "father" of behaviorism— rejected the then prevalent disease model of mental disorders as early as 1924. He maintained that faulty habits constituted

the basis of personality disturbances and that their cure consisted in retraining. Personality disturbances arise, he said,

from habit distortion—distortion carried to the point where compensatory factors (serviceable habits) are not sufficient to carry the individual along in society. . . . The proof that personality disturbances are due to long-continued behavior complications and not to organic disturbances appears from the fact that, in many cases, under new and suitable environments, the old reactions can be broken down and new ones entrained. . . . The retraining ("cure"), although more difficult, is neither more nor less mysterious and wonderful than teaching the infant to reach for candy and to withdraw his hand from a candle flame [1924, p. 449].

What is new today is that learning theory has gained wide acceptance both as an explanation of the ways in which abnormal behavior is acquired and as a rationale for treatment. There is now an extensive and rapidly growing body of literature on the effectiveness of the application of learning principles to the treatment of all types of behavior disorders (Kanfer and Phillips, 1970). The difficulty of conducting longitudinal studies on human subjects has limited research efforts to document the premise that behavior dis-

This photo series is from a study conducted by Bandura et al. (1963). The children first observed a film depicting a woman engaging in aggressive behavior (top frame). The lower two frames show a boy and a girl reproducing the behavior of the adult they had observed in the film.

orders are caused by deficits and errors in learning and maintained by current reinforcement procedures that perpetuate established behavior. Animal studies strongly support the hypothesis that abnormal behavior is learned in the same way that normal behavior is learned, although there is some question whether experimentally induced behavior disturbances in animals are valid analogues of human psychopathology.

Learning theory, however, poses two puzzling questions. At some time or other everyone is exposed to dramatic situations and makes undesirable responses that are reinforced. Why, then, doesn't everyone acquire fears, guilt feelings, and faulty habit patterns? Secondly, learning theory holds that "wrong" responses that lead

to negative reinforcement are supposed to "extinguish," or die out. Why do the maladaptive and distressing symptoms of the neurotic persist? One answer (suggested by Hollingworth, 1930, p. 95), is that there is more to a neurosis than the establishment of a faulty habit. "To be neurotic is above all to be the kind of person who is always forming such unserviceable or unsagacious habits even under circumstances or in a world where other people form useful ones." And perhaps to be neurotic is to cling to maladaptive habits that normal people outgrow or learn to discard. Genetic factors may predispose some people to acquire and retain maladaptive reaction patterns. After all, people exhibit wide individual differences in their innate capacity for learning most skills and behavior.

There is no reason why aptitude for learning how to cope effectively with problems in living should be an exception to the rule.

HUMANISTIC THEORIES

The humanistic approach extends the boundaries of psychopathology to include philosophical issues involving values, social interest, positive self-regard, authenticity, meaning, and self-actualization. Writers of this persuasion present a more explicitly favorable image of man than that suggested by the aggression and sex driven Freudian model or the mechanistic S-R model of learning theorists. Another distinguishing feature is their focus on the person as he is now and as he is becoming. Humanists are more interested in understanding the whole living person than in exploring the content of his unconscious or eliciting a chronology of his past learning and conditioning experiences.

Humanistic theories usually include elements of *phenomenology* and *existentialism*. Phenomenology is a school of philosophy which stresses the individual's subjective perception of himself and the outer world as the critical determinant of behavior. Existentialism is even more a philosophy of man than a specific personality theory. Its focus is on individual experience, individual freedom, and the uniqueness and worth of each person. Emphasis is placed on a person's right to be himself, to be guided by his own experience, and to accept responsibilities for his choices. Key importance is also attached to the individual "being-in-the-world"; for human existence to be meaningful there must be involvement and participation in one's social world. The personal frame of reference of existentialism has been explicitly stated by Rollo May (1961): "There is no such thing as truth or reality for a living human being except as he participates in it, is conscious of it, has some relationship to it."

Alfred Adler

Alfred Adler (1870-1937), a Viennese psychiatrist who was associated with Freud for a brief period, soon broke with psychoanalysis and founded his own school, which he called *individual psychology*. Adler (1929, 1939) maintained that the principal human motive was a striving for superiority or power. He interpreted this paramount striving as a compensatory reaction to underlying feelings of inferiority, which he assumed were universal and acquired early in life. The helpless infant, who is completely dependent on the whims and actions of adults, learns the meaning of inferiority while still in the crib. Feelings of inadequacy are further nurtured, according to Adler, by the presence of organic defects, parental overindulgence or rejection, and the child's ordinal position in the family.

The pampered, overindulged child is literally spoiled. He is of little value to himself or others once he leaves the protective hothouse atmosphere of his home. Unable to compete on equal terms with the outside world, he is susceptible to neurotic subterfuges. Or he may expect and demand the good things of life without any effort or sacrifice on his part. If he is denied, he feels justified in engaging in antisocial or criminal behavior to get what he imagines life owes him. The rejected child learns from daily home experiences that he is an inferior, unworthy person.

The only child usually has the same home experiences and shares the same difficulties as the spoiled child, unless he is an only child because his parents dislike caring for a child and take good care not to have another; in that case he is not only rejected, but lonely as well. The eldest child is in a favored position, but much is expected of him. His lead is constantly being threatened by younger siblings who are trying to catch up with and pass him. As the baby of the family, the youngest child may be pampered, ignored, or pushed around by the rest. Children of famous parents are particularly susceptible to inferiority feelings, since they may feel that more is expected of them than they can possibly deliver.

By the age of five, each child creates for himself what Adler referred to as a *style of life*. This is a relatively enduring pattern of behavior that is tailored to overcome the individual's inferiority complexes. A person's life style influences his approach to the three fundamental challenges of life: adjustment to society, vocation, and love. The normal individual develops a style of life and related goals that lead to realistic, effective, and socially useful solutions. He has real interest in other people, which makes him a cooperative and helpful friend, a responsible worker, and a considerate partner in love. The neurotic individual is deficient in social feeling, and his life style is egocentric and parasitic. Fearful of failure, he avoids competition and selects lofty or unrealistic goals that he cannot be expected to attain or that lead to hollow triumphs. Neurotic symptoms are unintentionally exploited to excuse failure, to gain the attention and services of others, or to exaggerate meager achievements. Since the neurotic does not dare to engage in any activity that may result in failure, he adopts a cautious yes-but attitude toward all life challenges. "I would like to go to college, but . . ."

Adlerian therapy is direct and short-term. It is aimed at helping the patient to gain insight into his style of life and fictional goals, to build up his self-confidence, and to encourage him to acquire more effective behavior patterns that will enable him to achieve realistic, socially useful goals. The conversational method is used. No attempt is made to uncover the unconscious. Transference is discouraged. The therapist adopts the role of an understanding but objective friend.

The major criticism of individual psychology is that it is too simple. All conflicts and disorders are reduced to the single formula of striving for superiority and egocentric goals to compensate for inferiority feelings. The chief merit of Adlerian concepts and practices is that they provide a rational common-sense approach to certain types of problems in children and adults for which counseling and guidance are often useful.

Carl Rogers

The best known of the phenomenological theories is the client-centered model developed by Carl Rogers (1959, 1974). Reality is defined in terms of the individual's perception and awareness of his experiences. Experiences that are perceived by the infant as favorable to the actualization of his inherent potentialities are evaluated positively and elicit approach responses. Those perceived as negating this objective are evaluated negatively and avoided.

As the child develops, selected experiences related to his awareness of being and functioning become organized and identified with the concept of self. As awareness of self emerges, the child soon learns that to be favorably regarded by parents and others is satisfying and rewarding. The internalization of this need for positive regard leads to the more important need of positive self-regard. If a person receives unconditional acceptance and approval from others, he acquires a sense of unconditional positive self-regard and personal worth. This fortunate experience leads to the development of an ideal or fully functioning person, one in whom there is no incongruence between self and potentialities, who has no defenses because he needs none, who is open to experience, spontaneous, self-reliant, and creative.

On the other hand, if the individual receives conditional positive regard—if he receives approval only occasionally and inconsistently—the outcome is less favorable. Disapproved experiences that are incongruent with the self-structure are either denied or distorted in such a way as to seem congruent with the self. Defenses are erected against these denied or distorted experiences. If these defenses prove unsuccessful, the resulting threat to the self-structure leads to anxiety and disorganized behavior. Associated symptomatic mani-

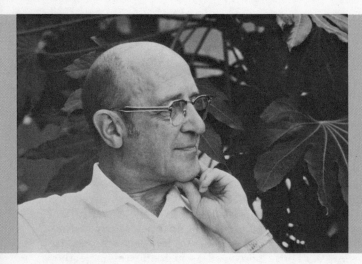

Carl R. Rogers, the founder of client-centered therapy and a vigorous exponent of the phenomenological approach. Rogers holds that empathy and positive regard of the client by the therapist facilitate treatment but that the client has the right and the capacity to solve his own problem.

festations may reflect emergency adjustments to the overt, direct expression of experiences hitherto distorted or denied.

Treatment involves a reversing of the defense process. Previously threatening experiences must be accurately symbolized in awareness and integrated into the self-concept. The client-centered therapist attempts to build up the patient's self-regard by genuinely offering unconditional positive regard in a context of empathic understanding. He tries to see the world from the patient's point of view, to sense and reflect his perceptions, distortions, strivings and feelings. The premise is that sincere acceptance and understanding of the patient as he is reduces his need for defenses. The client—this term is used to avoid the pejorative implications of "patient"—is thereby increasingly free to express his feelings and to experience and accept feelings and experiences previously denied to awareness. As he accepts ownership of formerly denied feelings, they are brought under greater voluntary control.

The final outcome, according to Rogers, is that the client sees himself and others more realistically and is more accepting of himself and of others. His positive self-regard is increased and his perception of his ideal self becomes more congruent with his actual self. Following therapy, his behavior is more productive, more adaptive, and more fully expressive of his own purposes and values.

In client-centered therapy the therapist is expected to be an active but noninterfering participant. His role is to listen attentively to the client and to convey his empathy and understanding by reflecting the feelings, attitudes, and ideas expressed. The rest is left to the client. The therapist refrains from offering interpretations, advice, or suggestions. A cardinal tenet of the Rogerian approach is that the individual not only has the right of self-determination, but—more important—has the capacity to make good decisions. The function of the therapist is to provide a climate that will facilitate the client's utilization of his vast inner resources for self-understanding, for altering his self-concept and attitudes, and for improving his behavior.

Client-centered therapy is not as simple as this may make it seem. The effective use of the approach is in great measure limited to therapists richly endowed with empathy and understanding, and to articulate, intelligent, and highly motivated clients who also are inner-directed. A commonly noted criticism is that the Rogerian approach tends to ignore the importance of aggressive feelings. On the plus side, client-centered therapy has found wide acceptance in counseling college students, pastoral counseling, and marriage counseling. Usually clients are seen on an individual basis, but the method has been effectively and extensively used with groups.

Existentialism

Most existential concepts have been European imports. Among the major contributors are Kierkegaard, Nietzsche, Heidegger, Jaspers, Sartre, Binswanger, Frankl, and Laing. Leading exponents in this country include Rollo May (1961), Paul Tillich (1952), and Abraham Maslow (1973). In keeping with the existential emphasis on personal experiences and individuality, these writers differ in their views, and each tends to use special terms of his own invention.

One of the common themes in existential writings is the human struggle between being and nonbeing. This struggle involves life versus death but it also includes being a person versus a nonperson, and full acceptance of one's self versus rejection or denial of parts of the self. A second and related conflict centers on being authentic vs. fraudulent. To be authentic a person must be honest with himself, make a commitment to life, and be willing to accept risks in expressing his freedom and actual-

izing his full potentialities. To do otherwise is to be a phony, to suffer loss of meaning and a reduction or alienation of self. The latter is considered to constitute the major basis for mental disorders.

Existential therapy is not distinguished by any specific techniques and the therapist may use any of the traditional approaches. What is important is his attitude of openness, to see and hear the patient as he is. The role of the therapist, as Adrian Van Kamp (1967) describes it, is to foster an atmosphere that will enable the patient to realize the unique meaning of his existence within his particular life situation, to face his personal responsibilities, and to accept both the joys and the unavoidable pain and suffering of human life. Rollo May (1961) defines the good therapist as one who is able to grasp the patient in his reality and whose own constructs are sufficiently flexible so that "he can listen in terms of the patient's constructs and hear in the patient's language."

The following summaries of some of the views expressed by Maslow, Frankl, and Laing provide a sampling of the scope of the existential perspective.

Maslow. In a paper originally published in 1956, Abraham Maslow (1973) tackled

---

SOME EXISTENTIAL TERMS

- Daseinsanalyse   Binswanger's term for existential analysis
- Existential   to stand out, emerge, become
- Essence   the converse of existential, with emphasis on fixed and universal characteristics
- Noögenic neurosis   Frankl's term for existential neurosis resulting from despair over the meaninglessness of life
- Ontological   related to the science of being; in Laing's usage, the same as being
- Logotherapy   Frankl's term for and approach to psychotherapy

Abraham Maslow (1908-1970), a leader in the development of humanistic psychology, which he called the "third force," the other two being behaviorism and psychoanalysis. Maslow stressed the positive attributes of man and especially his strivings for self-actualization.

the interesting problem of how children progress from *being* to *becoming*, from living for the moment to growth and self-actualization. He suggested that the answer is to be found in the spontaneous curiosity and creativity of children as they explore, manipulate, experience, and enjoy life. There is no need to assume foresight, purpose, or goal. When the child is satiated with his present pleasures, he becomes bored, and is ready to move on, and hopefully up. "Growth takes place when the next step forward is subjectively more delightful, more joyous, more intrinsically satisfying than the last."

Maslow assumed a hierarchy of needs. Starting with the satisfaction of physiological needs, the child moves on to a desire for safety, mastery, belongingness, love, esteem, and finally self-actualization. A further premise is that lower level needs must be gratified before the individual feels confident enough to move on to the next level; for example, the need for safety usually takes priority over the need for mastery. The healthy child does not have to be pushed to grow. He wants to go forward. It is only when he encounters frustration, failure, disapproval, or ridicule at

the next higher step that he fixates or regresses. If the arrest in growth persists, the frustrated individual may resort to neurotic compromises.

Utimately, each person must decide for himself whether to remain at his present level, move ahead, or fall back. The choice is not easy to make. Some conflict is inevitable since each individual has two sets of forces within him. One set clings to safety and defensiveness out of fear of taking chances and of losing what one already has; it is a fear of independence, freedom, and separateness. The other set of forces impels the individual forward toward wholeness and uniqueness of self and toward full functioning of all his capabilities.

Maslow shares the conviction of most humanists that if given a free choice, the child will choose wisely and move in a healthy direction of growth. The therapist can help by respecting and understanding the child's deficiency and growth needs and by being available when he is needed and getting out of the child's way when he is not. Parents and teachers can help by assuring gratification of the child's basic needs for safety, belongingness, love, and respect so he can take the necessary chances in moving toward fuller actualization of his potentialities.

Frankl. Viktor Frankl (1973) has focused on patients' frequent complaints that their lives are meaningless, empty, and futile. He has related this "existential vacuum" to the decline of historical traditions and values, which has left people in a quandary as to what they should do or become. To do what others do results in conformity; to do what others wish you to do makes for totalitarianism. A third possibility is a neurotic syndrome that Frankl refers to as *noögenic neurosis*. This is a neurosis deriving from despair over the apparent meaninglessness of life.

Frankl sees the "will to meaning" as more significant than Freud's striving for pleasure or Adler's will to power. He contends that man is constantly reaching out to encounter another person or for a meaning to fulfill. "Man is never concerned primarily with himself but, by virtue of his self-transcendent quality, he endeavors to serve a cause higher than himself or to love another person." This orientation makes for an open system, rather than a closed system based on the maintenance of equilibrium through the reduction of tension. Frankl rejects as futile the direct pursuit of pleasure. Pleasure for him is a side effect of fulfilling meaning or of a loving encounter with another human being. Self-actualization is also a side effect of fulfilling a meaning out in the world. The human search for meaning beyond self-gratification raises man above the level of a mere computer or an adaptive control system.

Laing. Ronald Laing (1965) has presented a perceptive analysis of the existential insecurity confronting a person who lacks a sense of continuous personal identity, of being a real, alive, whole person. This is the dilemma confronting the schizophrenic, who is uncertain whether he exists as a distinct entity and doubts whether other people have any substantial reality. When the sense of selfhood is tenuous, everyday difficulties threaten the individual

Ronald D. Laing, a British psychiatrist who favors an existential approach. He has suggested that from the point of view of the schizophrenic his seemingly bizarre behavior may represent a rational adjustment to the circumstances of his life.

with nonbeing. Any involvement or relationship with others lays him open to the dread that he may be engulfed and lose his wisp of autonomy and identity. To be engulfed by love, to be completely understood by another, is to be absorbed and destroyed. Isolation may be lonely and painful, but it is necessary if he is to gain a measure of safety.

The individual who has no sense of identity or of continuity as a person feels empty. He longs for the inner void to be filled. At the same time he is fearful that the implosion (penetrance and flooding) of outside reality will obliterate his identity. Another form of anxiety encountered by the person who doubts his existence as a real person is a fear of petrification, which is an extreme form of nonbeing, a dread of turning or being turned into an it, a robot, or a stone.

FAMILY SYSTEMS THEORIES

Family therapy is an approach to human problems; it is not based on any particular personality theory or school of psychopathology and it offers no distinctive therapeutic techniques. The approach consists in viewing the family as the patient and of treating family members conjointly. This approach follows from the premise that psychopathology in the individual is the product of family structure and interactions, and therefore changes in the individual can occur only if the family system changes (Haley, 1962). How many and which family members are seen in treatment sessions varies with the preferences of the therapist. Some therapists work only with the nuclear family, others try to include more distant relations. Young children may or may not be present. Some therapists work with groups of several families at one time. Most family therapists have a cotherapist, preferably one of the opposite sex, present at their meetings; others work alone.

This approach is not restricted to or dominated by any one professional discipline. The majority of family therapists are clinical psychologists, social workers, or psychiatrists, but persons affiliated with other disciplines and professions are also represented and an increasing number of lay persons are being trained as family therapists. The interdisciplinary composition of workers in the field has resulted in a blurring of the usual distinctions and hierarchies among professional groups. Functions and responsibility are primarily determined by competence.

Some family therapists favor psychoanalytic concepts, others think of themselves as Rogerians, Adlerians, gestalt therapists, behaviorists, communication experts, existentialists, or generalists. The particular orientation of the therapist influences the contents and activities of family sessions. The focus may be on uncovering the underlying causes of family friction, analyzing the power structure within the family, clarifying the communication system, or increasing familial interaction.

There are two points on which there is general agreement. One is that the function of family therapy is *not* to "bring the family closer together." The major problem is usually that family members are too deeply enmeshed and emotionally involved with one another; there is too much "we-ness"; there are too many gruesome twosomes. The goal of therapy is to promote the differentiation, individuation, and growth of each family member. In the words of Bowen (1966), the purpose of family therapy is "to separate the individual from the undifferentiated family ego mass." The second point of general agreement is the conceptualization of the family as a social system. Most people working along these lines refer to what they do as the family systems approach.

The Family as a Social System

The dominant influence in the emergence of a family systems theory is the general systems model developed by Ludwig von Bertalanffy (1969) and others. The applications of this model to family theory and therapy have been described by Olson (1970).

A basic feature of the general systems approach is a rejection of the mechanistic model of man as a robot whose actions are governed by simple stimulus-response connections. The model of man as a self-regulating, closed system designed to maintain a homeostatic equilibrium (a steady state through tension reduction) is also rejected. General systems theory views man as an autonomous, creative organism living in an open system. Thus his behavior is regulated by his whole family system. The whole is more than the sum of the parts, but the individual is an active participant, with a capacity for growth, development and spontaneous activity, and power to change both himself and the total system.

General systems theory stresses that man lives not in a universe of things but in a symbolic world of language, thought, and social entities. Family systems theory stresses the importance of communication. Family transactions are based on verbal and nonverbal communications. The individual learns through communication about his family system and the subtle family rules that regulate much of his behavior.

Another basic concept, borrowed from biology, is that of *progressive segregation*. Living organisms pass from a state of undifferentiated wholeness to one of differentiated parts. As applied to family theory, the goal of therapy is the differentiation of the separateness of each member. The individual should not be lost in, smothered by, sacrificed for, or made the scapegoat for his family.

Symptoms and Family Theory

An analysis of the origin and meaning of symptoms from a family systems perspective has been presented by James Framo (1972). He agrees with the traditional posi-

tion that the term "symptom" can be appropriately applied only to the behavior of individuals. However, he rejects the analytic idea that symptoms are the products of intrapsychic conflicts or surface manifestations of some disorder located within the individual. He maintains that symptoms are formed, selected, maintained, and reduced as a function of the familial context in which they are imbedded. He views them as "concomitants of the universal conflict between individuating, autonomous strivings and loyalty to the family relationship system."

Symptom choice is often determined by the role expectations imposed on the individual by his family ("the wild one," "the fighter," "the quiet one"). Other possibilities are that the deviant behavior of an individual may represent an acting out of some aspect of the family pathology or a reaction against it. Symptoms may be shared or exchanged within the family. Many seemingly bizarre symptoms make sense when viewed from the perspective of family interaction.

A dramatic example, described by Framo, is that of a schizophrenic girl who thought of herself as a ping-pong ball. She spent a good part of her time bouncing back and forth across the ward. Her parents had not spoken directly to one another for several years. The daughter served as the intermediary, and whenever her mother wished to communicate with her father, she would address the girl and instruct her what to tell him. The father would then relay his answer through the daughter. When parental exchanges were lengthy the daughter was figuratively batted back and forth.

Diagnosis and Family Theory

Family therapists question the validity of the mental illness concept and avoid assigning this traditional diagnostic label to individuals. Their objection has been forcefully expressed by Kelly (1971, p. 69).

I can no longer use the concept of illness to describe the social dysfunction of people struggling to operate in their cultural milieu as best they are able. —I cannot say to any of them with any conviction, "You are sick." I can say among other things, "You are unhappy, bewildered, disenchanted, betrayed, frustrated, frightened, trapped, enslaved, confused," but not simply "sick" unless I mean "sick and tired and fed up."

Instead of diagnosing individual members, the family therapist may attempt to formulate a general description of the family on the basis of information about the parents' families of origin, their marital relationship, their use of authority, the personality structures of individual members, their family values, their patterns of interaction, and other significant variables.

APPLICATIONS OF FAMILY THERAPY

Family therapy was initially tried out with schizophrenic patients and their families. The therapeutic success of the method with this population has been modest, but the procedure did expose some prevalent misconceptions regarding the nature of schizophrenia. When patients who gave every indication of being apathetic, withdrawn, and out of touch with their environment in a hospital ward were placed in a family therapy setting, they surprisingly behaved much like the "normal" members of the family. As soon as they returned to the ward, they reverted to their schizophrenic role.

Family therapy is currently extensively used in the treatment of marital problems, family crises, parent-child conflicts, neuroses, and other personality and behavior disturbances of children and adults. Research data on the effectiveness of the procedure are meager, in part because the usual criteria for evaluating outcome in individual patients are not applicable. As we noted earlier, family therapists are not particularly interested in the removal of symptoms in individual patients. Their goal is to improve the total system of family communication and interaction; if this is achieved, an improvement in the effectiveness and adjustment of each member of the family is supposed to come as a byproduct. According to Nathan Ackerman (1966), the procedure is contraindicated when there is evidence of an irreversible trend toward the breakup of the family or when one parent is afflicted with a progressive paranoid condition or manifests deeply rooted and intractable sociopathic traits.

FAMILY, GROUP, AND INDIVIDUAL THERAPY

Family therapy differs from group therapy in many respects. In group therapy, the members meet as strangers, and outside the therapy sessions they have no close contact with one another. There is no particular interest in the mental health of the group as a unit, since it is simply a device for facilitating the improvement of the individual members. In family therapy the members have a close past, present, and future association with one another. The concern is with the well-being of the total family.

Family therapy may be combined with individual therapy for certain members. An important difference between individual and family therapy is that in the former considerable emphasis is placed on the confidentiality of private communication, whereas in family therapy, secrets and feelings are openly shared. A unique feature of family therapy is that it provides a valuable source of nonverbal data. The postures, facial expressions, gestures, and preferred seating arrangements of the participants are often more meaningful than what is said.

SUMMARY

The various psychogenic theories are best considered as complementary rather than discrete. Each adds to and merges with the others to form an increasingly accurate description of man. The stark Freudian image of human behavior as dominated by primitive sexual and aggressive impulses and unconscious strivings is moderated by Adler's concept of social interest and brightened by the existentialists' addition of authenticity, self-fulfillment, and values. The emphasis of psychoanalysis on intrapsychic conflicts is balanced by the importance attached by Sullivan and others to interpersonal relationships and the stress placed by modern behavior theorists on the role of learning. The direct frontal attack on current symptoms favored by learning theorists offsets the analysts' preoccupation with the search of the past for insights that will explain present behavior.

All of these theories have one thing in common: none of them makes a sharp distinction between the determinants of normal and abnormal behavior. The basic processes underlying personality development and behavior are the same. Because of the complexity of the ingredients and the total operation, the end products differ. The more extreme variations that have unfavorable effects on the individual and his society are labeled abnormal.

References

Ackerman, N. *Treating the Troubled Family.* New York: Basic Books, 1966.

Adler, A. *The Practice and Theory of Individual Psychology.* New York: Harcourt, 1929.

————. *Social Interest.* New York: Putnam, 1939.

Allport, G. W. *Pattern and Growth in Personality.* New York: Holt, Rinehart & Winston, 1961.

Ansbacker, H., and Ansbacker, R. *The Individual Psychology of Alfred Adler.* New York: Basic Books, 1956.

Ayllon, T. "Intensive Treatment of Psychotic Behavior by Stimulus Satiation and Food Reinforcement." *Behavior Research and Therapy* 1 (1963): 53-61.

Bandura, A. "Social Learning Through Imitation." *Nebraska Symposium on Motivation,* ed. M. R. Jones, pp. 211-69. Lincoln: University of Nebraska Press, 1962.

————. *Principles of Behavior Modification.* New York: Holt, Rinehart & Winston, 1969.

Beels, C. C., and Ferber, A. "Family Therapy: A View." *Family Process* 8, no. 2 (1969): 280-318.

Berne, E. *Transactional Analysis in Psychotherapy.* New York: Grove Press, 1961.

————. *Games People Play.* New York: Grove Press, 1964.

————. *What Do You Say After You Say Hello?* New York: Grove Press, 1972.

Boszormenyi-Nagy, I., and Framo, J., eds. *Intensive Family Therapy.* New York: Harper & Row, 1965.

Bowen, M. "The Use of Family Theory in Clinical Practice." *Comparative Psychiatry* 7 (1966): 345-74.

Dunlap, K. *Habits: Their Making and Unmaking.* New York: Liveright, 1932.

Erikson, E. *Childhood and Society.* New York: Norton, 1963.

————. *Identity, Youth, and Crisis.* New York: Norton, 1968.

Eysenck, H. J. "The Effects of Psychotharapy." *International Journal of Psychiatry* 1 (1965): 99-142.

Ferber, A., Mendelson, M. and Napier, A. (eds.) *The Book of Family Therapy.* New York: Science House, 1972.

Ferster, C. B., and Perrot, M. C. *Behavior Principles.* New York: Appleton-Century-Crofts, 1968.

Framo, J. "Symptoms from a Family Transactional Viewpoint." In *Progress in Group and Family Therapy,* eds. C. Sager and H. Kaplan, pp. 271-308. New York: Brunner/Mazell, 1972.

Frank, G. H. "The Role of the Family in the Development of Psychopathology." *Psychological Bulletin* 64 (1965): 191-205.

Frankl, V. "Meaninglessness: A Challenge to Psychologists." In *Theories of Psychopathology and Personality,* ed. T. Millon, pp. 231-38. Philadelphia: Saunders, 1973.

Freud, S. *Beyond the Pleasure Principle.* London: International Psychoanalytic Press, 1922.

————. *New Introductory Lectures on Psycho-analysis*, trans. J. H. Sprott. New York: Norton, 1933.

————. *Autobiography.* New York: Norton, 1935.

————. *The Standard Edition of the Complete Psychological Works of Sigmund Freud.* London: Hogarth Press, 1956.

Fromm, E. *Man for Himself.* New York: Holt, 1947.

————. *The Sane Society.* New York: Holt, 1955.

Greenson, R. R. "The Classical Psychoanalytic Approach." In *American Textbook of Psychiatry*, ed. S. Arieti, vol. 2 pp. 1399–1416. New York: Basic Books, 1959.

Haley, J. "Whither family therapy." *Family Process* 1 (1962): 69–100.

Haley, J. ed. *Changing Families: A Family Therapy Reader.* New York: Grune & Stratton, 1971.

Hartmann, H. *Ego Psychology and the Problem of Adaptation*, trans. David Rapaport. New York: International Universities Press, 1958 (1939).

Hendrick, I. *Facts and Theories of Psychoanalysis.* New York: Knopf, 1939.

Hilgard, E. R., and Bower, G. H. *Theories of Learning.* New York: Appleton-Century-Crofts, 1966.

Hollingworth, H. L. *Abnormal Psychology.* New York: Ronald Press, 1930.

Holzman, P. S. *Psychoanalysis and Psychopathology.* New York: McGraw-Hill, 1970.

Horney, K. *New Ways in Psychoanalysis.* New York: Norton, 1939.

————. *Our Inner Conflicts.* New York: Norton, 1945.

Kelly, H. V. "Who Puts the Chronic into Chronic Mental Illness?" In *Systems Therapy*, ed. J. O. Bradt and E. J. Moynihan, 66-71. Washington, D.C.: Groome Child Guidance Center, 1971.

Kanfer, F. H., and Phillips, J. S. *Learning Foundations of Behavior Therapy.* New York: Wiley, 1970.

Laing, R. D. *The Divided Self: An Existential Study in Sanity and Madness.* Baltimore: Penguin Books, 1965.

Levitsky, A. and Perls, F. S. "The Rules and Games of Gestalt Therapy." In *Gestalt Therapy Now*, ed. I. Shepherd and J. Fagan. Palo Alto, Calif.: Science and Behavior Books, 1970.

Maslow, A. "Defense and Growth" (1956). In *Theories of Psychopathology and Personality*, ed. T. Millon. Philadelphia: Saunders, 1973.

————. *Toward a Psychology of Being.* Princeton, N.J.: Van Nostrand, 1962.

May, R. *Existential Psychology.* New York: Random House, 1961.

Medinnus, G. R., ed. *Readings in the Psychology of Parent-Child Relations.* New York: Wiley, 1967.

Mowrer, O. H. "Learning Theory and Behavior Therapy." in *Handbook of Clinical Psychology*, ed. B. B. Wolman, pp. 243-73. New York: McGraw-Hill, 1965.

Mullahy, P. "Harry Stack Sullivan's Theory of Schizophrenia." *International Journal of Psychiatry* 4 (1967): 492-521.

Olson, D. H. "Marital and Family Therapy: Integrative Review and Critique." *Journal of Marriage and the Family*, November 1970, pp. 501-538.

Pavlov, I. P. *Lectures on Conditioned Reflexes*, trans. G. V. Anrep. London: Oxford University Press, 1927.

Perls, F. *Gestalt Therapy Verbatim.* Lafayette, Calif.: Real People Press, 1969.

Resnick, J. H. "Effects of Stimulus Satiation on the Overlearned Maladaptive Response of Cigarette Smoking." *Journal of Consulting and Clinical Psychology* 32, no. 5 (1968): 501-5.

Rogers, C. R. "A Theory of Therapy, Personality, and Interpersonal Relationships, as Developed in the Client-Centered Framework." In *Psychology: A Study of a Science*, ed. S. Koch, vol. 3, pp. 184-256. New York: McGraw-Hill, 1959.

————. "In Retrospect: Forty-six years." *American Psychologist* 29 (1974): 115-23.

Sager, C. J. and Kaplan, H. S. eds. *Progress in Group and Family Therapy.* New York: Brunner/Mazel, 1972.

Satir, V. *Conjoint Family Therapy: A Guide to Theory and Technique.* Palo Alto, Calif.: Science and Behavior Books, 1964.

Skinner, B. F. *The Behavior of Organisms.* New York: Appleton-Century-Crofts, 1938.

————. *Verbal Behavior.* New York: Appleton-Century-Crofts, 1957.

Stampfl, T. G., and Levis, D. J. "Essentials of Implosive Therapy: A Learning-Theory-Based Psychodynamic Behavioral Therapy." *Journal of Abnormal Psychology* 72, no. 6 (1967): 496-503.

Sullivan, H. S. *Interpersonal Theory of Psychiatry.* New York: Norton, 1953.

Tillich, P. *The Courage to Be.* New Haven: Yale University Press, 1952.

Van Kamp, A. "The Goals of Psychotherapy from the Existential Point of View." In *The Goals of Psychotherapy,* ed. A. R. Mahrer. New York: Appleton-Century-Crofts, 1967.

von Bertalanffy, L. "General Systems Theory and Psychiatry—An Overview." In *General Systems Theory and Psychiatry,* ed. W. Gray, F. J. Duhl and N. D. Rizzo, pp. 33-46. Boston: Little, Brown, 1969.

Watson, J. B. *Psychology from the Standpoint of a Behaviorist.* Philadelphia: Lippincott, 1924.

———— and Rayner, R. "Conditioned Emotional Responses." *Journal of Psychology* 3 (1920): 1-14.

Yates, A. J. "The Application of Learning Theory to the Treatment of Tics." *Journal of Abnormal and Social Psychology* 56 (1958): 175-82.

6 · Biological Factors

Adam and Eve, Albrecht Dürer

Biological factors are involved in practically all facets of human behavior. They influence particularly the range and level of the organism's learning aptitudes, physiological drives, basic temperament, stress tolerance, adaptive resources, and response capabilities. Individual differences in these and other functions are partly due to individual variations in neurophysiological and biochemical traits. The major cause of biological individuality is the unique genetic endowment of each child. Other sources of biological individuality that have special psychiatric significance include brain damage incurred during the process of birth; nutritional deficiencies, particularly during infancy and early childhood; toxic substances produced within or taken into the body; and debilitating physical diseases.

In comparison with the elusiveness of the variables associated with psychogenic theories of psychopathology, the biological variables that are thought to have pathogenic significance are more tangible and more readily accessible to experimental study. For example, the role of genetic factors may be investigated by ascertaining whether the incidence of behavior disorders among the parents, children, and siblings of mental patients is significantly higher than chance expectancy. The importance of heredity may be further evaluated by comparing the relative incidence of specific types of maladaptive behavior among close versus distant relatives and for *monozygotic* (identical) versus *dizygotic* (fraternal) twins. Hypotheses regarding other biological variables may be conveniently tested by comparing the relative prevalence of psychopathology in persons with histories of birth injury, brain damage, or nutritional deficiencies with matched groups of normal control subjects.

The statistical findings of such studies are important in differentiating significant variables from incidental ones. But proof of a causal relationship between biological factors and psychopathology calls for more than supportive statistical evidence. What is needed is more specific information on (1) the ways in which genetic and other biological factors contribute to the development of abnormal behavior and (2) the reasons the effects of these variables differ so much from individual to individual. Variations in behavior commonly noted in identical twins and in persons with similar biological defects confirm the basic premise regarding the multiple interactive determinants of behavior.

GENES AND ABNORMAL BEHAVIOR

The child-to-be receives in full his genetic inheritance at the moment of conception, when the sperm cell contributed by the father penetrates and unites with the ovum provided by the mother to form a single fertilized cell or *zygote*. Along with the gift of life, each parent passes on, via the reproductive cells, one of each of his or her twenty-three pairs of chromosomes. When the twenty-three randomly assorted chromosomes received from the father are paired with the twenty-three received from the mother, the zygote has the normal human complement of forty-six chromosomes. As the zygote develops through cell division, each cell of the body receives a duplicate set of the original twenty-three pairs of chromosomes. Twenty-two of the paired chromosomes are referred to as

Karyotype (chromosomal map) associated with Klinefelter's syndrome, a genetic condition that occurs only in males. An extra X chromosome (XXY) is present, resulting in 47 instead of the usual 46 chromosomes. Characteristic physical features usually noted after puberty include underdeveloped testes, infertility, absence of beard, and enlarged hips. Mental retardation is common among XXY males but many have normal intelligence and are adequate in their general functioning.

autosomes. The remaining pair, identified by the symbols XX in females and XY in males, consists of the sex chromosomes.

Since all children born to the same parents receive a random assortment of the parental chromosomes, the chances of two siblings' receiving exactly the same set of chromosomes are considerably less than one in a billion. It is equally rare for siblings to have no chromosomes in common. The physical similarities noted among siblings are due to shared chromosomes.

Under suitable conditions, chromosomes may be seen with the aid of a high-powered microscope. Each of the paired autosomes has a somewhat distinctive rodlike appear-

ance. The Y sex chromosome is considerably smaller than the X. By enlarging photographs taken of the microscopic field and cutting out each chromosome, it is possible to match paired chromosomes and arrange the pairs in some systematic fashion on the basis of their size and shape. Taking advantage of these variations in appearance, geneticists have developed a standardized numbering system, ranging from 1 through 23, to identify specific pairs. The sex chromosome pair, for example, is numbered 23. Anomalies occasionally occur, so that a person has one less or one more than the standard forty-six chromosomes. Irregularities in the number and intactness of chromosomes are usually, but not always, accompanied by physical defects and mental retardation. *Down's syndrome* is a well-known example of mental deficiency associated with the presence of forty-seven chromosomes.

Genes

The chromosomes contain the genetic substance responsible for the transmission of inherited traits. Paired chromosomes have paired genes that serve similar functions. Both paired genes may be recessive or both may be dominant, or one may be recessive and the other dominant. The number of human genes is unknown but it is assumed that there are many, all of them capable of exact self-duplication. Recent discoveries have shown that the chemical composition of genes consists mainly of *deoxyribonucleic acid*, or DNA. In other words, genes are nucleic acid segments. The structure of the DNA molecule resembles a double spiral staircase twisted in the form of a helix. The spirals are made up of alternating sugar and phosphate units. The steps connecting the two spirals are formed by varied combinations of proteins called adenine, guanine, thymine, and cytosine.

The various arrangements of these chemical substances in a nucleic acid segment or gene provides a kind of molecular Morse Code. Chemical messages from the DNA are transferred to other molecules referred to as RNA, because of their *ribonucleic acid* composition. The RNA molecules move out into the cytoplasm of the cell and initiate reactions that lead to the synthesis of particular enzymes, as directed by the DNA code messages. These enzymes in turn influence chemical interactions that affect the structure and metabolic processes of the body. To the extent that the resulting bodily structures and metabolic processes influence behavior, genes may be credited with indirectly contributing to behavior.

Genotype and Phenotype

As we have seen, genes act as predisposing or contributory agents rather than as causal agents. It is a fundamental tenet of genetic theory that the action of any specific gene is influenced by its interaction with other genes and with the internal

Figure 6.1. Diagram to Show the Separation of DNA strands at the Beginning of Replication Followed by the Production of New Strands Along the Template of the Parent Strand (from Watson, 1965).

GENETIC PHYSICAL DISORDERS WITH ASSOCIATED BEHAVIOR DEFICITS

Down's syndrome is a more recent name for a type of mental deficiency that was formerly called "mongolism." The term *mongolism* was initially used by Langdon Down in 1866 to describe a type of mental deficiency characterized in part by a fold of skin continuing from the upper eyelid over the inner angle. The effect of this extra fold is a superficial Oriental appearance, but the condition has nothing to do with the Mongoloid race.

Earlier studies indicated that the disorder (1) was not present in the parents, (2) occurred with about equal frequency at all socioeconomic levels, (3) invariably affected both or neither of monozygotic twins, (4) rarely affected both members of dizygotic twin pairs, and (5) occurred more frequently in children born to older women but was unrelated to the age of the father. These data suggested that the disorder had some connection with the mother, had a genetic origin, but was not inherited in the usual sense that defective genes present in the parents were passed on to the child.

The etiological picture remained confused until 1959, when Lejeune, in France, discovered that children with Down's syndrome had forty-seven chromosomes instead of the standard forty-six. In terms of the identifying numbers assigned to human chromosomes, the anomaly usually consists of an extra chromosome 21 (three in place of the usual two).

The explanation for the extra chromosome, which is contained in the ovum, is attributed to the nondisjunction of a parent cell during meiotic division. Following the reduction process, one germ cell has twenty-four chromosomes and the other only twenty-two. The former, when fertilized by a germ cell having a normal complement of twenty-three chromosomes, results in a total of forty-seven in the offspring. The reason for the nondisjunction is not clearly understood. For mothers over forty-five, the risk of having a child with Down's syndrome is about 1 in 50.

Tests have been developed that make it possible to detect the presence of the gene defect in the fetus early in pregnancy. The birth of these handicapped children may now be prevented by medical intervention.

Phenylketonuria, or PKU, is an inherited metabolic disorder that accounts for about 1 percent of the population of institutions for mental defectives. The specific cause is the presence of a recessive gene that interferes with the normal production of an enzyme called phenylalanine hydroxylase, which is essential for oxidizing phenylalanine, an amino acid present in all proteins. Its faulty metabolism leads to the accumulation of phenylalanine in the blood and the excretion of phenylpyruvic acid in the urine. This metabolic disturbance somehow interferes with normal brain development during the crucial period of infancy. In addition to mental retardation, the disorder is marked by convulsions, temper outbursts, and rough skin.

A simple blood test, which is now required in many states, has been developed for detecting elevated phenylalanine levels in newborn infants. By placing affected infants on a special diet low in phenylalanine for several years, it is possible to prevent mental retardation from this cause. Although phenotypically normal with respect to intelligence, treated children retain their original genotype and pass on to their offspring the gene defect they acquired from their parents. Because of the recessive nature of the defective gene, the risk of mental deficiency may be reduced if persons known to be genetically susceptible to phenylketonuria marry into families free of the gene defect. Heterozygotic carriers are free of overt symptoms but have a reduced enzyme level, which can be detected by a test for tolerance of phenylalanine.

The success attained in the prevention of this disorder shows that the common belief that hereditary disorders are incurable is not necessarily correct. Far from being cause for pessimism, the establishment of a biochemical basis for a disorder may provide the key for its effective treatment and prevention.

Huntington's chorea is a progressive de-

Young woman with Down's syndrome (mongolism), a condition that results from a chromosomal abnormality, usually an extra chromosome 21. Victims typically show moderate to severe mental retardation.

generative disease of the central nervous system that is marked by diffuse brain atrophy. A single dominant gene is responsible for the disorder. Case histories indicate that 50 percent of the children of affected parents will also develop the disorder if they live long enough. Unaffected children are free of the dominant gene, so their children are unaffected.

The onset of overt neurological symptoms is usually delayed until the victim is between thirty and forty years old. The symptom picture is the same today as it was when it was originally described by Huntington in 1872.

Physical symptoms consist of irregular, involuntary, and uncontrollable movements of the face, neck, and extremities: facial grimaces, poorly articulated speech, shuffling gait, and jerky circular movements of the hands. The appearance of these symptoms may be preceded or accompanied by changes in personality and behavior. Common psychological symptoms include moodiness, irritability, apathy, obstinacy, irascibility, and paranoid trends. As the disorder progresses, there is a general mental deterioration. Suicide is not uncommon (Kolb, 1968). No treatment is known as yet.

and external environment. This tenet is expressed in the concepts of genotype and phenotype. The *genotype* is the particular combination of genes possessed by a particular individual. The *phenotype* consists of the observable physical and behavioral characteristics that arise from the interaction of the genotype and its environment. In different environments, one genotype may result in a variety of phenotypes. The extent of the limitation varies with the trait. For certain physical traits that are mainly dependent on the interaction of genes—eye color is one—the phenotypic variation is extremely restricted under usual environmental conditions. Consequently, the outcome is highly predictable in accordance with the principles of genetic inheritance. For physical traits that are more dependent on the external environment, the range and variety of the overt expression of innate predisposition are much greater.

For example, a person's genotype sets limits on the range of his possible physical height. Within this potential range, the person's actual maximum height (his phenotype) is greatly influenced by diet, physical illness, and socioeconomic factors. Similarly, biological inheritance may impose a limit on intellectual potentialities, but the individual's actual functioning abilities may be markedly influenced by environmental factors. *Phenylketonuria* serves as a good illustration of a genetically determined form of mental deficiency in which the actual phenotypic outcome may be drastically modified by diet.

Genes and Temperament

Genetic factors are largely responsible for individual variations in the raw materials from which all personalities are fashioned. The characteristics and properties of the biological building blocks set limits on the general design, complexity, and stability of the personality structures that may be built with them. The limits are broad and flexible, however, particularly among human beings. The particular personality actually developed by a child with a given genotype is greatly influenced by the molding pressures of his culture and his learning experiences within and outside the home. Because of the complex interaction of nature and nurture, it is often difficult to isolate their respective contributions. In general, however, heredity appears to be the more dominant factor in the determination of temperament traits, whereas the environment appears to be mainly responsible for attitudes, values, and social behavior. As Gordon Allport says (1961, p. 34):

Temperament refers to the characteristic phenomena of an individual's emotional nature, including his susceptibility to emotional stimulation, his customary strength and speed of response, the quality of his prevailing mood, and all peculiarities of fluctuation and intensity in mood, these phenomena being regarded as dependent upon constitutional make-up, and therefore largely hereditary in origin.

From the moment of birth infants exhibit wide individual differences in activity, intensity of reaction, adaptability, distractability, quality of mood, and other temperament qualities (Escalona, 1968; Thomas et al., 1968). Freud (1950, p. 316) recognized that "each individual ego is endowed from the beginning with its own peculiar dispositions and tendencies." Experimental data indicate that the early social behavior of infants is to a great extent controlled by innate predispositions. Monozygotic twins, who have the same genotype, show much greater resemblance than dizygotic twins with respect to the development of smiling, social orientation, and fear of strangers (Freedman, 1963). Individual differences in temperament noted during infancy tend to persist, in modified form, through childhood to adulthood. The consistency of temperament traits from infancy to later years has been amply demonstrated (Gesell et al., 1939; MacKinnon, 1942; Neilon, 1948; Schaefer and Bayley, 1963). One of the most dramatic findings has been that behavior exhibited during early childhood is a moderately good predictor of analogous behavior during early adulthood (Kagan and Moss, 1962).

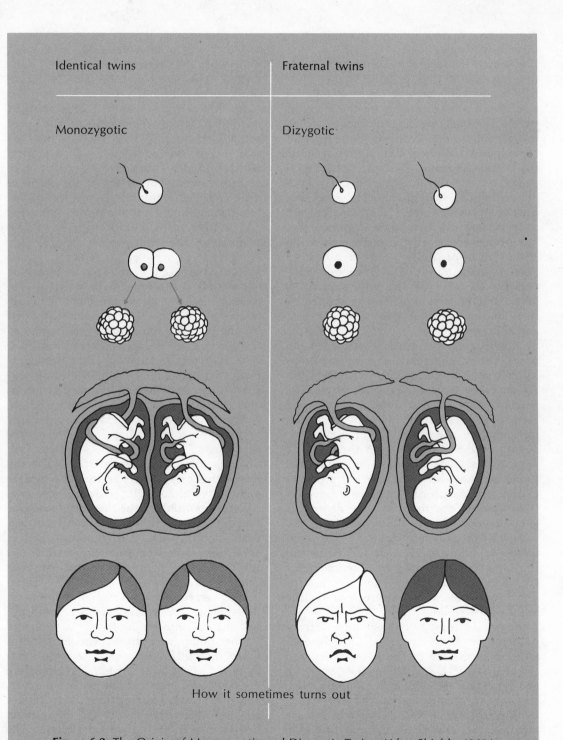

Figure 6.2. The Origin of Monozygotic and Dizygotic Twins. (After Shields, 1968.)

Twin Studies

The search for factual evidence to support the hypothesis that genetic factors contribute to temperament and personality disorders has relied mainly on the study of twins. The particular significance of twins for genetic studies rests on the fact that there are two kinds of twins: monozygotic (MZ) and dizygotic (DZ) pairs. MZ twin pairs have exactly the same genotype; DZ pairs differ in genotype. This biological distinction provides the rationale for the interpretation of twin data. Findings are interpreted as favoring heredity when the resemblances of MZ twins are significantly greater than those of DZ twins. Conversely, the role of the environment is given greater weight when the degree of resemblance is about the same for MZ and DZ twins.

Monozygotic or identical twins are the products of a single fertilized cell produced by the union of one sperm and one ovum. At an early stage in its development the single zygote divides, with the eventual birth of two separate infants. MZ twins have exactly the same set of genes, are always of the same sex, and usually look very much alike. Dizygotic or fraternal twins, on the other hand, are the products of the fertilization of two separate ova by two separate sperm cells. The degree of genetic similarity of DZ twin pairs is the same as for ordinary siblings. The main biological difference is that DZ twins are the same age; they may or may not be of the same sex, and they may resemble or differ from one another as much or as little as ordinary siblings.

About 1 in every 90 pregnancies terminates in the birth of twins. One-third of all twin births are of the MZ variety and two-thirds are DZ. Half of the latter are of the same sex. Blood grouping procedures are currently favored for determining whether twins of the same sex are identical or fraternal. Criteria used in earlier studies included fingerprint ridge count, similarity of eye color, and similarities and differences in other physical traits.

Most twin studies focused on the genetics of temperament have been conducted with normal subjects. The usual procedure has been to compare MZ and DZ twins for resemblances in scores attained on standardized temperament and personality tests. The twin method may be modified by the addition of sibling pairs, which provides a further check on the role of the environment. If the environment is the major determinant, the degree of resemblance should be about the same for MZ and DZ pairs, and DZ pairs should be more alike than siblings who differ in age. As a rule, degrees of agreement on test scores have been expressed in terms of correlation coefficients; high positive correlations indicate close agreement; low correlations indicate that the scores attained by one twin are unrelated to the scores of the other. High negative correlations indicate an inverse relationship. Since temperament and personality traits cannot be precisely measured, correlation coefficients of over .50 are generally regarded as high.

The results of a comparative study of twins and siblings that I conducted are summarized in Table 6.1. As is apparent, findings differ for specific traits. For the three traits most closely related to temperament, *general activity, restraint,* and *masculinity-femininity,* the intrapair correlation for MZ twins was signicantly higher than for DZ pairs. No significant differences were noted between the correlations for DZ pairs and siblings, and for both groups the correlations were low. These findings suggest that heredity is the main determinant for general activity, restraint, and masculinity-femininity.

The findings with respect to *ascendance, thoughtfulness,* and *personal relations* may best be interpreted as reflecting the combined effect of nature and nurture. For these traits, correlations were higher for MZ pairs than for DZ pairs, and higher for DZ pairs than for siblings. The correlation patterns for the remaining four traits suggest that they are determined principally by environmental factors. Age-related environmental factors appear to be relatively more important for *objectivity* and *emotional stability* than for *friendliness* and *sociability*. For the former two traits, the correlations for MZ and DZ twins were of the same magnitude; those for siblings were lower. No consistent differences were noted for the three groups with respect to friendliness and sociability.

In twin research involving behavior disorders, one starts by locating an otherwise unselected series of patients, each of whom has the disorder being investigated and has a living twin. A study is then made of the twins of these *index* or *proband* cases to determine the proportion of instances in which both members of a pair have the same disorder. It is generally assumed that the importance of heredity is confirmed if the *concordance rate* for a disorder (both twins similarly affected) is significantly greater for MZ than for DZ twin pairs. Higher concordance rates for MZ than DZ twins have been consistently noted for schizophrenia, affective psychoses, alcoholism, epilepsy, neuroses, and criminal

behavior (Essen-Moller, 1963; Rosenthal, 1970).

The significance of these findings has been clouded by the wide range of figures reported by various investigators with respect to the percent of co-twins similarly affected and the magnitude of the differences in concordance rates for MZ and DZ twins. This wide range is a result partly of differences in the composition of the populations studied and partly of differences in the strictness of diagnostic criteria. A valid criticism of most of the early twin studies on the genetics of mental disorders is that the subjects were selected from the resident population of institutions. The findings were therefore mainly applicable to severe chronic cases. Since 1965, investigators have deliberately attempted to avoid this sampling error by selecting proband cases from consecutive admissions to all types of treatment facilities.

The matter of the criteria used in diagnosis is more complicated. In the absence of objective and validated criteria for diag-

Table 6.1. The Differences Between Twins and Siblings (Product-moment Correlations for Same-sexed Pairs of MZ and DZ Twins and Siblings Less than Two Years Apart on the Guilford-Zimmerman Temperament Survey).

Traits	Correlation coefficient[a]		
	MZ (N = 25)	DZ (N = 26)	Sibs (N = 25)
General activity	.52	− .22	− .14
Restraint	.59	.16	.18
Masculinity-femininity	.51	.27	.33
Ascendance	.69	.39	.14
Thoughtfulness	.61	.43	.11
Personal relations	.58	.42	.14
Objectivity	.43	.41	.22
Emotional stability	.31	.33	− .19
Friendliness	− .22	.27	.28
Sociability	.57	.27	.46

[a]r of .38 and .49 are significant at the .05 and .01 levels respectively.

nosis, each investigator has developed his own criteria for the initial selection of suitable probands and for determining whether the twins should be classified as definitely concordant, doubtful or discordant. If—as is usually the case—the researcher knows in advance whether a particular set of twins is MZ or DZ, the subjectivity of his diagnosis may unwittingly result in decisions that favor his theoretical bias.

Shields and Gottesman (1972) have attempted to control for these two variables in evaluating cross-national findings for schizophrenia. Table 6.2 shows their "corrected" figures for recent studies conducted in five countries. In all five studies, proband cases were initially selected from a representative sample of the population. The "correction" for concordance involved re-examining the available information on subjects and arriving at a diagnosis on the basis of a standard set of criteria. The standardizing of diagnosis was helpful in reducing the spread of figures, but differences remained. For all studies combined, the extent of concordance was 46 percent

for MZ and 14 percent for DZ twins. For separate studies, the concordance rates for MZ were from two to five times higher than those for DZ pairs. The data clearly establish the importance of genetic factors in schizophrenia but leave open the question of its degree of importance. This same conclusion is also applicable to twin studies for affective psychoses. Findings with respect to neuroses and alcoholism are more controversial. The role of genetic factors in specific disorders will be considered in greater detail in subsequent chapters.

The fact that the concordance rates for MZ twins reported in Table 6.2 fall considerably short of 100 percent is not a valid reason for disregarding the contribution of heredity. As we noted earlier, a basic tenet of genetic theory is that the phenotype or overt expression of an innate predisposition is dependent upon the interactive effect of environmental factors. A person who has inherited a genotype associated with a particular disorder has a greater than chance expectancy of developing that disorder. Whether he actually ex-

Table 6.2. The Inheritance of Schizophrenia (Concordance Rates in MZ and DZ Twins in Five Countries).

Country (Investigator)	Number of twin pairs		Percent of Concordance (both similarly affected)	
	MZ	DZ	MZ	DZ
Norway (Kringlen)	69	96	45%	15%
Denmark (Fisher et al.)	25	45	56	26
Finland (Tienari)	20	23	35	13
U.S.A. (Cohen et al.)	121	131	43	9
United Kingdom (Gottesman and Shields)	26	34	58	12
Total	261	329	46	14

Adapted from J. Shields and I. I. Gottesman, "Cross-National Diagnosis of Schizophrenia in Twins." *Archives of General Psychiatry*, 39 (1972): 725-30.

hibits overt symptoms depends on the presence or absence of other significant modifying factors. Thus an individual may have an "abnormal" genotype but a "normal" phenotype. A person genetically predisposed to schizophrenia has a relatively high probability of developing the behavior traits associated with that disorder, but he will actually develop them only if he is exposed to adverse environmental experiences. Under more favorable circumstances, he may never exhibit overt symptoms, even though he retains the gene defect and transmits it unaltered to his offspring in accordance with genetic principles.

A final controversial issue associated with twin studies is the possibility that the higher concordance rates for MZ than DZ twins may be due to environmental rather than genetic factors. Opposing arguments on this point appear to be equally valid. MZ twins do, in fact, share a common environment to a greater degree than DZ twins (Smith, 1965). On the other hand, it may be argued that it is because of their common genetic endowment that MZ twins spend more time together, elicit similar responses from parents and others, and share more experiences than DZ twins. Conversely, the greater genetic disparity of DZ twins (which contributes to greater differences in physical traits, temperament, and aptitudes) may account for their greater dissimilarity in life experiences.

In any case, this is an academic issue. Most behavior scientists today recognize the futility of the nature versus nurture controversy. Behavior is the product of the continuous interaction of nature and nurture.

Temperament

If we assume that susceptibility to impaired psychosocial functioning is partly determined by heredity, the next step is to identify the nature of the innate predisposing factors. The most promising of the various proposed theories is that temperament attributes constitute the genetic component that often contributes most directly to vulnerability or resistance to psychopathology. This hypothesis has the advantage of including abnormal behavior within the general framework of normal behavior; it avoids the dubious practice of inventing a separate set of causes and explanations for deviant behavior. The temperament characteristics of prospective patients may be viewed as simply differing in degree from similar traits present in the general population. Temperament qualities associated with specific disorders include:

Neurosis: high anxiety level, rigidity, emotional overresponsiveness.

Schizophrenia: introvertive tendencies, low energy level, relative absence of spontaneity, relative incapacity for experiencing and expressing joy.

Manic-depressive psychosis: marked mood swings from elation to depression, low frustration tolerance, dependence.

Antisocial behavior: impulsivity, aggressiveness, restlessness, relative lack of social sensitivity, inadequate inhibitory controls.

Temperament deviations, however extreme, neither produce nor constitute behavior disorders. The main role of temperament is to create an emotional climate that influences the ways in which the individual acts toward others and others react to him. A timid, apathetic, inhibited child is apt to elicit a minimum of positive responses from parents, peers, and associates. In turn, the relative absence of social reinforcement will tend to discourage the child's subsequent efforts to relate to others. Repeated encounters of indifference, frustration, and rejection in interpersonal situations will tend to accentuate introvertive tendencies and lead to avoidance and distrust of other people.

Since one's self-image is influenced by the ways in which one is perceived and treated by others, the self-concept of the ignored and rejected child may remain relatively underdeveloped and be distorted by feelings of unworthiness and hopelessness. In extreme cases the individual may turn his back on the cold, unfriendly world and seek refuge in a private schizophrenic world of his own. Conversely, a sociable, outgoing, energetic, responsive child who elicits favorable responses from his family and peers is likely, as the result of repeated successful experiences, to acquire a favorable self-image, an optimistic outlook, and confidence in coping with daily problems. Temperament and environment work hand in hand to reinforce and stabilize innate predispositions.

The hypothesis that temperament is a major contributory cause of psychopathology has the merit of being subject to experimental testing. Thomas and his associates (1968) are currently conducting a comprehensive longitudinal study that is designed to investigate the relation of temperament characteristics observed in children during infancy to their subsequent personality development and susceptibility to behavior disorders. By the age of ten, 42 of the 136 children being studied had exhibited clinical signs of behavior disturbances. Most of the disturbed children had been described as "difficult" babies. During infancy they were distinguished by irregularity in biological function, predominance of withdrawal response or intense reactions to new stimuli, low adaptability, and frequent expression of negative moods. Behavior problems were rarely noted in children who had been "easy" babies. As infants these problem-resistant children were characterized by biological regularity, predominantly positive moods, rapid adaptability, and low to mild intensity of reactions. The authors are careful to note that no particular pattern of temperament as such results in or provides immunity against a behavior disturbance. Recognizing the multiple determinants of behavior, they conclude that deviant as well as normal development is the result of the interaction between given characteristics of temperament and significant features of the child's intrafamilial and extrafamilial environments.

In another longitudinal study (Fish et al., 1965), predictions were made as to possible schizophrenic outcome in a group of infants. Three out of a total of sixteen infants examined were judged to be vulnerable to schizophrenia on the basis of marked behavioral irregularities noted when they were a month old. All sixteen children were examined again when they were nine or ten. At that time all three of the "vulnerable" children exhibited behavior disturbances. The child who had shown the most severe impairment in infancy had developed an overt psychosis; the other two had developed less severe disorders. A third longitudinal study, involving older children, is being conducted by S. A. Mednick. Since his research has special significance for schizophrenia, his findings will be reported in Chapter 9, which is devoted to that disorder.

Neurobiochemical Defects

During the period when it was thought that mental disorders were analogous to physical disorders, serious attention was given to the theory that the genetic component of psychoses might consist of some neurophysiological, biochemical, or metabolic anomaly. The theory was kept alive by periodic positive findings. Unfortunately, on more careful reexamination these encouraging discoveries have invariably turned out to be accidental and nonreplicable or due to dietary deficiencies and other extraneous factors associated with a chronic institutionalized population. The search for specific neurobiochemical pathogenic agents has been all but abandoned. Current biological research is more concerned with the interaction between biochemical events and the behavioral variables that are involved in the organism's adjustment to its environment. Under normal circumstances, inborn metabolic variations and other biochemical predisposing factors are not sufficiently variant to produce significant disturbances in behavior, but they might do so under conditions of stress and other adverse environmental circumstances that induce more extreme biochemical changes (Russell, 1965).

Defects in Genetic Programming

In contrast to neurobiochemical theories, which are essentially based on the "engine" model, programming theories favor the more sophisticated "computer" model. Taking into consideration the basic concept of nature-nurture interaction, it is possible that impaired psychosocial functioning may result from:

1. Defects in genetic coding which lead to:
   (a) An absence of built-in programs for initiating certain critical actions or for appropriately handling certain kinds of input data.
   (b) Errors in programming that result in faulty analysis of input data.
2. Environmental errors, represented by:
   (a) A lack of a stimulus or response suitable to elicit programmed data, which interferes with or distorts the sequential pattern.
   (b) Faulty input data that fail to trigger available programs, set off "wrong" built-in programs, or lead to other erroneous responses.

Other possible sources of disordered functioning include the inherent incapacity of the organism to assimilate or cope with certain experiences, breakdown resulting from the overloading of the system, neural short-circuiting, feedback interference, absence of inhibitory controls, and defects in the biological filtering system that screens and regulates sensory input, associations, and responses.

A good illustration of genetic programming is the spontaneous occurrence of specific behaviors at certain stages in development. These critical-period behaviors —patterns specific to particular species of courtship, mating, nesting, infant care, and seasonal migration—are more evident in other organisms than in man. The successful mating of animals requires males and females to adhere to a genetically determined, species-specific sequence of courting behavior. Slight variations in the courtship patterns of related species interfere with the step-by-step sequence, stop the process, and thereby inhibit cross-breeding.

The presence of inherent programs in human beings is indicated by the spontaneous occurrence at certain age levels of speech sounds, smiling, negativism, acceptance of strangers, heterosexual impulses, and so on. Irregularities in the expression of these critical-stage responses or the failure of appropriate reinforcement may have unfavorable developmental consequences. A child whose smiles are never reinforced by the responding smiles of others soon stops smiling. Irregularities or deficiencies in the expression or reinforcement of heterosexual impulses may interfere with normal sexual development.

The adverse consequence of an environment that fails to nurture and reinforce innate behavior tendencies is most clearly apparent in neglected infants brought up in orphanages that provide nothing but custodial care. The effects vary, but most children reared from birth under such conditions, with a minimum of stimulation, fondling, and attention, show marked retardation in intelligence and language development (Yarrow, 1961). Frequently noted personality disturbances include social apathy, excessive crying, sporadic outbursts of rage, rigid posturing, stereotyped motor responses, and difficulty in establishing normal interpersonal relationships.

A somewhat related hypothesis is that human beings have an intrinsic need for a minimum level of sensory stimulation. Deprivation of or lack of variety in external sensory input may result in a compensatory intensification of internal mental activity—increased reverie, rehearsal of memories, and an upsurge of normally suppressed impulses with their accompanying affects. Thus the psychotic's break with outer reality may result in increased absorption with inner fantasies and impulses and an increased sensitivity to bodily sensations. The shift to internal stimulation may account for transient disturbances in psychological functioning frequently noted in laboratory experiments in which human subjects have been isolated and exposed for prolonged periods to conditions of either monotonous or markedly reduced sensory stimulation. The effects vary from subject to subject and are influenced by the instructions they receive and other factors, but perceptual errors, difficulty in thinking, disorientation, and confusion are commonly observed, and transient delusions and hallucinations occur occasionally (Solomon, 1961). Similar disturbances have been reported by seamen sailing alone on extended voyages, explorers, truck drivers on all-night trips, stratosphere pilots, and persons in solitary confinement.

There is a possibility that psychological disturbances may be directly or indirectly related to inherent defects in the inhibitory mechanisms of the organism (Diamond et al., 1963). Under usual circumstances, the organism is bombarded by a wide variety of stimuli. Some protective filter or inhibition of response is essential for concentration of attention, selective perception, logical thinking, and coherent speech. All behavior requiring choice involves the inhibition of alternatives. Defects in the filter or inhibitory mechanism may contribute to the hyperactivity and distractibility of the manic patient and to the word-salad speech and overinclusive thought processes of the schizophrenic. Massive inhibition, resulting in stimulus underload, may be related to the loss of feelings and the paralysis of thought and action characteristic of the depressed patient.

Some deficiency in genetic programming is highly probable in *autistic* children. These children are characterized from birth by a pathological absence of interest in and responsiveness to other human beings. Unlike normal children, who reach out for human contact and affection, autistic children experience outer reality as a source of intolerable irritation (Mahler, 1952). When social cues are forced on them, they either overreact or make no response at all. Autistic children do not welcome cuddling like normal babies, form no attachment to their mothers, are more interested in inanimate than animate objects, and treat people as if they were objects. Speech either never

develops or is severely limited. In a somewhat different context John Bowlby (1960) has suggested that there is a critical stage for primary attachment to the maternal figure. If this does not take place within a certain developmental period, the capacity is lost or impaired.

ANIMAL RESEARCH

Most of the experimental work on the genetics of behavior and disordered functioning has been carried out with animals. Our review would be incomplete without some mention of the findings of these studies. Animal research has demonstrated the presence and location of specific brain mechanisms that when stimulated produce sensations of pleasure or pain, induce feeding in satiated animals, initiate mating behavior, and evoke or inhibit rage reactions (Magoun, 1965).

Konrad Lorenz' observations on the *imprinting* of "following" behavior in ducks, which has been more systematically studied by Eckhard Hess (1959), have an important bearing on related human phenomena associated with critical development periods and irrational childhood fixations. Ducks are genetically programmed to follow a moving model. This program is effective for only a few hours after birth. Usually the mother is the only moving object around during this critical period, so the duckling follows her, and the action of following the mother becomes "imprinted" on the duckling. But if a person takes the place of the mother, the duckling follows him instead, and thereafter ignores its mother and other ducks as well. Other contributions of animal studies have consisted mainly of the confirmation, under better controlled experimental conditions, of observations and hypotheses initially derived from human data.

Harry Harlow's (1962) famous study of monkeys deprived of normal interactions (especially touch) between infants and mothers and among infants illustrates the

Harry F. Harlow, noted for his research on behavior pathology occurring in monkeys reared from infancy without normal interaction with others.

Harlow investigated the effects of separating monkeys at birth from their mothers. In the experiment illustrated here, infant monkeys were reared in isolation but had access to an artificial mother constructed of a wire frame covered with terry cloth.

relation of genotype to phenotype. More significantly, it identifies some of the environmental variables that—at least in monkeys—can transform a "normal" genotype into an "abnormal" phenotype. Monkeys separated at birth from their mothers and reared during the first year in wire cages that prevent any physical contact with other monkeys develop a variety of abnormal behavior patterns. In some respects their reactions resemble those of autistic children. They are mute, stare fixedly into space, rock back and forth, and exhibit sporadic, violent frenzies of rage. At the age of three, monkeys reared in isolation show infantile sexual behavior, absence of grooming, exaggerated aggression, and absence of affectional interaction with other monkeys. When physically mature, they resist heterosexual approaches or are clumsy and inept in mating.

Unmothered females that eventually submit to patient, experienced breeding males turn out to be terrible mothers. As Harlow describes them, they are helpless, heartless mothers, practically devoid of maternal feelings. The neglect and rejection experienced by the infants of these mothers have adverse effects on their phenotypic development. In comparison with infants who receive normal mothering, the infants of motherless mothers are deficient in social play and sexual behavior and are hyper-aggressive in interaction with their peers. (Arling and Harlow, 1967.)

Laboratory studies conducted with a variety of animals have consistently confirmed the importance of genetic factors in determining behavior traits in animals (Hall, 1941; Scott and Fuller, 1965). Starting with a heterogeneous population of a particular species, the experimenter finds it relatively simple, by selective breeding over two or more generations, to produce strains of animals that are predominantly fearful, stable, active, inactive, timid, or aggressive. These variations in temperament are correlated with differences in response patterns that are apparently largely genetic in origin. The environment seems to have relatively little effect in modifying the innate temperament of animals. Beagle puppies reared from birth with terrier litter mates grow up to be quiet, inhibited, shy, typical beagles; terrier puppies reared with beagles show the characteristic terrier traits of liveliness and excitability (James, 1951).

Another important contribution of animal studies has been the finding that genetic factors influence the impact of environmental stresses. The effects of the stimulation of infant rats on their subsequent emotionality as adults varies considerably with the genetic strain of the animals (Levine and Broadhurst, 1963). In his pioneer studies of experimentally induced neuroses in dogs, Pavlov (1927, 1941) noted that the inherent temperament of the dog appeared to be a critical factor in determining relative vulnerability to neurotic behavior.

Whether experimentally induced neuroses in animals are strictly analogous to neurotic behavior in humans is a moot question (Hunt, 1964). It has been argued that conditioned emotional reactions represent "normal" responses to unsolvable and inescapable problems. What is significant for our purpose is the marked variation in response made by different animals, whose emotional disturbance may be mild or severe, transient or permanent. Some animals become extremely agitated, others pass into a trance state marked by rigidity and negativism. Pavlov related response variation to the innate temperament of the dogs. Highly excitable (choleric) and inhibited (melancholic) dogs were considered to be highly susceptible to neuroses. Cheerful (sanguine) and calm (phlegmatic) dogs were regarded as constitutionally resistant to neuroses. Without necessarily subscribing to Pavlov's views on temperament, subsequent workers (Masserman, 1943; Liddell, 1944) confirmed the fact that some animals are highly susceptible to experimental neuroses while others are resistant to them. Gantt (1944) has reported on a detailed study of a dog named Nick who exhibited a lifelong neurosis following his exposure to a conflict situation, though other dogs exposed to the same situation

HOW TO MAKE A DOG NEUROTIC: PAVLOV'S EXPERIMENTAL DESIGN

In Pavlov's experimental design, a dog was restrained in a loose harness and subjected to a difficult discrimination problem that exceeded his capacity. In one variation, a conflict was produced between cortical excitatory and inhibitory responses. A circle of light was flashed on a screen and food was presented almost simultaneously, so that the circle became a signal for food and the dog was conditioned to salivate whenever he saw it. After this positive conditioned response had been established, an ellipse of light was substituted for the circle; but each time the ellipse was thrown on the screen, food was withheld. In effect, the dog was conditioned not to salivate at the ellipse. The dog readily learned to discriminate between the circle and the ellipse.

The experimenter then proceeded to make discrimination more difficult by using a series of ellipses that more and more approached a circle. The dog succeeded in making the proper discrimination as long as the axes of the ellipse were as 7 to 8. When the axes were as 8 to 9, the discrimination proved too fine for the dog and he broke down. All earlier established discriminations —even the easiest ones—were now lost. The dog salivated indiscriminately at the ellipse, the circle, the experimenter, and the laboratory apparatus. In addition, he was extremely upset and excited. He tore at the restraining harness, barked, whimpered, rejected food, and was generally unmanageable. Attempts to continue with the experiment on subsequent days were unsuccessful. Merely preparing the animal for experimentation reinstated the intense emotional excitement.

showed only mild agitation from which they soon recovered.

The case for heredity as a critical factor in psychopathology would be greatly strengthened if it could be shown that a substantial proportion of animals reared in their natural habitats spontaneously developed atypical, maladaptive behavior patterns that set them apart from the pack, herd, or flock. But this type of evidence is difficult to come by. Wild animals that are handicapped by behavior peculiarities and deficits soon die or are killed. The same fate awaits disturbed house pets and farm animals. Evidence for the spontaneous occurrence of psychopathology in animals is limited to a small number of cases reported by alert observers in animal research laboratories. Hebb (1947) has described two examples of neuroses occurring spontaneously in chimpanzees. One exhibited a phobic reaction; the other was subject to periods of depression. Since the known life experiences of the affected animals did not differ from those of their cagemates, Hebb concluded that the underlying cause must have been some constitutional defect.

Newton and Gantt (1968) reported on a detailed case history of a psychotic male French poodle. The dog was born in the laboratory. From an early age he was extremely timid, avoided contact with humans, and was easily intimidated by other dogs. His characteristic response to the presence of a person was a catatonic-like reaction marked by posturing and immobility. Other pecularities included homosexual tendencies and an atypical reaction to alcohol. The effect of alcohol on most dogs is to inhibit sexual activity; the catatonic dog reacted to alcohol with increased sexual activity, though in moderate doses alcohol improved his behavior so that he appeared almost normal. Newton and Gantt attributed the dog's abnormal behavior to inborn constitutional defects.

SUMMARY

Each organism's unique genetic endowment is a major determinant of its biological and behavioral individuality. The chemical codes contained in the genes initiate and in large measure regulate the complex biological processes associated with human growth and development. At every stage, however, the actual or phenotypic expression of genetic potentiality is subject to modification by environmental influences. The interactive contributions of the culture, the family, and personal learning experiences have marked effects on the style and content of psychological reactions.

As far as deviant behavior is concerned, the main contribution of genetic endowment appears to be in the area of temperament. The inherent temperament of the individual, as reflected in activity level, prevailing mood, adaptability, and intensity of reactions, does far more than influence his own reactions. The effect his behavior has on parents and other significant persons in large measure determines how others react to him. In other words, the individual tends to create his own social and emotional environment. The self-reinforcing interaction of the child and his environment may have desirable consequences if his innate temperament traits are positive, but if his innate traits are negative, their reinforcement by unfavorable interactions with others may result in extreme deviations. These deviant temperament characteristics, when combined with defensive symptomatic reactions, may be considered the main substance of the maladaptive behavior patterns that are referred to as mental disorders.

Although subject to other interpretations, the findings of long-term studies of children, twin data, and animal research are consistent with the hypothesis that innate temperament plays a stellar role in the etiology of behavior disturbances. Other possible biological contributions to psychopathology include various irregularities in genetic programming which lead to behavior deficiencies or to faulty handling of input data. Here also heredity is a contributory rather than an exclusive agent. Genes may set potential limits and factor certain reactions, but actual behavior is always the product of the interaction of nature and nurture.

References

Allport, G. W. *Pattern and Growth in Personality*. New York: Holt, Rinehart & Winston, 1961.

Arling, G. L., and Harlow, H. F. "Effects of Social Deprivation on Maternal Behavior of Rhesus Monkeys." *Journal of Comparative and Physiological Psychology* 64 (1967): 371-77.

Bowlby, J. "Separation Anxiety." *International Journal of Psychoanalysis* 41 (1960): 1-25.

Diamond, S.; Balvin, R.; and Diamond, F. *Inhibition and Choice*. New York: Harper & Row, 1963.

Escalona, S. *The Roots of Individuality*. Chicago: Aldine, 1968.

Essen-Moller, E. "Twin Research and Psychiatry." *Acta Psychiatrica et Neurologica* 39 (1963): 65-77. Reprinted in *International Journal of Psychiatry* 1 (1965): 466-75.

Fish, B.; Shapiro, T.; Halpern, F.; and Wile, R. "The Prediction of Schizophrenia in Infancy: III. A Ten-Year Follow-up Report of Neurological and Psychological Development." *American Journal of Psychiatry* 121 (1965): 768-75.

Freedman, D. "Heredity Control of Early Social Behavior." In *Determinants of Infant Behavior*, ed. B. M. Foss, vol. 3, pp. 149-53. New York: Wiley, 1963.

Freud, S. "Analysis, Terminable and Interminable." In *Collected Papers*, vol. 5, p. 316. London: Hogarth Press, 1950.

Gantt, W. H. *Experimental Basis for Neurotic Behavior*. New York: Hoeber, 1944.

Gesell, A., et al. *Biographies of Child Development*. New York: Harper, 1939.

Hall, C. S. "Temperament: A Survey of Animal Studies." *Psychological Bulletin* 38 (1941): 909-43.

Harlow, H. F. "The Heterosexual Affectional System in Monkeys." *American Psychologist* 17 (1962): 1-9.

Hebb, D. O. "Spontaneous Neuroses in Chimpanzees: Theoretical Relations with Clinical and Experimental Phenomena." *Psychosomatic Medicine* 9 (1947): 3-16.

Hess, E. H. "Imprinting." *Science* 130 (1959): 133-41.

Hunt, H. F. "Problems in the Interpretation of

'Experimental Neurosis.'" *Psychological Reports* 15 (1964): 27-35.

James, W. J. "Social Organization Among Dogs of Different Temperaments: Terriers and Beagles Reared Together." *Journal of Comparative and Physiological Psychology* 44 (1951): 71-77.

Kagan, J., and Moss, H. A. *Birth to Maturity: A Study in Psychological Development.* New York: Wiley, 1962.

Kolb, L. *Noyes' Modern Clinical Psychiatry,* 7th ed. Philadelphia: Saunders, 1968.

Levine, S., and Broadhurst, P. L. "Genetic and Ontogenetic Determinants of Adult Behavior in the Rat." *Journal of Comparative and Physiological Psychology* 56 (1963): 423-28.

Liddell, H. S. "Conditioned Reflex Method and Experimental Neurosis." In *Personality and Behavior Disorders,* ed. J. McV. Hunt, vol. 1, pp. 389-412. New York: Ronald Press, 1944.

MacKinnon, K. M. *Consistency and Change in Behavior Manifestation.* Society for Research in Child Development Monographs, no. 30 (1942).

Magoun, H. W. "Brain Mechanisms for Innate and Emotional Behavior." In *Handbook of Clinical Psychology,* ed. B. B. Wolman, pp. 181-96. New York: McGraw-Hill, 1965.

Mahler, M. S. "On Child Psychosis and Schizophrenia: Autistic and Symbiotic Infantile Psychosis." *Psychoanalytical Study of the Child,* vol. 7. New York: International Universities Press, 1952.

Masserman, J. H. *Behavior and Neurosis.* Chicago: University of Chicago Press, 1943.

Neilon, P. "Shirley's Babies After Fifteen Years: A Personality Study." *Journal of Genetic Psychology* 73 (1948): 175-86.

Newton, J. E. O., and Gantt, W. H. "The History of a Catatonic Dog." *Conditional Reflex* 3 (1968): 45-61.

Pavlov, I. P. *Lectures on Conditioned Reflexes,* trans. G. V. Anrep. London: Oxford University Press, 1927.

————. *Conditioned Reflexes and Psychiatry,* trans. W. H. Gantt. New York: International Publishers, 1941.

Rosenthal, D. *Genetic Theory and Abnormal Behavior.* New York: McGraw-Hill, 1970.

Russell, R. W. "Biochemical Factors in Mental Disorders." In *Handbook of Clinical Psychology,* ed. B. B. Wolman, pp. 197-215. New York: McGraw-Hill, 1965.

Schaefer, E. R., and Bayley, N. *Maternal Behavior, Child Behavior, and Their Intercorrelations from Infancy Through Adolescence.* Society for Research in Child Development Monographs, vol. 28, no. 3 (1963).

Scott, J. P., and Fuller, J. L. *Genetics and the Social Behavior of the Dog.* Chicago: University of Chicago Press, 1965.

Smith, R. T. "A Comparison of Socioenvironmental Factors in Monozygotic and Dizygotic Twins, Testing an Assumption." In *Methods and Goals in Behavior Genetics,* ed. S. G. Vandenburg, pp. 45-61. New York: Academic Press, 1965.

Solomon, P., ed. *Sensory Deprivation.* Cambridge: Harvard University Press, 1961.

Thomas, A.; Chess, S.; and Birch, H. *Temperament and Behavioral Disorders in Children.* New York: New York University Press, 1968.

Yarrow, L. J. "Maternal Deprivation: Toward an Empirical and Conceptual Re-evaluation." *Psychological Bulletin* 58 (1961): 459-90.

7 · Sociocultural Theories

An Alaskan medicine man, W. B. Styles

Most sociocultural theories either are of a global nature or deal with some specific factor such as the relation of psychopathology to economic status, social disorganization, and social change. A notable exception is the sociological theory of mental disorders outlined by Scheff (1966). As we saw in Chapter 1, Scheff prefers the term *residual deviant behavior* to *mental illness*. Residual deviant behavior consists of violations of certain social norms for which society has no precise name. He recognizes that the underlying causes of residual deviance may include a variety of biogenic, psychogenic, and sociogenic factors, but he maintains that most residual deviance is either denied or transitory. The most important single factor in the structuring and stabilization of mental illness is the reaction of society. In the crisis that occurs when a deviant is publicly labeled as a mental patient, the confused, disturbed person is highly suggestible and may see no alternative to the proffered role. More specifically, Scheff suggests that in many instances deviant behavior represents a normal reaction to a stress situation, and if it were only regarded in this light it would be transitory.

The labeling of such behavior as symptomatic of psychopathology and the pressure exerted on the disturbed person to seek treatment serve to accentuate and fix the disturbance. The medical tradition of playing it safe by diagnosing illness in cases of doubt contributes to this error. The questions asked and the answers expected during the psychiatric examination provide clues as to the way in which the person should behave to qualify as a mental patient. The culturally defined stereotypes of mental illness are further clarified and reaffirmed in interaction with members of his family and associates. The labeled deviant, whose behavior confirms the medical and societal diagnosis, may be rewarded and receive "sick" benefits for conforming to the conventionally accepted stereotype.

Once the label of mental patient has been publicly applied, the individual usually finds himself discriminated against when he seeks to return to normal status. He is treated with suspicion, distrust, and apprehension by his family, employer, and associates. If he accepts the role of deviant and thinks of himself as a "mental case," his ability to control and modify his own behavior may be impaired. His acceptance of therapy confirms his role as a mental patient. The longer the course of recommended therapy, the more the patient may perceive himself as a sick person in need of treatment. Thus psychotherapy, as Jerome Frank has also noted in a different context (1961, p. 7) may to some extent create the illness it treats.

SOCIOCULTURAL FACTORS

Culture and Personality

Culture is the total way of life of a people or social group. It may be thought of as a highly flexible mold. The shaping influences of a society contribute to similarities in personality, but they do not negate the role of biological and experiential factors that make for individual uniqueness. The range and variety of personality types is about the same in all cultures. At times a society may actually reinforce biological individuality by identifying at an early age persons who show promise of developing distinctive traits required for special

CULTURE AND PERSONALITY:
TWO CASES OF CONTRAST

Ruth Benedict (1934), an early advocate of the plasticity of human personality, contributed an interesting account of the role of culture in shaping personality differences between the savage Plains Indians and the quiet, restrained Pueblo Indians of North America. Historically the Plains Indians were buffalo hunters. The pattern of their culture encouraged dangerous living, emotional excesses, and violence. Mothers deliberately provoked their children to have temper tantrums to "make them strong." The toughening training of boys included exposure to hunger, thirst, and pain. Tribal ceremonies included orgiastic dances and the use of intoxicating drugs. The ideal man among the Plains Indians was brave, reckless, and cruel, and most Sioux and Crow warriors acquired these traits.

In contrast, the Pueblo Indians of the Southwest, as represented by the Pueblos, Hopis, and Zunis, cultivated the gentler traits of moderation, restraint, and mildness. Children were taught to be cooperative, flexible, and easygoing. They were treated with kindness and understanding and seldom scolded or punished. An orderly, even-tempered life, free of excesses, excitement, and violence, constituted the cultural ideal. Stimulating drugs had no part in their rituals, and their dances consisted of slow, monotonous thumping of the feet. Individualism, competition, greed, and aggressiveness were systematically discouraged and suppressed. Little importance was attached to possessions or success. The most valuable objects were the sacred things used in ceremonials; these were privately owned, but any qualified person was free to borrow them. If a man acquired more worldly goods than his neighbors, he was expected to redistribute his wealth during the great winter festivals.

Selfish strivings for power and authority were disparaged. A person who sought to be a leader was scorned and censured. Persistently ambitious individuals were hung by their thumbs until they were cured of this folly. If a man consistently won at running races, he was disbarred from competition in order to give others a chance to win. When high offices had to be filled, the group selected the best qualified man and forced him to accept. The selected person was expected to try to avoid the honor.

Another well-known example of the role of culture in shaping personality is the contrast reported by Margaret Mead (1935) between the gentle, cooperative Mountain Arapesh of New Guinea and the aggressive, distrustful Mundugumor. The two groups lived within a hundred miles of each other, but in culture and personality they were poles apart. The Arapesh culture in many respects resembled that of the Pueblo Indians. The Arapesh believed that the security of the individual and the group depended on mutual goodwill, cooperativeness, and interpersonal dependency. Their culture fostered personal warmth, kindliness, congeniality, and responsiveness to the requests of others. Social acceptance, rather than personal achievement, was the dominant motive. From infancy the child was trained to regard the outside world as friendly and helpful. Babies were wanted and pampered. They were breast-fed for years, and the breast was always available to comfort the older child when he was in pain or frightened. Children received no training in initiative or competition. There were no races, no games with opposing sides, no rewards for personal enterprise. Fighting between youngsters was not permitted.

The Arapesh solution to courtship and marriage was early residence of the future bride in the house of the parents-in-law. By the age of six or seven, all girls were betrothed and went to live in the households of their future husbands. The marriage was not consummated until the children grew up, but this arrangement provided a test of compatibility. If the betrothed children did not get along with one another, the girl went back to her family while there was still time to arrange for a more suitable trial marriage. Fathers avoided the potential conflict between the old and new generations by retiring from active life as soon as their eldest sons reached adolescence.

Family group of the Mountain Arapesh of New Guinea, studied by Margaret Mead. This culture fosters mutual goodwill, cooperativeness and absence of competition.

Mundugumor woman with child. The Mundugumor culture promotes feelings of distrust and hostility within the family group as well as with others.

The Mundugumor, on the other hand, encouraged feelings of hostility, mutual distrust, and violence. Every man, woman, and child was expected to look out for his own best interests. Babies were unwanted. Antipregnancy magic was practiced, and if pregnancy occurred anyway, each parent blamed the other. Mundugumor mothers suckled their children while standing up. The moment the infant stopped nursing, he was dropped into an uncomfortable basket. The child soon learned to fight for every drop of milk. He held on tightly to the nipple and sucked as rapidly as possible. As a result he frequently choked from trying to swallow too fast, much to the exasperation of both mother and child.

The fact that babies were unwanted was a result of local marriage customs. A man was permitted to have several wives, and the principal way of acquiring a new wife was to exchange one's daughter for the daughter of another man. The mother feared pregnancy because she might give birth to a daughter who could be used by her husband to acquire a new wife. The father feared pregnancy because if the child turned out to be a boy, he had fathered a potential rival. The principal way the son could acquire a wife was to trade his sister for the sister of another young man. The father tried to make home life as difficult as possible for his sons in the hope that they would run away at an early age and leave his daughters at his sole disposal. The mother sided with her sons against the father. The threat that a boy might grab off all the sisters and exchange them for wives for himself turned brother against brother. Daughters resented being marriage pawns and often expressed their hatred of mother, father, and brothers by eloping.

roles—the self-induced trance state of shamans, for example—and nurturing the maximum growth of these traits in selected individuals. The main thrust of society, however, is aimed at furthering the homogeneity of the group by promoting uniformity in personality and behavior.

Cultural anthropologists accept the genotype-phenotype model of biology with respect to the plasticity of personality development. A basic tenet of cultural anthropology is that each infant is born with potentialities for developing a variety of behavior characteristics. The molding influences of the culture into which an infant is born determine in great measure which of his inherent potentialities are realized and which are suppressed.

Some of the findings and implications of the extensive literature on culture and personality that have special significance for psychopathology are these:

1. The role of culture in shaping personality (and in producing personality types especially vulnerable to particular mental disorders) does not exclude the significance of genetic factors. Particularly in small, isolated, inbred societies, the emergence of a modal or basic personality type may be partly due to selective breeding. When a culture favors particular personality characteristics, individuals genetically endowed with potentialities for the desired traits will be preferred as mates. Over several generations, this selective marital factor, which in turn influences the number of children born with the favored potentialities, will result in a relatively homogeneous genetic population. Deviants will still occur, but their relative number will be gradually diminished. The effectiveness of selective breeding in creating desired behavior has been repeatedly demonstrated in animal studies.

2. As we can see by the examples we have examined and the study of the Hutterites, the molding influence of the culture is pervasive, consistent, and continuous throughout the life of the individual. The significance, if any, of a particular infantile experience depends on the extent to which it is an integral part of the total indoctrination and training program.

3. The success of culture (or heredity) in creating uniform or standard human potentialities is limited. Under favorable cir-

cumstances, culture and heredity working together may produce similar personality traits in a substantial proportion of a tribe or social group. A closer examination, however, indicates the highly individual character of each member (DuBois, 1944). Even the most rigid cultures produce an infinite variety of personalities. Furthermore, the personality types "typical" of certain cultures are found in all societies.

4. The fact that certain cultures, such as the Mundugumor, accept as normal some attitudes and traits that would suggest psychopathology in our culture again points to the unreliability of "symptoms" as cross-cultural indicators of psychopathology. Whether a person is distrustful or friendly, hated or loved by his family, in itself has nothing to do with his mental health. As long as he retains enough voluntary control over his impulses, emotions, and mental faculties to behave reasonably well and appropriately in accordance with the demands and expectations of his culture, he is a normal person from a psychiatric point of view and is so regarded by his society.

Culture and Psychopathology

The extensive literature on the role of culture in the development of mental disorders (reviewed by Linton, 1956; Leighton and Hughes, 1961; Wallace, 1967; and others) indicates that (1) no culture is free of mental disorders, (2) the major patterns of clinical syndromes are found in all large heterogeneous societies, and (3) the overt form or content of symptoms is mainly learned and hence culture-bound. The universality of mental disorders may be attributed to the presence of pathogenic influences in all cultures and to the inevitable pressures, frustrations, and conflicts of human life.

The occurrence of the major clinical syndromes in all advanced countries of the world has long been recognized. In the past, the labels have varied. More recently, most countries have accepted, with minor modifications, the eighth revision of the International Nomenclature and Classification System proposed by the World Health Organization of the United Nations. Wherever hospitals or clinics staffed by Western personnel have been established in underdeveloped countries, all of the major clinical syndromes have been observed in the native population. Earlier studies of primitive societies, based on casual field observations, emphasized the more dramatic and visible forms of psychopathology. The better controlled, more recent investigations have confirmed the occurrence of all of the major forms of mental disorders in primitive societies (Field, 1960; Toker, 1966; Elsarrag, 1968).

The simplest explanation for the presence of similar clinical syndromes in various cultures is that the major varieties of mental disorders represent characteristic human forms of maladaptive reactions to intolerable stress situations. Human beings characteristically react to the inevitable problems of life with the anxiety and rigidity associated with neurosis, the conversion symptoms of hysterics, the inner retreat of schizophrenics, the hopeless despair of the depressed, and the disorganized hyperactivity of manics.

Reasons for Mental Hospitalization

It is standard practice in mental hospitals throughout the world for the admitting officer to fill out a form for incoming patients which includes a description of the patient's behavior at the time and serves as a justification for admission. The information may be transmitted by an outside doctor but, whatever the original source, great reliance is placed on statements made by the patient's family and other concerned persons. This background information is a significant source of data for evaluating cultural criteria with respect to the more intolerable forms of psychopathology. The findings of two of my studies are summarized in Tables 7.1A and 7.1B. In both investigations, the data were based on consecutive male admissions, aged twenty-five to fifty, exclusive of persons diagnosed

CULTURE AND PSYCHOPATHOLOGY: THE CASE OF THE HUTTERITES

The Hutterites provide a good illustration of the influence of culture on psychopathology and personality. This religious sect of German origin dates back to the early sixteenth century. About 100 married couples and their children migrated to this country in 1875 and established culturally isolated settlements in the Dakotas, Montana, and the prairie provinces of Canada. Apart from adopting a highly mechanized form of agriculture, the Hutterites have preserved their original customs with minimal interaction with the outside world. All of the present population are descendants of the original immigrant group.

The Hutterites are farmers dedicated to simple communal living. They do not believe in education beyond grammar school. Radios, movies, television, jewelry, and other luxury items are taboo. Their homes consist only of bedrooms, all of which are furnished alike. Property is owned by the group rather than the individual, meals are served in common dining rooms, and elected group leaders assign work tasks. Every member is provided with a high level of social and economic security from birth to death.

The group takes such good care of its own that it was for a long time thought that the great security of their system resulted in the absence of mental illness. This was supported by the conspicuous absence of Hutterites in mental hospitals. However, a research team that gained the cooperation of the group and made a field study of the Hutterites in 1951 found that well over 2 percent of the group either had active symptoms of mental disorder or had recovered from some such disorder (Eaton and Weil, 1955). In attempting to account for the presence of so many disturbed persons, the investigators suggested that there may be

Hutterian women at work. The task is noodle-making, using a machine improved and rebuilt by colony technicians.

genetic, organic, or constitutional predispositions that will cause mental illness in any society, no matter how protective and stable it may be.

In most societies schizophrenia is far more prevalent than manic-depressive psychosis, but the reverse is true among the Hutterites. Since there is a definite tendency for manic-depressive psychosis to run in families, a possible explanation for this atypical finding is that some of the original immigrants had a genetic predisposition to manic-depressive psychosis that has been inherited by their inbred descendants. An alternate, but not necessarily contradictory, explanation is that the cultural pattern may favor depressive reactions. The indoctrination system of the Hutterites teaches its members to look for blame and guilt within themselves rather than in others. By precept and example, they are taught to repress aggressive impulses. The effectiveness of this training is shown by the fact that murder, arson, severe physical assault, sex crimes, and other forms of violence are extremely rare. Self-blaming starts at an early age. Melancholy moods are regarded by teachers as the primary emotional problem of Hutterite schoolchildren. When a person develops signs of mental disorder, the closely knit social group provides a highly therapeutic atmosphere by demonstrating strong support, guidance, tolerance, and love for him.

The predominance of depressive reactions fits in with the austere and puritanical customs of the sect. Security and stability are achieved through insistence on strict conformity to a predetermined and extremely narrow way of life. But, as the investigators noted, the rigid cultural mold has not resulted in stereotyped personalities. Despite uniformity in the externals of living, there are great variations in personality among the members of the sect. On projective personality tests, the Hutterites show strong antisocial and aggressive impulses, even though they effectively repress these feelings in daily life.

Hutterian men at work. The task is shingling a grain storage building.

as mentally defective, acutely alcoholic or brain damaged.

In the earlier study it was possible to make a specific comparison of symptoms for five European countries and the United States (Table 7.1A). The six countries dif-

Table 7.1. Reasons for Mental Hospitalization: International Comparisons.

A. Symptoms Noted in Five Countries.

Symptom	Percent of Admissions					
	United States	France	Italy	Spain	Portugal	Range
Delusions	60%	56%	66%	52%	54%	52-66%
Hallucinations	36	32	30	36	28	28-36
Hostile belligerence	72	52	60	58	66	52-72
Delusions and hostile belligerence	86	88	90	82	90	82-90
Suicide attempts	2	4	4	4	2	2- 4

Adapted from J. D. Page, "Cultural-National Differences in Symptomatology in Hospitalized Psychotic Patients." *Yearbook of the American Philosophical Society* (1965): 343-44.

Data are based on symptoms noted at time of hospitalization among fifty consecutive male patients, aged twenty-five to fifty, for each country, exclusive of persons diagnosed as mentally defective, acutely alcoholic, or brain damaged.

B. Behavior Deviations Noted in Six Countries.

Behavior deviations	Percent of Admissions						Mean		p
	Singapore N=150	Hong Kong N=100	Fiji N=50	New Zealand N=50	Australia N=50	Hawaii (Caucasian) N=50	Non-Western	Western	
Irrational/ incongruous[1]	79	80	90	68	52	66	83	62	<.001
Aggressive/ destructive threat to others[2]	69	56	70	44	32	46	65	41	<.001
Depressive, self-attack, suicidal[3]	27	20	14	46	48	36	20	43	<.001

[1] Irrational or incongruous behavior: delusions, hallucinations, ideas of persecution or grandeur, nonsensical or incoherent speech, extreme fearfulness, silly giggling, ideas of being possessed or bewitched, bizarre actions, talking to oneself.

[2] Aggressive or hostile actions: threats, assaultive behavior, violent explosive temper, murder, argumentativeness, shouting and cursing in public, indecent exposure, engaging in nuisance behavior in the neighborhood, property destruction, setting fires.

[3] Depressive states, suicidal tendencies, and self-inflicted injuries: despondency, depreciatory ideas against the self, and suicide attempts.

Data are based on symptoms noted at time of hospitalization among fifty consecutive male patients, aged twenty-five to fifty, for each country, exclusive of persons diagnosed as mentally defective, acutely alcoholic, or brain damaged.

fered markedly in the number of available hospital beds and admission regulations, but in all of them the two major symptoms cited as reasons for hospitalization were delusions and hostile belligerent behavior. One or both of these socially disturbing reactions were present in from 82 to 90 percent of consecutive male admissions. The general conclusion is that much the same criteria appear to be used in the United States and European countries in deciding the kinds of patients who are hospitalized.

The second study involved an examination of the hospital records of consecutive male admissions to public mental hospitals in Singapore, Hong Kong, Fiji, New Zealand, Australia, and Hawaii (Table 7.1B). In two of the nonwestern countries, the admission information consisted mainly of the statements of relatives, and the colloquial language used made cross-cultural comparison difficult. For this reason, the data were analyzed in terms of broad general categories.

In all six countries the presence of irrational or incongruous behavior was the main reason given for mental hospitalization. Percentage figures for this category were significantly higher for the three nonwestern countries than for the western countries. In the former the number of admissions described as showing aggressive or destructive behavior was significantly higher than those described as being depressed or engaging in self-injurious behavior. For male admissions to mental hospitals in New Zealand, Australia, and Hawaii, the frequency of depressive behavior was as great as that for aggressive or destructive behavior.

The greatest difference between western and nonwestern countries was the significantly higher occurrence of depressive reactions among hospitalized patients in the former. This finding is subject to various interpretations. One possibility is that because of the limited hospital facilities in Hong Kong, Singapore, and especially in Fiji, priority was given to patients showing "acting out" behavior that was disturbing to others. In western countries with more

adequate facilities, a more liberal policy may have existed with respect to subjectively disturbed but quiet patients. A second possibility is that in the less advanced countries, where belief in bewitchment is still prevalent, depressed patients may be more often referred to local specialists in curing spells or concocting charms. A final possibility is that in countries of a lower socio-economic level, depressive reactions may be more often expressed in acting out.

Culture and Symptom Form

The effect of culture on the outward form of psychopathology is most apparent in the content of symptoms. Whether a patient believes his thoughts and actions are being controlled by an evil spirit, a sorcerer or an electronic computer depends on his cultural background. Several studies (reviewed by Draguns and Phillips, 1972) have reported differences among cultures with respect to the relative incidence of particular symptoms and reaction patterns. One consistent finding has been the greater passivity of mental patients in Spanish-speaking countries as compared with those in the United States.

A number of studies have compared symptoms among Japanese patients in Tokyo and Hawaii with those in the mainland United States. The proportion of schizophrenic patients in Tokyo described as physically assaultive is much higher than among Japanese-Americans in Hawaii, and the latter, are in turn more physically assaultive than Caucasion schizophrenics in the continental United States (Schooler and Caudill, 1964; Maretski and Nelson, 1969). The highest incidence of hallucinations was noted among the Japanese in Hawaii and the lowest among the Tokyo patients. The high incidence of hallucinations among Japanese-Americans in Hawaii was confirmed in my 1970 study (Table 7.2); I also found paranoid ideas and suspiciousness to be significantly more common among Japanese than among Caucasians. The Japanese were more verbally assaultive than the Caucasian patients but no differences were noted in physical assaultiveness.

At a broader level, culture may be thought to influence the relative incidence of specific types of mental disorders. The incidence of toxic and brain disorders may be directly related to the prevalence of drug use, dietary deficiencies, syphilis, and other exogenous pathogenic factors. Alcoholism, for example, is rare in Islamic countries. The comparatively high recorded rate of schizophrenics in West Africa may be due in part to the prevalence of trypanosomiasis, a form of sleeping sickness that is transmitted by the bite of an infected tsetse fly and is associated with schizophrenic-like symptoms (Tooth, 1950).

There is some evidence that in cultures described by anthropologists as shame-oriented, psychiatric disorders are likely to take the form of antisocial, aggressive, acting-out behavior that is more disturbing to society than to the individual. In guilt-oriented cultures such as the Hutterite, on the other hand, there is a higher occurrence of depressive reactions. In David Riesman's (1950) terminology, shame cultures are "other-directed," since society at large controls and enforces moral conduct, whereas guilt cultures are "inner-directed," since the individual is expected to be responsible for his own conduct and to assume blame for his misdeeds.

The role of culture in shaping symptoms may be seen especially clearly in the unusual reactions observed in specific localities: amok and latah in Malaysia, koro in China, windigo among the Objibwa Indians, and piblokto among the Arctic Eskimo (Leighton and Hughes, 1961). Amok was a culture-bound type of rage reaction in which the disturbed individual would suddenly grasp his dagger and run about in a frenzy, madly slashing at anyone in his way. Latah, a condition mainly noted in women, has been described as an intense fear reaction marked by shuddering and the involuntary imitation of the actions and words of others. Koro was a form of sexual anxiety formerly noted among Chinese men; those who fell victim to it were convinced that their sex organs were shrinking and disappearing into their abdomens, and that when this happened they would die. Piblokto also appears to have been a dramatic fear reaction. The deranged Eskimo would run out naked in

Table 7.2. Symptoms Noted Among Japanese and Caucasian Patients in Hawaii (Based on 50 Consecutive Admissions in Each Category to Hawaii State Mental Hospital, 1970).

Symptom	Percent	
	Japanese	Caucasian
Physically assaultive	12	14
Grandiose ideas	6	8
Other irrational ideas	6	8
Use of alcohol and drugs	16	20
Depression, self-injury, suicide attempt	38	36
Anxiety, agitation, fearfulness	10	12
Verbal threats, abusive, destructive but no record of physical attack	38	20
Paranoid ideas, suspiciousness	52	32
Hallucinations	46	22

subzero temperatures and mimic the sounds of Arctic birds and animals.

These exotic disorders may at one time have been common in certain cultures, but they are now rare. Other, less dramatic cultural differences in surface symptoms are also disappearing. As rural, backward populations enter urban areas and become exposed to Western influences, the clinical manifestations of mental disorders begin to approximate those of the European white settlers (Wittkower, and Fried, 1959).

Culture and Incidence Rates

Whether certain cultures have a higher incidence of mental disorders than others is difficult to determine. A major obstacle is the absence of valid criteria for deciding how "sick" a person must be before he is counted as deranged. The extreme variations in the prevalence rates of psychological disorders noted in epidemiological studies conducted in various parts of the world are mainly due to variations in the conception of mental disorder (Dohrenwend and Dohrenwend, 1965). This variability applies mainly to mild disorders and most authorities agree that the incidence of severe disorders (psychoses) is about the same in all cultures, tribal as well as Western (Kiev, 1964).

On the basis of a survey of mental disorders among the natives of the South Pacific, Eric Berne (1960) concluded that the same proportion of every large population, whether Anglo-Saxon, Polynesian, or Melanesian, develops a psychosis each year. Differences in the recorded number of patients in various cultures are related to such incidental factors as the availability of doctors and hospital facilities and the societies' relative tolerance of various forms of deviant behavior. In support of this hypothesis, Berne noted that the incidence rates of first admissions to mental hospitals in New Zealand were the same for people of European stock and for Maoris. This finding is consistent with earlier reports. Some years ago it was noted that mental disease was as prevalent in Samoa as in rural areas of the United States (Winston, 1934). Lin (1953) observed that the incidence of psychosis among the natives of Formosa was on a par with that of central Germany.

In determining whether the incidence of mental disorders is increasing, we must make a distinction between severe and mild disorders. For admissions to mental hospitals, which are limited to the more severe disorders, there is conclusive evidence that the admission rate per 100,000 population for ages under fifty is about the same today as it was in 1840 (Goldhamer and Marshall, 1949; Page and Landis, 1943; Dunham, 1966). In other words, the transition from the horse-and-buggy era to the jet age has not resulted in any noticeable increase in admissions to mental hospitals. It is reasonable to assume that the proportion of unhospitalized psychotic patients has also remained about the same over the past century. The available data thus refute the popular belief that the pressures and strains of modern life have resulted in an increase in severe mental disorders. It is quite possible that cases of neuroses and other mild disorders have increased, but in the absence of valid long-range comparative data, the hypothesis remains unproved.

Social Factors

Socioeconomic status, social disorganization, and social change are also thought to be related to mental disorders. Occasionally, as in times of war, economic depression, and transition from tribal to city living in developing countries, it is possible to evaluate the significance of these variables separately. As a rule, however, they are closely interrelated. For example, low-income areas tend to be more disorganized, to have a higher population turnover, and to include a higher proportion of migrant and immigrant residents than high-income areas.

A rough measure of the relation of socioeconomic status to diagnosis is provided by a comparison of first admissions to high-cost private hospitals with first admissions to publicly supported state hospitals in the United States. A higher proportion of first admissions to public hospitals than private hospitals are diagnosed as senile, psychotic with arteriosclerosis, drunk or alcoholic, and drug addicted. The proportions of persons with schizophrenic reactions and personality disorders other than alcoholism are about the same in public and private institutions. The percentage of first admissions diagnosed as psychoneurotic is three times as great in private mental hospitals as in public institutions. Manic-depressive and psychotic depressive reactions also constitute a higher proportion of admissions to private mental institutions.

The interpretation of these and the related findings of field studies is not easy. The possibility that socioeconomic background either has a direct effect on the relative incidence of specific disorders or is influential in favoring the development of certain symptom patterns cannot be ruled out. On the other hand, reported class differences in the relative distribution of specific disorders may be a result of (1) examiner bias (the doctor may tend to assign more "favorable" labels to better educated and wealthier patients), (2) class differences in defining and recognizing a psychiatric problem, and (3) differences between classes in available or preferred procedures for handling certain types of deviant behavior.

The higher proportion of disturbed elderly persons admitted to public rather than private mental hospitals, for example, may be related to the greater prevalence of biological defects among the more poorly educated and less economically successful members of society, the harder life of the culturally disadvantaged, the higher incidence of nutritional deficiencies that contribute to impaired mental functioning in the indigent aged, and the inability of the less affluent to care for incompetent aged relatives at home or to place them in nursing homes. Examiner bias has long been recognized. In 1932 Pierre Janet, the French psychiatrist, wrote:

If the patient is poor he is committed to a public hospital as psychotic; if he can afford the luxury of a private sanitarium he is put there with a diagnosis of neurasthenia; if he is wealthy enough to be isolated in his own home under constant watch of nurses and physicians he is simply an indisposed eccentric.

A major limitation of hospital admission data is that they are based on restricted samples. Even in countries that provide adequate facilities, the number of unhospitalized persons exhibiting neurotic and psychotic behavior is as great as or greater than the number of hospitalized mental patients. More comprehensive data are provided by field studies that attempt to count or estimate the total number of treated and untreated cases for a whole population in a specified geographical area. But this approach introduces other problems. There is no objective and valid test that can be routinely administered to a large population to differentiate between disturbed and normal persons. The criteria used have been loose, and investigators often include doubtful cases that more stringent screening would exclude.

Another limitation is that almost all field studies have been concerned with the prevalence rather than the incidence of mental disorders. *Incidence rates* include only new cases that have developed during a designated period of time (usually a year). *Prevalence rates*, which run much higher than incidence figures, are determined by counting all mental patients in the population on a particular day or year and dividing this number by the total population. Prevalence rates are loaded in favor of chronic, long-term cases. Prevalence rates are actually better measures of the effects of socioeconomic status on the duration of mental illness than of its occurrence.

In fourteen out of eighteen field studies on the relation of prevalence rate to socioeconomic status (Dohrenwend and Dohrenwend, 1965), maximum rates were found at the lowest social stratum. Minimum rates were reported for the lowest social stratum in three studies, in the middle social group in five studies, and in the highest stratum in ten studies. This inverse relationship between social class and the prevalence of mental disorder applied to all psychological disorders combined. When investigators focus on specific disorders, field studies indicate that the total prevalence of neurosis and psychosis, treated and untreated, is not related to social class; maximum and minimum rates have been reported for these two forms of disorder about as often in the lowest socioeconomic group as in other classes (Dohrenwend and Dohrenwend, 1967). Psychosis in children has also been found to be unrelated to social class (McDermott et al., 1967).

The higher prevalence rate for all disorders combined at the lowest social stratum is partly due to the disproportionate number of alcoholics, asocial personalities, and persons with other character disorders reported at this socioeconomic level. In ten of the thirteen field studies reviewed by the Dohrenwends (1967), the highest rates of character disorders were found in the lowest social class.

Social Disorganization and Change

Early studies indicated that the incidence of schizophrenia was higher in deprived neighborhoods than in middle-class urban areas. However, more recent reports, in which corrections were made for the greater mobility and population turnover in the deprived areas, have reduced the difference to a statistically insignificant point. The only disorder that does appear to have a higher corrected incidence in disorganized communities is sociopathy (Dunham, 1966).

Social changes, in particular the changes accompanying migration, the transitions from war to peace and from peace to war, and the increased urbanization of developing nations, do not in themselves appear to constitute hazards to mental health (Murphy, 1961). Most studies report no increase in the rates of admission to mental hospitals in the civilian population during war-

time and no increase in the incidence of psychoses among military personnel. There is a decrease in the rate of mental disorders among prisoners of war. Repeated air raids may lead to an increase in neurotic and psychosomatic complaints in civilian populations, however. Combat soldiers and pilots, exposed to prolonged stress, also tend to show an increase in neuroses and psychosomatic reactions (Reid, 1961).

Anomie and Mental Disorders

Kleiner and Parker (1966) have investigated the relationship between mental illness, social mobility, and Emile Durkheim's four characteristics of *anomie*: lack of integration with significant reference groups, inability to perceive realistic barriers to achievement, high status aspirations, and low self-esteem. Their findings, based on the results of a study of almost three thousand members of an urban Negro population, are in partial conflict with Durkheim's theory of an invariant relationship between social mobility, anomie, and deviant behavior. Kleiner and Parker found that mobility and mental illness are correlated at some strata in the social hierarchy but not at others. Their data show that rates of mental disorder are higher among downwardly mobile individuals in low-status occupations and upwardly mobile individuals in high-status positions than among their nonmobile peers. In addition, both upwardly and downwardly mobile individuals exhibit the characteristics of anomie.

Social Class and Therapy

A number of studies (Hollingshead and Redlich, 1958; Reissman et al., 1964) indicate a definite relationship between social class and the source of referral for treatment, the type of treatment offered and accepted, and the duration of treatment. The majority of psychotic patients in the highest socioeconomic groups are self-referred or referred by family and friends. Most middle-class patients are referred by physicians, and most psychotic patients in the lowest socioeconomic class are referred by the police, the courts, and social agencies. Upper-class and upper-middle-class neurotics attending outpatient clinics are more often assigned to senior staff members and receive intensive "depth" treatment, whereas lower-middle-class and lower-class neurotics are more often assigned to junior staff members and receive "directive" therapy and medication. Lower-class psychotic patients stay in hospitals longer than upper-class patients, but neurotic lower-class patients tend to discontinue outpatient or private office treatment much sooner than do patients from higher classes.

Apart from the cost factor, the early withdrawal from treatment of the lower-class neurotics appears to be due to their dissatisfaction with the traditional "talking out" forms of psychotherapy, which stress self-understanding and personality reconstruction. Most of them want the doctor to tell them what to do or give them something that will make them well. Many uneducated neurotic patients believe they are physically ill and expect pills and needles, along with the sympathy usually given the sick. Freud (1950, p. 401) foresaw the special therapeutic problems that might be posed by the poor and suggested a possible remedy:

We shall probably discover that the poor are even less ready to part with their neuroses than the rich because the hard life that awaits them when they recover has no attraction, and illness in them gives them more claim to the help of others. Possibly, we may often be able to achieve something if we combine aid to the mind with material support.

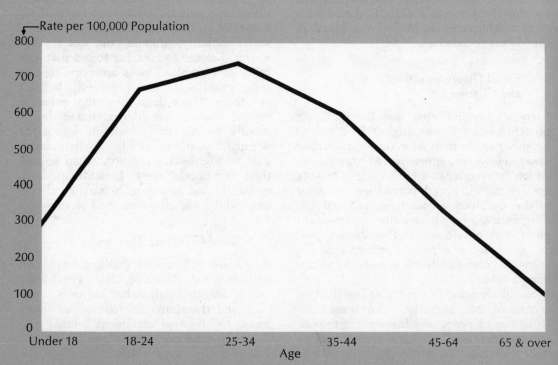

Figure 7.1. Admissions to Outpatient Psychiatric Services by Age (United States, 1969).

SOURCE: National Institute of Mental Health, Survey and Statistical Reports, Statistical Notes 26-50, September, 1971.

DEMOGRAPHIC DATA

Age

Since the development of a mental disorder is a gradual process, precise information on age of onset is difficult to obtain. Data are available with respect to the age of persons attending outpatient clinics during a particular year and the age of first admissions to state and county hospitals. The age distribution of admissions to outpatient clinics, expressed in terms of rate per 100,000 population, is shown in Figure 7.1. The admission statistics include children and adults, new cases and persons with prior histories of treatment. For this outpatient population, the admission rate rises sharply from ages eighteen to twenty-four, peaks between the ages of twenty-five and thirty-four, and then shows almost a straight-line decrease to age sixty-five and over.

The age pattern for first admission to mental hospitals is quite different (Figure 7.2). For 1969, the rate per 100,000 population increased sharply from age fifteen to twenty-four. Apart from a small rise from thirty-five to forty-five, the rate remained fairly stable through age sixty-five and over. The significance of social policy on this pattern is indicated by the contrast between the curves for 1962 and 1969. In 1962 the highest admission rate was for the age group sixty-five and over. As a result of the policy of discouraging the admission of elderly persons to mental hospitals there has been a drop in this rate from 164 to 101 per 100,000. The first admission rate for all other ages has increased.

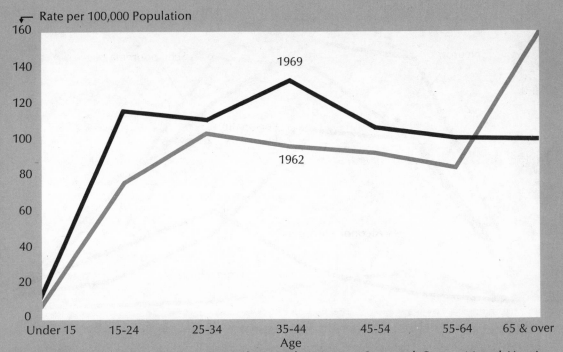

Figure 7.2. Changes Over Time in Rate of First Admissions to State and County Mental Hospitals by Age (United States, 1962 and 1969).

SOURCE: National Institute of Mental Health, Survey and Reports Section, Statistical Note 55, May, 1971.

One of the puzzling aspects of psycho-pathy is that each disorder mainly occurs during a particular age period. Data on this point for admissions to outpatient clinics are shown in Figure 7.3. Each disorder has its own peak age and the overall distribution patterns tend to be bell-shaped. The age specificity of specific disorders may be related to biological defects that "mature" or are expressed at different times. But the age correlation may also be accounted for on the basis of psychosocial factors, as, for example, the high rate of drug abuse among persons of college age.

Sex

Learning and behavior disorders in children occur at least three times more often in boys than in girls (Kessler, 1966). The greater incidence of reading and other learning problems in boys may be related to their slower rate of maturation (Bentzen, 1963). The greater aggressiveness of boys and their tendency to "act out" emotional difficulties may account for the sex differences noted in the incidence of behavior disorders during the preadolescent years. There are some indications that emotional problems of a neurotic nature are more prevalent among adolescent girls than adolescent boys.

At the adult level, field studies reviewed by the Dohrenwends (1965, 1967) report (1) no consistent sex differences in the prevalence of total psychological disorder, psychoses, or schizophrenia; (2) a tendency for affective disorders to occur more often in women than in men; (3) consistently higher rates of neurosis for women; and

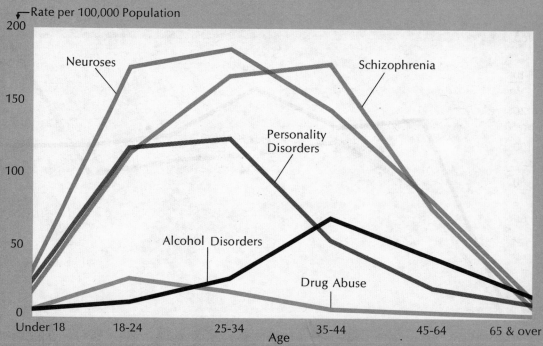

Figure 7.3. Admissions by Age and Diagnosis to Outpatient Psychiatric Services (United States, 1969).

Adapted from National Institute of Mental Health. Survey and Reports Section. Statistical Notes 65-50. September, 1971.

(4) consistently higher rates of character disorders for men. These findings suggest that males and females are equally vulnerable to psychological disorders and equally susceptible to gross schizophrenic disorganization. In the case of milder disorders, however, the two sexes tend to react differently to life problems. Females in our society more often react by becoming depressed, nervous, or emotional. Males more often turn to alcohol or engage in aggressive or some other form of socially unacceptable behavior.

Males and females also vary in their use of psychiatric facilities. The total number of men and women seen in treatment is about the same, but males more often are admitted to state and county mental hospitals, whereas a larger number of females are seen in private mental hospitals, community mental health centers, and inpatient services associated with general hospitals. The sex ratio with respect to specific disor-

ders also varies markedly in terms of the psychiatric facilities used. In general, the sex ratio in favor of males for alcohol disorders, drug abuse and organic brain syndromes is more marked for public mental hospitals than other psychiatric facilities. For depressive disorders and neuroses, more women than men are admitted to all types of facilities. For personality disorders, the sex ratio shifts markedly with type of facility (Table 7.4).

The different use of various types of facilities is partly due to the preferential treatment accorded women in the United States. Psychologically disturbed males are more often treated in public mental hospitals whereas disturbed women are more often treated in higher cost mental hospitals and in general hospitals. The differences noted in sex ratios are also partly due to sex differences in the relative incidence of specific disorders. Males and females tend to react differently to life problems.

Table 7.3. Sex Differences in Use of Treatment Facilities (Ratio of Male to Female Admissions by Diagnosis, by Type of Facility, United States, 1970).

Sex and Diagnosis	Total	Type of Facility				
		State and County Mental Hospital	Private Mental Hospital	Community Mental Hospital Center	General Hospital Inpatient Psychiatric Unit	Outpatient Psychiatric Service
		Sex Ratio (Males per 100 Females)				
Total (All Diagnoses)	96	149	69	88	69	99
Alcohol Disorders	381	568	254	286	306	272
Disorders Related to Drug Abuse	197	267	139	214	135	202
Organic Brain Syndromes (Excluding Drug and Alcohol Intoxication)	107	115	74	106	89	124
Schizophrenia	82	95	62	82	64	86
Depressive Disorders (Psychotic and Neurotic)	43	51	48	42	41	42
Other Neuroses	80	74	87	57	52	65
Personality Disorders	109	216	81	110	77	103
Transient Situational Disturbance	99	113	66	88	64	109

SOURCE: National Institute of Mental Health. "Differential Utilization of Psychiatric Facilities by Men and Women, United States 1970." Survey and Reports Section, Statistical Note 81, June 1973.

Under stress, women more often react by becoming depressed, anxious, and by showing other neurotic symptoms. Men more often turn to alcohol and drugs.

Marital Status

Among patients admitted to state mental hospitals, the incidence of mental disorders is lowest for married people and highest for the divorced and separated. The admission rates for the single and widowed fall about midway between those for the married and divorced (Landis and Page, 1938; Thomas and Locke, 1963). One possible explanation for these findings is that marriage contributes to the prevention of mental disorders. An alternative explanation is that marriage acts as a selective factor. Unstable individuals are less successful in finding marriage partners; if they do marry, they tend to be divorced fairly soon (Loeb, 1966).

Still another explanation is that marital status is unrelated to the real incidence rate; the lower hospital admission rate for married individuals may be simply due to the fact that if a disturbed person is married, he has a far greater chance of being cared for at home than does a person with no one to care for him. This advantage, to a lesser degree, would be shared by widowed and single individuals living with their families.

SUMMARY

Sociocultural theories are concerned with a variety of related but independent issues. One theory that has virtually gained the status of law holds that society acts as the arbiter in deciding what types of norm violations indicate behavior disorders. Scheff (1966) suggests that the main criterion is residual deviance. The label of "neurotic" or "psychotic" is applied to persons exhibiting disturbing, socially unacceptable behavior that does not fit other culturally recognized categories of deviance. Thus a person is not usually considered mentally disordered if his deviant behavior can be described as drunkenness, sex perversion, criminality, stupidity, prejudice, or bad manners.

Labeling a person as neurotic or psychotic has two major consequences. First, he is expected to conform to local stereotypes of mental illness. If he does so, thus permitting his symptoms to become fixed, he is granted the privileges and benefits associated with the "sick" role. If he fails to do so, society washes its hands of any responsibility for his care. He is dismissed as a troublesome person. Second, he is isolated and treated as a social outcast. Long after he has recovered, he is still regarded by associates with apprehension and distrust.

Research on the hypothesis that sociocultural factors directly cause mental disorders has been essentially negative. The best guess is that the total incidence of psychopathology is about the same in all cultures. Culture mainly influences the content of symptoms, the attitude of the group toward mental deviants, and treatment procedures. This does not preclude the possibility that certain clinical forms of psychopathology are more prevalent in some cultures than in others. Field studies of socioeconomic factors suggest that the total prevalence of psychopathology may be higher at the lowest social stratum than among other classes. This finding appears to be due mainly to the disproportionate number of alcoholics, antisocial personalities, and other types of mild deviance found at the lowest socioeconomic level. The source of referral and type of treatment given a mental patient is related to his socioeconomic status.

Demographic data indicate that the total prevalence of psychopathology is about the same for males and females. Females tend to have higher prevalence rates for neurosis and affective psychosis, whereas men have higher rates for character disorders. These findings suggest sex differences in ways of reacting to problems. Under stress women more often become nervous, depressed, and emotionally upset, while men more often resort to alcohol, become aggressive, and engage in other forms of acting-out behavior. The incidence of admissions to mental hospitals is lowest for the married population and highest for divorced and separated persons.

References

Benedict, R. *Patterns of Culture.* Boston: Houghton Mifflin, 1934.

Bentzen, F. "Sex Ratios in Learning and Behavior Disorders." *American Journal of Orthopsychiatry* 33 (1963): 92-98.

Berne, E. "A Psychiatric Census of the South Pacific." *American Journal of Psychiatry* 117 (1960): 44-47.

Dohrenwend, B. P., and Dohrenwend, B. S. "The Problem of Validity in Field Studies of Psychological Disorder." *Journal of Abnormal Psychology* 70 (1965): 52-69.

————. "Field Studies of Social Factors in Relation to Three Types of Psychological Disorders." *Journal of Abnormal Psychology* 72 (1967): 369–78.

Draguns, J. G. and Phillips, L. *Culture and Psychopathology: The Quest for a Relationship.* Morristown, N.J.: General Learning Press, 1972.

DuBois, C. *The People of Alor.* Minneapolis: University of Minnesota Press, 1944.

Dunham, H. W. "Epidemiology of Psychiatric Disorders as a Contribution to Medical Ecology." *Archives of General Psychiatry* 14 (1966): 1-19.

Eaton, J. W., and Weil, R. J. *Culture and Mental Disorders: A Comparative Study of the Hutterites and Other Populations.* Glencoe, Ill.: Free Press, 1955.

Elsarrag, M. E. "Psychiatry in the Northern Sudan: A Study in Comparative Psychiatry." *British Journal of Psychiatry* 114 (1968): 945-48.

Field, M. J. *The Search for Security.* Evanston, Ill.: Northwestern University Press, 1960.

Frank J. D. *Persuasion and Healing.* Baltimore: Johns Hopkins Press, 1961.

Freud, S. *Collected Papers,* vol. 2 pp. 401-2. London: Hogarth Press, 1950.

Goldhamer, H., and Marshall, ·A. *Psychoses and Civilization.* Glencoe, Ill.: Free Press 1949.

Hollingshead, A. B., and Redlich, F. C. *Social Class and Mental Illness.* New York: Wiley, 1958.

Janet, P. *La force et la faiblesse psychologiques.* Paris: Moloine, 1932. Quoted in K. Menninger et al., *The Vital Balance,* p. 29. New York: Viking Press, 1963.

Kessler, J. W. *Psychopathology of Childhood.* Englewood Cliffs, N.J.: Prentice-Hall, 1966.

Kiev, A., ed. *Magic, Faith, and Healing.* New York: Free Press, Macmillan, 1964.

Kleiner, R. J., and Parker, S. *Mental Health in an Urban Negro Community.* New York: Free Press, Macmillan, 1966.

Landis, C., and Page, J. D. *Modern Society and Mental Disease.* New York: Rinehart, 1938.

Leighton, A. H., and Hughes, J. M. "Culture as a Causative of Mental Disorder." *Milbank Memorial Fund Quarterly* 39, no. 3 (1961): 446-88.

Lin, T. "A Study of the Incidence of Mental Disorder in Chinese and Other Cultures." *Psychiatry* 16 (1953): 313.

Linton, R. *Culture and Mental Disorders.* Springfield, Ill.: Charles C Thomas, 1956.

Loeb, J. "The Personality Factor in Divorce." *Journal of Consulting Psychology* 30 (1966): 562.

Maretzki, T., and Nelson, L. D. "Psychopathology among Hawaii's Japanese: A Comparative Study." In *Mental Health Research in Asia and the Pacific,* ed. W. Caudill and T. Lin, pp. 164-77, Honolulu: East-West Center, 1969.

McDermott, J. F., Jr., et al. "Social Class and Mental Illness in Children: The Question of Childhood Psychosis." *American Journal of Orthopsychiatry* 37 (1967): 548-57.

Mead, M. *Sex and Temperament in Primitive Cultures.* New York: Morrow, 1935.

Murphy, H. B. M. "Social Change and Mental Health." *Milbank Memorial Fund Quarterly* 3 (1961): 385-445.

Page, J., and Landis, C. "Trends in Mental Disease," *Journal of Abnormal and Social Psychology* 38 (1943): 518-24.

Reid, D. D. "Precipitating Proximal Factors in the Occurrence of Mental Disorder: Epidemiological Evidence." *Milbank Memorial Fund Quarterly* 2 (1961): 229-45.

Reissman, F.; Cohen, J.; and Pearl, A., eds. *Mental Health of the Poor.* New York: Free Press, Macmillan, 1964.

Riesman, D. *The Lonely Crowd: A Study of Changing American Character.* New Haven: Yale University Press, 1950.

Scheff, T. J. "A Sociological Theory of Mental

Disorders." In *Approaches to Psychopathology*, ed. J. D. Page, pp. 250-68. New York: Columbia University Press, 1966.

Schooler, C. and Caudill, W. "Symptomatology in Japanese and American Schizophrenics," *Ethnology* 3 (1964): 172-77.

Thomas, D. S., and Locke, B. Z. "Marital Status, Education, and Occupational Differentials in Mental Illness." *Milbank Memorial Fund Quarterly* 41, no. 2 (1963): 145-60.

Toker, E. "Mental Illness in the White and Bantu Population of the Republic of South Africa." *American Journal of Psychiatry* 123 (1966): 55-65.

Tooth, G. *Studies of Mental Illness in the Gold Coast.* London: H. M. Stationery Office, 1950.

Wallace, A. F. C. "Anthropology and Psychiatry." In *Comprehensive Textbook of Psychiatry*, ed. A. M. Freedman, H. I. Kaplan, and H. S. Kaplan, pp. 195–201. Baltimore: Williams & Wilkins, 1967.

Winston, E. "The Alleged Lack of Mental Disease Among Primitive Groups." *American Anthropologist* 36 (1934): 234-38.

Wittkower, E. D., and Fried, J. "Cross-cultural Approach to Mental Health Problems." *American Journal of Psychiatry* 116 (1959): 423-28.

8 · Schizophrenic Reactions

Des Malades Mentales,
Jean Etienne Esquirol

If the concept of schizophrenia did not exist, it would be necessary to invent an equivalent diagnosis to provide a broad-range label for the most severe and most perplexing forms of disorganized human behavior. Periodic attempts have been made to delineate schizophrenic reactions on the basis of gross disturbances of association, impaired thinking, delusions and hallucinations, and profound breakdown in interpersonal relations. In practice, however, schizophrenia has been and remains a catch-all diagnosis for diverse psychotic reactions exclusive of the more clearly defined manic-depressive states.

Table 8.1 includes a partial listing of the bewildering array of dysfunctions presumed to be symptomatic of schizophrenia. The concurrent presence of several of these symptoms is usually required to establish a diagnosis of schizophrenia. Another critical but necessarily delayed diagnostic sign is limited improvement or response to treatment. Sooner or later the label of schizophrenia is assigned to most chronic mental patients who are free of obvious brain pathology.

In the United States the concept of schizophrenia is broadly interpreted to include several borderline categories, involving a combination of schizophrenic features and symptoms associated with some other disorder. For example, *a schizo-affective reaction*, which is one of the clinical types recognized in the 1968 APA classification, is a combination of schizophrenic symptoms and pronounced depression or elation. American psychologists also use diagnoses such as *ambulatory schizophrenia* and *pseudoneurotic schizophrenia*, which are not included in the APA classification system. Patients so designated usually present a mixture of neurotic and schizophrenic symptoms. This broad interpretation affords a more optimistic outlook with respect to prognosis. In addition, it tends to accentuate the importance of psychosocial factors in the etiology of schizophrenia.

Many European psychiatrists favor a more restricted concept, placing greater emphasis on the significance of organic pathology and genetic defects. This narrower concept acknowledges the variability of outcome. Some patients go on to become chronic deteriorated cases; the symptoms of others are arrested at a mild stage or show good clinical improvement following a severe psychotic episode. However, it is thought that complete recovery, with full restitution of functions, is rare, and that the disorder almost invariably has residual effects. A good clinical description of this more restricted concept is provided by Slater (1968, p. 15):

Schizophrenia is an illness affecting the mind and the personality of the patient in a way which is seldom completely resolved; after an attack of illness there is nearly always some degree of permanent change of personality, and if there are several attacks this change will become more and more marked. This change is one that de-individualizes and dehumanizes the patient, and leaves him, above all, with impaired capacities for normal affective responses. While an attack of illness is proceeding there will be one or more of a series of distinctive symptoms: hallucination in a clear state of consciousness, passivity feelings, primary delusional experiences, and rather typical forms of thought disorder. After recovery, often only partial, some of these symptoms may persist; but principal disabilities will be in the form of various psychological defects.

Aberrant reactions that correspond closely to modern descriptions of schizophrenia were recorded in ancient civilizations and have been observed in all known primitive societies. Epidemiological data indicate that the rate of occurrence of

Table 8.1. Clinical Signs Associated with Schizophrenic Behavior.

Clinical signs	Characteristics
Anhedonia	Impaired ability to experience or integrate feelings of pleasure
Ambivalence	Concurrent love-hate feelings for the same person or object
Attention interference	Impaired capacity for maintaining a mental set of readiness; difficulty in focusing attention on a specific topic; inability to exclude irrelevant material
Autism	Thinking and behavior dominated by wishes, fears, and fantasies; marked subjectivity of interpretations
Chaotic sexuality	Confusion as to gender; strange sexual fantasies
Cognitive slippage	Disorganized, overinclusive, or underinclusive association of ideas
Disturbances in affect	Inappropriate moods; apathy; intense anxiety; blunting of affect
Disturbances in volition	Blocking, inhibition, negativism, indecision
Hypersensitivity	Oversensitivity and overresponsiveness to others; easily hurt feelings
Interpersonal difficulties	Lack of skills or capacity for relating to others, emotional distance; distrust of others
Lack of insight	Inability to realize or denial that one's behavior is abnormal
Loss of ego boundaries	Identity confusion; blurring of boundaries between self and external world; belief that others can invade and control one's inner life
Loss of voluntary control	Spontaneous and unpredictable appearance and expression of thoughts, sensations, impulses, and reactions, independently of voluntary decision and choice
Motor disturbances	Motionlessness; rigidity; waxy flexibility; echopraxia; stereotyped movements; grimaces; stupor
Perceptual disturbances	Hallucinations; illusions; errors in estimating size, time intervals, etc.
Progressive deterioration	Increase in intensity and frequency of symptoms; a critical sign, but cannot be considered significant until one or more years after onset of symptoms
Reality-testing impairment	Difficulty in distinguishing fantasies from real life experiences; misperception and misinterpretation of external events; ideas of reference
Social withdrawal	Isolation and insulation from social environment; turtle-like retreat into one's shell; preoccupation with self
Speech disturbances	Incoherent, rambling speech; muteness; stilted speech; "word salad": neologisms, echolalia, private language
Thinking disturbances	Bizarre delusions; irrational thought; shift from abstract to concrete thinking

schizophrenia has been relatively stable for the past hundred years. The expectancy rate is about the same in all countries. With minor allowances made for variations in the strictness of the criteria used, the findings for the United States, several European countries, and Japan agree that about 1 percent of the general population may be expected to develop the disorder during their lifetimes (Slater, 1968). The number of new cases that develop each year, whether hospitalized or not, runs about 150 per 100,000 general population.

The onset of schizophrenic behavior usually occurs during late adolescence and early adulthood. In a substantial number of cases the disorder persists for many years. The resulting accumulation of patients in hospitals and in the community pushes up the prevalence rate. At any point in time, the combined rate for chronic and recent cases is at least 300 per 100,000 population (Mishler and Scotch, 1963; Crocetti and Lemkau, 1967). In the United States about 20 percent of first admissions to public mental hospitals and 50 percent of the resident populations of these hospitals are classified as schizophrenic. Close to 75 percent of all annual first admissions diagnosed as schizophrenic are from fifteen to forty years old, with the peak incidence rate between twenty-five and thirty-five. Since several years may intervene between the occurrence of the disorder and the initial hospitalization, the actual age of onset is somewhat earlier than these figures indicate.

No significant sex differences have been noted in the incidence or prevalence of schizophrenia. For hospitalized patients the median age at time of initial admission is slightly lower for males than for females; however, this is probably due to a greater delay in hospitalizing female patients than to real sex differences in the age of onset of symptoms. In our culture, many of the early signs of schizophrenia (social withdrawal, passivity, and preoccupation with fantasies) are more tolerated in adolescent girls than in boys, and in any case parents are inclined to postpone for a longer period the hospitalization of psychologically disturbed daughters than sons.

ORIGINS OF THE CONCEPT OF SCHIZOPHRENIA

The symptom patterns of schizophrenia have been described for thousands of years. Up to the end of the eighteenth century, however, all psychoses were either grouped together under the general heading of madness or separated into two categories, melancholia and mania. Depressed patients were considered to be suffering from melancholia and all others were classified as maniacs. In 1801 Pinel added the category of *dementia*, which he identified as a disorder in thinking. His description of dementia corresponds very closely with contemporary descriptions of schizophrenia. Among its symptoms he noted impaired thinking, defective judgment, insulated ideas that followed one another without connection, broken sentences, diminished sensibility to external impressions, disparity between emotions and ideas, withdrawal, and inattentiveness.

In 1849 John Conolly described a condition mainly present in young persons, in which "the intellect, the affections, the passions, all seem inactive and deadened, and the patients become utterly apathetic" (Noyes and Kolb, 1963, p. 326). The term *dementia praecox* (literally, premature dementia) was first used by Morel in 1860. He applied this diagnosis to a fourteen-year-old boy who had formerly been bright and cheerful, and for no apparent reason became withdrawn, sullen, morose, forgetful, and extremely hostile toward his father. In 1871 Hecker used the term *hebephrenia* to designate a mental disease of puberty and adolescence that quickly terminates in mental deterioration. In 1874 Kahlbaum contributed the term *catatonia* to describe a condition in which the patient is mute, motionless, stares fixedly into space, shows no reaction to sensory impressions, and sometimes exhibits a waxy flexibility of the body. At about the same time, several other investigators independently described a *paranoid* form of mental illness, marked by delusions of persecution.

In 1896 Kraepelin brought together under the general heading of *dementia praecox* the disorders of catatonia, hebephrenia (a disorder marked by silliness, delusions, and hallucinations) and some of the paranoid psychoses. He maintained that these three reactions represented different manifestations of the same disease. Later on he added a fourth subtype, *simple schizophrenia,* which had been originally described by Diem in 1903. Kraepelin maintained that these four seemingly unrelated disorders were all caused by some as yet unspecified metabolic disease of early adolescence that led to progressive mental deterioration.

In 1911 Eugen Bleuler suggested that the term *schizophrenia* be substituted for dementia praecox. Bleuler considered the latter term misleading, since the condition was not limited to young persons and did not always lead to progressive deterioration. His observations, as well as Kraepelin's data, indicated that many patients showed marked clinical improvement. His choice of a new label was intended to call attention to what he regarded as the key feature of the group of schizophrenias: a "splitting" of the psychic functions. What he meant by this was not the polarization of two different personalities, as occurs in neurosis, but a disunity of personality functioning: fragmentation of ideas, incongruence between ideas and emotions, rapid shift and change of ideas, mental blocking, and other signs of intrapsychic disharmony and contradictory tendencies.

Bleuler shared Pinel's view that schizophrenia essentially represented a disturbance in thinking. He distinguished between primary and secondary symptoms. Primary symptoms included a loosening of associations, autistic thinking, disturbances of affect, and ambivalence, and were related to a possible underlying morbid somatic process. Secondary symptoms, which in-

Eugen Bleuler (1857-1939), Swiss psychiatrist, who introduced and described the concept of schizophrenia.

cluded hallucinations and delusions, were considered to represent psychological attemps at adaptation to the primary disturbance. In later revisions of his basic textbook, Bleuler distinguished between "process" and "reactive" forms of schizophrenia. By "process schizophrenia" he meant an endogenous progressive disease. The term "reactive" implied that the schizophrenia was reversible and induced by situational factors. This distinction has been refined and extensively studied by subsequent investigators.

Another important early contributor to the concept of schizophrenia was Adolf Meyer. As early as 1906 he criticized the concept of dementia praecox as a disease entity. He believed that the clinical picture of schizophrenia was more logically seen as a set of maladaptive reactions to the

EMIL KRAEPELIN: A CASE OF DEMENTIA PRAECOX (1894)*

You have before you to-day a strongly-built and well-nourished man, aged twenty-one, who entered the hospital a few weeks ago. He sits quietly looking in front of him, and does not raise his eyes when he is spoken to, but evidently understands all our questions very well, for he answers quite relevantly, though slowly and often only after repeated questioning. From his brief remarks, made in a low tone, we gather that he thinks he is ill, without getting any more precise information about the nature of the illness and its symptoms. The patient attributes his malady to the onanism he has practised since he was ten years old. He thinks that he has thus incurred the guilt of a sin against the sixth commandment, has very much reduced his power of working, has made himself feel languid and miserable and has become a hypochondriac. Thus, as the result of reading certain books, he imagined that he had a rupture and suffered from wasting of the spinal cord, neither of which was the case. He would not associate with his comrades any longer, because he thought they saw the result of his vice and made fun of him. The patient makes all these statements in an indifferent tone, without looking up or troubling about his surroundings. His expression betrays no emotion; he only laughs for a moment now and then. There is occasional wrinkling of the forehead or facial spasm. Round the mouth and nose a fine, changing twitching is constantly observed.

The patient gives us a correct account of his past experiences. His knowledge speaks for the high degree of his education; indeed, he was ready to enter the University a year ago. He also knows where he is and how long he has been here, but he is only very imperfectly acquainted with the names of the people round him, and says that he has never asked about them. He can only give a very meagre account of the general events of the last year. In answer to our questions, he declares that he is ready to remain in the hospital for the present. He would certainly prefer it if he could enter a profession, but he cannot say what he would like to take up. No physical disturbances can be definitely made out, except exaggerated knee-jerks.

At first sight, perhaps the patient reminds you of the states of depression which we have learned to recognise in former lectures. But on closer examination you will easily understand that, in spite of certain isolated points of resemblance, we have to deal with a disease having features of quite another kind. The patient makes his statements slowly and in monosyllables, not because his wish to answer meets with overpowering hindrances, but because he feels no desire to speak at all. He certainly hears and understands what is said to him very well, but he does not take the trouble to attend to it. He pays no heed, and answers whatever occurs to him without thinking. No visible effort of the will is to be noticed. All his movements are languid and expressionless, but are made without hindrance or trouble. There is no sign of emotional dejection, such as one would expect from the nature of his talk, and the patient remains quite dull throughout, experiencing neither fear nor hope nor desires. He is not at all deeply affected by what goes on before him, although he understands it without actual difficulty. It is all the same to him who appears or disappears, where he is, or who talks to him and takes care of him, and he does not even once ask their names.

This peculiar and fundamental want of any *strong feeling of the impressions of life,* with unimpaired ability to understand and to remember, is really the diagnostic symptom of the disease we have before us. It becomes still plainer if we observe the patient for a time, and see that, in spite

* Case originally published in Kraepelin, E. *Lectures in Clinical Psychiatry* (1894), trans. T. Johnstone. London: Baillière, Tindale & Cox, 1904. Reprinted in *Documentary History of Psychiatry*, ed. C. E. Goshen, pp. 201–205. New York: Philosophical Library, 1967.

of his good education, he lies in bed for weeks and months, or sits about without feeling the slightest need of occupation. He broods, staring in front of him with expressionless features, over which a vacant smile occasionally plays, or at the best turns over the leaves of a book for a moment, apparently speechless, and not troubling about anything. Even when he has visitors, he sits without showing any interest, does not ask about what is happening at home, hardly even greets his parents, and goes back indifferently to the ward. He can hardly be induced to write a letter, and says that he has nothing to write about. But he occasionally composes a letter to the doctor, expressing all kinds of distorted, half-formed ideas, with a peculiar and silly play on words, in very fair style, but with little connection. He begs for "a little more *allegro* in the treatment," and "liberationary movement with a view to the widening of the horizon," will "*ergo* extort some wit in lectures," and "*nota bene* for God's sake only does not wish to be combined with the club of the harmless." "Professional work is the balm of life."

These scraps of writing, as well as his statements that he is pondering over the world, of putting himself together a moral philosophy, leave no doubt that, besides the emotional barrenness, there is also a high degree of *weakness of judgment* and *flightiness,* although the pure memory has suffered little, if at all. We have a *mental and emotional infirmity* to deal with, which reminds us only outwardly of the states of depression previously described. This infirmity is the incurable outcome of a very common history of disease, to which we will provisionally give the name of *Dementia Praecox.*

The development of the illness has been quite gradual. Our patient, whose parents suffered transitorily from "dejection," did not go to school till he was seven years old, as he was a delicate child and spoke badly, but when he did he learned quite well. He was considered to be a reserved and stubborn child. Having practised onanism at a very early age, he became more and more solitary in the last few years, and thought that he was laughed at by his brothers and sisters, and shut out from society because of his ugliness. For this reason he could not bear a looking-glass in his room. After passing the written examination on leaving school, a year ago, he gave up the *vivâ voce,* because he could not work any longer. He cried a great deal, masturbated much, ran about aimlessly, played in a senseless way on the piano, and began to write observations " 'On the Nerve-play of Life,' which he cannot get on with." He was incapable of any kind of work, even physical, felt "done for," asked for a revolver, ate Swedish matches to destroy himself, and lost all affection for his family. From time to time he became excited and troublesome, and shouted out of the window at night. In the hospital, too, a state of excitement lasting for several days was observed, in which he chattered in a confused way, made faces, ran about at full speed, wrote disconnected scraps of composition, and crossed and recrossed them with flourishes and unmeaning combinations of letters. After this a state of tranquillity ensued, in which he could give absolutely no account of his extraordinary behavior.

Besides the mental and emotional imbecility, we meet with other very significant features in the case before us. The first of these is the silly, vacant *laugh,* which is constantly observed in dementia praecox. There is joyless humor corresponding to this laugh; indeed, some patients complain that they cannot help laughing, without feeling at all inclined to laugh. Other important symptoms are *making faces* or grimacing, and the fine muscular twitching in the face which is also very characteristic of dementia praecox. Then we must notice the tendency to peculiar, distorted turns of speech—*senseless playing with syllables and words* —as it often assumes very extraordinary forms in this disease. Lastly, I may call your attention to the fact that, when you offer him your hand, the patient does not grasp it, but only *stretches his own hand out stiffly to meet it.* Here we have the first sign of a disturbance which is often developed in dementia praecox in the most astounding way.

patient's life experiences and he advocated the study of the patient's total life history as a means of learning the origin and accumulation of faulty reaction habits. Following the lead of Sullivan (1953), many contemporary psychologists and psychiatrists agree that much schizophrenic behavior consists of ineffective and socially unacceptable patterns of interpersonal reaction.

TRADITIONAL CLINICAL TYPES OF SCHIZOPHRENIA

Simple Schizophrenic Reaction

The typical development of simple schizophrenic reaction consists of an insidious pattern of gradual social withdrawal, reduction of interest in external events, and indifference to the usual social amenities. The fundamental wish of people exhibiting this reaction is apparently to be left alone to do nothing. Personal hygiene is neglected; patients rarely bathe, and they are untidy in appearance and dress. Motor responses are slow, and speech is more or less restricted to grunts and monosyllables. The disorder is usually stationary and chronic. Delusions and hallucinations do not occur. If left alone and permitted to do as they please, these patients cause relatively little trouble; but if thwarted or pushed into action, they may be irritable and nasty.

Hebephrenic Schizophrenic Reaction

Hebephrenic reactions represent one of the more extreme chronic forms of personality disorganization. Characteristic symptoms include impaired thinking, disconnected speech, shallow and inappropriate affect, inappropriate giggling, facial grimaces, and stereotyped mannerisms. Delusions and hallucinations, if present, are bizarre and disorganized. When hebephrenic patients are not under medication, they contentedly spend hours talking and smiling to themselves or conversing with imaginary persons.

Catatonic Schizophrenic Reaction

Catatonic reaction is marked by either stupor or extreme excitement. The onset of acute symptoms may be abrupt, but there is usually a long history of poor social adaptation. In the stuporous or withdrawn state, the patient is uncommunicative and unresponsive. Some assume peculiar postures and maintain them for long periods. They may sit or stand rigidly without seeming to move a muscle for hours at a time. In an extreme case the withdrawn catatonic may be mute, inaccessible, and literally helpless. Some patients show extreme rigidity of the body and others manifest a waxy flexibility of the limbs. Catatonic excitement is characterized by diffuse excitement and hyperactivity, but the patient usually remains rooted in one spot. Speech, if present, is incoherent, and repetitive. There appears to be a serious disturbance in volition. Some patients are extremely passive and robot-like in their responses to commands, while others are extremely negativistic and contrary. Particularly if a patient is bedridden and rigid, he may seem dead to the world, but later he may give a good account of everything that went on around him. Impulsive suicide attempts are occasionally noted, but as a rule the intent is not so much to die as to be reborn.

Paranoid Schizophrenic Reaction

Paranoid reactions are marked by poorly organized delusions of persecution or grandeur, hallucinations, and ideas of reference (the assumption that the words and actions of other people refer to oneself). Patients tend to be suspicious, aloof, sensitive, and egocentric. The prevailing theme is that people are hostile and are maltreat-

SCHIZOPHRENIA: CASE REPORTS

Simple Schizophrenic Reaction

A young man, until committed to a mental hospital at the age of twenty-one, had impressed his neighbors and teachers as being a quiet, well-behaved, calm youngster. In fact, he was considered a model child. A careful scrutiny, however, revealed a long history of maladjustment. All his life the patient had chewed his bedsheets in his sleep. He wet the bed until the age of fourteen. As a child he rarely played with other children, and he never had any close friends. During his high school years he would periodically lock himself in his room for several hours at a time and refuse to come out even for meals. During adolescence he avoided girls. He was a good student until about the tenth grade, but after that his work began to decline. His high school teachers complained that he spent too much time daydreaming. He attended college for one semester but went to classes infrequently and rarely handed in assignments. After dropping out of college, he bummed around the country for a few months and then returned home. At the insistence of his mother, he sought employment, but was fired from three jobs in the space of a month.

He then stopped looking for work and stayed in his room. Most of his time was spent lying in bed or staring vacantly out of a window. He rarely spoke to members of the family. He ate by himself and refused to shave or take baths. Whenever his mother tried to get him to change his clothes or take a walk—anything at all except lie in bed staring out of the window—he would call her obscene names until she left him alone. On one occasion he became so enraged that he struck her to "shut her up." This led to his being committed to a mental hospital.

Hebephrenic Schizophrenic Reaction

An unmarried woman of thirty who had always been considered somewhat odd gradually became clumsy in her housework and erratic in her behavior. As time went on she started to listen to imaginary voices. Periodically she would laugh and giggle to herself for no apparent reason. She would frequently go about the house half undressed. On one occasion she attempted to seduce a much younger brother. She was hospitalized shortly after she took to walking naked in the garden at night under the impression that the man in the moon was her secret lover. When interviewed on admission to the hospital she stated that through her sexual union with the moon, heaven and earth had been united.

Catatonic Schizophrenic Reaction

A young woman, recently married, was rushed to the hospital by her husband after she had made a pseudo attempt at suicide by inflicting superficial cuts on the *outside* of her wrists. She was somewhat excited when admitted to the hospital, so she was given a sedative and put to bed. During the night she became very disturbed, threw objects around, and banged her head savagely against the wall. She was then transferred to a mental hospital, where she soon lapsed into a catatonic stupor. In going through her bureau, the husband came across a note written by his wife entitled "The Perfect Suicide." The plan outlined was a disappearance act rather than a suicide. The would-be suicide was supposed to leave her home in the middle of the night and travel by train to a distant town. She was to take nothing with her. After arriving at a large city, she was to buy a complete new wardrobe. Her traveling clothes were to be destroyed, since they might be identified and traced. The next step was to dye her hair, change her features through plastic surgery, and develop a new personality.

Paranoid Schizophrenic Reaction

A veteran attending college wrote several lengthy, rambling, and incoherent letters to the college president, of which the general idea seemed to be that the student was the human depository for the A-bomb formula.

He blamed enemy agents for his frequent absences from classes. He stated that several of his alleged classmates were actually enemy agents who had been assigned to get him drunk so that they could obtain the A-bomb secret from him. His psychology professor was accused of reading his mind and forcing him to do things against his will. Here and there the letters contained veiled threats. The school authorities got in touch with the student's father, who took his son home. After a few days the family decided that they were unable to take care of him at home and arranged for his admission to a veteran's hospital.

ing or plotting against them. The delusions of persecution may be reinforced by hallucinations, which are usually auditory; patients hear their enemies call them bad names, talk about them, and threaten them. Other common hallucinations include staring faces, unusual body sensations that are attributed to the actions of enemies, and peculiar odors. Their grandiose ideas are extravagant, but they are in much better contact with their environment and are more responsive to it then nonparanoid schizophrenics (Silverman, 1964). Their sensory input is augmented by extensive scanning behavior. In contrast, nonparanoid schizophrenics tend to be indifferent to novel stimuli and inattentive to the environment. They show limited scanning and have a more restricted sensory input.

Other Schizophrenic Reactions

The APA classification includes a condition referred to as *acute schizophrenic episode*. This reaction is often associated with confusion, perplexity, ideas of reference, emotional turmoil, dreamlike dissociation, and generalized excitement. Many patients recover within a few weeks. Sometimes the disorganization is progressive and takes on the characteristics of catatonic, hebephrenic, or paranoid schizophrenia.

A more internationally accepted category is *schizo-affective reaction*. This diagnosis is applied to patients showing a mixture of schizophrenic symptoms and pronounced elation or depression. In Scandinavian countries, the distinguishing label of *schiz-ophreniform psychosis* is often used to describe schizophrenic reactions characterized by acute onset, clear-cut precipitating factors, and a relatively good prognosis.

Psychoses occurring in children are sometimes referred to as *childhood schizophrenia*. There is considerable doubt, however, whether these reactions should be considered schizophrenic at all. The symptoms associated with psychosis in infants and young children differ from those seen in adults. Furthermore, genetic studies indicate that it is rare for so-called childhood schizophrenic reactions to occur in the children of schizophrenic parents. Severe personality and behavior disturbances occurring during childhood are more appropriately referred to as infantile autism when they occur in infants and child psychosis in older children.

THE PROCESS-REACTIVE CONTINUUM

The traditional subdivision of the schizophrenias into simple, hebephrenic, catatonic, and paranoid types rests on observed differences in clinical symptoms. An alternate approach is to divide schizophrenics into two main subgroups on the basis of poor or good prognosis. This approach is best represented by the widely accepted concepts of *process* and *reactive* schizophrenia. Other dichotomous terms that at one time or another have been suggested to differentiate patients with poor chances for recovery from those with good chances include nuclear and peripheral schizophrenia, chronic and episodic or acute schizophrenia, true schizophrenia and schizophreniform psychosis, and dementia praecox and schizophrenia. These pairs of terms are similar to but not necessarily synonymous with the process-reactive concept.

Although specifically concerned with poor versus good outcome, the process-reactive dichotomy also implies a differential course of development. By definition, the term "process" refers to a gradual step-by-step development. The typical process patient has a long premorbid history of maladjustment going back to early childhood. The appearance of frank psychotic symptoms during adolescence is only a continuation of preexisting behavior patterns. In reactive schizophrenia, on the other hand, the early personality development is, on the surface at least, reasonably normal. The onset of symptoms is sudden and often precipitated by some traumatic experience or conflict. Kantor and Herron (1966) have suggested that process schizophrenia is associated with a failure to develop a structured self-image during early childhood. The self-image remains unformed or is very primitive. In reactive schizophrenia an adequate self-image is formed, but some specific stress precipitates a breakdown in later years.

The greater severity, longer premorbid history of maladjustment, and poorer outcome of process schizophrenia suggest the possibility that genetic factors are relatively more important in its etiology than in that of reactive schizophrenia. Some support for this inference is provided by schizophrenic twin studies, but the evidence is far from conclusive (Kringlen, 1968; Gottesman, 1968). The available data suggest that different genes are involved in the etiology of process and reactive schizophrenia but the genetic loadings are of about the same magnitude.

Process-Reactive Scales

A number of rating scales and self-report questionnaires for measuring the process-reactive dimension have been developed. Four of the better known instruments are the Elgin or Wittman, Kantor et al., Phillips, and Ullmann-Giovannoni Scales. The scales have good interrater reliability. Despite differences in the kinds of behavior sampled, scores on the four tests show high intercorrelations. In addition, it has been found that all four measures are correlated with marital status. For patients over twenty-five, marital status alone is about as good a predictor of favorable outcome as any of the scales (Ullmann, 1967; Meichenbaum, 1969). A cogent explanation for the agreement of the various scales is that they all measure what may be referred to as general social competence (Zigler and Phillips, 1962). Experimental studies indicate that the performance level of process schizophrenics on varied tasks is inferior to that of reactive schizophrenics. This finding is hardly surprising, since the relative adequacy of behavior constitutes the main criterion for initially differentiating the two groups.

The extensive literature on the process-reactive continuum and the related issue of good versus poor prognosis in schizophrenia (Garmezy, 1965; Offord and Cross, 1969) points to the conclusion that process and reactive types do not constitute two discrete groups. All tests and measures indicate that schizophrenic reaction is a continuous dimension. The "typical" process schizophrenic is at one end of the continuum and the "typical" reactive schizophrenic is at the opposite end of the same continuum. Most schizophrenics are located somewhere between these two extremes. The main advantage of the process-reactive concept is that it enables investigators, by selecting patients at either end of the continuum, to obtain comparatively homogeneous groupings. This advantage is an important consideration in research studies.

MEASURES OF PROCESS AND REACTIVE SCHIZOPHRENIA

The four measures most commonly used to assess process and reactive schizophrenia are the Elgin or Wittman Prognostic Scale, the Kantor-Wallner-Winder List of Criteria, the Phillips Scale, and the Ullmann-Giovannoni Self-Report Scale. All four scales yield continuous distributions of scores. Most schizophrenic patients cluster in the middle range; extreme scores on one end are considered indicative of process schizophrenia and on the other end are considered indicative of reactive schizophrenia.

The Elgin Prognostic Scale

The Elgin Scale was devised by Wittman in 1941, and subsequently revised by Becker and Steffy (Becker, 1956; Steffy and Becker, 1961.) Items on the Elgin Scale consist mainly of factors thought to have prognostic significance. Information for scoring is obtained from case-history data. The Becker revision provides for scaled ratings on (1) defect of interests versus definite display of interests, (2) insidious versus acute onset, (3) degree of difficulty in social adjustment during childhood, (4) extent of heterosexual contact, (5) careless indifference versus worry and self-consciousness, (6) duration of psychosis, (7) extent of hebephrenic symptoms, and (8) presence or absence of precipitating conditions. The major difficulty with this scale is that the wording of the descriptive labels is imprecise. Not much of the information needed for scoring the numerous items is available in the typical case history. Factor analytic studies indicate that the test mainly measures withdrawal behavior and reality distortion. Interrater reliability is quite high, but the test has low predictive significance regarding outcome (Garmezy, 1965). Watson and Logue (1969) have reported intercorrelations of .45 and .70 between the Elgin Scale and the Ullmann-Giovannoni and Phillips scales respectively. Soloman and Zlotowski (1964) have reported an overall correlation of .87 between the Elgin and Phillips scales.

The Kantor-Wallner-Winder List of Criteria

Kantor and his associates have reported a developmental scale based on the presence or absence of certain designated forms of maladjustment or pathological signs in the case history of a patient. Indicators of process schizophrenia during childhood include early psychological trauma and prolonged physical illness. Process indicators

Characteristics of Process Schizophrenia

Clinical features:

1. Insidious, gradual development as contrasted with acute onset.
2. Early age of first hospitalization.
3. Absence of any relevant external precipitant.
4. Mild neurological signs suggestive of minimal brain damage.
5. Presence of marked disturbances in thinking.
6. Flat affect, absence of tension, confusion, anxiety, neurotic symptoms.
7. Turning against others rather than self-depreciatory or depressive trends.
8. More severe psychopathology than the average hospital admission.

Social and personal history factors:

1. Poor schoolwork.
2. Difficulties in peer-group adjustment starting in early childhood.
3. Introverted rather than extroverted personality.
4. Slight if any dating behavior during early adolescence.
5. Absence of any satisfying love attachment.
6. Failure to marry.
7. Poor employment record.
8. History of schizophrenia in the family.

for the period from the fifth year to adolescence include difficulties in school, introverted behavior, sudden changes in behavior, and an overprotective or rejecting mother. Indicators during the adolescent period are failure to develop heterosexual interests, insidious onset of psychosis, and poor response to treatment. Adult characteristics associated with process schizophrenia include massive paranoia, low tolerance for alcohol, somatic delusions, loss of normal inhibitions ("indecent" behavior), and absence of depressive features. This scale has not been used much, and data on its reliability and validity are limited.

The Phillips Scale

The scale developed by Phillips (1953) has been the most widely used. Originally it had three subsections dealing with premorbid history, possible precipitating factors, and clinical signs of disorder. More recently the abbreviated Phillips Scale, limited to premorbid history, has become more common. The items included on this scale deal mainly with social factors: past and present sexual adjustment, friendships or the lack of them, leadership qualities, and general interpersonal adjustment. The information required for scoring is usually readily obtainable from case-history data and interviews with the patient and his parents. Data summarized by Garmezy (1965) indicate that the scale is a highly reliable instrument. Interrater correlations of .90 have been reported in several studies. The scale has been found to be valid in differentiating patients with good prospects for recovery from those for whom the prognosis is poor. As might be expected from the content of the items, scores on the premorbid scale are highly correlated with marital status. High intercorrelations with other process-reactive measures have usually been noted.

The Ullmann-Giovannoni Scale

Ullmann and Giovannoni (1964) have prepared a simple self-report measure of the process-reactive continuum. The inventory consists of a list of twenty-four questions that are asked directly of the patient. The test is essentially a measure of social competence. Social items deal with marital status, level of education, duration of employment, the ability to make and keep friends during the teen years, social interactions, duration of hospital stay, and so forth. Watson and Logue (1969) have reported correlations of .45 between the Ullmann-Giovannoni and Elgin scales and .60 between the Ullmann-Giovannoni and Phillips scales.

RESEARCH FINDINGS AND RELATED THEORIES

Two points should be kept in mind in evaluating the extensive clinical and experimental literature on schizophrenia. The first is that no specific finding holds for all schizophrenics. Deficits noted in some patients are absent in others. Actually, it is a rare symptom or trait that occurs in even a bare majority of schizophrenics. Only about a third of them, for example, report hallucinations. Second, behavior deviations associated with schizophrenia are not limited to schizophrenics. Similar disturbances in psychosocial functioning are noted in more moderate and better controlled form in normal individuals.

Furthermore, reactions like those of schizophrenia occur in a wide variety of other conditions. Several infectious diseases are accompanied by behavior disturbances that mimic schizophrenic reactions. Disturbances in association and thinking, hallucinations, delusions, distortions in body image, perceptual aberrations, and other typical schizophrenic behavior may result from taking LSD and other drugs, sensory deprivation, prolonged loss of sleep, and oxygen deprivation (Chapman, 1969). There is, however, an important difference. As soon as a person recovers from an infectious disorder or the immediate effect of drugs, loss of sleep, or sensory deprivation, his schizophrenic-like reactions disappear. In schizophrenia, the disturbances in functioning are the disorder.

Sensory and Intellectual Functions

Schizophrenics show no impairment in hearing, vision, and other sensory functions, and their intellectual capacity is comparable to that of the general population. Reported lowered performance on intelligence tests prior to and following the onset of the psychosis may be accounted for on the basis of population selection factors (Lane and Albee, 1968) and disturbances in motivation, attention, affect, and spontaneity (De Luca, 1967). Under proper conditions, the preservation of intellectual functions can be demonstrated even in chronic cases (Bleuler, 1950; Hamlin, 1969).

Social Withdrawal

Process schizophrenia, particularly in chronic cases, is characterized by extreme social withdrawal. These patients are frequently described as shut in, introverted, detached, and apathetic. Therapists find it difficult to establish contact with them and to gain their confidence. The usual psychoanalytic procedure is not applicable, since these patients fail to develop the essential transference relationship.

Schizophrenics are particularly sensitive to social stimulation. They appear fearful of emotional involvement with others. The withdrawal and social aversion of schizophrenics is usually attributed to a series of experiences, beginning in childhood, that has convinced them that the social world is hostile. People are never to be trusted, only feared, fought, or ignored. The basic distrust may be related to parental rejection, inconsistent discipline, ridicule, unreasonable demands, violation of

confidences, overdomination, and so on. Withdrawal provides a defense against further hurts and threats. Jan Hartog's colorful description (1966, p. 336) of withdrawal behavior in a fear situation is applicable to schizophrenic withdrawal:

I stood there petrified with wordless, incomprehensible fear. . . . I felt all initiative, all desire to resist slowly drain out of me, and I began to be overcome by a drowsy indolence, a fatalistic resignation, a dreamy feeling of unreality. I seemed to withdraw, slowly, into a small secret hiding place within myself, a warm, secure, utterly intimate contentment that grew into somnolence as I slowly drifted out of reach of reality and all its threats and horrors. I could be attacked, brutalized, tortured, shot; I knew that as long as I managed to stay hidden in that secret place inside myself, so snug and safe and yet with such feeling of space and solitude about it that it seemed as large as the world, I would feel no pain, no terror, no despair, nothing, just this inexpressible sense of well-being and remoteness.

Unpredictability of Behavior

A general characteristic of schizophrenics is a high rate of unpredictable reactions in daily life and in clinical and experimental situations. When we speak of the unpredictability of schizophrenic behavior we are referring not to any qualities of individuality or originality in the behavior, but simply to the fact that it is erratic and inappropriate. Schizophrenics as a group have a tendency to overrespond to small stimuli and not to respond strongly enough to large stimuli. They may react to incidental stimuli and ignore those that are significant, or they may fail to differentiate between irrelevant and relevant stimuli. The same kind of stimuli in totally different contexts may elicit the same perseverative response. Familiar situations may be reacted to as if they were new and new situations as if they were old. David Shakow (1967, p. 63) has attempted to explain this as the result of some defect in an assumed central control system that interferes with

SCHIZOPHRENIC WORD SALAD AND NEOLOGISMS

The incoherence, disconnectedness, and seeming irrelevance of schizophrenic speech is illustrated in this excerpt from a transcribed interview:

Maybe I will sacrifice . . . The old test will start over again. In fact, it's glorifying. Wait a minute, will you please? I don't like this, it kind of chokes me; will you please undo it, Daddy? I like nature. If you get cold nothing can affect it, it won't rust. Hair, it might be robin redbreast. I like my conscience, though. They have tried in every generation. I love you. Ivory complexions. Whiskey, darling—that wasn't whiskey that calmed me, but the milk; that was the only thing that saved me. Summer is passing, so far we have gone. If God said I want to make the world perfect then they will have to do it themselves. There isn't a hole in my head. Joan of Arc, was she your daughter too? I like gingerbread but I like milk too. You hurt that nerve, didn't you? Oxygen, will you please give me that? I'm going to stop your heart with it. Chop the arteries off and your heart stops. A snake can't swallow but it can climb up the family tree if they have the trees they want.

The tendency of some schizophrenics to create new words or neologisms is not, of itself, strange. Many normal individuals enjoy coining new words. The difference is that "normal" neologisms can be readily deciphered. They are usually produced by condensing two familiar words into one. Often the intent is to create a new term that adds a humorous twist to a familiar word: "reminusances," "brunch," "sinema." The origin of schizophrenic neologisms is usually obscure. The coined terms appear to be private words whose meaning is known only to the patient.

Schizophrenic neologisms	Patient interpretation of word
bedrudgers	persecutors
iava	supper
gruesor	gruesome and sorrowful
poive	pleasant saying

Some schizophrenic monologues consist almost exclusively of such neologisms and are completely incomprehensible to anyone who has not painstakingly learned the patient's private language—which the schizophrenic is not likely to permit.

the integration of stimuli and the maintenance of a regulating mental set:

In schizophrenia there is a distinct weakening of the control center that serves the integrating and organizing function of the interrelated affective and cognitive processes and makes possible the establishment of "generalized" or major sets. Accompanying this weakening is a tendency for "segmented" patterns to come to the fore and become inordinately important.

Motivation

The schizophrenic's poor performance on complex experimental tasks is frequently attributed to his low motivation. It would be more accurate to say that schizophrenics as a group are less responsive than normal people to social types of incentives, but are fully as responsive to reinforcing agents that directly affect their physical well-being and personal interests. One survey of the literature concluded that verbal praise and urging have relatively little effect on the test performance of schizophrenics (Buss, 1966). This finding is consistent with early observations (Cameron's, 1938) that schizophrenics are little concerned with other persons' reactions to them. However, when the experimental situation is structured so that a "correct" response leads to the elimination of electric shock, white noise, or other noxious stimuli, the performance of schizophrenics shows as much improvement as that of normal persons, or even greater improvement. Fontana and Kline (1968) found that the patient's speed of response on a simple reaction-time test was greatly influenced by his perception of the outcome of his performance: if he thought a good performance would facilitate the attainment of his current goals within the hospital, he responded much more quickly than if he thought his personal goals would be hindered.

Speech Disturbances

The majority of schizophrenics are uncommunicative. They rarely initiate conversation. If asked a direct question, they may give a brief answer, remain silent, or make some cryptic and seemingly irrelevant response. Since speech is a medium of interpersonal communication, the sparse or mystifying speech of the schizophrenic may reflect his alienation and his disinterest in his social environment. Deluded patients may refrain from speaking because they are afraid to express their inner thoughts or are ordered by voices to keep silent. In contrast with their limited social speech, some schizophrenics do a lot of talking to themselves. Sometimes their private speech is inaudible; at other times it is loud and clear. Their outpouring of words is more likely to be reflexive than deliberate, a disorganized monologue rather than a medium of communication (Matarazzo, 1962).

The ideas expressed in schizophrenic speech appear to consist of free associations and the spontaneous verbalization of fleeting inner thoughts. The net result is a kind of word salad that is as confusing to other schizophrenics as it is to normal individuals, though it may occasionally be quite poetic or suggest some profound but elusive meaning. One schizophrenic spoke of "a bonfire of delight" and "the attainment of ethereal bliss through polytechnical science and soul exploration."

Thought Disturbances

Disturbances in association and thinking are generally regarded as the outstanding characteristics of schizophrenic behavior. Diagnosis usually rests on the presence of delusions or the patient's tendency to give irrelevant, illogical, or peculiar responses to questions (Hunt and Arnhoff, 1955). Interestingly, most patients show no significant impairment in their ability to generate ideas, to use abstract concepts, or to solve problems. Particularly in the early stages, schizophrenics often complain of too many thoughts running through their heads at the same time (McGhie and Chapman, 1961). They exhibit a high degree of ingenuity or idiosyncrasy in interpreting proverbs, sorting out objects, and evolving concepts.

What distinguishes schizophrenics is the seeming irrationality and bizarreness of their thoughts. An outstanding feature of their thinking, which Norman Cameron (1938) has called *overinclusiveness*, consists of failure to stay within the boundaries of an assigned task and to exclude irrelevant or inappropriate material. Research findings (Payne et al., 1966) indicate that overinclusive thinking is present in about 50 percent of acutely schizophrenic patients. Among chronic patients the frequency of its occurrence is about the same as for the general population.

When a young female patient was asked to report her associations to the word "day," she answered, "Night, April fifteenth, immaculate conception." To the question "Are you married?" she responded, "Yes. There are many bad women in the world who should be punished. The Lord is the father of my child." If one knows the patient's case history, it is sometimes possible to follow the train of thought. In this case, the strange responses were probably due to the intrusion of inner ideas. About a year before the patient was admitted to the hospital she had had a brief love affair with a young man. They had only one sex experience, but she became pregnant. Shortly afterward the young man married another girl.

Sometimes the derailment of associations appears to be related to the patient's response to the dominant meaning of a word instead of its contextual meaning (Chapman, Chapman and Miller, 1964). A classical example has been reported by Bleuler (1950). The patient was asked if there was

Louis Wain, a wellknown English painter, developed clinical signs of schizophrenia in middle age. Changes in his drawings of cats during his psychiatric episode reflect the perceptual distortions associated with schizophrenia.

something weighing heavily on his mind. The response was: "Yes. Iron is heavy." Sometimes the omission of significant connections results in the appearance of fragmentary or unduly concrete thought. Thus a patient may define a donkey as "big ears." Under further questioning, however, the answer can usually be improved to "a horselike animal with big ears." When asked to sort objects into categories—any sort of groupings that may occur to them—schizophrenics can and do utilize the conventional categories of color, size, shape, and function, but in addition they frequently make other, private sortings: objects they like and objects they don't like, or objects that have some personal significance to them and others that have no special meaning (McGaughren and Moran, 1956).

A variety of theories has been proposed to account for the disordered cognitive processes of schizophrenics. Since reactions similar to schizophrenic disturbances in association and thinking are commonly noted in normal persons under stress, no unique interpretation may be required. The disordered mental functioning of schizophrenics may be attributed to their highly aroused state, their preoccupation with or avoidance of inner problems, and their unconcern with whether their reactions make sense to others.

However, the eccentricity of schizophrenic thinking and the persistence of the disturbance have led workers in the field to favor more elaborate theories (reviewed by Boren, 1968). Most theories presume the presence of some developmental, psychological, or neurophysiological defect that results in difficulties in processing complex stimuli, response interference, loss of inhibitory control, or regression to childhood styles of thinking. Paul Meehl (1962) has suggested that some neural integrative defect of genetic origin may be responsible for the "cognitive slippage" of schizophrenics. Fisk (1961) has proposed that overactivity of the reticular activating system might account for the distractability of schizophrenics.

Several investigators (Payne, 1966; Yates, 1966) have attributed disturbances in association and thinking to defects in a postulated filter system. This hypothesis was originally introduced by Broadbent (1958) to explain the selectivity of attention and perception in normal individuals. Some selective mechanism is necessitated by the fact that the nervous system can process only a very small part of the total stimuli bombarding the organism from within and without at any moment. When functioning properly, the filter system limits sensory input to a manageable number of messages that are pertinent to the organism in its current state. The irrelevant associations and overinclusive thinking of schizophrenics, then, could be related to filter defects that result in the indiscriminate passage of an excessive number of stimuli. Conversely, the paucity of ideas and constricted thinking noted in some patients might be due to a clogged or closed filter system that excludes stimuli. Family studies of schizophrenics (Lidz et al., 1965; Singer and Wynne, 1965) indicate that in comparison with the parents of normal controls, the parents of schizophrenics have greater difficulties in conceptual thinking and have more blurred and fragmented styles of thinking and communication.

These data may be interpreted as supporting a learning theory or a genetic theory or both. Wynne and Singer explicitly state that both gene-determined and intrafamilial factors may contribute to the development of disordered thinking in schizophrenics. They also note that deviant responses on various psychological tests, which indicate disturbances in association and thinking, are not restricted to the families of schizophrenics. The same type of responses also occur in nonschizophrenic families, but less frequently.

Affective Disturbances

Schizophrenics exhibit the full gamut of human emotions. They may be tender, brutal, loving, cold, hostile, elated, depressed, sensitive, callous, excited, or apathetic. In general, however, they differ from the normal population in three principal ways: (1) their emotional reactions are inappropriate to known external events, (2) they appear to be relatively deficient in their capacity to experience joy and pleasure, and (3) they are unduly anxious. As far as outsiders can judge, the silly giggling of hebephrenics, the hostile belligerence of paranoids, the extreme excitement or panic reactions of the acutely disturbed, and the detached indifference of simple and chronic schizophrenics bear no relationship to external reality. Ambivalence of feelings—the simultaneous expression of love and hate—are more commonly noted in schizophrenics than in normal persons.

Sandor Rado (1956, 1962) believes that a diminished capacity for experiencing pleasure, which is partly genetic in origin, is a major differentiating characteristic of persons who develop schizophrenia. The deficiency is referred to as *anhedonia*. The schizophrenic's relative incapacity for enjoyment makes for an empty, meaningless existence. He derives little satisfaction from his accomplishments or talents. Unable to enter and share the emotional life of others, and with diminished capacity to express warmth and affection, he is left out in the cold. He responds to his outsider status with fear and rage. Having so few sources of pleasure, the potential schizophrenic cannot afford any loss. The suffering caused by the death of a parent, the loss of a friend, or a broken love affair, which an emotionally richer person can overcome, may be a catastrophic experience for a schizophrenic. Rado favors a modified psychoanalytic treatment in which emphasis is placed on emotional reeducation.

On an experimental basis, R. G. Heath (1964) has investigated the possibility of providing the schizophrenic with increased pleasurable sensations by means of electrical stimulation of the pleasure center of the brain. The technique, modeled after experiments conducted with animals, consists in implanting an electrode in the pertinent area of the brain. The patient can activate the electrode at will and give himself a shot of pleasure by pressing a button. The procedure works temporarily, but it is not considered a definitive cure for schizophrenia.

The high anxiety level of schizophrenics is inferred from their emotional hyperresponsiveness. Obvious signs of intense emotional arousal are frequently noted during the early, acute stages. The anxiety of chronic, nondeluded patients is less apparent; most of them, on the surface at least, appear to be unresponsive, listless, and apathetic. But beneath the surface there is tension. Studies of the psychophysiological reactions of these patients to experimentally induced stress situations indicate a higher than normal degree of cortical and autonomic arousal (Venables, 1966). Perhaps the surface apathy of chronic schizophrenics serves as an inhibitory defense against overstimulation. Differences of opinion exist as to whether the extreme anxiety of schizophrenics is a learned reaction or an expression of innate temperament. There is, however, considerable clinical and experimental evidence that schizophrenia-prone individuals have long histories of emotional instability dating from early childhood.

S. A. Mednick (1958) has utilized the anxiety of the preschizophrenic as the cornerstone of his theory of schizophrenia. In essence, the theory holds that the disturbances in association and thinking that distinguish schizophrenia represent learned stratagems for avoiding anxiety. Starting in childhood, the hyperresponsive preschizophrenic learns to avoid arousal stimuli by switching his attention to some neutral or distant association or thought. The substituted thought enables him momentarily to avoid the arousal stimulus. The maneuver results in a reduction in arousal level, which serves to reinforce the association between the arousal stimulus and the avoidant thought. The reduction in arousal resulting from pairing arousal stimuli with avoidant thoughts increases the probability that the individual will resort to avoidant thoughts on subsequent occasions when he is confronted with arousal stimuli. After many such reinforced learning trials, the individual acquires a repertoire of conditioned avoidance responses (irrelevant thoughts) that can help him to control his autonomic hyperresponsivity. When these responses become so spontaneous that they interfere with sustained thought processes and dominate the individual's thinking, he may be classified as schizophrenic. Mednick and Schulsinger (1968) have reported experimental data indicating that high-risk children of schizophrenic mothers show greater autonomic hyperresponsiveness and quicker rates of recovery from autonomic imbalance than control subjects. However, the hypothesis of conditioned avoidance responses is difficult to test and remains unconfirmed.

Self-Concept

The clinical impression that schizophrenics have a somewhat fragmented and unstable concept of self has received some experimental confirmation. It has been shown that the schizophrenic's self-concept is more readily disrupted by experiences of failure than the normal person's (Guller, 1966). There is some evidence that schizophrenics show greater deviation in sex-role patterns than the general population. Female schizophrenics tend to react assertively and aggressively, in a manner usually thought of as masculine, whereas schizophrenic males tend to be sensitive, quiet, and withdrawn, as the "typical" female is thought to be (McClelland and Watt, 1968). A number of male schizophrenics report delusions of undergoing a change of sex, of being a woman or neuter (Gittleson and Levine, 1966). A small percentage of schizophrenics experience distortion in body image, either overestimating or underestimating the size of body parts and sensations of body change. Similar disturbances in body image occasionally occur in normal subjects undergoing unusual stress (Fisher, 1964).

CONTRIBUTORY ETIOLOGICAL FACTORS

The causes of schizophrenic behavior are multiple, cumulative, and interactive. The unraveling and isolating of specific contributory factors and the analysis of their interaction remain a challenge for the future. Considerable progress has been made in identifying some of the major components, however. Current data support the following general conclusions:

1. The relative probability that a person will manifest overt schizophrenic behavior is directly related to the closeness of his genetic kinship with a known schizophrenic. The highest risk is shared by a monozygotic twin of a schizophrenic and a child whose mother and father are both schizophrenics. The morbidity risk is about the same for dizygotic twins, siblings, parents, and children with one schizophrenic parent. The expectancy rate is considerably lower for half-siblings, uncles, nieces, cousins, and other more distant relatives.

2. It is probable that the hereditary component in schizophrenia consists of two or more genes (polygenes) rather than a single gene.

3. The phenotypic or overt expression of a schizophrenic genotype is quite variable. About 40 percent of the monozygotic twins of schizophrenics also develop schizophrenia. Another 30 to 40 percent of the twins exhibit schizophreniform reactions, character disturbances, or neurotic symptoms; the remainder are symptom-free and essentially normal. When both twins develop schizophrenia, differences are often noted with respect to specific symptoms and prognosis. In short, the overt outcome of a genetic predisposition is greatly influenced by the facilitating, modifying, or inhibitory interacting influence of nongenetic variables.

4. What specifically is transmitted by the gene defect is unknown. The general presumption is that coding errors embedded in the chemistry of one or more

genes lead to the development of some neurobiochemical condition that in turn influences the individual's relative predisposition to schizophrenic behavior. The presence of the gene defect is considered a necessary prerequisite for schizophrenia, but the nature of the disturbance in functioning that actually occurs, if any, depends on the interactive effects of other adverse psychosocial and biological factors. One consistent finding that may have some etiological significance is that the great majority of persons who in later life develop schizophrenia are characterized from early childhood by certain seemingly inborn temperament traits. Specifically, potential schizophrenics appear to be constitutionally more passive, introverted, and emotionally hypersensitive than the normal population.

5. Family pathology is considered the main environmental agent in the etiology of schizophrenia. Earlier studies emphasized the role of the mother. The hypothesis was that possessive, overcontrolling, domineering mothers contributed to the development of schizophrenic offspring by preventing the growth of their children as independent and autonomous persons. But research findings have brought this concept into question. Similar patterns of restrictive mothering have been observed in studies of physically ill and mentally retarded children. It would appear, then, that preschizophrenic children, along with other handicapped and problem children, require and elicit maternal protectiveness and control. Thus the inadequacies and dependency needs of preschizophrenic children may be the cause rather than the result of their mothers' attitudes.

A more general hypothesis is that marital conflicts, family disorganization, and confused communication between parents and children may contribute to the development of schizophrenic behavior. Pathogenic styles of perception and contradictory modes of communication within families, for example, may lead to the acquisition of behavior patterns associated with schizophrenia. It is also possible that

children may model their behavior after that of disturbed parents, share their delusions and distortions, or serve as scapegoats for the displacement of family pathology. The significance of these familial factors has recently been challenged by studies of adopted children. Children of schizophrenic mothers who have been reared from birth in foster homes by normal adoptive parents show about the same incidence rate for schizophrenia as children who have been reared by their own schizophrenic mothers.

6. Psychodynamic theories stress the etiological significance of early unfavorable parent-child experiences that burden the preschizophrenic with feelings of insecurity, distrust, hostility, and despair. The child's prospects of adjustment are further weakened by a vaguely defined and essentially negative self-concept. He perceives himself as inadequate, unworthy, unappreciated, and unlovable.

7. Attempts to demonstrate a causal relationship between socioeconomic status and vulnerability to schizophrenia have been unsuccessful. Schizophrenia appears to be randomly distributed at all socioeconomic levels, with one notable exception: in large industrialized cities a disproportionately large number of schizophrenics are found in the lowest socioeconomic group. The available evidence suggests that this finding is due to the downward social drift of schizophrenics.

8. Data on the relative incidence of schizophrenia in different cultures are fragmentary and inconclusive. The alienation of the schizophrenic from his culture may be interpreted as a symptom, a result, or a cause of his disordered behavior.

9. A number of theories have been proposed linking schizophrenia with a variety of neurological, biochemical, and metabolic factors (Hamwich et al., 1967; Zubin and Shagass, 1969). Further research may eventually indicate that some specific neurobiological defect is associated with certain selected patients. So far, however, the findings of experimental studies have been more suggestive than conclusive.

TREATMENT AND OUTCOME

The availability of antipsychotic drugs that control acute symptoms plus changing public attitudes toward mental patients have encouraged the increased use of general hospitals, community organizations, and home care in the treatment of schizophrenics. The most commonly used drug in treating schizophrenic symptoms is *chlorpromazine*, but many other drugs are available for patients who show undesirable side effects or are unresponsive to this medication. In many cases, however, and particularly in process-reactive cases where patients have long histories of progressive impairment in psychological functioning and social behavior, it is difficult to say exactly what constitutes improvement or recovery. In terms of release rates of drug-treated patients, about 75 percent of the schizophrenics admitted to mental hospitals are returned to the community within a few months and another 10 to 15 percent are discharged after a longer stay. Many are readmitted once or twice and a small percentage become permanent residents.

The findings of a three-year follow-up study of 588 patients admitted to veterans' hospitals (Sherman et al., 1964) are representative of the prognosis for hospitalized schizophrenics. The treatment process was considered an unqualified success in 23 percent of the cases: they left the hospital after a short stay and were not readmitted to a VA hospital. Ten percent remained continuously hospitalized over the three-year period and hence were considered clear therapeutic failures. At one time or another 90 percent of the initial group left the hospital. At the end of the three-year period 66 percent of the total group were out and 34 percent were in the hospital. Again married patients showed a better prognosis than those who remained single. A paradoxical but understandable observation noted by Morris Carstairs (1967) is that discharged patients who go to live with strangers, where emotional involvement is minimal, have a better outcome than those who return to their own families.

Psychotherapy

The literature on the applicability of psychotherapy to schizophrenia is inconsistent. Many therapists feel that they are too withdrawn, distrustful and uncooperative to respond to psychotherapy. Freda Fromm-Reichmann (1950) agrees that it is difficult to treat schizophrenics but believes that with patience and understanding a therapist can establish rapport with them, and she has reported several therapeutic successes. One of her former patients, H. Green, has written a sensitive autobiographical account of her recovery from schizophrenia, called *I Never Promised You a Rose Garden*.

A comprehensive research study on the application of client-centered therapy to schizophrenics (Rogers et al., 1967) showed that as far as overall outcome was concerned, the results were about the same for the intensively treated patients and the matched control group, which had been exposed only to the general hospital program. There was some evidence that the nature of the therapeutic relationship had an effect on income. Those patients who perceived a high degree of harmony with their therapists were independently rated as showing the greatest positive change. Therapist-client relationships rated high in empathy ranked second in degree of personality change. The control group followed next. Patients whose relationships with their therapists were marked by little or no agreement or empathy showed no change or even regressive change.

Individual psychotherapy seems to be much less effective than drugs in the treatment of first admissions to large state hospitals (May, 1968). Ninety-five percent of those treated with drugs only were released within a year, whereas the release rate for those receiving psychotherapy alone was 64 percent. The duration of hospital stay for patients in the latter group was longer than for drug-treated cases. The cost of treatment (from admission to release) was 70 percent higher for patients given psychotherapy alone than for those treated with drugs alone. A possible criticism of this study is that the psychotherapy was conducted by inexperienced residents. A more recent study (Karon and Vandenbos, 1970) showed that experienced psychotherapists are much more effective than inexperienced clinicians in the treatment of schizophrenics.

Good and Poor Therapists

Betz and Whitehorn (Whitehorn and Betz, 1960; Betz, 1967) have demonstrated that some therapists are far more effective than others in achieving immediate results with schizophrenics. Good or *A* therapists had a 75 percent improvement rate, as contrasted with poor or *B* therapists, who had a 27 percent improvement rate. The more successful *A* doctors differed from their *B* colleagues in more frequently (1) grasping the personal meaning and motivation of the patient's behavior, (2) interacting more freely and actively with the patient, and (3) setting limits on the kind and degree of obnoxious behavior they would permit, but not seeking to interpret or instruct. *B* doctors were either passively permissive or pointed out the patient's mistakes and misunderstanding in an instructional style.

On the Strong Vocational Interest Inventory, the *A* physicians had interest patterns similar to those of lawyers and certified public accountants, while *B* therapists had interest patterns similar to those of printers and teachers of mathematics and the physical sciences. The difference in interest patterns suggests that *A* therapists had a more problem-solving and less mechanical approach than *B* doctors. An interesting footnote is that eventually time, the great healer, almost evened the score. Follow-up data collected five or more years after discharge indicated that 65 percent of the patients treated by *B* doctors

were improved, compared with 77 percent of the patients of *A* doctors.

Reinforcement Therapy

Reinforcement techniques have been found to be highly effective in modifying or eliminating specific symptoms of schizophrenic patients (Ullmann and Krasner, 1969). The usual procedure in such experiments is first to determine the base rate of some frequently emitted specific symptom. Subsequent responses that are in the direction of the desired change are then selectively reinforced. For example, if the target objective is to decrease bizarre verbalizations, the experimenter will smile and make some encouraging comment whenever the patient makes a coherent or sensible remark. As a rule, incoherent or "sick" talk is ignored, but shock or some other negative reinforcement may be used to decrease the frequency of bizarre speech. Success is measured by the amount of decrease in the frequency of the symptom response and increase in the frequency of desired behavior.

Operant conditioning principles have been found to be particularly helpful in modifying the ward behavior of chronic patients. Many hospitals have established token economy wards where the environment is carefully controlled so that patients receive systematic reinforcement for appropriate behavior. Members of the staff promptly hand out tokens to patients whenever they exhibit any desired behavior. Since tokens are required to "pay" for the necessities as well as for the luxuries of hospital life, patients are motivated to learn to conform to the rules of the game. The rules are modified somewhat from patient to patient so that the earning of tokens is kept within each patient's capability. In essence, patients are paid for assuming responsibility for self-care and "normal" behavior.

Although operant conditioning and token economy programs have demonstrated their effectiveness in improving the ward behavior of schizophrenics, it should be added that the procedures have negligible curative value. The stability of induced behavior changes is dependent on the continuation of reinforcement. When reinforcement is discontinued, there is a relapse and a return of symptoms.

Community Care

The effectiveness of home care for schizophrenics has been experimentally explored. (Pasamanick et al., 1967). The study involved an eighteen-month follow-up of outcome in three comparable groups of schizophrenic patients: a group treated at home with drugs, a group given placebos while being cared for at home, and a hospital-treated control group. The drug and placebo groups were visited regularly in their homes by public health nurses, and these visits and the drug medication were the principal ingredients of the treatment program. Only the project director knew whether the home-care patients were receiving drugs or placebos.

An evaluation made at the end of the project showed that 77 percent of the drug-treated group were able to remain continuously at home as compared with 34 percent of those receiving placebos. Over the total follow-up period, the drug-treated patients were home 90 percent of the time, the placebo cases 80 percent, and the hospital control group 75 percent. Failures in the home-care program usually occurred within six months. When patients treated at home had to be removed to a hospital, it was usually because they exhibited bizarre or dangerous behavior or because the responsible relatives could no longer cope with the patient and his needs. In general, patients cared for at home showed greater improvement in mental status, psychological test performance, domestic functioning, and social participation than those who received routine hospital care. Most of the improvement in performance occurred during the first six months of the study. Improvement was limited to a return of functioning to the prepsychotic level.

SUMMARY AND AN ATTEMPTED SYNTHESIS

Schizophrenia is a broad description label applied to persons marked by gross personality disorganization and severe impairment in psychosocial functioning. About 1 percent of the general population in all countries exhibit psychosocial deficits associated with the disorder at some time during their lives. The onset of overt symptoms usually occurs between the ages of fifteen and forty.

The heterogeneity of reactions and of persons included within the vaguely defined boundaries of schizophrenia has long been recognized. No satisfactory rationale or set of criteria has yet been formulated for what Bleuler has referred to as "the group of schizophrenias." There is little evidence that the traditional clinical subtypes (simple, hebephrenic, catatonic, and paranoid) have any basis in reality as separate disorders or that they represent different manifestations of a single disease entity. About all that patients assigned to the same subcategory have in common is some similarity in surface symptoms.

The process-reactive concept has some value in differentiating persons with a relatively favorable prior history of social interaction, who tend to have a relatively favorable prospect for recovery, from patients with a prior history of social inadequacy, for whom the prognosis is poor. It seems, however, that the symptoms of the patients in these two groupings differ more in degree than in kind. Process schizophrenia and reactive schizophrenia represent end positions of a single continuum rather than discrete disorders.

The more basic issue of what constitutes or distinguishes schizophrenic behavior remains unresolved. A tentative hypothesis is that the crucial element is social withdrawal. The multiple determinants of social withdrawal as a mode of adjustment or life style will be considered in the following chapter, which is concerned with the origins of schizophrenic behavior. Our present interest is in seeing how many pieces of the puzzle of schizophrenia can be put together if the following premises are accepted as valid: (1) from early childhood the preschizophrenic has experienced difficulty in relating to others and in establishing satisfying interpersonal relationships; (2) with each succeeding year the gulf separating him from other human beings is widened; (3) alone and friendless, he withdraws more and more within himself; (4) a point is finally reached where in despair or protest he gives up the seemingly hopeless task of being understood and accepted by others, and shuts the door on the outer world and retreats into a private inner world.

The transition is neither planned nor deliberate. Some persons experience acute panic as they sense they are losing control of their ability to move freely from one world to the other and are no longer able to distinguish outer-world experiences from inner-world fantasies; others have feelings of profound relief when they at last give up the unequal struggle to cope with reality and shut it all away from them. By the time the patient is diagnosed as a schizophrenic, the priority of the inner world has been established. Safe within the fortress of the self, the schizophrenic may look out at the world, but his interest is limited to those external events that have personal significance for him.

Under these conditions, the behavior of the schizophrenic, when evaluated in accordance with the expectations and standards of his society, is erratic and unpredictable, apathetic, undermotivated, and unresponsive. No longer interested in keeping up appearances to impress others, the schizophrenic may become careless in his grooming and manners and indifferent to social amenities. Coherent speech and logical thinking require both concentrated attention and interest in effective social communication; the schizophrenic who is preoccupied with his inner world couldn't care less if others find his speech incomprehensible and his thoughts confusing. His disorganized speech and thoughts may actually serve as a protective barrier against intrusion. Since the self-concept is to a great extent a product of the reflected opinions and evaluations of significant others, the limited interpersonal involvement of the preschizophrenic accounts in large part for his fragmented self-concept.

Social withdrawal involves more than making no demands on others that might lead to rebuffs. The individual must maintain a constant state of alertness to protect himself against possible threats from the external world. Interpersonal and new situations, in particular, provoke anxiety in him. But social withdrawal does not solve all of his problems. He is still left with his frustrated sexual urges, his social needs, his unfulfilled aspirations, and his painful memories of real or imagined wrongs. These still pressing problems are expressed in wild fantasies, delusions, and hallucinations. If in acting out or reacting to his delusions and hallucinations the individual inadvertently breaks the rules of society, his behavior may be perceived by others as bizarre, annoying, and occasionally dangerous.

Although the schizophrenic prefers to have as little as possible to do with the outside world, he is aware of external events. His functioning capacity is not significantly impaired. When it serves his purpose, he can effectively perform tasks that result in the elimination of painful stimuli. He can learn to modify his symptoms and "normalize" his behavior to earn tokens that can be exchanged for desired objects. This adaptability, however, does not extend to placing trust in a therapist or readily confiding his secrets. Psychotherapy is difficult and often unrewarding to both patient and therapist. Sensitive therapists with extraordinary understanding, empathy, and patience may slowly effect positive changes. Those who lack these gifts may do more harm than good.

Unless a schizophrenic is a real source of danger to himself or others, commitment to a mental hospital is best avoided. The patient perceives his "incarceration" as one more proof of his rejection by society. After he gets over his initial resentment, he may realize that permanent hospitalization ideally serves his objective of social withdrawal and resignation from life. The development of drugs that are highly effective in reducing inner turmoil and alleviating overt symptoms has made it possible to care for patients at home and in the community. Neighborhood day-care centers where schizophrenics can be taught social skills in a friendly, acceptive, club-like atmosphere may be more effective than talking-out or confrontational forms of therapy.

References

Becker, W. C. "A Genetic Approach to the Interpretation and Evaluation of the Process-Reactive Distinction in Schizophrenia." *Journal of Abnormal and Social Psychology* 53 (1956): 229-36.

Betz, B. J. "Studies of the Therapist's Role in the Treatment of the Schizophrenic Patient." *American Journal of Psychiatry* 123 (1967): 963-71.

Bleuler, E. P. *Dementia Praecox or the Group of Schizophrenias* (1911). New York: International Universities Press, 1950.

Boren, W. E. *Schizophrenia Research and Theory.* New York: Academic Press, 1968.

Broadbent, D. E. *Perception and Communication.* London: Pergamon Press, 1958.

Buss, A. H. *Psychopathology.* New York: Wiley, 1966.

Cameron, N. "Reasoning, Regression, and Communication in Schizophrenics." *Psychological Monographs* 50, no. 1 (1938).

Carstairs, G. M. "Social Factors Influencing the Genesis and Outcome of Schizophrenia." In *The Origins of Schizophrenia*, ed. J. Romano, pp. 270-75. New York: Excerpta Medica Foundation, 1967.

Chapman, L. J. "Schizomimetic Conditions and Schizophrenia." *Journal of Consulting and Clinical Psychology* 33 (1969): 646-50.

———, Chapman, J. P., and Miller, G. A. "A Theory of Verbal Behavior in Schizophrenia." In *Progress in Experimental Personality Research*, ed. B. A. Maher, pp. 49-77. New York: Academic Press, 1964.

Crocetti, G. M., and Lemkau, P. V. "Schizophrenia, 11: Epidemiology." In *Comprehensive Textbook of Psychiatry*, ed. A. M. Freedman, H. I. Kaplan, pp. 599-603. Baltimore: Williams & Wilkins, 1967.

De Luca, J. M. "Direct Measurement of Differential Cognitive Deficit in Acute Schizophrenia." *Journal of Abnormal Psychology* 72, no. 2 (1967): 143-46.

Fisher, S. "Body Image and Psychopathology." *Archives of General Psychiatry* 10 (1964): 5-29.

Fisk, F. A. "A Neurophysiological Theory of Schizophrenia." *Journal of Mental Science* 107 (1961): 828-38.

Fontana, A. F., and Kline, E. B. "Self-preservation and the Schizophrenic 'Deficit.'" *Journal of Clinical and Consulting Psychology* 32 (1968): 250-56.

Fromm-Reichmann, F. *Principles of Intensive Psychotherapy.* Chicago: University of Chicago Press, 1950.

Garmezy, N. "Process and Reactive Schizophrenia: Some Conceptions and Issues." In *Classification in Psychiatry and Psychopathology*, ed. M. M. Katz, J. O. Cole, and W. E. Barton, pp. 419-66. Washington, D.C.: U.S. Government Printing Office, 1965.

Gittleson, N. L., and Levine, S. "Subjective Ideas of Sexual Change in Male Schizophrenics." *British Journal of Psychiatry* 112 (1966): 779-82.

Gottesman, I. I. "Severity/Concordance and Diagnostic Refinement in the Maudsley-Bethlehem Schizophrenic Twin Study." In *The Transmission of Schizophrenia*, ed. D. Rosenthal and S. S. Kety, pp. 37-48. New York: Pergamon Press, 1968.

Guller, I. "Stability of Self-concept in Schizophrenia." *Journal of Abnormal Psychology* 71 (1966): 275-79.

Hamlin, R. M. "The Stability of Intellectual Function in Chronic Schizophrenia." *Journal of Nervous and Mental Disease* 149 (1969): 496-503.

Hamwich, H. E.; Kety, S. S.; and Smythies, J. R. *Amines and Schizophrenia.* London: Pergamon Press, 1967.

Hartog, J. D. *The Captain.* New York: Atheneum, 1966.

Heath, R. G. "Pleasure Response of Human Subjects to Direct Stimulation of the Brain: Physiologic and Psychodynamic Considerations." In *The Role of Pleasure in Behavior*, ed. R. G. Heath, pp. 219-43. New York: Harper & Row, 1964.

Higgins, J., and Peterson, J. C. "Concept

of Process-Reactive Schizophrenia: A Critique." *Psychological Bulletin* 66 (1966): 201-6.

Hunt, W. A., and Arnhoff, F. N. "Some Standardized Scales for Disorganization in Schizophrenic Thinking." *Journal of Consulting Psychology* 19 (1955): 171-74.

Kantor, R. E., and Herron, W. G. *Reactive and Process Schizophrenia.* Palo Alto, Calif.: Science and Behavior Books, 1966.

———, Wallner, J. M., and Winder, C. L. "Process and Reactive Schizophrenia." *Journal of Consulting Psychology* 17 (1953): 157-62.

Karon, B. P., and Vandenbos, G. R. "Experience, Medication, and the Effectiveness of Psychotherapy with Schizophrenics." *British Journal of Psychiatry* 116 (1970): 427-28.

Kringlen, E. "An Epidemiological-Clinical Twin Study on Schizophrenia." In *The Transmission of Schizophrenia*, ed. D. Rosenthal and S. S. Kety, pp. 49-63. New York: Pergamon Press, 1968.

Lane, E. A., and Albee, G. W. "On Childhood Intellectual Decline of Adult Schizophrenics: A Reassessment of an Earlier Study." *Journal of Abnormal Psychology* 73 (1968): 174-77.

Lidz, T.; Fleck, S.; and Cornelison, A. R. *Schizophrenia and the Family.* New York: International Universities Press, 1965.

McClelland, D. C., and Watt, N. F. "Sex-Role Alienation in Schizophrenia." *Journal of Abnormal Psychology* 73, no. 3 (1968): 226-39.

McGaughren, L. S., and Moran, L. J. " 'Conceptual Levels' versus 'Conceptual Area' Analyses of Object-Sorting Behavior of Schizophrenic and Neuropsychiatric Groups." *Journal of Abnormal and Social Psychology* 52 (1956): 43-50.

McGhie, A., and Chapman, J. "Disorders of Attention and Perception in Early Schizophrenia." *British Journal of Medical Psychology* 34 (1961): 103-16.

Matarazzo, J. D. "Prescribed Behavior Therapy: Suggestions from Interview Research." In *Experimental Foundations of Clinical Psychology*, ed. A. J. Bachrach. New York: Basic Books, 1962.

May, P. R. A. *Treatment of Schizophrenia.* New York: Science House, 1968.

Mednick, S. A. "A Learning Theory Approach to Research in Schizophrenia." *Psychological Bulletin* 55 (1958): 316-27.

——— and Schulsinger, F. "Some Premorbid

Characteristics Related to Breakdown in Children with Schizophrenic Mothers." In *The Transmission of Schizophrenia*, ed. D. Rosenthal and S. S. Kety, pp. 267-91. New York: Pergamon Press, 1968.

Meehl, P. E. "Schizotaxia, Schizotypy, Schizophrenia." *American Psychologist* 17 (1962): 827-38.

Meichenbaum, D. H. "Validation Study of Marital Status and the Self-report Scale for Process-Reactive Schizophrenia." *Journal of Consulting and Clinical Psychology* 33 (1969): 351-56.

Mishler, E. G., and Scotch, N. A. "Sociocultural Factors in the Epidemiology of Schizophrenia." *Psychiatry* 26 (1963): 315-51.

Noyes, A. P., and Kolb, L. C. *Modern Clinical Psychiatry.* Philadelphia: Saunders, 1963.

Offord, D. R., and Cross, L. A. "Behavioral Antecedents of Adult Schizophrenia: A Review." *Archives of General Psychiatry* 21 (1969): 267-83.

Pasamanick, B.; Scarpetti, F. R.; and Dinety, S. *Schizophrenics in the Community: An Experimental Study in the Prevention of Hospitalization.* New York: Appleton-Century-Crofts, 1967.

Payne, R. W. "The Measurement and Significance of Overinclusive Thinking and Retardation in Schizophrenic Patients." In *Psychopathology of Schizophrenia*, ed. P. H. Hoch and J. Zubin, pp. 77-97. New York: Grune & Stratton, 1966.

Phillips, L. "Case History Data and Prognosis in Schizophrenia." *Journal of Nervous and Mental Disease* 117 (1953): 515-25.

Pinel, P. *A Treatise on Insanity* (1801). New York: Hafner, 1962.

Rado, S. *Psychoanalysis of Behavior*, 2 vols. New York: Grune & Stratton, 1956, 1962.

Rogers, C. R., ed., with Gendlin, E. T., Kiesler, D. J.; and Truax, C. B. *The Therapeutic Relationship and Its Impact: A Study of Psychotherapy with Schizophrenics.* Madison: University of Wisconsin Press, 1967.

Shakow, D. "Some Psychophysiological Aspects of Schizophrenia." In *The Origins of Schizophrenia*, ed. J. Romano, pp. 15-26. New York: Excerpta Medica Foundation, 1967.

Sherman, L. J.; Mosley, E. C.; Ging, R.; and Bookbinder, L. J. "Prognosis in Schizophrenia: A Follow-up Study of 588 Patients." *Archives of General Psychiatry* 10 (1964): 123-30.

Silverman, J. "Scanning Control Mechanism

and 'Cognitive Filtering' in Paranoid and Nonparanoid Schizophrenia." *Journal of Consulting Psychology* 28 (1964): 385-93.

Singer, M. T., and Wynne, L. C. "Thought Disorder and Family Relations of Schizophrenics: IV. Results and Implications." *Archives of General Psychiatry* 12 (1965): 201-12.

Slater, E. "A Review of Earlier Evidence on Genetic Factors in Schizophrenia." In *The Transmission of Schizophrenia,* ed. D. Rosenthal and S. S. Kety. New York: Pergamon Press, 1968.

Solomon, L., and Zlotowski, M. "The Relationship Between the Elgin and the Phillips Measures of Process-Reactive Schizophrenia." *Journal of Nervous and Mental Disease* 138 (1964): 32-37.

Steffy, R. A., and Becker, W. C. "Measurement of the Severity of Disorder in Schizophrenia by Means of the Holtzman Inkblot Test." *Journal of Consulting Psychology* 25 (1961): 555.

Stephens, J. H.; Astrup, C.; and Mangrum, J. C. "Prognosis in Schizophrenia." *Archives of General Psychiatry* 16 (1967): 693-98.

Sullivan, H. S. *Conceptions of Modern Psychiatry.* New York: Norton, 1953.

Ullmann, L. P. *Institution and Outcome: A Comparative Study of Psychiatric Hospitals.* New York: Pergamon Press, 1967.

—— and Giovannoni, J. M. "The Development of a Self-report Measure of the Process-Reactive Continuum." *Journal of Nervous and Mental Disease* 138 (1964): 38-42.

—— and Krasner, L. *A Psychological Approach to Abnormal Behavior.* Englewood Cliffs, N.J.: Prentice-Hall, 1969.

Venables, P. "Psychophysiological Aspects of Schizophrenia." *British Journal of Medical Psychology* 39 (1966): 289-97.

Watson, C. G., and Logue, P. E. "Interrelationships of Several Process-Reactive Measures." *Journal of Consulting and Clinical Psychology* 33, no. 1 (1969): 120-22.

Whitehorn, J. C., and Betz, B. J. "Further Studies of the Doctor as a Crucial Variable in the Outcome of Treatment with Schizophrenic Patients." *American Journal of Psychiatry* 117 (1960): 215-23.

Wittman, P. "A Scale for Measuring Prognosis in Schizophrenic Patients." *Elgin State Hospital Papers* 4 (1941): 20-33.

Wynne, L. C. "Methodological and Conceptual Issues in the Study of Schizophrenics and Their Families." In *The Transmission of Schizophrenia,* ed. D. Rosenthal and S. S. Kety, pp. 185-99. New York: Pergamon Press, 1968.

Yates, A. J. "Psychological Deficit." In *Annual Review of Psychology,* ed. P. R. Farnsworth, 1966, pp. 111-44.

Zigler, E., and Phillips, L. "Social Competence and the Process-Reactive Distinction in Psychopathology." *Journal of Abnormal and Social Psychology* 65 (1962): 215-22.

Zubin, J., and Shagass, C., eds. *Neurobiological Aspects of Psychopathology.* New York: Grune & Stratton, 1969.

9 · Origins of Schizophrenic Behavior

Guernica, Pablo Picasso

Schizophrenic behavior is the end product of the interaction of biological, experiential, and sociocultural factors. The role of any specific factor can be evaluated only in the context of its interaction with other significant variables. The relative importance of particular pathogenic agents may vary considerably from patient to patient, but in no case is any single factor the sole determinant.

THE GENETICS OF SCHIZOPHRENIA

The principal research methods used to investigate the genetic component of schizophrenia are the family method, the twin method, longitudinal studies of high-risk children, and comparative studies of children reared in their biological families and in adoptive homes. Studies of families, twins, and high-risk children indicate the importance of genetic factors by demonstrating the degree to which the incidence rate for schizophrenia is directly correlated with the degree of consanguinity. Findings may be considered to support the genetic hypothesis if schizophrenia occurs more frequently among closely related people than among distant relatives. This interpretation has been challenged by the observation that people who are closely related are more likely to share a common environment than those more distantly related. Twin data, most of which indicate significantly higher concordance rates (both twins schizophrenic) for monozygotic than dizygotic pairs, provide good support for the genetic hypothesis, al-

though the fact that both types of twins are reared together in the same family does not completely rule out the possible importance of environmental factors. As we noted earlier, in addition to having an identical set of genes, monozygotic twins tend to have more similar life experiences than dizygotic twins. The occurrence of schizophrenia in both twins of MZ pairs reared apart provides dramatic evidence in favor of heredity, but only a small number of such cases have been reported. The most conclusive genetic data have come from the study of children of schizophrenic parents reared in foster or adoptive homes.

Family Studies

Family studies begin with the selection of a representative group of patients whose clinical history and behavior meet predetermined criteria warranting a diagnosis of schizophrenia. These individuals are referred to as *index cases*. Investigators then conduct careful individual studies of close and distant relatives of the index cases to determine the presence or absence of schizophrenic behavior and other forms of pathology. An age correction is usually made in calculating expectancy rates for young persons, presently free of overt symptoms, who have not yet attained the age when the onset of symptoms usually occurs.

The extensive literature on family studies has been reviewed by Slater (1968), and a concise summary of his findings is presented in Table 9.1. The figures refer to definite schizophrenics. If doubtful or borderline cases were added, the reported percentages would be increased about 25 percent. A further correction would have to be made to include other forms of pathology.

So far as definite schizophrenics are concerned, the data clearly indicate that the morbidity risk is directly related to the closeness of blood ties. As compared with a chance expectancy rate of 1 percent for the general population, the average expectancy rates among the relatives of schizophrenics range from 2-3 percent for nephews, cousins, and grandchildren to 37 percent for the children of two schizophrenic parents.

These findings are consistent with genetic principles, but they cannot be regarded as conclusive evidence that schizophrenia has a solely genetic origin, since behavioral similarities in relatives may be due to the influence of nurture rather than nature or a combination of the two. The most objective conclusion is that the data reflect the interactive effect of both nature and nurture. However, a slight weighting in favor of genetic influence may be inferred from the fact that the expectancy rate for a child with one schizophrenic parent is the same whether the father or the mother is schizophrenic. From a genetic point of view, the child's risk should be the same, but it is difficult to reconcile this finding with environmental theories that emphasize the greater role of the mother in child rearing and home management.

Another finding that may be interpreted as favorable to the genetic rather than the environmental position is that the expectancy rate for siblings is three times greater than for half-siblings. The close agreement of expectancy rates for parents, children, and siblings (11 to 14 percent) is consistent with the fact that these three groups have the same degree of genetic overlap.

The observation that the children of two schizophrenics have a 37 percent risk of developing the disorder requires some elaboration. This figure does not accurately reflect the combined effect of nature and nurture. Only 22 percent of these children remained in continuous residence at home with one or both parents up to the age of fifteen. The remainder were reared by rela-

Table 9.1. Expectation of Schizophrenia for the Relatives of Schizophrenics.

Relationship		Percentage of expectation
Parents		11%
Children	Both parents schizophrenic	37
	Mother schizophrenic	14
	Father schizophrenic	14
Siblings	Neither parent schizophrenic	9
	One parent schizophrenic	12
Half-sibs		3
Grandchildren		3
First cousins		3
Nephews and nieces		2

Adapted from E. Slater, "A Review of Earlier Evidence on Genetic Factors in Schizophrenia," in *The Transmission of Schizophrenia*, ed. D. Rosenthal and S. S. Kety (New York: Pergamon Press, 1968), pp. 15-26.

tives or placed in foster homes or under agency care for varying periods of time (Erlenmeyer-Kimling, 1968). A large proportion of the nonschizophrenic children developed other disorders. Only about a third succeeded in making a reasonably normal adjustment (Rosenthal, 1967).

Twin Studies

The twin approach requires (1) the selection of a number of known schizophrenic patients (index cases) who have living twins, (2) tracing the co-twins and examining them for the presence or absence of schizophrenia or some other disorder, and (3) determining by blood tests or other criteria whether the twins are of the monozygotic or dizygotic variety. In earlier twin studies the index cases were chosen mainly from the resident populations of mental hospitals, and therefore included an unduly large number of severe chronic cases. More recent investigators have attempted to correct for this error by gathering data on total populations or on consecutive admissions to clinics and hospitals.

The findings of both early and recent studies agree that the concordance rate for monozygotic twins is about four to five times higher than for dizygotic twins. As Table 9.2 indicates, however, the absolute magnitude of concordance rates for both types of twins was considerably higher in the older studies than in the more recent ones. In data gathered prior to 1962, the mean concordance rate for identical twins was 64 percent, as compared with 14 percent for dizygotic twins. The comparable figures for more recent studies, exclusive of those reported by Tienari, show concordance rates of 36 percent for monozygotic and 8 percent for dizygotic twins.

The contrast in concordance rates for the two types of twins confirms the importance of genetic factors in the development of schizophrenic behavior. Most investigators agree that several genes, rather than one

Table 9.2. Concordance Rates for MZ and Same-sexed DZ Twins.

Investigator	Country	Number of pairs		Percentage of concordance	
		MZ	DZ	MZ	DZ
Earlier reports:[a]					
Rosanoff (1934)	U.S.A.	41	53	61%	13%
Essen-Moller (1941)	Sweden	11	27	64	15
Kallmann (1946)	U.S.A.	174	296	69	11
Slater (1953)	U.K.	37	58	65	14
Inouye (1961)	Japan	55	11	60	18
Recent studies:					
Harvald and Hauge (1965)[a]	Denmark	7	31	29	6
Gottesman and Shields (1966)[a]	U.K.	24	33	42	9
Tienari (1968)[b]	Finland	17	—	6-36	—
Kringlen (1968)[c]	Norway	55	90	38	10

[a] I. I. Gottesman and J. Shields, "Contributions of Twin Studies to Perspectives on Schizophrenia," in *Progress in Experimental Personality Research,* ed. B. A. Maher (New York: Academic Press, 1966), vol. 3, pp. 1-84.
[b] P. Tienari, "Schizophrenia in Monozygotic Male Twins," in *The Transmission of Schizophrenia,* ed. D. Rosenthal and S. S. Kety (New York: Pergamon Press, 1968), pp. 27-36.
[c] E. Kringlen, "An Epidemiological-Clinical Twin Study on Schizophrenia," in ibid., pp. 49-63.

dominant one, are involved. Interestingly, the concordance rate for monozygotic twins noted in recent studies is practically identical with the incidence rate for the children of two schizophrenic parents.

The findings that only about one-third of monozygotic pairs are concordant for schizophrenia have sometimes been misinterpreted as minimizing the significance of heredity. Proponents of heredity as the decisive factor are not particularly bothered by this criticism, since genetic theory assumes that the overt expression of a genetic predisposition is greatly influenced by other factors. In this connection it may be added that another 40 percent of monozygotic co-twins of schizophrenics develop other disorders. That still leaves a substantial number who are "normal" from a psy-

chiatric standpoint (Kringlen, 1968).

Twins discordant for schizophrenia provide a valuable source of material for investigators studying the significance of other factors in the modification of genetic predispositions. Some of the earlier studies suggested that the concordance rate for female pairs was higher than that for male pairs. Better controlled recent investigations, which report the same concordance rates for male and female twins, have ruled out the possible significance of sex (Shields, 1968). The co-twins of schizophrenics who later became schizophrenic themselves often had difficult relationships with their fathers and were overprotected by their mothers in childhood (Kringlen, 1968).

Some of the more significant findings of a comprehensive review of research on the

Table 9.3. Early Characteristics of 100 Pairs of MZ Twins Discordant for Schizophrenia.

Characteristic	Outcome of co-twins	
	Schizophrenic	Nonschizophrenic
Neurotic as child	16	1
Submissive	37	4
Sensitive	38	5
Serious; worrier	22	4
Illness of central nervous system as child	17	4
Birth complication (any)	24	6
Asphyxia at birth	12	3
Dependent	12	3
Quiet, shy	25	8
Stubborn	20	7
Weaker than co-twin	27	11
Dominant	14	30
Outgoing, lively	13	35
Spokesman for pair	7	22
Better at school than co-twin	8	29
More intelligent than co-twin	—	16

Adapted from W. Pollin and J. R. Stabenau, "Biological, Psychological, and Historical Differences in a Series of Monozygotic Twins Discordant for Schizophrenia," in *The Transmission of Schizophrenia*, ed. D. Rosenthal and S. S. Kety (New York: Pergamon Press, 1968), pp. 317-32.

early childhood characteristics of monozygotic twins discordant for schizophrenia are reported in Table 9.3 (Pollin and Stabenau, 1968). A higher proportion of the twins who later became schizophrenic had histories of birth complications and diseases of the central nervous system. As children the schizophrenic twins were described as more neurotic, submissive, sensitive, and dependent. A co-twin who did not become schizophrenic was more likely to have been the leader and spokesman for the pair during childhood, more outgoing, and more intelligent.

Twins Reared Apart

A total of sixteen cases have been reported in which schizophrenia occurred in monozygotic twins reared apart (Slater, 1968). Fourteen of the pairs were separated soon after birth or during infancy; the other two were separated at the ages of three and seven. Ten of the sixteen cases, or 63 percent, were concordant for schizophrenia. In the remaining six cases only one of the twins of each pair developed the disorder. These figures are in agreement with those obtained in earlier comparable studies for monozygotic twins brought up together. The fact that the concordance rates are the same for twins reared together and apart suggests that genetic factors are largely responsible for the development of schizophrenia.

Longitudinal Studies

Practically all information available on schizophrenia is based on studies of patients *after* the onset of the disorder. These data have two major drawbacks: (1) when distinctive psychological or biological characteristics are noted, it is difficult to decide whether these represent causal factors or incidental byproducts of the disorder; (2) attempts to assess the etiological significance of childhood experiences are vulnerable to the unreliability of memories of events that happened twenty years ago or more. Ideally, information should be gathered on patients prior to the onset of the disorder. There is, of course, no sure way of predicting who will develop a mental disorder, but the odds can be improved somewhat by studying the offspring of schizophrenic parents, since as a group, children with one schizophrenic parent have about a 15 percent risk of developing the disorder. This approach is being utilized by S. A. Mednick (1967) in his longitudinal study of high-risk and low-risk children. In selecting high-risk children, Mednick chose only those whose mothers had definite histories of process schizophrenia, as confirmed by prolonged hospitalization. Children whose mothers had no psychiatric history were chosen for the low-risk group. Both groups were matched on other pertinent variables.

In 1962, when the study was started, the average age of the children was fifteen years, and Mednick plans to follow up these children for twenty years. The investigation is being conducted in Denmark, where a central national register is kept of every psychiatric hospitalization. The population being studied consists of 207 high-risk children and 104 low-risk children (normal controls). Each of the high-risk children is paired with another high-risk child. The assumption is that at most only one of each pair will actually become schizophrenic. It will therefore be possible to compare high-risk children who become schizophrenic with those who do not become schizophrenic. Each low-risk child is matched with a pair of high-risk children to form a triad. The expectation is that about 15 percent of the high-risk children and about 1 percent of the low-risk children will become schizophrenic.

Preliminary results indicate that as a group the high-risk children differ in many ways from the low-risk children. On all measures, however, the two groups show considerable overlap. A substantial proportion of high-risk children do not exhibit the traits and reactions identified with their group. Table 9.4 lists the significant findings noted for the two groups with respect to school behavior. During their school years, high-risk children tend to be withdrawn, sensitive, easily upset, and passive. They are loners who are avoided or rejected by their classmates. The descriptive picture derived from school behavior agrees well with other available data. The findings suggest that observations by teachers can be conveniently used for the early identification of children who have a high risk of becoming schizophrenic in later years.

Mednick and Schulsinger (1968) have also reported some other interesting preliminary findings:

1. There is a general trend for the births of high-risk subjects to have been attended with difficulties.

2. The high-risk group consistently shows a shorter period of latency of galvanic skin response (GSR) to stress stimuli than low-risk children. This shorter latency suggests that the high-risk group is characterized by a volatile autonomic nervous system that is easily and quickly aroused by mild stress. The high-risk group also shows faster autonomic recovery from the effects of stress stimuli.

3. Disorders of association, which are characteristically associated with schizophrenia, to some extent also are characteristic of high-risk children. As a group they tend to give more idiosyncratic and fragmented responses on single-word association tests.

4. The home lives of the high-risk children are more often characterized by frequent parental quarrels. The mother is seen as the dominant parent, and the children often see her as scolding, unreliable, and not to be trusted with their confidences. (But it must be remembered that the high-risk group was chosen from among children whose mothers, not fathers, were schizophrenic. It is reasonable to assume that this finding might be reversed if it were the fathers who were schizophrenic.)

Table 9.4. School Behavior of High-risk and Low-risk Children (As Reported by Teachers Without Knowledge of the Children's Group Membership).

	Percent "yes"	
Items on which groups differed at .05 level	High-risk	Low-risk
Was pupil left back?	10%	3%
Was pupil seen by psychologist?	13	1
Is pupil passive, taking no initiative?	52	36
Is pupil a loner, avoiding his classmates' activities?	33	21
Is pupil rejected by his classmates?	18	8
Does pupil get upset for almost no reason?	23	12
Does pupil become withdrawn when excited?	22	8
Is pupil abnormally active?	63	80
Is pupil abnormally subdued?	24	15
Is pupil abnormally sensitive?	22	18
Is pupil nervous?	37	14
Do you think the pupil will have a serious psychiatric illness in the future?	19	4
Did pupil attend any special classes (for retarded, for poor readers, etc.)?	24	12

Adapted from S. A. Mednick, "The Children of Schizophrenics," in *The Origins of Schizophrenia*, ed. J. Romano (New York: Excerpta Medica Foundation, 1967), pp. 179-200.

5. During adolescence, high-risk children show some early signs of functioning impairment. Their performance on intelligence tests is slightly below the performance of low-risk children. Tests that require concentration and effort show particular impairment. The high-risk child tends to have a restricted social life. These findings suggest the beginning of a pattern of withdrawal under stress.

Five years after the onset of the study, when the children were at an average age of twenty, follow-up data indicated that twenty of the high-risk children, or close to 10 percent, had manifested severely abnormal behavior. Of these disturbed children, thirteen had been admitted to psychiatric facilities or placed under psychiatric care. The remaining seven manifested bizarre symptomatic behavior or were described as schizoid, delinquent, or alcoholic.

Although these findings are limited to a few cases, preliminary data indicate that the high-risk disturbed children differ in several respects from matched high-risk children who so far have behaved normally. In comparison with the normal group, the disturbed children were separated from their mothers earlier because the mothers required hospitalization for psychiatric treatment. Perhaps the most significant finding to date is that the high-risk children who have already developed schizophrenia or some other psychiatric abnormality had a much higher incidence of complications during gestation or birth. Seventy percent of the disturbed high-risk group had histories of anoxia, prematurity, prolonged labor, umbilical cord complication, mother's illness during pregnancy, breech presentation, etc. Only 15 percent of the normal high-risk group had experienced complications during gestation or birth.

Although the hypothesis is still tentative, Mednick (1970) suggests that brain damage during pregnancy and birth, in combination with genetic and environmental factors, may be responsible for the development of some forms of schizophrenic behavior. The twin data in Table 9.3 provide significant confirmation of this hypothesis. When only one member of a pair of MZ twins develops schizophrenia, the affected twin more often has a history of asphyxia following delivery, birth complications, or central nervous system illness during early childhood. The implication that brain damage associated with pregnancy and birth complications may be a contributory factor raises the interesting possibility that the incidence of schizophrenia might be significantly reduced through improved prenatal and delivery care.

Intrafamilial Interactions

Adverse parent-child relationships, marital discord, confused communication, and other signs of intrafamilial disturbances have been repeatedly noted in studies of schizophrenics. The interpretation of these findings is another matter. Before serious consideration can be given to the idea that family pathology is the cause of schizophrenic behavior, it must be demonstrated that (1) the incidence of pathology is significantly higher in schizophrenic than in nonschizophrenic families, (2) the observed pathology is not the result of or a reaction to special problems created by the presence of one or more disordered members within the family, and (3) removal of a child from the assumed pathogenic influences of a schizophrenic family would decrease the risk of his developing the disorder.

The issue is still not fully resolved. It is generally recognized that the family environment is an important contributory factor in the personality structure and the general adjustment level of any individual. However, research data offer little support for the specific hypothesis that a pathological parental attitude or family disorganization is the direct cause of schizophrenic behavior. The basic contribution of the family to schizophrenia appears to be the transmission of defective genes from disturbed parents to their vulnerable offspring.

Parental attitudes. The popular stereotype of the domineering schizophrenic mother and the weak, ineffectual father is admittedly an oversimplification. The father is often the dominant parent (Fontana, 1966). The range of individual differences in the feelings and reactions of parents toward their preschizophrenic children and in their styles of child rearing is probably as great as among the general population. Fleck (1963) has suggested that the parent-child relationship varies with the sex of the patient. The mothers of schizophrenic sons tend to be dominant, intrusive, and engulfing, while the fathers are passive and ineffectual. In the case of schizophrenic daughters, the mothers are uninvolved and emotionally distant while the fathers are often paranoid and narcissistic. They are disparaging of the opposite sex, but at the same time may behave seductively toward their daughters. In other words, the same-sexed parent fails to provide an attractive model for identification, and the model presented by the parent of the opposite sex arouses distrust and hostility. The net effect is that identification with either parent is precluded (Caputo, 1963).

The variability of parent-child interactions in schizophrenic families makes it difficult to attach great causal significance to any particular interaction pattern. On the other hand, too many studies have described the mothers of chronic schizophrenics as possessive, overcontrolling, restrictive, and intrusive to allow us to dismiss the stereotype casually. Even if this description were found to fit only a relatively small proportion of schizophrenics, it would still be significant if these traits were more characteristic of the mothers of schizophrenics than of other mothers. But the evidence on this point is negative. In studies in which an attempt has been made to control for the possibility that the presence of a "problem" child may influence the mother's behavior, the results have been consistent and unequivocal: no significant differences in maternal overprotection, overcontrol, and related attitudes have been found between the mothers of schizophrenics and the mothers of brain-injured, retarded, or delinquent children and of psychologically normal children who are diabetic or physically handicapped. In his review of these studies, Mednick (1967) suggests that the family discord associated with schizophrenia, as well as the pathological attitudes of the mother, are the result rather than the cause of the disorder.

Marital discord. Although marital discord is by no means unknown in "normal" families, *schism* between husband and wife is especially characteristic of schizophrenic families (Lidz et al., 1965). In marriages that exist in a chronic state of disequilibrium and discord there is little or no sharing of problems and satisfactions. Each spouse is caught up in his or her own difficulties and in pursuing egocentric objectives. The disregard of the needs of the partner leads to increasing ill will, recurring threats of separation, and mistrust. Communication consists primarily of coercive efforts and defiance. Husband and wife compete in undercutting each other in the eyes of their children. This may be done to gain the children's sympathy and loyalty or simply to hurt and spite the marital partner. In this struggle the wife usually has an advantage of sorts. She spends more time with the children than the husband does, and the husband's frequent assumption that she and the children alike are naturally subordinate to him tends to arouse in her a resentment that the children find it easy to share. Human beings who are defined as inferior show a strong tendency to resent those who define themselves as superior, and to form a united front against them. The more the husband reduces his wife to the instrumental role of household servant, the more he is himself reduced to the instrumental role of provider of financial support. This is a game in which there can be no winners, only losers—not least the children of this sorry pair.

The term *marital skew* has been used to describe another mutually destructive pat-

ORIGINS OF SCHIZOPHRENIC BEHAVIOR

Gregory Bateson, a social anthropologist, who has called attention to the confused communication in schizophrenic families and especially to the "double bind" phenomenon.

tern, in which the psychopathology of the dominant partner is accepted and supported by the healthier spouse. This arrangement appears to satisfy the dependency or masochistic needs of the weaker partner. The accord presented by the parents leaves the children little choice but to go along with the *folie en famille*. The maintenance of the illusion that abnormality is normal requires adroitness in evading too close an examination of certain issues. A double set of standards may be required, one for home life and another for adjustment outside the home.

The double bind. The "double-bind" hypothesis has been advanced by Gregory Bateson and his associates (1956). The basic premise is that much of the irrational and disorganized behavior of schizophrenics is the result of their prolonged exposure during their formative years to a confusing pattern of contradictory messages. The prospective schizophrenic is required to make some response, but since the messages he is receiving are contradictory, whatever he says or does is bound to be "wrong"—an impossible situation. A child may be asked to come and sit on his mother's lap, for example, but her tone makes it clear that she hopes he won't.

It is usually assumed that the child is the victim and the mother the creator of the bind. However, children also are adept at putting their parents in situations in which they can't win no matter what they do.

The double bind consists essentially of three orders or injunctions. The primary message is usually verbally expressed and consists of an order to do or not to do something. This primary message is accompanied by a secondary contradictory communication that is usually expressed indirectly by posture, gesture, or tone of voice. The third message is an injunction, usually unexpressed but nevertheless quite clearly communicated, prohibiting the victim from escaping from the field. Since the messages are contradictory, no appropriate reaction is possible. The individual may have difficulty in recognizing that the messages are contradictory because one communication is verbal and the others are nonverbal and hence not clearly defined. If the child does understand that the messages are contradictory, and says so, he is simply told that he is mistaken. Bateson tells of a young schizophrenic who had made a fairly good recovery when he was visited in the hospital by his mother. He welcomed her by impulsively putting his arms around her shoulders, whereupon she stiffened. When the young man, sensing her hostile reaction, withdrew his arms, she asked, "Don't you love me anymore?" The son blushed, and the mother said, "Dear, you must not be so easily embarrassed and afraid of your feelings." When he returned to the ward, the patient promptly assaulted an aide.

Jay Haley (1960) has suggested a modification of the double bind that has the same result of confused communication. Members of the schizophrenic's family are observed to be constantly qualifying and disqualifying their own statements and the statements of the others. They say one thing and do another. The letters of mothers of schizophrenics contain interesting examples of this incongruence (Weakland and Fry, 1962). In writing to her hospitalized schizophrenic son, a mother may caution him against the dangers of smoking, and then add in a postscript that she is mailing him a carton of cigarettes.

The child as victim. The family theories of schizophrenia require some modification to take account of the fact that only about 15 percent of the children and siblings of schizophrenics manifest overt signs of the disorder. One possibility is that the deleterious effects of family pathology are restricted to those members of the family who are genetically predisposed to mental disorder.

Those favoring an environmental point of view have argued that the differential outcome in children of the same family may be due to the fact that the parents have a closer relationship with the schizophrenic child than with the others. The standard explanation (offered by Lu, 1961, 1962; Wynne and Singer, 1963; and others) is that from infancy the child who later becomes schizophrenic is more deeply involved in the family's emotional life than his nonschizophrenic siblings. The potential schizophrenic submits to the mother's domination, while the normal sibling rebels. The vulnerable child is confined to the constricted, pathological atmosphere of the home; the normal sibling enjoys greater

freedom and becomes more involved with the outside world. To a greater degree than his siblings, the preschizophrenic child accepts the contradictory parental expectations that he be dependent and at the same time strive for perfection and high achievement.

The child "selected" as a victim may be the most docile one, the biologically weakest, or the child who happens to be born during a period of maximal marital conflict or family crisis (Stabenau and Pollin, 1968). On the basis of their retrospective study, Prout and White (1956) conclude that the preschizophrenic child has been more sensitive, more dependent, and less outgoing than his healthier sibling from infancy. His greater need for attention and support may have invited maternal overprotection.

Family therapists have suggested that the dynamics and needs of the family system may require different children to play different roles. Thus one child may be selected to serve as the "sick" or "bad one," another the "healthy one," and a third the "conscience of the family." Lidz and his co-workers (1965) question whether many of the children of schizophrenic families are actually unaffected. They agree that only about 15 percent of the siblings are clinically schizophrenic, but claim that a large additional number suffer from a variety of other mild or borderline conditions.

The assumption of a family etiology of schizophrenia has certain implications for treatment. According to Lidz (1967), a basic aim is to free the individual of his symbiotic ties with his parents and to help him become a person in his own right, with his own separate identity. Distortions in behavior are interpreted not as personal defenses but rather as learned distortions that have been imposed upon him by his parents as they attempted to work out their own problems. An important function of the therapist is to encourage the patient to accept and trust his own feelings and ideas, and to question the ideas and feelings he has acquired from his parents.

Adoption Studies

The strongest evidence against the importance of family environment as the cause of schizophrenia comes from studies of children of schizophrenic mothers who have been reared from infancy in foster or adoptive homes. L. L. Heston (1966) reported the pioneer investigation in this area, and a more detailed analysis of findings has been presented by Heston and Denney (1968). The experimental subjects were forty-seven children born to hospitalized schizophrenic mothers. Fifty control subjects were selected from the records of the same foundling homes that received the experimental subjects. The mothers of the control children had no history of psychiatric disorder. All of the children in both groups were considered physically normal at birth. The two groups were matched individually for sex, length of time in child-care institutions, and type of eventual placement (adoptive home, foster home, or institution). The psychiatric outcome was determined when the children in the two groups had reached an average age of thirty-six years.

The results strongly support a genetic etiology for schizophrenia. Five of the forty-seven children of schizophrenic mothers, or 11 percent, also became schizophrenic. None of the control group of adopted children of normal parents developed schizophrenia. Another 44 percent of the experimental group had histories of other forms of psychopathology, including neurosis, sociopathic personality, and criminal behavior. Only 18 percent of the control group had histories of some type of psychiatric or social disability other than schizophrenia. The divorce rate was the same for the two groups. One other interesting finding was that the experimental group had more colorful life histories. As adults, the normal children of schizophrenic mothers were more spontaneous, had more imaginative hobbies, and were engaged in more creative work than the normal children of normal mothers.

Heston's main conclusion, that children of schizophrenic mothers reared in adoptive homes have about the same expectancy of becoming schizophrenic as children reared by their biological mothers, has been confirmed by other studies (Karlson, 1966; Rosenthal et al., 1968). Karlson studied outcome among the siblings of schizophrenics who had been adopted before the age of one and reared apart from their biological parents. He found that six out of twenty-nine siblings of schizophrenics who had been reared in adoptive homes also became schizophrenic. This represents a total of 21 percent, which is slightly higher than the figure usually found for siblings of schizophrenics reared in their parental homes. None of the foster siblings reared in the same homes as the adopted children became schizophrenic. Rosenthal and his associates compared the adopted children of schizophrenic parents with the adopted children of nonschizophrenic parents, and found that out of a total of thirty-nine in the former group, three were eventually diagnosed as schizophrenic and another six were considered borderline schizophrenics. Out of a total of forty-seven children of nonschizophrenic parents, none were diagnosed as schizophrenic and only one was considered a borderline case.

PSYCHODYNAMIC THEORIES

Recent psychodynamic approaches are represented in the writings of Sylvano Arieti and Ronald Laing. Arieti (1967) has outlined four stages in the development of schizophrenia. The first stage, in early childhood, is the seeding period. The future patient is raised in a home environment that offers him only a modicum of security and trust. Early relations with his parents are characterized by intense anxiety and devastating hostility. The child is forced to sustain the impact of intense negative emotions, of tension, fear, and anxiety. He tends to participate as little as possible in the unpleasant external reality, and escapes into an overdeveloped

Sylvano Arieti, a psychiatrist, whose postulated four stages in the development of schizophrenia are a significant contribution to the psychodynamic interpretation of that disorder.

fantasy world. For a longer period than the average child, he interprets the world, life, and himself on the basis of images, symbols, magical wish fulfillment, and other primary processes. Ideas of causality are confused. He believes that whatever occurs is brought about by unpleasant clusters of images that represent his parents, and especially his mother. With the development of language, he tends to interpret the world "paleologically." Similarity is confused with identity. Certain characteristics of his mother or his ways of dealing with her are unconsciously generalized to all women. His self-identity is very shaky.

Despite the emotional turmoil of this period, most of these children go on to the second stage, in which behavior is more realistic and appropriate. The child becomes aware that the family does not constitute the whole world, and he begins to build up hope for his own future. Although he may still harbor serious doubts about his personal worth, he is able to construct a more stable self-image. In the majority of cases the process of disorder stops at this stage, so that a psychosis never develops. The individual more or less succeeds in adjusting to life.

If the defenses acquired during the second stage are ineffective, the child proceeds to the third stage, which has its onset around the time of puberty. Sexual maturity, with its implications of broader life problems with which the individual will be expected to cope, may be a precipitating factor. If handicapped by defects in his early development, the young person may come to believe not only that his family is unwilling to accept his inadequacy, but that the world at large finds him wanting. Adolescents who later become schizophrenic tend to select concepts and categories that have a gloomy emotional tone. They see these concepts as final; they permit no exceptions. The future patient acquires a negative self-image. Particularly in the sexual realm he sees himself as inadequate, as having no definite sexual identity, as a homosexual or undesirable as a sexual partner. He perceives his future as bleak and hopeless. As long as he lives he will be unacceptable to others. He does not fit; he is alone. His self-image is so unfavorable that he may become unacceptable to himself. It is at this point that *preschizophrenic panic* occurs. There is an upsurge of the repressed early experiences of the first stage. The individual sees himself as totally defeated, worthless, and with no possibility of redemption.

Unless this inner demoralization is arrested, the individual goes on to the fourth or psychotic stage. The psychosis represents a defense against his terrifying and devastating self-image. The paranoid process frees him from the need for self-accusation. "Other people" now call him names, accuse him, and ridicule him. The "external" persecution causes fear and anxiety, but this is more bearable than self-blame. One can defend oneself against external danger, deny external accusations, fight back against persecutors, but there is no defense or escape from self-accusation. During the period of panic, everything "inside" the patient appears in a state of turbulent change. This too is externalized during the psychotic stage, when the outside world appears difficult and strange.

Laing (1965) has presented an existential-phenomenological interpretation of schizophrenia. His main point is that the schizophrenic has failed to develop a firm and cohesive sense of personal identity. His insecurity concerning his existence as a real person is traced to early childhood, when he felt unloved, unnoticed, or rejected. Because of his tenuous concept of self, he cannot cope effectively and as an autonomous person with the problems of life. The psychosis represents an attempt to preserve the self. The bizarreness and obscurity of behavior often noted in schizophrenics is their way of protecting themselves from intrusion. The schizoid person feels exposed and vulnerable to others, different, lonely, isolated, and filled with despair. He is frightened of the world, afraid that any contact with others will be penetrative, fragmenting, and engulfing. His self-concept is so limited that he believes that if he shares anything of himself with others, he will be depleted and sucked dry. Despite his longing to be loved for his real self, the schizophrenic is extremely afraid of being loved. Any form of understanding by others is a threat to his defensive system, which is distorted and subjective.

To Laing, the schizophrenic suffers from a divided self. One part consists of a secret self that is characterized by an inner withholding of compliance and passive defiance of the outer world. The other part is a false outer self that represents the patient's surface compliance with the expectations of significant others in his life. The false self serves to maintain the appearance of normality. When a psychosis is fully developed, the veil of the false self is removed and we see the secret true self.

SCHIZOTAXIA, SCHIZOTYPE, AND SCHIZOPHRENIA

Paul Meehl (1962) has outlined a comprehensive theory of schizophrenia that takes account of the interaction of genetic and environmental factors. For Meehl, the significant diagnostic indicators of schizophrenia are (1) disturbances in thinking or "cognitive slippage"; (2) interpersonal aversiveness—the patient's distrust of social involvement because of fear of rejection; (3) anhedonia, or defect in the capacity to experience pleasure; and (4) ambivalence or affect confusion, characterized by simultaneous feelings of love and hate.

Meehl starts with the assumption that the genetic predisposition to schizophrenia consists of some defect in neural integration. This inherited neural defect, which he calls *schizotaxia*, is the essential prerequisite. Persons lacking this genetic neural defect have little or no risk of developing schizophrenia, but all schizotaxic individuals develop *schizotypic* personalities regardless of the favorableness of their social learning histories. Schizotypic personalities exhibit in varying degrees the four behavior traits listed above. Whether the process stops at this level or goes on to an actual psychosis depends on several additional factors. Schizotypic persons who have the good fortune to inherit little readiness for anxiety, physical vigor, and strong resistance to stress, and whose interpersonal learning experiences are favorable, become well-compensated "normal" schiz-

Paul E. Meehl, a distinguished clinical psychologist. His innovative contributions include the concepts of schizotaxia, schizotype, and schizophrenia.

otypes. The minority of schizotypics, who inherit great readiness for anxiety, little physical vigor, and low resistance to stress, and who are subjected to an ambivalent regime imposed by a domineering, possessive, "cold" parent, go on to develop the clinical signs of schizophrenia.

SOCIAL AND CULTURAL FACTORS

Social Class

In 1939 Faris and Dunham reported an inverse relationship between social class and incidence rates of schizophrenia as reflected in first admissions to mental hospitals serving the Chicago area. Subsequent investigations have consistently reported an excessive rate of schizophrenia in the lowest (Class V) social group for large industrialized urban communities (Mishler and Scotch, 1963). However, for Classes I through IV (professional to semiskilled workers), the occurrence of schizophrenia is about the same (Dunham, 1964). It has

also been found that the concentration of schizophrenia in the lowest social class does not occur in small towns and in rural communities (Kohn, 1968).

Two theories have been suggested to account for the unusually high rate of schizophrenia in the lowest socioeconomic strata of large urban communities. The first is that schizophrenia is produced by the conditions of poverty, mobility, and social isolation that prevail in disorganized slum areas. The alternate explanation, which is often referred to as the "social selection" or "drift" hypothesis, is that the general social incompetence of potential schizophrenics causes them gradually to drift down to the bottom of the socioeconomic strata.

Most of the evidence favors the latter interpretation. As early as 1953, Gerard and Houston noted that the inverse relationship of social class to schizophrenia did not hold for patients admitted directly to mental hospitals from their own family settings. The excess of schizophrenics with low socioeconomic backgrounds was due entirely to the disproportionate number of young schizophrenics who had left home to live in rented rooms and cheap lodging houses. Similar findings have been reported in England (Hare, 1956). The downward drift of schizophrenics has been most clearly demonstrated in studies comparing the occupational levels of schizophrenic males with those of their fathers. In another study conducted in England, the occupational levels of the fathers of schizophrenics were found to be on a par with those for the general population (Goldberg and Morrison, 1963). However, the sons who developed schizophrenia showed a downward drift in occupational status as compared with their fathers. A similar decline in the occupational and social status of schizophrenic sons has been confirmed by studies in Norway (Grunfeld and Salvesen, 1968) and in Rochester, New York (Turner and Wagenfeld, 1967).

Once the schizophrenic drops to the bottom of the heap, he stays there. In addition, a substantial proportion of his children who inherit a predisposition to schizophrenia fail to move up, so they too eventually contribute to the heavy representation of schizophrenic patients at the lowest socioeconomic level in large urban areas.

Isolation and Alienation

The underlying causes of the schizophrenic's estrangement from his social environment may be traced to an innate temperament that favors introvertive behavior and unfavorable parent-child experiences. Once started, however, the alienation process itself is an important factor in developing and sustaining symptomatic behavior. The more the child avoids interaction and involvement with others, the less opportunity he has to acquire the skills necessary for harmonious interpersonal relationships. In addition, the isolated child has limited opportunity to acquire the beliefs, values, rules, and practices of his social group. His perceptions of himself, his peers, and the outer world are increasingly shaped by inner fantasies. The absence of friends and interpersonal communication deprives him of feedback that might correct his distorted perceptions and idiosyncrasies.

The preschizophrenic is often keenly aware of his growing estrangement and may make vacillating efforts to relate to others, but his social incompetence, basic distrust, and lack of empathy make him open to rebuffs, which reinforce his tendency to withdraw. The breach between the preschizophrenic and the larger community is progressively widened, and he eventually abandons whatever social amenities he may have acquired (Millon, 1969). He is increasingly mystified by the rules of interpersonal relations and experiences difficulty in making sense of the actions of others. Perplexed and bewildered, he feels doomed to wander alone in a strange and frightening world.

Cultural Differences

The impact of the culture in shaping the overt symptoms of schizophrenia is generally accepted. Whether cultural factors affect the incidence rate is less certain. Murphy (1968) has questioned the validity of earlier reports of the low incidence of schizophrenia among the Hutterites. On the other hand, he has presented some evidence that the incidence of schizophrenia is excessively high among Irish Catholics, the people of northwest Croatia, and the Tamil-speaking people of south India and Ceylon. The most clear-cut data relate to the latter group. Several studies have reported a higher incidence of schizophrenia among Tamil university students in Singapore than is found among Chinese and Malay students. In addition, the rate of mental disorder in the Indian army has been found to be significantly higher among Tamil soldiers than among soldiers coming from other regions of the country. Murphy attributes the excessive rates in these three ethnic groups to cultural conflicts rather than to any specific social factor.

WHAT CAUSES SCHIZOPHRENIA?
The Case of the Genain Quadruplets

The multiple interacting causes of schizophrenia may best be illustrated by a case study. This case is unusual in that it involves the occurrence of schizophrenia in all four members of a set of identical quadruplets. The study of the Genain quadruplets, reported by Rosenthal and his colleagues (1963), is a model of comprehensive coverage.

Myra, Nora, Iris, and Hester all exhibited schizophrenic behavior by the age of twenty-four. Their shared symptoms included catatonic posturing, hallucinations, panic reactions, social withdrawal, irritability, crying, screaming, vomiting, multiple aches and pains, confusion, blurred vision, and exhaustion. Each of the girls also exhibited certain distinctive reactions of her own, however, and they showed considerable variability in the severity of their psychoses and in its outcome. Myra, the healthiest one, made a good recovery and married. At last report, when the quads were in their thirties, she was living in the community. The other three girls have shown a progressive downward pattern. All were in state hospitals at the time the study was concluded. Of the three, Nora had the most favorable prognosis and Hester the least favorable; Hester, in fact, was considered a hopeless chronic case.

On the basis of the wealth of data collected on the quads, confirmation could be found for practically all theories of schizophrenia. The father's family included several members with histories of psychosis. Atypical electroencephalographical records, suggesting brain damage, were observed in the father and all of the girls. The turbulent home atmosphere and unwholesome interaction of the various members of the family provide support for social learning theories of schizophrenia. Parental quarrels were frequent and severe. The mother was domineering and overcontrolling. The father was a dependent, ineffectual person who periodically reacted against his inadequacy with violence, rage, and threats. Both parents were intrusive and denied the girls any privacy.

Both parents were unduly concerned with their health. The parental hypochondriacal model may have contributed to the host of somatic symptoms that the quads also manifested. For the mother, who was a frustrated nurse, the home was her hospital and later a private psychiatric ward. She was fearful of the health of the quads, constantly giving them medication and putting them to bed for long periods when they showed signs of the slightest fatigue. All the girls were periodically enuretic, even during adolescence.

From early childhood the quads exhibited traits identified with the premorbid personality of schizophrenics. They were described by their teachers as introverted, frail, anxious, reserved, stand-offish, precise, proper, and lacking in initiative, spontaneity, and drive. In part these characteristics might have reflected inborn temperament qualities, but the parents did everything possible to reinforce them. The quads were often literally fenced in, denied outside contacts, and made to keep to themselves as a self-contained and impenetrable unit. They were deprived of opportunities to form associations and contacts outside the home, to learn what other people were like and how to behave with them. Even after they had grown up the girls were treated as children. All the members of the family were symbiotically involved with one another. Their attitude toward the outside world was one of apprehensive distrust. This attitude was particularly encouraged by the father, who saw threats everywhere. On occasions he patrolled the premises as an armed guard.

The secluded, socially isolated family unit provided abundant examples of irrational behavior to serve as models for the quads. The paternal grandmother, who lived with the family until the children were seven years old, was a highly unstable, irrational, suspicious, superstitious person, who drove the quads' mother almost to the point of suicide. The father was ill-tempered, expressed homicidal threats, drank to excess, had black-out spells, and heard voices. At times he would attempt to gain the sympathy of the quads by feigning illness. More often he would express his inadequacy as a parent by violent shouting and fault-finding. As soon as one of the daughters became mentally disordered, he would concentrate his criticisms and verbal abuse on another, until all were disturbed.

As the strong member of the family, the mother used her position to keep the girls completely dependent on her. Her unresolved problems created difficulties for all the girls. Hester, the troublesome rebel, was crushed and rejected. The other three were prevented from developing personalities of their own and were assigned roles that represented some component of the mother's personality. Communication within the family was fuzzy, indirect, and often provided a classic example of the double bind. An unusual feature that illustrates both the poor communication and the symbiotic relationship was the phenomenon of echoing. When one of the girls was asked a question by an outsider in the presence of the mother, the mother would answer and the girl addressed would then echo her response. The isolated, restricted life of the quads prevented them from exploring, testing, and checking their perceptions and misconceptions of themselves and the outside world. In a way, irrational behavior was the standard within the family. Healthy members were resented and put under pressure until they too conformed.

The scapegoat theory of schizophrenia, which assumes that the family unconsciously selects and exploits one of its members as the victim for its latent pathological components, is supported by the history of Hester. Why was Hester selected? As the last-born baby, the frailest, shortest, oddest, slowest to develop, and least intelligent of the quads, she was the natural victim. The selection appears to have been made mainly by the mother, who was critical of Hester from her first day because she cried all the time, was a feeding problem, and apparently was less docile than the other quads. According to the mother, Hester was always a problem to her. When she was young, it was cry, cry, cry. Later she was difficult to manage. If the mother tried to correct her, she became obstinate, fought back and broke things. Gradually the mother came to identify Hester's hostility and sexuality with her disliked husband. She described Hester as an extremely troublesome, unappreciative, deceiving, destructive child. Hester was also the chief target for the father's hostility. Her sisters accepted the designation of Hester as the "bad child" and the "baby," and were somewhat ashamed of her because of her masturbation and poor schoolwork.

The onset of Hester's mental illness probably occurred before the age of fourteen, but her behavior was considered symptomatic of badness rather than of mental disorder. The early onset of her psychosis is suggested by the fact that by the age of fourteen her IQ test score had dropped from 105 to 77. Because of poor grades, she dropped out of high school in her junior year. All of her sisters graduated from high school and later obtained employment as secretaries. Hester was assigned the role of kitchen maid, the Cinderella who was picked on by everyone and expected to do all the dirty work. She accepted this negative image and acted accordingly. She was in fact bad tempered, destructive, and aggressive.

Hester was the personification of her mother's negative feelings toward belligerence and sexuality. But she was not the only one to be treated as an extension of some component of the mother's personality. Each daughter internalized and attempted to live out her assigned role, and in so doing sacrificed her own personality. Iris represented the mother's repressed drives. She was assigned the role of the unappreciated, neglected child, whose demonstrated competence was never rewarded or even acknowledged. The mother's positive feelings were reserved for Nora and Myra. Nora, the firstborn and the healthiest during infancy, was expected to be the sweet, dependent child who was attached to the mother so completely that she could have no inner life of her own. Myra represented a projection of the mother's emotional needs for independence. In later years, Myra supplanted Nora as the mother's favorite.

Chaotic sexuality prevailed in the Genain home. The father, who became impotent by the time the girls were ten years old, frequently accused his wife of promiscuity. He refused to permit the girls to go out on dates, even when they were grown up and working, for fear they would become sexually involved. At the same time, he would pat their buttocks, feel their breasts, and enter their rooms to watch them dress and undress. The mother, who had had an illicit love affair when she was sixteen, was preoccupied with real or imagined sexual misconduct on the part of others. She was particularly concerned with the sexuality of Hester, who started masturbating at the age of three. The mother considered Hester a bad, oversexed girl. She attributed Hester's subsequent breakdown to an unsubstantiated confession she forced from her to the effect that Hester had on numerous occasions been sexually molested by the school janitor.

Despite severe punishment, Hester continued to masturbate, and was soon followed by Iris. When they were twelve, Hester and Iris were discovered by their mother engaging in mutual masturbation. A doctor was consulted about the problem, and he recommended that both girls be circumcised. The parents went along with his recommendation. The hospital records indicate that Iris and Hester were admitted for circumcision and the release of adhesions about the clitoris. The mother later reported that the doctor removed "all the mucous membrane to the uterus." Both girls resisted the operation and broke their stitches. Acting on the doctor's orders, the mother tied the girls' hands to their beds for thirty nights. This traumatic experience did not stop the masturbation, however.

According to the mother, three of the girls had a terrifying sexual experience shortly before the onset of psychosis. Within a span of two years, one after another of the girls allegedly found herself alone with a man (in an elevator, an office, a washroom). The man exposed himself, pushed the girl against the wall, and tried to undress her. In each instance the girl escaped being raped by fighting back and screaming. The exception was Hester. The mother was pretty sure that Hester had had a similar experience, but did not complain because she liked it, and probably even encouraged the fellow.

In summary, the quads probably inherited a genetic predisposition to schizophrenia from their father. Under more favorable circumstances, one or all of them might have avoided becoming psychotic. The unwholesome home atmosphere and the personality defects of the parents did more than activate an inherent predisposition. From infancy onward, the quads were exposed to adverse environmental and learning experiences that reinforced and augmented their inherent vulnerability. The eventual schizophrenic outcome was the product of the complementary interaction of genetic and environmental factors. The variation in severity of the quadruplets' psychoses may be attributed to variations in the prenatal as well as the postnatal environment. At birth Hester and Iris weighed much less than the other two girls.

SUMMARY

Research data have clearly established that genetic factors are of key importance in predisposing an individual to the development of schizophrenic behavior. However, the phenotypic expression of the genetic predisposition is dependent on the interactive effect of other factors. In the absence of additional unfavorable agents, the genetic predisposition is not activated, but it is transmitted to offspring in full strength. The genetic component appears to consist in part of an introverted temperament. There is growing evidence that a contributory biological agent in some instances is mild brain damage resulting from complications during pregnancy and delivery. The confused status of findings with respect to the role of the family may reflect the significance of the varying forms of interaction of the child and his parents. If the parents have psychological problems of their own, as they frequently do in schizophrenic families, their pathological interactions with one another and with the child may contribute to the development of schizophrenic or other abnormal reactions in their relatively more vulnerable children. Conversely, the defective functioning of the genetically predisposed, introverted, and mildly brain-damaged child may promote pathological emotional ties between the child and his biological or adoptive parents.

References

Arieti, S. "New View on the Psychodynamics of Schizophrenia." *American Journal of Psychiatry* 124, no. 4 (1967): 453-58.

Bateson, G.; Jackson, D.; Haley, J.; and Weakland, J. "Toward a Theory of Schizophrenia." *Behavioral Science* 1 (1956): 251-64.

Caputo, D. V. "The Parents of the Schizophrenic." *Family Process* 2 (1963): 339-56.

Dunham, H. W. "Social Class and Schizophrenia." *American Journal of Orthopsychiatry* 34 (1964): 634-42.

Erlenmeyer-Kimling, L. "Studies on the Offspring of Two Schizophrenic Parents." In *The Transmission of Schizophrenia*, ed D. Rosenthal and S. S. Kety, pp. 65-83. New York: Pergamon Press, 1968.

Faris, R., and Dunham, H. W. *Mental Disorders in Urban Areas.* Chicago: University of Chicago Press, 1939.

Fleck, S. "Comparison of Parent-Child Relationships of Male and Female Schizophrenics." *Archives of General Psychiatry* 8 (1963): 1-7.

Fontana, A. "Familial Etiology of Schizophrenia: Is a Scientific Methodology Possible?" *Psychological Bulletin* 66 (1966): 214-27.

Gerard, D., and Houston, L. G. "Family Setting and the Social Ecology of Schizophrenia." *Psychiatric Quarterly* 27 (1953): 90-101.

Goldberg, E. M., and Morrison, S. L. "Schizophrenia and Social Class." *British Journal of Psychiatry* 109 (1963): 785-802.

Gottesman, I. I., and Shields, J. "Contribution of Twin Studies to Perspectives on Schizophrenia." In *Progress in Experimental Personality Research*, ed. B. A. Maher, vol. 3, pp. 1-84. New York: Academic Press, 1966.

Grunfeld, B., and Salvesen, C. "Functional Psychoses and Social Status." *British Journal of Psychiatry* 114 (1968): 733-37.

Haley, J. "Direct Study of Child-Parent Interactions." *American Journal of Orthopsychiatry* 30 (1960): 460-67.

Hare, E. H. "Mental Illness and Social Conditions in Bristol." *Journal of Mental Science* 102 (1956): 349-57.

Heston, L. L. "Psychiatric Disorders in Foster-Home-Reared Children of Schizophrenic Mothers." *British Journal of Psychiatry* 112 (1966): 819-25.

———— and Denny, D. "Interactions Between Early Life Experience and Biological Factors in Schizophrenia." In *The Transmission of Schizophrenia*, ed. D. Rosenthal and S. S. Kety, pp. 363-76. New York: Pergamon Press, 1968.

Karlson, J. *The Biological Basis of Schizophrenia.* Springfield, Ill.: Charles C Thomas, 1966.

Kohn, M. L. "Social Class and Schizophrenia: A Critical Review." In *The Transmission of Schizophrenia*, ed. D. Rosenthal and S. S. Kety, pp. 155-73. New York: Pergamon Press, 1968.

Kringlen, E. "An Epidemiological-Clinical Twin Study on Schizophrenia." In *The

Transmission of Schizophrenia, ed. D. Rosenthal and S. S. Kety, pp. 49-64. New York: Pergamon Press, 1968.

Laing, R. D. *The Divided Self: An Existential Study in Sanity and Madness.* Baltimore: Penguin Books, 1965.

Lidz, T. "The Influence of Family Studies on the Treatment of Schizophrenia." *Psychiatry* 32 (1967): 235-51.

———, Fleck, S., and Cornelison, A. R. *Schizophrenia and the Family.* New York: International Universities Press, 1965.

Lu, Y. "Mother-Child Role Relationships in Schizophrenia: A Comparison of Schizophrenic Patients with Nonschizophrenic Siblings." *Psychiatry* 24 (1961): 133-42.

———. "Contradictory Parental Expectations in Schizophrenia." *Archives of General Psychiatry* 6 (1962): 219-34.

Mednick, S. A. "The Children of Schizophrenics." In *The Origins of Schizophrenia*, ed. J. Romano, pp. 179-200. New York: Excerpta Medica Foundation, 1967.

———. "Breakdown in Individuals at High Risk for Schizophrenia: Possible Predispositional Perinatal Factors." *Mental Hygiene* 54, no. 1 (1970): 50-61.

——— and Schulsinger, F. "Some Premorbid Characteristics Related to Breakdown in Children with Schizophrenic Mothers." In *The Transmission of Schizophrenia*, ed. D. Rosenthal and S. S. Kety. New York: Pergamon Press, 1968.

Meehl, P. E. "Schizotaxia, Schizotypy, Schizophrenia." *American Psychologist* 17 (1962): 827-38.

Millon, T. *Modern Psychopathology.* Philadelphia: Saunders, 1969.

Mishler, E. G., and Scotch, N. A. "Sociocultural Factors in the Epidemiology of Schizophrenia: A Review." *Psychiatry* 26 (1963): 315-51.

Murphy, H. B. M. "Cultural Factors in the Genesis of Schizophrenia." In *The Transmission of Schizophrenia*, ed. D. Rosenthal and S. S. Kety, pp. 137-55. New York: Pergamon Press, 1968.

Pollin, W., and Stabenau, J. R. "Biological, Psychological, and Historical Differences in a Series of Monozygotic Twins Discordant for Schizophrenia." In *The Transmission of Schizophrenia*, ed. D. Rosenthal and S. S. Kety, pp. 317-32. New York: Pergamon Press, 1968.

Prout, C. T., and White, M. A. "The Schizophrenic's Sibling." *Journal of Nervous and Mental Disease* 123 (1956) 162-70.

Rosenthal, D. "An Historical and Methodological Review of Genetic Studies of Schizophrenia." In *The Origins of Schizophrenia*, ed. J. Romano, pp. 15-26. New York: Excerpta Medica Foundation, 1967.

——— et al. *The Genain Quadruplets.* New York: Basic Books, 1963.

———; Wender, P. H.; Kety, S. S.; Schulsinger, F.; Welner, J.; and Ostergaard, L. "Schizophrenics' Offspring Reared in Adoptive Homes." In *The Transmission of Schizophrenia*, ed. D. Rosenthal and S. S. Kety, pp. 377-91. New York: Pergamon Press, 1968.

Shields, J. "Summary of the Genetic Evidence." In *The Transmission of Schizophrenia*, ed. D. Rosenthal and S. S. Kety, pp. 95-126. New York: Pergamon Press, 1968.

Slater, E. "A Review of Earlier Evidence on Genetic Factors in Schizophrenia." In *The Transmission of Schizophrenia*, ed. D. Rosenthal and S. S. Kety, pp. 15-26. New York: Pergamon Press, 1968.

Stabenau, J., and Pollin, W. "Comparative Life History Differences of Families of Schizophrenics, Delinquents, and 'Normals.'" *American Journal of Psychiatry* 124 (1968): 1526-34.

Tienari, P. "Schizophrenia in Monozygotic Male Twins." In *The Transmission of Schizophrenia*, ed. D. Rosenthal and S. S. Kety, pp. 27-36. New York: Pergamon Press, 1968.

Turner, R. J., and Wagenfeld, M. O. "Occupational Mobility and Schizophrenia: An Assessment of the Social Causal and Social Selection Hypotheses." *American Sociological Review* 32 (1967): 104-13.

Weakland, J. H., and Fry, W. F. "Letters of Mothers of Schizophrenics." *American Journal of Orthopsychiatry* 32 (1962): 604-27.

Wynne, L., and Singer, M. "Thought Disorder and Family Relations of Schizophrenics: A Research Strategy." *Archives of General Psychiatry* 9 (1963): 191-98.

Melencolia,
Albrecht Dürer

Affective psychoses are distinguished by extreme disturbances of mood, either elation or deep depression, which dominate mental life to such an extent that a person's feelings, ideas, and attitudes are relatively unaffected by rational considerations and factual data. The euphoric individual continues to express grandiose ideas and to proclaim his supreme happiness even after his uncontrolled behavior has caused him to be hospitalized. The depressed patient is convinced of the seriousness of imaginary or trivial misdeeds and the hopelessness of his future. The pervasiveness of the distorted emotional perspective seriously interferes with the individual's capacity to cope with the ordinary demands of daily life in a reasonably effective and appropriate fashion. Affective psychoses account for approximately 6 percent of first admissions to public mental hospitals in the United States and 15 percent of first admissions to private hospitals. Some countries make more frequent use of this diagnostic category than we do. About 80 percent of patients hospitalized for affective disorders are depressed. The remaining 20 percent are characterized by elation or alternating periods of elation and depression.

The three major types of affective psychoses listed in the 1968 *Diagnostic Manual* of the American Psychiatric Association are manic-depressive psychosis, involutional melancholia, and psychotic depressive reaction. The terms "mania" and "melancholia" have long histories. Both diagnoses were included in the ancient Hippocratic classification of mental disease. When Kraepelin developed his nomenclature system in 1896, he proposed that the diagnoses of manic-depressive psychosis and involutional melancholia be restricted to emotional disturbances without demonstrable brain pathology and for which the prognosis was relatively favorable. Other "functional" psychotic reactions, marked mainly by disordered thinking, early onset of symptoms, and poor prognosis, were assigned to the new category of dementia praecox.

Kraepelin's original description and differentiation of manic-depressive psychosis and involutional melancholia have been retained in the 1968 APA classification. Depressions that begin after the age of forty-five are classified as involutional melancholia. Agitation, feelings of guilt, and somatic complaints are commonly associated with the depression of involutional melancholia. The diagnosis of manic-depressive psychosis is applied to spontaneously occurring mood disturbances that begin during early adulthood and are marked by either elation and hyperactivity or depression and retardation of mental and motor activity. The concept of *psychotic depressive reaction* is of more recent origin. This diagnosis is favored when the individual has no prior history of affective disturbances and the depressive mood is attributable to some obvious loss or misfortune.

The relative frequency of occurrence of the three affective disorders, as noted among admissions to outpatient psychiatric services, is shown in Table 10.1. Approximately 40 percent of admissions are classified as manic depressives. Psychotic depressive and involutional melancholia patients each account for about 30 percent of admissions with affective psychoses. Four times as many women as men are diagnosed as psychotic depressives. For the other two affective disorders, the sex ratio is 3 to 2 in favor of women.

MANIC-DEPRESSIVE REACTIONS

The hypothesis that the symptoms of mental disorders represent extreme variations of normal personality traits is particularly applicable to manic-depressive reactions. Many normal individuals have periodic mood swings. For no apparent reason they are sometimes energetic, enthusiastic, optimistic, and highly confident. At other times they go to the opposite extreme and are mildly depressed, discouraged, relatively uncommunicative, self-deprecatory, and listless. When mood swings remain within acceptable limits, these individuals are referred to as *cycloid* or *cyclothymic* personalities.

A manic attack is an extreme upswing, accompanied by excessive elation, hyperactivity, accelerated speech, and flight of ideas. A depressive attack is an extreme downswing, marked by a pervasive mood of sadness, motor retardation, poverty of ideas, and a slowing of mental activity.

Manic attacks generally occur at an earlier age than depressive reactions, and they are usually of shorter duration. Prior to the discovery of effective remedies for relieving symptoms, the average duration of manic attacks was about three months and depressive reactions lasted about six to eight months. With modern drugs, overt manic symptoms can be brought under control in a week and depressive symptoms controlled in ten to fifteen days. Drug therapy is continued for several months. If medication is discontinued too soon there is a return of symptoms. Following the termination of the attack, the individual typically shows no aftereffects and becomes his old self again. Months or years later he may have one or more subsequent attacks. The disorder has been called an intermittent psychosis because of the frequent recurrence and disappearance of symptoms. Initial and later attacks may be either of the manic or depressive type.

The frequently noted fact that a person may on one occasion exhibit a manic reaction and later on be depressed is the basis for considering manic-depressive psychosis a single clinical entity. Aretaeus, a famous physician of ancient Rome, is credited with first recognizing the dual nature of the disorder. In 1854 Falret suggested the name

Table 10.1. Frequency of Occurrence of the Three Affective Disorders (Admissions to Outpatient Psychiatric Services, by Sex, United States, 1969).

Diagnosis	Total Number	Percent by Sex	
		Male	Female
Manic depressive	12,174	41	59
Psychotic depressive	8,970	19	81
Involutional melancholia	8,053	43	57
Total	29,197	35	65

Adapted from National Institute of Mental Health. "Admissions to Outpatient Psychiatric Services by Age, Sex and Diagnosis, United States, 1969." Survey and Reports Sections, Statistical Notes: 26-50, September 1971.

"circular madness." Occasionally patients show a mixture of symptoms; the prevailing mood may be one of dejection but the individual is hyperactive and talkative. In older patients, recurring attacks are usually of the depressive variety.

Reactions characterized by alternating manic and depressive phases are referred to as circular or bipolar. Usually there is an intervening normal period between attacks. The term "unipolar" is applied to cases in which recurring attacks are limited to periodic shifts from a normal to a manic state or from a normal to a depressive state. The latter sequence is more common. The frequency of recurring attacks varies considerably from patient to patient. In a follow-up study of 138 carefully selected manic-depressive patients, Rennie (1942) found that 22 percent had no subsequent attacks, 23 percent had two attacks, 25 percent had three attacks, 15 percent had four attacks, and another 15 percent had five or more. The overall figure of two or more attacks in 78 percent of the cases is somewhat higher than that reported in other studies. This finding may be due to the heavy preponderance of initial depressive reactions in the Rennie sample. The probability of recurrence is greater for depressive reactions than for manic reactions. Data reported by Perris (1968) indicate that the number of recurring episodes is significantly higher in bipolar than in unipolar cases. Perris noted no sex differences in the total number of episodes or the relative predominance of manic or depressive attacks. Most studies agree that the initial and subsequent attacks are more often depressive than manic.

Incidence of Manic-Depressive Psychosis

In 1933 manic-depressive psychosis was diagnosed in 13 percent of all first admissions to mental hospitals in the United States. By 1968 the figure had dropped to 2 percent. No comparable decline has been noted in other countries. In some countries, such as England and Italy, the number of hospital first admissions classified as manic-depressive in recent years is about the same as for schizophrenia. There is a possibility that the decline in recorded cases of manic-depressive psychosis in the United States represents an actual decrease in the prevalence of this disorder, but it is more probable that the noted decrease is due to changing diagnostic practices and a trend toward treating manic-depressive patients in the community.

Initial attacks may occur at any time between the ages of twenty and sixty; the peak age of first hospital admissions is forty to forty-five. Since many of these patients have histories of earlier mild attacks, the actual peak age of onset may be closer to thirty-five. Women are usually younger than men at the time of initial hospitalization, which represents a reversal of the sex pattern observed in schizophrenia (Landis and Page, 1938). In addition, manic-depressive psychosis is more prevalent among women than men. About 65 percent of all manic-depressive patients admitted each year to private and public mental hospitals are women. The reason that the incidence rates for all affective psychoses are lower for men may be that men have a greater tendency than women to resort to alcohol when they feel depressed, and many of them are classified as alcoholics instead. A study of hospitalized alcoholics noted that 70 percent of consecutively admitted patients reported mild to deep depression as measured by a standardized self-destructive depression scale (Weingold et al., 1968).

Manic Reactions

The prevailing mood of the manic person is one of elation. He is expansive, humorous, optimistic, and carefree. He describes himself as being on top of the world and full of pep. He radiates exuberance and vitality. He reaches out for attention by trying to be entertaining and friendly, sharing intimate confidences, making jokes, and so on. At times his striving for attention leads to braggadocio, profanity, and indecencies.

MANIC REACTIONS: TWO CASES

The circumstantial speech, impaired thinking, critical attitude, and superficial exalted ideas typical of *hypomania* can be seen in the following interview:

How are you today?

Oh, I'm superperfect. The state's only wasting their money keeping me here. How about a steak dinner tonight with peppermint ice cream? The service here is too slow. Why, there isn't a good nurse here. I could work circles around them.

Are you a nurse?

Well, I don't have my R.N. yet, but I have all of my requirements. You see, I'm too clever for you. Say, who's that nice young doctor you have here? Boy, I could go for him. I think I'll marry a doctor, a rich psychiatrist, and then open up four or five private hospitals so I could retire at thirty. I work fast. I could be the scrub nurse in the operating room and the superintendent of the joint. I want to be the big shot. My sister is a very brilliant girl. Her estimate is about ninety-five percent. She's a senior in college. She admires medical men, any man with a brain. My mother's father was a doctor, a horse doctor, so you see it all traces back.

Would you tell me something about yourself?

Have I got to dig that up again? I hope, I hope, I hope. Do I like men? Do I enjoy going to parties? I don't believe in falling for a guy. I think I'm better than any guy, anyway. I don't think much of myself, do I? I'm very conceited and very fussy and I don't eat things unless they're in courses, either.

What led to your being brought to the hospital?

I'm trying to tell you. I went to interview Mrs. Johnson for a job. I was working at Dr. Smith's house just to get acquainted with things and get a line-up of positions. I thought I might work into a clue even though I'm not a graduate. So anyway, I got a job through a telephone call. She never saw me or anything. Her husband was a nice-looking guy. He had had some money but he lost it through drinking. I only drink to be sociable. Mrs. Johnson liked my appearance and personality and she said I would do, as I looked neat. I don't care if I go out with a medical man or a factory man. I can still adjust myself to the environment. She liked me so well she invited me to accept a date with her son, who is a licensed engineer. They have a beautiful house; you should see it. She got married a second time, to a Greek. She asked me to come down and take her daughter out horseback riding because I go in for all kinds of sports. I have a regular outfit I wear. Of course, I said I would, but I was so busy I didn't get a chance to. I haven't a license but I do drive. I only know four policemen in town and if I got caught I probably would be in a jail instead of in this jail, but they couldn't catch me because I'm awfully smart.

How did you happen to come here?

I'm coming to that. I went over to the house to be interviewed for a job. I just walked in and observed the joint to see if I thought I'd like it. I saw a big fat bug last night. She took all my references and all that stuff. She almost took my prenatal record. I started to work and worked from one to six without stopping. She has a lot to learn. I left there that night and started out to see my friend. He's a six-footer. We make a nice couple. Last year we won a dance contest.

The second speech sample illustrates the extreme distractibility, disorganized association of ideas, and increased inner pressure that is characteristic of *acute mania*. This unchecked word deluge was released when the examiner asked the patient, "Why are you in this hospital?" The content is partly relevant. The patient was divorced and her former husband had recently remarried. She had two sons. A secretary was present to record the interview.

I came here to see the light. I want you to see with your eyes what you saw at night, by the light in the white night. How could you be a child and go into the wild? Kind sir, why are you so kind? Why did you drive a car to Buffalo on Route Twenty? You are twenty years old. Tell me, why did you send that card through the mail? Why do you look up? Why do gentlemen prefer blondes? Do you love your wife? You're beginning to get a little bald. You know babies are born without hair. Do you know why Leo the lion, l-i-o-n, was lionhearted? Do you have a heart? Do you know what you're doing? Doctor, listen, doctor, doctor, doctor, d-o-c-t-o-r. Don't make mothers go suffering on. Don't go near the fireplace over there. Listen. You heard it in West Bloomfield. You saw the bloom in the fields. Why was the light blooming in the fields at night? You have got to have tools to work. Don't we need fish once in a while? Why do you write ABCs on the blackboard? You can see white and black. Say, listen, listen, listen, l-i-s-t-e-n, I can see your tiepin. It isn't right. Listen, pins, pins, pins, p-i-n-s. Look at that girl write down.

A car just went by. There is a calendar. Time, time, time, t-i-m-e, give you all you want. Do you see the saw? Do you hear the buzz? The busy bee, the ABC. Say, listen, don't go away. I put Margie where she belonged. It was just like your hand. Is your hand still working? I was sitting on that chair. Why did you just write the alphabet, daddy, because you are going to become a daddy and daddy knew that if he kept cleaning and cleaning and working and who was Jack? There are so many kinds of jack. Jack and the beanstalk, jack in your pants, jackpot, Jack and Jill. Daddy was

kind to us, he was kind, he was kind. Weren't you good? You were working awfully hard. You understand you must look at a map. There was a girl and she was a bad girl and she had a bad map and this is what she did to me. She made me say something I wouldn't say and that's why I was still in school. Did you know they had stills in school? Just listen to the ABCs. Oh, the most beautiful thing, roses in bloom, roses in bloom. Is your name Rosenbloom?

I'll tell you a story and this is going to be a short-short story and that's just fiction. You must listen. They don't want you to get up until the sun gets up. What time do my sons get up? What time does my one son get up? What time do my two sons get up? What time do my three sons get up? Doctor, tell me when does the sun get up? I wish you were a nurse. I can see the sun coming through those ABCs the hard way. I want to see it over for you and I want a new husband. People all over the whole universe do not understand the situation, and they don't want mothers all over the world to go on twisting that ring on their finger. Please listen carefully. You have to hear more than that, doctor. Why did you send on Christmas Day of all days in that old calendar? Why must you sit down and write? Why did you have to write so beautifully? Why didn't you do it, but why did you send it and when I said that you didn't, you said to me, "I am sending you a line, just a line to let you know that we are married."

No, this was the way it had to be. You understand why you have those children, my two boys? I don't see quite far enough and I started to look up but you see, there is a cage up there. You will see a cage now. Don't you see how wrong you are? Don't you see how you done, Mr. and Mrs., and used her name? Don't we need a plane? There is a drawer in there under that desk. Who is that woman just sitting there? Does she have a name? And is she on my plane?

The fact that he is usually not much disturbed by the discrepancy between his euphoric state and his awareness of being a patient in a mental hospital suggests that he vaguely realizes that his gaiety is a facade, a kind of desperate whistling in the dark. The surface thinness of the euphoria becomes apparent when the patient experiences some real or imagined slight or frustration. Then elation quickly gives way to irritability, arrogance, anger, and rage. The friendly manic may be temporarily transformed into a violent maniac.

The manic patient lives in the immediate present. Passing thoughts and urges are expressed instantly. In the middle of the night he may phone friends or public officials about trivial matters. He may impulsively engage in ruinous business undertakings. His lack of restraint may lead to sexual indiscretions or illegal acts. He is too busy rushing off in all directions to take time to eat and too excited to sleep. Loss of weight is common. The physical exhaustion of the manic, his impulsive actions, and his belligerent behavior when he is thwarted are largely responsible for his being referred for treatment. Hospitalization is a protective measure.

The manic's manner of speaking reflects his excited, pressured state. His speech is accelerated, and he shifts rapidly and unpredictably from one topic to another. It is possible to understand what he is saying, however, and to follow his erratic train of thought. In this respect the speech of the manic differs from the bizarre, idiosyncratic speech of the schizophrenic. When asked a question, the manic starts to give an appropriate answer, but his distractability soon leads to detours away from the original topic. Sentences are rarely completed. In the middle of a sentence he may go off on another thought, respond to some incidental external stimulus, play with the sound of words (puns, rhymes), or get lost in rambling details. The flight of ideas is suggestive of a camouflage or unconscious ruse designed to direct his own attention away from sensitive areas. The excited manic is apt to report perceptual errors that usually are more accurately described as illusions than as hallucinations. Impairment of attention and concentration may interfere with memory. Judgment is defective.

Depending on the relative intensity of symptoms, distinctions are made among hypomania, acute mania, and delirious mania. Patients may progress from one stage to the next or remain in a state of mild excitement. *Hypomania* is characterized by moderate elation, increased psychomotor activity, faulty judgment, and impulsiveness. Lack of restraint may lead to spending sprees, promiscuity, and annoying boisterous behavior. In *acute mania* behavior is less controlled, and *delirious mania* is marked by a complete loss of control. The patient is wildly excited, disoriented, incoherent, and violent. Hallucinations and delusions are usually present. Sedation or physical restraint is required to avoid exhaustion and to prevent the patient from harming himself or others.

Depressive Reactions

The core syndrome of the depressive phase of manic-depressive psychosis consists of (1) feelings of sadness, helplessness, despair, and hopelessness; (2) low self-esteem, pessimism, guilt feelings, and self-blame; and (3) behavior changes marked by disinterest, apathy, psychomotor retardation, and reduced mental activity. Concomitant physical symptoms include chronic fatigue, restless sleep, anorexia, weight loss, dry mouth, constipation, and reduced sex drive. Other common symptoms, which reflect individual personality variables, include anxiety, agitation, irritability, obsessive-compulsive tendencies, rigidity, immobility, demands for attention and love, impaired concentration, hypochondriacal complaints, and psychosomatic ailments.

A large number of rating scales have been developed for obtaining quantitative measures of the intensity and frequency of depressive symptoms. Some of the scales (Hamilton, 1960; Cutler and Kurland,

Aaron T. Beck, noted University of Pennsylvania psychiatrist, whose recent research in depression indicates that distorted thinking plays a major role in depression. According to Beck, the depressed patient's negative view of himself, the outside world, and the future lead to the familiar symptoms of depression: sadness, despair, "paralysis of the will," and suicidal wishes.

1961) call for observer ratings of depressed mood, guilt, suicidal tendencies, somatic symptoms, and so on. Others consist of similar items prepared in the form of a questionnaire that is filled out by the patient (Zung, 1965; Beck, 1967; and Pilowsky et al., 1969). The scales have been found to give highly consistent scores, and therefore are considered to have good reliability. However, there is considerable overlap in the scores attained by depressed patients and patients assigned other diagnostic labels.

Factor analytic studies (Grinker et al., 1961; Wittenborn, 1962; Friedman et al., 1963; and Lorr et al., 1967) have identified five reaction patterns:

1. Depressive mood: dejection, despair, suicidal ideas, loss of interest in people and in usual activities.
2. Anxious self-blame: high anxiety level, self-castigation.
3. Retardation: slowing of action, thought, and speech.
4. Impaired functioning: loss of energy and drive; difficulty in making decisions; inability to get started, to concentrate, and to work.
5. Somatic symptoms: lack of appetite,

weight loss, disinterest in sexual activity, gastrointestinal symptoms.

These feelings, attitudes, and behavior changes are obviously not restricted to psychotic depressions. Normal individuals in mourning and depressed neurotics exhibit essentially similar reactions. The similarities in feelings and behavior of depressed normal, neurotic, and psychotic individuals illustrate again the artificiality of traditional psychiatric categories based on the medical model of separate and distinct disorders.

THE CONTINUUM CONCEPT OF DEPRESSIVE REACTIONS

Normal, neurotic, and psychotic persons are all subject to periodic depressions. When they are depressed, persons in all three groups exhibit similar reactions. The differences consist largely in the relative severity and duration of depressive behavior, the relative appropriateness of the mood change to its known precipitating cause, the degree of voluntary control of feelings and actions, and the extent to which the depressive state interferes with general functioning. The continuity concept does not rule out differences in the etiology of normal, neurotic, and psychotic depressions. The greater severity and bizarreness of symptoms manifested by the psychotic (delusional ideas, preoccupation with suicide, strange somatic complaints, and gross impairment in functioning) suggest that his inherent adaptive resources are less effective than those of the normal or neurotic person. Family and twin studies indicate that genetic determinants are relatively more important in psychotic than in nonpsychotic depressive reactions.

Normal Depression

Many individuals, described as "normal cyclothymes," are subject to periodic mood swings. Mild periods of depression, which may alternate with periods of increased energy and optimism, occur more or less spontaneously. During "letdown" periods, which may last for several days, the individual continues with his usual activities. His pace is slowed but his performance level is unaffected. He may be described by associates as unusually quiet, reserved, or moody. A more typical example of normal depression is the transient state of despondency and lethargy following some significant disappointment or misfortune. A period of mourning is an expected and normal reaction to the loss of a loved one.

Depressive reactions associated with bereavement may be as intense and prolonged as in neurotic and psychotic depressions. A person undergoing a normal depressive reaction retains considerable control of his feelings and actions. When the situation demands it, he can temporarily dry his tears and set aside his heavy burden of sorrow and despair so that his general behavior and functioning remain reasonably effective and appropriate. The expression of grief is largely personal and private. Interest in the outside world may be reduced, but the individual is aware of and responsive to his social environment. Guilt feel-

ings and loss of self-esteem are minimal. The individual may be extremely unhappy and at times quite irritable, but he is not a threat to himself or a source of intolerable concern or annoyance to others. Relatives and friends understand and respect the sorrow of a person in mourning. Actually they would be more disturbed, and quite properly so, if he showed no grief following the death of a child or a spouse. The question of psychotherapy seldom arises. It is recognized that a person who has suffered a major loss needs and should be given time to work through his bereavement at his own pace. Acute grief reactions usually subside within a month or two, but a period of a year or more may be required to complete the mourning process in full.

Lindeman (1944) and Parkes (1965) have examined the relation of normal grief reactions to psychiatrically recognized depressive disorders. Both investigators concluded that despite the close similarity in symptoms, the two conditions are independent. A formal diagnosis of mental disorder was considered valid for very few of the bereaved persons seen in treatment. This finding casts doubt on the importance often attached to the death of a close member of the family as *the* cause of mental disorder.

Shakespeare has provided an insightful description of the depressive mood, self-devaluation, and envious thoughts often experienced by normal individuals when everything seems to be going wrong. He has also included an antidote or balancing factor. His well-known twenty-ninth sonnet is preceded by the lines: "But day doth daily draw my sorrows longer, and night doth nightly make grief's strength seem stronger."

When, in disgrace with fortune and men's eyes,
I all alone beweep my outcast state,
And trouble deaf heaven with my bootless cries,
And look upon myself, and curse my fate,
Wishing me like to one more rich in hope,

Featured like him, like him with friends
  possesst,
Desiring this man's art, and that man's scope,
With what I most enjoy contented least;
Yet in these thoughts myself almost despising,
Haply I think on thee,—and then my state,
Like to the lark at break of day arising
From sullen earth, sings hymns at heaven's
  gate;
    For thy sweet love remember'd such
      wealth brings,
    That then I scorn to change my state
      with kings.

Neurotic Depression

The onset of *neurotic depressive* symptoms is usually precipitated by some significant event. The neurotic has less control over his feelings and actions than the normal individual, but with effort he is capable of coping with his usual responsibilities. He lacks the fortitude and self-sufficiency of the depressed normal individual. He is more inclined to feel sorry for himself and to complain of his painful dejection, his loss of capacity for pleasure, his chronic fatigue and poor health. He is more demanding of love and attention and has a greater need for outside help. There is usually some impairment in work efficiency and productivity. Unlike the psychotic, the neurotic is free of delusions and does not make bizarre interpretations of his condition. He realizes that his depressive symptoms are part of his neurosis and that they will subside when he recovers. Hope is not lost; he tries to fight his depression. He looks forward to the time when he will be his normal self again. The neurotic may experience guilt, but he does not torture himself with remorse over imaginary misdeeds. He is not so likely to commit suicide as the depressed psychotic.

Psychotic Depression

When the psychotic person first experiences symptoms of depression, he typically does not know why he feels as he does. If pressed for an explanation, he or his family can usually recall some adverse experi-ence that he suffered in the recent or distant past, but the relevance of the offered explanation is often questionable. Financial worries and marital difficulties, which are frequently blamed, are fairly common human problems, and even genuinely traumatic experiences seldom wait for years to produce symptoms. Significantly, the depression is unrelated to external changes. The patient may attribute his despondency to the illness of some member of his family or to the loss of employment, but his symptoms continue unabated long after the relative makes a complete recovery or he is offered a good position. The patient may have had several previous attacks from which he recovered in a few months, but he is convinced that this time his condition is hopeless and incurable.

The psychotic accepts his depression as an integral part of his being. He lives his depression. Feelings and behavior are controlled by delusions that cannot be altered by appeals to reason. Despite factual evidence to the contrary, he clings to sincerely held beliefs that he is guilty of unnameable sins, that he has ruined his family and violated the trust others placed in him, and that the world would be better off if he were dead.

In attempting to account for the loss of appetite and energy and the general sluggishness of bodily processes that are often associated with depressive feelings, the psychotic may introduce bizarre details: his blood has turned to water, his bones have decayed, his internal organs have disintegrated. His pervasive pessimistic outlook and morbid self-blame may make suicide an attractive solution. The profound inhibition of thought and action may lead to gross impairment in functioning, muteness, and immobility. The reduced mental productivity that is characteristic of psychotic depressions mainly reflects the patient's state of mind. The individual feels too exhausted, too incompetent, and too apathetic to do much of anything. If he is asked to perform some task, he may complain that he is too tired or that the task is beyond his capacity. There is usually no actual loss of mental abilities, however. When the patient's protests are casually ignored and the examiner treats him as if he were competent, most depressed patients show slight, if any, impairment in cognitive, perceptual, or psychomotor tests (Friedman, 1964).

Suicidal tendencies. The depressed psychotic places his family and therapist in a difficult bind. If they are attentive to his complaints and respond sympathetically to his obvious suffering, they unwittingly reinforce "sick" behavior. If they refuse to listen to his endless woes or are critical of his behavior, he may be driven to develop symptoms so severe that his audience cannot ignore them.

Suicidal thoughts afford a striking example of this dilemma. About 75 to 80 percent of depressed psychotic patients express suicidal ideas, 15 to 25 percent make actual attempts at suicide, and an estimated 10 percent eventually succeed. The threat is too real to be ignored. The more concern and alarm the family shows in response to talk of suicide, the more the patient dwells on the subject, since it is guaranteed to elicit attention. If in desperation the family arranges for his compulsory hospitalization as a safety measure, he may interpret their action as proof of rejection or abandonment, and thus as justification for putting an end to his miserable, lonely existence. If comments about "ending it all" and "being better off dead" are not taken seriously, he may feel compelled to try to kill himself to prove he is not simply seeking attention and sympathy.

The depressed psychotic's preoccupation with suicide is genuine. He sincerely believes in the hopelessness of his condition. Life has no meaning or purpose for him. His present anguish is intolerable, the future is nonexistent or bleak, and the past is a painful reminder of his guilt, his unworthiness, and his failures (Arieti, 1959). A few patients carefully conceal their suicidal intent from their families so that they will not interfere. During the acute phase these patients may lack the energy to carry out their plans. Suicide frequently occurs when the patient appears to be on the road

to recovery and family and hospital vigilance are relaxed. Usually the depressed patient takes only his own life, but occasionally a distraught father, worried about the fate of his wife and children when he is no longer there to look after them, will kill them too. Young depressed mothers may kill their children before killing themselves, but they are not so likely as men to consider their spouses incapable of getting along without them.

Types of psychotic depression. Two main approaches have been used in attempts to separate psychotic depressives into homogeneous subgroups. One is based on the relative predominance of certain symptom clusters as determined by clinical observations and factor analytic studies. The three principal syndromes thus delineated are (1) depressive mood with mental and psychomotor retardation; (2) depressive mood with agitation, guilt, and self-blame; and (3) depressive mood with self-pity, hypochrondriacal complaints, and psychosomatic symptoms.

The second approach, which is favored in traditional diagnosis, is based on the relative severity of symptoms. The three levels generally recognized are simple depression, acute depression, and depressive stupor.

Simple depression consists of relatively mild reactions with no clear-cut delusions. A characteristic feature is a marked loss of feelings, interests, and drive. Inhibition or retardation of thought and action is common. The individual wakes up early and dull from a restless sleep. Ahead lies another gloomy, hopeless day. The mere thought of getting out of bed and dressing is exhausting. With effort he can care for his basic needs, but every movement is painfully slow. If someone asks him a question, he pauses for a long time before making a brief reply in a low, tired voice. Communication is clear, however, and he constructs his sentences in his usual fashion. Feelings and responses are inappropriate to the reality of the situation but consistent with the depressed mood. The occurrence of suicidal ideas is usually the main reason for hospitalization.

A CASE OF SIMPLE DEPRESSION

The following excerpt from an interview with a middle-aged female patient illustrates many of the salient traits of simple depression (Page, 1947).

Have you been in a mental hospital before?
Yes.
How many times?
Twice.
How are you feeling now?
Well, sort of sad and low in spirits.
Can you compare your present feelings with how you feel when you are well?
When I was well, I woke up in the morning and was eager to get up and do my work. Now I find it very hard to do anything.
How do you feel when you awake in the morning?
Well, I want to stay in bed and have to force myself to get up and dress.
How do you feel after you are up and dressed?
Why, I just want to stay in one place and do nothing.
Do you sleep well?
Yes. It sometimes takes a little time to get to sleep, that's all.
Do you have a good appetite?
No, I'm not very interested in eating.
Why is that?
Well, the food has no taste, for one thing.
What ideas run through your head now?
I just feel as if I didn't care about going on.
What do you mean?
Oh, I'd be better off dead.
Would you tell me more about that?
Oh, I never tried to do anything. I merely thought of it as an escape.
Escape from what?
I don't know. Just from myself, from the despondency.
What makes you despondent?

I don't know.
Did anything happen to upset you?
No.
Do you have many worries?
Oh, I worry some about myself, just trivial things.
What do you mean?
Oh, just about my appearance.
Is this a recent worry?
No, I've always worried about that.
What do you do all day?
Not very much.
Do you read?
No, I look at the headlines sometimes.
Did you read when you were at home?
Yes, I belong to the Book-of-the-Month.
Why don't you read here?
I try to, but I can't get interested in what I read.
Do you think you are as mentally alert as when you were well?
No. I can't retain what I read and I find it difficult to discuss anything with other people.
Can you explain that a little more?
The words don't come as easily as they did before.
Anything else?
I don't grasp things like I did before.
Do you enjoy listening to music?
I used to.
And now?
I have no feeling for it.
Is your husband responsible for your being here?
No, I suggested that he bring me here.
Why?
I was despondent and felt I needed some protection.
Do you think you would have harmed yourself if you had stayed home?
I really don't know.
Do you want to get well?
Why, certainly!
How does the future look to you now?
Not very bright.

Acute depression may progress from simple depression, or the transition from normal behavior may be direct and abrupt. The chief characteristic is the presence of obvious psychotic features. The patient is completely absorbed in his symptoms. The impairment of functioning is pronounced. Symptoms associated with simple depression may occur in more intense form. In addition, the patient may express deluded ideas of having inflicted ruin and disgrace on his family. Death is sought as a punishment for his misdeeds. There is a marked loss of appetite resulting in a considerable weight loss. Constipation is common. The patient may refuse food on the ground that he is not entitled to it or that his stomach has atrophied.

Depressive stupor is characterized by a massive paralysis of thought and action. The patient may be aware of what is going on about him but he does not respond to questions and is more or less immobilized. Severe cases may be confined to bed and may require spoon feeding.

OTHER DIAGNOSES OF SEVERE DEPRESSIVE REACTIONS

As we noted earlier, the 1968 APA classification lists involutional melancholia and psychotic depressive reaction as separate disorders, both of which are considered distinct from the depressive phase of manic-depressive psychosis. The seeming decline of manic-depressive psychosis in the United States is due in part to increasing use of these other two diagnoses. Each accounts for a larger number of first admissions to mental hospitals than the category of manic-depressive psychosis.

The principal designated feature that sets *involutional melancholia* apart from other depressions is the fact that the symptoms first occur during the climacteric period (ages forty-five to sixty-five), when significant biochemical and psychosocial changes typically take place in human beings. The menopause in women was once considered an important contributory factor. Other assumed identifying characteristics include a prepsychotic personality marked by rigidity, compulsive behavior, agitation, delusional ideas, feelings of guilt, severe insomnia, and somatic symptoms.

Psychotic depressive reaction, unlike the depressive phase of manic-depressive psychosis, is considered to be directly related to some signicant loss or misfortune. By definition, then, this diagnosis is applied only to persons who have no history of earlier depressions or of marked cyclothymic mood swings. If a subsequent attack occurs, the original diagnosis is changed to manic-depressive psychosis. Genetic factors are thought to be less pronounced in psychotic depressive reactions.

The validity of the assumption that involutional melancholia and psychotic depressive reaction constitute distinctive clinical entities has long been questioned by qualified experts. The symptom pattern, course, treatment, and prognosis of each of these disorders do not differ significantly from those of the depressive phase of manic-depressive psychosis. The latter, in turn, differs mainly in severity of dysfunction from the depressive reactions observed in neurotic and normal persons. The criteria cited in defense of the use of separate diagnoses are artificial and arbitrary. Variations in age of onset, frequency of episodes, and type of personality before the occurrence of symptoms are more reasonably interpreted as manifestations of incidental individual differences than as diagnostic signs of separate disorders.

The relevance of the precipitating cause is a highly subjective matter. What others may regard as an insignificant event (the death of a pet, the loss of a job) may have critical symbolic significance to the patient. From my own point of view, too much emphasis has been placed on the importance of some loss as the key to depressive behavior. The explanation is too simple and too pat. If disappointments, failures, and the deaths of loved ones were the direct and only causes of psychotic depression, practically everyone would have recurring attacks. Depressive reactions, like other so-called mental disorders, are the end products of multiple interacting psychobiosocial factors. They represent characteristic ways in which certain types of individuals (mainly extraverted, cyclothymic, and compulsive personalities) usually respond when the cumulative stresses of life exceed innate and acquired adaptive resources.

In order to justify the "loss" interpretation, it is frequently necessary to assume that a depression represents a delayed reaction to some disturbing event that occurred years ago. Such an explanation requires considerable twisting to account for the common observation that the onset of depression may follow a promotion, the birth of a wanted baby, or some outstanding success. The sequence of events is less paradoxical when viewed from the broader perspective of the total life history of the individual. The final attainment of some objective that a person has been steadily pursuing for most of his life may be a crushing disappointment if it falls short of his unrealistic aspirations or if it fails to offset the accumulated failures, mistakes, and deprivations of the past. Under such circumstances life may indeed appear hopeless.

Winokur and Clayton (1966) and Hopkinson and Ley (1969) have proposed a division of all affective disorders into two types, distinguished by the genetic and clinical differences noted in family histories. One type, which resembles manic-depressive psychosis of the bipolar variety, is characterized by early age of onset (twenty to forty), a tendency to recurrence, and a relatively high incidence of affective disorders among other members of the family. Attacks are often of the manic type. The second type usually occurs in families in which the incidence of affective disorders among first- and second-degree relatives is comparatively low. This type has a late age of onset and is less likely to recur or to manifest itself in manic symptoms. Clinical impressions derived from other sources suggest that the first type is more often associated with a cyclothymic prepsychotic temperament, whereas compulsive features are more prevalent in the second type. More research is needed to confirm preliminary findings and to rule out the possibility that the noted differences between the two types are not artificial by-products of the inclusion of depressed, brain-damaged elderly persons in the late-onset group.

ETIOLOGICAL FACTORS IN AFFECTIVE DISORDERS

The occurrence of the reaction patterns traditionally associated with affective disorders is an established fact. Whether the clinical syndromes represent one or more separate mental disorders and whether they are sharply differentiated from normal behavior are controversial issues. The meanings assigned to the labels of manic-depressive psychosis and involutional melancholia have important etiological implications. Acceptance of the concept of separate disorders includes a commitment to the premise that all persons diagnosed as suffering from one or another of these behavior disturbances are distinguished by certain pathogenic agents that are absent in normal individuals and in patients suffering from other disorders. If the diagnostic terms are interpreted as convenient labels that simply describe extreme variations in certain kinds of human behavior, the futile search for unique determinants is avoided. All that is necessary is to account for the greater than normal variation in mood, psychomotor activity level, and related reactions. This unfortunately is easier said than done.

The greater than usual variations in mood and behavior associated with affective psychosis are probably due to a combination of factors. From a genetic point of view, there is a good probability that manic-depressive patients are distinguished by a greater instability of the biological mechanisms that regulate emotions and activity level. Under favorable conditions, this genetic predisposition is phenotypically expressed in mild mood swings and increased activity. Normal persons exhibiting these traits are often described as extraverts or cyclothymes. Some individuals who are genetically predisposed to mood swings impose rigid controls on their emotions. A more stable mood is thus achieved at the cost of compulsive defenses and inhibition of feelings.

The risk of marked mood swings, and especially of severe depressive reactions, is increased when genetically predisposed individuals are taught at an early age to place great value on conformity or achievement. In order to earn the love of his parents (especially of his mother) during his formative years, the child must conform to her standards of proper behavior and success. In later years, other authority figures and the impersonal "they" are substituted for the mother. The individual remains other-directed and dependent on external approval. Failure to live up to idealized and often unrealistic standards leads to periodic discouragement. The individual's acceptance of social values and his dependence on the goodwill and support of others preclude his blaming them too openly for his failures and shortcomings. His high aspirations, strong social needs, and basic temperament rule out schizophrenic resignation from human society. The remaining alternative is self-blame and oppressive gloom or a massive defense expressed in pseudoelation, expansiveness, and frenzied hyperactivity.

The onset of despair or compensatory overoptimism is usually delayed until adulthood, when the individual is confronted with the responsibility of converting aspirations into realities and encounters disappointment. The pain of failure is aggravated by the fact that it is unexpected—and from his point of view undeserved. During childhood and early adolescence, his life experiences reinforce his favorable self-image. Parents and teachers are impressed by his high energy level, his buoyant spirits, his emotional expressiveness and sociability. His willingness to do what is expected of him leads to praise. He shows promise. The same qualities promote a surface popularity with his peers. As children, persons who later develop affective disorders appear to be well adjusted. They are rarely referred to child guidance clinics or juvenile courts. As adults they typically have good occupational records and are respected members of their communities. Having done all the "right"

things, they feel entitled to appropriate rewards. The shattering threat of failure and loss of self-esteem, combined with their innate tendency toward lack of emotional control, leads to pervasive despair.

When such a person is young and still retains hope and vigor, he may put on a brave front. Mainly for his own benefit he attempts to conceal his desperate plight by erecting a facade of confidence and optimism. He is elated, boastful, and full of plans that must be executed immediately. The older person temporarily gives up the struggle and attempts to enlist the sympathy of others by making known his dejection and self-devaluation. The misfortunes and misdeeds he proclaims may be factual or imaginary. It doesn't really matter, since they are red herrings that he unconsciously drags across the path to divert attention from his real failure—the failure to live up to his personal expectations. This explains the inappropriateness of his reactions to his reported misfortunes and sins, and the fact that he makes no effort to remedy past misdeeds. His guilt and self-blame are genuine, but his denial of the real reasons and his exploitation of convenient substitutes make observers question his sincerity and regard his reported feelings and ideas as delusions.

The Importance of Heredity

The significant role of genetic factors in severe mood disturbances has been repeatedly confirmed in family and twin studies of manic-depressive patients. Some studies have combined manic-depressive with other affective disorders. One comprehensive review of the extensive international literature on the subject indicates that the incidence of manic-depressive psychosis in the general population can be placed at approximately 0.7 percent (Rosenthal, 1970). This probability estimate represents the median figure of the incidence rates found in ten separate studies in various countries. Comparable expectancy rates for twins and relatives of manic-depressive patients (index cases) are shown in Table 10.2.

These figures clearly indicate that manic-depressive and affective reactions occur much more frequently among first-degree relatives of index cases than among the general population.

In general, the relative risk is directly related to the closeness of genetic ties. If a monozygotic twin develops an affective disorder, the chance that his twin will develop a similar disorder (the concordance rate) is an impressive 70 percent. The rate drops to 20 percent for dizygotic pairs. The risk of similar disorders in parents, siblings, and children of manic-depressives is more than ten times greater than for the general population. The expectancy rate found for siblings in some studies is as high as that noted for DZ twins in other studies, but most investigators have reported lower rates for siblings. In this respect the genetic data for manic-depressive psychosis differ from those for schizophrenia. The higher expectancy rates for DZ co-twins of manic-depressives than for their siblings suggest that environmental factors may be relatively more important in the development of manic-depressive psychosis than of schizophrenia.

Various studies (reviewed by Mendels, 1970) indicate that siblings of index cases have a greater probability of developing manic-depressive psychoses if their early childhood environments are unfavorable. For more distant relatives—aunts, uncles, and grandchildren—the risk of developing affective disorders is about 3 percent. This figure, like all the others that have been cited, represents the median finding of several studies. The marked differences in rates reported in various studies (the range is shown in Table 10.2) are partly due to incidental factors. In a few of the twin studies, the number of cases was too small to permit us to consider the findings valid. Some investigators corrected for age in calculating expectancy rates for siblings and children; others did not. Some studies were more carefully controlled than others with respect to the selection of "pure" manic-depressive index cases, the diagnostic criteria applied to relatives, the elimination of doubtful cases, and so on.

The specific nature of the genetic component in manic-depressive psychosis is unknown. Biochemical changes have often been noted in mood-disordered patients. These findings are inconclusive, however, since it is difficult to decide whether the observed changes are the cause or the result of the emotional disturbance (Mendels,

Table 10.2. The Importance of Heredity (Expectancy Rates for Affective Disorders among Relatives of Index Cases Diagnosed as Manic-depressives or Affective Psychotics.)

Kinship	Number of studies	Median expectancy rate	Percentage range
MZ twins	6	70%	50-93%
DZ twins	6	20	0-38
Parents	10	8	3-23
Siblings	9	9	3-23
Children	6	11	6-24
Uncles and aunts	2	3	1-4
Grandchildren	2	3	2-3

1970). Electroencephalographic studies indicate that manic and depressed patients show no consistent abnormalities in the resting alpha rhythm. Samuel Kraines (1966) has advanced the theory that the manic-depressive syndrome is related to disturbances in the functioning of the hypothalamus, and this ties in neatly with the fact that the hypothalamus regulates mood, appetite, sleep, sexual activity, and drive. Manic reactions are presumed to be due to periodic hyperactivity of the hypothalamus, which leads to overresponsiveness of the emotional circuit, an increase in energy level and related changes. Depressive reactions are attributed to inhibition of hypothalamic function, which in turn limits sympathetic outflow and results in a general reduction of emotional responsiveness, drive, and activity. The hypothesis merits further research, but at present remains highly speculative.

Psychoanalytic Theory

Psychoanalysts view the "manic-depressive character" as a particular style of relating to others and reacting to anxiety-arousing situations. They attribute the development of this behavioral pattern to the interaction of innate constitutional factors and certain parental ways of child rearing. The following account is a summary of observations and inferences made by Cohen et al. (1954) on the basis of their intensive study of a small group of manic-depressive patients.

Persons prone to manic-depressive psychosis are usually brought up in families that are set apart from the surrounding social environment. The isolation of the family may be due to membership in a minority group, recent loss of status due to reduced income, higher status than other families in the neighborhood, a broken home, or anything else that separates it socially from its neighbors. The family is distressed by this social difference, and an all-out attempt is made, particularly by the mother, to improve the family's acceptability in the community by fitting in with "what the neighbors think." In this attempt the children are used as instruments. They are inculcated with a strict and conventional concept of good behavior, and are taught that they have a family obligation to get good grades in school, to win prizes, and through their achievements to be considered by the community as a credit to their parents. The child who later becomes a manic-depressive is often the one selected as the chief bearer of the burden of gaining acceptance for the family. The chosen one is usually the brightest, the best-looking, the most gifted, or in some other way outstanding.

The driving force behind the striving of the family is usually the mother. The child recognizes her as the authority in the family. She is feared and regarded as cold and unloving. At the same time, since she is the source of all rewards, her approval is desired and sought. The child sees the father as weak and unreliable but lovable. The contemptuous attitude of the mother toward the father serves as an example to the child of what might happen to him if he should fail to achieve the goals she sets.

But this driving woman was not always cold and unloving. She was tender and affectionate while the child was a helpless, dependent baby. His early infancy was normal, and he developed an awareness of himself as a distinct person. (In this respect the prospective manic-depressive differs from the schizophrenic, who has a sketchy, blurred self-image.) By the end of the first year, however, the mother of the child destined to be a manic-depressive starts to take firm measures to check his growing independence and rebelliousness. Strong pressure is put on him to conform to her wishes and to abstain from "bad" behavior. The abrupt shift from a loving, all-gratifying mother to a tyrannical, punitive authority lays the groundwork for his later ambivalent attitude toward authority figures.

The child's acceptance of the task of winning social acceptance for the family makes him feel responsible for whatever hardships or failures the family experiences. This feeling of responsibility and blame is carried over to his own family when he marries. As adults, persons susceptible to manic-depressive psychosis are conscientious, conventionally well behaved, hardworking, and often successful. They are outgoing and friendly, but their interpersonal relations lack depth. The cyclothyme's good humor, liveliness, and social facility gain him a wide circle of acquaintances but few intimate friends. In exchange for being pleasant, entertaining, and ingratiating, he expects that others will gratify his need for love, attention, and success.

But the concept of reciprocity is missing. The person with a manic-depressive character structure has little to give. He is insensitive to the needs and feelings of others. His style is to establish dependent relationships with strong authority figures and thereby become the recipient of their assistance. Success and promotion may be perceived as threats if they involve the loss of a dependency relationship. The demandingness and exploitativeness of the potential manic-depressive eventually leads others to avoid or reject him. The harder he tries, the more annoyed they become and the less they give. When all hope is lost and he is faced with the crushing blow of abandonment, he enters into a psychotic state.

His symptoms represent an exaggeration of his characteristic behavior when he is in a healthy interval. While he is psychotic, his inner emptiness and dependence on others are openly expressed by a display of misery, appeals for attention and reassurance, ideas of personal bankruptcy, and so on. Difficulties with others are denied, so that he has no one to blame but himself.

Psychoanalysts interpret manic behavior as a defensive structure that the individual erects as a more tolerable substitute for feelings of despair and self-devaluation. It is better to pretend to be important than to admit to being nothing.

Learning Theory

Reinforcement theory as such cannot account for the vulnerability of certain individuals to severe mood disturbances, but the choice and persistence of symptoms may in great measure be explained in terms of learning principles. The loss of interest, feelings of futility, and reduced activity level of the depressive may be attributed to a relative absence of positive reinforcements and a relative predominance of losses, frustrations, and other aversive stimuli. His unresponsiveness to his social environment leads to a decrease in external stimulation, which in turn confirms the dreary emptiness of his existence and sustains his low level of responsiveness. The sympathy and reassurance periodically elicited by a dejected appearance, self-accusations, and somatic complaints contribute to their recurrence and persistence. The elation of the manic is self-reinforcing. His uninhibited, jovial behavior is a source of welcome attention. As a result of successful past experiences, the manic-prone individual may learn to rely on periodic spurts of hyperactivity to cope with his problems.

Sociocultural Factors

Manic-depressive and related depressive reactions appear to be more or less randomly distributed at all socioeconomic levels. Where differences have been noted, incidence rates have been slightly higher among the upper classes. Affective psychoses constitute a larger proportion of first admissions to private than public mental hospitals. Cross-cultural studies (Murphy et al., 1967; Zung, 1969) indicate that the prevalence of depressive reactions and the range of their symptoms are about the same throughout the world. However, the relative occurrence of specific symptoms is influenced by the particular culture, local religious beliefs, social class, and geography. Guilt feelings and self-accusation, for example, are strongly related to the Judeo-Christian tradition. Theatrical grief and self-neglect tend to be more characteristic of lower-class than upper-class populations.

Recent studies have refuted earlier claims that depressions are rare among primitive people (Prince, 1968). The discrepancy between earlier and later reports appears to be partly due to the failure of older studies to take account of cultural differences in ways of expressing feelings. In African rural societies, depressive states are more often expressed in somatic complaints and ideas of persecution than in guilt and self-blame (Collomb, 1967). In former years, too, primitive people referred only troublesome persons for treatment at mission hospitals and clinics. Depressed persons, who were usually considered victims of bewitchment, were treated by native practitioners skilled in such matters.

THE TREATMENT OF AFFECTIVE DISORDERS

By definition, manic-depressive and other psychotic depressive reactions are characterized by spontaneous recovery. About 80 percent of the attacks terminate well within nine months. As previously indicated, modern drugs can usually bring symptoms under control in a week or two. If symptoms persist over a year, the original diagnosis is often changed. In depressive cases, general psychomotor retardation is considered a favorable prognostic sign and somatic complaints are regarded as unfavorable signs (Kay et al., 1969). The main objectives of therapeutic intervention are to moderate the severity of symptoms, shorten the duration of attacks, and decrease the risk of exhaustion in manic patients and of suicide in depressed patients.

The two favored treatments for severe depressions are electroconvulsive shock (ECT) and antidepressant drugs. ECT involves the brief passage of an electric current across electrodes placed at the patient's temples. The current is of sufficient voltage to produce instant unconsciousness and what resembles an epileptic seizure. The usual treatment consists of a series of ten to fourteen convulsions spaced over a period of time. Prior to inducing the convulsion it is customary to administer a muscle relaxant or a short-acting anesthesia to control the severity of the muscular contractions during the seizure. ECT produces temporary amnesia, disorientation, and confusion. These unfavorable after-effects usually disappear spontaneously within a month or two following discontinuance of shock treatments.

Comparative studies (Zung, 1968) suggest that ECT is slightly more effective than antidepressant drugs in the treatment of depressions, and the faster speed of action of ECT in moderating depressions is an important advantage in suicidal cases. Antidepressant drugs generally take effect only after two weeks of treatment.

The drug most often used in the treatment of manic states is *lithium carbonate* (Gattozzi, 1970; Baldessarini and Stephens, 1970). Acute manic symptoms generally are brought under control by lithium in from five to ten days. Some psychiatrists recommend starting the treatment of highly disturbed manic patients with antipsychotic drugs and then switching to lithium. Supplementary psychotherapy is advised after the acute symptoms of mania or depression have been brought under control. The action of drugs is limited to the regulation of symptoms, so medication must be continued for the duration of the attack, which may last several months. The possibility of preventing the recurrence of attacks by keeping the patient under constant medication is currently being investigated. Preliminary findings, covering a follow-up period of two years, indicate that continued lithium medication is effective in preventing both manic and depressive episodes. *Imipramine*, an antidepressant, has been found effective in preventing the recurrence of depressive episodes (Prien et al., 1974).

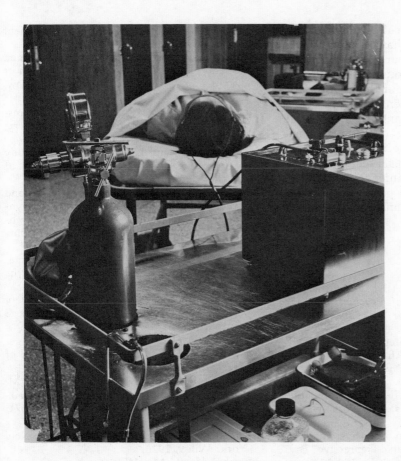

Electroshock therapy is widely used in the treatment of severe depressions.

No satisfactory explanation has been advanced for the action of either ECT or of the antidepressant drugs. Dies (1968) has proposed a social learning theory interpretation for ECT in which the punishment aspect of the seizure is seen as negative reinforcement. It has also been suggested that the temporary amnesia produced by ECT may have some therapeutic significance.

SUMMARY

Severe affective disturbances distinguished by extreme deviations in mood have traditionally been subdivided into the categories of manic-depressive psychosis, psychotic depressive reaction, and involutional melancholia. Further clinical subdivisions of manic-depressive reactions have been suggested on the basis of (1) bipolar and unipolar types, (2) severity of manic reactions (hypomanic, hypermanic, and delirious reactions), and (3) severity of depression (simple, acute, and stuporous depressions).

It has recently been proposed that psychotic affective disturbances be divided into two separate disorders: bipolar and predominantly manic reactions characterized by early age of onset (twenty to forty), in which there is a strong genetic loading, and depressive reactions occurring relatively late in life, in which the genetic loading is less pronounced. An alternate approach is to disregard the historical concept of separate disorders and view affective psychoses as extreme variations of the mood swings characteristic of normal individuals described as cyclothymes. The continuum concept is particularly applicable to the similarities of behavior observed in normal mourning, neurotic depressions, and psychotic depressions. The continuum concept does not rule out the appropriateness of medical treatment.

ECT and antidepressant drugs are highly effective in controlling depressive symptoms. Lithium is a specific drug for the treatment of manic states. Preliminary findings suggest that maintenance doses of lithium are effective in preventing the occurrence of either manic or depressive episodes.

References

Arieti, S. "Manic Depressive Psychosis." In *American Handbook of Psychiatry*, ed. S. Arieti, pp. 419-54. New York: Basic Books, 1959.

Baldessarini, R. J., and Stephens, J. H. "Lithium Carbonate for Affective Disorders." *Archives of General Psychiatry* 22 (1970): 72-77.

Beck, A. T. *Depression: Clinical, Experimental, and Theoretical Aspects*. New York: Harper & Row, 1967.

Cohen, M. B., et al. "An Intensive Study of Twelve Cases of Manic-Depressive Psychosis." *Psychiatry* 17 (1954): 103-37.

Collomb, H. "Methodological Problems in Cross-cultural Research." *International Journal of Psychiatry* 3 (1967): 17-19.

Cutler, R. P., and Kurland, H. D. "Clinical Quantification of Depressed Reactions." *Archives of General Psychiatry* 5 (1961): 280-85.

Dies, R. R. "Electroconvulsive Therapy: A Social Learning Theory Interpretation." *Journal of Nervous and Mental Diseases* 146 (1968): 334-42.

Friedman, A. S.; Cowitz, B.; Cohen, H. W.; and Graneck, S. "Syndromes and Themes of Psychotic Depression." *Archives of General Psychiatry* 9, (1963): 504-12.

———. "Minimal Effects of Severe Depression on Cognitive Functioning." *Journal of Abnormal and Social Psychology* 69 (1964): 237-43.

Gattozzi, A. A. *Lithium in the Treatment of Mood Disorders*. National Clearinghouse for Mental Health Information publication no. 5033. Washington, D.C.: U.S. Government Printing Office, 1970.

Grinker, R. R.; Miller, J.; Sobshin, M.; Numm, R.; and Nunnally, J. C. *The Phenomenon of Depressions*. New York: Harper & Row, 1961.

Hamilton, M. A. "A Rating Scale for Depression." *Journal of Neurology, Neurosurgery, and Psychiatry* 23 (1960): 56-62.

Hopkinson, G., and Ley, P. "A Genetic Study of Affective Disorder." *British Journal of Psychiatry* 115 (1969): 917-22.

Kay, D. W. K.; Garside, R. F.; Roy, J. R.; and Beamish, P. "Endogenous and Neurotic Syndromes of Depression: A Five- to Seven-Year Follow-up of 104 Cases." *British Journal of Psychiatry* 115 (1969): 389-99.

Kraines, S. H. "Manic-Depressive Syndrome: A Psychologic Disease." *Diseases of the Nervous System* 27 (1966): 3-19.

Landis, C., and Page, J. D. *Modern Society and Mental Disease*. New York: Farrar & Rinehart, 1938.

Lindeman, E. "Symptomatology and Management of Acute Grief." *American Journal of Psychiatry* 101 (1944): 141-48.

Lorr, M.; Sonn, T. M.; and Katz, M. M. "Toward a Definition of Depression." *Archives of General Psychiatry* 17 (1967): 183-86.

Mendels, J. *Concepts of Depression*. New York: Wiley, 1970.

Murphy, H. B. M.; Wittkower, E. D.; and Chance, N. A. "Cross-cultural Inquiry into the Symptomatology of Depression: A Preliminary Report." *International Journal of Psychiatry* 3 (1967): 6-15.

Page, J. D. *Abnormal Psychology*. New York: McGraw-Hill, 1947.

Parkes, C. B. "Bereavement and Mental Illness: Part I. A Clinical Study of the Grief of Bereaved Psychiatric Patients." *British Journal of Medical Psychology* 38 (1965): 1-12.

Perris, C. "The Course of Depressive Psychoses." *Acta Psychiatrica Scandinavia* 44 (1968): 238-48.

Pilowsky, I.; Levine, S.; and Boulton, D. M. "The Classification of Depression by Numerical Taxonomy." *British Journal of Psychiatry* 115 (1969): 937-45.

Prien, R. F., Klett, C. J. and Caffey, E. M. "Lithium Prophylaxis in Recurrent Affective Illness." *American Journal of Psychiatry* 131 (1974): 198-202.

Prince, R. "The Changing Picture of Depressive Syndromes in Africa: Is It Fact or Diagnostic Fashion?" *Canadian Journal of African Studies* 1 (1968): 177-92.

Rennie, T. A. C. "Prognosis in Manic-Depressive Psychoses." *American Journal of Psychiatry* 98 (1942): 801-14.

Rosenthal, D. *Genetic Theory and Abnormal Behavior.* New York: McGraw-Hill, 1970.

Weingold, H. P.; Lachin, A.; Bell, H.; and Coxe, R. C. "Depression as a Symptom of Alcoholism: Search for a Phenomenon." *Journal of Abnormal Psychology* 73 (1968): 195-97.

Winokur, G., and Clayton, P. "Family History Studies: I. Two Types of Affective Disorders Separated According to Genetic and Clinical Factors." *Recent Advances in Biological Psychiatry* 9 (1966): 35-50.

———. "Family History Studies: II. Sex Differences and Alcoholism in Primary Affective Illness." *British Journal of Psychiatry* 113 (1967): 973-79.

Wittenborn, J. R. "The Dimensions of Psychosis." *Journal of Nervous and Mental Disease* 134 (1962): 117-28.

Zung, W. K. "A Self-rating Depression Scale." *Archives of General Psychiatry* 12 (1965): 63-70.

———. "Evaluating Treatment Methods for Depressive Disorders." *American Journal of Psychiatry* 124 (1968): 40-48.

———. "A Cross-cultural Survey of Symptoms in Depression." *American Journal of Psychiatry* 126 (1969): 116-21.

11 · Neurotic Reactions

Lady Macbeth,
W. C. Wilson

Symptom patterns associated with neurosis include acute anxiety, irrational fears, psychogenic blindness, amnesia, dual personality, obsessive thoughts, compulsive rituals, depressive mood, chronic exhaustion, feelings of unreality, and undue concern with the state of one's health. What do these varied reactions have in common to justify their being grouped in the same category? One common characteristic that is particularly helpful in differentiating neurotic behavior from sociopathy is that in neurosis the main victim is the patient. The neurotic has been described as his own worst enemy. He is not a martyr or a masochist who enjoys suffering. He desperately wants to enjoy life and to be happy, but his peace of mind is shattered by nameless fears, doubts, ideas of guilt, confused identity, frustrated aspirations, inferiority feelings, and somatic concerns.

A second common characteristic of neurotic reactions is the absence of delusions, hallucinations, and other bizarre behavior associated with psychosis. Neurotics do not grossly misinterpret outer reality and they do not exhibit significant personality disorganization. The neurotic sees himself and is perceived by others as standing much closer to the normal than to the psychotic end of the mental health continuum. His symptoms may restrict his activity, reduce his efficiency, and cause him acute personal anguish, but he is aware of the way society expects him to behave, and by and large, his behavior remains within socially acceptable limits in work performance, interpersonal relations, and everyday activities.

Basically, the neurotic's alignment with the normal is due to the fact that he recognizes his symptoms *as* symptoms. Unlike the psychotic, who accepts his delusions as real and lives them, the neurotic is capable of distinguishing his "sick" from his normal behavior. He is aware of the senselessness of his anxiety and his self-defeating, defensive reactions. He would like nothing better than to be rid of his irrational fears, obsessions, compulsions, guilt feelings, and somatic ailments. But, try as he will, he is unable to do so. At best, he can with extreme effort moderate and regulate their expression so that his overt behavior does not appear to casual observers as irrational or obviously peculiar. His relative inability to control his symptoms accentuates his anxiety by raising the haunting specter that he is losing his mind. The neurotic's awareness of the maladaptiveness of his reactions and the futility of his subterfuges is a major source of personal unhappiness. The unfavorable attitudes of close associates, who often regard his behavior as attention-getting, foolish, or annoying, add to his problems.

With respect to the continuum of psychopathology, neurotic symptoms represent moderate deviations whereas psychotic symptoms represent extreme deviations from similar traits observed in normal individuals. The differences consist mainly in the degree to which specific behavior is subject to voluntary control and rational interpretation, which in turn influences the relative appropriateness and adequacy of psychosocial functioning. The contrasts noted in the previous chapters in the ways in which normal, neurotic, and psychotic individuals manage depressive feelings also hold for other traits.

Compulsive tendencies, for example, are present in all three groups. Many normal persons rigidly adhere to a fixed and highly predictable pattern of behavior. They resist changes in their scheduled lives, but when circumstances demand it, they can and do alter their usual routines and customary ways of doing things. The neurotic is less flexible and adaptive. He may recognize the ridiculousness of his compulsive behavior but he experiences great difficulty in modifying established habits or in inhibiting impulses for prolonged periods. He retains sufficient control and judgment, however, to keep his behavior within reasonable bounds. Unlike the psychotic, he does not attribute his compulsive acts to a plot by enemies who are controlling his thoughts and impulses with the aid of some diabolic machine and forcing him to engage in repetitive rituals against his will.

All human beings periodically experience vague aches and pains that are unrelated to specific or treatable illness. Normal individuals learn to ignore these incidental and transient symptoms; the neurotic may dwell upon them and exaggerate their significance; the psychotic may imagine that his body is undergoing a radical change or that certain organs are wasting away. Finally, neurotic behavior is more responsive than psychotic behavior to changes in the individual's life situation and more amenable to psychological forms of treatment. The neurotic's greater adaptability is related to his maintaining closer contact with his social environment.

Anxiety Theory of Neurosis

The main rationale for considering the diverse forms of neurotic behavior as a single clinical entity is based on the anxiety theory of neurosis. A distinction is made between normal and neurotic anxiety. Both varieties consist of general unrest and vague feelings of apprehension. The normal individual is usually aware of the cause of his anxiety and is motivated by its presence to engage in problem-solving activity that will eliminate the underlying cause. In neurosis, the individual is unaware of the cause of his dread and anxiety level is considerably higher. For no

apparent reason he is periodically overwhelmed by a massive, diffuse emotional reaction. Concomitant physiological sensations (palpitation, difficulty in breathing, cold sweat) intensify his state of alarm and apprehension.

The next step in the anxiety theory of neurosis is more speculative. It is assumed that as a defense against the direct experience of terrifying anxiety attacks, the neurotic may unconsciously develop "substitute" symptoms that serve to alleviate, displace, or otherwise regulate the intensity of anxiety. These defensive measures are more reflexive than reflective. The resulting substitute symptoms constitute other recognized forms of neuroses. To the extent that they succeed in warding off anxiety, they are self-reinforcing and in time become firmly established, stereotyped habit responses that are not under the full control of the individual (Pfeiffer, 1968). The circumvented source of the anxiety, meanwhile, remains unresolved and unassimilated.

The American Psychiatric Association recognizes eight principal types of neurosis: anxiety neurosis, hysterical neurosis, phobic neurosis, obsessive-compulsive neurosis, depressive neurosis, neurasthenic neurosis, depersonalization neurosis, and hypochondriacal neurosis. It seems to many psychologists, however, that these are more appropriately regarded as descriptive names identifying certain kinds of reactions than as separate disorders.

Anxiety Neurosis

Anxiety is the emotion of uncertainty. To a greater or lesser degree, it is present whenever a person is confronted with an unsolved problem or challenge that is vital to his well-being and for which he has no readily available solution. What makes neurotic anxiety an acutely frightening experience is that it is all-pervasive and yet objectless and nameless. The neurotic is sporadically seized with a feeling of impending but unidentifiable disaster. Since

ANXIETY NEUROSIS: THE CASE OF MR. A

Mr. A. achieved considerable success in college as a student and as a campus personality. After graduation he married and accepted one of several attractive positions he was offered. But he left his job after six weeks on the grounds that it was too nerve-racking, and he gave up his next position after two weeks because it was too dull and had no future. Shortly after starting on his third job, he began to complain that he was unhappy there too. He felt that his employer didn't like him and that his co-workers were unfriendly. On several occasions he asked his employer and fellow workers to tell him how he was doing on the job, but (he said) they never gave him a straight answer. Since he had already changed jobs twice within two months, his wife insisted that he stay with his present job.

Shortly thereafter he began to develop acute anxiety symptoms. For no apparent reason, he would periodically feel dizzy, break out in a cold sweat, and tremble. At such times his stomach would churn, and it seemed that his heart was skipping beats. He went to see two physicians, both of whom assured him that he was in good physical condition. For a time he sought relief from his mounting tension through frequent intercourse, but by the time he made an appointment for a psychological examination, he had lost interest in sex. His wife stated that on two recent occasions he had been impotent. His wife was beginning to regret her marriage. She referred to her husband as a baby who needed a mother to take care of him, rather than a wife. Mr. A. had always been very strongly attached to his mother, and since his marriage he had gone to see her at least three times a week. The mother had high hopes for her son. She had objected to his marriage on the grounds that he was too young. She also objected to the girl her son married, because she was not a college graduate and had no money. After Mr. A. developed nervous symptoms, his mother blamed his wife for his condition. Therapy was discontinued after two visits because of a crisis precipitated by his wife. She gave him the choice of a divorce or moving to the West Coast, to get as far as possible from his mother. With great reluctance, Mr. A. agreed to move.

he is not clearly aware of the cause of his anxiety and is therefore uncertain about what he should do, the anxiety remains free-floating and diffuse. He is apprehensive but is unable to account for his uneasiness. His state of alarm impairs concentration, reduces efficiency, increases irritability, and interferes with sleep. Physiological disturbances associated with emotional overreaction, which may include cardiac irregularities, breathing difficulties, excessive perspiration, tremors, and nausea, may be misinterpreted as signs of heart failure and impending death. Anxiety attacks occur unexpectedly, under any circumstances. During sleep they may be expressed in nightmares. Between attacks the person is relatively free of symptoms.

Hysterical Neurosis

A distinction is made between *hysterical conversion* and *hysterical dissociative reactions*. Both types may be interpreted as representing spontaneous, unplanned attempts to avoid anxiety by the exclusion of part of the self. Conversion reactions involve the exclusion of some bodily function, whereas dissociative reactions involve the exclusion of some components of the personality. In conversion reactions, it is assumed that the emotional energy associated with anxiety is transformed or "converted" into physical symptoms primarily involving the loss of sensory and motor functions. The disability is psychological; there is no relevant neurological or physical injury. Characteristic symptoms include paralysis, blindness, deafness, aphonia (loss of voice), and disturbances in sensations.

The psychological nature of these somatic symptoms is particularly apparent in neurotic paralysis, anesthesia, and parasthesia, in which the area of the body affected conforms to popular conceptions rather than to neurological boundaries. For example, a hysterical paralysis of the arm typically stops abruptly at the shoulder, although any damage to the nerves of the arm would inevitably affect the shoulder area as well. An unusual feature of conversion reaction is the neurotic's apparent lack of concern about his symptoms. This attitude of *belle indifférence* was formerly considered to be an identifying characteristic. More recent studies suggest that only about one-third of hysterical patients are indifferent to the loss of sensory or motor function (Stephens and Kamp, 1962).

According to psychoanalytic theory, the choice of symptom has a symbolic significance. The sacrificed function may represent a defense against a forbidden impulse or self-punishment for having such an impulse. Thus a paralysis of the hand may represent a defense against masturbation. In accord with the biblical injunction, "If thine eye offend thee, pluck it out," blindness may constitute a self-imposed punishment for observing a forbidden scene.

Dissociative reactions represent unconscious attempts to escape from conflicts by isolating or separating inner sources of discord. Dissociative reactions include *somnambulism*, *amnesia*, *fugue states*, and *dual personalities*. In somnambulism, or sleepwalking, the major portion of the personality sleeps on while the dissociated segment reenacts some disturbing experience or attempts to reach some happier or safer place. In cases of amnesia, the patient retains most of his memory; he remembers practically all of his vocabulary, the social mores, the names of objects, and so on. Loss of memory is usually limited to personal identity and to specific life experiences of a traumatic nature. Fugue states are characterized by amnesia plus a flight from usual surroundings. A person with a fugue reaction literally runs away from personal problems by traveling to another town, taking on a different name, and starting a new life, oblivious of his former identity. Months or years later, he may suddenly recall his former identity and previous life and be at a loss to explain his present circumstances.

Dual personalities are relatively rare. The creation of two alternating personalties presumably resolves conflicts between "good" and "bad" impulses. When the "good" person is in control, the "bad" person is absent, and vice versa. Usually there is a third personality who is in touch with and a blend of the other two. The "good" person is well behaved, restrained, somewhat depressed, conscientious, and highly moral. The "bad" person is naughty, fun-loving, uninhibited, and infantile. In Freudian terminology, the good personality is dominated by the superego, the bad personality is controlled by the pleasure-seeking id, and the third personality represents the coordinating, reality-oriented ego. Once established, each of the multiple personalities exhibits distinct and consistent characteristics. The spontaneous transition from one personality to another may occur at any time during sleep or when the person is awake. One personality recedes and is immediately replaced by another, whose actions, speech, values, and temperament are clearly different. The personality in charge at the moment may ridicule or offer apologies for the conduct of the other.

In contrast with fugue states, which are largely confined to men, nearly all of the few cases of multiple personality reported have been young women. The clinical picture is much the same in all cases. A classical study is that of Miss Beauchamp (Prince, 1908), who exhibited three personalities, referred to as "The Saint," "The Devil," and "The Woman." The Saint was reserved, idealistic, conscientious, and sad. The Devil, also known as Sally, was a mischievous, fun-loving, troublesome imp.

MULTIPLE PERSONALITY: THE SIXTEEN SELVES OF SYBIL

The case history of Sybil, reported by Schreiber (1973), records three main personalities. There was Sybil herself, a timid, constrained, saintly woman; Peggy, an aggressive, uninhibited, fun-loving girl; and Victoria, a poised and sophisticated woman of the world. In addition, other facets of the personality were personified to create a multiple personality consisting of a total of sixteen alternating selves. Multiple personalities on this scale are no longer fashionable, but in former centuries it was common for disturbed persons to claim that they were possessed by several demons, each of whom had a separate name and distinctive characteristics.

Sybil's story is unusual with respect to the severity of family pathology. On the other hand, her strange case beautifully illustrates the basic principle that pathological reactions represent extreme variations of similar behavior commonly noted in normal persons. At one time or another nearly every girl has wished she were a blonde, a brunette, a redhead, a sophisticated woman of the world, a pixie, a motherly person, a perpetual adolescent, or even a competent handyman.

Other basic principles illustrated by the case of Sybil are: (1) the multiple determinants of psychopathology, (2) the vague boundaries separating severe neurosis from psychosis, (3) the persistent human striving for identity and unity of self, (4) the meaningfulness of symptoms in relation to a person's developmental history, and (5) the everpresent possibility of recovery or marked improvement, even in seemingly hopeless cases.

The story, as told by Schreiber (1973), starts in a midwestern town when Sybil was sent home from college at the age of twenty-two because of a nervous condition. Her basic problem was that she was worried about periodic losses of memory. All her life, people said that she had done things she had no memory of having done. She was seen by Dr. Wilbur, who later was to play an important part in her life.

After two years at home, Sybil returned to college and graduated with a major in art. During her last year at college her mother died. Following graduation, she returned home, got a job, and lived with her father, a building contractor. At the age of thirty-one she went to New York to continue her education. A more personal reason for going to New York was to resume her treatment with Dr. Wilbur, who was now practicing there as a psychoanalyst. For the next eleven years she was in analytic treatment with Dr. Wilbur.

In the course of treatment she exhibited sixteen separate personalities. The three main characters were Sybil Isabel Dorsett, Peggy Baldwin, and Victoria Antoinette Scharleau. Sybil, the prevailing personality, was a very constrained, inhibited, fearful, depleted person, who was unable to express anger. She took life seriously, was very religious, and worried all the time. Sybil had no awareness of the other personalities. Peggy was an aggressive, tough, uninhibited, fun-loving, energetic woman. Unlike Sybil, she enjoyed playing cards, buying pretty dresses, and being the life of the party. Peggy knew about Sybil but was not too familiar with the other personalities. Victoria, or Vicky, was a self-assured, sophisticated woman of the world, who was familiar with all of the personalities.

Each of the three personalities, as well as the other thirteen, differed in style of speaking, movements, and facial expressions. Each was perceived as having distinct physical characteristics. Mary was plump and brown-haired, Vanessa was a tall redhead, and Marjorie was a small willowy brunette. The list of characters sharing the same body also included two male selves, Mike and Sid. Each of the characters had particular skills denied the others. Peggy was the mathematician, Vanessa could play the piano, Sybil was the best artist, and so forth.

The multiple personalities started appearing when Sybil was three and a half years old. During the periods when one or another personality was in charge, Sybil would have no memory of the others' activities. These memory gaps would result in perplexing experiences. Persons Sybil had never seen before would insist they knew her. She would find dresses she had not bought hanging in her closet. She would sometimes return to a painting she had started and find that someone else had completed it in a style different from her own. Occasionally Peggy took trips on her own. Days later, Sybil would reappear to find herself in a strange city with no idea how she got there.

Sybil was the victim of unfavorable heredity, traumatic early experiences, and a pathogenic mother. Her parents were forty years old when she was born. She was an only child. Her mother had a long record of bizarre behavior. She had been seen by a psychiatrist and diagnosed as a schizophrenic, but she refused treatment. Two other members of the mother's family suffered from hysterical dissociation. The father's family also included psychotic members. A paternal aunt frequently dressed in men's clothing and exhibited other peculiarities.

Sybil's early years were a literal nightmare. Until she was nine years old she slept in a crib in her parents' bedroom and was an unwilling captive audience for the sights and sounds of her parents' active sex life. And there was much more. From the time Sybil was six months old until she was six, her mother used her as an outlet for her psychopathology. In one morning ritual, the mother placed Sybil on the kitchen table and inserted a variety of objects into the child's vagina: a flashlight, a small empty bottle, a buttonhook, a handle of a dinner knife, a small silver box. Sybil's vagina was permanently scarred. Sybil was often forced to drink a glassful of milk of magnesia (a laxative) and then put to bed. The inevitable

result was that Sybil soiled herself, and her mother would then punish the child for doing what she made her do. On one occasion she struck Sybil so hard that the child suffered a dislocated shoulder. At other times she burned Sybil's hand with a hot flatiron, put the child in a trunk and closed the lid, and stuffed cotton in her nose until she lost consciousness.

These tortures occurred when the mother and daughter were alone. The father would occasionally observe that the child had been injured, but he accepted without question the mother's explanation that Sybil had fallen or hurt herself accidentally. As often happens in such cases, he preferred not to know what was going on. He realized his wife was odd and had been diagnosed a schizophrenic, but felt it was her responsibility to care for the child.

According to Dr. Wilbur, the spontaneous division of Sybil's personality into a number of selves served as a protective device against the horrors and dangers of reality. At least parts of Sybil would be "away" and unaffected by traumatic experiences. Most of the personalities denied that Sybil's mother was their mother also. Interestingly, Sybil made a distinction between her fear and hatred of the instruments of torture and the torturer. Her mother repeatedly told Sybil that she was the best mother in the world, and in some ways she did show a motherly interest in the girl. The turning point in therapy occurred when Sybil gave up the pretense of having had a good mother and a happy childhood. The ghost of the mother was exorcised when Sybil finally acknowledged openly to herself and her therapist that she had often wished her mother dead and even had strong impulses to kill her.

The main procedure used in treatment was Freudian psychoanalysis. During a critical period when Sybil was suicidal, electric shock convulsions were administered to control her depression and suicidal tendencies. *Sodium pentothal* was used for a while to facilitate the recall of childhood memories. In the latter part of treatment, hypnosis proved a useful aid in the integration of the multiple personalities into one. The new Sybil, an amalgam of the other sixteen personalities, emerged when Sybil was forty-two years old.

By the time her life history appeared in book form, eight years later, Sybil had made great strides and had begun to establish herself as an artist and art teacher. The excellent adjustment she attained, after forty years of inner turmoil, is eloquent testimony of the human striving toward growth, wholeness, and fulfillment despite seemingly insurmountable barriers.

THE MULTIPLE PERSONALITIES OF SYBIL AND THEIR DATES OF BIRTH

Sybil Isabel Dorsett (1923): a depleted person; the waking self.

Victoria Antoinette Scharleau (1926), nicknamed Vicky; a self-assured, sophisticated, attractive blonde; the memory trace of Sybil's selves.

Peggy Lou Baldwin (1926): an assertive, enthusiastic, and often angry pixie, with a pug nose, a Dutch haircut, and a mischievous smile.

Peggy Ann Baldwin (1926): a counterpart of Peggy Lou with similar physical characteristics; she is more often fearful than angry.

Mary Lucinda Saunders Dorsett (1933): a thoughtful, contemplative, maternal, home-loving person; she is plump and has long dark-brown hair parted on the side.

Marcia Lynn Dorsett (1927), last name sometimes Baldwin; a writer and painter; extremely emotional; she has a shield-shaped face, gray eyes, and brown hair parted on the side.

Vanessa Gail Dorsett (1935): intensely dramatic and extremely attractive; a tall redhead with a willowy figure, light-brown eyes, and an expressive oval face.

Mike Dorsett (1928), one of Sybil's two male selves; a builder and carpenter; he has olive skin, dark hair, and brown eyes.

Sid Dorsett (1928), the other of Sybil's male selves; a carpenter and general handyman; he has fair skin, dark hair, and blue eyes.

Nancy Lou Ann Baldwin (date undetermined): interested in politics as the fulfillment of biblical prophecy and intensely afraid of Roman Catholics; fey; her physical characteristics resemble Peggy's.

Sybil Ann Dorsett (1928): listless to the point of neurasthenia; pale and timid with ash-blonde hair, an oval face, and a straight nose.

Ruthie Dorsett (date undetermined): a baby; one of the lesser developed selves.

Clara Dorsett (date undetermined): intensely religious; highly critical of the waking Sybil.

Helen Dorsett (1929): intensely afraid but determined to achieve fulfillment; she has light-brown hair, hazel eyes, a straight nose, and thin lips.

Marjorie Dorsett (1928): serene, vivacious, and quick to laugh; a tease; a small, willowy brunette with fair skin and a pug nose.

The Blonde (1946): nameless; a perpetual teenager; has blonde curly hair and a lilting voice.

The New Sybil (1965): the seventeenth self; an amalgam of the other sixteen selves.

SOURCE: F. R. Schreiber, *Sybil* (Chicago, Ill.: Regnery, 1973. Also Warner Paperbook Library, 1974.)

Sally liked to play tricks on the Saint—undoing her knitting, hiding her money, sending her boxes containing spiders. On occasion Sally would get drunk and leave the Saint with the hangover. The Woman personified the ambitions, self interest, frailties of temper, and usual behavior of an average person. With the aid of hypnosis and suggestion, the real Miss Beauchamp was eventually put together by merging the Saint and the Woman and suppressing Sally.

Thigpen and Cleckley (1957) have described a similar dissociation of personality in their well-known case study of *The Three Faces of Eve*. Eve White was a demure, sad, conscientious, inhibited young lady who sought treatment for blinding headaches and periodic blackouts. Eve Black, who unexpectedly put in an appearance during one of the early therapy sessions, was gay, seductive, adventuresome, carefree, and uninhibited. Jane, the third personality, who later changed her name to Evelyn, represented a composite of Eve White and Eve Black.

Phobic Neurosis

Phobias consist of irrational, intense, persistent fears of specific objects or situations that are recognized by the individual, as well as by others, as inherently harmless. There are all kinds of fears, but only a few qualify as neuroses. To be afraid of dangerous animals and hazardous situations is normal and wise. Isolated specific fears that do not greatly inconvenience or disturb the individual—mild fear and avoidance of dogs, insects, escalators, public speaking, or air travel—are more appropriately referred to as idiosyncratic reactions than as neuroses. These nonneurotic fears, which may persist for long periods, are often the products of simple conditioning experiences during childhood. Neurotic phobias are more serious. A fear of crowds is indicative of a neurosis if the individual is so dis-

SOME COMMON PHOBIAS

Acrophobia	fear of high places
Agoraphobia	fear of open places
Ailurophobia	fear of cats
Aquaphobia	fear of water
Astrophobia	fear of thunder and lightning
Claustrophobia	fear of closed places
Cynophobia	fear of dogs
Hematophobia	fear of blood
Mysophobia	fear of germs or contamination
Monophobia	fear of being alone
Nyctophobia	fear of darkness
Ochlophobia	fear of crowds
Pyrophobia	fear of fire
Xenophobia	fear of strangers
Zoophobia	fear of animals

turbed by the close presence of others that he is unable to use public transportation to travel to work, to shop in a crowded store, to attend parties, and so on. Characteristic reactions of phobic neuroses include feelings of apprehension, heart palpitations, nausea, fatigue, and faintness. If escape is not possible, panic may result.

A widely accepted theory is that phobias represent the displacement of anxiety from its real source to some symbolic substitute object or situation. The advantage of this mechanism is that the person can now express his anxiety without being disturbed by awareness of its real cause. Thus anxiety associated with the repression of sexual temptation may be displaced to a fear of germs or a dread of bodily contact. A conflict involving the acting out of hostile impulses may be expressed in a morbid fear of knives or guns.

The specificity of the phobia permits the person to regulate somewhat his exposure to the externalized feared object. As long as he avoids it, he can enjoy relative peace. However, the underlying anxiety remains and must be afforded periodic outlet. To be useful, the substitute object must be readily available. The popularity of phobias involving high places, open places, closed places, darkness, crowds, and germs is due to the fact that they ideally serve this purpose. With the passage of time, the underlying cause may fade and the phobia continue as a residual habit. Under these circumstances, the simple elimination of the surface phobic symptom is all that is required for a complete cure.

Obsessive-Compulsive Neurosis

Obsessions consist of spontaneously recurring words, thoughts, ideas, and impulses that a person is unable to exclude from his mind. He may be persistently plagued by unanswerable questions regarding the meaning of truth, repeatedly assailed by doubts regarding the correctness of past actions, or troubled by persistent impulses to shout obscenities or engage in some aggressive act. Compulsions overlap with obsessions, but they more specifically involve repetitive motor acts: compulsive hand-washing, complicated rituals of dressing and undressing, the repeated touching of parts of the body, and so on.

Like fears, not all obsessive-compulsive reactions are symptomatic of neurosis. Mild obsessive-compulsive tendencies may result in an orderly, efficient style of life. Persons obsessed with great ambitions may be highly productive and in the process find contentment and fulfillment. Neurotic obsessive-compulsive behavior serves no constructive purpose, is highly distressing to the individual, and often seriously impairs his functioning. The obsessive-compulsive neurotic realizes the senselessness of his behavior, but he has no choice. If he tries to suppress or resist unwanted thoughts or impulses, he experiences acute anxiety. His obsessive-compulsive reactions constitute a kind of magic that wards off inner tension. It is easier and more comforting to carry out the magic ritual than to face the underlying problem. The inconvenience of staying awake half the night counting one's pulse to prove that one is still alive is a small price to pay if this activity closes off thinking about committing suicide. The mechanisms underlying obsessive-compulsive behavior include displacement reaction formation, and undoing, as in Lady Macbeth's repeated washing of her hands to cleanse them of the blood of the murdered king.

Depressive Neurosis

Neurotic depressive reactions are mood disorders in which anxiety is often mixed with guilt. Characteristic symptoms include feelings of dejection, helplessness, self-depreciation, hopelessness, restlessness, irritability, and insomnia. Unlike psychotic depressions, neurotic depressions are usually precipitated by some identifiable cause, such as the death of a loved person, the loss of some cherished possession, or personal failure; but they are less well controlled than normal sorrow or grief reactions, more prolonged, and more often complicated by feelings of self-reproach. Thus a wife who has frequently wished for her husband's death may be troubled by a mixture of neurotic depressive and guilt feelings when he actually does die. Secondary symptoms in the form of self-depreciation and feelings of remorse may represent ways of allaying guilt or inflicting self-punishment.

Seligman (1973) has called attention to parallels between experimental studies leading to learned helpless behavior and the major symptoms of reactive depression. He advances the theory that depressive reactions are precipitated by traumatic experiences over which the individual has no control, such as death, physical disease, financial loss, and growing old. The effect of these inescapable and uncontrollable calamities on certain vulnerable persons is to create a belief in their helplessness that pervades all their behavior. Many of the actions of depressed neurotic patients fit the helplessness model. Typical complaints are paralysis of will, marked loss of confidence, passivity, and dependence.

Neurasthenic Neurosis

The dominant feature of *neurasthenia* is chronic exhaustion. Beard (1880), the American psychiatrist who originally coined the term, attributed neurasthenia to a general weakening of the nerve cells produced by overwork. Though the term has been retained, Beard's definition has been discarded. Neurasthenia is now considered to result from persistent nonadjustive emotional reactions. Typical complaints include feelings of weakness, undue fatigability, loss of interest, vague aches and pains, and difficulty in thinking. Since the symptoms are related to underlying anxiety, they are not affected by rest or relaxation. There is also a tendency for the fatigue to be selective. The neurasthenic may be completely worn out by a few minutes of work, but he may experience no difficulty in dancing all night.

Unlike hysterics, who tend to ignore their physical symptoms, neurasthenics are acutely aware of their ailments. They describe their symptoms in great detail to all who will listen, and are constantly seeking treatment. The neurasthenic often goes the rounds from clinic to clinic, from physician to faith healer to dispenser of patent medicines. Each new remedy brings about some temporary improvement; then there is a relapse, and off he goes in search of another cure. In his approach to his aches and problems, the neurasthenic tends to be dependent. When he consults a physician, he expects him to assume responsibility for his health, happiness, and success.

As Weiss and English (1943, p. 552) have noted, the message communicated by many neurasthenics is: "There's my story, Doctor. Now you pat me and rub me and feed me medicine and take my pains away and give me a good appetite and an easy bowel movement and a good night's sleep, and give me inspiration and happiness and tell me how to be successful. And while you're about it, get my mother-in-law out of the house and I'll pay you when I get a job."

Depersonalizaion

Depersonalization is a dreamlike state of haziness and estrangement. Everything seems unreal, different, and strange. The person may not be quite sure of the boundaries separating the self from the outside world. The self may be viewed with the detachment of an outside observer. A related phenomenon, called *déjà vu*, is the feeling that something seen for the first time has already been seen before. The content of the two reactions differs but both are experienced as hazy, dreamlike states. Normal individuals may experience momentary feelings of depersonalization and the syndrome is also noted in other disorders. Depersonalization is considered a neurotic reaction if it persists for several days or weeks and the individual is aware of the unreality of the experience. If he accepts the depersonalization as real, a diagnosis of psychosis is more appropriate.

Hypochondriacal Neurosis

Hypochondriasis consists of exaggerated concern with one's physical or mental health when there is no detectable cause for worry. Despite repeated reassurance, the hypochondriac remains convinced that he has some disease. He is acutely sensitive to any irregularities in physical or mental functioning and may go to extreme measures to safeguard his health. The preoccupation is wholly mental; there is no loss or impairment in bodily functions. A concern with imaginary ailments may represent a displacement or substitution of anxiety related to some underlying emotional problem. Hypochondriasis appears to be more common among children and the aged than in other age groups (Kenyon, 1965). This age factor may be related to the typical occurrence of marked physical changes at the extremes of life. Care must be taken to differentiate hypochondriacal neurosis from somatic delusions, which are frequently present as secondary symptoms in psychoses.

Other Forms of Neurosis

The advantage and limitation of the APA classification system is that it is based on clinically observed symptom clusters. Specific diagnoses rest solely on descriptive differences. The issue of possible etiological differences is avoided. It is tacitly assumed that the causes for the varied reactions are much the same. Special diagnostic labels have been periodically introduced to identify and differentiate certain selected cases that seemingly have a particular etiology or explanation. An added implication in these special cases is that therapy, to be effective, should be tailored to fit the presumed underlying cause. Two of the older, more established special labels are war neurosis and occupational neurosis. A more recent addition is existential neurosis.

Existential neurosis. This disorder of contemporary life resembles neurasthenia and depression, but basically it consists of a state of alienation from self and society. Its key characteristics are a pervasive sense of the meaninglessness of one's life, loneliness, apathy, boredom, and aimlessness. Existential neurosis is associated with a personality devoid of psychological or humanistic identity (Maddi, 1967). The individual considers himself as nothing more than a player of social roles and an embodiment of biological needs. He accepts his social roles and biological needs as given, and may be quite successful in expressing them, but his development as a real person, with strong feelings, involvement, purpose, and direction, is stunted. An existential neurosis is precipitated when the individual is confronted with environmental or interpersonal stresses that interfere with the enactment of his roles and the satisfaction of his needs, or which expose his inadequacy as a human being. Good examples of existential neuroses are found in the literary works of Albert Camus and Arthur Miller.

Occupational neurosis. Strictly defined, an occupational neurosis consists of some impairment in the sensory and motor functions that are directly related to one's occupation—a singer's laryngitis, an athlete's sore back—especially when these ailments precede a scheduled performance rather than follow it. In most instances, the traditional diagnosis would be conversion hysteria. However, the designation of occupational neurosis may be extended to include a wider variety of neurotic reactions that follow industrial accidents or are attributed to hazards associated with one's vocation. Presumed contributing factors include dissatisfaction with one's job, desire for disability compensation, hurt feelings, desire for attention and sympathy, and other assorted personal motives. Common complaints in accident compensation cases are anxiety, depression, headache, dizziness, poor memory, inability to concentrate, and conversion symptoms. Patients are often irritable, stubborn, and argumentative. They actually experience the symptoms they report, feel entitled to compensation, and resent any suggestion that they may be malingering. The granting of compensation or the termination of litigation usually results in some clinical improvement, but symptoms may persist long afterward.

A related rare disorder, one that is a product of confinement rather than occupation, is known as *Ganser's syndrome*. The condition is mainly noted in prisoners. The individual appears alert and normal but gives approximate, pseudo-stupid answers to questions. Thus he may say that two plus two equal five, call a hammer a saw, and so on. As a rule these people show spontaneous recovery within a few days or weeks. Ganser's syndrome may represent a mild dissociation state in which the prisoner unconsciously behaves as he thinks a mental patient would behave.

War neurosis. The causes of neurosis in combat troops are as varied and complex as the causes of neurosis in civilians during peacetime, but the immediate precipitating sources of stress are more obvious in war neurosis. The diagnostic labels of "shell-shock" and "combat fatigue," which were extensively used during the First and Second World Wars respectively, are self-explanatory. The real stress, of course, was not the sound of exploding shells or the fatigue of combat, but the threat to existence posed by the inescapable risks of battle. The range and variety of symptoms noted in war neurosis correspond to those of civilian life (Janis, 1951), but certain types of reaction are perhaps more prevalent in war neurosis, particularly during its early stages: recurring nightmares, startle reactions to loud noises, exhaustion, tremors, and a vacant, staring expression (Sargent and Slater, 1940).

No simple relationship has been observed between a prior history of personality disturbance and vulnerability to war neurosis. In many instances, the stresses of combat apparently serve to reactivate past conflicts and lead to a recurrence of old symptoms. However, a large proportion of individuals with histories of prior neurosis show a high level of tolerance to war stresses, and many persons with records of good adjustment to civilian life develop symptoms, which often are transient

(Raines and Kolb, 1943). The decisive factor may be the relative severity or duration of stress.

One important lesson learned during the Second World War was that when men exhibited signs of acute stress reaction, supportive therapy aimed at an early return to duty and administered in forward areas was far more effective than hospitalization. Hospitalization, which implied that the soldier was "sick," often led to chronic disability. A second lesson learned during the Korean and Vietnamese wars was that setting time limits on tours of combat duty, so that men could depend on being withdrawn from stress by some definite date, made the stress more tolerable and prevented many breakdowns (Brill, 1967). The favorable long-term outcome of most war neuroses has been shown in a study reported by Brill and Beebe (1955). Five years later, only 14 percent of the patients with histories of war neurosis reported that they were unable to work full-time because of continued symptoms. The great majority were either free of neurotic symptoms or had only mild complaints.

CHOICE OF NEUROSIS

Attempts to account for the development of a particular type of neurosis have focused primarily on the preexisting personality of the neurotic. Symptoms are regarded as intensified manifestations of characteristic modes of reacting and adjusting to difficulties. As Robert White has said (1964, p. 277), "Choice of symptom syndrome is by no means a 'decision' that is made at the last minute, when neurotic breakdown becomes unavoidable. There is an integral relationship between the symptoms finally produced and certain more general characteristics of the patient's personality which have been present for a long time."

According to Hans Eysenck (1961a), an inherited autonomic lability that is expressed in emotional overresponsiveness is

Combat fatigue. An exhausted and emotionally drained soldier holds his head in his hands and stares into space following his return from a mission during the Vietnamese War.

the major etiological factor in all neuroses. The type of neurosis is related to the individual's relative position on the introversion-extraversion continuum. Persons high on neuroticism (emotional instability) and high on introversion are prone to develop anxiety, obsessive-compulsive, and depressive reactions. Hysterics are more extraverted than other types of neurotics, but they do not differ significantly from normal persons with respect to introversion-extraversion. It appears that the more extraverted hysterics acquire conditioned responses slowly, fail to learn social inhibitions, and are therefore impulsive and undersocialized. Introverts are quick to be-

come conditioned and slow to build up reactive inhibition. They tend to become oversocialized and inhibited.

Norman Cameron (1963) differentiates between obsessive-compulsive and depressed patients on the basis of general orientation. The obsessive-compulsive patient is oriented toward gaining independence. He is obstinate, self-sufficient, and self-assertive. He is action-centered and tries to go it alone. The depressed patient, on the other hand, wants to be taken care of. He is oriented toward other people. He seeks reassurance, understanding, love, and help from others, but at the same time he resents his need of them.

David Shapiro (1965) has related choice of neurosis to the individual's characteristic style of thinking, perceiving, feeling, and acting. The obsessive-compulsive style is distinguished by rigidity in thinking. Attention is narrowly focused, to the exclusion of new facts and different points of view. The dogmatic style serves as a way of overcoming doubt and uncertainty. For the obsessive-compulsive person, life is earnest. He is constantly under pressure to be engaged in some purposeful activity. He feels uncomfortable with any degree of freedom. Decisions are avoided, since the act of deciding carries with it a certain freedom of choice. When forced to choose, he is apt to invoke some rule or principle to provide the "right" or "proper" answer. His inability to relax restricts playfulness, spontaneous activity, and emotional expression.

The hysterical style presents a sharp contrast. Hysterical behavior is dramatic, theatrical, romantic, vivid, provocative, diffuse, and global. The hysteric's inability to maintain persistent concentration leads to distractibility. Other investigators have reported similar observations. Female hysterics in particular have been described as egocentric, emotionally shallow, exhibitionistic, disorganized, immature, and sexually inhibited but flirtatious. Although partially valid, these and other observations on the relation of personality to type of neurosis are far from conclusive. Many kinds of personality are found in all forms of neurosis. Personality types associated with a particular neurosis also occur in other neuroses (Foulds and Caine, 1959; Stephens and Kamp, 1962; Rosenberg, 1967).

Choice of neurosis may be related to learning experiences associated with early home training. One possibility is that the child may imitate the parental model. There is no certainty that if the mother characteristically reacts to stress by developing nervous headaches, becoming depressed or fearful, or seeking escape in invalidism, the child will eventually do likewise; but the example is there and ready-made for adoption. A leaning toward hypochondriasis

might be expected in a child reared in a health-conscious home where he is daily cross-examined on possible ailments, fed pills and health foods, routinely questioned on the regularity of his eliminative process, and required to have his temperature taken whenever he sneezes or looks listless. Cold, rigid, systematic, overconscientious parents who insist that their children assume responsibility for their actions at an early age and who set puritanical standards for them may foster obsessive-compulsive tendencies. Parents may contribute to a hysterical personality in a child by rewarding dependency, exhibitionism, coquetry, and histrionic behavior.

All these examples are plausible; but as White (1964) has noted, the role of parental attitudes and training in symptom choice remains hypothetical. Carefully controlled longitudinal studies of children and their families are needed to provide more definite answers.

THE ETIOLOGY OF NEUROSES

A neurosis is an integral part of the total personality. It consists essentially of the individual's more maladaptive attitudes, traits, and habit patterns. Along with the more adaptive attitudes, traits, and habit patterns of normal persons, the symptoms of neurotics are the products of the cumulative interaction of biological factors, environmental influences, and learning experiences. The content, severity, modification, and remission of neurotic behavior are therefore subject to maturation changes and new experiences. In other words, there are no specific single causes. The particular combination of co-determinants may vary considerably from patient to patient.

Age and Sex

Neuroses occur at all ages, but the peak age for initial treatment is between twenty and forty. The total number of treated and untreated neurotics, regardless of age of onset, also is highest during the period between adolescence and early middle age (Shepherd and Gruenberg, 1957). Rates for women tend to be slightly higher in all age groups. This sex difference may be due to a tendency in our culture to view emotional symptoms as signs of weakness. We consider it "feminine" to express emotions openly, so girls are not taught to hide their feelings to anywhere near the extent that boys are. To be "manly" is to suppress most emotions and to be aggressive, so men are more likely than women to "act out" their personal difficulties and thus are more frequently classified as suffering from character or personality disorders.

Genetic Factors

Most authorities who give full weight to the hereditary components of behavior consider that persons susceptible to neuroses inherit one or more polygenetically determined temperament traits associated with emotional instability. Whether behavior becomes sufficiently disordered to warrant a diagnosis of neurosis depends on the degree and nature of the stresses encountered by the individual. Since neurotic symptoms are exaggerations of preexisting traits and differ more in degree than in kind from similar traits common among normal persons, the diagnosis of neurosis is far from an exact science.

In the few studies in which concordance rates of monozygotic (MZ) and dizygotic (DZ) twins have been compared, the findings have been inconsistent. Overall, however, they support the hypothesis of a hereditary determinant. When the findings of the five studies reviewed by Essen-Moller (1965) are combined, the concordance rate for neurosis is found to be 43 percent for forty-seven MZ pairs and 23 percent for fifty-six DZ pairs. Of more significance than the actual figures is the observation made by Shields and Slater (1961) that when both members of a pair were neurotic, there was much greater intrapair similarity in symptoms if the twins were monozygotic than if they were dizygotic.

The specificity of genetic predisposition is further suggested by family studies that have shown a tendency for the parents and siblings of neurotics to develop the same type of neurosis. The averaged findings of several studies indicated that 36 percent of the parents of anxiety patients and 17 percent of their siblings had histories of anxiety neuroses (Slater, 1964). Comparable figures for obsessive-compulsive patients were 18 percent for parents and 12 percent for siblings. The averaged findings of several studies of hysteria indicated that 10 percent of the parents of hysterics and 7 percent of their siblings had the same disorder. These results may, of course, also be interpreted as due to the common home environment of the patients, parents, and siblings.

The possibility of *assortative mating*, which would have the effect of concentrating the genes associated with neuroticism, has been raised by Slater and Woodside (1951). In comparing a series of normal and neurotic soldiers and their wives, these investigators found that the wives of neurotics were themselves more neurotic and came from more neurotic families than the wives of normal soldiers. Some evidence of assortative mating on the basis of correlations obtained between fathers and mothers on the Minnesota Multiphasic Personality Inventory (MMPI) scale has also been reported (Gottesman, 1965). However, of the three scales that are considered to measure the traits that constitute the neurotic triad—hypochondriasis, hysteria, and depression—a statistically significant positive intraparent correlation was found only for hypochondriasis.

Data on the inheritance of neurotic tendencies, as measured by the personality test scores of nonpatient populations, are more conclusive. The surprising 1937 findings of Newman, Freeman, and Holzinger, that separated MZ twin pairs were slightly more alike in emotional instability than MZ twins reared together, have been more recently confirmed by Shields (1962). In the earlier study, the intrapair correlations were .58 for the separated MZ pairs, .56

for the nonseparated MZ twins, and .37 for DZ twins. The corresponding figures reported by Shields were .53 for separated MZ twins, .38 for MZ twins reared together, and .11 for DZ pairs. These findings are difficult to interpret. One possibility is that when MZ twins are reared together one may bear the brunt of life experiences. When they are reared apart, the supportive influence of the twin is removed so that each manifests his genetic potentialities more fully. Significantly higher MZ than DZ intrapair correlations with respect to neuroticism have been reported in several studies (Carter, 1933; Eysenck and Prell, 1951; Vandenberg, 1966; and others). Twin studies also provide some evidence of hereditary components associated with the relative responsiveness of the autonomic nervous system (Vandenberg, 1966).

Developmental Factors

Most psychological theories of neurosis stress the importance of parent-child relationships and early life experiences as contributing influences in the development of personality flaws that predispose the child to neurotic behavior in later years. Supporting evidence consists mainly of retrospective case-history data. The presumed pathogenic determinants cover a broad range:

1. Sex conflicts induced by early indoctrination in puritanical standards or unresolved oedipal bonds. Parental exploitation of the child's love needs as a means of control or other disappointing earlier experiences may cause a child subsequently to avoid becoming emotionally involved with other persons.
2. Inferiority feelings resulting from unfavorable comparisons with siblings, belittlement, unrealistic expectations and goals set by parents, or past failures.
3. Conflicts regarding the expression of aggression related to strong parental disapproval and withdrawal of affection whenever the child attempted to assert himself, resist domination, or express hostile feelings.
4. Insecurity feelings resulting from overprotection, parental inconsistencies, separations, or the expression of affection by the parents only when the child was "good."
5. Traumatic experiences during childhood that were either dismissed or ridiculed by parents or could not be discussed with parents. These unresolved fears may form the nucleus for subsequent phobias.
6. Dependence and immaturity resulting from parental domination and indulgence; the sacrifice of autonomy and self identity as the price paid for retaining parental affection and the security and safety thus provided.
7. Identification with and adoption of a parental model of neurotic behavior. For varied reasons, parents may actually encourage and reinforce hypochondriacal, compulsive, hysterical, and fearful behavior in their children.

Clinical observations have repeatedly confirmed the occurrence of these and other developmental defects in neuroses. A plausible explanation of the patient's present symptoms can often be deduced from his earlier adverse learning experiences. However, the etiological significance of these developmental factors is challenged by the fact that many children who have histories of similar parent-child relationships or early life experiences do not become neurotic. The great majority of the brothers and sisters of neurotics do not manifest overt signs of neurosis as adults. Since no two children have exactly the same relationship with their parents, the presence of subtle individual variations may account for the differential outcome of similar patterns of rearing and parent-child interaction.

The more marked predisposition of certain persons to neurosis may also be due to the timing or particular combination of unfavorable experiences, the greater intensity or duration of conflicts, or the relative absence of favorable balancing factors within or outside the home. There is also the possibility that adverse environmental and learning experiences do not in themselves produce a neurosis. The interactive effect of an innate low threshold of anxiety and unfavorable life experiences may be required before neurosis can occur. And the inherent emotional instability of the potential neurotic not only may influence his reactions to situations, but may also affect the attitudes and behavior of his parents and the home atmosphere.

Psychoanalytic Theory

Psychoanalytic theory considers that every neurosis results from a faulty resolution of the Oedipus complex, and hence is rooted in early childhood. The basic assumption is that anxiety originates from the inability or failure of the ego to control id impulses. Conflicts in later life reinstate this early anxiety. Symptoms represent defenses against a threatened breakdown of repression and the emergence of anxiety.

In anxiety reactions, the underlying feelings of apprehension are overtly manifested. In phobias, the fears expressed represent an externalization and displacement of anxiety on specific objects. Obsessive-compulsive symptoms represent prohibitions against, atonements for, or disguised gratifications of repressed sexual or aggressive impulses. The primary purpose of compulsive ceremonials is to avoid awareness of the source of anxiety. The traumatic experience is presumably isolated from its affect and associated connections so that it is not readily accessible to recall. Depressive reactions are attributed to guilt feelings resulting from the superego's disapproval of the ego's failure to inhibit id impulses. Hysteria is interpreted as a denial of sexual conflict. It is assumed that the conversion of libidinal energy into physical symptoms provides an indirect expression of erotic impulses.

In summary, neurotic symptoms constitute defenses designed to ward off anxiety resulting from intrapsychic unconscious conflicts, mainly sexual in nature, that are traced to repressed unfavorable parent-child relationships. The aim of therapy is to uncover the origin and resolve the underlying problem, and thereby remove the basic cause of symptoms.

Learning Theory

Dollard and Miller (1950) attempted to translate psychoanalytic concepts into the language of learning theory. They accepted the basic premise that inner conflicts constituted the main cause of neurosis, but for the traditional psychoanalytic concepts they substituted primary drives, acquired drives, reinforcement, stimulus generalization, and higher mediating mental processes. More recent advocates of the application of modern learning theory to neurosis have completely discarded psychoanalytic concepts. (Lazarus, 1971).

Eysenck and Rachman (1965) describe three stages in the development of a neurosis. The first consists of a traumatic event or a series of traumatic events that produces strong unconditioned autonomic reactions. The immediate emotional reaction to traumatic events may be highly disruptive, but in normal individuals the effects are usually transitory. Because of innate autonomic instability, the potential neurotic's response to trauma tends to be stronger and more lasting. The second stage is reached if conditioning takes place, and previously neutral stimuli connected with the unconditioned stimuli now serve as signals that elicit the original maladaptive emotional behavior.

As a rule, these conditioned reactions clear up spontaneously over a period of time. If the individual is repeatedly exposed to a conditioned stimulus that is not followed by the repetition of traumatic events, the absence of reinforcement leads to the gradual extinction of conditioned responses. Under certain circumstances, however, spontaneous remission or extinction does not occur. This brings us to the third stage, which is marked by an avoid-

THE CASE OF LITTLE HANS: THREE INTERPRETATIONS

In 1905, Sigmund Freud published his only account of a child analysis. The subject was Little Hans, a five year old boy with a phobia about horses. He was afraid to go out in the street for fear a horse would bite him. The case is regarded in psychoanalytic circles as a classical illustration of sex in the development of phobias. It is also considered confirmatory evidence of the oedipal complex. The importance attached to the case of Little Hans has served as a challenge to adherents of other schools. Wolpe and Rachman (1960) have suggested a learning theory explanation for the boy's fear and Maurer has proposed an existential interpretation. Detailed notes of Hans' behavior and conversations made by his father, which he reported to Freud, provide the basis for all three interpretations. Each interpretation is based on the selective use of information supporting the analytic, behavioral, and existential viewpoints.

1. Freud only saw Hans once. Treatment was carried out by the boy's father, who corresponded regularly with Freud and applied his suggestions. Freud's interpretation was that the real basis of Hans' fear was that he wanted to go to bed with his mother and was afraid of retaliatory action by his father. The evidence cited in support of this interpretation was Hans' lively interest in sex and his asking his mother on one occasion to touch his "widdler" (urine maker) while she was bathing him. Another bit of evidence was that Hans described the feared horse as having "a black thing around his mouth" (a leather muzzle) and the father had a black moustache. On several occasions, the father suggested to his son that he was really afraid of the horse's large penis but Hans dismissed this idea by noting that

widdlers don't bite. Hans also repeatedly said and showed by his behavior that he was fond of his father. The only threat of castration had been made by the mother when she caught Hans playing with his widdler.

2. Wolpe and Rachman (1960) offer a simpler explanation based on conditioning. The fear of horses started shortly after Hans had witnessed an accident in the street. A horse pulling a bus fell and, while on its back, kicked out wildly with its feet. Hans subsequently related an earlier experience that involved the father of a playmate, warning the playmate not to touch a horse standing in the street lest it bite her. In accord with learning principles, the fear of horses was generalized to include all large animals that Hans was familiar with from visits to the zoo. A final observation that fits the learning model is that Hans cured himself of his fear by playing with toy horses, pretending to be a colt, and riding horseback on a cooperative maid. In short, he desensitized his fear.

3. According to A. Maurer (1964) the horse incident precipitated for Hans an existential fear of death. He also was afraid of drowning; he was terrified that his mother might release her hold on him while she was giving him a bath and he would be washed down the drain. At age three, Hans had entered his mother's room shortly after she had delivered a baby sister. On this occasion he had been upset by the bloodstained bedpan and the basins filled with water and blood. He was afraid of guns. He was also afraid that his mother might desert him as she had once threatened. Freud was not unaware of this aspect of Hans' problem. In his analysis he makes the passing comment that Hans "is occupied not only by the riddle of life but with the riddle of death."

ance of the conditioned stimulus, which in turn prevents extinction. If a person who has been in a plane accident subsequently avoids air travel and hence is rewarded or effectively reinforced by having no further contact with the feared object, there is no

opportunity for extinction to occur. The three-stage theory is particularly applicable to phobic reactions, anxiety states, and obsessive-compulsive disorders.

Learning theory agrees with psychoanalytic theory in stressing the importance of traumatic experiences and faulty learning in the etiology of neuroses. Beyond this point, however, they differ. Freud attributed the origin of all neuroses to fixation at the oedipal period of early childhood. Learning theory sets no age limits; traumatic experiences following persistent conditioned responses may occur at any time. Freudian theory assumes the existence of some repressed intrapsychic conflict that is the source of surface symptoms. Until the underlying conflict is uncovered and resolved, symptoms will persist. The treatment of symptoms per se is considered futile, since other symptoms would soon be substituted. Learning theory attaches no importance to unconscious conflicts. There is no need to unravel the past. The symptom is the neurosis; get rid of the symptom, and there is no neurosis, no substitution of symptoms.

Behavior therapy based on learning theory is concerned with present maladaptive habits. It focuses on the modification of behavior directly through learning and unlearning procedures, rather than insights gained by exploring and interpreting the unconscious.

Stress and Conflict

Studies of combat personnel exposed to the hazards of war provide a natural source of data for evaluating the role of stress in the etiology of neurosis. The overwhelming and inescapable strain imposed on airmen during World War II has been graphically described by Grinker and Spiegel (1945). In some overseas units it was a mathematical certainty that only a few men of each squadron would finish a tour of duty. In addition to the dangers of enemy activity, there was the ever-present risk of mechanical and structural failure of the planes on which the pilots' safety depended. Conflicts between the demands of duty and safety were augmented by identification with and loyalty to crew members. Many airmen stated that they suffered more when their crews were flying without them on combat missions than when they

went along themselves. The spectre of death was pervasive. In the words of Grinker and Spiegel (1945, p. 35):

The men suffer not only from the sense of bereavement, but from having seen the anguish of bloody and painful death. They cannot look away when the ship flying on their wing receives a direct flak hit and bursts into flame. The sight of their tentmates bailing out with burning parachutes, or exploded out of a disintegrating ship, becomes stamped on their memory. The empty beds in the tent at night reflect this memory, which does not disappear with the sending home of their buddy's clothes and personal effects. The grief persists and, though it is dulled by time, new losses may be added to it. In addition, the loss of friends stimulates increased anxiety. What happened to his buddy may well happen to himself, since they are so much alike,

The threat to life is not the only stress experienced by combat troops. Other associated pressures include lack of sleep, physical exhaustion, extremes of temperature, hunger, separation from families, injuries, illness, excessive responsibility, uncomfortable living conditions, and so on. What effect do these multiple stresses have on the incidence of neurosis? The main conclusion that may be drawn from the literature is that the impact of stress varies markedly with the individual. Some men break under mild stress, others tolerate prolonged, intense pressure without showing overt signs of emotional disturbance. The finding of some studies indicate that men with a prior psychiatric history are relatively more vulnerable to neurosis; other studies show that neurotic civilians often make excellent soldiers. With respect to more general findings there appears to be agreement that the incidence of neurosis among combatants tends to be related to the casualty risk. One of the better controlled studies on this point is that reported by Tompkins (1959). As is apparent from the summary of his data reported in Table 11.1, the incidence of neurosis among flyers is directly related to their degree of danger as measured by casualty figures.

For civilian populations exposed to

bombing, the psychological effects appear to be variable and transient. Janis (1951) has reported a comprehensive analysis of the psychological effects of air war on the civilian populations of Britain, Germany, and Japan during World War II. His main conclusions are:

1. The havoc produced by A-bomb attacks on Hiroshima and Nagasaki had no noticeable effect on the occurrence of psychosis, neurosis, and other severe disorders. The dominant reaction among the survivors was transient acute fear or anxiety. In some cases the emotional disturbance took the form of an acute depressive reaction.

2. Under conditions of severe and continued bombing, there was a marked incidence of temporary emotional shock, even among persons who were previously stable. Transient symptoms consisted mainly of excess anxiety, mild depression, and apathy. These reactions were most likely to occur among those who had undergone near-miss experiences. Markedly predisposed persons with prior histories of neurosis often showed an exacerbation of their former symptoms. Some chronic neurotics improved. Most psychotic patients showed no essential change in their clinical condition.

3. Following heavy air attacks, there was a slight but definite increase in psychosomatic disorders. Peptic ulcers were most common. Other noted reactions were coronary insufficiency and menstrual difficulties.

4. Children exposed to the dangers and destruction of air raids were most apt to become emotionally disturbed if their parents or other adults exhibited overt signs of emotional upset in their presence. This observation supports Bandura and Walters' view (1963) of the importance of the influence of adult models on the behavior of children.

5. People exposed to a series of air raids tended to adapt and show increased capacity to withstand the stress of subsequent attacks. Spontaneous reactions, which probably contributed to emotional adjustment, included sightseeing in damaged areas, increased social interaction, and the development of fatalistic attitudes, rituals, and superstitions. The presence of other persons in communal shelters tended to lessen anxiety.

Sociocultural Factors

The fact that neuroses occur in all cultures, including those in which the free expression of the sexual drive is limited only

Table 11.1. Danger and the Incidence of Neurosis among Combat Fliers.

Duty	Relative incidence of neurosis	Flying hours per casualty
Night bombing	12.0%	160
Day fighting	6.0	188
Night fighting	3.4	231
Coastal reconnaissance	3.3	360
Training	1.1	1,960

Adapted from V. H. Tompkins, "Stress in Aviation," in *The Nature of Stress Disorder*, ed. J. Hambling (Springfield, Ill.: Charles C Thomas, 1959), pp. 73-80.

by the incest taboo, brings into question the importance attached by psychoanalysts to sexual conflicts. There is some evidence that hysterical-conversion reactions are relatively more common and obsessive-compulsive reactions less common in primitive than in more advanced cultures. In our own culture, field reports (Dohrenwend and Dohrenwend, 1967) indicate that the maximum prevalance rate for treated and untreated cases combined occurs about as often in the lowest social stratum as in other classes. At any one time, the number of neurotic patients in treatment is greatest in the highest socioeconomic class; but the incidence rate, or number of new cases that develop each year, is about the same at all social levels (Hollingshead and Redlich, 1958). The lower rate of neurotic patients in treatment in the lower classes may be due as much to a tendency of those with little education to view neurotic symptoms as manifestations of physical disease, for which medication and rest are required, as to their inability to afford psychotherapy.

Symptoms appear to be somewhat related to social class. In general, higher socioeconomic groups more often manifest vague psychological symptoms, whereas the lower classes tend to show a predominance of physical and behavioral symptoms. As the psychiatrist sees it, "The Class V [lowest socioeconomic group] neurotic behaves badly, the Class IV aches physically, the Class III patient defends fearfully, and the Class I-II patient is dissatisfied with himself" (Hollingshead and Redlich, 1958, p. 240). More often than not, physicians go along with the bodily aches and complaints of the verbally inarticulate lower-class patient and prescribe medication, whereas the Class I patient is treated by subtle and prolonged psychotherapy.

TREATMENT OF NEUROSES

The method of choice in the treatment of neuroses is psychotherapy, which may be broadly defined as including any psychological or behavioral approach that is intended to contribute to some beneficial change in the client's personality and behavior. Treatment may be conducted by professionally trained mental health personnel or others; it may be highly structured or informal. A comprehensive handbook of psychotherapy covering theory, methods, goals, and outcome has been edited by Bergin and Garfield (1971).

Increasing use is being made of group and family therapy but the basic principles are more conveniently discussed in relation to individual therapy. Inquiry into the nature of the client's problem typically marks the beginning of individual therapy. The extent and nature of the inquiry, the processes or techniques used, and the kinds of changes sought vary markedly with the therapist's orientation and the patient's clinical condition and financial resources. The inquiry phase may range from one or two interviews devoted to a statement of the complaint and relevant case-history data to the hundreds of sessions required by psychoanalysis for the comprehensive unraveling and critical examination of the conscious and unconscious components of the personality. During the inquiry, as well as during later phases, the patient is encouraged by the understanding and nonjudgmental attitude of the therapist to speak freely and frankly on personal matters.

The briefer the period of inquiry, the more use is made of a conversational, semistructured, question-and-answer type of interview, aimed at identifying the specific problem as quickly as possible so the therapist can proceed to corrective measures. When the inquiry is intensive, extensive, and prolonged, the sessions are less structured. The patient is encouraged to tell his story in his own way and at his own pace, to report dreams, make free associations, and so on. The recognized purpose of the treatment sessions, reinforced by occasional comments by the therapist, serves to direct communication on more or less relevant topics.

*Albert Ellis, founder of rational psychotherapy,
who urges clients to think well of themselves,
refrain from derogatory self-messages, and
engage in positive actions.*

Advocates of intensive inquiry maintain that the procedure itself has therapeutic value. It is commonly observed that patients experience a tremendous sense of relief at discussing honestly their fears, inadequacies, hates, and guilt feelings, or at revealing for the first time in their lives some secret shameful act or thought. This cathartic effect is usually transient and of limited therapeutic significance. Of greater importance is the fact that the repressed or hitherto avoided sources of anxiety are brought out in the open, where they can be dealt with objectively and rationally. Now that he can take a long look at his early experience with adult eyes, the patient may himself realize that he has been exaggerating the uniqueness and severity of his "sinful" or "depraved" behavior during childhood and adolescence. The seeming horrendousness and unpardonableness of one's misdeeds and faults may be further lessened by the therapist's lack of surprise or shock at the "awful" disclosures and his continued unconditional acceptance of the patient as a person of worth. The therapist does not condone, forgive, or minimize past mistakes. They did occur. Memory traces

of the events along with associated affects are permanently imprinted on the patient's nervous system and subject to recall. What many therapists try to do is to help the patient distinguish between the unique self, worthy of esteem, and his actions, some of which may have been or still are undesirable and in need of correction.

Counseling Procedures

Alfred Adler (1929), George Kelly (1955), E. L. Phillips (1956), and others have noted that the rigid, maladaptive behavior of neurotics often appears to be causally related to faulty attitudes, unrealistic expectations and goals, and discrepancies between the individual's real and imagined ideal self. With some variations, these authors have recommended counseling to reevaluate patients' personal constructs, aspirations, and value systems; to explore and try out alternate possibilities; and to trim expectations and goals to fit their capabilities and life circumstances. In principle, the counseling process involves an objective discussion and appraisal of possible alternatives, with the final decision left to the patient. In practice, the patient tends to follow the cues and adopt the value systems of the therapist.

One counseling procedure that borders on behavior therapy is *rational-emotive psychotherapy*, founded by Albert Ellis (1967). One of his basic tenets is that neurotics needlessly create anxiety and anger by accepting uncritically certain irrational hypotheses: that it is essential to be loved or approved by virtually every significant person one meets; that to be considered a worthwhile person one should be competent in all respects; that it is catastrophic if one does not discover the solution to human problems. Ellis also holds that neurotics constantly, both consciously and unconsciously, tell themselves irrational, nonsensical things that keep them continually upset and impede their performance. Thus a person who is uneasy in social situations may constantly tell himself that people do not like him, that they speak disaparagingly about him, that he is inferior to just about everyone he has ever met.

The therapist explains the general mechanisms of emotional disturbances, gives the patient some literature to read, and may direct him to engage in certain specific activities outside of therapy. Patients are seen once a week or less and encouraged to work out their own problems with significant people in their lives. The therapist repeatedly demonstrates that the maladaptiveness of the patient's behavior is not due to external events, but rather to his irrational interpretation of his experiences and his defeatist attitude that he is incapable of winning the acceptance of others because he doesn't measure up to them.

The aims of rational therapy are to increase the patient's confidence and independence and to train him to react to life circumstances with a minimum of anxiety and hostility. The patient is taught that it is possible to accept himself as a worthwhile human being just because he exists. All that is expected of him is that he make some kind of interesting, satisfying life for himself and to have some commit-ment to something outside himself, whether to people, things, or ideas. His intrinsic value is not dependent on external criteria of popularity, achievement and the opinions of others. This down-to-earth approach works with some patients. Others prefer and respond better to therapies that encourage them to strive for maximum self-realization, to move toward people, to be less egocentric, and to establish genuine bonds of affection with others.

Psychoanalytic Therapy

As we have seen, psychoanalytic therapy is aimed at strengthening the ego at the expense of the id by "lifting" repressed material from the unconscious to the conscious, where it can be interpreted and integrated with the rest of conscious content. Wih the aid of free association and dream analysis, the therapist facilitates the recall and assimilation of repressed material while maintaining a relatively objective, nonevaluative attitude. The interpretation and resolution of the transference phenomenon contributes to cognitive insight. Transference represents a repetition of the infantile neurosis, with the analyst serving as a convenient target for the expression of feelings and attitudes the child originally had for his parents. The fact that the analyst does not react to the projected feelings and attitudes as the parents did forces the patient to reexamine and correct his infantile reaction patterns.

Up to this point, most analysts are in accord. But many of them disagree on the necessary length of treatment, the desirability of countertransference, and the relative emphasis that should be placed on current rather than past difficulties. The traditional belief that the probability of recovery is directly related to length of treatment has been challenged by several analysts. Prolonged treatment over several years has not been found to be any more effective than shorter treatment. A more serious criticism is that prolonged therapy often leads to dependency and regressive attitudes. Franz Alexander (1963) favored the periodic interruption of treatment to give the natural recuperative powers of the human personality a chance to function. During temporary interruptions, the patient often discovers he can take over his own management, an important step in gaining self-confidence. The orthodox view that the analyst should strive to remain a "blank screen" has been rejected by many analysts as unrealistic. Two-way interaction between therapist and patient is a more natural procedure, and many analysts have found it more effective.

The classical Freudian emphasis on the reconstruction of the patient's childhood history is important in giving him an understanding of the source of his difficulties, but he is really more concerned with his present problems, and Alexander maintains that is where the analyst's focus should be. Understanding the past should be related to and subordinated to the patient's circumstances here and now. Finally, many analysts today are interested in combining the insights of psychoanalysis with the principles of learning theory. Analytic therapy may be regarded as an educational process aimed at the unlearning of the reactions of childhood and the acquisition of new, more effective, and more satisfying adult response patterns. The nonreinforced repetition of the infantile neurosis during transference may be interpreted as facilitating extinction. *Countertransference*, or an increase in the analyst's involvement with the patient, encourages and rewards the emergence of new, more adaptive responses.

Behavior Therapy

The terms *behavior therapy* and *behavior modification* refer to a variety of techniques that use learning concepts to produce a desired change in behavior. Behavior therapy focuses on observable and measurable changes in specific responses. When the therapist seeks case-history information, his main concern is with the disturbing behavior or the specific symptom that is to be changed. Detailed infor-

mation is obtained during the initial interviews on the types of stimuli or situations that elicit, aggravate, or ameliorate the symptom response, and the learning contingencies that have influenced and shaped the response and currently support it.

The early sessions may be devoted to a general discussion of the patient's problem and to explanations and reassurances. Patients under pressure to talk about their difficulties are permitted to do so, but this sort of traditional procedure is mainly used for purposes of clarification and the establishment of rapport. No attempt is made to identify the childhood determinants of neurosis or to help the patient gain insight and resolve intrapsychic conflicts. Since a basic premise of behavior theory is that neurotic symptoms represent persistent acquired habits that can be unlearned, the therapy proper starts with the application of some learning process. Certain techniques are favored for specific types of problems, but the general approach is one of experimentation. If one technique does not work, another is tried. The principal behavior modification procedures are *counterconditioning, systematic desensitization, operant conditioning, role rehearsal* associated with *assertive training* and *implosive therapy*.

Counterconditioning. In 1924 M. C. Jones demonstrated the applicability of conditioning procedures in the treatment of a phobia. The subject in this now classic study was Peter, a three-year-old who had a great fear of furry objects. Treatment consisted of associating the sight of a rabbit with the pleasurable experience of eating. While Peter was happily eating, a rabbit in a cage was introduced at the far end of the room. On subsequent days the rabbit was brought closer and closer as Peter had his lunch. Care was taken to maintain a safe distance, so that the positive relaxed state associated with eating was stronger than the fear response. Under these conditions, Peter learned to accept and react favorably to the rabbit. By the end of the experiment he was able to stroke the rabbit without signs of fear.

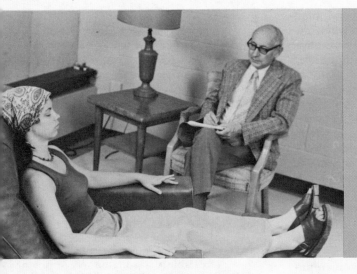

Joseph Wolpe, a psychiatrist who pioneered in the development of behavior therapy in this country. This scene with a patient illustrates the procedure of systematic desensitization which he favors in the treatment of phobias.

Moreover, the acquired positive response to the rabbit was generalized to other animals and furry objects.

Two other early proponents of counterconditioning in the elimination of fears were W. H. Burnham (1924) and H. L. Hollingworth (1930). E. R. Guthrie (1935) proposed that the basic rule for breaking a habit was to practice other responses to the cues that initiated the habit. In 1958 Joseph Wolpe introduced his concept of *reciprocal inhibition* as the general principle underlying the counterconditioning of anxiety responses.

The elimination of anxiety-response habits always seems to require the inhibition of anxiety by a competing response. The formal process is the establishment of conditioned inhibition through what has been called the "reciprocal inhibition principle": If a response inhibitory of anxiety can be made to occur in the presence of anxiety-evoking stimuli, it will weaken the bond between these stimuli and the anxiety [Wolpe and Lazarus, 1966, p. 12].

Systematic desensitization. There is a danger in the application of counterconditioning procedures: the anxiety response to a stimulus may be greater than the planned inhibitory response. The solution proposed by Wolpe and Lazarus is to break the

anxiety-response pattern into small units that can be eliminated one by one. Using information obtained from the patient, the therapist establishes an anxiety hierarchy consisting of anxiety-evoking stimuli or situations arranged in descending order of intensity of reaction. An abbreviated hierarchy of stimuli related to a fear of flying, for example, might be:

1. Being airborne in a plane.
2. Sitting in a plane.
3. Going to an airport for the purpose of taking a trip by air.
4. Planning a trip by air.
5. Thinking about flying.
6. Watching an airplane in the sky.
7. Seeing a picture of an airplane.

The patient is given detailed instructions and practice in *progressive relaxation.* After he has attained the capacity to calm himself at will and is in a relaxed state, he is asked to imagine the scene or situation that is least anxiety-provoking. If this does not arouse any significant anxiety, the next scene in the hierarchy is presented. Usually three or four steps in the hierarchy are presented during an individual session, until the patient can imagine the most anxiety-provoking scene without becoming upset. When fear has been generalized to related stimuli, it may be necessary to work through several hierarchical sets. It is inferred that when desensitization is successful, the relaxation responses become connected to stimuli that formerly evoked anxiety. The goal, of course, is to generalize clinical improvements made in the therapeutic setting to real-life situations. Wolpe (1961) has reported complete or almost complete freedom from phobic reactions outside of the therapeutic setting in twenty-seven of thirty-nine randomly selected patients, or approximately seventy percent of the cases.

Operant conditioning. This procedure is based on the principle of reinforcement, which holds that behavior is largely controlled by its consequences and that it can be modified and maintained by manipulating the consequences. More simply stated, there is a high probability that "rewarded" behavior will be repeated whereas ignored or "punished" behavior will be discontinued. An important advantage of operant conditioning is its wide range of applicability. Autonomic as well as voluntary responses may be modified by appropriate reinforcement.

The therapist may increase the frequency of a desired response by being more attentive or making some favorable comment whenever the patient spontaneously emits the response. Under the direction and supervision of the therapist, members of the patient's family may continue the reinforcement program at home. This extension contributes to the generalization of desirable responses to other persons and other situations. Conversely, the therapist and family members may decrease the frequency of undesirable behavior by deliberately ignoring the behavior and the patient whenever he exhibits it. To be effective, reinforcement must immediately follow the behavior selected for modification. Conditioning is more rapid and permanent if reinforcement is occasionally omitted. Ideally, reinforcement should be confined to a specific target, a particular kind of behavior. When this has been corrected, the procedure may be applied to other targets in turn.

OPERANT CONDITIONING: HOW TO MAKE A PATIENT EAT

Bachrach, Erwin, and Mohr (1965) have reported an interesting example of control of eating behavior in an anorexic patient by operant conditioning techniques. Because of a pathological loss of appetite, the patient had lost 73 pounds over a number of years—and she weighed only 120 to begin with. Now thirty-seven years old and weighing forty-seven pounds, she was in imminent danger of death by starvation if normal eating behavior was not quickly restored.

The first step in the treatment procedure was to establish a suitable environment. Before operant conditioning was begun, the patient was installed in an attractive hospital room with radio, television, books, records, and magazines readily available and with free access to visitors. Since she seemed to enjoy receiving visitors, playing records, and watching television, it was decided to use these as reinforcing contingents.

Without warning or explanation the patient was now transferred to a barren room overlooking the hospital courtyard and furnished only with a bed, night stand, and chair. Here she would stay, deprived of all pleasurable activities, unless she ate. Her family, the hospital administrators, and the nursing staff cooperated in this unusual procedure, but the patient herself was told nothing of the plan. Arrangements were made for a member of the training staff to eat each meal with her. The initial shaping schedule called for rewarding the patient for any activity associated with eating. If she lifted her fork toward the food, the experimenter would talk to her about something of interest. Step by step, the response required to attract the experimenter's attention and conversation was increased to lifting food toward her mouth, chewing, and so on.

Other reinforcements were gradually introduced. At first the patient was permitted the use of a radio, television, or phonograph after a meal if she had eaten any part of it. If she ate nothing, nothing would be done in the way of reinforcement, and she would be left alone until the next meal. Gradually she was required to eat more and more of the meal in order to have access to the radio or television set. Meals were slowly increased in caloric value, and the patient was allowed her choice among alternative menus. As her weight began to rise, other reinforcements were added: the company of other patients in her room at mealtime, walks around the grounds, increased visits by members of her family, hair care, and so on. When it was discovered that although the patient was now eating, she was no longer gaining weight, the situation was changed to permit reinforcement only if there was a gain in weight, however slight.

After two months she had gained fourteen pounds. She was discharged from the hospital then, but continued to return at regular intervals for outpatient care. The assistance of the family was enlisted in carrying out a reinforcement program at home. She made a fairly good social adjustment in the community, but a year later she was readmitted to the hospital and the same reinforcement regimen was applied. When she was discharged a month later she had gained seven pounds, bringing her weight to eighty-eight pounds. She was offered a job as a general practical nurse in the hospital where she had been a patient, and she worked there for a year. When she quit her job—the hours were too demanding, she said—her weight had dropped to seventy-eight pounds.

A victim of anorexia nervosa. (From Bachrach et al., 1965).

Assertive training. Assertive training is recommended in the treatment of neurotics who have difficulty in expressing their feelings of anger and resentment when they are criticized or dominated by their parents, their employers, their husbands or wives, or other associates. The individual typically endures injustices and exploitation without standing up for his rights, and as a result, anxiety builds up and generalizes. The basic strategy, as proposed by Wolpe and Lazarus (1966), is to convince the patient of the virtue of asserting his rights and to point out the emotional and social repercussions of inhibiting his anger. Citing some of the patient's own interpersonal experiences, the therapist shows how the cumulative effects of anxiety and tension can be avoided by dealing spontaneously with each situation as it arises. Play-acting, or behavior rehearsal, as behaviorists prefer to call it, affords the patient an opportunity to learn and practice adaptive responses in "safe" situations. Incidents are reenacted, with the therapist and the patient frequently switching roles so that each plays the part of the "other person." By playing the role of the patient, the therapist provides examples of assertive responses for the patient, who may need help in defining the rights he may reasonably demand in a given situation and in distinguishing between assertive and aggressive responses.

The conquest of anxiety depends on the consequences of the individual's attempts at self-assertion. If his efforts result in punitive retaliation, he will be reluctant to make further attempts. The therapist tries to avoid this by starting with a mild counteraction to domination that has a high probability of successful outcome. Each successful attempt reinforces the assertive role. As the patient gradually gains confidence and acquires a more favorable perception of himself, the need for role-playing diminishes.

Implosive therapy. This technique is based on the principle that repeated exposure to disturbing scenes and stimuli will eventually result in the extinction of associated emotional responses. The basic steps have been described by Stampfl and Levis (1973). The first two sessions are devoted to diagnostic interviews. The objective is for the therapist to identify the conditioned aversive stimuli that are presumed to generate the anxiety, anger, depression, or other emotional responses that are determinants of the patient's symptoms. Lists are prepared of aversive internal stimuli (ideas, thoughts, impulses) and of external stimuli (phobic objects, social situations, parental arguments). In the second step (third session), the patient receives training in "neutral" imagery. The therapist instructs him to close his eyes and visualize in detail various "neutral" scenes such as watching TV or eating a meal. This step is to acquaint the patient with the procedure of imagining scenes and events and becoming sensitive to evoked responses. If the patient reacts emotionally during this trial session, the scene is quickly changed by his being asked to think of something else.

The treatment proper starts with the fourth session. The therapist directs the patient to imagine scenes, which on the basis of earlier interviews are known to generate strong emotional responses. The therapist attempts to maximize emotional arousal (*flooding*) by describing the aversive stimuli as vividly and realistically as possible. "Any attempt on the part of the patient to avoid the imagined aversive stimuli is prevented by the therapist. The essence of the procedure is to force repeated exposures to the aversive stimuli that underlie the patient's difficulties." The idea is that repeated exposure in imagery to the disturbing stimuli will lead to the eventual extinction of the associated emotional responses. Homework assignments are given in which the patient is asked to practice in imagery the aversive scenes used during the treatment session. Treatment continues until the conditioned aversive stimuli elicit little or no emotional arousal.

As the patient acquires understanding

of the principles of extinction and becomes more skillful in the use of the method, he may apply the procedure at home by himself to further extinction of emotional responses and to new problems as they occur. The procedure is still regarded as experimental. Preliminary findings on four published reports indicate the technique is highly effective in producing favorable changes in behavior and personality.

Drug Therapy

Tranquilizers and antianxiety drugs are extensively used in the treatment of neurosis. Their main advantage is that by relieving symptoms they permit the patient, at slight cost in money and effort, to cope more effectively with his problems and responsibilities. On the other hand, the reduction in tension thus induced lowers motivation for seeking and continuing with psychotherapy, which offers the possibility of providing a solution to the client's problem and a cessation of symptoms.

Treatment Outcome

Earlier reviews of studies of neurotic adults (Eysenck, 1961b) and children (Levitt, 1971) showed that about two-thirds of treated patients recover or show marked improvement within two years. The figure is quite stable regardless of the type of patient or the method of therapy. However, there is some doubt whether this favorable finding can be credited to the effectiveness of psychotherapy. The recovery rate of untreated patients also runs about 65 to 70 percent. The terms "treated" and "nontreated" are misleading. Relatively few neurotics are treated by professionally-trained specialists. Most so-called untreated patients discuss their problems with physicians, clergymen, nurses, relatives, or friends. Therefore, a more correct statement is that informal treatment by laypersons or nonspecialists is about as effective as treatment by professionals.

This finding does not necessarily rule out the possibility of the greater effectiveness of professional therapists. Most of the earlier studies of both treated and untreated populations were poorly controlled. A major methodological difficulty is the problem of matching the relative severity and kinds of problems presented by treated and untreated patients and by patients given different forms of therapy. The absence of valid, uniform criteria for evaluating improvement constitutes another major difficulty. Various criteria that have been used and suggested include the client's self-evaluation, the therapist's subjective evaluation, and changes in the results obtained on objective and projective adjustment-measurement tests administered before and after therapy (Strupp and Bergin, 1969). Criteria of improvement in overt behavior include the absence of symptoms formerly present, increased productiveness, more efficient use of potentialities, improved interpersonal relationships, and more positive, hopeful attitudes (Bergin and Garfield, 1971). Frank (1974), equates successful therapy with the restoration of morale.

There is some evidence (Truax and Carkhuff, 1967; Bergin, 1966) that over a period of time most untreated patients show slight to moderate improvement, whereas the effects of therapy are more variable. Some patients get much better following therapy, and others become worse. The variable effects of treatment may be due to the application of the wrong procedures to specific patients or the ineptitude of the therapist. A recent rise in awareness that psychotherapy as currently practiced is not a unitary process applied to a unitary problem has led to a restatement of the issue. We need to ask not whether psychotherapy is effective, but rather which specific therapeutic interventions are effective in producing what specific changes in which specific patients under what specific conditions. Recent studies have indicated that behavior therapy may be more effective than other forms in the treatment of phobic reactions. More studies are required before a final evaluation can be made. It is characteristic of advocates of new approaches to report initial optimistic results. Experience may indicate that behavior therapy is particularly effective in treating certain types of neurosis but is not necessarily the treatment of choice in all neuroses.

EXPERIMENTAL NEUROSIS IN ANIMALS

Some aspects of neurosis are restricted to man. Only human beings can describe the personal content of their neuroses and the subjective feelings associated with them. But the development of techniques for inducing neurotic disturbances of behavior in lower animals has afforded an opportunity for examining under controlled laboratory conditions the more overt or objectively observable components of neurosis. Animal research has been particularly helpful in evaluating the importance of constitutional factors, the role of stress, the nature of neurotic symptoms, and the relative effectiveness of certain forms of treatment. The significance of inherent constitutional factors in the relative vulnerability of individual animals to induced neurotic behavior has already been discussed (in Chapter 6).

The Role of Stress

The usual procedure for producing an experimental neurosis is to subject the animal to a conflict situation from which there is no escape. Restraint of activity and compulsory decision-making are essential. Exposing the animal to an unsolvable maze-learning problem that permits freedom of movement or avoidance of any response does not lead to neurosis. In the classical Pavlovian model, the animal is restrained by a harness and is required to discriminate between two conditioned stimuli that initially are readily differentiated but gradually become indistinguishable.

A procedure utilized by H. S. Liddell (1944) begins by conditioning the animal to flex its foreleg when it hears a slow metronome beat. This is done by repeatedly pairing the sound of the beat with a mild shock to the foreleg. When the slow beat has become established as a dependable conditioned stimulus for eliciting the flexing of the leg, the metronome beat is speeded up. The quick beat is never accompanied by shock. Following repeated nonreinforced trials, the fast beat becomes a negative stimulus that serves as a cue for inhibition of the leg flexion. After the animal has learned to make the correct discriminatory response, the two beats are gradually made more and more alike until the animal can no longer differentiate the positive or excitatory stimulus from the negative or inhibitory stimulus. At this point, disorganization occurs. The animal shows obvious signs of emotional distress, tears at the restraining apparatus, responds erratically to incidental stimuli, loses the capacity to make even simple discriminations, and may assume a rigid, cataleptic posture. This disorganization in behavior, with its accompanying autonomic disturbances, is persistent and resistant to treatment. Symptoms tend to be less pronounced outside the laboratory, but cues associated with the traumatic experience reinstate the emotional excitement and deviant behavior.

Neurotic sheep studied by Liddell were less gregarious than other sheep in the pasture. When startled, they would flee in the opposite direction from the rest of the flock. When dogs got into the pasture, it was invariably the neurotic sheep that were killed. The neurotic ewes had a higher abortion rate and often failed to establish adequate relations with their newborn offspring. W. H. Gantt (1944) has reported a detailed case history of a neurotic dog that manifested continued and varied symptoms over a twelve-year period, even though most of its years were spent on a farm. In short, exposure to stress produces enduring neurotic behavior in animals that previously were symptom-free.

Pavlov (1941) attributed the production of neurosis to a clash between cortical excitations and inhibitions or to an over-straining of the excitatory or inhibitory capacities of the animal. Jules Masserman (1943) has demonstrated that it is possible to produce neurotic behavior in cats and other animals by creating a conflict of motives. As a first step, a cat is trained to respond to a signal of light by opening a food box to obtain a pellet of food. The animal is then trained to depress a switch that permits him to operate the feeding signal at will. After this self-feeding pattern has been established, a conflict is induced by subjecting the cat at irregular intervals to a mild shock or blast of air as he reaches for the food. Following several such experiences, the conflict resulting from the contraposing of the animal's needs and the unpredictability of results when he tries to satisfy them leads to a variety of maladaptive neurotic behavior patterns. Responses noted in a number of animals include trembling, rigid crouching, fast-pounding pulse, refusal of food leading to starvation, stereotyped or ritualistic movements, diarrhea, deviant sexual behavior, extreme timidity, and unpredictable aggression.

As we noted in Chapter 6, genetic differences in temperament may account for some of the variations in the severity of behavior disorganization of animals under stress. But other factors are also important. Masserman (1961) found that cats that had been given free run of their quarters, permitted to mate at will, catch mice, and so on, were less adversely affected by exposure to stress than isolated cats confined to cages. And he goes on to draw a human parallel: people with multiple interests can better withstand frustration and conflict than those whose existence centers about a single vulnerable adaptation.

Studies conducted with rats and mice on the effects of infantile stimulation on adult emotionality point to a U-shaped relationship. Exposure to a moderate amount of stress during infancy (handling or shock) reduced adult emotionality, whereas animals that had never been handled and those that had been subjected to extreme infantile stimulation tended to show increased emotionality in adulthood (Myers, 1965; Adler, 1966).

The possibility that the prenatal emotional state of mothers may influence the emotionality of their offspring has been investigated (Hockman, 1961, and Thompson et al., 1962). Both researchers found that female rats subjected to stress experiences during pregnancy gave birth to offspring that were more emotional than control groups.

The Nature of Neurotic Symptoms

The similarity between neurosis in humans and neurotic reactions experimentally induced in animals provides further evidence that neuroses differ mainly in degree and duration from normal reactions to stress. No disease entity is involved. Neurotic reactions in animals, like those in humans, are involuntary, relatively uncontrollable, maladaptive, and obviously distressing to the organism. Two constant factors are diffuse emotional excitement or anxiety and rigid, inflexible, repetitive behavior (Wilson, 1963).

Animal studies have helped clarify what has been referred to as the neurotic paradox (Mowrer, 1948): the fact that neurotic behavior seemingly defies common-sense pleasure-pain motivation theories and the laws of learning. The normal expectation is that actions that have favorable net effects are reinforced and repeated, whereas those that have unfavorable consequences are extinguished, inhibited, and abandoned. The neurotic persists in engaging in self-defeating, detrimental behavior month after month and year after year. Furthermore, as Freud has emphasized (1933), the neurotic will seek treatment at great sacrifice in time, money, and effort, but at the same time he will vigorously resist therapeutic efforts to free him of the symptoms that cause him and those about him so much suffering.

Alexander and French (1946) suggested that the persistence of stereotyped neurotic behavior is related to the individual's avoidance of the problem. In normal development, new experiences modify past patterns. When the problem is too disturbing to face, no new learning occurs. An experimental confirmation of this possibility has been reported by Mowrer (1948). A rat is put at the left end of an alleyway about four feet long with high sides and ends. The floor of the alley consists of a grill that can be used for administering shock. Ten seconds after being placed at the left end of the alley, the rat is shocked by an electric charge that is run through the entire length of the grill. In the course of trial-and-error activity, the shocked rat discovers an opening at the extreme right end of the alley that leads into a small compartment where there is no shock. On subsequent trials the process is repeated. The rat is placed at the left end of the alley and shock is administered ten seconds later. After a few trials the rat learns to escape shock by running to the safe compartment within the ten-second period of grace.

When this escape pattern has been well established, the procedure is revised by permanently charging the right half of the grill and leaving the grill at the left end uncharged. Upon being placed into the now "safe" left end, the rat promptly runs across the charged grill at the right to get to the compartment. This voluntary exposure to shock goes on for hundreds of trials. To cure the animal, the investigator blocks the entrance to the safety compartment. To escape from the charged right end of the alley, the rats retreats to the uncharged left end. Finding that this end is now safe, the rat discontinues his flight into shock.

A somewhat similar series of studies based on traumatic avoidance learning in dogs was conducted by Solomon and Wynne (1954). Their apparatus consisted of a shuttle box divided into two compartments by a barrier. A dog was placed in one compartment, which had a gridded floor. Ten seconds after the animal was placed in the compartment, a shock was

administered through the grid. The animal soon learned to jump over the barrier, usually within two seconds after he had been placed in the compartment. This pattern continued through hundreds of extinction trials. If the barrier was raised so that it was not possible for the dog to jump over it, the animal exhibited signs of intense anxiety. Since the animal had not been in the gridded portion of the box long enough to know that shock was no longer being administered, no new learning occurred, and the gridded compartment itself (the conditioned stimulus) continued to arouse anxiety, which was relieved by the instrumental response of jumping.

Unlike the dog, a human neurotic may realize that his symptoms are irrational and self-defeating, but as long as they are effective in relieving anxiety, they serve an important function, as the dog's do for him, and are self-perpetuating. Normal individuals avoid this dilemma by facing former areas of trauma and, in the light of more favorable or neutral subsequent experiences, learning new and more adaptive responses. Animal studies (Sandler, 1964) have shown that self-punishing or masochistic behavior can be explained on the basis of standard learning principles, without recourse to inferred concepts of guilt or superego conflicts. Through the proper manipulation of stimuli and reinforcement agents, animals may be trained to tolerate severe electric shock with no overt signs of pain or distress, to administer self-punishment over long periods for meager and uncertain rewards, and even to work for punishment alone.

The initial adaptiveness of neurotic behavior is illustrated by Norman Maier's (1949) experimental studies of frustration. He placed a rat on a jumping stand and confronted it with two cards placed side by side in the windows of a vertical screen. One card showed a black circle against a white background and the other a white circle against a black background. The cards could be latched in place or left free so they could be easily knocked over. The rat was required to jump at the cards.

If the "correct" response was made, the card fell over and the animal landed on a platform, where it found food. If the "incorrect" response was made, the animal hit the latched card with his nose and fell into a protective net.

When the problem was solvable—when food was always obtained by jumping at the card with the white circle, for example, regardless of its position—the animal had no difficulty in learning the correct symbol. But when the problem was made unsolvable by latching the cards in random order, the animal soon refused to jump at all. If it was forced to do so by being shocked or exposed to a blast of air, the rat tended to settle eventually on a position stereotype. Most rats exposed to this situation consistently jumped at the card on the left or the card on the right, no matter which card it happened to be. Since this solution permitted a 50 percent chance of success, the stereotyped response actually assured maximum success. Also indicative of the adaptiveness of the response was the observation that once the fixated response had been acquired, the animal jumped more readily than he had before, appeared less nervous, and had fewer seizures.

As long as the problem remained unsolvable, the animal could not be faulted for its stereotyped response pattern, which in fact represented the best solution under the circumstances. But the persistence of the fixed-position response when the situation was altered so that a more effective solution was possible was suggestive of neurotic behavior. Animals that had acquired the habit of consistently jumping at the card on the right continued to do so even when the window to the left was kept open with food in plain sight. Like human neurotics, these animals apparently knew better, but persisted in their self-defeating behavior just the same. When placed on the jumping stand, they would appropriately turn and face the open window on the left, sniff the food, and then jump at the locked door on the right. This irrational response continued over numerous trials. Neither punishment nor extinction techniques were effective in eliminating the fixated response. When the fixated response was prevented, however, so that the animal had no alternative to the "correct" response, it was possible to train the animal to choose the reward card in five to ten trials.

SUMMARY

Neurotic reactions are distinguished from psychosis by the absence of severe impairment in psychosocial functioning and of gross distortion of external reality. The neurotic experiences no delusions, hallucinations, or personality disorganization. He can usually carry on his work and meet his personal and social responsibilities with reasonable adequacy. The core problem is excessive anxiety, which may be expressed directly or in substitute reactions that are considered to be defenses against anxiety: hysterical conversion, hysterical dissociative, phobic, obsessive-compulsive, depressive, neurasthenic, depersonalization, and hypochondriacal reactions. The neurotic does not understand the nature or meaning of these reactions, but he does realize they are symptoms for which he should seek treatment. Neurotic reactions that appear to have some specific etiological background are sometimes assigned special labels: existential neurosis, occupational neurosis, war neurosis.

Proposed contributory causes include genetic endowment, autonomic instability, developmental flaws, unresolved intrapsychic conflicts associated with the Oedipus complex, unfavorable learning experiences, and exposure to overwhelming stress situations. The techniques of treatment tend to be related to the presumed dominant cause. About 65 to 70 percent of neurotic patients show good clinical improvement, whether or not they have received formal treatment. This somewhat surprising finding may be due to variations in the competence of therapists and the tendency of each therapist to have a favored approach that he uses with most of his patients. It is quite probable that highly qualified therapists who work only with certain kinds of problems or who adapt their methods to the patient obtain much better results than the statistical average.

References

Adler, A. *The Practice and Theory of Individual Psychology.* New York: Harcourt, Brace, 1929.

Adler, R. "Frequency of Stimulation During Early Life and Subsequent Emotionality in the Rat." *Psychological Reports* 18 (1966): 695-701.

Alexander, F. "The Dynamics of Psychotherapy in the Light of Learning Theory." *American Journal of Psychiatry* 120 (1963): 440-48.

Alexander, F., and French, T. M. *Psychoanalytic Therapy.* New York: Ronald Press, 1946.

Bachrach, A. J.; Erwin, W. J.; and Mohr, J. P. "The Control of Eating Behavior in an Anorexic by Operant Conditioning Techniques." In *Case Studies in Behavior Modification,* ed. L. P. Ullmann and L. Krasner, pp. 153-63. New York: Holt, Rinehart & Winston, 1965.

Bandura, A., and Walters, R. H. *Social Learning and Personality Development.* New York: Holt, Rinehart & Winston, 1963.

Beard, G. M. *A Practical Treatise on Nervous Exhaustion.* New York: Wood, 1880.

Bergin, A. E. "Some Implications of Psychotherapy Research for Therapeutic Practice." *Journal of Abnormal Psychology* 71 (1961): 235-46.

———— and Garfield, S. L. *Handbook of Psychotherapy and Behavior Change.* New York: Wiley, 1971.

Brill, N. Q. "Gross Stress Reactions: Traumatic War Neurosis." In *Comprehensive Textbook of Psychiatry,* ed. A. M. Friedman, H. I. Kaplan, and H. S. Kaplan, pp. 1031-35. Baltimore: Williams & Wilkins, 1967.

———— and Beebe, G. W. *A Follow-up Study of War Neuroses.* Veterans' Administration medical monograph. Washington, D.C.: U.S. Government Printing Office, 1955.

Burnham, W. H. *The Normal Mind.* New York: Appleton, 1924.

Cameron, N. A. *Personality Development and Psychopathology.* Boston: Houghton Mifflin, 1963.

Carter, H. D. "Twin Similarities in Personality Traits." *Journal of Genetic Psychology* 43 (1933): 312-21.

Dohrenwend, B. S., and Dohrenwend, B. P. "Field Studies of Social Factors in Relation to Three Types of Psychological Disorders." *Journal of Abnormal Psychology* 72 (1967): 369-78.

Dollard, J. and Miller, N. E. *Personality and Psychotherapy.* New York: McGraw-Hill, 1950.

Ellis, A. "Goals of Psychotherapy." In *The Goals of Psychotherapy,* ed. A. R. Mahrer. New York: Appleton-Century-Crofts, 1967.

Essen-Moller, E. "Twin Research and Psychiatry." *International Journal of Psychiatry* 1 (1965): 466-75. Originally published in *Acta Psychiatrica et Neurologica* 39 (1963): 65-77.

Eysenck, H. J. "Classification and the Problems of Diagnosis." In *Handbook of Abnormal Psychology,* ed. H. J. Eysenck. New York: Basic Books, 1961 (a).

————. "The Effects of Psychotherapy." In *Handbook of Abnormal Psychology,* ed. H. J. Eysenck. New York: Basic Books, 1961 (b).

———— and Prell, D. B. "The Inheritance of Neuroticism: An Experimental Study." *Journal of Mental Sciences* 97 (1951): 441-65.

———— and Rachman, S. *The Causes and Cures of Neurosis.* San Diego, Calif.: Knapp, 1965.

Frank, J. D. "Psychotherapy, the Restoration of Morale." *American Journal of Psychiatry* 131 (1974): 271-74.

Foulds, G. A., and Caine, T. M. "Symptom Clusters and Personality Types Among Psychoneurotic Men Compared with Women." *Journal of Mental Science* 105 (1959): 469-75.

Freud, S. *New Introductory Lectures on Psychoanalysis,* trans. J. H. Sprott. New York: Norton, 1933.

————. "Analysis of a Phobia in a Five-Year-Old Boy." In *Collected Papers,* vol. 10, pp. 5-149. London: Hogarth Press, 1957.

Gantt, W. H. *Experimental Basis for Neurotic Behavior.* New York: Hoeber, 1944.

Gottesman, I. "Personality and Natural Selection." In *Methods and Goals in Human Behavior Genetics,* ed. S. G. Vandenberg, pp.

63-80. New York: Academic Press, 1965.

Grinker, R. R., and Spiegel, J. P. *Men Under Stress*. New York: McGraw-Hill, 1945.

Guthrie, E. R. *The Psychology of Learning*. New York: Harper, 1935.

Hockman, C. H. "Prenatal Maternal Stress in the Rat: Its Effects on Emotional Behavior in the Offspring." *Journal of Comparative and Physiological Psychology* 54 (1961): 679-84.

Hollingshead, A. B., and Redlich, F. C. *Social Class and Mental Illness*. New York: Wiley, 1958.

Hollingworth, H. L. *Abnormal Psychology*. New York: Ronald Press, 1930.

Janis, I. L. *Air War and Emotional Stress*. New York: McGraw-Hill, 1951.

Jones, M. C. "A Laboratory Study of Fear: The Case of Peter." *Journal of Genetic Psychology* 31 (1924): 308-15.

Kelly, G. A. *The Psychology of Personal Constructs*. New York: Norton, 1955.

Kenyon, F. E. "Hypochondriasis: A Survey of Some Historical, Clinical, and Social Aspects." *British Journal of Psychiatry* 38 (1965): 117-34.

Lazarus, A. A. *Behavior Therapy and Beyond*. New York: McGraw-Hill, 1971.

Levitt, E. E. "Research on Psychotherapy with Children." In *Handbook of Psychotherapy and Behavior Change*, ed. A. E. Bergin and S. L. Garfield, pp. 474–494. New York: Wiley, 1971.

Liddell, H. S. "Conditioned Reflex Method and Experimental Neurosis." In *Personality and Behavior Disorders*, ed. J. McV. Hunt, vol. 1, pp. 389-412. New York: Ronald Press, 1944.

Maddi, S. R. "The Existential Neurosis." *Journal of Abnormal Psychology* 72 (1967): 311-25.

Maier, N. R. F. *Frustration: The Study of Behavior Without a Goal*. New York: McGraw-Hill, 1949.

Masserman, J. H. *Behavior and Neurosis*. Chicago: University of Chicago Press, 1943.

———. *Principles of Dynamic Psychiatry*. Philadelphia: Saunders, 1961.

Maurer, A. "Did Little Hans Really Want to Marry His Mother?" *Journal of Humanistic Psychology* 14 (1964): 139-48.

Mowrer, O. H. "Learning Theory and the Neurotic Paradox." *American Journal of Orthopsychiatry* 18 (1948): 571-610.

Myers, E. "Effects of Different Intensities of Postweaning Shock and Handling on the Albino Rat." *Journal of Genetic Psychology* 106 (1965): 51-58.

Newman, H. H.; Freeman, N.; and Holzinger, K. J. *Twins: A Study of Heredity and Environment*. Chicago: University of Chicago Press, 1937.

Pavlov, I. P. *Conditioned Reflexes and Psychiatry*, trans. W. H. Gantt. New York: International Publishers, 1941.

Pfeiffer, E. *Disordered Behavior*. London: Oxford University Press, 1968.

Phillips, E. L. *Psychotherapy: A Modern Theory and Practice*. New York: Prentice-Hall, 1956.

Prince, M. *The Dissociation of a Personality*. New York: Longmans, 1908.

Raines, G. N., and Kolb, L. C. "Combat Fatigue and War Neurosis." *Naval Medical Bulletin* 41 (1943): 923-36.

Rogers, C. *Client-Centered Therapy*. Boston: Houghton Mifflin, 1951.

Rosenberg, C. M. "Personality and Obsessional Neurosis." *British Journal of Psychiatry* 113 (1967): 471-77.

Sandler, J. "Masochism: An Empirical Analysis." *Psychological Bulletin* 62 (1964): 197-204.

Sargent, W., and Slater, E. "Acute War Neuroses." *Lancet*, July 6, 1940, pp. 1-2.

Seligman, M. E. "Fall into Helplessness." *Psychology Today*, June 1973.

Schreiber, F. R. *Sybil*. Chicago, Ill.: Regnery, 1973. Also Warner Paperbook Library, 1974.

Shapiro, D. *Neurotic Styles*. New York: Basic Books, 1965.

Shepherd, M., and Gruenberg, E. M. "The Age for Neuroses." *Milbank Memorial Fund Quarterly* 3 (1957): 258-65.

Shields, J. *Monozygotic Twins, Brought Up Apart and Brought Up Together*. London: Oxford University Press, 1962.

——— and Slater, E. "Heredity and Psychological Abnormality." In *Handbook of Abnormal Psychology*, ed. H. J. Eysenck, pp. 298-343. New York: Basic Books, 1961.

Slater, E. "Genetic Factors in Neurosis." *British Journal of Psychology* 55 (1964): 265-69.

——— and Woodside, M. *Patterns of Marriage*. London: Cassell, 1951.

Solomon, R. L., and Wynne, L. C. "Traumatic Avoidance Learning: The Principles of Anxiety Conservation and Irreversibility." *Psychological Review* 61 (1954): 353-84.

Stampfl, T. G. and Levis, D. J. *Implosive Therapy: Theory and Technique*. Morristown,

N. J.: General Learning Press, 1973.

Stephens, J. H., and Kamp, M. "On Some Aspects of Hysteria: A Clinical Study." *Journal of Nervous and Mental Disease* 134 (1962): 305-15.

Strupp, H. H., and Bergin, A. E. "Some Empirical and Conceptual Bases for Coordinated Research in Psychotherapy: A Critical Review of Issues, Trends, and Evidence." *International Journal of Psychiatry* 7 (1969): 19-90.

Thigpen, C. H., and Cleckley, H. M. *Three Faces of Eve*. New York: McGraw-Hill, 1957.

Thompson, W. R.; Watson, J.; and Charlesworth, W. R. "The Effects of Prenatal Maternal Stress on Offspring Behavior in Rats." *Psychological Monographs* 76, no. 38 (1962).

Tompkins, V. H. "Stress in Aviation." In *The Nature of Stress Disorder*, ed. J. Hambling, pp. 73–80. Springfield, Ill.: Charles C Thomas, 1959.

Truax, C. B., and Carkhuff, R. R. *Toward Effective Counseling and Psychotherapy: Training and Practice*. Chicago: Aldine, 1967.

Ullmann, L. P., and Krasner, L. *Case Studies in Behavior Modification*. New York: Holt, Rinehart & Winston, 1965.

Vandenberg, S. G. "Contributions of Twin Research to Psychology." *Psychological Bulletin* 66 (1966): 327-52.

Weiss, E., and English, O. S. *Psychosomatic Medicine*. Philadelphia: Saunders, 1943.

White, R. W. *The Abnormal Personality*. New York: Ronald Press, 1964.

Wilson, R. S. "On Behavior Pathology." *Psychological Bulletin* 60 (1963): 130-46.

Wolpe, J. *Psychotherapy by Reciprocal Inhibition*. Stanford, Calif.: Stanford University Press, 1958.

———. "The Systematic Desensitization Treatment of Neuroses." *Journal of Nervous and Mental Disease* 132 (1961): 189-203.

———. *The Practice of Behavior Therapy*. New York: Pergamon Press, 1969.

——— and Lazarus, A. A. *Behavior Therapy Techniques*. New York: Pergamon Press, 1966.

——— and Rachman, S. "Psychoanalytic Evidence: A Critique Based on Freud's Case of Little Hans." *Journal of Nervous and Mental Disease* 131 (1960): 135-48.

The Desperate Man, Albrecht Dürer

The continuum concept of psychopathology assumes an intermediate or borderline state between normal and definitely abnormal behavior. The category of personality disorders bridges the gap between normal and neurotic or psychotic behavior. Personality disorders may be more accurately described as personality types marked by deeply ingrained maladaptive behavior patterns. The "disorder" consists essentially of flaws in the basic personality structure. More specifically, it involves defects in temperament, perception of self and others, general orientation to life, and characteristic mode of response. A diagnostic label of schizoid, compulsive, paranoid, hysterical, or antisocial personality indicates both the nature of the maladaptive behavior and its presumed relationship to more severe disorders.

The concept of personality types is, of course, an artifact of convenience. Each individual is unique. For purposes of classification and clinical study, however, it is helpful to group together persons who share certain behavior characteristics in varying degrees. It is understood that the categories overlap and that persons placed in the same category show wide individual differences even in the traits they share. An

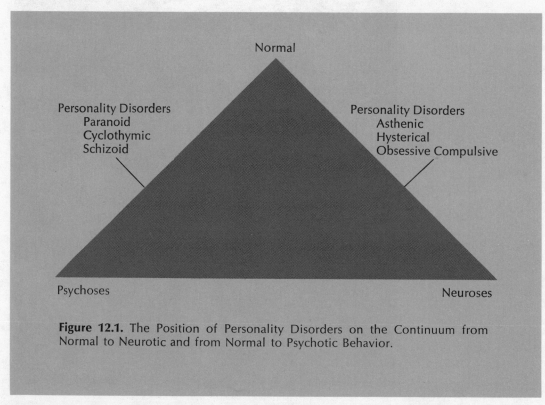

Figure 12.1. The Position of Personality Disorders on the Continuum from Normal to Neurotic and from Normal to Psychotic Behavior.

analogous practice is the stratagem of arbitrarily differentiating among individuals, for rough descriptive purposes, on the basis of outstanding physical characteristics: tall and thin, short and stocky, tall and heavy, and so on.

The adult personality types described in the *Diagnostic and Statistical Manual* (DSM-11) of the APA are listed in Table 12.1. The diagnostic terms proposed for use with children in the 1966 classification prepared by the Group for the Advancement of Psychiatry (GAP) are more general but cover essentially the same personality types. Both classification systems recognize or imply that:

1. Personality disorders are distinguished by a restricted repertoire of behavior patterns. An individual diagnosed as having a personality disorder typically exhibits the same sort of behavior in all situations. He makes little or no attempt to vary his behavior to fit the circumstances. Thus he may be consistently aggressive,

detached, suspicious, or dependent. The inappropriateness of such rigid response is self-defeating and leads to poor social adjustment.

2. The person who has a personality disorder accepts his behavior pattern as "normal" for him. He is not unduly disturbed either by the nature of his personality traits or by the frequent occurrence of interpersonal difficulties resulting from the inappropriateness of his stereotyped feelings, thoughts, and actions. He rarely seeks treatment on his own initiative. If his family or others insist on therapy, he is usually uncooperative. His unresponsiveness to therapy is understandable, since it poses a threat to his one and only way of behaving.

3. The personality type is fashioned through the complex and cumulative interaction of genetic, environmental, and experiential determinants. The biological endowment of the infant (activity level, responsiveness, adaptiveness, stability of affect) is often a critical factor in influenc-

Table 12.1. Two Proposed Lists of Personality Disorders (Personality Types).

American Psychiatric Association	Group for the Advancement of Psychiatry
Paranoid	Mistrustful
Cyclothymic	
Schizoid	Isolated
Explosive (aggressive)	Impulse-ridden
Obsessive-compulsive	Compulsive
Hysterical (histrionic)	Hysterical
Asthenic	
Antisocial (sociopathic)	Tension discharge
Passive-aggressive	Oppositional
Inadequate	
Passive-dependent	Overly dependent Overly independent

ing the direction of development. The infant's distinctive reactivity pattern elicits distinctive counterreactions from his parents and others. Inherent constitutional tendencies thus shape the nature of the experiences to which the child is exposed. The circular interaction between the child's biological constitution and his restricted and repetitive environmental experiences leads to the acquisition of distinctive modes of perceiving, feeling, thinking, and behaving. Each year the pattern is more deeply etched. By adolescence or even earlier it is firmly established and highly resistant to change.

4. Since cultural factors also influence personality development, certain types of pathological personalities may be more prevalent in some cultures or subgroups than in others, but all types occur in all cultures and socioeconomic groups.

5. The recognized personality types are neither pure nor homogeneous. Persons with the same diagnosis show wide individual differences. Mixed types are common. An individual may exhibit both schizoid and paranoid features, or hysterical and antisocial behavior.

6. As a rule the pathological process is arrested at the level of personality disorder. It does not automatically progress to a clearly defined neurosis or psychosis. The individual experiences varying degrees of difficulty in interpersonal adjustment, but competence of functioning in school and work is usually not significantly affected. There is one exception: the inadequate personality.

7. Although most persons with disordered personalities do not go on to develop a neurosis or psychosis, the rigidity and nonadaptiveness of their behavior makes them highly vulnerable to stress. If they do "break" and are forced to resort to more desperate coping devices, the choice of neurosis or psychosis is influenced by the premorbid personality. A schizoid personality is more apt to manifest a schizophrenic than a depressive syndrome. In the case of mixed personality types, the direction of

further disorder is less predictable.

The reactions of mild pathological personalities tend to be more extreme than similar behavior patterns in normal individuals. Normal behavior is more diversified, more flexible, and hence more adaptive. Under appropriate circumstances it is normal to be aggressive, suspicious, dependent, detached, passive, and even antisocial.

The boundaries of personality disorders are vaguely defined. The diagnosis is often used as a catchall for personality, character, and behavior deviations that do not fit neatly into other recognized categories. With some justification the diagnosis may be extended to include antisocial personalities and mild or early stages of psychosis or borderline neurosis. Its application to sexual deviance, excessive drinking, and drug misuse is less defensible. When these behavior patterns are excluded, personality disorders account for about 10 percent of first admissions to public mental hospitals and 6 percent of admissions to private mental hospitals and general hospitals with separate inpatient psychiatric units. The peak age of first admissions is between fifteen and twenty-four. Males assigned this diagnosis outnumber females among admissions to public mental hospitals, but females outnumber males among admissions to private mental hospitals and general hospitals. The duration of hospital stay is brief. Personality disorders constitute a small fraction of 1 percent of the resident populations of public mental hospitals (*Patients in Mental Institutions, 1965*).

PARANOID PERSONALITY

Characteristic traits of the paranoid personality include unwarranted suspicion, jealousy, envy, general distrust of others, rigidity, hypersensitivity to slights, and exaggerated feelings of self-importance. Judging others by himself, the paranoid person takes it for granted that others feel hostile toward him. His readiness to perceive deceit and aggression lead to repeated social difficulties and counteraggression, which confirm and reinforce his distrust (Millon, 1969). Safety lies in independence and self-reliance. The resulting isolation and limited communication deprives the paranoid of reality checks that might modify his distorted views. As part of his defensive posture the paranoid projects blame for mistakes and shortcomings on others.

Paranoid Personality and Psychosis

When ideas of distrust and suspicion are so distorted and magnified that the individual is convinced he is being watched, followed, exploited, and persecuted by enemies, a diagnosis of psychosis takes precedence over paranoid personality. An obvious requirement is that the persecutory theme is a delusion with no factual basis or that it represents a gross and uncorrectable misinterpretation of some actual event or series of events. Diagnosis is frequently simplified by the added presence of delusions of grandeur, which may be incorporated into the persecutory theme. Thus the patient may attribute the enmity of his persecutors to their presumed resentment at his superior abilities or to attempts to discredit his rightful claim to some valuable property or invention.

Three types of paranoid psychosis have been differentiated. Patients characterized by bizarre and poorly organized delusions of persecution, hallucinations, disturbances in thinking, and significant impairment in general functioning are classified as *paranoid schizophrenics*. It is presumed that in these cases the underlying personality is more schizoid than paranoid.

When the delusional system is carefully elaborated, internally consistent, and more or less encapsulated, leaving the rest of the personality intact, a differentiation may be made between paranoia and paranoid state. *Paranoia* is extremely rare. It is characterized by the gradual development over many years of an elaborate paranoid system that is based on the misinterpretation

or overextension of the implications of an actual event. If the fundamental premise is granted, the rest proceeds logically. In these cases it is often difficult to say how much of the patient's story of deception, intrigue, and exploitation is true and how much is elaboration.

Paranoid state is more common than paranoia but also comparatively rare. The delusional system is less well organized than in paranoia and more improbable. However, the ideas expressed are not altogether farfetched. The relative intactness of the rest of his personality enables the patient to carry on with his work and usual activities.

As long as the paranoid is guarded in the overt expression of his delusions or confides only in sympathetic listeners, his distorted perspective is discounted or tolerated. The social rule of reciprocity provides that everyone is entitled to a few harmless peculiarities or quirks. In the interest of peace, families may put up with obviously irrational behavior. Difficulties arise when the paranoid feels that he has suffered in silence long enough and starts to accuse or attack his persecutors. Psychiatric referral may follow direct threats, acts of aggression, appeals to authorities for help, the initiation of endless lawsuits, and so on. On occasion the paranoid person may become convinced that his enemies are closing in for the kill, and he may panic. Fortunately, such extreme reactions are rare. Most paranoid individuals quickly learn how far they can go before getting into trouble with society. The retention of control helps keep their behavior within acceptable bounds.

Paranoia and paranoid states together account for less than 1 percent of first admissions to public and private mental hospitals. The prevalence rate is about the same for males and females. Paranoid patients tend to be brighter and better educated than most persons hospitalized with other diagnoses, but all socioeconomic levels are represented. The median age at the time of hospital admission is about fifty.

PARANOID PERSONALITIES: THREE CASES

A suspicious husband

1. The disruptive effect of a paranoid orientation on interpersonal relations is clearly seen in the report of a middle-aged woman, recently married for the first time, who sought professional advice on how to cope with her extremely jealous husband. During the courtship period she had been unable to understand why he had had difficulty in his previous two marriages, both of which ended in divorce. He was completely devoted to her. He was interested in everything she did, accompanied her everywhere, and gave the impression that he loved her so much that he couldn't let her out of his sight.

His attentiveness and interest continued after they were married, but now his wife found them stifling. She had to account for everything she did while he was away at work. If he phoned during the day and she failed to answer, she had to face a cross-examination that night. If she casually looked at another man when they were out together, he would accuse her of flirting. If she received any mail he would accuse her —all in fun, he would later claim—of having a lover, until in desperation she would permit him to read the letter. He was very critical of the way she dressed. If she ever made a disparaging remark about him, he would become angry and sulk for days. The only way she could get along with him was to humor and flatter him. On occasions when her saturation point had been reached and she threatened to leave him, he would proclaim his need and love for her and plead for another chance. For a while he would improve, but soon he would revert to his old pattern of jealousy and suspicion.

A distrusting wife

2. The distinctive features of the paranoid state also can be seen in the case of a man who initially requested a clinic appointment to discuss a marital problem. His wife refused to come with him but demanded a separate interview to check on her husband's story. She was granted her interview, but after hearing her husband's story and telling her own, she refused to return for treatment.

Apart from variations in subjective interpretation, husband and wife agreed on the main facts. At the time of their interviews the husband was fifty-five years old and the wife was fifty. They had been married twenty-two years and had a daughter who had recently married. A current complaint of the wife was that the husband had given the daughter a generous check to help with the purchase of furniture. The wife did not object to the gift, but felt it should have been given jointly. She cited this incident as an example of her husband's sneaky behavior. The husband's story was that he couldn't very well discuss the gift with his wife, since they had more or less stopped talking to one another, even though they were living together and at his wife's insistence still shared the same bed. The wife saw no point in discussing her earlier his-

Paranoid State and Prejudice

In many ways a paranoid state is analogous to a firmly entrenched prejudice in which there is strong ego involvement. By carefully selecting supportive evidence and ignoring or distorting contradictory facts, an otherwise sensible person may be sincerely convinced of the validity of his prejudice. The presence of false beliefs and irrational attitudes need not interfere with judgment or competence with respect to other subjects.

As in the case of prejudices, a dominant person may impose his delusions on some submissive member of the family. The terms *folie à deux* and "psychosis of association" have been proposed to identify situations in which two people, usually but not necessarily members of the same famtory. Her sole concern was to expose her husband's inadequacies and infidelity.

A hostile wife

3. This marital history corresponds with that of a similar case described by Dupont and Grunebaum (1968). Both husband and wife were serious-minded and hard-working persons. During the period when the wife was manifesting paranoid symptoms, she continued with her routine shopping and domestic duties. Their social life since their marriage had been limited. Their home life, prior to recent events, was described as "normal," but "dull and empty" would be a more accurate description. The wife had insisted on discontinuing sexual intercourse following the onset of menopause when she was forty-two. The husband had passively given in to her wishes. In recent years he had spent as little time as possible in her company. On returning home from the office he occupied himself with gardening and refinishing furniture.

The wife first accused him of infidelity five years prior to their clinic visits. The husband, who apparently was innocent, protested in vain. She could tell that he was seeing other women, she said, by the look in his eye, his general behavior, and his lack of sexual interest in her. Shortly after her accusation she hired a detective to collect evidence for a divorce. In his report the detective described several incidents that were essentially casual contacts the husband had with girls in his office, acquaintances in restaurants, and so on. Armed with this evidence, the wife started divorce proceedings.

The husband contested the divorce to prove his innocence. The divorce petition was denied. The wife claimed that her lawyer had "sold her out" and the judge had been bribed.

Following the divorce failure, the wife became increasingly abusive and hostile. She spread stories about her husband's illicit affairs in the neighborhood. On several occasions she phoned her husband's employer to complain about his unfaithfulness. The husband sought revenge and refuge in silence. Next the wife took to cutting out articles in newspapers and magazines about wives who had murdered their husbands, and placed the clippings in his coat pockets. Finally she put a kitchen knife under her pillow, just in case her husband might attack her while she was asleep.

It was this episode that persuaded the husband that his wife was mentally ill, and he urged her to arrange for psychiatric treatment. To his surprise, she agreed. If he would fill out the necessary commitment papers, she would go along with "being framed" and go to a mental hospital. After a brief stay she would convince the hospital authorities that she had made a complete recovery and they would have to discharge her. (She had read an article on current policies of discharging patients as soon as possible.) Following her release from the hospital, she would kill her husband and get away with it on the grounds of a temporary recurrence of her psychosis. It was at this point that the husband arranged for a clinic appointment to discuss his marital problem.

ily, concurrently share the same delusional system (Gralnick, 1942). This rare condition usually occurs in socially isolated families in which the submissive person (usually a wife or mother) has very limited contact with persons other than the paranoid. The submissive partner relies on the dominant one for reinforcement. Separation usually results in the gradual extinction of imposed delusional ideas in the de-

pendent partner. The paranoid, like the prejudiced person, hangs on to his false beliefs. Treatment is usually ineffective. The general distrust of others includes the therapist.

Contributory Factors

Paranoid personality and paranoid state have traditionally been regarded as reaction patterns rather than as distinct disorders. No serious attempt has been made to relate paranoid behavior to any specific gene defect, biochemical defect, or brain pathology. Contributory factors are complex and may vary somewhat from patient to patient.

It is generally assumed that the process of acquiring a paranoid outlook starts early in life and develops gradually over thirty or more years. During infancy the potential paranoid fails to acquire what Erikson has referred to as a sense of basic trust in the good will of his social environment. Basic distrust of the intentions and motives of others may stem from parental rejection, undependability of parental response to early needs, the presence of a more favored sibling in the home, or some other situation that makes it impossible for the child to have confidence in others' intentions toward him. Inherent tendencies of temperament that make for independence and aggressiveness may contribute to unfavorable early social experiences in and outside the home and favor the emergence of a chip-on-the-shoulder attitude.

Whatever the cause, from childhood the paranoid is committed to a pattern of self-reliance and distrust of others. The world is perceived as a cold, hostile place. The best course is to go it alone, confide in no one, and keep up one's guard. This approach leads to seclusiveness, a lack of understanding of others, and a defensive hypersensitivity to slights and humiliations.

The potential paranoid's perspective is narrow and egocentric. He has neither interest nor facility in putting himself in other people's shoes and seeing things from their point of view. Perhaps because of inherent aggressiveness, the paranoid-prone person reacts to failure and threats by attack rather than by schizophrenic retreat, depressive despair, or neurotic compromise. Favorable self-evaluation is protected by the projection of blame and fault on others. The individual's suspiciousness and aggressiveness tend to elicit rejection and counteraggression on the part of others, so that in effect he creates by his own actions a cold, hostile social environment.

The Freudian thesis that paranoia is associated with latent homosexuality offers an explanation for the clinical observation that the persecutor is usually a member of the paranoid's own sex. The assumption of a causal relationship between paranoid behavior and homosexuality has little foundation, however. There is no conclusive evidence that latent homosexuality (a slippery term to define) is more prevalent among paranoids than in the general population. Many paranoids show no homosexual tendencies, and most overt homosexuals never develop paranoid delusions. The paranoid's poor heterosexual adjustment is more probably due to suspicion and distrust than to sexual deviation.

According to Norman Cameron (1959), psychotic delusions of persecution represent a desperate attempt to justify suspicions, to account for failure, and to explain the spying and persecution of others. All the pieces fall neatly into place with the invention of a *pseudocommunity*. The paranoid pseudocommunity, as Cameron defines it, is an imaginary organization of real or imagined persons who are united in a plot against the patient. An advantage of the pseudocommunity is that it brings the threat into focus. Instead of being confronted with a blurred, nameless "they," the patient with a clearly defined delusional system knows who the enemy is and can take appropriate defensive or offensive measures. His resistance to treatment is understandable, since a "cure" would require him to give up his all-purpose rationalization.

CYCLOTHYMIC PERSONALITY

Persons described as cyclothymic are characterized by recurring or alternating periods of mild depression and mild elation. Because of the mildness and short duration of their mood changes these individuals are considered to be basically normal. When in

CYCLOTHYMIC PERSONALITY: THE CASE OF DOCTOR B.

The potential adjustment difficulties of cyclothymes may be seen in the case of Dr. B., who married and opened an office in his home shortly after graduating from a school of optometry. To supplement his income while waiting for his practice to grow he obtained a position working two days a week for another optometrist. This still left him with some free time, so he opened a second office in a suburban town where he was the only optometrist. This venture worked out so well that he discontinued his part-time position and opened a third office in another suburb. He obtained a substantial bank loan to purchase equipment and a second car.

By dividing his time between his three offices and working evenings, Dr. B. managed to earn an excellent income, but it brought small joy to his wife. She saw little of him, and that little was too much. He constantly found fault with her poor management, lack of ambition, and failure to give him 100 percent cooperation. On weekends he felt he should lead an active social life to compensate for his long working hours. His wife dreaded going out to parties with him, since he irritated friends with his boasts, arrogance, and practical jokes, which were often in poor taste. Then too there were periods when he was depressed and worried about his financial obligations and his unhappy marriage. But, as he constantly reminded everyone who would listen, he was a "success."

an elated state, the individual is energetic, enthusiastic, confident, and in good spirits. The world is his oyster. All things are possible. While in a depressed period, he is listless and pessimistic. His former good humor and optimism are replaced by worry, a sense of futility, and irritability. As in manic-depressive reactions, mood changes may be bipolar or unipolar. The onset of elation or depression may be independent of external circumstances.

The omission of a cyclothymic personality in the GAP classification of personality disorders in children is consistent with the psychodynamics of this personality type. Cycloid personalities tend to be dependent, pliant, submissive, and friendly. They strive to bolster basic feelings of insecurity by forming a strong attachment to one or two persons. In exchange for affection, loyalty, and subservience, they expect that the person with whom they have identified will take care of them. In order to gratify their strong needs for attention and approval, they conform to rules and social expectations and make themselves pleasant, cooperative, and amusing.

During childhood these attributes are assets. Difficulties arise during late adolescence and early adulthood, when the individual is expected to be independent and self-reliant. At this point he may resent his dependency but feel powerless to do anything about it. Doubts as to the dependability of the person who serves as his anchor lead to anxiety and worry. The individual may sporadically lash out against the person who has failed him. Most commonly, hostility is turned against the self and expressed in dejection and feelings of unworthiness. If the expected rewards of social conformity and compliance do not materialize, the individual feels betrayed and deserted, but usually he dares not openly vent his anger against those upon whom he is still dependent for attention and approval. Instead he attacks and blames himself. As a reaction against despondency or as a means of regaining favor, the individual may become more assertive, gregarious, and hyperactive. Artificial optimism may mask hopelessness, surface gaiety be substituted for despair, and boasts conceal feelings of inadequacy.

SCHIZOID PERSONALITY

Schizoid personality is differentiated from schizophrenia by the absence of delusions, hallucinations, and thought disorders. Persons with schizoid personalities are detached from reality but not out of touch with it. This critical distinction places them in the normal or borderline-normal category. They are typically described as shy, seclusive, emotionally cold, introverted, and reserved. They avoid situations in which they may be required to compete with others. The daydreams and inner emotional lives of schizoid personalities may be rich and intense, but their overt behavior is devoid of spontaneity and warmth.

Ernst Kretschmer (1936) described several subtypes of schizoid personalities. Some are stiff, formal, and meticulously proper in social situations. Others give the impression of being fragile, delicate, and hypersensitive. Some are exclusively preoccupied with vague philosophical problems, impractical schemes, and futile missions. Some are recluses and eccentrics who from choice live alone and discourage visitors. Schizoid personalities may be highly creative and productive in occupations that permit them to work alone, but more often they are employed at simple jobs that are below their abilities.

In his description of the detached-avoidant personality, which corresponds to the schizoid personality, Theodore Millon (1969) notes that these individuals are not deficient in their capacity for experiencing emotions, nor are they insensitive to the moods and feelings of others. Many are oversensitive to the actions of others and very alert to censure. Their detachment is a defensive reaction against unfavorable interpersonal experiences in the past: parental rejection, depreciation, belittlement.

The GAP classification favors the term "isolated personality" to describe children who tend "to exhibit distant, detached, cold, or withdrawn attitudes toward family and friends." The isolated child is typically unable to form warm and meaningful interpersonal attachments. His usual pattern of passivity and shyness may be periodically broken by unpredictable outbursts of rage, contrariness, or sadistic behavior. The surface behavior of overly inhibited children may superficially resemble that of schizoid personalities, but they may be distinguished by the fact that though they seem to wish for close interpersonal relationships, they are prevented from achieving them by their inhibitions, rather than by the schizoid's fear and ambivalence. In their own homes and with a few close friends they may be much less inhibited.

OBSESSIVE-COMPULSIVE PERSONALITY

Individuals with obsessive-compulsive personalities are characterized by rigid conformity, orderliness, strict conscience, and undue inhibition. Compulsive personalities tend to irritate associates with their attention to petty details, insistence on perfection, and inordinate scrupulousness. Their lack of tolerance, adaptability, and flexibility may cause them to be passed over for promotion to supervisory positions. Their need for regularity may be expressed in a preoccupation with bowel movements and a rigid sleep schedule. Many are obsessed with cleanliness, dental hygiene, special diets, and physical fitness. The compulsive pattern in children is similar to that of adults. The orderliness and conformity of children may be misinterpreted as a kind of pseudomaturity. A distinction is made between transient periods of compulsive rituals engaged in by many children and a compulsive personality.

Compulsive persons are usually industrious, reliable, and efficient, but they show a lack of spontaneity, imagination, and creativity. There is a grimness in their approach to work. Security and absence

SCHIZOID PERSONALITY: THE CASE OF PRINCESS ANNE'S KIDNAPPER

Usually schizoid personalities passively accept their isolation and seeming rejection by society. On occasion, they express their hostility toward the unfriendly world by acts of violence. Ian Ball was diagnosed as a schizoid personality when he was nineteen. He sought psychiatric treatment off and on until he was twenty-one. In 1974, when he was twenty-six years old, he tried to kidnap Princess Anne of England. During the attempted abduction, he shot and killed two police officers and wounded two other men. He was arrested, and when later tried in court, he pleaded guilty and was sentenced to a mental institution for an indefinite period.

Newspaper accounts of Ball's developmental history, as presented during the court hearing, indicated a long history of maladjustment. From early childhood he felt himself to be an outcast. He had no friends in school and left when he was sixteen years old. By this time he had broken contact with his mother. His father died when he was five. He changed jobs frequently. He was unable to concentrate on his work and could not communicate with others. He was on public welfare for two years prior to the abduction attempt, during this period he occasionally heard voices and considered suicide. He also had fantasies about getting a lot of money, which would make it unnecessary for him to work and would also make him more attractive to girls.

His thinking ability apparently was unimpaired. In the fall of 1973 he vacationed in Spain, where he bought two guns that he planned to use in his abduction attempt. On his return he rented a house where he intended to hide the princess. By phoning the press office at Buckingham Palace, he obtained all the information he needed with respect to Princess Anne's movements. Prior to the attempted abduction he wrote a ransom letter, which was found on him, indicating that a ransom of over $7 million was to be paid in unmarked, consecutively numbered five-pound notes that had not been sprayed with any traceable chemical substance. In addition, he had prepared documents listing his conditions for the release of the princess. Among other conditions he was to be granted a full pardon for any criminal acts he had committed and permitted to leave the country with the money.

Ian Ball in the hands of London police.

of conflict lies in strict adherence to fixed routines, rules, and procedures. Relations with others are correct, objective, and impersonal. Careful attention is given to personal boundaries and rights.

The parents of compulsives frequently have similar traits and serve as models for imitation. Parental child rearing practices are heavy on discipline. Emphasis is placed on conformity, self-control, self-responsibility, and independence. Home life lacks warmth; frivolous play and impulse gratification are frowned upon.

HYSTERICAL PERSONALITY

The *hysterical* behavior pattern is mainly noted in adolescent girls and young women but may also be found in males. The adjective "histrionic" expresses the essence of the personality. The hysterical person is self-dramatizing, self-centered, excitable, unstable, and often a player of roles. The artificiality of emotions is illustrated by the seductiveness often noted in hysterical women. When men respond to their provocative behavior, they are usually surprised and frightened. Experienced men are well aware of the underlying frigidity of coquettes. In defense of histrionic females it must be said that their flirting is not a deliberate strategy to tease and frustrate. From their perspective, men misinterpret their signals. Their intent is simply to attract male interest and attention.

The GAP description of the hysterical personality in children and adolescents is very similar to that for adults:

This group of children shows tendencies toward flamboyant, overdramatic, overaffective, oversuggestible, and coy behavior. They often appear to be overly dependent upon the environment for the establishment of their own independent identities. Despite their often misleading overt heterosexual behavior, they give evidence of unusual repression of sexual impulses and of difficulties in the

establishment of their sexual identities and relationships. Masochistic needs for the experiencing of suffering or pain may be present unconsciously. Individuals in this category may be strongly manipulative or demanding in a passive-aggressive fashion.

Millon (1969) has emphasized the gregariousness and dependence of the hysterical personality. The two key traits are interlocked. Devoid of inner resources, the hysteric is heavily dependent on his social environment for stimulation, approval, and affection. In the pursuit of these objectives, he takes the initiative. He actively "courts" others by being vivacious, charming, agreeable, and seductive. He may develop an exquisite sensitivity to the moods and thoughts of others, but his own actions and feelings are shallow, simulated, and manipulative. He is a fraud, a player of games.

The hysteric's capacity for self-deception is strikingly illustrated in more severe hysterical neurotic reactions that include loss of memory, blindness, and paralysis. In his discussion of factors contributory to the development of the hysterical personality, Millon lists histrionic parental models, rivalry among siblings for parental attention, parental failure to provide a consistent and stabilizing set of values, reinforcement in the home of showoff behavior, and the presence during infancy of a variety of caretakers who supplied the child with intense, short-lived stimulus gratifications at irregular intervals.

PASSIVE-AGGRESSIVE PERSONALITY

The *passive-aggressive* personality is also referred to as the *oppositional syndrome* and the *negativistic personality*. The passive-aggressive person is given to procrastination, stubbornness, refusal to talk, intentional inefficiency, contrariness, negativism, noncooperativeness, and general obstructionism. He may be chronically sullen and complaining, or he may disguise his negativism beneath a surface charm and agreeableness, so that it is only after a series of increasingly frustrating encounters that other people are able to recognize the hidden obstructionism of his behavior. These covert styles of expressing resentment and hostility are especially characteristic of insecure, dependent persons who dare not express their aggression openly. Reactions of this type can be more exasperating than direct attacks. A parent may feel justified in punishing a child who talks back or is destructive, but be at a loss how to discipline a child who refuses to eat, doesn't hear when called, "accidentally" breaks a prized cup when asked to help with the dishes, or sabotages parental aspirations by failing in school.

The oppositional syndrome should not be confused with normal resistance to excessive demands or the child's healthy strivings toward self-direction and independence. Passive aggressiveness is the life style of the person, his typical way of behaving in most situations.

The frequent occurrence of passive-aggressive behavior in several members of the same family may be attributed to shared learning experiences or shared genes. Family discord, exploitation of children to gratify parental needs, and contradictory communications that make it impossible for any response to be "right" (the double bind) may all contribute to the development of passive-aggressive behavior. A follow-up study of a large group of passive-aggressive patients (Small et al., 1970) has indicated that when contrary interpersonal behavior is part of the character structure rather than merely a manipulative technique, it is resistant to change. With advancing age there is an increase in anxiety and manifestations of depression. Thought processes become more constricted and tangential, but these persons do not develop delusions or hallucinations. Over time, somatic complaints became more pronounced and persistent.

ANTISOCIAL OR SOCIOPATHIC PERSONALITY

As a psychiatric concept the diagnosis of *antisocial personality* is loosely applied to a heterogeneous group of individuals whose life style is marked by the immediate gratification of impulses and egocentric desires without regard or concern for the feelings and welfare of others. In the pursuit of these objectives, sociopaths may engage in unethical, immoral, or criminal behavior. These are the people who in earlier times were referred to as rogues, ne'er-do-wells, black sheep, and scoundrels. They have no sense of loyalty or responsibility to family, friends, or society. Other people are regarded as dupes and suckers, to be used and exploited by the sociopath.

Successful antisocial personalities or sociopaths may be quite charming, persuasive, and socially adroit. When caught in some misdeed, they may skillfully extricate themselves by lying, blaming others (including the victim), begging forgiveness, and making a show of remorse. The true sociopath, however, does not experience genuine anxiety, guilt, or remorse for the anguish and suffering he causes others. Punishment has no deterrent effect. All that is learned from past experience is to be more circumspect next time.

The impulsiveness, low frustration tolerance, and lack of empathy for the feelings of others suggest inherent temperamental defects. The restless search for excitement and new experiences which characterizes many sociopaths (Quay, 1965) may also be related to inherent temperament. The sociopath's egocentricity makes him incapable of affection or love for others. On the other hand, the sociopath may be acutely sensitive to others' desire for a show of affection, which he can turn to his own profit. Cleckley (1964) has suggested that many sociopaths may actually be psychotic.

Definitions of Sociopathy

J. C. Prichard is credited with being one of the first to recognize sociopathy as a separate clinical entity. In 1837 he delineated a behavior pattern that he referred to as *moral insanity:*

There is a form of mental derangement in which the intellectual faculties appear to have sustained little or no injury, while the disorder is manifested, principally or alone, in the state of feelings, temper or habits. In cases of this nature, the moral and active principles of the mind are strongly perverted or depraved; the power of self-government is lost or incapable, not of talking or reasoning upon any subject proposed to him, for this he will often do with shrewdness and volubility, but of conducting himself with decency and propriety in the business of life.

Here is the DSM-11 definition of antisocial personality:

This term is reserved for individuals who are basically unsocialized and whose behavior pattern brings them repeatedly into conflict with society. They are incapable of significant loyalty to individuals, groups, or social values. They are grossly selfish, callous, irresponsible, impulsive, and unable to feel guilt or to learn from experience and punishment. Frustration tolerance is low. They tend to blame others or offer plausible rationalizations for their behavior. A mere history of repeated legal or social offenses is not sufficient to justify this diagnosis.

The GAP classification includes antisocial personalities in the category of tension-release disorders. More specifically, the diagnosis is applied to children described as *impulse-ridden:*

These children show shallow relationships with adults or other children, having very low frustration tolerance. They exhibit great difficulty in control of their impulses, both aggressive and sexual, which are discharged immediately and impulsively, without delay or inhibition and often without any regard for the consequences. Little anxiety, internalized conflict, or guilt is experienced by most of these children, as the conflict remains largely external, between society and their impulses. . . . The basic defect in impulse controls appears to be reinforced by a deficit in conscience or superego formation, with failure to develop the capacity for tension storage and for the postponement of gratifications. Such children ordinarily exhibit primitive defense mechanisms, with strong denial of dependent or other needs, projection of their hostile feelings onto adults or society, and rationalization of their own behavior. . . . Stealing, firesetting, vandalism, destruction, aggressive attack, and other antisocial acts may frequently occur, and behavior may shift at times from one form to another or several others; addiction is not infrequent in older children and adolescents. Although their judgment and time concepts are poor, they usually have adequate intelligence and their reality testing in certain areas is quite effective.

Differential Diagnosis

Although the distinctions are sometimes finely drawn, diagnostic differentiations are made among sociopathic personality, criminal behavior, and the antisocial reactions sometimes noted in neuroses and psychoses. One basic premise is that sociopathic behavior is related to some basic defect in the personality of the individual. This inference was explicitly indicated in the former diagnosis of *constitutional psychopathic personality.*

A large proportion of delinquents and criminals may be technically described as antisocial personalities, but many forms of criminal behavior represent chosen vocations. Particularly in the case of culturally disadvantaged individuals, certain types of criminal behavior may be regarded as desirable or acceptable ways of earning a livelihood. Within the social values of the subculture, the professional criminal may be regarded as loyal and dependable. Unlike the sociopath, the "normal" criminal is capable of establishing relationships of warmth and trust with others. His criminal antisocial behavior is frequently restricted to a particular type of activity. In other respects his behavior may conform to expected standards. A racketeer, for example, may be a good father and husband.

Neurotics who engage in antisocial behavior are differentiated by the fact that they typically exhibit anxiety and guilt for their actions. Neurotic antisocial behavior is not an expression of some basic personality defect, but represents the impulsive acting out of conflicts and tensions. A further distinguishing characteristic is that acting-out neurotics are capable of empathy and of forming meaningful affectional relationships with others.

Antisocial behavior in a psychotic is interpreted as an incidental symptomatic manifestation of his disorder. This interpretation is confirmed by the relative absence of overt antisocial behavior prior to and following the psychotic episode.

In brief, the diagnosis of adult offenders as antisocial personalities is based on (1) case-history data that indicate the repeated occurrence from early childhood of incorrigible, harmful, and authority-defying behavior in the home, in school, at work, and in the community; (2) the seeming absence of anxiety, guilt, or concern for the feelings of others; and (3) the absence of symptoms identified with other psychiatric disorders (delusions, mental retardation, and alcoholism). It is inferred from the persistence of wrongdoing (despite awareness of the rules, repeated warnings, and punishment) that these individuals are deficient in moral scruples and social feelings. The prevailing punitive attitude toward sociopaths of members of their own families as well as of society at large rests on the premise that these individuals knowingly, callously, and willfully violate established rules of social conduct because they are interested only in the immediate gratification of egocentric impulses and desires. An alternate, more objective viewpoint is that inherent and acquired personality defects are mainly responsible for the long-term persistence of antisocial behavior.

Epidemiology

The overlap with criminal behavior, alcoholism, and other diagnostic categories makes it difficult to estimate the prevalence of antisocial personalities. A conservative guess is that the label may be appropriately applied to about 1 percent of the total male population and about 0.50 percent of the female population. The pattern is more frequently noted in lower socioeconomic groups but occurs at all class levels.

Developmental History

Manifestations of sociopathy occur at an early age. These children are distinguished by impulsiveness, destructiveness, aggressiveness, and defiance of authority. Commonly noted antisocial activities include stealing, incorrigibility, truancy, lying, and running away from home. Sex experiences of a promiscuous and often deviant nature start early. The severity of antisocial behavior during childhood is the best predictor of adult sociopathy. L. N. Robins (1966) found that 43 percent of the children referred to a psychiatric clinic who were found to have ten or more antisocial symptoms were diagnosed as antisocial personalities thirty years later. For children with fewer than three antisocial symptoms, the risk of adult sociopathy was only 4 percent.

Practically all sociopaths have had several encounters with the police and courts by the time they reach adulthood. Other typical findings among adult patients include excessive use of alcohol and drugs, wanderlust, frequent change of jobs, poor military records, many somatic complaints, and a high incidence of divorce, separation, and marital conflict. After the age of thirty, about a third of these patients show some moderation of overt antisocial behavior, but interpersonal relations continue to be marked by irritability and hostility (Robins, 1966). The decline in antisocial behavior appears to be mainly a function of aging. Patients rarely attribute their improvement to help received from professional workers. The reasons most commonly offered for their improvement are maturity, marriage, increased responsibilities, and fear of imprisonment.

Treatment

R. D. Hare (1970) has presented a cogent analysis of reasons for the failure of traditional forms of therapy with sociopathic individuals. The effectiveness of psychotherapy is influenced by personal distress on the part of the patient, a strong desire to change, the establishment of a warm, trusting relationship with the therapist, and the mutual expectation of beneficial results. Since the sociopath sees nothing wrong with his behavior, which he finds rewarding at least in the short run, he has no incentive to change and no interest in establishing an emotional relationship with the therapist, of which he is incapable in any case. The therapist, for his part, has been conditioned by his training and experience to regard sociopathy as incurable.

Research Data on Sociopathy

In contrast to the paucity of research data on other deviant personality types the literature on antisocial personalities is extensive. The major conclusion that may be drawn is that the determinants of sociopathy are complex and interactive. The significance of specific variables is limited. A second general conclusion is that for meaningful results the concept of antisocial personality must be sharply and clearly defined, with emphasis on objectively observable and measurable characteristics. The common practice of selecting subjects from reformatories and prisons is highly questionable since these individuals constitute a restricted and biased sample.

Heredity. No genetic studies have been reported of persons clinically diagnosed as antisocial personalities. Composite figures from six twin studies conducted with institutionalized criminals and delinquents indicate a concordance rate of 66 percent for MZ twins and 32 percent for DZ twins (Essen-Moller, 1963). To what extent these findings are applicable to antisocial personalities is unknown.

The discovery a few years ago that about 2 percent of the males in maximum security institutions had an unusual XYY chromosome pattern stimulated a transient flurry of interest in the possibility that extreme sociopathy might be associated with this genetic anomaly. This hypothesis has now been discarded (Fox, 1971; Hook, 1973). Studies of randomly selected antisocial personalities, patients in mental hospitals, and inmates of regular prisons have established that the incidence of the XYY chromosome in these male groups is the same as that for the general population, about 1 per 1,000. The 2 percent rate among inmates of institutions for the criminally insane, defective delinquents and disturbed sex offenders appears to be a result of administrative policies. Most XYY persons are neither antisocial personalities nor criminals. If they should commit crimes, their offenses are no more serious or violent than those of normal XY males. But XYY persons have two strikes against them: they are unusually tall (over six feet) and many show poor control of their impulses. These traits make them seem dangerous and increases the probability that they will be sent to maximum security institutions.

Family setting. Data on the early childhood experiences of adults are subject to faulty recall and retrospective distortion. Robins (1966) avoided this pitfall by starting with a large group of 524 children seen in a child guidance clinic and then investigating their psychiatric status thirty years later. The median age of the children at referral was thirteen years. Since many of the children were initially referred for antisocial behavior, it was predicted that a substantial number would be diagnosed as sociopathic personalities as adults. In point of fact, ninety-four were so diagnosed on the basis of a standard set of criteria, independently of their early clinic records. After the diagnoses had been made, the child clinic records were examined to determine correlates and predictors of subsequent sociopathy. The psychiatric status of a control group of one hundred children was also investigated after thirty years had passed. The control group was matched for pertinent variables. Two main requirements for inclusion in the control group were that the child had not repeated a full grade and had no record of expulsion from school or transfer to a correctional institution.

The popular belief that low socioeconomic status contributes heavily to sociopathy was not confirmed. Both groups of children lived in the same lower-class neighborhood, but only 2 percent of the control children were diagnosed as sociopathic personalities as adults, compared with 22 percent of the clinic-referred children. Careful study of the role of "bad companions" led to the conclusion that the greater availability of antisocial children in some neighborhoods was of minor importance. Antisocial children tend to seek each other out because of their common interests and their rejection by others. Antisocial boys who participated in gangs were neither more nor less likely to be sociopathic adults than were nonparticipants. Boys without severe antisocial behavior rarely grew up to be sociopaths, whether or not they joined gangs.

The adjustment of the mother was found to have no direct effect on the risk of adult sociopathy. The presence of an antisocial father in the home, however, was a highly significant predictor of adult antisocial behavior. His presence was considered the chief underlying factor in the prevalence of family discord, inadequate supervision, and inconsistent discipline noted in the early histories of children who later were diagnosed as sociopathic personalities. Fathers who were cold, strict disciplinarians tended to have fewer sociopathic children. Broken homes, no matter what was responsible for the absence of the missing parent, did not differentiate children who became sociopaths from those who developed other disorders.

The effect of parental rejection of a child was difficult to evaluate. Sometimes repudiation resulted from the parent's irresponsibility and at other times from the fact that the child's behavior was intolerable. Bell (1968) and Wiggins (1968) have called attention to the effect of the child's behavior on parental attitude and mode of disciplining. A probem child may cause his parents to shift back and forth between overindulgence and strictness, to be indifferent, or to reject him. The interaction, of course, works both ways. Disturbed parents may elicit adverse reactions in their children.

Neurophysiological correlates. As Hare (1970) has noted in his comprehensive review, research findings in this area are more suggestive than conclusive. The hypothesis that sociopathy is associated with cortical immaturity is based on the frequent observation of a slow alpha EEG rhythm in adult sociopaths. A similar brain-wave pattern is characteristic of young children. There is some evidence that antisocial persons tend to show diminished autonomic activity, as measured by electrodermal and cardiac changes. Autonomic underactivity has been noted both in the resting state and in response to stress. The low cortical and autonomic arousal of sociopaths has been considered related to their apparent lack of anxiety and their hunger for stimulation and excitement, but physiological findings are inconsistent with these inferences and make their validity questionable.

Social learning deficit. The ineffectiveness of punishment as a deterrent plus the sociopath's apparent failure to acquire the social values of his culture have led to the hypothesis that antisocial behavior is related to an inherent inability to learn tasks that are dependent on fear for reinforcement. Some support for this theory has been demonstrated in experiments in which subjects were shocked for making wrong responses. Sociopaths tend to be less efficient than others in learning to avoid punishment, but they show no deficit in learning complex tasks under stressful conditions (Hare, 1970) or when monetary rewards are used as incentives (Schmauk, 1968). The poor learning of sociopaths in shock experiments may be due to a negative reaction to punishment.

OTHER PERSONALITY TYPES

Asthenic Personality

The *asthenic* behavior pattern is characterized by low energy level, easy fatigability, and absence of zest in living. These individuals tend to be complacent, apathetic, and distant.

Inadequate Personality

The *inadequate* individual is not mentally deficient, but he seemingly never does anything right. His behavior is characterized by ineptness, poor judgment, ineffectual responses to emotional and social demands, lack of stamina, and absence of drive. Like the diagnoses of other personality types, the label of inadequacy represents a social value judgment. The individual may have little interest in the achievement standards of his culture. In the context of his perspective and objectives, he may consider his behavior adequate and adaptive. The diagnosis is mainly applied to persons of low socioeconomic status. The general inadequacy is suggestive of the personality and behavior of simple schizophrenics.

Passive-Dependent Personality

The *passive-dependent* person is typically docile, plaintive, mildly dejected, clinging, and submissive. He tends to avoid giving an opinion, since he can seldom be sure he will not offend someone. He resists the assumption of responsibilities that require independent judgment, since this too entails the risk of giving offense, and in any case he has little faith in his own judgment. He wants to be told what to do and how to do it. When his docility and "goodness" fail to bring him the rewards he expects, he experiences a sense of personal failure and simultaneous resentment at those who not only do not reward him, but themselves obtain rewards he feels they do not deserve. Not surprisingly, he is prey to a variety of physical ailments, which arise from or are exacerbated by the suppression of his conflicting emotions. Poor physical health serves to justify his failure to win the rewards he feels are otherwise due him.

Explosive Personality

The explosive personality is also called an aggressive personality and emotionally unstable personality. As long as everything is going smoothly, the individual may appear well adjusted, but when he is frustrated or confronted with some minor stress, he loses control. Aggressive impulses are directly and forcefully expressed, either verbally or physically. Outbursts of rage are suggestive of infantile temper tantrums in their unpredictability and intensity. At the adult level, these uncontrolled and irrational attacks provoke anxiety and hostility in others and may have serious social repercussions. When calm is restored, the individual usually regrets his actions, but this does not prevent their repetition when he is frustrated again.

PSYCHOANALYTIC INTERPRETATION OF PERSONALITY DISORDERS

The term "character disorders" is preferred to "personality disorders" in the psychoanalytic literature. The meaning is about the same. The term "character" refers to the basic personality structure of the individual and his customary mode of perceiving, reacting, and adapting. Maladaptive traits and behavior patterns that fall somewhere between normal functioning and neurosis on a morbidity scale are labeled character disorders.

Psychoanalysts recognize the contribution of genetic and environmental factors in shaping personality, but they maintain

Erich Fromm, a social psychologist and psychoanalyst who is widely known for his many books dealing with man's struggle to cope with the loneliness and isolation of modern society.

that character formation is closely related to psychosexual development. Fixation at a particular stage of early sexual development is thought to result in the relative predominance and persistence of personality and behavior traits associated with that stage (Fenichel, 1945; Blum, 1953). Thus fixation at the early oral stage leads to an *oral character*, marked by extreme dependence, which may be expressed in demanding behavior. Overcompensation may lead to an exaggerated independence. Overindulgence during infancy favors the development of such traits as optimism, self-assurance, and generosity. Deprivation may lead to selfishness, pessimism, and a sadistic attitude toward others.

Adult character traits that are presumed to be related to early anal fixation include frugality, obstinacy, and orderliness. The *anal character* is also associated with excessive cleanliness, compulsive behavior, and sadistic tendencies. Fixation at the oedipal level is associated with the *urethral character* and the *phallic character*. The urethral character, which is identified with an earlier age period than the phallic, is marked by ambition and competitiveness. The phallic character is characterized by recklessness, aggressiveness, and narcissism.

FROMM AND CHARACTER ORIENTATION

Erich Fromm (1947) has distinguished four maladaptive syndromes that he has labeled *nonproductive character orientations*. The character orientations indicate for each individual his method of acquiring and assimilating the things he needs to satisfy his needs and his style of relating himself to other people and the world. The advantage of a relatively permanent character system is that it enables the individual to act consistently without having constantly to make new decisions. The character a child develops is influenced by his innate temperament, the impact of personal experiences, and especially the character of his parents. In his description of nonproductive character orientations, Fromm stressed their negative aspects.

The receptive orientation. Persons with a receptive orientation feel that all the good things in life come from the outside and are provided by others. Their own role is to encourage a continued supply of love, food, drink, information, and helpful services from others by being grateful, friendly, loyal, and agreeable. The resulting paralysis of independent action and critical abilities makes these people increasingly dependent on others. They are always in search of helpers, the more the better. They feel lost, anxious and helpless when alone or forced to make decisions or do things on their own.

The exploitive orientation. The basic premise of this orientation is the same as that of the receptive type to the extent that the source of all good things is thought to be outside the self. The difference is that the exploitive individual expects to take what he wants from others by force or cunning rather than to passively wait to be given what he wants. Even though he may be capable of productivity, the exploitive person prefers to grab what he wants. His motto appears to be "Stolen fruits are sweeter." An extreme example is the pleasure that kleptomaniacs derive from stealing things they can afford to buy. People are judged in terms of their usefulness for exploitation. In contrast to the receptive type, who tends to be confident and optimistic, the exploitive type is usually suspicious, cynical and envious.

The hoarding type. The hoarding type does not expect to get much from the world. His security is based on hoarding and saving. He regards love as essentially a possession. The miserliness of this orientation includes feelings and thoughts as well as money and material things. These individuals frequently are tight-lipped, orderly, pedantic, punctual, and rigid. Many are obsessed with compulsive washing and cleanliness. They make a sharp distinction between mine and thine.

The marketing orientation. Individuals of this type are mainly concerned with the market value of their personality and behavior. "The character orientation is rooted in the experience of oneself as a commodity and of one's value as exchange value." The marketing type acquires and exhibits whatever personality traits and attitudes are required of him to succeed in the marketplace. His motto is "I am whatever you desire of

me." He is more concerned with his salability and success than with his happiness, self-esteem, or individual identity.

SUMMARY

The concept of personality disorder fits in neatly with our basic premise that the behavior patterns associated with neurosis and psychosis represent extreme variations of reactions noted in normal individuals. These maladaptive personality patterns may be regarded as mild to moderate deviations from the normal. Deviations may be arrested at this level or proceed to more extreme and more disturbing reactions, identified as neuroses or psychoses. Many of these personality types correspond to the premorbid personalities of psychotic and neurotic patients. If a person develops a neurosis or psychosis, his symptoms will in all probability consist largely of an accentuation of his preexisting faulty modes of perceiving, thinking, feeling, and reacting.

The principles and processes regulating the development of deviant and normal personalities are the same. From the moment of birth a continuing complex, reciprocal, and cumulative interaction occurs between the child and his social environment. The inherent and distinctive temperament of the infant influences the kinds of responses he elicits from his parents. In turn, the attitudes, feelings, temperaments, and behavior of the parents affect the infant's reactions. As the child's sphere of activity is enlarged, siblings, peers, and significant others become involved in the biosocial molding pattern. During the early formative years there may be considerable trial-and-error experimentation as child, parents, and others try out different roles and techniques in their interactions for gaining their respective objectives.

The fluidity of the interactive process and the unpredictable occurrence of fortuitous learning experiences permit considerable variability in personality outcome.

In principle, a child may develop any one of a wide variety of behavior patterns. In actuality, the range of potential variation is limited. One limiting factor is the child's genetic endowment, which influences his activity level, the intensity of his feelings and reactions, his prevailing mood, general competence, and adaptability. The established personality characteristics of his parents, which influence parent-child relations, constitute a second major restriction. The available models and reinforcement contingencies in the home and community set further restrictions.

Within the limits imposed by these biosocial factors, the child endeavors to structure, interpret, and adapt to his environment. The behavior patterns acquired may not be ideal, but they may be the best available at the time. The tendency to react to new situations on the basis of previously acquired patterns leads to consistency of behavior and of response by others. Through frequent repetition, maladaptive as well as effective traits become deeply ingrained and relatively fixed. The rigidity of the behavior set interferes with the introduction of new responses, which, if favorably reinforced, would alter the pattern.

References

American Psychiatric Association. *Diagnostic and Statistical Manual of Mental Disorders* (DSM-11). Washington, D.C., 1968.

Bell, R. A. "A Reinterpretation of the Direction of Effects in Studies of Socialization." *Psychological Review* 75 (1968): 81–95.

Blum, G. S. *Psychoanalytic Theories of Personality.* New York: McGraw-Hill, 1953.

Cameron, N. "The Paranoid Pseudocommunity Revisited." *American Journal of Sociology* 65 (1959): 52-58.

Cleckley, H. *The Mask of Sanity,* 4th ed. St. Louis: Mosby, 1964.

Dupont, R. L., and Grunebaum, H. "Willing Victims: The Husbands of Paranoid Women." *American Journal of Psychiatry* 125 (1968): 151-59.

Essen-Moller, E. "Twin Research and Psychiatry." *Acta Psychiatrica et Neurologica* 39 (1963): 65-77. Reprinted in *International Journal of Psychiatry* 1 (1965): 466-75.

Fenichel, O. *Psychoanalytic Theory of Neurosis.* New York: Norton, 1945.

Fox, R. G. "The XYY Offender: A Modern Myth?" *Journal of Criminal Law, Criminology, and Police Science* 62 (1971) 59-73.

Fromm, E. *Man for Himself.* New York: Holt, Rinehart & Winston, 1947.

Gralnick, A. "Folie à deux: The Psychosis of Association." *Psychiatric Quarterly* 16 (1942): 230-63.

Group for the Advancement of Psychiatry. *Psychopathological Disorders in Childhood: Theoretical Considerations and a Proposed Classification.* New York, 1966.

Hare, R. D. *Psychopathy: Theory and Research.* New York: Wiley, 1970.

Hook, E. B. "Behavioral Implications of the Human XYY Genotype." *Science* 179 (1973): 139-50.

Kretschmer, E. *Physique and Character.* London: Routledge & Kegan Paul, 1936.

Millon, T. *Modern Psychopathology.* Philadelphia: Saunders, 1969.

Montague, A. "Chromosomes and Crime." *Psychology Today* 2 (1968): 42-49.

Patients in Mental Institutions, 1965. Public Health Service publication no. 1597. Washington, D.C.: U.S. Government Printing Office, 1968.

Prichard, J. C. *Treatise on Insanity.* Philadelphia: Haswell, Barrington, & Haswell, 1837.

Quay, H. C. "Psychopathic Personality as Pathological Stimulation Seeking." *American Journal of Psychiatry* 122 (1965): 180-83.

Robins, L. N. *Deviant Children Grown Up.* Baltimore: Williams & Wilkins, 1966.

Schmauk, K. "A Study of the Relationship Between Kinds of Punishment, Autonomic Arousal, Subjective Anxiety, and Avoidance Learning in the Primary Sociopath." Unpublished Ph.D. dissertation, Temple University, 1968.

Small, I. F.; Small, J. G.; Alig, V. B.; and Moore, D. F. "Passive-Aggressive Personality Disorder: A Search for a Syndrome." *American Journal of Psychiatry* 126 (1970): 973-81.

Wiggins, J. "Inconsistent Socialization." *Psychological Reports* 23 (1968): 303-36.

13 · Alcoholism

Gin Lane, William Hogarth

Alcoholism is and has long been the major drug problem of the United States and most of the Western world. For a brief period during the 1960s it looked as if college students in their revolt against the establishment would replace the mind-blurring intoxicant of the past with newer drugs. But alcohol won out. Among youth today alcoholism is a far more serious and prevalent problem than opiates, hallucinogens, stimulants, and sedatives. Most young people on other drugs also drink to excess.

Alcohol is a psychoactive drug. The traditional practice of differentiating between alcohol and other drugs is in great measure due to the fact that most societies accept alcohol more than opiates and other psychoactive drugs. Laws regulating the use of alcohol are much more tolerant than those for other drugs and the penalties for their infraction are far milder. The common denominator in all psychoactive drugs is that they are toxic substances. Moderate doses produce a blurring of conscious awareness that serves as a satisfying "time out," during which anxieties and problems are temporarily set aside and the individual can relax, become "high," or experience what is euphemistically referred to as a transcendent state. Very large doses lead to a comatose condition and the possibility of a permanent escape from the pressures of life.

Having acknowledged that alcohol and drug use are in the same general class, we can proceed to perpetuate the time-honored custom of considering alcoholism as a separate problem. The main justification for this procedure is that alcohol and other drugs are treated separately in the research literature. Little attention has been given to the fact that many chronic alcoholics also take other drugs.

ALCOHOLISM

Figures on the extent and severity of alcohol use are very unreliable. A rough estimate is that about one-third of the adult males in the United States are teetotalers. Another third are casual or social drinkers. Some of the members of this middle group drink only at parties and on special occasions; others may take one to two drinks daily, usually at mealtime. The remaining third may be described as heavy drinkers. Some drink excessive amounts each day. Others restrict their consumption to sporadic over-indulgence on weekends and on special occasions. Most of the men in this latter group do not consider themselves alcoholics, and this judgment is shared by their associates. From a psychiatric point of view, a diagnosis of alcoholism is restricted to those for whom drinking constitutes a relatively serious chronic problem in their personal, family, social, and occupational adjustment. A substantial proportion of heavy drinkers may come to this state after years of drinking. At any one time, however, less than 5 percent of the total adult male population definitely qualify as alcoholics.

Almost four times as many men as women are admitted each year to some type of psychiatric facility in the United States for the treatment of alcoholism (Table 13.1). The sex ratio in favor of males varies with type of facility from a high of over 5 to 1 for public mental hospitals to less than 3 to 1 for private mental hospitals and outpatient psychiatric clinics. Since women more often than men confine their drinking to the privacy of their homes and are more protected, it is quite possible that the published figures exaggerate the magnitude of sex differences. If all female alcoholics were counted, the corrected sex ratio might well be about 2 to 1, which is the ratio for other drug abuse disorders.

Women who become alcoholics generally begin serious drinking at a later age than men, but once started, they progress rapidly to a state of alcoholic addiction. The symptoms and drinking habits of alcoholic women differ somewhat from those of alcoholic men (Wanberg and Horn, 1970). Female drunks are very rarely seen on Skid Row.

Alcoholics are found in all walks of life, at all educational and intelligence levels, in all social classes, and in all occupations. Alcoholism is as much a medical, sociological, and economic problem as it is a psychiatric problem. The death rate of alcoholics from various organic diseases and from suicide is much higher than that for the general population. Alcoholism is a major contributing factor to injuries and deaths associated with automobile accidents. The annual cost to industry in absenteeism, injuries, defective products, and reduced work output runs into the billions of dollars. Alcoholism is a major cause of family discord, broken homes, desertion, and divorce. It is also an important contributory factor in delinquency and crime.

About 25 percent of all annual admissions to state and county mental hospitals are diagnosed as acute or chronic alcoholics. The peak age of hospital admissions is during the prime years between thirty-five and forty-five. Drinking, however, starts much earlier. Studies based on the prevalence of alcoholism in the general population indicate that the highest prevalence of drinking problems occurs among males 21 to 25 years of age (Cahalan and Room, 1974). The main sufferer is the alcoholic himself, whose uncontrollable drinking results in loss of health, employment, family, self-respect and hope.

Table 13.1. Sex Differences in Alcohol and Drug Abuse (Admissions by Type of Treatment Facility, U.S., 1970).

Type of facility	Sex ratio: males per 100 females	
	Alcohol disorders	Drug abuse disorders
State and County mental hospital	568	267
General hospital inpatient psychiatric unit	306	135
Community mental health center	286	214
Outpatient psychiatric service	272	202
Private mental hospital	254	139
Total	381	197

SOURCE: National Institute of Mental Health. "Differential Utilization of Psychiatric Facilities on Men and Women. United States 1970." Survey and Reports Section, Statistical Note 81, June 1973.

Definition of Alcoholism

Our general definition of psychopathology is also applicable to alcoholism. Like other forms of abnormal behavior, alcoholism is relatively independent of voluntary control, causes significant impairment in psychosocial functioning, and causes the individual to be a liability, threat, or source of distress to himself and others. As in other forms of psychopathology, impairment of voluntary control is the critical criterion. Some people are unable to abstain from drinking, others are unable to control the amount they drink, and once started, drinking continues until the individual is intoxicated.

Our definition is very similar to that proposed by the report of the Cooperative Commission on the Study of Alcoholism (Plaut, 1967, p. 39): "Alcoholism is defined as a condition in which an individual has lost control over his alcoholic intake in the sense that he is consistently unable to refrain from drinking or to stop drinking before getting intoxicated." Fox (1967) has defined alcoholism as a behavioral disturbance in which the excessive intake of alcohol interferes with the physical or mental health of the individual and is usually accompanied by an impairment in interpersonal relationships. She also adds the important point that alcoholism is a form of addiction that is marked by an emotional and physiological dependence on alcohol.

Intoxicating Liquors

Ethyl alcohol, the active ingredient in beer, wine, and whiskey, is a colorless, relatively odorless liquid. "Alcohol breath" is due to additives mixed with the alcohol. Ethyl alcohol is absorbed into the blood mainly from the small intestines, and some absorption also occurs from the stomach and lungs. The speed of absorption depends on the type and amount of food the drinker has consumed and his emotional state. Carbon dioxide speeds up the absorption rate, which explains the quick high obtainable from champagne. Alcohol is oxidized by the liver at a steady rate. It takes about an hour to oxidize an ounce of whiskey. A person may drink all day and remain sober if he limits his intake to an ounce of whiskey per hour. During the oxidation process, alcohol is converted into harmless acetic acid.

Methyl alcohol, also known as wood alcohol, has the same toxic effect as ethyl alcohol, but differs from it in two respects: (1) the rate of oxidation is much slower, which results in a much longer period of intoxication, and (2) the oxidation of methyl alcohol results in a highly toxic substance that damages the optic nerve and leads to blindness.

A third intoxicating agent, which shares with alcohol the essential characteristic of inducing anesthesia, is ethyl ether. Ether is obtained from the action of sulfuric acid on alcohol. Ether drinking was quite popular in Ireland, and to a lesser degree in England and Scotland, during the latter part of the nineteenth century. A fascinating account has been given by Kerr (1890). Half a wineglass of ether rapidly produces intoxication in the average person. As a substitute for alcohol, ether has the advantage of allowing one to proceed from a sober state to marked inebriation and back to sobriety in a period of a couple hours. The rapidity of its effects and of recovery from it permit a person to get drunk and become sober again six times a day. The physiological and psychological effects of ether are about the same as those of alcohol. A side effect of ether drinking consists of chronic and distressing inflammation of the stomach.

Reasons for Drinking

The consumption of alcohol is a voluntary act engaged in for the explicit purpose of exchanging a state of sobriety for one of mild to severe intoxication. The general objective is a temporary change of consciousness and behavior. Mild inebriation is usually accompanied by a feeling of *euphoria*. More severe intoxication produces a hazy state that facilitates an escape from self and reality. The often-reported pleasant feeling while under the influence of alcohol consists essentially of an absence of negative feelings. Social drinking is usually characterized by a designated time limit during which the individual is expected to relax and have fun. By tacit agreement, participants at drinking parties are not only permitted but encouraged to be more outgoing than usual and to give freer expression to their impulses. The cocktail hour is often referred to as the happy hour, when individuals can say and do things without being held strictly accountable for them.

For the more habitual drinker, who often starts drinking in the morning, the hazy state induced by alcohol may serve a variety of purposes, depending on his particular needs. Thus alcohol may constitute a form of self-medication for moderating feelings of depression, reducing anxiety, and neutralizing resentment. Alcohol may provide an escape from the emptiness and futility of one's existence. It may serve as an unconscious means of expressing self-destructive tendencies. The individual persists in drinking because by and large alcohol fulfills whatever psychological function it is called upon to perform. It is also readily available. In the long run the results are harmful, but the immediate effects are satisfying. Once the habit is firmly established, it is self-perpetuating. The chronic alcoholic who says that he drinks because he is an alcoholic is not being evasive. Whatever reason he may have originally had for drinking may no longer be pertinent. The established habit is reason enough for drinking.

Developmental Stages of Alcoholism

The usual progression is from social drinking to a psychological dependence on alcohol to a physiological dependence. Physiological dependence is marked by a loss of control over drinking, a "craving" for alcohol, adaptive cell metabolism, and withdrawal symptoms. The sequence from psychological to physiological dependence may

be rapid or may proceed slowly over a period of ten or more years.

E. M. Jellinek (1952) has outlined four stages of alcoholism. The first or *prealcoholic* phase is marked by an intensification of social drinking. The individual drinks to excess and begins to show signs of emotional or psychological dependence. The second or *prodromal* phase is marked by increased tolerance, surreptitious drinking, and preoccupation with alcohol. Periodic blackouts may occur. When the individual sobers up the following day, he may be unable to remember what he did while he was drunk. Guilt feelings are common, but the individual is unable to resist his compulsive desire for alcohol.

The third or *crucial* phase marks the transition to a true state of alcoholism. Social drinking is largely replaced by solitary drinking. Behavior is alcohol-centered. The person starts drinking regularly in the morning and is unable to control his alcoholic intake. Alcohol takes precedence over friends, occupation, and family. Behavioral disturbances include persistent remorse, marked aggressive behavior, unfounded jealousy, and self-pity. During this phase the individual may lose his job, leave home, and experience his first hospitalization or imprisonment for alcoholism. Since his diet may consist largely of alcohol, he may suffer from nutritional deficiencies. Alcohol is now needed to counteract hangover symptoms: headache, diarrhea, and acute thirst. The final or *chronic* phase is marked by prolonged periods of intoxication that may last for several weeks. By this time most drinkers are homeless drunks.

The *Diagnostic and Statistical Manual* of the American Psychiatric Association recognizes three categories of alcoholism: episodic excessive drinking, habitual excessive drinking, and alcohol addiction. Persons who become intoxicated four to twelve times a year are described as episodic excessive drinkers. Those who are under the influence of alcohol more than once a week or who are intoxicated more than twelve times a year are classified as habitual excessive drinkers. The diagnosis

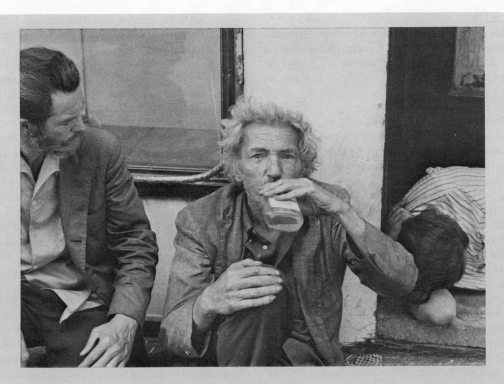

Skid Row: A scene on the Bowery in New York City

of alcohol addiction is restricted to persons who are dependent on alcohol. Signs of dependence include an inability to go one day without drinking, the presence of withdrawal symptoms, and periods of heavy drinking that continue for three months or more.

Patterns of Alcoholism

For purposes of identification, the three principal patterns of drinking behavior have been labeled Alpha, Delta, and Gamma (Jellinek, 1960).

Alpha alcoholism is limited to psychological dependence. The individual drinks too much at the wrong time, but he does not progress to the point where he loses control of his drinking. He retains the ability to abstain and to regulate the amount he drinks. Drinking mainly serves as a means of reducing tension and bod-

ily pain. Although relatively controlled, his persistent drinking leads to impairment of work efficiency and disturbed interpersonal relations.

Delta alcoholism is distinguished by an inability to abstain. The individual drinks practically every day, though he can regulate the amount and time of drinking. This pattern is frequently noted in beer- and wine-drinking countries such as Germany and France. The drinking pattern involves both psychological and physiological dependence. Withdrawal symptoms and craving occur if the person abstains.

Gamma alcoholism is mainly characteristic of Anglo-Saxon and Scandinavian countries, where whiskey is the favorite beverage. Gamma alcoholism is marked by a loss of control with respect to the amount of alcohol consumed. The Gamma drinker may go for weeks or months without touching a drop, but once he starts drinking he is unable to stop until he passes out. Gamma alcoholism also involves physiological dependence and withdrawal symptoms.

Effects of Alcohol

Intoxication. The behavioral signs of intoxication are due to the depressing effect of alcohol on the nervous system. Alcohol acts as a general anesthetic. As the concentration of blood alcohol increases, there is progressive impairment or reduction of normal brain functions. The stages of intoxication are described in Table 13.2. An important function of the cortex of the brain is to inhibit impulsive activity and emotional instability. The impairment of this cortical function accounts for the increase in excitement and the relative loss of restraint commonly noted in mild to moderate levels of intoxication. Disturbances in sensation, perception, speech, motor coordination, memory, and judgment more directly reflect the anesthetic effect of alcohol on the nervous system. When drinking is spaced out, the induced drowsi-

ness tends to limit excessive intake. Large amounts consumed over a brief period may result in coma or death.

Loss of inhibitions. MacAndrew and Edgerton (1969) have criticized the popular view that alcohol, through its effects on the brain, temporarily breaks down the normally operative inhibitions in man with a consequent release of repressed sexual and aggressive impulses. They agree that alcohol, if taken in sufficient quantity, invariably results in impairment of the sensory and motor functions, but they maintain that the behavioral effects of alcohol vary with the individual, with the occasion, and especially with the attitudes and traditions of a particular society. Where drunkenness is an accepted excuse for disorderly behavior and reduced responsibility, alcohol use often leads to increased aggression, violence, sexual promiscuity, and other forms of misconduct. In other societies with different cultural rules and customs, people may consume prodigious amounts of alcohol without engaging in unruly, belligerent, or immoral behavior. A wealth of anthropological observations

Table 13.2. The Effects of Alcohol.

Blood alcohol concentration	Behavioral effects
0.05%	Relaxation of restraints, talkativeness, informality, mild memory impairment.
0.10	Feeling of well-being, slurred speech, clumsiness, impulsiveness, poor coordination.
0.20	Unsteady gait, distortion of sensations (double vision), impaired speech, disjointed conversation, poor judgment, drowsiness. High accident risk if driving car.
0.40	Impaired perceptions, stuporous or comatose.
0.60	Loss of consciousness. High possibility of death due to cessation of breathing and heartbeat.

indicates that in some societies drunkenness is characterized by increased self-preoccupation, social detachment, joviality, or friendliness.

Delirium tremens. Delirium tremens is the most dramatic withdrawal reaction of alcoholism. It usually occurs only in habitual drinkers, either after sustained intoxication or following a period of relative abstinence. Early symptoms include restlessness, irritability, and disturbed sleep accompanied by terrifying dreams. The delirious phase is marked by profound confusion, tremor, illusions, and visual hallucination. The patient "sees" insects, bugs, and small animals crawling over him, and his usual reaction is one of acute fear. Other symptoms include tremors, rapid and irregular pulse, excessive perspiration, indistinct speech, disorientation, and heightened distractibility. Convulsive seizures occasionally occur. The reaction usually lasts from three to five days. Good nursing care is required to cope with the patient's extreme psychological and physiological disturbance. Sedation and restraints are not indicated, but paraldehyde and tranquilizers are usually administered to quiet the patient. Nutritional deficiencies are treated with vitamins and a diet high in carbohydrates.

Acute alcoholic hallucinosis. Acute hallucinosis occurs primarily in individuals with schizoid traits. Apparently the prolonged use of alcohol serves to release latent schizophrenic tendencies. The key symptom consists of auditory hallucinations. Frequently the voices accuse the person of sexual misconduct: males tend to be accused of homosexuality and females of promiscuity. Victims may angrily protest their innocence or be too terrified to answer at all. Depressive feelings are common. In addition to the fact that these hallucinations are auditory rather than visual, acute alcoholic hallucinosis differs from delirium tremens in several respects. Persons with delirium tremens tend to be confused, disoriented, and out of touch with their environment; those with acute hallucinosis are usually well oriented and experience no distortion of perception. Some persons with acute hallucinosis respond favorably to tranquilizers, antidepressants, and vitamins; others go on to manifest typical schizophrenic reactions that may persist for several months.

Korsakoff-Wernicke syndrome. The vitamin deficiency that frequently accompanies prolonged alcoholism may result in degeneration of the nerves. The condition is called Korsakoff's syndrome if the degeneration is largely confined to the cerebrum and peripheral nerves, and Wernicke's disease if the brain stem is the site of the degenerative process. Psychiatric symptoms include amnesia, falsification of memory, and disorientation in time and place. To fill in memory gaps, the individual may report fictitious but plausible memories. He is seemingly unaware of his fabrication. In most instances he is quite jovial. Since the condition is caused by nutritional deficiencies, many cases respond well to a vitamin-enriched diet and clear up in a month or two. In other cases there is a more or less permanent impairment in psychological functioning (Noyes and Kolb, 1963).

Somatic symptoms. Prolonged use of alcohol may lead to cirrhosis of the liver, peripheral neuritis, endocrine disturbances, and other physical symptoms. Most of these organic disorders are due to nutritional deficiencies resulting from the alcoholics unbalanced diet.

Direct observations. In an interesting study, four male alcoholics were directly observed over a sustained period of experimental intoxication (Tamerin and Mendelson, 1969). The subjects, who ranged in age from thirty-seven to forty-six, all had long histories of chronic alcoholism. During the ten weeks of the experiment the men were restricted to a closed research unit. The schedule consisted of a two-week observation period, three weeks during which the men were periodically provided with liquor, a ten-day withdrawal period, a three-week period of free access to liquor, and a final ten-day withdrawal period.

THE AUTOBIOGRAPHY OF AN ALCOHOLIC

I took my first drink during my freshman year at college, the night I was initiated into my fraternity. One of the boys sold me on the idea that it was the thing to do in order to show I was a good sport. That first drink wasn't especially memorable. After all, one doesn't become a drunk overnight. I was a social drinker all during my college days. I've had many good times and suffered to some extent on the mornings after. In those days it never occurred to me to drink in the morning. I couldn't bear the sight of the stuff. I don't think it affected my scholarship much. In any event, I graduated—not brilliantly, but I did get my degree.

After college I began to drink more seriously. It was about two years after my school days that I took my first drink in the morning. I can see now that that morning was the beginning of the end. By then I was married and the father of a young son, but this added responsibility didn't seem to make any difference. Drinking was no longer a minor sport for me—I was becoming a pro. Now I drank every morning if I had had anything the night before—and I usually had.

Mysteriously enough, I managed to hold my first job for eleven years, but finally my boss reached the end of his endurance, and at almost the same time, so did my wife. Why go into all the details? Happy moments, yes, but terrible hours, too. Unbearable embarrassments, loss of friends, even jail. By this time, of course, I was really trying my damnedest to quit drinking. I spent hundreds of dollars on psychiatrists, and when I lost my job I went away to a private sanitarium for a month. This was an impressive experience, but it did me no good. I had the idea that this was a chance to build myself up physically, and when I got out I'd be able to start all over again—and this time I could handle it. I would never under any circumstances get drunk again.

From there I went to New York City and got a new job without much trouble. I started drinking again, but not the same way I had before. I'd have a couple of drinks, and then the next day it would be three, and the next day maybe four. This would go on for four or five weeks, and all this time I'd be going to work every day and managing not to make too many mistakes. Then the morning would come when I just couldn't make it to the office. For three or four days I'd stay in my apartment and drink. I wouldn't go out at all except to lay in another supply of the sauce. Eventually the time would come when I'd be so weak and jittery that I knew I'd have to quit or I'd die—so I'd quit. Because when I was drinking I wasn't eating, I knew I ought to eat at least a little during these jags, and I'd fix a sandwich or something, but then I'd look at it and the thought of actually eating it was enough to make me sick. I was living alone and I didn't know anyone in New York well enough to ask for help, so the upshot was that I generally went to a hospital for a few days. Then I'd come out sober and repentant, and I'd be all right for a month or so, and then I'd start the whole thing over again.

Finally, after losing my job again, I decided that the first thing I had to do was go somewhere where I wouldn't be able to get a drink for a long time. And I did. The particular details aren't important, but what I've discovered about this whole business is: first, we problem drinkers must realize that we can never become moderate drinkers. The "reformed drunk" who becomes a moderate drinker never was a drunk in the true sense of the word. The real reformed alcoholic becomes a teetotaler. Second, and most important of all, we must decide that we don't *want* to become moderate drinkers. So long as the alcoholic persists in admiring the moderate drinker, so long as he wants to be a moderate drinker himself, sooner or later he's going to try it, and the only possible result is disaster. (Adapted from "Can the Alcoholic Become a Moderate Drinker?")

During the observation period the men reported that they expected to be more relaxed, more comfortable, and less depressed once they started drinking. And so, in fact, they were—at least in the beginning. But after a brief period of pleasure, continued drinking had the opposite effect. Even though the experiment sanctioned drinking, the men experienced more distress when they were drunk than when they were sober. They felt remorseful and guilty and worthless, they cried, they thought of suicide. These adverse reactions were intensified during the free-access period, when the men drank more over a shorter period and hence were more intoxicated. The total amount consumed during the free-access period was about the same as during the more spaced-out programmed drinking period.

When sober, the men were polite to each other but distant, inhibited, and bored. Left to themselves, they kept busy with aimless repetitive activities. Their behavior was described as rigid and restrictive. Intoxication stimulated group interaction. When they were drunk they became increasingly aggressive and open, freely expressed disapproval and hostility, and engaged in heated discussions. They were more interested in one another, and more interesting. There was a great deal of mutual support. At the same time they were more irritable and exhibited a childish demandingness. Incoherent, rambling speech and social regression set in as intoxication increased. By the end of each drinking period the men were uniformly unshaven, unkempt, and sloppy. With their return to sobriety, they resumed their formal, distant relationships.

Observations with respect to the popular hypothesis that alcoholics have strong latent homosexual tendencies were inconclusive, as usual. While they were drunk the men were more affectionate and engaged in closer physical interactions, but homosexuality was never directly expressed, and in fact the men manifested greater heterosexual interest. When they were sober they treated the female nurses with the same distant politeness they showed toward each other; when they were drunk they sought greater physical contact with them. This could be interpreted as a general reaching out for human contact, male or female, in men who when sober led lonely, isolated lives.

Determinants of Alcoholism

The magical, all-purpose placebo effect of alcohol offers a more adequate explanation for its use than for its abuse. Most people who drink stop short of incapacitating intoxication. The great majority of excessive drinkers somehow manage to regulate and control both their drinking patterns and their behavior while under the influence of alcohol so that their functioning is not grossly impaired. What differentiates the chronic alcoholic, whose life is dominated and wrecked by alcohol? There is no simple explanation on which everyone can agree. The following summary of contributory factors represents the general trends of thought to be found in the extensive literature on the subject, but the formulation is more theoretical than factual.

Tension reduction. Alcohol is one of many means invented and exploited by man to alter his self-perceptions and behavior and to help him cope with life problems. A major attraction of alcohol is that it quickly produces a hazy, relaxed state that is usually highly effective in temporarily reducing conscious awareness of anxiety, discontent, depression, and other negative feelings. This "therapeutic" function has been confirmed by animal studies. In their pioneer investigation of the effects of alcohol on emotionally disturbed animals, Masserman and Yum (1946) first induced neurotic reactions in cats by exposing them to an unsolvable approach-avoidance conflict. Whenever the hungry cat approached the food box, he received an electric shock. Given a choice of fluids, neurotic cats showed a greater preference for alcohol than did normal cats. While they were under the influence of alcohol, their neurotic symptoms diminished. Conger (1951) has demonstrated that alcohol resolves experimentally induced conflicts in animals by decreasing the intensity of fear-motivated avoidance responses.

Sociocultural factors. Social and cultural factors influence the extent of alcohol consumption, patterns of drinking, and the incidence of alcoholism (Bates, 1946; Jellinek, 1960). Where the use of alcohol is prohibited, as among the Moslems and Mormons, the incidence rates of drinking and of alcoholism are very low. During the early years of national prohibition in the United States, the incidence of alcoholic first admissions to mental hospitals dropped sharply. The use of alcohol need not be related to alcoholism, however. The attitudes and customs of a culture may favor the use of alcoholic beverages but be strongly opposed to drunkenness. Among orthodox Jews, for example, drinking wine is an integral part of religious observances but excessive drinking is considered a desecration, the diversion of a sacred function to a profane purpose. The more secular use of alcohol by the Irish as a lubricant for all social occasions may contribute to the high incidence of alcoholism among them.

Italy has one of the highest rates of alcohol consumption in the world and one of the lowest rates of alcoholism. Italians regard wine as a mealtime beverage. The pattern is established early in life. During dinner, the young child may be served a glass of very diluted wine, and the concentration is gradually increased as he gets older. Excessive drinking or the use of alcohol except as an accompaniment of food or on special occasions is frowned upon. A person who drinks for the sake of drinking or who is frequently intoxicated is regarded as "vulgar," a low order of glutton.

France shares with Italy a high rate of alcohol consumption, with wine as the main beverage. In contrast to Italy, however, France has a much higher rate of alcoholism. A contributory factor is the more permissive and indulgent attitude of the French toward drinking. Particularly among the working class, a man may start drinking a little at breakfast and continue with an occasional drink throughout the day and evening. In Italy, drinking is a respected personal option. A Frenchman runs the risk of giving offense if he declines a drink.

In countries where drinking is accepted, wide variations in the use of alcohol may be noted with respect to geographical area, religious affiliation, and socioeconomic status. Data based on surveys in the United States indicate higher rates of drinking in northern and coastal states than in the south-central states. Members of liberal Protestant denominations drink more than those affiliated with evangelical and nontraditional churches (Christian Scientists, Jehovah's Witnesses, and so on). In large cities, drinking is more prevalent among higher socioeconomic groups.

Genetic factors. The popular belief that alcoholism runs in families has been substantiated by several studies (Rosenthal, 1970). About one-fourth of the brothers and fathers of male alcoholics are also alcoholics. This figure is from three to five times greater than the incidence of alcoholism in the general male population. One of the best predictors of problem drinking in males is a family history of heavy drinking fathers (Cahalan and Room, 1974). The incidence of alcoholism in the mothers and sisters of alcoholics appears to be considerably lower and more variable, but female relatives also have a greater than chance risk of becoming alcoholics. The limitation of family studies is that there is no way of determining whether the high occurrence rates of similar forms of deviant behavior are due to genetic factors, imitative learning, or shared environmental experiences.

More specific genetic information is provided by twin and adoption data. Two studies have been reported comparing the concordance rates of alcoholism in MZ and DZ twins, one in Sweden and the other in Finland. Both investigators concluded that genetic factors were implicated in at least certain aspects of alcoholism (Rosenthal 1970). A more recent study of adopted children (Goodwin et al., 1973) found that 18 percent of the male children whose biological parents were alcoholic became alcoholics themselves, whereas only 5 percent of the adoptees whose biological parents were nonalcoholic developed an alcoholic problem. The much higher rate observed in the adopted sons of alcoholics justifies the conclusion that genetic factors may contribute to the development of alcohol problems. The fact that 82 percent of the high risk children did not become alcoholic leaves ample elbowroom for environmental, cultural, and experiential influences.

The genetic component, if confirmed, may be associated with vulnerability to general behavior pathology, or may be associated with a specific biochemical imbalance or neurophysiological defect. Animal studies have shown that certain strains of mice show a marked preference for alcohol whereas other strains avoid it.

Individual factors. The innate and acquired characteristics of the individual are critical in the etiology of alcoholism. The social environment may exert great pressure on a person to drink or abstain, but the final decision rests with the individual. If he is persuaded or wants to try alcohol, in itself a selective factor, his next step depends on the effect the total experience has on him. Reactions to the use and the effects of alcohol vary considerably. Some people take to alcohol immediately: it's just what they are looking for. Others gradually learn to enjoy drinking, or turn to it in a crisis. Still others, in part because of biological factors, may find that alcohol does nothing for them. Drinking only makes them dizzy, sick, or unable to stay awake. Some of these people experience the usual "release" effects of alcohol, but discontinue drinking because it makes them behave in ways they later regret—or because they're afraid it might.

If a person does continue drinking, individual factors influence the amount he will drink and the frequency with which he will drink. Drinkers with emotional problems and those handicapped by feelings of inadequacy may reasonably be expected to make more extensive use of alcohol and to become more dependent on it than others. Psychiatric studies of chronic alcoholics usually reveal the existence of other personality problems (De Vito et al., 1970). Frequently recorded diagnoses include passive-aggressive personality, explosive personality, schizoid personality, and antisocial personality. Depressive reactions are common. A small number of alcoholics are classified as neurotic or psychotic. Alcohol appears to facilitate and increase the "acting out" of aggressive tendencies, especially in deviant personalities.

Personality test data confirm the wide diversity of personality characteristics noted among alcoholics in clinical studies. Alcoholics tend to attain higher scores for anxiety and sociopathy and lower scores for frustration tolerance than normal controls (MacAndrew and Geertsma, 1964; Meneker, 1967). However, there is no evidence of a distinctive alcoholic personality. The main difference between normal persons and alcoholics is that the latter report more traits indicating general maladjustment (Goss and Morosko, 1969). Even this general finding may more accurately describe the alcoholic's personality when high than when sober. John Partington (1970) has demonstrated that alcoholics tend to think of themselves in dualistic ("Dr. Jekyll-Mr. High") terms. Their own evaluation of their sober self is much more favorable than their description of their high self. Many of the unfavorable psychological traits observed in alcoholics disappear when they become consistently abstinent (Fox, 1965).

A more scientific approach to studying the personality of alcoholics is to obtain personality measures for a large sample of boys and subsequently to compare the early personality traits exhibited by those who later became alcoholics with the early traits of those who did not. Two such longitudinal studies have been reported (McCord and McCord, 1960, and Jones, 1968). The population in one study consisted of lower-class Boston youths, and the other was composed largely of middle-class boys in California. The findings were the same. At the time of initial study, boys who in later years became alcoholics were characterized by inadequate control of their impulses, underlying dependency, and compensatory overemphasis on masculinity. In their national survey studies Cahalan and Room (1974) also noted a high incidence of impulsivity and acting-out behavior during youth among adult males with drinking problems. The consistency of results obtained with these diverse groups strongly indicates that these traits may serve as predisposing factors. Yet not all boys who have these traits grow up to become alcoholics. Some develop other types of problems, and others are indistinguishable from the general population. The final outcome depends on the cumulative interaction of multiple biological, social, and psychological variables.

The determinants of alcoholism, then, are complex and varying. Nevitt Sanford (1968) has suggested that the personality correlates of alcoholism may vary with the motives for and patterns of drinking. The person who uses alcohol as self-indulgence or to obtain relief from personal problems may have little in common with the man whose heavy drinking is a continuation of a long established family custom and who derives a great deal of satisfaction from the feeling of group solidarity associated with drinking.

Treatment of Alcoholism

Practically every conceivable medical, punitive, and psychotherapeutic technique has been tried in the treatment of alcoholism. Multidisciplinary and comprehensive approaches have been recommended to deal with the medical, social, family, personal, and legal problems associated with this behavior (Fox, 1967; Catanzaro, 1968). The shotgun approach makes it difficult to isolate the effectiveness of specific techniques, but this is a minor matter. No single method can claim much success. Often the difference between failure and success depends on the chance establishment of a satisfying relationship between the alcoholic and another person, a new position, or a serious illness.

Detoxification. Following a prolonged period of intoxication, many patients show symptoms of alcohol poisoning (Salzberger, 1967): restlessness, confusion, irritability, belligerence, fright, tremors, nausea. About half of the hospitalized alcoholics have hallucinations, delusions, and memory loss. About 15 percent have delirium tremens. Treatment includes withdrawal of alcohol, vitamins, and a diet high in carbohydrates. Drugs commonly used to quiet the patient and provide relief from distress include paraldehyde, tranquilizers, and antidepressants. Toxic symptoms generally subside within two or three days.

Drug therapy. Alcoholics who remain in treatment beyond the acute stages of intoxication usually continue to receive tranquilizers or antidepressants. Antabuse (disulfriam) is sometimes used to help motivated, cooperative patients resist the temptation to drink. Persons who tend to commit crimes when intoxicated may be placed on probation rather than sent to jail if they agree to take antabuse. The offender is required to swallow a pill each day in the presence of his probation officer as a condition for continued probation. In all cases the alcoholic must be fully informed beforehand of the disastrous consequence of drinking while on antabuse. The presence of antabuse in the body interferes with the usual metabolism of alcohol (Billet, 1968). If an alcoholic drink is taken within four days after an antabuse pill has been swallowed, a toxic substance called acetaldehyde is formed, which induces a throbbing headache, flushing of the face, spasms of coughing, vomiting, heart palpitation, labored breathing, and blurred vision. One such experience suffices. The limitation of the method is that a person can resume drinking whenever he wishes simply by discontinuing the antabuse.

Some experimental studies have been reported on the use of LSD (lysergic acid diethylamide) in the treatment of alcoholics. Generally LSD has been used to facilitate recall and self-awareness as an adjunct to a psychodynamically oriented therapy (Ditman, 1967). Most experts object to the procedure on the ground that the potential harm of LSD outweighs whatever value it may have as a therapeutic aid.

Behavior modification. Aversive conditioning and other techniques based on learning principles have been employed since 1930 in the treatment of alcoholics (Frank, 1967). Earlier studies utilized a nausea-inducing emetic as the aversive stimulus. The alcoholic was injected with a quick-acting emetic. A minute or two before the onset of nausea he was asked to drink one of a variety of alcoholic beverages, which he promptly vomited up. The experience was repeated several times over a period of a week or more to establish a conditioned association between the sight, taste, and smell of alcohol and vomiting.

More recent studies have used electric shock as the aversive stimulus. The alcoholic is instructed to sip or sniff alcohol. As he does so, he receives a shock of controlled intensity. Periodically a glass of orange juice or some other nonalcoholic drink is substituted for alcohol, with no accompanying shock. Avoidance conditioning is thus restricted to alcoholic beverages. This approach may be augmented by other behavior modification techniques. McBrearty et al. (1968) have described a broad-spectrum approach that includes didactic training, relaxation, and desensitization.

Individual therapy. Traditional forms of individual psychotherapy that involve talking out problems, a search for underlying causes, and patient self-understanding have not fared well in the treatment of alcoholism. Alcoholism interferes with the establishment of an effective patient-therapist relationship. For psychotherapy to succeed, the therapist and patient must work together in an atmosphere of mutual trust, confidence, and positive regard; alcohol dissolves interpersonal relationships far more readily than it cements them. Most therapists, for their part, find it difficult to establish and maintain a feeling of em-

pathy with the alcoholic. They weary of his denials, become discouraged with his relapses, and end up questioning the sincerity of his motivation. The alcoholic then feels more misunderstood and rejected than ever. The failure of insights gained through therapy to prevent his drinking convinces him of the hopelessness of his condition. In any case, alcoholism is as much a family problem as an individual problem.

Family therapy. If his family is still interested in the alcoholic, family therapy is often effective in moderating his drinking, reducing home friction, and alleviating his burden of guilt and remorse. Though women are often blamed for driving men to drink, the wife of the alcoholic is not responsible for his alcoholism. This is his own doing, and often she is an innocent victim. It sometimes happens, however, that a woman originally selects her husband because his drinking satisfies her own neurotic needs. After marriage her need to dominate, control and punish him or to be a long-suffering martyr may push him deeper into alcoholism. In these cases, family therapy may provide the assistance she needs in resolving her own problems. When the wife is an innocent victim, family therapy may be helpful in improving the discordant relationship created by the recurring family crises resulting from excessive drinking.

Group therapy. Group therapy is considered to be one of the more effective approaches to alcoholism (Thomas, 1968). Usually the group consists of about ten alcoholics who meet once or twice weekly. The structure and direction of sessions vary with the leader. The alcoholic who has long experienced isolation and rejection finds acceptance and identification in the company of others who share a common problem. The supportive atmosphere facilitates candid discussion of personal experiences, failures, and resentments. Since all the members are experts in the use of denial, rationalization, and projection, they are quick to expose these defensive maneuvers. The individual is forced to face the truth about his drinking. The success of

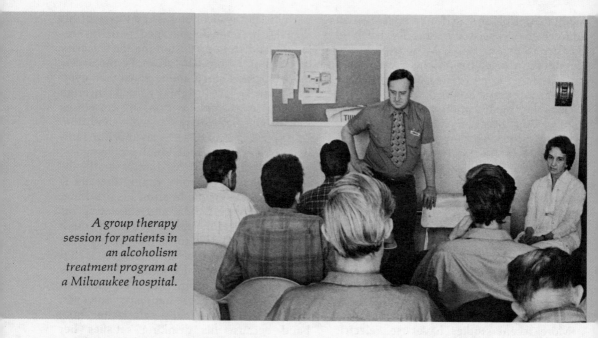

A group therapy session for patients in an alcoholism treatment program at a Milwaukee hospital.

any member in abstaining offers encouragement to the others.

Alcoholics Anonymous. Alcoholics Anonymous is an informal organization of men and women run by alcoholics for alcoholics. The only requirement for membership is an honest desire to stop drinking. There are no dues or fees. Local groups in cities and towns throughout the country meet regularly to share their experiences in order to gain strength to resolve their common problem and to help others. Instead of depending on alcohol, members are encouraged to depend on each other.

A.A. offers the alcoholic fellowship and direction. Although the movement is nonsectarian, great stress is placed on spiritual values and reliance on God for guidance and assistance. At meetings each member publicly confesses that he was and is an alcoholic. One of the twelve steps that constitute the guiding principles of A.A. calls for the individual to admit to God, to himself, and to another human being the exact nature of his wrongdoings. Each member is urged to make a list of all the persons he has harmed and to try to make amends whenever possible.

There are no valid statistics on the effectiveness of A.A., but the viability and growth of the organization suggest that it serves a useful function for some alcoholics. Its emphasis on a higher power makes it relatively ineffective for those who do not respond to this approach. A.A. has sponsored an auxiliary organization, called Al-Anon, for members of alcoholics' families.

Outcome and aims. The extreme heterogeneity of the alcoholic population makes it very difficult to evaluate the outcome of alcoholism. The prognosis tends to be favorable for alcoholics who have not progressed beyond the stage of psychological dependence and who are still employed and living in a family setting. The prognosis is very poor for homeless Skid Row derelicts. When alcoholism is associated with severe personality disorganization, outcome is less favorable than when the personality is relatively intact. A second complicating variable is the strictness of the criteria employed in evaluating outcome. From 40 to 60 percent of treated alcoholics have sober periods lasting six months or longer. The number of "cured" alcoholics who maintain total and complete sobriety for life is quite small. Most authorities agree that few alcoholics succeed in going back to moderate social drinking.

M. E. Chafetz (1967), however, has questioned the desirability of insisting on permanent abstinence as the only criterion of successful treatment. As he sees it, adherence to this strict goal hinders therapy. When relapses occur, as they almost invariably do, the therapist is disappointed, the patient is disturbed by feelings of guilt and failure, and his family loses hope. A more rational approach is to aim for a reduction of alcoholic behavior by concentrating on family adjustment, occupational effectiveness, and social adequacy. In the evaluation of the effectiveness of treatment, account must be taken of the possible development of substitute symptoms during periods of abstinence.

Lovibond and Caddy (1972) have described a treatment procedure designed to train the alcoholic to become a moderate drinker. The first phase consists in teaching the subject to discriminate his own blood alcohol concentration (BAC). This is done by providing him with a scale of the behavioral effects that typically accompany different concentration levels. For example, a BAC of .04 is usually experienced as a feeling of warmth and relaxation and a concentration of .08 is associated with a sense of loss of social inhibitions. The subject is then asked to consume pure alcohol in fruit juice and to estimate his blood alcohol. Every fifteen to twenty minutes a Breathalyzer reading is taken, the subject is asked to estimate his BAC, and his actual BAC is immediately fed back to him by means of a large meter in front of him. Each time an actual BAC reading is presented he is encouraged to associate his present subjective state with the meter reading. Subjects quickly learn to estimate their BAC with reasonable accuracy.

Before the start of the second phase, the subject is given a detailed account of the nature and aims of the treatment procedure. He is told he can drink with impunity during the treatment session as long as his BAC, as indicated by meter feedback information, remains below .065 (a level typically reached after two quick double martinis). Beyond the .065 level he will receive an electric shock on the face or neck at irregular intervals while drinking. The subject is required to continue drinking beyond the .065 level so that aversive conditioning will be experienced. Treatment is conducted on an outpatient basis and continued for six to twelve sessions (about fifty shocks).

The short-term results of this procedure showed that twenty-one of the twenty-eight subjects who completed the treatment could be regarded tentatively as successes in that their drinking rarely exceeded the .065 level. Three of the remaining seven exhibited some improvement. The other four were failures. Ten percent of the original experimental group dropped out early in the program. A much longer follow-up period is required to evaluate the effectiveness of the treatment. Preliminary observations indicate a reduction in the subject's desire to continue drinking beyond two or three glasses. As stated by the investigators, "treatment typically produces a motivational change rather than merely a conditioned fear reaction." In addition to their reduction in alcohol intake, most of the treated subjects showed dramatic improvement in general health, well-being, and self-respect.

The Prevention of Alcoholism

The Cooperative Commission on the Study of Alcoholism has outlined a comprehensive program for the prevention of alcoholism (Plaut, 1967). One broad approach aims at improving the general mental health of the population. Sources of environmental stress would be reduced if we improved the quality of family life and created a more humane society that afforded ample room for diversity and for individual self-realization. The use of alcohol as a self-prescribed remedy for problems in living might be lessened through the development of programs designed to help people acquire better ways of coping with difficulties and also through increasing the availability of community facilities and crisis centers geared for the prompt treatment of disturbed individuals and families.

A second broad approach aims at changing attitudes toward drinking and drinking patterns through large-scale educational endeavors and concurrent changes in laws and rules. With the cooperation of government agencies, the schools might contribute to this endeavor by providing students with factual information on the roles and effects of alcohol. In a predominantly drinking society it is futile to aim for the abolition of alcohol. This was demonstrated by the failure of the 1920-1933 prohibition experiment. The objective of the educational program should be to correct current misconceptions regarding drinking and to substitute a rational attitude for the currently widespread emotionalism. Drinking is neither a sign of moral weakness nor a test of manliness or sophistication. Excessive drinking is harmful, but mild to moderate drinkers derive pleasure and comfort from the relaxing effects of alcohol. There should be no pressure to drink, and abstinence should be respected, but neither should there be any pressure to make beer and wine unavailable. A repressive attitude toward drinking tends to encourage its use by adolescents as a form of rebellion.

Drinking for its own sake should be discouraged. When drinking is acceptable to the persons concerned, it should be integrated with other activities, such as family dinners and social functions. Serving beer and wine in college cafeterias and at college social functions might tend to discourage excessive drinking off campus. The rules of hospitality need revision. Both host and guests should share the responsibility of seeing to it that no one drinks so much that his behavior becomes objectionable or dangerous to others. The dangers of driving while under the influence of alcohol must be stressed in driver education courses.

SUMMARY

Alcoholism is currently the major drug problem in the United States among the young as well as adults. The major psychological effect of alcohol, which explains its wide attraction, is that it produces a transient blurring of conscious awareness that serves as a convenient "time-out" period from daily cares and pressures and from one's usual self. Most societies reinforce this function of alcohol by adopting a more permissive attitude toward people's behavior while they are under its influence. The Bacchanalian festivals of former centuries and the carnivals and the cocktail parties and beer busts of today are institutionalized forms of the use of alcohol for "time out" behavior.

The use of alcohol qualifies as a form of behavior pathology when the individual is unable to control when and how much he drinks. The impairment in psychosocial functioning associated with alcohol abuse results in the individual becoming a threat and source of distress to himself, his family, and others. About 5 percent of the male population and 2 percent of the female population in this country have a serious alcohol problem.

There is some evidence that genetic factors contribute to vulnerability to alcoholism but patterns of drinking and the amount of consumption appear to be more directly related to sociocultural and religious factors. Personality traits frequently noted in boys who later become alcoholics include inadequate control of impulses, underlying dependency, and a compensatory overemphasis on masculinity.

About 50 percent of alcoholics have sober periods lasting six months or longer. The number who stop drinking permanently is unknown but is believed to be quite small. The traditional insistence on complete abstinence as the only criterion of successful treatment has recently been challenged on the grounds that a reduction of alcohol use is a more realistic goal.

References

Anonymous. "Can the Alcoholic Become a Moderate Drinker?" *Mental Hygiene* 23 (1939): 80–86.

Bates, R. F. "Cultural Differences in Rates of Alcoholism." *Quarterly Journal of Studies on Alcohol* 6 (1946): 480-99.

Billet, S. L. "Antabuse Therapy." In *Alcoholism: The Total Treatment Approach*, ed. R. J. Catanzaro, pp. 90-104. Springfield, Ill.: Charles C Thomas, 1968.

Cahalan, D. and Room, R. *Problem Drinking among American Males.* New Haven, Conn.: College and University Press, 1974.

Catanzaro, R. J., ed. *Alcoholism: The Total Treatment Approach.* Springfield, Ill.: Charles C Thomas, 1968.

Chafetz, M. E. "Alcoholism." In *Comprehensive Textbook of Psychiatry*, ed. A. M. Freedman and H. I. Kaplan, pp. 1011-26. Baltimore: Williams & Wilkins, 1967.

Conger, J. J. "The Effects of Alcohol on Conflict Behavior in the Albino Rat." *Quarterly Journal of Studies on Alcohol* 12 (1951): 1-29.

De Vito, R. A.; Flaherty, L. A.; and Mozdzierz, G. T. "Toward a Psychodynamic Theory of Alcoholism." *Diseases of the Nervous System* 31 (1970): 43-49.

Ditman, K. S. "The Use of LSD in the Treatment of the Alcoholic." In *Alcoholism: Behavioral Research*, ed. R. Fox, pp. 256-71. New York: Springer, 1967.

Fox, R. "Psychiatric Aspects of Alcoholism." *American Journal of Psychotherapy* 19 (1965): 408-16.

————. "A Multidisciplinary Approach to the Treatment of Alcoholism." *American Journal of Psychiatry* 123 (1967): 769-78.

Frank, C. M. "Behavior Modification and the Treatment of the Alcoholic." In *Alcoholism: Behavioral Research*, ed. R. Fox, pp. 186-203. New York: Springer, 1967.

Goodwin, D. W.; Schulsinger, F.; Hermansen, L.; Gruze, S. B.; and Winokur, G. "Alcohol Problems in Adoptees Raised Apart from Alcoholic Biological Parents." *Archives of General Psychiatry* 28 (1973): 238-43.

Goss, A., and Morosko, T. E. "Alcoholism and Clinical Symptoms." *Journal of Abnormal Psychology* 74 (1969): 682-84.

Jellinek, E. M. "Phases of Alcohol Addiction." *Quarterly Journal of Studies on Alcohol* 13 (1952): 673-78.

————. *The Disease Concept of Alcoholism.* New Haven, Conn.: Hillhouse Press, 1960.

Jones, M. C. "Personality Correlates and Antecedents of Drinking Patterns in Adult Males." *Journal of Consulting and Clinical Psychology* 32 (1968): 2-12.

Kerr, N. "Ether Drinking." *New Review* 3 (1890): 536-46. Also reprinted in National Institute of Mental Health, *Drug Dependence*, pp. 15-19. Washington, D.C.: U.S. Government Printing Office, 1969.

Lovibond, S. H., and Caddy, G. "Discriminated Aversive Control in the Moderation of Alcoholics' Drinking Behavior." *Biofeedback and Self-Control 1971*, ed. J. Stoyva et al., pp. 545-52. Chicago: Aldine, 1972.

MacAndrew, C., and Edgerton, R. B. *Drunken Comportment: A Social Exploration.* Chicago: Aldine, 1969.

———— and Geertsma, R. "A Critique of Alcoholism Scales Derived from the MMPI." *Quarterly Journal of Studies on Alcohol* 25 (1964): 68-76.

McBrearty, J. F.; Garfield, Z.; Dichter, M.; and Heath, G. "A Behaviorally Oriented Treatment Program for Alcoholism." *Psychological Reports* 22 (1968): 287-98.

McCord, W., and McCord, J. *Origins of Alcoholism.* Stanford, Calif.: Stanford University Press, 1960.

Masserman, J. H., and Yum, K. S. "An Analysis of the Influence of Alcohol on Experimental Neuroses in Cats." *Psychosomatic Medicine* 8 (1946): 36-52.

Meneker, T. "Anxiety About Drinking in Alcoholics." *Journal of Abnormal Psychology* 72 (1967): 43-49.

Noyes, A. P., and Kolb, L. C. *Modern Clinical Psychiatry.* Philadelphia: Saunders, 1963.

Partington, J. T. "Dr. Jekyll and Mr. High: Multidimensional Scaling of Alcoholics' Self-evaluation." *Journal of Abnormal Psychology* 75 (1970): 131-38.

Plaut, T. F. A. *Alcohol Problems: A Report to the Nation by the Cooperative Commission on the Study of Alcoholism.* New York: Oxford University Press, 1967.

Rosenthal, D. *Genetic Theory and Abnormal Behavior.* New York: McGraw-Hill, 1970.

Salzberger, G. J. "The Acute Alcoholic Debauch." *Diseases of the Nervous System* 28 (1967): 387-89.

Sanford, N. "Personality and Patterns of Alcohol Consumption." *Journal of Consulting and Clinical Psychology* 32 (1968): 13-17.

Tamerin, J. S., and Mendelson, J. H. "The Psychodynamics of Chronic Inebriation:

Observations of Alcoholics During the Process of Drinking in an Experimental Group Setting." *American Journal of Psychiatry* 125 (1969): 886-99.

Thomas, M. "The Group Therapies." In *Alcoholism: The Total Treatment Approach*, ed. R. J. Catanzaro, pp. 127-45. Springfield, Ill.: Charles C Thomas, 1968.

Wanberg, K. W., and Horn, J. L. "Alcoholism Symptom Patterns of Men and Women: A Comparative Study." *Quarterly Journal of Studies on Alcohol* 31 (1970): 40-61.

14 · Drug Use and Abuse

A Midnight Modern Conversation, William Hogarth

From prehistoric times, man has sought magic substances that, in Shakespeare's words, would "pluck from the memory a rooted sorrow, raze over the written troubles of the brain, and with some sweet oblivious antidote cleanse the stuff'd bosom of that perilous stuff which weighs upon the heart." The search has been highly productive. A wide variety of drugs have been discovered in nature or created in the laboratory that have the power to blur conscious awareness, shut off the demands and pressures of reality, increase energy, alleviate anxiety, and open the door to strange new experiences. These mind-altering drugs are usually classified in four main categories.

1. **Opiates.** Also referred to as narcotics, these drugs relieve physical and psychic pain, induce a state of euphoria in some individuals, and lead to drowsiness and sleep. The primary drug is opium; morphine, heroin, and codeine are derived from it.

2. **Hallucinogens.** Here is included a variety of drugs that produce perceptual alterations, illusions, visual hallucinations, euphoria, and mood changes. The best known are marijuana, hashish, and lysergic acid diethylamide (LSD). Others are mescaline, which is obtained from the dried buttons of the peyote cactus, and psilocybin, which is the active ingredient of a vivid red-capped mushroom. Peyote is used in religious rites among the American Indians of the Southwest, and the "sacred mushroom" serves a similar function among certain Indian groups in Mexico.

3. **Stimulants.** The more technical name is analeptics; the slang term is "uppers." With the exception of cocaine, which is obtained from the coca leaf, these stimulants are synthetic chemicals. Collectively known as amphetamines, they include Benzedrine, Dexedrine, and Methedrine. Amphetamines increase the energy level and have an exhilarating effect. Prior to the discovery of their mind-altering function, they were extensively used as medical aids in weight reduction, to diminish fatigue, and to repel sleep.

4. **Sedatives.** Here are included the habit-forming barbiturates ("downers"), which in mild doses have a relaxing effect and in moderate doses induce sleep. Large doses are lethal. A recent nonbarbiturate addition is methaqualone.

Drug Effects

The effects of all these drugs vary with their purity, dosage, method of administration, personality variables, setting, and the expectations of the user. Mild doses may have no harmful effects, but massive doses lead to delirium, confusion, or death. Amphetamine pills taken orally produce a mild to moderate exhilaration. When injected intravenously, the same drug may precipitate psychotic-like reactions. Drugs that have little or no effect on normal individuals may lead to panic and acute psychotic episodes in more unstable individuals.

Users who anticipate behavior changes or who take drugs for the specific purpose of becoming high usually report more marked reactions than skeptical persons who question the ability of drugs to dominate them. On different occasions the same person may show considerable variation in behavior following the use of the same drug. Good trips on LSD may be interspersed with bad trips. The effects of most drugs are enhanced when they are taken in group situations, in which the participants provide mutual stimulation and reinforcement. The solitary marijuana smoker does not experience the same feeling of warmth and friendliness toward his fellow man as do group users who sit in a circle and pass a cigarette or pipe from person to person.

The effects of drugs are greatly influenced by the expectations of the user. Cues and suggestions offered by experienced users influence the reactions anticipated by beginners and thereby produce and perpetuate certain patterns of reactions to specific drugs. Thus drug behavior may to a considerable degree be interpreted as the acting out of expected roles with variations introduced by the particular needs and characteristics of the individual (Coe and Sarbin, 1966).

The effects of mental set and expectation on drug behavior are phenomena common to many other sensory experiences as well. Laboratory experiments have repeatedly demonstrated that they may lead to unusual reactions in normal persons. Orne and Scheibe (1964) compared the reactions of experimental and control groups to sensory deprivation. Both groups spent an equal amount of time in an isolation chamber. The experimental group was asked to report any visual imagery, unusual feelings, difficulties in concentration, hallucination, and the like; they were told that such experiences were not unusual in the conditions to which they were to be subjected. Experimental subjects were also informed that by pressing a red button labeled "Emergency Alarm," they could obtain immediate release. The control subjects were given no instructions that might lead them to expect unusual reactions.

Under these conditions, the experimental group more frequently reported perceptual distortions, restlessness, spatial disorientation, anxiety, and unpleasant emotions. Some of their reactions were similar to those commonly experienced by drug users: visions of multicolored spots, wavering walls, and the spontaneous movement of inanimate objects. Some thought they had been left behind or trapped in a burning building. One experimental subject pressed the panic button and gave "disorganization of senses" as his reason for ending the experiment. One of the control subjects also became upset and signaled to be let out of the room.

The complexities of drug behavior may be simplified by distinguishing between the physiological changes induced by drugs and the user's interpretation of and reactions to these changes. The direct effects of drugs are essentially restricted to changes in conscious awareness and in sensory, motor, and autonomic functions. Some drugs are stimulants that lead to increased activity and alertness. Others are depressants that result in a relaxed or drowsy state—a feeling of floating. Some drugs act on the visual system and produce hallucinatory sensations consisting mainly of changing colors and forms. When this happens, the individual in characteristic human fashion tries to make sense of these strange experiences or to structure them in some meaningful way. The basic process is no different than "seeing" specific objects or scenes in cloud formations or in ink blots. Since the stimuli are internal, their interpretation is generally based on personal feelings and thoughts. The setting and expected effects contribute to the imposed perception and reaction.

In brief, drugs are not directly responsible for the visions of celestial beauty, the paranoid reactions, the oceanic tranquility, the horrors, the rapturous colored music, the fears, or the illuminating insights reported by drug users. These psychological side effects are contributed by the individual.

Motives for Drug Use

There are as many reasons for using drugs as for using alcohol, and most of them are the same. The overlap in motives is apparent from the fact that drugs and alcohol are usually used concurrently. The combined use of alcohol and drugs has been suggested as a possible explanation for the

WHY DO PEOPLE TAKE TO DRUGS? CASE STUDY OF A HEROIN USER

John, a twenty-four-year-old graduate student, had been mainlining heroin (injecting it directly into the veins) off and on for five years. He was raised by well-educated and doting parents. His main complaint about his mother was that her love for him seemed contingent upon his performance and achievement. "In the course of treatment, a picture emerged of an indulgent mother-child relationship, in which the mother seemed to have been constantly ready and eager to meet her son's dependency needs and spare him unnecessary frustrations. The description that the patient provided of his total dependence on the drug, which seemed to gratify his every need, corresponded precisely to the perception of his attachment to his mother."

His mother saw him as a brilliant and gifted Adonis, qualities that he knew realistically he did not possess. "He felt he had been denied the experience of facing and accepting the pain of his own limitations. Instead he had grown up always fearing that he might disappoint his mother and lose her love if she discovered his actual shortcomings."

As he entered adolescence he became increasingly uneasy about his capacities as a student, his ability to make friends, and his success with girls. He felt a nameless dread, a vague feeling of rejection, of living in an emotional void. His introduction to heroin seemed to solve all his problems. There was no pleasure comparable to the experience of shooting heroin. With the drug in his system, his fear of rejection was replaced with a feeling of solidarity with other drug users. He felt self-confident, at ease, and free of pain, distress, and depression. At such times he would share phantasies with his addict friends of a romantic vagabond existence. (Adapted from Khantzian et al., 1974).

high incidence of unexplained deaths among drug addicts. Drug abuse is not limited to youth. Long before college students discovered drugs, their parents' generation was dependent on barbiturates, amphetamines, and to a lesser degree on medically prescribed opiates.

The sudden epidemic of drug abuse on college campuses and in high schools during the 1960s coincided with the general student revolt against the establishment. In this context, the apparent preference of young people for drugs rather than alcohol could be interpreted as a rejection of the intoxicants of the older generation. The new drugs (LSD, marijuana, speed, heroin) were their own thing. With the decline of the spirit of revolt, college students have again returned to alcohol. The drug scene on campuses has faded considerably, with some residual use of marijuana and a few of the milder drugs.

There remains the problem of explaining the appeal of drugs to youth. High on the list of motives is curiosity, a desire for new experiences. The more adventuresome may be challenged by the drama and danger associated with the more potent drugs. To the usual reasons of escape from problems and alleviation of tension are added the thrill of adventure and the heady experience of jousting with social authority and even with death. There is also an element of magic, of being suddenly transformed into a new person or transported to a new world of strange sensations and experiences. Particularly among adolescents, the tremendous pressure of the peer group may lead to the periodic use of drugs as a passport to social acceptance through conformity. For alienated and isolated persons the camaraderie and feeling of togetherness of the drug subculture may help to satisfy social needs.

Khantzian et al. (1974) have suggested

that heroin use may represent a way of coping with life problems for a person who has failed to develop other means of adapting to stress. In addition, the subculture of addicts may help fill the person's social vacuum and provide an alternative to the establishment of meaningful relationships with other people.

The Extent of the Problem

In the 1960s there was a tremendous increase in the use of drugs of all types. Data on arrests for drug offenses in England are representative of similar increases in other countries. The number of marijuana offenses in the United Kingdom increased from 235 in 1960 to 3,071 in 1968. During the same period, drug offenses involving the use of heroin and other potent drugs jumped from 28 to 1,099 (see Table 14.1). These figures do not include the much larger number of unrecorded offenses. In the United States the explosion in the use of drugs by relatively affluent young people first started on college campuses during the early 1960s. More recently drug use has become common in high schools and even in the lower grades. There has also been an increased use of drugs among adults in the more liberal sectors of the middle and upper classes.

Although multiple drug use is common, the choice of drugs is related to age and socioeconomic class. Among college students marijuana is by far the most popular, followed by the amphetamines. Heroin continues to be most prevalent in lower socioeconomic groups and particularly among minority groups. In some cities many young children have taken to sniffing glue and drinking cough medicines for kicks. Barbiturates have traditionally been associated with middle-class adults, but their use has spread to younger age groups. At one time drug use was largely restricted to cities, but it has spread to small towns

Table 14.1. The Recent Increase in Drug Abuse (Drug Offenses in the United Kingdom, 1960-1968).

Year	Opium	Marijuana	Heroin and related drugs
1960	15	235	28
1961	15	288	61
1962	16	588	71
1963	20	663	63
1964	14	544	101
1965	13	626	128
1966	36	1,119	242
1967	58	2,393	573
1968	73	3,071	1,099

Number of drug offenses

Adapted from H. B. Spear, "The Growth of Heroin Addiction in the United Kingdom," *British Journal of Addiction*, 64 (1969): 245-55.

and rural areas. One indication of the extent of the problem is that most preadolescents and adolescents are quite familiar with the argot of drug users.

The Labels of Addiction

The pejorative attitude of society toward those who use drugs for pleasure is reflected in the immoral and illegal connotations of the term "drug addict." In the argot of users, drugs are occasionally assigned favorable labels (jolly beans, blue angels), but heavy users are unfavorably described as "hooked," "potheads," "acid heads," and "speed freaks." The indiscriminate application of the label of drug addict to all users has led to confusion and controversy. At the present time, an otherwise normally functioning student who takes a few puffs of pot once or twice a month at parties is technically a drug user. If apprehended and found to be in possession of a fraction of an ounce of marijuana, he is subject to arrest in many states. Yet he is obviously not in the same class as the drug addict whose whole life revolves about obtaining and using heroin.

More precise terms are needed to differentiate the harmless from the harmful use of drugs. The usefulness of such a change of labels may be seen in the recent substitution of the terms "psychological dependence" and "physiological dependence" for the unsatisfactory concept of drug addiction. The substituted terms are not perfect, since "dependence" may be easily misconstrued as implying some defect in character. But when "psychological dependence" is used as intended, it indicates a learned reaction pattern acquired and sustained through reinforcement, and thus falls in the same category as other habits and acquired tastes and is subject to the usual learning principles involved in habit-breaking. Physiological dependence is more complicated. It is signaled by physical withdrawal symptoms when the user stops taking the drug to which he is addicted. The source of the problem is a change in cell metabolism, which necessitates a period of time for metabolic readjustment. Tolerance is also a physiological matter. The body quickly adapts to the presence of certain drugs, so that increasing amounts are required to produce the reactions formerly produced by small doses.

The Consequences of Drug Use

As with alcohol, the harmful effects, if any, of drug use vary with the product used, the amount consumed, the individual characteristics of the user, and other factors. The abuse of drugs by young people has a long list of consequences, none of them favorable: early dropping out of school; inability to obtain or hold a job; disruption or severing of family ties; conflict with the law; malnutrition; high risk of infectious disorders through use of unsterile preparations, syringes, and needles; increased exposure to venereal diseases; precipitation of psychotic episodes; and shortening of life through physical neglect, accidental overdose, or suicide. In contrast with alcoholics, who often have records of twenty years or more of heavy drinking, most addicts have relatively short histories of drug abuse. They either stop or die.

Although the findings are inconclusive, there is some evidence that LSD produces chromosomal changes that may lead to genetic defects in the infants of parents who have taken the drug at any time prior to the pregnancy of the mother. It is an established fact that when a woman takes heroin during pregnancy, the child is born with a physiological dependence on the drug and at birth exhibits typical withdrawal symptoms: excessive yawning, tremors, diarrhea, hyperactivity, excess mucus, and sneezing.

Opiates

Opium. Opium is the name of the juice obtained from the flower pod of a particular type of poppy. On exposure to the air, the juice coagulates to form a gum. The pain-killing and soporific effects of opium have been known for centuries.

SOME SLANG TERMS RELATING TO DRUG ABUSE

Acid	LSD, LSD-25 (lysergic acid diethylamide)
Bang	Injection of drugs
Barbs	Barbiturates
Bennies	Benzedrine, an amphetamine
Blank	Extremely low-grade narcotic
Blast	Strong effect from a drug
Blue angels	Amytal, a barbiturate
Bombita	Amphetamine injection, sometimes taken with heroin
Bum trip	Bad experience with psychedelic drugs
Busted	Arrested
Chipping	Taking narcotics occasionally
Cokie	Cocaine addict
Cold turkey	Sudden withdrawal of narcotics
Cop out	Quit, take off, confess, defect, inform
Cut	Dilute drugs by adding milk, sugar, or another inert substance
Dexies	Dexedrine, an amphetamine
Downers	Sedatives, alcohol, tranquilizers, narcotics
Dynamite	High-grade heroin
Fix	Injection of narcotics
Floating	Under the influence of drugs
Freakout	Bad experience with psychedelics; also, a chemical high
Good trip	Happy experience with psychedelics
Goofballs	Sleeping pills
Grass	Marijuana
Hash	Hashish, the resin of cannabis
Hearts	Dexedrine tablets (shape)
Hooked	Addicted
Horse	Heroin
Joint	Marijuana cigarette
Jolly beans	Pep pills
Kick the habit	Stop using narcotics
Lemonade	Poor heroin
Mainline	Inject drugs into a vein
Meth	Methamphetamine (also known as Methedrine, Desoxyn)
Pot	Marijuana
Reefer	Marijuana cigarette
Roach	Marijuana butt
Run	An amphetamine binge
Scag	Heroin
Snow	Cocaine
Speed	Methedrine, an amphetamine
Stick	Marijuana cigarette
Strung out	Addicted
Uppers	Stimulants, cocaine, psychedelics
Weed	Marijuana
Yellowjacket	Nembutal, a barbiturate

Since ancient times it has been smoked or eaten in the Near and Far East to induce a tranquil, relaxed state of mind conducive to pleasant dreams while still awake. In comparison with its chemical derivatives, opium is a relatively mild drug, but it is no less habit-forming. Increasing amounts are required to compensate for the tolerance that is built up and to prevent withdrawal symptoms. Gradually the chronic user drifts into an idle life of indifference in which his sole concern is opium.

Morphine. A German druggist isolated the active chemical ingredient in opium in 1803. Appropriately, he named his discovery morphine, after Morpheus, the Greek god of sleep and dreams. The invention in 1855 of the hypodermic syringe provided the means of maximizing the effects of morphine through intravenous injection. The extensive use of morphine as a pain reliever during the Civil War resulted in the addiction of many soldiers. The continued medical use of the drug during the early decades of the twentieth century caused many treated patients unwittingly to acquire the morphine habit. The availability of morphine contributes to its excessive use by physicians. About 1 percent of physicians become addicted to opiates at some time during their professional lives.

Heroin. Heroin is a derivative of morphine. For many years after its discovery in 1898, it was considered a safe substitute for morphine for medical purposes. Unfortunately, it has turned out to be far

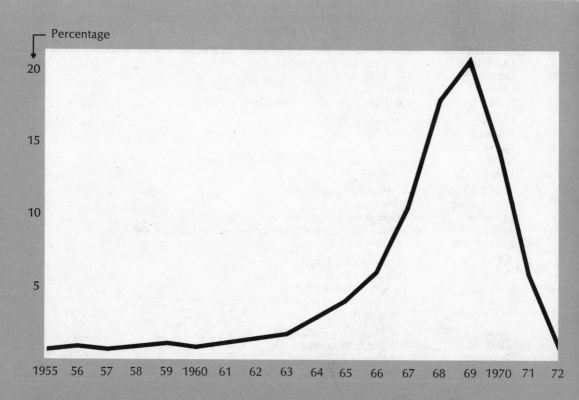

Figure 14.1. Year of First Use of Heroin (13,000 Patients).

SOURCE: R. L. DuPont and M. H. Greene, "The Dynamics of a Heroin Addiction Epidemic." *Science* 181 (1973): 716-22.

more potent and much more harmful.

Heroin is the drug of choice for 90 percent of the users of narcotics. The sharp and sudden increase in heroin use in this country between 1966 and 1970 and the equally dramatic dwindling away of the epidemic starting in 1971 have been graphically illustrated by Du Pont and Greene (1973). Their data (Figure 14.1) were based on 13,000 heroin users in Washington, D.C., who entered the comprehensive national treatment program between 1969 and 1973. The victims of the epidemic were mainly youths between the ages of sixteen and twenty (Figure 14.2); this age group accounted for 55 percent of all new addicts. The inclusion of persons twenty-one to twenty-five raises the total to over 75 percent.

Du Pont and Greene attribute the decrease in new cases after 1971 to stricter law enforcement in reducing the supply of heroin, the greater availability of treatment, and the development of an anti-heroin attitude in the community. On the latter point they note, "Heroin is now out. No longer is the pusher seen as a glamorous individual, a fabulously successful business man. He has become a parasite in the community. Youngsters in the susceptible age group have become more aware of the dangers of addiction and, therefore, less willing to experiment with heroin."

The heroin epidemic, unfortunately, cannot be relegated to history. A large number of users have died, but there remain thousands who will need rehabilitation and

Figure 14.2. Age at First Use of Heroin.

SOURCE: R. L. DuPont and M. H. Greene, "The Dynamics of a Heroin Addiction Epidemic." *Science* 181 (1973): 716-22.

treatment for many years to come. For those who refuse treatment there are the ever-present risks of imprisonment and the financial problems of obtaining the large amount of money required each day to support their habits. The risk remains that new generations of youth and regional groups formerly unaffected may become users.

The high induced by heroin consists of a pleasant, drowsy state that lasts about four hours. When an addict is in this state he is said to be "nodding," because a characteristic reaction is a sleepy nodding of the head. When junkies get together there are no outbursts of hilarity or aggression and little sexual activity. The frequently-heard stories of orgies and sexual attacks by addicts are myths. The use of heroin blocks the sex impulse. Users tend to be inadequate, passive-dependent persons. Their one topic of conversation is drugs. They exchange experiences, compare notes on the relative merits of combining heroin with other drugs, and discuss sources of supply. The future is limited to the next fix. This is a serious matter, since the dreaded withdrawal symptoms appear twelve to sixteen hours after the last shot.

Once a heroin user becomes thoroughly hooked, he no longer experiences the euphoria he enjoyed in the beginning. Now he needs the drug simply to function normally and avoid withdrawal symptoms. These symptoms tend to be quite uniform. Early reactions include frequent yawning, dilation of the pupils, profuse sweating, restlessness, and a watery flow from the eyes and nose. The hair on the skin stands erect. If heroin is taken then, the symptoms subside; if not, the addict goes on to suffer violent cramps, frequent vomiting, diarrhea, chills, aches, agitation, and insomnia. The skin characteristically resembles that of a plucked chicken; hence the expression "cold turkey" for sudden withdrawal of drugs. The expression "kick the habit" also is related to withdrawal symptoms. The later stages of withdrawal include muscular twitches and spasmodic kicking of the feet.

The withdrawal period usually lasts a week. The severity of symptoms is greatest between the second and third days. The symptoms may be moderated by a gradual reduction in the intake of drugs rather than sharp withdrawal. This procedure extends the withdrawal period over two or more weeks (Maurer and Vogel, 1967).

Hospitalization is sometimes recommended for the treatment of withdrawal symptoms, particularly if the addict is among the 20 to 30 percent of heroin users who are also addicted to barbiturates. Sudden withdrawal of barbiturates usually results in severe convulsions. Practically all patients can be cured of physiological dependence in a matter of weeks. The elimination of psychological dependence is more difficult. About 90 percent of users discharged as "clean" following hospital treatment become readdicted within six months of their return to their home territory (Hunt and Odoroff, 1963).

Several methods have been proposed for preventing readdiction and furthering rehabilitation:

1. **Substitution of methadone for heroin.** Methadone is a synthetic pain-killer that provides "cross-tolerance" to heroin. The patient receives a daily oral dose that is gradually increased until full tolerance is reached. Once he is able to tolerate a full dose of the substitute without experiencing any effect from it, continued daily doses block the action of heroin. The patient feels no need for heroin as long as he keeps taking the substitute, and if he does take heroin or some other opiate, it has no effect on him. Thus no purpose is served by the continued use of heroin. The addict is able to function normally without them.

The patient who has built up a tolerance to methadone experiences no sedative or euphoric effect from it. However, the drug leads to physiological dependence and to withdrawal symptoms if its use is discontinued. The substitution of one addictive drug for another raises a serious ethical issue. The pragmatic justification is that by eliminating the stranglehold of narcotics

Heroin injection. The unsanitary conditions associated with heroin abuse are mainly responsible for the high death rate of street users.

and freeing the addict of the ever-pressing need to obtain funds by whatever means, the substitute drug helps the addict to resume a productive role in society if this is what he really wants. The daily doses of the substitute cost only a few cents each. Favorable results in selected cases have been reported by Dole and Nyswander (1968).

2. Total and continued treatment. Brill and his associates (1963) have described a comprehensive community-centered program for the rehabilitation of the addict following his withdrawal from physiological dependence on drugs. During the course of a five-year experiment, a number of social agencies cooperated in providing former addicts with vocational training, aid in finding jobs and housing, financial assistance, family counseling, casework, psychiatric therapy, and other services. One general conclusion was that addiction should be regarded as a chronic disorder. Permanent abstinence is too much to ex-

pect, at least right away. A more feasible goal is to help the addict hold a job and abstain from drug use as long as he can. A second general conclusion was that the usual methods of social work are not applicable to the drug addict. The caseworker must reach out to help the addict and be highly flexible in his approach. He can't sit in his middle-class office and wait for the addict to come in to discuss his problems. It is not enough to make community facilities available to the addict; he requires a great deal of help to make use of the services offered. The long-term results of such a community-centered program have not yet been reported.

3. Treatment by former addicts. Considerable interest has recently been expressed in the treatment of addicts by former addicts. Charles E. Dederich, a former alcoholic, started the movement known as Synanon in 1958 on the West Coast (Yablonsky, 1965). Not all people who seek help at Synanon in building meaning-

Group session at Synanon, a mutual-aid reeducation center in California for drug addicts and alcoholics. Group meetings, which are an important feature of the program, stress direct confrontation and candid give-and-take exchanges.

ful lives are drug addicts, but most of them are. A similar East Coast program was established at Daytop Lodge in 1963. Since then, other centers have been opened in several cities. All of these centers provide live-in therapeutic communities, staffed by former addicts or others who have experienced related problems.

Characteristics of narcotics users. In a comparative study of young narcotics users in the United States and the United Kingdom (Willis, 1969), the social class backgrounds of the English subjects were found to be more varied and generally higher than the class backgrounds of the American subjects, most of whom came from underprivileged socioeconomic environments. The English group also had a better work history. In other respects, however,

the two groups were essentially similar. When compared with a control group of nonaddicts, the American and English users were found to have higher incidences of parental loss through death or separation, family psychiatric disturbances, persistent truancy during childhood, impotence, delinquency, and criminal behavior.

Willis' overall impression that the drug users in both national groups were highly disturbed individuals is consistent with other findings. Gilbert and Lombardi (1967) compared the test scores on the Minnesota Multiphasic Personality Inventory (MMPI) of a group of young male addicts with the scores of a nonaddicted group of similar socioeconomic status. Psychopathy indicators were found to be more widespread among the addicts. Traits

ADDICTS TREATING ADDICTS: DAYTOP LODGE

Shortly after a newcomer's arrival at Daytop Lodge he is interviewed by a team of clean-cut, conventionally dressed young men who start questioning him in a kindly, sympathetic manner. After he has fed them the usual line given to professional workers in the mental health field, the interviewers cut him short. In blunt, four-letter words they tell him that he is talking sheer drivel. In this and subsequent interviews the message is forcefully conveyed that the addict alone is responsible for his addiction. The only valid explanation is that he is stupid. He is not sick. He simply has no more sense or responsibility than a three-year-old. If he wants to grow up and become a man, he can stay. Otherwise, the door is open and he can get lost. If he decides to stay, he must do as he is told. Certain primary rules are strictly enforced: no use of drugs or alcohol, no physical violence, no shirking of responsibility. There can be no more lying or cheating. The watchwords are honesty and reliability.

Treatment consists largely of group therapy. The usual explanations based on intellectual theories, childhood deprivations, and so on are hooted down. The focus is kept on present behavior. Members of the group interact at gut level. They critically examine each other and take each other apart. At marathon encounters that may last twenty-four hours, the search for the naked truth about oneself is relentlessly pursued. Supplementary programs, including weekly parties with invited outside guests, are aimed at resocialization. The length of treatment is usually a year or more, but members may leave whenever they wish, and some stay on indefinitely, eventually assuming staff responsibilities and making a career of the movement. Many addicts have been helped by this approach but no reliable figures on the results of treatment are available (Shelly and Bassin, 1965).

noted more frequently in the addicted group included depression, tension, insecurity, feelings of inadequacy, and difficulty in forming lasting and warm interpersonal relationships. Hill and his associates (1960) noted that adolescent and adult hospitalized addicts exhibited similar deviant personality characteristics. On the MMPI scale both age groups showed high Pd (psychopathy) scores.

Follow-up studies. There are degrees of heroin abuse. Many individuals experiment with the drug sporadically or on weekend parties and then discontinue its use voluntarily. No follow-up data are available for these individuals. Studies of formerly hospitalized narcotics users indicate that a substantial majority discontinue use for varying periods of time (Duvall et al., 1963). Winick (1962) has noted a tendency for a decrease of narcotics addiction with maturation after the age of thirty-five. A more recent study (Vaillant, 1973) shows that there is no consistent age at which addicts become abstinent. This study is of special interest in that it provides a comparison of the effectiveness of the older methods of hospitalization and imprisonment with the current use of compulsory community supervision (parole) or methadone maintenance. The report concludes that the current procedures are far more effective. The study involved a twenty-year follow-up of 100 narcotic addicts first admitted to the U.S. Public Health Service Hospital in Lexington, Kentucky in 1952. During the intervening twenty years, 23 percent died, mostly of unnatural causes. As of 1970 about 40 percent had achieved stable abstinence and another 10 percent were doubtful successes. The remaining 25 percent were known to be still using drugs.

Preliminary reports on methadone maintenance programs suggest that weaning established addicts from continued methadone medication is difficult. Methadone withdrawal usually results in client requests for an increase in dosage or their return to heroin. A brief follow-up of sixty-one heroin addicts in a methadone maintenance program (Scott et al., 1973) showed that at the end of three years, 64 percent of the original group were still in the program, 23 percent had returned to drugs or had been imprisoned, 10 percent had died, and 3 percent had been discharged as free of drugs.

Hallucinogens

Marijuana, hashish, LSD, mescaline, and psilocybin are more accurately described as phantasmagorogenic than hallucinogenic drugs. The perceptual experiences of colors and designs induced by these drugs are similar to hallucinations in the fact that they originate within the person rather than in external reality, but they differ from true hallucinations, as experienced by psychotics, in the fact that the drug user realizes that they are not real experiences but special effects produced by the drug. He knows that when the action of the drug wears off, the show will be over. The dictionary definition of "phantasmagoria" neatly fits the drug experience: "a shifting series of illusions or deceptive appearances, as in a dream, in which figures increase or diminish in size, dissolve, pass into each other, etc." The term "psychedelic" may serve as well as any to identify and distinguish these drugs and their effects.

The intended objective in taking LSD and related drugs is not to blank out the mind but to open it to new experiences. The illusion of being more alert and creative accentuates the desired effect. Mood changes are incidental: the psychic event is the goal. Psychedelic drugs may be considered introvertive drugs. The high consists of an intensification of subjective experiences, of increased self-absorption and detachment, of passive euphoria. The "hashish laughter" occasionally noted in extravertive persons is a personal rather than a social reaction. Psychedelic drugs are often taken in group settings, but boisterous gregariousness is not part of the scene. Continued use of any of the hallucinogenic drugs studied so far leads to psychological dependence, but there is no increase in tolerance and no evidence of withdrawal symptoms following the discontinuance of drug use.

Marijuana. Of all the drugs taken for their pleasurable effects, marijuana is the most widely used in the United States today. Fortunately, it is also the mildest. A conservative estimate is that about 50 percent of college students have smoked marijuana at least once and that about 25 percent do so at least once a month. A slight impairment in psychological functioning may occur while it is being smoked, but periodic use has no known harmful effects. The major objection to marijuana is that its frequent use by young people may lead to their loss of interest in schoolwork and early dropping out of school. Heavy use leads to psychological dependence. A small percentage of marijuana users go on to stronger drugs. It has been speculated that they would probably have done so even if they had not started with pot, but there is no way of reaching a final judgment on this.

Marijuana consists of a crude mixture of the flowery tops, leaves, seeds, and stems of female plants of Indian hemp. The taller male plant contains very little of the active ingredient and is used mainly in making rope. The sticky resin exuded by the tops of the female plants is known as hashish, which is much more potent than marijuana. The active ingredient in the resin has been synthesized. It is known as trans-tetrahydrocannabinol (THC). Marijuana is usually smoked; hashish is smoked or eaten.

Persons who have smoked marijuana characteristically report a feeling of mental relaxation accompanied by physical languor. Mental alertness is retained but there is a diminution of interest in mental and physical activity. The "cool" of the marijuana smoker is a quiet, passive state. Time seems to pass slowly. Some users experience an intensification of sensory

Marijuana plants growing in a
Chicago back yard.

A display of
marijuana
paraphernalia.

HOW THE MARIJUANA MARKET WORKS

The wholesale importing of marijuana is usually arranged by semi-independent entrepreneurs with criminal backgrounds. Shipments are divided and passed on to big dealers. The big dealers sell to small dealers, who in turn break up their purchases into pound packages that are sold to user-sellers. The user-sellers usually sell one-ounce packages (enough to make about 40 joints) to regular users. The buyer of a one-ounce package may sell some of his supply to more moderate users. The quantity involved is so small, however, that the profit motive at this level is incidental; sales of less than an ounce are largely accommodations or favors to friends. Marijuana is often shared with friends in much the same way as a bottle of liquor. More is given away, especially to female friends, than is sold. Periodic users rarely purchase the drug. They depend on being offered some at parties or when they visit regular users.

The average user smokes about two joints a day, which brings the cost to less than a dollar a day. The monetary aspect is too small to encourage stealing to support the habit. In contrast to the heroin addict, who typically consumes all he can purchase within twenty-four hours or less, the marijuana user spaces out the consumption of his supply over several days or weeks and usually keeps some on hand as a reserve (Goode, 1969).

impressions. Perceptual distortions are more characteristic of hashish than of marijuana. In a carefully controlled experimental study on the clinical and psychological effects of marijuana (Weil, Zinberg, and Nelson, 1968), comparisons were made of the reactions of regular and naïve users—persons who had had no prior experience with marijuana—who smoked marijuana or placebo cigarettes in a neutral laboratory situation. The placebo cigarettes were made from the chopped stalks of male hemp plants, which contain no active ingredient. The study resulted in a number of interesting findings:

1. The intoxicating properties of marijuana varied with the mental set or the psychological expectation of the subject. All chronic users who knew they were smoking high-grade marijuana became high. The naïve subjects showed no definite intoxication from smoking marijuana cigarettes, with one exception: a naïve subject who had previously expressed a desire to get high became markedly euphoric. He laughed continuously while taking his first battery of tests.

2. Naïve subjects showed impaired performance on simple intellectual and psychomotor tests after smoking marijuana. Regular users showed either mild impairment or some slight improvement in performance.

3. Marijuana smoking resulted in a moderate increase in heart rate and caused a reddening of the conjunctivae of the eyes. No changes were noted in pupil size or blood sugar level.

4. The psychological and physiological effects of marijuana approach a maximum within a half hour of inhalation. The effects were diminished after one hour and completely dissipated by the end of three hours.

LSD. The natural source of lysergic acid diethylamide is a purple fungus (ergot) that infects rye plants. Some of the incidents of mass hysteria of former times may have occurred when members of a community ate baked goods prepared with infested grain. In its synthetic form LSD is an odorless, colorless liquid of tremendous potency. A gram supplies thousands of doses. All that is required to launch a person on a fantastic eight-hour trip into inner space is a sugar cube or a piece of paper containing a tiny amount of the drug.

LSD reached its peak of popularity about

1965. Since then its use among college students has declined sharply, largely because of increased awareness of the frequency of bad trips and of the spontaneous recurrence (flashback) of hallucinatory and related experiences months after the last dose, the occasional onset of a schizophrenic-like psychosis following an LSD experience, and fear of chromosomal defects and brain damage (Smart and Bateman, 1967). The experimental data on chromosome and brain damage are inconclusive. A difficulty in assessing the specific effect of LSD on the brain is that most acid heads also take a variety of other drugs.

Cohen and Edwards (1969) have concluded that there is no evidence that the heavy use of LSD results in a generalized psychoneurological dysfunction. The only difference they found between the performance of LSD users and a matched control group in a wide variety of psychological tests was that the users showed impairment of their spatial visual orientation. Each of the users had a history of having used LSD on more than fifty occasions, and most had also used other drugs, but none of them was on drugs at the time of testing. An inverse relationship was noted between general intelligence and frequency of LSD use. This finding is subject to two interpretations. Excessive use may have caused intellectual impairment, or low intelligence may have led to frequent use of LSD.

Although specific reactions to LSD are greatly influenced by personal factors and the setting in which it is taken, the drug itself appears to have certain specific effects. Most users report unusual and constantly changing distortions in perception and apperception. A second common reaction is a feeling of detachment. It is as though the individual were watching a show in which everything is somewhat unreal and the improbable is ordinary. He is overwhelmed with the spontaneous spectacle of brilliant colors and intricate designs. In kaleidoscopic fashion, real and imagined objects and persons change, flow, and merge together. Synesthesia, or the mixing of sensory modalities, often occurs: a color may not only be seen, but heard and tasted and felt. People commonly feel a surge of creativity while on LSD, but their actual performances show no increase in creative ability, and often show a distortion of the creative process (Cohen, 1964). Katz, Waskow, and Olsson (1969) noted the presence of intense but contradictory emotions in their subjects. Characteristic physiological reactions include pupillary dilation, excessive perspiration, tremors, alternating hot and cold flashes, increased heart rate, and a rise in blood pressure.

Other hallucinogens. Mescaline, the active ingredient of peyote cactus buttons, and psyilocybin, the active ingredient of the "divine mushroom," have the same general effects as LSD. The hallucinogenic mushrooms of Mexico and their religious significance for native users have been discussed by R. G. Wasson (1959). An early account of the effects of mescaline reported by S. Weir Mitchell in 1896, is of interest for the light it casts on the constancy of reactions and the importance of individual factors. Mitchell was one of the first to test the validity of the feeling of increased mental ability associated with hallucinogenic drugs. He found that mescaline improved neither his mental competence nor his creativity. His visions were described in dramatic terms. He reported seeing "a tall, richly finished Gothic tower," "an abrupt rush of countless points of white light, as if the unseen millions of stars in the Milky Way were to flow in a sparkling river before the eye," "rippled purples, half transparent, and of ineffable beauty," and "huge precious stones, but uncut, some being more like masses of transparent fruit." The visions of his less imaginative medical colleague Dr. Eshner consisted of stars, crescents, points of light, and mosaics.

Stimulants

Cocaine. The Incas of Peru chewed coca leaves for their invigorating effect, and their descendants still do. The active ingredient, cocaine, was isolated in 1855. Applied externally, cocaine is a local anesthetic. When it is swallowed, sniffed, or injected, it has a stimulating effect. As the exhilarating effects wear off, there is a counterreaction of depression and irritability. Large doses of cocaine sometimes result in a characteristic hallucinatory experience: the user sees and feels minute bugs crawling under the skin. Tolerance for cocaine increases, but there are no withdrawal effects. Frequent inhalation of cocaine results in raw, red nostrils.

Amphetamines. During the Second World War, both sides made extensive use of the stimulant action of amphetamines to counteract fatigue and exhaustion. After the war, the drugs were used in nasal inhalants for the relief of cold symptoms. The public soon discovered that amphetamines were effective pep-up and stay-awake pills. This discovery led to their popularity among students preparing for examinations and among long-distance truck drivers. Drug users found other applications for them.

The three most widely used amphetamines are Benzedrine (bennies), Dexedrine (dexies), and Methedrine (speed). Amphetamine use quickly leads to psychological dependence. When taken orally and in moderate doses, these drugs increase activity level and have an exhilarating, mildly euphoric effect. When they are injected intravenously, these reactions are sharply accentuated.

The effects of mainlining Methedrine in a group setting have been described by Carey and Mandell (1968). The drug lives up to its slang name. Almost before the needle is withdrawn, the user experiences a rush or flash of sensation. This initial reaction has been compared to an electric shock, a multiple orgasm, and being splashed suddenly by cold water. Afterward the individual feels extremely alert and full of energy. A person on a long run may stay awake two or more days. During this period he feels heightened restlessness, engages in compulsive aimless activity, ex-

periences rapid mood changes, and reacts to quite ordinary situations with unexpected aggressiveness. For some the racing world produced by speed gets out of control and may lead to a freakout or temporary psychosis marked by panic, delusions, and hallucinations. Chronic excessive users gradually develop a paranoid outlook. When high they report hearing police running down the hall to arrest them or see little men with machine guns moving in for the kill. During such episodes the person high on speed can be very dangerous. Believing himself about to be attacked, he may decide to attack first.

But what goes up must come down, and the speed freak comes down with a crash. Following an interval of sleep the individual is highly irritable, belligerent, and impulsive. The aftereffects are so unpleasant that the individual either gives up Methedrine or quickly turns to it again to regain the feeling of being high. The chronic Methedrine mainliner is unemployed, has no friends except other users, and is dependent on theft for money to purchase his supply. Only the young use Methedrine in this way; older persons can't stand the pace. Neither can the young, but many of them don't live long enough to find it out.

Sedatives

Sedatives and tranquilizing drugs of various types are extensively used as medicines. When taken in the small doses prescribed by physicians, these drugs are useful in relieving tension and inducing sleep. High doses produce toxic effects, physiological dependence, and withdrawal reactions. A major group of sedatives, often misused by drug addicts, are those derived from barbituric acid.

Barbiturates. Among the commonly used barbiturates are Amytal (called blue heavens), Luminal (purple hearts), Nembutal (yellow-jackets), and Seconal (red devils).

There are two distinct groups of chronic users. One is composed of middle- and upper-class persons, often unhappy house-

An array of amphetamines and barbiturates seized in a narcotics raid.

wives, who usually start taking a barbiturate for insomnia. The mind-dulling effect of the drug is gradually exploited as a universal remedy for emotional problems. The second group consists of drug addicts who use barbiturates as supplements to other drugs or as more readily available substitutes. Barbiturates are commonly used to accentuate the effects of heroin and to moderate the stimulating actions of amphetamines. Barbiturates act as central nervous system depressants. General reactions include drowsiness, mental confusion, and impaired motor coordination. The associated loss of control may lead to overt belligerence in passive-aggressive users. Barbiturates are dangerous in two ways: an overdose results in death, and withdrawal symptoms are severe. These symptoms, which last about a week, may include delirium, delusions, hallucinations, and convulsions.

Methaqualone. Methaqualone is a nonbarbiturate, sedative-hypnotic drug. It was first synthesized in India in 1955. The drug was widely used and abused in Japan, Australia, and England before its introduction in 1965 to the United States under the trade name of Quaalude. The phenomenal sales of Quaalude soon led other drug houses to market methaqualone under various trade names (Sopor, Parest, and Somnafac). The major selling point of methaqualone as a medicine is the claim that it is a safe, nonaddicting drug that is as effective as the more dangerous short-acting barbiturates in reducing tension and producing natural sleep. An added attraction of the drug claimed by "street users" is that it has aphrodisiac properties.

Methaqualone is an effective sedative and relaxant, but the other claims for it have been challenged by research findings (Bridge and Ellinwood, 1973; Inaba et al., 1973). Studies reported in Japan, Europe, and the United States show that continued and heavy use of methaqualone may result in physiological as well as psychological addiction. Withdrawal symptoms following abstinence include headache, anorexia, nausea, abdominal cramps, and convulsions. Overdosing may lead to a toxic psychosis, coma, or death. The common practice of taking a number of drugs and combining drugs with alcohol makes it difficult to isolate the specific effects of methaqualone.

In England, methaqualone is listed with other dangerous drugs under the British Drug Prevention of Misuse Act. As of 1974, the United States had taken no steps to restrict its manufacture or sale. The ready availability of the drug through prescription by doctors and cooperative pharmacists has contributed to the quiet epidemic of methaqualone abuse. Informal surveys suggest that in 1973 the three favored drugs among teenage users were alcohol, marijuana, and methaqualone. The three are often used concurrently or alternately.

Interviews with college students and others of similar age who take methaqualone for non-medical reasons suggest that the effects and motives for "luding out" are very similar to those of alcohol (Gerald and Schwirian, 1973). One user stated, "Quaalude produces intoxication without all the calories of booze." About half the users combine drinking with pill-taking. Their commonly reported reasons are "to get high," "to relax," "to escape from problems." As with alcohol, the alleged aphrodisiac effect of methaqualone is a myth based on self-fulfilling expectations and wishful thinking. As with alcohol, too many pills may increase desire while decreasing performance. The onset of methaqualone's action usually occurs after thirty minutes, and the effects continue for about four hours. Many users report "a tingling of the body," dizziness, chills, and feelings of disorientation. Aftereffects include headache, hangover, and a feeling of "losing one's mind." A few users report impairment of memory, irritability, and hostile impulses.

Drugs and the Law

The rationale for drug laws is that it is the responsibility of society to prohibit the importation, manufacture, sale, and use of objects that endanger the health, safety, and welfare of its members. The principle behind the laws is clear and universally recognized, but their interpretation and implementation raise a number of questions. How harmful must a drug be before its prohibition is warranted? If an individual has been informed of the risk involved in taking a dangerous drug and still desires to use it, should he be permitted to do so if his use does no harm to others? Should a person who persists in taking a prohibited drug be treated as a criminal or as a sick person?

Most societies have preferred to play it safe and prohibit the use of drugs that may have harmful effects, even if as in the case of marijuana their harmfulness has not been established beyond dispute. Past experiences support this decision. Time and again drugs that were considered to be innocuous or even beneficial have turned out to be harmful. Once the use of a drug is widely accepted, it is extremely difficult to enforce its prohibition. When potentially harmful drugs have beneficial medical values, it must be determined whether they do more good than harm, and this is not always easy. A case in point is the use of methadone, which currently may be legally obtained on a medical prescription, as a substitute for heroin in the treatment of addicts. This is a medical and social problem, and a serious one; but to make it a moral issue is to add to the problem, not to solve it.

Most countries have adopted sterner measures against the importers, distributors, and sellers of illicit drugs than against users. When a user of drugs also sells them, he is more likely to be arrested for selling than for possession. The legal distinction between a punishable and nonpunishable offense is sometimes a fine one. The fact that a person is known to be an addict is not legal grounds for arrest. If an addict voluntarily applies for treatment or is hospitalized because of his physical or psychological reactions following drug use, no criminal charges are pressed against him. But possession of even a small amount of an illicit drug is legal grounds for arrest.

In England, physicians may prescribe narcotics for registered addicts but not for nonregistered addicts. If a registered addict is found to be in possession of an illicit drug other than the one for which he is registered, he is subject to arrest and punishment. Recently England has sharply curtailed the right of physicians to prescribe drugs for registered addicts because of abuses of the system. Too many registered addicts applied for and received excessive amounts of drugs, which they then sold on the black market or shared with friends, who in turn became addicted. The failure of the English plan is not an isolated case. A similar program for providing addicts with drugs under medical supervision was tried in the United States during the early 1920s and was a total disaster.

The current policy in the United States, as defined by federal, state, and local laws, is that the possession or sale of illicit drugs constitutes a criminal offense. In the case of first or mild offenders, however, the present trend in most jurisdictions is for judges to impose a fine or to place the offender on probation rather than to impose a jail sentence. The emphasis is on treatment rather than punishment.

This attitude is reflected in the Narcotic Addict Rehabilitation Act, which was passed by Congress in 1966. An important provision of the act is that persons charged with a violation of federal law who are determined to be addicted to narcotic drugs "should, in lieu of prosecution or sentencing, be civilly committed for confinement and treatment designed to effect their restoration to health and return to society as useful members." Under the terms of the act, certain criminal charges against an addict are dismissed if he completes a comprehensive treatment program that may last three years. During most of this time the addict lives and works in the community but is required to participate in an intensive rehabilitation program tailored to fit his needs. Also, his urine is tested at frequent but unpredictable intervals ensuring that any use of drugs may be quickly detected.

SUMMARY

Opiates, hallucinogens, stimulants, and sedatives have long been used by man. The recent epidemic of "hard drug" abuse by the young has abated but several problems still remain. One neglected problem is the social, economic, and educational rehabilitation of the thousands of young people who dropped out of high school and college because of drug use. A second problem is the development of better methods of treating heroin addicts than inducing a lifelong dependence on methadone.

The larger issue is concerned with prevention. The experience of the past decade has demonstrated both the vulnerability of youth from all social classes to the lure of drugs and the ineffectiveness of current countermeasures. The present trend of substituting alcohol for other drugs is a poor remedy. The prevention of drug abuse will not be easy. For many maladjusted persons, drugs provide an expedient and satisfying escape from problems in living. They deliver what is expected of them and with a high degree of dependability. Opiates and sedatives induce a pleasant and relaxed state, amphetamines increase the energy level and have exhilarating effects, and hallucinogens produce novel subjective experiences and mood changes. The transitory nature of their effects is easily corrected by a repeat dose. As an extra dividend, today's "high" helps an individual to forget his regrets for the past and the bleakness of his future.

The logical goal of prevention is the correction of the factors leading to susceptibility to drug abuse. Some progress has been made in identifying significant variables associated with high risk vulnerability. Research data indicate that a large proportion of drug users are characterized by unstable family backgrounds, unresolved dependency conflicts, and poor social adjustment during their formative years. The elimination of these pathogenic influences is mainly the responsibility of the family and the community. Legal measures may be helpful in reducing the availability of drugs but punishing the user will not solve his underlying maladjustment.

References

Barber, T. X., and Calverley, D. S. "An Experimental Study of 'Hypnotic' (Auditory and Visual) Hallucinations." *Journal of Abnormal and Social Psychology* 68 (1964): 13-20.

Bridge, T. P. and Ellinwood, E. H. "Quaalude Alley: A One Way Street" *American Journal of Psychiatry* 130 (1973): 217-19.

Brill, L., et al. *Rehabilitation in Drug Addiction.* U.S. Department of Health, Education, and Welfare mental health monograph no. 3. Washington, D.C.: U.S. Government Printing Office, 1963.

Carey, J. T., and Mandell, J. "A San Francisco Bay Area 'Speed Scene.'" *Journal of Health and Social Behavior* 9 (1968): 164-74.

Coe, W. C., and Sarbin, T. R. "An Experimental Demonstration of Hypnosis as Role Enactment." *Journal of Abnormal Psychology* 71 (1966): 400-6.

Cohen, S. *The Beyond Within: The LSD Story.* New York: Atheneum, 1964.

——— and Edwards, A. E. "LSD and Organic Brain Impairment." In National Institute of Mental Health, *Drug Dependence*, pp. 1-4. Washington, D.C.: U.S. Government Printing Office, December 1969.

Dole, V. P., and Nyswander, M. E. "The Use of Methadone for Narcotic Blockade." *British Journal of Addiction* 63 (1968): 55-57.

Duvall, H. J.; Locke, B. Z.; and Brill, L. "Follow-up Study of Narcotic Drug Addicts Five Years after Hospitalization." *Public Health Reports* 78 (1963): 185-93.

Gerald, M. C., and Schwirian, P. M. "Nonmedical Use of Methaqualone." *Archives of General Psychiatry* 28 (1973): 627-31.

Gilbert, J. G., and Lombardi, D. N. "Personality Characteristics of Young Male Narcotic Addicts." *Journal of Consulting Psychology* 31 (1967): 536-38.

Goode, E. "The Marijuana Market." *Columbia Forum* 12 (1969): 4-8.

Hill, H. E.; Haertgen, C. A.; and Glaser, R. "Personality Characteristics of Narcotics Addicts as indicated by the MMPI." *Journal of Genetic Psychology* 62 (1960): 127-39.

Hunt, G. H., and Odoroff, M. E. *Follow-Up Study of Narcotic Drug Addicts After Hospitalization.* U.S. Public Health Service report no. 77. Washington, D.C.: U.S. Government Printing Office, 1963.

Inaba, D. S.; Gay, G. R.; Newmeyer, J. A.; and Whitehead, C. "Methaqualone Abuse." *Journal of the American Medical Association* 224 (1973): 1505-09.

Katz, M. M.; Waskow, I. E.; and Olsson, J. "Characterizing the Psychological State Produced by LSD." *Journal of Abnormal Psychology* 73 (1969): 1-14.

Khantzian, E. J.; Mack, J. E.; and Schatzberg, A. F. "Heroin Use as an Attempt to Cope: Clinical Observations." *American Journal of Psychiatry* 131 (1974): 160-64.

Maurer, D. W., and Vogel, V. H. *Narcotics and Narcotic Addiction.* Springfield, Ill.: Charles C Thomas, 1967.

Mitchell, S. W. "Remarks on the Effects of Anhelonium lewinii (The Mescal Button)." *British Medical Journal* 2 (1896): 1625-28. Also reprinted in National Institute of Mental Health, *Drug Dependence*, pp. 12-19. Washington, D.C.: U.S. Government Printing Office, 1969.

Orne, M. T., and Scheibe, K. E. "The Contribution of Nondeprivation Factors in the Production of Sensory Deprivation Effects." *Journal of Abnormal and Social Psychology* 68 (1964): 3-12.

Scott, N. R.; Oryen, W.; Musillo, C.; and Cole, P. T. "Methadone in the Southwest: A 3-Year Follow-up of Chicano Heroin Addicts." *American Journal of Orthopsychiatry* 43 (1973): 355-61.

Shelly, J. A., and Bassin, A. "Daytop Lodge: A New Treatment Approach for Drug Addicts." *Corrective Psychiatry and Journal of Social Therapy* 11 (1965): 186-95. Also reprinted in *Behavior Disorders*, ed. O. Milton and R. G. Wahler, pp. 289-97. Philadelphia: Lippincott, 1969.

Smart, R. G., and Bateman, K. "Unfavorable Reactions to LSD." *Canadian Medical Association Journal* 97 (1967): 1214-21.

Spear, H. B. "The Growth of Heroin Addiction in the United Kingdom." *British Journal of Addiction* 64 (1969): 245-55.

Vaillant, G. E. "A 20-Year Follow-Up of New York Narcotic Addicts." *Archives of General Psychiatry* 29 (1973): 237-41.

Wasson, R. G. "The Hallucinogenic Mushrooms of Mexico." *Transactions of the New York Academy of Sciences* 21 (1959).

Weil, A. T.; Zinberg, N. E.; and Nelson, J. M. "Clinical and Psychological Effects of

Marijuana in Man." *Science* 162 (December 13, 1968): 1234-42.

Willis, J. H. "Drug Dependence: Some Demographic and Psychiatric Aspects in United Kingdom and United States Subjects." *British Journal of Addiction* 64 (1969): 135-46.

Winick, C. "Maturing Out of Narcotic Addiction." *Bulletin of Narcotics* 14 (1962): 1-7.

Yablonsky, L. *The Tunnel Back: Synanon.* New York: Macmillan, 1965.

15 · Psychopathology and Sex

The Metamorphoses of Ovid, Auguste Rodin

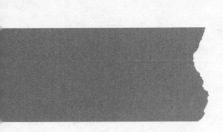

Irregularities in psychosexual development and functioning are commonly noted in the life histories of persons officially diagnosed as suffering from neuroses, psychoses, and other recognized mental disorders. In these cases, the sexual inadequacy or distortion may be appropriately considered and treated as an integral part of the total personality disturbance. Sexual irregularities are also frequently observed in persons whose general adjustment—apart from difficulties that may be associated with their unusual or unconventional sex behavior—is essentially within the normal range. For example, *homosexuals* may be troubled by or angry with their outcast state, but most manage to lead satisfying and useful lives. Some are highly successful and respected doctors, lawyers, teachers, artists, and writers. Most *transvestites* and *transsexuals* compare favorably with the general population with respect to their moral values, productivity, and competence in coping with problems in living. Exhibitionists and peepers are more clearly distinguished by their sexual inadequacy than by the social harmfulness of their actions.

There is no satisfactory label for classifying these atypical, specific, and usually circumscribed kinds of behaviors. The legal term "sex offenses" and the medical term "sex disorders" are inappropriate and misleading. The fact that a person's sex behavior differs from that of the majority does not warrant regarding him as a criminal or a sick person. On the other hand, the mere designation of "variations from the norm" is too mild and neutral. These behaviors not only vary from the expected and the usual, but from the point of view of much of society they are considered to be undesirable, harmful, or morally wrong.

The favored term "sex deviation," which includes the connotation of "different" and "undesirable," is an expedient compromise. The term may be criticized in that behavior may be different from the norm without being undesirable or harmful. There is no harm in a transvestite man slipping into sexy female clothing in the privacy of his home, if his wife has no objection. Many homosexuals strenuously object to being ostracized and discriminated against merely because their needs for sex, affection, and love can be fully expressed only through contact with members of their own sex. With justification, they feel that their atypical sex preferences should be accepted and respected as long as their affairs are restricted to consenting adult partners and carried on with a proper regard for the social proprieties.

A possible solution consists in limiting the undesirable and harmful connotation of "sex deviations" to those kinds of behavior that cause great personal distress or significantly interfere with the rights, welfare, and safety of others. This interpretation is consistent with our definition of psychopathology in this book. The American Psychiatric Association has recently taken a similar position with specific reference to homosexuality. Following a conference on the subject (Stoller, et al., 1973), the Association's Board of Trustees adopted a resolution eliminating homosexuality as a psychiatric disorder from the APA nomenclature. When the individual is functioning normally and is satisfied with his condition, homosexuality will be considered an irregular form of sexual behavior. The problems of those who seek professional help because

DEFINITIONS OF SEX TERMS

Bestiality   The use of animal contact for sexual gratification.

Cunnilingus   Stimulation by the tongue of the clitoris and other parts of female genitalia.

Exhibitionism   A mild sex deviation in which the person derives erotic gratification from exhibiting and attracting the attention of others to his sex organs. The condition is essentially limited to males who exhibit their penises to females who are strangers and involuntary viewers.

Fellatio   The use of the mouth as a receptor organ for the penis for purposes of sexual gratification.

Fetishism   A mild sex deviation in which an inanimate object by itself serves as a source of sexual arousal and gratification. Essentially restricted to males.

Frottage   A mild form of sexual assault in which a person derives sexual gratification by intentionally rubbing against the body or parts of the body of another individual without the latter's consent.

Heterosexuality   Sex life oriented toward persons of the opposite sex. Male-female relations definitely preferred as more stimulating and gratifying.

Homosexuality   A sex orientation in which the person feels more strongly attracted to and derives greater erotic satisfaction from contact with members of his or her own sex than with members of the opposite sex.

Incest   Sexual intercourse between father and daughter, mother and son, or brother and sister.

Masochism   A sex variation in which an individual attains sexual arousal and gratification from being subjected to physical pain or otherwise mistreated.

Necrophilia   A morbid sex deviation marked by sexual interest in corpses.

Partialism   A sex bias in which an individual is especially stimulated by some specific part of the body, as for example the hand, the buttocks, the breasts, and so forth. Differs from fetishism, which involves inanimate objects.

Pedophilia   A sex deviation in which an adult derives sexual gratification from the use of children as sex objects. Essentially restricted to males.

Sadism   A sex variation in which an individual derives erotic arousal and gratification through inflicting physical or psychic pain on another person.

Transsexuality   A deviation in sex role, in which the person has the secondary physical characteristics of one sex but thinks of himself as a member of the opposite sex.

Transvestism   A sex variation mainly found in males, in which the man feels sexually stimulated by dressing in the clothes of the opposite sex. Most transvestites have a heterosexual orientation.

Voyeurism   A mild sex deviation most often noted in males. The "peeper" derives sexual stimulation and gratification from surreptitiously looking at other persons when they are undressing, nude, or engaging in sexual activities.

of internal conflicts or social pressures would be classified as *deviations in sexual orientation.*

DEVIATIONS, VARIATIONS, DYSFUNCTIONS

The restriction of the term "deviation" to sexual behavior that is both different from the norm and undesirable frees the term "sex variation" for behavior that differs from the norm but is not significantly harmful or undesirable. On occasion, the distinction may be a fine one, with the decision resting on the age of the participants, current value systems, social custom, mutual consent, and other subjective factors. In the absence of voluntary choice and partner agreement, most sex variations qualify as deviations. This holds for heterosexual as well as homosexual irregularities in behavior. If a wife objects to wearing high heels or a leather jacket when having intercourse with her husband, his *fetish* is a disturbing sex deviation. Oral-genital stimulation is a normal variation when acceptable to and enjoyed by both partners, but when it is distasteful and distressing to one partner and the other insists on it, the latter's behavior may be perceived as a deviation by the unwilling victim.

The omission of any mention of *impotence, premature ejaculation,* or *frigidity* (orgasmic deficiency) in the preceding discussion is intentional. These are forms of *sex dysfunction* which represent failures in performance rather than deviations from the accepted social norm. The intent, mode, and choice of partners are normal. Owing mainly to emotional blocks the individual is either unable to complete the conventional sex act or does not find the experience as satisfying as he or she would like. The participants may be acutely distressed. Outsiders are typically unaware of failures in sex performance. If they were, they might be sympathetic but they would not consider such behavior socially undesirable, immoral, or harmful. In short, sex dysfunctions do not represent either variations or deviations in sex behavior. They are essentially psychosomatic disturbances that are more appropriately described and discussed in a later chapter on psychophysiological reactions.

THE CONCEPTS OF SEX VARIATION AND DEVIATION

One important advantage of the concepts of variation and deviation is the implication that behavior so designated differs mainly in frequency of occurrence and degree of desirability from the norm. Thus *nymphomania* and *satyriasis* are more correctly perceived as extreme variations in the relative intensity of the human sex drive than as unique disorders expressed in insatiable lust. The uninvited *voyeur* is not alone in deriving erotic pleasure from looking at sex objects or scenes; many normal individuals share a similar interest that is more appropriately expressed. The *exhibitionist* is the less attractive brother of the streaker and the bikini girl. Heterosexuals as well as homosexuals may be emotionally attracted to members of their own sex; the main difference is that the attraction is much stronger and more exclusive for homosexuals. Normal males differ from males with fetishes in being more stimulated by the package than the outside wrapping, but they too may be highly partial to some detail such as color of hair, size of breasts, or buttock shape. In the case of dating couples, even rape may be considered an extreme and undesirable variation of the norm, since the male is expected to be aggressive and persistent and the female is expected to protest and resist.

A second though more controversial advantage of the concepts of variation and deviation is that they provide a convenient medium for classification. Homosexuality may be described as a deviation in sex orientation and transsexuality as a deviation in sex role. Animal contact, fetishism, and pedophilia may be grouped together as deviations in the choice of sex objects. Deviations in sex mode would include exhibitionism, voyeurism, sadism, masochism, and transvestism.

There is some merit in thus identifying the nature of deviations but the classification categories are arbitrary. Homosexuality, for example, could with equal justification be considered a deviation in the choice of sex object. The different types of behavior included in a particular category are unrelated with respect to content, cause, severity, or recommended treatment. The same criticisms are applicable to Freud's early distinction between deviations in sex object and aim, and Gagnon and Simon's (1967) differentiation of "normal" sexual variations (masturbation, premarital sex), abnormal sexual deviations (harmful sexual offenses), and socially organized deviations (homosexuality, prostitution). In view of the artificiality of categories, each form of deviation will be considered separately. The same plan will be followed for "normal" and minor variations.

CLASSIFICATION OF NORMAL, VARIANT, AND DEVIANT SEX BEHAVIOR

Orientation, Partner, and Method	Normal: Socially Approved to Accepted	Variation/Deviation: Socially Disapproved Mildly to Severely
Sex orientation or role	Heterosexual	Transsexual Bisexual Homosexual
Choice of partner or sex object	Spouse, lover, or other consenting adult of opposite sex Self	Promiscuity Prostitution Same-sex partner Nonconsenting partner Pedophilia Incest Bestiality Necrophilia
Mode or method of stimulation	Coitus Masturbation Oral-genital (heterosexual)	Transvestism Fetishism Anal intercourse Voyeurism Exhibitionism Masochism Sadism Sexual assault (forcible rape)

THE ELUSIVE SEX NORM

The concept of deviance presumes the existence of a recognized cultural norm. This assumption is valid in principle but confusing on specifics. Most societies have historically accepted the procreative function of sex as the most important criterion. Normal sex behavior has thus been equated with heterosexuality and more or less limited to human coital intercourse between a physiologically mature male and female, other than incestuous relationships. Other local restrictions have frequently been added to safeguard the stability of the family unit and the legitimacy of children. This narrow view accounts for society's long delay in acknowledging the obvious harmlessness and personal pleasure of masturbation and society's strong rejection of homosexuality and other deviations that preclude male-female intercourse.

The stress on heterosexuality reflects reality. Cultural indoctrination may reinforce and channel the expression of heterosexuality but most males and females are genetically programmed to be sexually responsive to members of the opposite sex. Postpubertal biochemical changes intensify and sustain the orientation. The biosocial process works. Heterosexual outlets accounted for over 75 percent of the total sex behavior of the sexually active adult males and females interviewed by Kinsey (1948, 1953). The addition of masturbation with heterosexual fantasies would increase the figure to over 90 percent (Table 15.1).

The confusion associated with the sex norm is not in differentiating deviant from normal behavior. The distinguishing, culture-free characteristic of most deviant behavior is that it cannot serve the procreative function of sex. This fixed criterion covers homosexuality, transsexuality, exhibitionism, voyeurism, animal contact, molestation of young children, and the exclusive use of noncoital variations in technique that are ends in themselves. Difficulties in defining the sex norm are mainly due to the lack of clear and stable criteria for differentiating socially acceptable from socially prohibited heterosexual acts, all of which are performed in normal fashion. The prohibition may be related to marital status, frequency of intercourse, number of partners, degree of voluntary consent, and so forth. Apart from universal social approval of marital intercourse, the rules governing acceptable and prohibited heterosexual behavior vary from society to society and from one generation to the next.

The contemporary revolution in sexual attitudes provides a good illustration of both the changeableness of standards and the fact that changes are largely confined to which of the "normal" heterosexual variations are prohibited or accepted. The current era of increased permissiveness has resulted in a moderation of society's punitive attitude toward sex deviants, but behavior that in the past was described as deviant is still so regarded. The main impact of change has been an increased public acceptance of the normality of masturbation, female sexuality, premarital sex, extramarital affairs, and variations in sexual technique. The repeal of prohibitions has encouraged those interested in such behavior to start earlier and indulge more frequently.

Interestingly, the "sex revolution" has not led to a sharp increase in the percentage of the population engaging in formerly prohibited "normal" behavior. The increase in incidence rates for masturbation, premarital sex, and extramarital sex has been mild to moderate and largely associated with the greater sex freedom of females. Corresponding rates for males have shown little change. Similarly, there is no evidence of any significant increase in the incidence of homosexuality or other recognized forms of deviant behavior. The one possible exception is forcible rape, which is more directly related to the general increase in crime rates than to changes in sex standards. For personal reasons, many males and female prefer to abide by the traditional standards of sex morality. An analogous situation is voluntary abstinence in the use of alcohol in a society where drinking is socially accepted.

Changes in social attitudes have primarily resulted in a greater openness and straightforwardness about sexual activities that were formerly engaged in furtively, and often with an accompanying sense of shame or guilt. No longer required to deny, repress, or conceal their natural sex feelings, women can take a more active and egalitarian role. The superior male position in coitus, which implies that the female is or ought to be passive and submissive, is

Table 15.1. Sex in the United States (A Summary of the General Findings Reported by the Kinsey Group).

Behavior	Percent or Usual Frequency	
	Female	Male
Premarital coitus		
Accumulative incidence	50%	92%
Masturbation		
Accumulative incidence	62%	93%
By age 20	33%	92%
Age change after 25	increase	decrease
Marital coitus		
Usual frequency per week		
Age 21-35	2-3	2-3
Age 36-55	1-2	1-2
Leading to Orgasm (average)	70-77%	100%
Extramarital coitus		
By age 40	26%	50%
Oral-genital (active heterosexuals)		
Stimulation of female genitalia	46-57%	—
Stimulation of male genitalia	—	43-57%
Homosexual experience		
Some experience by age 45	20%	50%
To orgasm by age 20	3%	22%
To orgasm by age 45	13%	37%
Animal contacts		
Cumulative incidence	3.6%	8.0%
Erotic response	3.0%	8.0%
To orgasm	0.4%	8.0%

SOURCE: Kinsey et al. (1948) (1953).

A sampling of ads for swingers and other sex seekers, from a nationally distributed magazine.

no longer considered the only appropriate behavior. Because of differences in population samples and methodology, the findings of recent studies on the prevalance of premarital intercourse are not directly comparable to those reported earlier findings, but the available data confirm the absence of startling change. In 1953, Alfred Kinsey found that 71 percent of boys between the ages of sixteen and twenty had had premarital intercourse. A 1973 report by R. C. Sorensen placed the incidence of premarital sex among boys between the ages of sixteen to nineteen at 72 percent. Twenty percent of the females interviewed by Kinsey (1953) reported having had premarital coitus between the ages of sixteen and twenty. More recent figures by Kantner and Zelnick (1972) indicate that 28 percent of unmarried white girls between the ages of fifteen and nineteen have had premarital intercourse. Sorensen's (1973) much higher rate of 57 percent for females still indicates that nearly half the unmarried adolescent girls in the United States are virgins.

Swinging and Swingers

The greater openness of sex today is dramatically illustrated by the phenomenon of "swinging" (Smity and Smity, 1972). Swinging specifically refers to married couples' sharing extramarital sex through mate swapping. But sex outside of marriage is not new; fifty percent of the grandfathers and 26 percent of the grandmothers of the present generation secretly engaged in extramarital coitus (Kinsey, 1953). What is new about swinging is that husband and wife mutually agree to have sex relations outside the marital bond and are willing to do so in the presence of each other, and this equality is a far cry from the historical double standard. Usually the husband takes the initiative in suggesting swinging, but after a few experiences the wife is usually more interested in continuing than the husband.

The motives are the same as in the past, namely, to seek greater variety and excitement in one's sex life, to demonstrate attractiveness and potency, and to restore jaded interest in sex. The advantage of swinging is that it avoids deceit, jealousy, and the complications of starting and terminating an illicit affair. Everything is open and aboveboard. What might become awkward personal involvement with outside partners is easily avoided by not exchanging with the same couple more than once or twice.

Studies of swingers (Ramey, 1972; Cole and Spaniard, 1974) indicate that most participants are middle class individuals. Apart from their atypical sex interest, they are conservative in their attitudes and have conventional value systems. Surveys suggest that about 2 percent of the married population have engaged in mate-swapping and an additional 7 percent would be interested if the opportunity arose. The movement has its own communication network, rules of conduct, and special meetingplaces. Beginners can easily and inexpensively get started by answering or inserting ads in national magazines and local publications.

Swinging consists of two and occasionally three couples meeting together. The setting provides an opportunity for voyeurism and exhibitionism as well as mate-switching. Choice of activities and change of partners are optional and subject to individual consent. Drinking may occur but drugs are usually prohibited. It is understood that if pregnancy occurs, the husband is expected to assume the obligations of paternity. If a couple decides to have a child, they usually drop out of swinging. Swinging may also consist of a couple incorporating a single male or single female, with the latter more common. Ads frequently specify that the single woman should be "versatile," i.e., interested in both male-female and female-female sex play. The excitement of swinging and group sex is usually short-lived. Most participants drop out after a couple of years.

Liberalizing factors

The more liberal sex norms of today are the product of many interacting influences. Kinsey's startling mid-century findings on the actual sex experiences of normal people had a profound effect in making the public aware of the need to bring their standards more in accord in reality. The incongruity of regarding the common practice of masturbation as harmful was readily resolved by redefining it as harmless. However, as long as contraceptive methods were unreliable and there were no available cures for venereal diseases, society could not afford to relax its prohibitions against premarital and extramarital sex. With the discovery of more effective drugs for treating disease and the development of more reliable and convenient contraceptive techniques, the traditional arguments against sex permissiveness were weakened. These developments, combined with the spirit of the time, made greater sex freedom feasible.

SEX OFFENSES AND THE LAW

The terms "sex offense" and "sex offender" are arbitrary legal designations that have no meaning outside the law. The interpretation of certain deviant sex acts as sex offenses is related to the police power of society to enact and enforce legislation to protect the public from harm. A sex offender is a person who has been legally convicted of the commission of an overt sex act that constituted a punishable violation of a statute. Most sex offenses are defined by state laws, and a deviation that is punishable in one state may not be so regarded in a neighboring state. Local regulations also determine the severity of punishment stipulated for specific offenses. Most states have an accumulation of unrepealed laws dating from a more moralistic era which, if enforced, would make most of the population liable to arrest. Fortunately, active prosecution is generally limited to public acts of indecency, sex solicitation in public places, child molestation, and forcible rape.

The present social climate is one of tolerance toward most forms of deviant sex behavior that are committed in private by consenting adults. The courts are also less punitive. In disposing of arrests involving charges of peeping or exhibitionism, many judges today question whether the actual harmfulness or danger to others of such behavior warrants stiff jail sentences. Forcible rape of innocent strangers remains a serious criminal offense but judges have become more lenient in cases where an adult female was well-acquainted with her attacker and put up only token resistance. The courts are making increasing use of suspended sentences or probation when a convicted offender has no prior criminal record and the victim suffers no serious physical or mental harm.

Since about 1938, many states have enacted special legislation that provides for the compulsory treatment of certain sex offenders as an alternative to imprisonment. This option is restricted to those who qualify as "treatable sexual psychopaths." The concept of sexual psychopathy is strictly a legal invention. It is somewhat analogous to the legal definition of insanity in criminal proceedings, in that neither exists outside of lawbooks. Psychiatric classifications of mental disorders do not recognize sexual psychopathy as a distinctive clinical syndrome or as a separate mental disorder. The purpose of the legal concept is to take account of the possibility that some sex offenders are more "sick" than "bad." In such cases the courts still have the responsibility of protecting society, but justice is better served by providing for the compulsory treatment of offenders than by punishing them with imprisonment.

Procedures and regulations governing sexual psychopathy vary somewhat from state to state. As a rule the offender, his attorney, or others may request a mental examination at the time of arrest or conviction. The judge then may arrange for the offender to be examined by qualified experts, who typically are experienced professionals in the field of psychiatry or clinical psychology. Their assignment is to determine whether, in their opinion, the offender is a sexual psychopath. The assessment process is admittedly subjective. In general, clinicians favor a diagnosis of psychopathy when behavior appears to be compulsive, repetitive, or bizarre (Gebhard et al., 1965). A man with a long record of offensive homosexual activities or an exhibitionist whose exposure occurs under circumstances that appear to invite arrest is far more apt to be described as a sexual psychopath than an armed rapist convicted of a single offense against an adult female. The judge is not bound by the experts' positive report of psychopathy. If he goes along with their assessment, he may commit the offender to a hospital for observation or arrange for other coercive trial therapy to ascertain if the offender is amenable to treatment. A "no" decision on the latter point by the hospital or therapist results in the offender's return to the court for routine sentencing.

Studies of sexual psychopaths indicate that clinicians are biased in their evaluation of "treatable" offenders (Gebhard et al., 1965). Offenders are seen as treatable if they are reasonably bright, well educated, young, and have emotional problems marked by inhibition rather than aggression. In short, preference is shown for offenders who are more like the kinds of patients that are typically seen in private practice. This bias tends to exclude the most dangerous as untreatable. It has the advantage of providing treatment for those with the best prognosis. There are no controlled studies of the relative effectiveness of treatment vs. incarceration in preventing subsequent offenses. On humane grounds alone, the treatment alternative represents an important forward step. The coercive nature of treatment does pose ethical and practical problems, but these are minor compared with the punitive and degrading alternative of incarceration.

The importance of sex offenses in relation to other crimes depends on the basis of comparison. Sex offenses account for less than 5 percent of all reported crimes. This low percentage is due to the fact that about 90 percent of all serious crimes consist of offenses against property. Of the approximately 10 percent of crimes committed against the person each year, about half involve sex offenses. As compared with other types of criminals, sex offenders have a much lower recidivism rate; only about 15 percent have a record of two or more arrests (Mohr, 1972).

The great majority of sex offenders are not dangerous. On the other hand, some are violent and sadistic. Newspaper accounts of brutal and multiple sex murders are not uncommon, and Jack the Ripper and the Boston Strangler are familiar objects of fascinating dread. Multiple sex murders are often associated with the acting out of delusional ideas by a psychotic individual. If apprehended, the offender is usually certified as insane and committed for life to a maximum security institution.

SEX AND PSYCHOPATHOLOGY

Psychopathology is directly concerned with those aspects of sex behavior that cause distress, offense or harm to the individual, his or her partner, and others. Three overlapping topics of relevant interest are the understanding of sex problems, their prevention, and their treatment. The scientific study of sex variations and deviations remains a challenge for the future. Much of the work thus far has been devoted to clearing the field of time-encrusted myths and misconceptions, so that this long buried facet of human behavior could be examined with objective eyes rather than through the distorted lenses of moralists. Two outstanding contributors have been Sigmund Freud and Alfred Kinsey. Freud (1905) demolished the myth of childhood innocence of sex and went on to make infantile sexuality the cornerstone of psychoanalysis. Kinsey (1948, 1953) replaced fantasies with facts by providing comprehensive statistical data on the real sex lives of more than 20,000 persons. His scholarly approach made sex research re-

spectable. Each pioneeer also may be credited with formulating a basic theory about the origin and course of sex deviations.

Theories of Sex Deviation

Freud attributed sex deviations to arrested psychosexual development. He maintained that sexual development, under normal circumstances, follows a biologically predetermined timetable. The individual progresses step by step from the oral-anal-phallic sequence of early childhood through the latent period and on to the final destination of genital heterosexuality. According to Freudian theory, sex deviations are due to fixations at or regressions to the phallic or oedipal stage, when the four- to six-year-old child is working through his mother-love and father-rivalry relationships and is haunted by castration fears. At this stage, sex feelings are diffuse and confused as to aim and object. Fixation may result in the continuation of some aspect of childhood sex behavior into adulthood. In normal sex development, these childish manifestations would become integrated with and subordinate to the adult stage of heterosexual genital primacy. Freud's explanation of sex deviations is essentially similar to his theory of neurosis. Both conditions are associated with faulty resolution of the Oedipus complex.

A logical subsequent modification of Freud's theory is the contemporary psychoanalytic view that sex deviations represent symptomatic manifestations of larger and more basic personality disorders. The latter interpretation shifts the focus of attention and treatment to the total personality. The symptom viewpoint has been emphasized by Salzman (1972), who regards all sex deviations as evidence of failure or deficiency in interpersonal function. The basic problem is that the individual is incapable of a loving, trusting, intimate involvement with another human being. In this context, some sex deviations may have little to do with sex. Their main function may be to relieve anxiety, fulfill neurotic needs, overwhelm others, avoid

Alfred C. Kinsey, (1894-1956), a noted zoologist and sex researcher, who shares with Freud major credit for advancing our knowledge of human sexuality.

areas of conflict, or express hostility. For example, the excessive but seldom gratifying sex activities of the nymphomaniac and the Don Juan may be based on a compulsive neurotic need endlessly to prove one's adequacy or superiority. This interpretation, of course, is not applicable in those instances where these labels are loosely and incorrectly applied to persons whose perfectly normal sex desires are above average or greater than those of their partners.

Kinsey favored a learning theory to explain variations and deviations in sex behavior. Compared with the psychoanalytic interpretation, which focuses on the *why*, learning theory attempts to explain *how* sex deviations are acquired. According to Kinsey (1953), the capacity for sexual arousal and response is physiological and inborn. Innate or neurophysiological factors may also account for individual variations in intensity of the sex drive. All other aspects of human sexual behavior are the products of learning and conditioning.

The child learns from accidental contacts that certain tactile stimulations are pleasurable. The cultural model of approved and disapproved sex behavior helps mold his attitudes and his acceptance or avoidance of particular types of overt activity. His first sex experiences, and more particularly the pleasure, pain, or disappointment associated with the initial experience, influence the repetition or discontinuance of the activity. Depending on his particular experiences the individual acquires preferences with respect to choice of outlet, partner, and mode of gratification. The standard processes of learning and conditioning are equally applicable to normal and deviant sexual activitiy. Behavior that on the surface may appear bizarre and irrational is understandable in terms of the individual's past experiences. The greater prevalence of deviant behavior among males may be explained as due to the greater responsiveness of males to a wider variety of psychological stimuli, which in turn increases the probability of their acquiring a greater variety of conditioned responses.

In recent years, increasing attention has been given to the importance of learning and conditioning in the acquisition of normal and deviant sex behavior. John Gagnon and William Simon (1973) stress the significance of social factors in providing the scenario or script of normal and deviant sex roles which the individual learns and acts out on appropriate occasions. Many modern psychoanalysts see no conflict in substituting the concept of faulty early conditioning for the Freudian concept of childhood fixation in order to explain the avoidance of heterosexual contacts by adults. The importance of biological factors has been downgraded, with the notable exception of a continuing interest in the search for a neuroendocrine basis for transsexuality and homosexuality.

Prevention

Psychopathologists strongly support the establishment of rational social standards of sex behavior that recognize the realities of human sex needs and the broad range of individual differences in intensity of sex drive, mode of expression, and preferred sex object. They also endorse sex education programs in the school systems. However, they realize that the main hope of preventing pathological behavior rests with sound sex training in the home. As long as parents provide unsatisfactory male and female models for the child, confuse the sex identity of infants by rearing girls as boys and boys as girls during their early years, or promote attitudes of disgust, shame, and fear toward sex; the incidence of deviance will not be significantly diminished.

Treatment

Psychoanalysis, group therapy, and other traditional approaches are still being used in the treatment of sex deviations. The current trend, however, is to favor behavior modification techniques that have the advantage of focusing on specific activities. Preliminary findings (Feldman, 1966; Barlow, 1973) suggest that these techniques are somewhat more effective than the older psychotherapeutic methods, but the results are more encouraging than conclusive. Most reports have been based

only on single cases or small samples with limited follow-up information. Aversive therapies in particular, have been criticized on the grounds that while they may be temporarily effective in inhibiting the occurrence of deviant behavior in cooperative subjects, they rarely result in any increase in acceptable or normal behavior. The individual is left with the alternative of leading a sexless existence or of reverting to former outlets. The addition of supplementary conditioning procedures designed to reinforce positive normal responses is desirable but usually of little help. It is extremely difficult to elicit dependable, normal, heterosexual responses in persons whose behavior repertoire or capability is deficient in this area.

The use of hormonal therapy to increase heterosexual feelings and response in homosexuals and transsexuals has proven more disturbing than beneficial and has been discontinued. Increasing use is being made of surgery in the sex reassignment of transsexuals who insist on a change in their physical gender. In these cases hormonal treatment is effective in initiating and maintaining sexual features associated with the other (preferred) sex.

The castration of sex offenders is legal and used in selected cases in Denmark and a few other European countries (Stürup, 1972). This extreme treatment is voluntary. Applicants are essentially restricted to convicted or institutionalized sex offenders who have a choice of long-term incarceration or a high possibility of parole within a short period following castration, when presumably they are no longer a threat to society. The authorities carefully screen applicants to select candidates otherwise suitable for release to the community. Selected applicants are fully informed as to the nature and the permanent effects of the operation. Castration typically results in a significant diminution of sex drive and sexual aggressiveness. The decline in sex capacity following castration is gradual and usually takes a year or more before impotence is established. About a third of the younger castrates remain capable of coitus for several years after the operation. Sex deviations that do not require penile erection are unaffected. Follow-up studies indicate that about 90 percent of the castrates are satisfied with the results. About 2 percent are subsequently arrested for sex offenses, and this is considerably lower than the recidivism rate for nonoperated sex offenders.

The ethical and moral issues associated with castration may be sidestepped by the use of drugs that are highly effective in producing impotence in males (incapacity for penile erection) and reducing sex drive. As with castration, this drastic treatment is voluntary and recommended only for sex offenders whose self-regulation of unacceptable sex behavior is so severely impaired that the only alternative is long-term incarceration (Money, 1970). The advantage of desexualization by drugs is that the effects are transient and reversible. The individual gains a period of respite from his pressing sex demands. Time and conventional therapies may eventually decrease the intensity of socially unacceptable urges or increase self-control so that drug medication can be discontinued.

SUMMARY

Normal sex behavior has traditionally been identified with the procreative function of sex. This restricted view accounts for society's traditional disapproval of masturbation, homosexuality, transsexuality, and "sterile" variations in technique. Cultural prohibitions against premarital and extramarital sex have been mainly concerned with the preservation of the family unit and infant care. Other sex irregularities have been condemned on the grounds that they constituted an unwarranted invasion of privacy, were deemed offensive, or posed a threat to the safety and welfare of others. These sex offenses include exhibitionism, voyeurism, animal contact, child molestation, and rape.

The recent sex revolution has resulted in a broadening of the "accepted normal" range to include masturbation, premarital sex, and extramarital relations. In the United States homosexuality has been removed from the officially recognized list of sex disorders. The appropriateness of applying the disease-connoting label of "sex disorder" to any form of sex variation and deviation is being seriously questioned. Increasing use is now made of the concept of variation from the norm as a replacement for the more pejorative concept of sex deviation. There has been a moderation in the punitive attitude of the courts toward sex offenders whose actions are more annoying than harmful.

The causes of atypical sex behavior are not known. According to psychoanalytic theory, sex deviations are due to arrested psychosexual development at the oedipal level. Learning theory favors the importance of conditioning. Biological factors may be involved in transsexuality and homosexuality.

The "sickness" model of sex deviations, which implies a need for corrective treatment, is on the wane. Treatment is recommended only when the individual is subjectively disturbed by his atypical sex behavior or when his actions lead to interpersonal difficulties or social conflict. In these selected cases, the reasonable rights of society must be protected, but within this restriction, the current practice is to leave the goal of therapy to the individual. Since it is extremely difficult by the use of accepted therapeutic procedures to alter a person's sex style against his will, the therapist actually has little choice. For example, he can either refuse to treat a disturbed homosexual who wants to become a better adjusted homosexual or he can try to help him accept his homosexuality and regulate his actions so that social conflict is minimized.

References

Barlow, D. H. "Increasing Heterosexual Responsiveness in the Treatment of Sexual

Deviations: A Review of Clinical and Experimental Evidence." *Behavior Therapy* 4 (1973): 655-71.

———, Leitenberg, H., and Agras, W. S. "Experimental Control of Sexual Deviation Through Manipulation of the Noxious Scene in Overt Sensitization." *Journal of Abnormal Psychology* 74 (1969): 596-601.

Cole, C. L., and Spaniard, G. B. "Comarital Mate-Sharing and Family Stability." *Journal of Sex Research* 10 (1974): 21-31.

Feldman, M. P. "Aversion Therapy for Sexual Deviations: A Critical Review." *Psychological Bulletin* 65 (1966): 65-79.

Freud, S. "Three Essays on the Theory of Sexuality" (1905). In *The Standard Edition of the Complete Psychological Works of Sigmund Freud*, vol. 7. London: Hogarth Press and the Institute of Psycho-Analysis, 1953.

Gagnon, J. H., and Simon, W., eds. *Sexual Deviance*. New York: Harper & Row, 1967.

———, and Simon, W. *Sexual Conduct: The Social Sources of Human Sexuality*. Chicago: Aldine, 1973.

Gebhard, P. H.; Gagnon, J. H.; Pomeroy, W. B.; and Christenson, C. V. *Sex Offenders: An Analysis of Types*. New York: Harper & Row, 1965.

Kantner, J. F., and Zelnick, M. "Sexual Experience of Young Unmarried Women in the United States." *Family Planning Perspectives*, 4 (1972): 9-18.

Kinsey, A. C., and Gebhard, P. H. *Sexual Behavior in the Human Female*. Philadelphia: Saunders, 1953.

Kinsey, A. C.; Pomeroy, W. B.; and Martin, C. E. *Sexual Behavior in the Human Male*. Philadelphia: Saunders, 1948.

Mohr, J. W. "Evaluation of Treatment." In *Sexual Behaviors*, ed. H. L. P. Resnick and M. E. Wolfgang, pp. 413-28. Boston: Little, Brown, 1972.

Money, J. "The Therapeutic Use of Androgen-Depleting Hormone." *Journal of Sex Research* 6 (1970): 165-74.

Ramey, J. W. "Emerging Patterns of Behavior in Marriage." *Journal of Sex Research* 8 (1972): 6-30.

Salzman, L. "The Psychodynamic Approach to Sex Deviations." In *Sexual Behaviors*, ed. H. L. P. Resnick and M. E. Wolfgang, pp. 207-26. Boston: Little, Brown, 1972.

Smity, J. R., and Smity, L. G., eds. *Co-Marital Sex: Recent Studies of Sexual Alternatives in Marriage*. Boston: Little, Brown, 1972.

Sorensen, R. C. *Adolescent Sexuality in Contemporary America*. New York: World Publishing Co., 1973.

Stoller, R. J.; Marmor, J.; Bieber, I.; Gold, R.; Sacarides, C. W.; Green, R.; Spitzer, R. L. "A Symposium: Should Homosexuality be in the APA Nomenclature?" *American Journal of Psychiatry* 13 (1973): 1207-1216.

Stürup, G. K. "Castration: The Total Treatment." In *Sexual Behaviors*, ed. H. L. P. Resnick and M. E. Wolfgang, pp. 361-82. Boston: Little, Brown, 1972.

The Penitent, Albrecht Dürer

All sex behavior that differs in mode, aim, or object from the culture-defined model of "normal" sex behavior is appropriately described as a *variation*. The latter designation simply indicates that the behavior is atypical, unusual, or different. The *deviation* label, on the other hand, has definite negative connotations. The term is generally applied to sex variations that are evaluated by society as offensive, disturbing, or harmful to the individual or others. The distinction is admittedly often hazy. The same behavior which under some circumstances is accepted as a "normal" variation may be judged as deviant under other conditions. For example, masturbation in private is a normal variation whereas masturbation in public before an objecting audience is considered deviant behavior. Atypical sex activities may be tolerated as permissive variations when engaged in by consenting adults, while the same actions may be interpreted as deviations when one partner is a child or an unwilling adult who finds the experience distressing or harmful.

In short, there are no fixed or separate categories of sex variations as opposed to sex deviations. The evaluation of the behavior in the total context in which it occurs (including prevailing social values) is usually the deciding factor. Furthermore, there is no logical rationale for classifying or grouping specific behaviors on the basis of their surface manifestations, relative severity, or social evaluation. Each of the main recognized forms of variant or deviant behavior will therefore be discussed independently with no particular significance attached to their order of presentation or their evaluative status.

MASTURBATION

Masturbation consists of intentional self-stimulation for sexual gratification, which may or may not include orgasm. As generally used, the term implies solitary self-gratification. When genital self-stimulation occurs in conjunction with other activities between sex partners, it is usually considered part of the larger pattern. Male masturbation is largely confined to direct manual stimulation of the penis. Female masturbation is more diversified and more individualistic. In addition to manual or mechanical stimulation of the genitalia, it may include caressing the breasts and the tensing of muscles. Both male and female masturbation are frequently accompanied by sex fantasies, which typically reflect the sex orientation, prior experiences and desires of the individual. Heterosexuals have heterosexual fantasies, homosexuals have homosexual fantasies. Fantasy content may be far more imaginative, extreme, and deviant than the person's actual experiences.

Society's negative attitude toward masturbation is indicated by the meaning of the Latin word of origin: *masturbatio*, meaning "to defile or pollute by hand." Onanism is sometimes incorrectly used as a synonym for masturbation but more specifically refers to *coitus interruptus*, in which the male withdraws during intercourse prior to orgasm to avoid impregnation. The biblical origin of the latter term can be traced to the story of Onan, who was asked by his mother to sleep with his brother's wife in order that she might have children. Onan shirked his duty by spilling his seed on the ground whenever he slept with his brother's wife.

Age-old superstitions associating masturbation with all kinds of mental and physical harm were partly invented to reinforce Judeo-Christian teachings, which equated sexual self-indulgence with sinfulness. A second and more basic explanation is related to society's vague apprehension that in the absence of a strong masturbation taboo, children and adolescents would discover and enjoy the pleasure that could be obtained from this readily available sexual outlet. As adults they might continue the practice and thereby feel less inclined to seek heterosexual activities that would result in marriage and reproduction.

This apprehension was based on a lack of understanding of the biology, sociology, and psychology of human sexuality. Human beings, along with other animals, are genetically programmed to produce special hormones when they reach maturity. These hormones increase the intensity of the sex drive and also increase sensitivity and responsiveness to heterosexual stimuli. The biological heterosexual orientation is reinforced by cultural pressures and especially by complex psychological needs for intimacy and love. Given a choice, most adolescents and adults find heterosexual activities more rewarding and fulfilling than being one's own best sex partner. The interpersonal relationship is also preferred to solitary masturbation by homosexuals and others with atypical tastes.

Whatever the underlying reasons, society's campaign against masturbation has been successful. As recently as 1900, psychiatrists, physicians, and educators as well as the general public sincerely believed that masturbation, particularly by children, resulted in imbecility and mental illness. The list of harmful effects was often extended to include skin disorders, blindness, physical weakness, and sterility and impotence in later years. Public acceptance of the alleged sinfulness and harmfulness of "self-abuse" has been more effective in

creating intense feelings of guilt, depression, and self-condemnation than in preventing its occurrence.

Most persons today realize that masturbation is harmless, but the taboo lingers on. Many persons with limited education still believe masturbation is wrong or unnatural. The better educated are uneasy about "excessive" masturbation, which is conveniently defined as "more than one's current practice." In some instances, self-stimulation is intellectually accepted as harmless, but the individual is concerned with his lack of will power to break the habit. Society still has reservations about approving or ignoring masturbation. Teachers, parents, and family physicians rarely discuss the topic with children. It remains a secret practice that the growing child must learn about on his own through accidental discovery, observation of others, peer communication, reading books, or being masturbated by someone with more experience. Even today there are college girls who, although aware of masturbation, do not know that they can achieve orgasm through self-stimulation.

The early Kinsey figures (1948, 1953) have been confirmed and revised upward by more recent studies (Abramson, 1973; Clifford, 1974). At least 95 percent of American males and 70 percent of females admit to having had some masturbatory experiences. The median age of onset for boys is about fourteen years of age; girls begin a little later. Frequently females start out with heterosexual experiences and later engage in masturbation as a substitute for coitus (Gagnon and Simon, 1970; Gebhard et al., 1970). During the adult years, masturbation accounts for a higher proportion of female than male total sex outlets.

Until recently, clinicians have regarded masturbation as a substitute for heterosexuality or as a sign of immaturity of age or psychosexual development. This view is changing. Professionals in the field of sex education are emphasizing the value of masturbation as a positive experience in its own right, in that it provides a convenient

THE PENALTIES OF SELF-ABUSE

The following is excerpted from the *Ladies' Guide,* a popular reference book of the 1890s.

Effects of Solitary Vice in Girls

The victim of this evil habit is certain to suffer sooner or later the penalty which nature invariably inflicts upon those who transgress her laws. Every law of nature is enforced by an inexorable penalty. This is emphatically true respecting the laws which relate to the sexual organs.

Wide observation has convinced us that a great many of the back-aches, side-aches, and other aches and pains of which girls complain, are attributable to this injurious habit. Much of the nervousness, hysteria, neuralgia, and general worthlessness of girls originates in this cause alone.

The period of puberty is one at which thousands of girls break down in health. The constitution, already weakened by a debilitating, debasing vice, is not prepared for the strain, and the poor victim drops into a premature grave.

Signs of Self-Abuse in Girls

Mothers should always be on the alert to detect the first evidences of this vice in their daughters, since later nothing but almighty power seems competent to loosen its grasp. The only positive evidence is detection of the child in the act. A suspected child should be watched under all circumstances with unceasing vigilance.

[But] aside from positive evidence, there are other signs which may lead to the discovery of positive evidence.

• *A marked change in disposition.* When a girl who has been truthful, happy, obliging, gentle, and confiding, becomes peevish, irritable, morose, and disobedient, she is under the influence of some foul blight.

• *Loss of memory and loss of the love for study.* The nervous forces are weakened, giving place to mental weakness and inactivity.

• *Unnatural boldness in a little girl.* If she has previously been reserved, this is just ground for the suspicion of secret vice.

• *A forward or loose manner in company with little boys.* Girls addicted to this habit are guilty of the most wanton conduct.

• *Languor and lassitude.* In a girl who has possessed a marked degree of activity and energy, this should give rise to earnest solicitude on the part of the mother for the physical and moral condition of her child.

• *An unnatural appetite.* Sometimes children will show an excessive fondness for

and enjoyable means of obtaining release of sex tensions. Other claimed advantages include relief from boredom and loneliness, help in falling asleep, a greater sense of self-control, and a greater feeling of independence.

Females especially may find masturbation a highly effective method for attaining as many orgasms as they need for satiation. Kinsey (1953) and Masters and Johnson (1966) have noted that females can attain more intense orgasms with greater rapidity and with far greater reliability through masturbation than from partner-induced stimulation. This observation has recently been applied in the treatment of women suffering from orgasmic deficiency. Marquis (1970) has recommended the deliberate use of masturbation by women who have never experienced an orgasm. In this way, these women become familiar with the sensation of orgasm. Once they realize they are capable of this experience and have learned to recognize its occurrence, their inhibitory fear of anticipated failure is reduced and their newfound confidence may be transferred to intercourse.

mustard, pepper, vinegar, and spices. Little girls who are very fond of cloves are likely to be depraved in other respects.

• *The presence of leukorrhoca.* Self-abuse occasions a frequently recurring congestion of the parts, together with the mechanical irritation accompanying the habit

• *Ulceration about the roots of the nails.* This especially affects one or both of the first two fingers of the hand, the irritation of the fingers being occasioned by the acrid vaginal discharge.

• *Biting the fingernails.* The irritation of the fingers, which gives rise to the habit of biting nails, grows out of the irritable condition of the nails mentioned above.

• *The expession of the eyes.* The dull, lusterless eye, surrounded by a dark ring, tells the tale of sin.

• *Palpitations of the heart, hysteria, nervousness, St. Vitus's dance, epilepsy, and incontinence of urine, giving rise to wetting the bed.*

How to Cure Vicious Habits

The habit of self-pollution is one which when thoroughly established, is by no means easily broken. The victim of this most terrible vice is held in the most abject slavery, the iron fetters of habit daily closing the prisoner more and more tightly in their grasp. The effect is to weaken the moral sense perhaps more rapidly than any other vice, until there is little left in the child's character to which an appeal can be made.

The mother should first carefully set before the child the exceeding sinfulness of the habit, its loathsomeness and vileness, and the horrible consequences which follow in its wake. But in most cases, the evil is not so easily mastered. The little girl should be kept under constant observation every moment of her waking hours. Care should be taken that the child does not feign sleep for the purpose of gaining an opportunity to avoid observation.

It is much more difficult to cure this soul-destroying vice in girls than in boys. They are seldom as ready to confess their guilt as are boys, and then are less easily influenced by a portrayal of its terrible consequences. Sleepless vigilance must be coupled with the most persevering patience.

In obstinate cases, severe means must be adopted. We were once obliged after every other measure had failed, to perform a surgical operation [clitoridectomy] before we were able to break the habit in the case of a girl of eight or ten years who had become addicted to the vice to a most extraordinary degree.

FETISHISM

The technical distinction between partialism and fetishism illustrates the continuity of variations in sex behavior. Partialism, which is commonly noted in normal males, is an exaggerated sex interest in some part of the female anatomy. For example, a male may be especially aroused by large breasts, small hands, or legs of a certain shape. Women who have that specific physical trait are preferred to others even though they might be less attractive in other respects. Male fetishists, on the other hand, are turned on by articles of female attire, such as bras, panties, stockings, shoes, and other inanimate objects. Some are content simply to collect these articles and use them in their masturbatory activities. Their preference for a particular kind of garment that has actually been worn by a woman may result in their breaking into houses or apartments to steal the coveted objects. Others are interested in more direct female contact, provided the female is wearing the fetish object or the male is holding it in his hand. Thus a man may insist that his sex partner wear a raincoat or high-heeled shoes while he is having intercourse with her. Without the fetish he may be impotent or incapable of having an orgasm.

The explanation of this behavior in terms of learning theory is that the fetish object is somehow associated in the man's mind with a gratifying early sex experience. Initially the object may have had special significance because it was in the stimulus field at the moment of his first gratifying sex experience with a female. Each subsequent repetition of the pairing of the fetish with a sex response reinforces the bond and increases its effectiveness as a stimulus or symbol. Psychoanalysts interpret fetishes as defenses against castration anxiety or against the anxiety experienced by the child when he is separated from his mother. Objects worn by the mother are used by the son to maintain union with her.

Greenacre (1970) has proposed that the fetish (some article of the mother's clothing) may serve as a transition object that connects the son with the mother and is external to both. The fetish may be rooted in the oedipal stage but generally it is manifested during the latency period or early adolescence. The mixed-up erotic son-mother relationship may be expressed in the use of the mother's pants by the son while masturbating. There is a possibility that fetishists who seek the intensive type of therapy provided by psychoanalysis are a select group. Case studies reported by psychoanalysts indicate that fetishism is typically associated with a wide range of other unusual sex behaviors.

SADISM AND MASOCHISM

In the heat of heterosexual passion, males and females may engage in mild biting, scratching, or pinching. When enjoyed by both, sex may include a certain amount of rough play. Those who indulge in fantasies during intercourse may occasionally imagine dramatic scenes in which they play the role of attacker, victim, or both. These aggressive components of sex are normal. The terms "sadism" and "masochism" refer to more extreme behavior in which inflicting or experiencing pain is as important as the sex act and in fact may be substituted for it.

Sadism and masochism frequently go together. The partners may take turns whipping and being whipped, burning and being burned by a lighted cigarette, or otherwise torturing and being tortured. Humiliating and degrading acts may be substituted for physical pain. Cooperative partners are usually sought in full-service houses of prostitution, which include specialists in these activities. In today's more open society, interested parties may advertise in special magazines for "bondage and discipline" partners. The sex act may involve the use of costumes and special equipment. Relatively few individuals engage in extreme sado-masochistic behavior. A generous estimate is that about 5 percent of males and females engage in one or two mild experiences out of curiosity. The number of those who prefer and persist in such activities appears to be less than 1 percent.

The fusion of aggression and sexuality has long been recognized by students of animal as well as human behavior, but the relationship remains an unsolved enigma. Especially among birds, courting rituals often bear such a striking resemblance to aggressive behavior that the courting male must add special signals to reassure the female that his intent is not really hostile. Normal heterosexual behavior between human beings also resembles aggressive behavior to the untutored eye. It is common for children who inadvertently witness intercourse between their parents to interpret it as a physical attack by the father on the mother. Thus, although the etiology of sadism and masochism is difficult to unravel, they appear to be two more examples of normal reactions carried to deviant extremes.

SEX ROLE PROBLEMS

Although often confused with one another, homosexuality, transsexuality and transvestism are three separate forms of atypical sex behavior. Their common feature, which accounts for much of the confusion, is that in all three conditions the sex role of the person is at variance with his or her sex gender. Homosexuals prefer sex partners of their own gender. Transsexuals also find members of their own gender to be sexually more attractive but for different reasons. They firmly believe that they are normal heterosexual persons who by a quirk of nature have been assigned "wrong" external sex organs and inappropriate secondary sex characteristics. The female transsexual feels she is a male in all respects except her physical self. The male transsexual feels he is a female trapped in a male body. The transvestite male gets his erotic pleasure from dressing in female attire.

The common practice of classifying all three kinds of behavior as deviations in sex identity is misleading. The persons concerned do exhibit sex behavior that is more characteristic of members of the opposite gender, but the deviation is in their sex role rather than in their sex identity. The male homosexual knows he is a male, thinks of himself as a male, and wants to be regarded and treated by others as a male person whose sexual orientation differs from that of most men. The lesbian is similarly aware of her sex gender. She may feel that her life would be easier if she had the same sex interests as other women but she experiences no confusion or conflict with respect to her personal sex identity. The inner torment of the transsexual male is mainly due to his acute awareness of the discrepancy between his true sex identity and his contrasting anatomy. He is absolutely convinced that apart from his masculine physical characteristics he is a female person. The transsexual female is equally convinced that she is a male person with an unwanted female body. The transvestite male knows he is a male, wants to be a male, and functions adequately as a male in his sex relations with women.

HOMOSEXUALITY

Homosexuality is the most prevalent and the most controversial of the sex variations and deviations. It has also been the most extensively studied. Weinberg and Bell (1972) have compiled an annotated bibliography of more than twelve hundred publications dealing with some aspect of this baffling problem. Some of the confusion associated with the subject is semantic. The prefix "homo" is derived from a Greek word meaning "the same," so "homosexual" is equally applicable to sex activities between men or between women. Female homosexuals are more generally referred to as *lesbians*, a name derived from the homosexual practices of the Greek poetress Sappho (ca. 600 B.C.) and her coterie of young women on the island of Lesbos. The adjective "homosexual" has different connotations when applied to (1) specific acts, (2) a person's sex orientation, or (3) an individual's total sex behavior.

A homosexual act may be defined as any physical act between members of the same gender that is perceived as sexual in nature by one or both partners. In societies where men or women kiss and embrace one another as a friendly gesture on meeting, their behavior is not homosexual, unless there is additional erotic intent or response. The occurrence of orgasm is confirmatory but not essential. The homosexual act may consist of exhibitionism, kissing, general body contact, oral or manual manipulation of the partner's genitalia, or anal intercourse.

The fact that an individual engages in one or more homosexual acts does not make him or her a homosexual person. If the person's basic orientation is heterosexual and members of the same sex are used as substitutes for heterosexual sex objects for reasons of expediency or convenience, the individual is and remains a heterosexual. Most of the homosexual experiences of preadolescents, students in sex-segregated schools, prisoners, and others isolated for long periods from members of the opposite sex fall in this category. Given opportunity and choice, these individuals prefer partners of the opposite sex. Heterosexual persons may also occasionally engage in incidental homosexual behavior out of curiosity, in search of thrills, while under the influence of alcohol, or when inadvertently caught in a demanding situation.

The designation of a person's sex orientation as homosexual is another matter. Persons so described may or may not engage in overt homosexual acts. The situation is analogous to that of men or women who are definitely heterosexual in their orientation but who from choice, religious commitment, or lack of opportunity have no significant direct sex experiences with members of the opposite sex. What is meant by a homosexual orientation is that the individual is sexually attracted to persons of the same sex, desires physical contact with them, and finds such experiences to be erotically exciting and gratifying. For these individuals, romance and love are literally unisexed. They may enjoy the company and friendship of the opposite sex, but intimate physical contacts are flat or repugnant.

Typically the homosexual orientation starts before puberty. Early adolescent fantasies usually have a homosexual content. Because of social pressures, the individual may deny or repress his inclinations and evade facing the fact that he is "different" until adulthood or even middle age. It is not uncommon for homosexuals to marry, have children, and then decide that the time has come to be their real selves. To complicate matters, there are degrees of homosexual orientation. Some individuals are exclusively or predominantly homosexual, others are bisexual or mildly homosexual.

This variation in degree brings us to the third meaning, which is concerned with the relative predominance of homosexual outlets in the total sex behavior of the person at any particular period in his or her life. Kinsey's figures indicate that 50 percent of males and 25 percent of females have one or more psychological or physical homosexual responses after puberty. Thirty-seven percent of males and 13 percent of females have overt homosexual contacts to the point of orgasm. About 4 percent of white males and 1 to 3 percent of single females are exclusively homosexual in their psychological responses and overt experiences.

Misconceptions about Homosexuality

Contrary to popular belief, it is impossible to differentiate homosexuals on the basis of their appearance, style of dress, or mannerisms. A small proportion of male homosexuals, referred to as "queens," are effeminate in manner and may on occasion wear female attire (appearing "in drag"). These individuals, who produce an unfavorable public image for the group, are frowned upon by their peers. Most male homosexuals are conventionally masculine in appearance and behavior. Many prefer highly masculine types as partners. Some lesbians, referred to as "butches," adopt masculine styles of behavior; others, known as "femmes," are feminine in appearance and personality. Butches tend to prefer femmes as partners; femmes may or may not prefer butches.

A second related misconception is the identification of certain occupations with homosexuality. Some male hairdressers, masseurs, interior decorators, poets, and artists are homosexual in their orientation; others are not. A homosexual may be a doctor, lawyer, merchant, or thief. He may also be a steelworker, minister, professional athlete, policeman, lumberjack, or psychologist. Lesbians are also found in all occupations.

A third misconception is that the individual homosexual consistently plays either an active or a passive role. He may, but by no means necessarily. It is more usual for the homosexual to play alternating roles, sometimes being the active partner, at other times or with other persons assuming the passive role.

A fourth misconception is that homosexual behavior is always a matter of choice: the homosexual simply prefers partners of his own sex. This seems to be true of some homosexuals, but not of all. The individual who turns to members of his own sex for sexual and emotional satisfaction because he is unable to respond to the opposite sex, for whatever reason, cannot be said to have a choice.

A fifth misconception has to do with the stereotype of the male homosexual who is constantly on the prowl in public toilets and gay bars. This type does exist, but the same can be said of certain heterosexual young men who are constantly on the lookout for pickups in "straight" bars and other public places. Neither is representative of the total male homosexual or heterosexual population. Most "closet" homosexuals lead a very restricted sex life. Male as well as female homosexuals may establish what is essentially a stable marital relationship with a congenial person of the same sex. Their quiet, inconspicuous life

KINSEY'S HETEROSEXUAL-HOMOSEXUAL RATING SCALE

Rating	Description	Percent of Total Population at Age 25 White Male
0	Exclusively heterosexual with no psychological or overt homosexual reactions	79
1	Predominantly heterosexual with single incidental homosexual experience	4
2	Predominantly heterosexual in orientation and response, but with some homosexual experiences	5
3	Equally heterosexual and homosexual	3
4	Predominantly homosexual, but more than incidentally heterosexual in activity and erotic response to members of the opposite sex	2
5	Predominantly homosexual, with only occasional experience with or response to members of the opposite sex	2
6	Exclusively homosexual	3

SOURCE: Kinsey (1948).

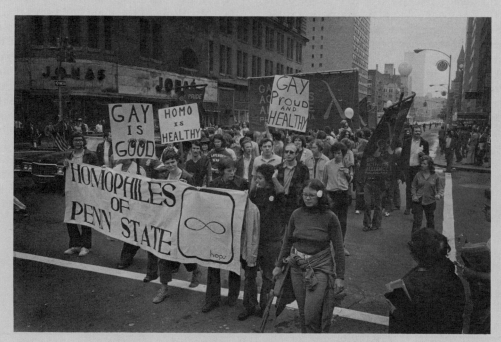

A street demonstration that reflects the more open contemporary attitude toward homosexuality.

style may be unnoticed or casually accepted in the community.

A sixth misconception is that homosexuality is contagious. Persons who associate with known homosexuals may be suspected of having similar inclinations. However, the fear that exposure to or association with homosexuals will result in the conversion of heterosexuals is as naïve as the idea that the cure for homosexuality is marriage.

Changing Social Attitudes

No contemporary society accepts homosexuality as normal behavior. The main effect of recent changes has been the emergence of a more tolerant attitude toward those who differ from the norm in their sex orientation. More specifically, society has become more understanding and somewhat more accepting of the right of the homosexual to live his own sex life without being branded as a criminal, a moral degenerate, or a mentally ill person. Considerable progress has also been made in decreasing the risk that disclosure will automatically result in social ostracism, discrimination, or loss of employment. The cultural and legal rules regulating heterosexual behavior, of course, also apply to homosexuals. Sex relations must be confined to consenting adults and conducted with regard for the sensibilities of others. Open solicitation, public lewdness, rape, child molestation, and related offenses by homosexuals are prohibited. Homosexuals engaging in such behavior are still subject to arrest, imprisonment, or compulsory psychiatric treatment. On the other hand, police harassment of "law-abiding" homosexuals has generally been discontinued in most western countries, including the United States. This change is mainly of importance to men. Lesbians have historically been free of criminal arrest or prosecution.

The improvement in society's attitudes

toward the homosexual is relative. Firmly established cultural stereotypes are not easily changed. College students, who might be expected to be most responsive to the new sex climate, still retain a negative attitude toward homosexuals. A 1974 report by Steffensmeier and Steffensmeier showed that two-thirds of college students agree with the stereotype that homosexuals are psychologically disturbed or sick. Twenty percent of the female and 38 percent of the male students see homosexuals as dangerous. The more the students agree with the "sick" and "dangerous" stereotypes, the more they reject homosexuals. Consistent with earlier studies, male and female students were found to be far more intolerant of male than of female homosexuals. Male students especially reject male homosexuals. The authors of this report conclude that continued social rejection and condemnation of the "developing" homosexual may accentuate his feelings of failure, shame, and low self-esteem. Restricted interaction with others is apt to push him into a homosexual subculture with consequent intensification, perpetuation, and self-acceptance of his deviant behavior.

Female Homosexuals

Kenyon (1966a, 1966b) and Saghir and Robins (1969) have conducted comprehensive studies of female homosexuals living in the community. Subjects were selected on the basis of membership in homophile (homosexual) organizations. Women who join such organizations are not necessarily representative of the total lesbian population and may differ in significant ways from lesbians who prefer anonymity; but with this caveat we can gain useful insights from these investigators' findings.

1. Homosexual emotional attachments, awareness, and experience typically occurred before adolescence. The pattern of orientation was well established by the end of adolescence.

2. About two-thirds had had sexual intercourse with men. Most gave it up as unsatisfactory after a few tries.

3. About 25 percent had been married, but with rare exceptions these marriages soon terminated in divorce.

4. About one-half engaged in masturbation when they were not involved in homosexual affairs.

5. The most common homosexual practice was mutual manual stimulation of the genitals. Cunnilingus ranked second. Other practices, which were infrequent, included insertion of an object into the partner's vagina, full body contact, and the kissing and caressing that are common among heterosexual couples.

6. Homosexual women tended to be more successful than homosexual men in establishing relationships that lasted a year or more—frequently much more. As long as the affairs lasted, the overwhelming majority were faithful to each other.

7. Lesbians reported poor relationships with their parents more often than control groups of "straight" women, and a higher proportion of lesbians reported unhappy childhoods.

8. Histories of psychopathology and of homosexuality were more frequent in the families of lesbians than in those of control subjects. A substantial number of lesbians reported periodic depressive moods.

9. Twenty percent of the lesbians reported that they believed they had not been brought up and treated as girls by their parents. None of the control subjects made such a report.

10. Seduction during early childhood appeared to be unrelated to subsequent homosexuality.

Male Homosexuals

The composite clinical portrait that emerges from studies of male homosexuals is similar in some respects to that of lesbians, but there are several differences. Research studies reported by Bieber (1967), Apperson and McAdoo (1968), and Saghir and his associates (1969, 1970) indicate the following:

1. Homosexual self-identity and orientation start before adolescence and are

well established by the end of adolescence. About two-thirds never experience heterosexual fantasies.

2. Homosexual men report extremely active sex lives. The usual pattern is four or more sexual encounters with other males each week, supplemented by masturbation four or more times per week.

3. Homosexuals tend to be promiscuous and unfaithful. Their affairs are largely casual and impersonal—pickup contacts that end when the sex act is completed. Relationships lasting more than a year occur, but they are usually characterized by much casual infidelity. There are, of course, exceptions. Love affairs between homosexual men, as among lesbians, may be as affectionate and enduring as those of heterosexual persons.

4. Before the age of fifteen, mutual masturbation is the most common practice. After fifteen, fellatio occurs most frequently. Next in order of frequency at the adult level is anal intercourse.

5. A considerably smaller percentage of homosexual men than homosexual women have had heterosexual experiences or have tried marriage. Fear of impotence in heterosexual relationships or complete lack of sexual response to women may account for this difference.

6. About an equal number of male and female homosexuals have received therapy (roughly 20 percent), generally without success. Depressive reactions and excessive drinking tend to be more characteristic of homosexual than control subjects.

7. Childhood seduction by adult males does not appear to be an important contributory factor.

8. The majority of the mothers of male homosexuals are described as overly possessive, overly controlling, seductive, and emasculating. The fathers of homosexuals are described as distant, cold, and often hostile. As children, homosexual men tended to be submissive and closely involved emotionally with their mothers. Fathers were usually feared and disliked. Not all studies agree with these parental characteristics; fathers may be strong, lov-

ing persons and mothers may not fit the indicated stereotype.

The Search for Causes

The heterogeneity of the homosexual population makes it extremely difficult to conduct meaningful research into the causes of this behavior. As previously noted, many persons who engage in homosexual acts are basically heterosexual or bisexual in their orientation. The frequency of homosexual acts may range from one or two experiences to several hundred. A person may be exclusively homosexual for a period of years and then switch to heterosexuality, or vice versa. A small percentage of males and a considerably smaller percentage of females are exclusively or predominantly homosexual most of their lives, but there is no way of identifying beforehand who will remain exclusively homosexual. Given this situation, it is not surprising that research has been more successful in demonstrating the absence than the presence of significant differences between homosexual and heterosexual persons. Where differences have been noted, the data have been inconsistent and inconclusive.

Heredity. No chromosomal abnormalities have been found to be associated with homosexual behavior. The importance of genetic factors has been examined by comparing concordance rates among MZ and DZ twins for homosexual behavior. In six separate studies, all conducted with male subjects, the median concordance rate (both co-twins homosexual) is 50 percent for MZ and 14 percent for DZ twin pairs (Rosenthal, 1970). The difference is impressive, but difficult to interpret. The small number of subjects examined in most studies introduces the possibility of sampling errors. The grand total of subjects in all six studies was fifty-five MZ and thirty-nine DZ twins. Many of the homosexual subjects were located in mental hospitals or prisons. In these cases the higher MZ than DZ concordance rate for homosexuality may have been mainly due to some

A homosexual marriage ceremony in Los Angeles.

more fundamental psychopathology. The most that the researchers themselves have claimed is that genetic imbalances may increase vulnerability to whatever environmental factors may be associated with the development of a homosexual orientation. In short, the explanation for homosexuality is the same as for heterosexuality, i.e., the interaction of genetic and environmental factors (Kallmann, 1952; Heston and Shields, 1968).

Biochemistry. The hypothesis that homosexual males may be deficient in male sex hormones has been investigated by comparing the level of glandular secretions (plasma testosterone) of homosexual and heterosexual males. The results have been inconsistent. Some investigators have noted no differences; others have reported higher or lower testosterone levels in homosexuals (Brodie et al., 1974). Earlier attempts to redirect the sex orientation of homosexual men by injecting them with male sex hormones have proven ineffective. This type of hormonal treatment has been discontinued because it may create added difficulties by increasing the sex drive without altering the homosexual aim.

Parent-child relations. Homosexual sons and daughters have all types of parents and come from all kinds of homes. When a father is cold, distant, and hostile and the mother is seductive, overcontrolling, and emasculating, a son may find little attraction in becoming like his father and looking forward to marrying someone like his mother. Mother-daughter conflict, combined with an unsatisfactory father figure or a disruptive home situation, might turn a girl against the conventional female role.

For women who object to the culture-imposed inferior status of females, homosexuality may be a way out. In the words of Simone de Beauvoir, the author of *The Second Sex*, "Homosexuality can be for a woman a mode of flight from her situation or a way of accepting it." Data on the rejection of the traditional heterosexual role because of adverse parent-child relations or family disturbances are more suggestive than conclusive. The parents of homosexual offspring also rear heterosexual children. The pathogenic family factors that are often associated with homosexuality are also characteristic of other forms of psychopathology, and are also noted in children who find their way to normality.

Socioeconomic factors. On this point the evidence is unequivocal. The distribution of homosexuality in the population is truly democratic. Homosexuals are found in all ethnic and social classes, among the educated and uneducated, the poor and the wealthy, and in all conceivable occupations (Kinsey, 1948, 1953).

Treatment

As long as the homosexual is free of significant personal or social conflicts, there is no obvious need for therapy. Therapeutic intervention under such circumstances may actually be undesirable. When a homosexual seeks therapy because of subjective distress or is forced to do so by social pressure, most therapists today leave the critical issue of the goal of therapy up to the patient. If he desires to move in the direction of heterosexuality, the therapist will try to help him do so. On the other hand, the therapist is equally willing to help him accept his homosexuality or modify the overt expression of his continuing homosexual behavior so that his actions do not bring him into open conflict with society. These options are both humane and practical. Sex orientation cannot be redirected without the voluntary and full cooperation of the individual. Even when he is motivated to shift to heterosexuality, the results are unimpressive. Reported outcome figures indicate that from one-fourth to one-third of homosexuals

treated for two or more years with psychoanalysis (Bieber et al., 1962) or group psychotherapy (Hadden, 1972) become exclusively heterosexual. These figures probably err on the side of optimism, since "successful" outcomes were based on the impressions of the therapist and information supplied by the patient at the close of therapy. No follow-up data are available. All patients who improved had had prior heterosexual experiences; many were bisexuals. Changes from exclusive homosexuality to exclusive heterosexuality are extremely rare.

It is too early to say whether aversive conditioning is more effective in "converting" willing and cooperative homosexuals. Data have so far been restricted to individual case reports and small selected samples. No long-term follow-up studies have been reported. Two main procedures have been used. One consists in showing a male subject pictures of attractive nude males. As soon as he reports or exhibits signs of erotic arousal he is given a mild shock that serves as the aversive stimulus. The shock is terminated when the picture of the nude male is replaced by a picture of an attractive nude female (Rachman and Teasdale, 1969).

The second procedure is intended to avoid objections to the use of shock. There are limits to the amount of shock that can ethically be administered in the guise of therapy, yet if the shock is too mild it may lose its aversive significance. K. L. Mandel (1970) has suggested an alternative aversive stimulus for use with male homosexuals. The subject is first shown a color slide of a very attractive nude male. As soon as he indicates that he feels sexual arousal, the therapist superimposes another image on the first from a second projector. The patient is asked to focus his attention on those regions of the body that are now covered with sores, and to signal when the picture has aroused a feeling of disgust. At his signal the juxtaposed images are removed from the screen and replaced by a color slide showing an attractive nude woman. The patient is asked to relax and

TRANSSEXUALITY

concentrate on the "relief" stimulus. If the patient shows no erotic feelings within a minute, the picture of the woman is removed. If arousal occurs, the heterosexual stimulus is removed after a few seconds.

In those cases where the subject opts to remain homosexual and desires help to become better adjusted, therapeutic outcome may be more favorable. For various reasons, therapists have been reluctant to report either successes or failures in this area. A reasonable inference is that the effectiveness of therapy will depend in great measure on whether daily life experiences reinforce or undo therapeutic gains.

TRANSSEXUALITY

Transsexualism represents a deviance in sex role. The individual has the physical attributes of one gender but is convinced that his feelings, desires, interests, and sex orientation are those of a person of the opposite sex. The fact that a person with male physical characteristics is interested in male lovers does not mean he is homosexual; his orientation is actually heterosexual since he thinks of himself as female (and the reverse, for female transsexual). This strange confusion is rare in either sex, but appears to be more common among males than females. The incidence has not been definitely established. A rough estimate is that about 1 per 100,000 males in the general population and 1 per 400,000 females are sufficiently disturbed by their misidentification in sex gender to seek corrective surgery. Clinical studies of transsexuals have been reported by Pauly (1968), Green and Money (1969), Baker (1969), and Money (1972).

The male transsexual has the standard anatomical, biological, and hormonal equipment of his sex. From early childhood, however, he perceives himself as a female. In contrast to the homosexual male, who is interested in his male sex organ and derives pleasure from its use and admiration

by other males, the transsexual is ashamed of his male organ. He wants to be a female, and indeed believes that in all essential respects, except for a few unfortunate anatomical details, he *is* a female. In sexual relations with males, the transsexual male always assumes the receptor role. Anal intercourse is regarded as a substitute for vaginal intercourse. The transsexual male prefers to have sexual relations with non-homosexual men. In his erotic fantasies he may visualize himself with large breasts, a vagina, long hair, and feminine body contours. Since the male organ is denied, transsexual males rarely masturbate, and may not have erections while having sexual relations with males. Stimulation of the penis by sex partners is unpleasant and undesired. During sex play the transsexual male attempts to minimize any attention his partner may focus on the rejected organ. The personality profiles of male transsexuals are more typical of women in our society than of men. They have interests that the culture identifies as feminine, and describe themselves as submissive rather than aggressive (Money and Primrose, 1968).

The female transsexual is indistinguishable in physical appearance and biochemistry from other females. However, she thinks of herself as a male in all characteristics except for the unfortunate presence of breasts and female sex and reproductive organs. Most transsexual women trace their male self-image back to their preschool years. As children most of them were tomboys, enjoyed fighting, and preferred boys' games and activities. As they grew up they found they had little interest in boys but were sexually attracted to females. In their love-making as adolescents and adults, they consistently preferred the more aggressive male role in their relationships with female partners. As compared with homosexual women, who are comfortable with and may take pride in their feminine bodies, the female transsexuals are ashamed of their breasts and try to minimize their size. In their sex fantasies, female transsexuals see themselves as male, flat-chested, broad-shouldered, and complete with penis (Money and Brennan, 1968).

Interpretation

Three related explanations have been advanced. One is that hormonal disturbances during the prenatal period are responsible for the confusion in sex gender. The second is sex role confusion resulting from the treatment of girls as boys and of boys as girls by their parents during infancy and early childhood. A third explanation is that normal individual variations may account for these extreme conditions. Studies of sex differences in temperament and interests have demonstrated that males show wide individual variations in traits defined as masculine and that women differ markedly in the degree to which they exhibit traits defined as feminine. Some men are more "feminine" than most women and vice versa. Transsexual individuals may thus be understood as persons in the overlapping middle area of the male-female continuum who are highly motivated to do something about their ambiguous sex status. Prenatal hormonal imbalance and parental reinforcement of cross-sexual identity may contribute to these extreme variations in temperament and interests.

Treatment

Psychotherapeutic and counseling procedures aimed at leading the transsexual to accept the gender identity of his anatomy are of little value. What these individuals want and seek is a physical change in which their anatomy will correspond with their gender preference. Male transsexuals want to be converted to females and female transsexuals want to become males. Both of these radical changes can be produced through surgery. The first sex change operation was performed in Europe about 1930. Public interest in the operation dates from 1952, when the conversion of George to Christine Jorgensen was widely publicized in the newspapers. Sex change surgery in the United States started about 1965 at Johns Hopkins Hospital, and other university hospitals throughout the country now provide this service. The exact number of operations performed in the United States is unknown. A rough estimate is that about 500 males and 250 females change their sex anatomy each year.

The recommended psychiatric and medical procedure is to have applicants wait a year before making a final decision on surgery. During the waiting period applicants are given hormonal treatment to effect secondary sex changes. Males receive estrogen and progestin injections to enlarge the breasts and soften the skin. Females receive androgen to deepen the voice and stimulate beard growth. Applicants for surgery are encouraged to try out their desired sex role for a year or two prior to the irreversible operation. Men are urged to dress as women, wear makeup, and live and work as women. Women are encouraged to adopt the dress and work patterns of men. If the trial period is successful and there are no contrary indications, surgery may be performed.

In the conversion of a male to a female, the penis and testicles are amputated and an artificial vagina is created. When tissues are taken from the scrotum and the penis in creating the artificial vagina, the person may retain local erotic sensitivity so that the sensation of orgasm is possible.

The conversion from female to male is more difficult. The obvious female symbols can be eliminated through removal of the breasts and a hysterectomy. The difficulty comes in providing the newly created male with an adequately functioning penis. By freeing the clitoris from its connective tissues it is sometimes possible to provide the former female with a miniature penis. An artificial penis may be created by skin grafts and silicone injections, but it is too soft for intercourse. Female transsexuals are advised to forgo the complicated surgery required to create an artificial penis and to be satisfied with a strapped-on dildo for use in intercourse.

CONUNDRUM: THE CASE OF
JAMES/JAN MORRIS

In an autobiographical book, appropriately entitled *Conundrum*, Jan Morris (1974) described with candor, insight, and humor the dilemma of being a transsexual and the process of becoming a woman after living to middle age as a man. In her former male existence as James Morris, "she" had a distinguished career as a soldier, globetrotting correspondent, and writer. As a reporter attached to Edmund Hillary's group, James attained fame by scooping the world on the conquest of Mount Everest. But James first realized at the age of four that he should really be a girl and had been born in the wrong body. For the next twenty years he kept this thought a personal secret, shared only with God. He ended his nightly prayers during childhood with the plea, "Please, God, make me a girl."

Long before he was aware of the implications of his dilemma, he sensed that he was different from others, that there was a piece missing in his makeup. He was at a loss to explain his condition. He had a happy childhood and had not been treated as a girl during infancy. He did not look or act effeminate, but his schoolmates and later his army mates sensed his femininity and went out of their way to be protective toward him. As a young man he enjoyed the company of girls but had no desire to go to bed with them. He was unable to understand the importance men gave to the sex act. Intercourse seemed to him a reproductive device. At a higher level it represented a symbolic act of absolute interdependence, a kind of sacrifice. In his middle twenties he fell completely in love and married a most understanding woman. Love, marriage, and a family of five children (one daughter died early) saved him from social isolation and self-destruction.

The sense of purpose provided by marriage and family did not suffice to still his restless quest for completeness, for unity of gender and sex. With increasing age, episodes of melancholy became more severe; he was troubled with fierce migraine attacks and became more preoccupied with thoughts of suicide. His devotion and responsibility to his family precluded an operation while the children were still young. However something had to be done. At thirty-five he started to take massive doses of female sex hormones. Over the next ten years the hormone treatment gradually led to the development of secondary female sex characteristics. During the latter years of this transition period he was literally half male and half female. He had the soft skin and breasts of a woman and the offensive sex organs of a male. Sometimes he dressed and lived as a woman and at other times as a man. At age forty-six he could wait no longer and arranged for surgery, followed soon thereafter by divorce.

The operation closed the door on maleness and opened wide the door to womanhood. James became Jan on passport, social security papers, driver's license, bankbooks, and other identity documents. Jan started to emerge as a person and as a woman in her own right. Compared with James, she had more variable moods, cried more easily, was less forceful, more passive, and more self-contained. The more people reacted to her as a woman, the more womanly she became. Her experiences confirm the hypothesis that the perceptions others have of us soon shape our self-perception. If it was assumed that she was incompetent in backing a car, she became incompetent. An object too heavy for a woman to lift became too heavy an object. The more men expected her to be helpless and uninformed, the more she obliged by acting the part. Her interest in large world affairs declined and she became more interested in people, in clothes, and incidental day-to-day experiences. Her long dormant sex urges were revived.

At the time she wrote her autobiography, she felt attracted to men and inordinately pleased with their interest in her. She had no immediate plans for marriage. She was still closely attached to, loved, and admired her former wife, with whom she had established a sister-in-law relationship. Jan is now the loving aunt of children "he" fathered when still James.

Most transsexuals who have undergone a conversion operation have been pleased with the results. Particularly in the case of males, the completeness of the anatomical change permits the person to lead a fairly complete life as a female. Most states today permit males who have had the operation to change their names legally and amend their birth certicates so their gender is indicated as female. Except for her inability to bear children, the female can function as a wife, and she can be a mother to adopted children. Transsexual females who have changed their sex gender may also legally change their names and sex identity and establish households in which their role is that of husband and father of adopted children.

What drives the transsexual relentlessly to the operating table? Neither sex gratification nor preference for the life style of the opposite gender is a satisfactory explanation. These objectives could be attained without surgery through homosexual activities and transvestism. The true transsexual finds homosexuality repugnant and derives no pleasure from wearing the clothes of the other sex. The answer is to be found in the tenets of existentialism for wholeness, meaning, and authenticity. The transsexual sees himself as a divided self. His half male, half female status makes him a nonperson, excluded from full membership in either the male or the female world. He also sees himself as a phony or an impostor. He knows beyond a shadow of a doubt that he is a woman who is being untrue to himself and deceiving others by passing himself off as a male. His agonizing conflict can be solved only through hormone treatment and surgery. These drastic measures are his only hope for reconciling his true gender with his anatomy and uniting in a harmonious whole his body and soul.

There is obviously no guarantee that sex reassignment will bring fulfillment and happiness. Men and women whose gender matches their anatomy also have their share of disappointment and problems. The transsexual is not deterred by the realization that he may not be any happier after the operation or that the sex change may result in professional, economic and social penalties. The overriding compulsion to be made whole justifies the risk to life, the pain, the body mutilation, the social censure, and even the breakup of the family in the case of married persons.

TRANSVESTISM

Transvestism is the practice of wearing the clothing of the opposite sex. Since the label is rarely applied to females, we shall limit our discussion to males who dress in female attitre. A distinction must be made between the transvestite, the homosexual, and the transsexual, all of whom may cross-dress. The homosexual disguises himself in female clothing to be more attractive to the minority of homosexuals who are interested in men who appear feminine. The transsexual dresses as a female because he feels more comfortable wearing apparel consistent with his psychological sex identity; he is not sexually excited by dressing as a woman. The true transvestite is usually masculine in appearance and behavior and heterosexual in his sex identity and orientation. He dresses as a woman because the touch of intimate feminine clothing is sexually stimulating to him.

This behavioral peculiarity is usually isolated, so that it does not interfere with the individual's overall adjustment. The transvestite typically wears female attire only in private, often as part of a masturbation ritual. The transvestite puts on his feminine clothes and then masturbates while looking at himself in a mirror. In effect, he has sexual intercourse with himself. He is male and female, a completely self-sufficient heterosexual unit. After the sex act, he changes back to his usual male clothing and goes about his regular affairs.

Transvestism may start as a fetish. The teenaged boy may use some article of female clothing to provide friction while masturbating. Other articles are gradually

TREATING A TRANSVESTITE: A CASE REPORT

A graduate student who had served successfully in the infantry during the Vietnamese War was 28 at the time he was referred for treatment. His dressing as a woman, which started at age ten, was often associated with fantasies of being captured by a woman, forcibly dressed in a tight-fitting female garment, having his ears pierced and his legs shaved. He referred himself for treatment after a woman friend was shocked and distressed to learn of his behavior.

Treatment was aimed at reversing the masochistic aspects of his fantasy by encouraging more assertive behavior in his relations with women. While relaxed, he was asked to imagine that he was an aggressive male who controlled, dominated, and humiliated a woman. His girl friend cooperated in his greater assertiveness during intercourse. After twenty-nine treatment sessions over a seven month period, he reported no further temptation to dress as a woman and no further masochistic or sadistic fantasies (after Rhoads and Feather, 1974).

added until he has a complete outfit. He always remains aware of his masculinity, however, and his sex experiences are heterosexual. Most transvestites marry and have children, and their peculiarity of dress is usually concealed from the children. Some wives object to their husband's behavior; others apparently do not. The latter may feel less threatened by a husband who comes to bed wearing frilly female clothing, but functions as an adequate male during intercourse. Some transvestites have early histories of being punished by women by being made to dress in girl's clothing (Buckner, 1970; Stoller, 1971).

Studies of the personal characteristics of transvestites indicate that they are less aggressive than normal men, are more restrained, prefer passive activities to excitement and change, and are relatively withdrawn from social involvement. They describe themselves as self-reliant and independent (Bentler and Prince, 1969).

Marks and Gelder (1967) have reported the successful treatment of transvestites by aversion training. Shock was administered to the forearm or leg of the patient while he was in the process of dressing or imagining scenes involving women's clothing. The criterion for the effectiveness of treatment consisted of diminished erection responses to actual or imagined cross-dressing.

EXHIBITIONISM

The exposure of sex organs to persons of the opposite sex for purposes of self-gratification or for provoking an emotional response is a common occurrence. In the course of petting or coitus, lovers often deliberately call attention to their physical sex attributes. Body display is the name of the game for strippers, streakers, topless waitresses, and nudists. These harmless, voluntary, and situationally appropriate examples of exhibitionism are generally accepted as falling within the socially tolerated range of normal variations.

Exhibition is considered a form of sex deviation when the act of exposure is repetitive, appears to be the expression of a compulsive urge, is inappropriate to time and place, and involves subjecting an unwilling and innocent viewer to an offensive and possibly disturbing experience. Deviant exhibitionism is restricted to males. Incidents typically occur on the street or some other public place, where the exhibitionist waits in a secluded spot until he sees a female approaching. He then catches her attention, flashes open his raincoat to reveal his erect penis, and hopefully waits for some response on her part that indicates her awareness of his masculinity. Reactions of shock, fright, or disgust intensify the exhibitionist's pleasure, but her hurried flight is what is most satisfying.

For the exhibitionist, the exposure is the sole desired end. The last thing he wants is for the female to show some positive interest and move toward him. The rules are: "Look, be alarmed, react, but don't come closer or touch." If the female showed signs of interest and started to close the distance gap carefully set by the exhibitionist, nine out of ten would panic and run away. The inappropriateness, maladaptiveness, and disturbing nature of this type of behavior would most likely result in its being considered deviant or at least most peculiar even in societies where nudity is casually accepted. A reasonable inference is that the repeated occurrence of such incidents indicates an underlying personality problem.

One suggested interpretation is that the exhibitionist is a sexually insecure person who feels compelled to prove that he is a man and a heterosexual. On the other hand, he dares not put his manliness to the crucial test of actual physical intimacy. The momentary exposure serves as a convenient compromise solution to this approach-avoidance conflict. The exhibitionist demonstrates that he is a heterosexual male by approaching and confronting females with obvious proof of his maleness. The sexual gratification resulting from this encounter serves to reinforce the act and thereby increases the probability of its repetition. At the same time, the inappropriateness of the setting and the selection of strangers as involuntary accomplices assures the avoidance of direct physical contact. This avoidance of intimate sexual relations may be related to feelings of sexual inadequacy, fear of intercourse, or dislike of females.

The reported incidence of exhibitionism is a function of law-enforcement practices. Mohr et al. (1964) estimate that exhibitionists comprise about one-third of all sex offenders who appear before the courts

"INDECENT EXPOSURE": A CASE REPORT

The patient is a thirty-three year old married man who was referred for treatment following his arrest for "indecent exposure." The patient reported a record of seven similar charges over the years. His early home life was uneventful. He has two older brothers and a younger brother and sister. The family was a close-knit group and he got along well with his parents and siblings. He had average grades in school, leaving at the age of fifteen. While in school he preferred solitary sports such as cycling and swimming. At age fourteen, he suffered a head injury in a cycling accident and was unconscious for two or three days. Sex was never openly discussed in the family, and the patient never saw members of his family undressed. He expressed an intense dislike for nudism and obscene language. He seldom drinks alcoholic beverages.

He married his first wife at age twenty. Prior to marriage he had had no sex experiences. Sex relations with his wife were poor. She had poor health and spent several months each year in the hospital. When at home she nagged the patient incessantly. There were three children born to the couple. At age twenty-five, the patient started his exhibitionism. This coincided with the terminal phase of his wife's illness. At first he exposed himself in more remote areas outside the city, but later he began to use one of the parks within the city. He was caught but discharged.

Following his wife's death, the patient remarried at age twenty-nine. The following

each year. Because of the relative harmlessness of most exhibitionists, many are discharged, so that they constitute a much smaller proportion of all convicted sex offenders. Of the 1,356 convicted male offenders whose case histories were obtained by the Kinsey Institute for Sex Research, only about 10 percent were exhibitionists.

Detailed findings based on the latter group have been reported by Gebhard et year he began exposing himself with increasing frequency. The pattern was always the same. At nightfall he would go to the same place each time, undress in the bushes, and wait until a young woman passed on the other side of the fence. He would then expose himself and feel intensely gratified if the woman responded with evidence of shock. He enjoyed planning the act in advance. During the exposure he felt much more aroused than he did while having intercourse with his wife. On those occasions when the victim was amused or made an aggressive approach he felt frustrated and fled, dressing "on the wing."

At age thirty, he was admitted to a psychiatric unit for assessment. An electroencephalogram at the time was reported normal. A minor tranquilizer was prescribed, but the patient discontinued taking it after discharge. Within a few weeks the patient resorted to his exhibitionistic practices and ignored arrangements for continuing psychiatric help. Despite a regular patrol of relatives he exposed himself every two or three weeks. His wife was apparently unaware of the nature of his behavior. She believed that he occasionally felt a compulsive need to undress and was seen only inadvertently by others. The second wife has had two children by the patient and is stepmother of the other three children.

The present referral for treatment occurred when the patient was thirty-three years old. By this time the police had acted on ten complaints received over the previous two months. On initial examination the patient expressed concern about his ex-

hibitionism and gave a full account of his activities. He described himself as a lonely, isolated person. He thought that as compared with his brothers he was less successful in life. The patient works regularly as a football referee in his spare time. However, he never associates with players after a match, and he never showers with the team. He prefers to go to a hotel and shower alone. He expressed an intense dislike of nudism. He seldom undresses in the presence of his wife, and his children have never seen him undressed. Medical and psychological examinations indicated no evidence of brain damage and no clinical signs of depression. His intelligence was average.

Treatment included aspects of negative practice, implosive therapy, and symptom scheduling. The negative practice technique consisted in having the subject undress on several occasions in the presence of a therapy team of mixed sex. The idea was to extinguish the subject's pleasurable feelings associated with seeing female victims fleeing in alarm. During the undressing sessions, the therapy team was instructed to show no embarrassment but to keep looking at the subject and his genitals in a natural manner. During the exposure sessions the therapy team asked the patient intimate questions to keep his anxiety level high (implosive therapy). Video tape replays of the undressing and other techniques were also used concurrently. After twelve sessions, treatment was discontinued. A follow-up a year later indicated no known recurrence of exposure (After Stevenson and Jones, 1972).

al. (1965). Their main conclusion was: "The exhibitionists do not manifest many salient traits, but those which do exist all point toward some deficiency or difficulty in heterosexual adjustment." Sixty-four percent of the exhibitionists had married, compared with 85 percent of nonoffenders of similar age. Single or married, most exhibitionists relied mainly on masturbation and prostitutes for their sexual outlets. The availability of wives and other females

is not sufficient to offset the compulsive urge to exhibit, which is usually triggered by some emotional stress. The exhibitionist's restriction of his audience to strangers may be regarded as another sign of his feelings of sexual inadequacy. If he exposed himself to his wife or a female friend, she might cooperate sexually and thereby put his masculinity to the test.

Gebhard et al. (1965) agree that most exhibitionists are not dangerous and are "to be pitied rather than feared." They are careful to add that there are exceptions. About one in ten of the convicted exhibitionists in their study group had attempted or seriously contemplated rape.

The results of individual and group psychotherapy with exhibitionists have for the most part been discouraging. Treated and untreated subjects show about the same rate of recidivism (Mohr et al., 1964). The newer behavior therapies are promising, but so far reports have been limited to single cases with brief follow-up. One advantage of behavior therapies is that several techniques may be used concurrently in a kind of shotgun approach. Stevenson and Jones (1972) have reported an interesting application of a combination of behavioral therapy techniques in the successful treatment of an exhibitionist. A brief summary of this particular case is presented above.

VOYEURISM

Voyeurism is considered a mild form of sexual deviation when it involves a person surreptitiously looking into windows, rooms, or other places in the hope of seeing someone undressing or in the nude. Typically the person being observed is a stranger. This type of behavior is generally limited to males, who are known as "peeping Toms."

Voyeurs are a mixed group. Some are adolescent boys who engage in this behavior for a short time prior to heterosexual experiences. More often, voyeurs are older, insecure, lonely men who either have no interest in the sex act or are too fearful of rejection or impotence to approach women directly. As a rule, the peeper confines his activities to looking. If he is fortunate enough to catch sight of an undressing or partially nude woman, he may double his pleasure by masturbating while looking. When the show is over, he silently steals away. A few, who are more aggressive, may tap on the window to attract the atten-

tion of the female, and thereby add to the excitement of the encounter. The term voyeurism is also applied to male or female interest in watching others engaging in sex activities.

ANIMAL CONTACT

Folk tales and myths of females having sex relations with swans, apes, horses, snakes, goats, and other animals are mainly the products of male imagination and wishful thinking. Females rarely fantasize about or actually engage in significant animal contacts. Only one of the 5,793 females interviewed in the Kinsey (1953) study reported actual coitus with an animal. Less than 25 females reported an occasional contact leading to orgasm as the result of masturbating the animal or having the animal manipulate their genitalia with its mouth. For the remaining 3 percent of females who reported one or more experiences of sexual arousal involving animals, contact was limited to general body contact or momentary touching of the animal's genitalia. Contacts were restricted to dogs and cats who were household pets.

Sexual contact with animals by males is more common. About 8 percent reported one or more orgasmic experiences with animals, and for farm-reared boys the figure is 17 percent (Kinsey 1948). Convicted sex offenders, who are a select group, report somewhat higher incidence rates (Gebhard, 1965). Male experience with animals is essentially confined to the teenage period and is completely discontinued as soon as sexual activity with humans is established. Much of the early teenage male experience with animals is prompted by curiosity or humor or is accidental. Where penile insertion occurs for sexual gratification, the act usually has no more psychological significance than the use of the animal as a modified form of masturbation. Availability determines the choice of animal, and the list includes dogs, horses, calves, sheep, and large birds.

Boys and girls who use animals as convenient sex outlets are not unduly disturbed by their behavior at the time of its occurrence. In later years, when they learn of society's condemnation of animal contact, they may have mild feelings of regret or guilt but their main concern is that others should not find out about their childhood misbehavior. From a psychiatric point of view, animal contact is not considered a significant symptom except when an adult, through choice or compulsion, restricts his sexual behavior to repeated animal contacts involving penile penetration of the body of either partner. In such instances, which are extremely rare, the individual usually exhibits other signs of severe psychopathology. The courts, on the other hand, may deal harshly with an adolescent or adult accused of sexually abusing an animal, regardless of the seriousness or frequency of occurrence of the offense.

CHILD MOLESTATION

Society's abhorrence of sex offenses committed by adults against children is more clearly expressed by the designation of "child molestation" than by the technical term *pedophilia*, which, literally translated, means "love of children." Adult exploitation of young children as sex objects is not an act of love. Such behavior is typically used for purely selfish gratification by frustrated males who are too inadequate to compete at the adult level. A large number of offenders against children are mental defectives, psychotics, amoral delinquents, alcoholics and impulsive opportunists. With children under ten, their offenses are usually limited to petting, manipulation of the child's genitals, and exhibitionism. Oral-genital stimulation, coitus, or sodomy may occur or be attempted with older children.

The molesters of young children include a few senile men, but their average age is about thirty-five. The molesters of older children average about ten years younger. In their study of convicted heterosexual offenders against children, Gebhard et al. (1965) differentiated between nonaggressive and aggressive offenders. Nonaggressive offenders, who make no use of force or violence, frequently are acquainted with the child or are friends of the family. This is by far the most common pattern. Most nonaggressive offenders are psychosexually immature males who only feel sexually comfortable with children (Cohen and Seghorn, 1969). Aggressive offenders are usually unacquainted with their victims. They tend to be the most criminal and recidivistic of all sex offenders, and there is always some risk they may end up murdering the child.

Women as well as men may misuse children as sex objects, but the reported incidence of pedophilia among women is very low. About twice as many girls as boys are the victims of child molestation. The selection of boys by male offenders is more a matter of opportunity than of homosexual inclination. Aggressive male offenders typically select boys for the release of their aggressive and sexual impulses. In these cases, the physical violence appears to be essential for sexual excitement. Aggressive offenders are usually given prison sentences whereas nonaggressive offenders are more often referred for psychotherapy or committed to a mental hospital.

INCEST

Most incestuous relationships are between father and daughter; intercourse between mother-and-son is rare. The occasional occurrence of coitus between brother and sister is usually limited to encounters during the teenage period that mainly express curiosity and sexual experimentation. A concise summary of theories and data about incest has been provided by Ferracuti (1972). Incest is proscribed in almost all cultures, and the taboo is as strictly enforced in tribal as in modern societies.

Almost all theories stress a social rather than a biological or moral basis for the taboo. The prohibition of incest forces the individual outside of the family circle for sexual satisfaction, which serves to decrease the risk of rivalries within the family, to further the socialization of the individual, and to prevent the isolation of the family unit by extending its relationships with other kinship groups.

Incest occurs at all socioeconomic levels in our society, but most findings have been based on the study of lowerclass families where the father was convicted and imprisoned. For this population, alcoholism and crowded living conditions are often associated with incestuous behavior. Convicted fathers range in intelligence from dull to normal. They frequently have poor work histories and exhibit assorted character defects. On the other hand, they rarely have prior criminal records.

Marital discord and sexual frustration are common in these families. The mother is often absent from the home much of the time, and frequently she is aware of the father-daughter relationship but is passively acquiescent. The father may look upon the daughter as a replacement for his wife and court her as he once courted the mother. While he may make use of his parental authority to overcome the daughter's resistance, the actual use of force appears to be uncommon. The daughters often are sexually precocious, provocative, eager to assume the adult role or to use the incestuous relationship to express hostility toward their mother. Their resistance to the sex act is often mild and, at the time, they rarely feel guilty about it. The psychological harmfulness of the experience with respect to the daughter's subsequent sexual or personal adjustment appears to be highly variable. As a rule the incestuous relationship is of short duration. Referral to and intervention by the police and social agencies usually results in the immediate termination of the affair. In other cases, the daughter, after a time, either refuses further participation or feels she must leave home.

RAPE

Males seldom, if ever, complain to the police of having been raped by an aggressive female. Rape may therefore be defined as a sex offense that is restricted to men who seduce or force nonconsenting females to submit to intercourse and other sex acts. The legal scope of rape is usually confined to the sexual violation of adolescent and adult females who are not related to the offender. This limitation serves to exclude incest, pedophilia, and acts of sexual aggression committed by a husband against his unwilling wife.

An important distinction is made by the courts between *statutory rape* and *forcible rape*. The critical factor in statutory rape is the age of the girl. From a legal point of view it is assumed that females under the age of seventeen (or older in some states) are too young to give meaningful consent. If they are "persuaded" or "seduced" to have sex relations with a man, they may later accuse him of rape even though at the time they were seemingly willing and active participants and there was no threat or use of force. Unless the accused can prove that he did not have sexual relations with an underage partner, he is automatically guilty. In adjudging such cases, the court may take into account the reputation of the accused and the accuser, the nature of their relationship, the girl's prior sex experience, and her degree of consent or protest. However, the age factor alone suffices for conviction and the imposition of a prison sentence.

Gebhard et al. (1965) have drawn a composite personality profile of adult offenders convicted of sexual contact, without the use of force or threat, with females aged sixteen and over. The profile fits many males convicted of statutory rape. As a group they are strongly heterosexual and take advantage of every opportunity to gratify their sexual desires. While deficient in moral values, they are not actually antisocial. Most would not consider forcible

RAPE: A CASE REPORT

This man had been preoccupied with fantasies of rape since puberty. A favorite teenage fantasy was that of breaking into a house at night and tearing the clothes from a girl. She at first would resist, later become sexually aroused, and finally cooperate. His first overt assault occurred at age fifteen. While engaged in window peeping he happened to see a woman undress and go to bed. He became aroused, entered the house, and struck the woman with the handle of a knife, hoping to make her unconscious and available for intercourse. The woman, however, screamed and the subject ran away. No other known aggression occurred for the next seven years. At age twenty-two, he broke into the house of a neighboring woman whose husband was away. He found her asleep in bed, nude. He warned her to be quiet and began to caress her. According to his story, she acted out his teenage fantasy. She became aroused and cooperative during consequent coitus. Her story is not available, but her actions suggest a lack of mutual desire. The woman informed the police, who arrested the young man the next morning. However, she refused to press charges and he was released.

He married at age twenty-two. During the two years of his marriage he seized females at night on at least two occasions, but their screams caused him to abandon his efforts. On two other occasions he entered a house at night but left when he discovered the females were not alone. Following the breakup of his marriage, he made three attempts at rape. On one occasion he grabbed a girl in a residential area but fled when she screamed. On the second occasion he attempted to pull a woman into his car. Her cries and struggles attracted passers-by and he let her go. He drove around until he saw a lone female in another car. He followed her and watched her enter her apartment. When he thought she was asleep he entered by way of her window. He found the woman in bed, put his hand over her mouth, told her to be quiet, and began caressing her. She informed him that she was menstruating and showed him evidence of it. This caused him to lose his erection. He left under the impression that the woman would welcome his return when she was no longer menstruating. When he did return some nights later he was welcomed by the waiting police. He was surprised that the woman bore him any ill will. His wishful self-delusion had led him to believe that she would want to see him again (After Gebhard et al., 1965).

rape, pedophilia, or serious crimes. On the other hand, they see nothing wrong in making passes at any girl and taking their pleasure when and where they find it. They are impulsive opportunists who believe in immediate self-gratification and let the future take care of itself. Their careless disregard of the age of potential sex partners is consistent with their simple approach to life. A high proportion were married at the time of their arrest.

Charges of rape are more difficult to substantiate or refute when the victim is over the statutory age limit. Conviction rests on three key points: (1) the offender's use of force or threat; (2) the extent of the victim's protest and resistance; and (3) supportive medical evidence of vaginal penetration and other injuries. These legal technicalities are somewhat simplified when offender and victim are total strangers to one another. About 50 percent of all rape cases referred to the police are of this type. The stranger relationship does not eliminate the possibility of female enticement or voluntary compliance but the burden of proof of participation by the victim is on the accused.

The old argument, that it is practically impossible to have intercourse with a healthy adult female who is determined to prevent it, is irrelevant. When a woman is faced with the alternative of submitting or being slashed, knocked unconscious, or brutally beaten, she can hardly be said to have a choice. Under these circumstances, yielding and quickly terminating the experience may be the wisest thing to do. Another possibility is that when suddenly confronted by a physically stronger or armed rapist, the woman may be so frightened and confused that she is unable to scream or fight back effectively until it is too late.

The fears of women attacked by strangers are not baseless. Gebhard et al. (1965) noted in their study of convicted heterosexual aggressors against adults that many who attacked strangers engaged in unnecessary violence. It is apparently easier to be cruel when the victim is an unknown face in the dark. A few had sadistic tendencies, some were emotionally unstable, and others were asocial individuals who couldn't care less about the welfare of their victims. The latter group literally used women as impersonal sex objects. Whenever they felt a need for a woman, they grabbed one—anyone. Age and other physical attributes were unimportant.

Another group of rapists, as illustrated in the above case report, have the delusion that women would welcome being assaulted, enjoy the experience, and arrange for return visits. Cohen and Seghorn (1969) also found similar patterns of aggression, impulsiveness, and deluded narcissistic thinking in their study of convicted rapists. Many random attackers of females are antisocial persons with histories of criminal behavior. Rape is frequently accompanied by theft or robbery.

In about half the reported rape cases the offender and victim are not strangers. Some are dating friends, others are neighborhood acquaintances or recent pickups. A prior social relationship has always presented legal complications, and in recent years the greater sex freedom of women plus the courts' increasing interest in the contributing role of the victim in sex offenses has compounded the difficulty (Amir, 1972). The adversary system of the law further blurs the distinction between the accused and accuser by subjecting the victim to sharp cross-examination. In effect, the victim is put in the embarrassing and seemingly unfair position of proving her innocence. She may be blamed for precipitating the attack if she permitted or encouraged the man's preliminary advances and then changed her mind at the last minute, if she arranged to meet the accused at his or her home when she knew no one else would be there, if she had some drinks with him at a bar and then voluntarily left with him, and so forth. In these cases, the reputation of the girl, the use of brute force or threats, and the degree of resistance are important considerations in the court's disposition of the complaint.

When the victim is viewed as having been partially responsible for putting herself in a compromising position or otherwise contributing to the assault, the accused man is frequently acquitted. Under these conditions it is understandable why the majority of rape victims are reluctant to file a futile complaint that would only serve to call attention to their experience and expose them to public shame and possible retaliation by the assailant.

For the victims, rape is typically a traumatic experience. Some women are more adversely affected than others. The wide range of individual variations in immediate reactions and residual effects may be related to the specific circumstances of the incident, the personality and adaptive resources of the victim, her prior sex history, the degree of emotional support provided by her family and others, and her subsequent life experiences. Research on these and related topics is sparse, and the few available studies are mainly concerned with immediate or short-term reactions.

A report by Sutherland and Scherl (1970) is of special interest in that it attempts to identify the successive stages of adjustment frequently observed in victims between the ages of eighteen and twenty-four. The first phase, which may last for several days following the event, is one of acute distress. Reactions may include shock, confusion, agitation, anger, emotional instability, and disbelief. The second phase is a period of pseudo-adjustment, in which the victim resumes her regular activities and reports that all is well. This facade of normalcy is a temporary protective period when extensive use is made of the defense mechanisms of denial, suppression, and rationalization.

The third phase consists in facing the temporarily shelved traumatic event and coming to terms with it. The victim must realistically appraise her degree of complicity and resolve her anger and resentment toward her assailant. This phase is often marked by depression, obsessive thinking about the experience and repetitive talking about it. The third phase may be regarded as a form of self-therapy. The depression serves as an expiation for real or imagined complicity while the obsessive and verbal preoccupation with the experience are excellent means of desensitization. The third phase ends when the victim accepts and integrates the experience into her self-structure.

Uniform Crime Report statistics prepared by the FBI indicate that there are about 30,000 rape victims a year in the United States. This is a conservative estimate. In large cities rape accounts for 1 percent of all arrests for serious crimes. About two-thirds of apprehended rapists are between fifteen and twenty-five years of age, and most of the remaining one-third are under forty-five. Victims may be of any age, but most are under twenty-five, with a median age of approximately twenty. Additional facts and figures have been summarized by Amir (1972). The incidence of rape is highest in high-crime areas. Far more lower- than upper-class males are convicted of rape. Usually the victim and the offender live in the same area and are of the same race. About 50 percent of all reported rapes occur in the victim's home. In large cities approximately 20 percent of the victims have police records. Only about one-fourth of the victims, most of whom are older women, put up strong resistance.

SUMMARY

Sexual outlets in man range from the normal variation of masturbation to the pathological offenses of child molestation and forcible rape. Attitudes toward masturbation have recently upgraded it from a harmless substitute for coitus or a sign of immaturity to a positive experience in its own right. Preliminary studies suggest that masturbation may be helpful in the treatment of women with orgasmic deficiency.

Fetishism is related to partialism and transvestism, but is different from both. Partialism refers to a biased sex interest in some physical feature of the opposite sex. For example, a male may be partial to the hair color or the size of breasts of females. The male fetishist is more interested in articles of female attire than female anatomy, and is excited by bras, panties and other related symbols. Unlike the transvestite, he does not wear these articles; he uses them as visual and tactile stimuli for erotic arousal.

The elements of aggression, which are often associated with sex, are present in extreme form in sadism and masochism. The substitution of physical acts of violence for coitus suggests an avoidance of sexual intimacy. The avoidance of physical intimacy may also be a factor in exhibitionism and voyeurism. The exhibitionist is mainly interested in shocking his victim, while the voyeur is content to be a passive observer.

The legal concept of criminal sex offenses is particularly applicable in cases of child molestation, incest and rape. All three may be described as physical assaults against persons who because of their age or other conditions are incapable of meaningful voluntary consent or who are forced against their will to submit.

Homosexuality refers to erotic preference for members of the same sex, so the term is equally applicable to women and to men. Homosexual individuals may engage in heterosexual acts. The critical factor is that the homosexual is more sexually attracted to members of the same than of the opposite gender and finds sexual contact with them more exciting and gratifying. The reversal of sex orientation typically starts before puberty. There are wide individual differences with respect to the relative degree and persistence of homosexual preferences. In recent years society has become more tolerant of homosexuals, to the extent that they have felt free more openly to admit their different sex style without fear of arrest or loss of employment. However, the general public (including college students) still retain an unfavorable attitude toward homosexuals. Homosexuality is no longer considered a disorder for which treatment is automatically recommended. For persons who voluntarily seek therapy, the choice of goal is left to the individual.

Transsexuality is a much less common form of deviance in sex role. The individual has the external physical characteristics of one gender but is absolutely convinced that his or her real personality is that of a person of the opposite gender. The male transsexual desperately wants to be made a whole female through the surgical removal of his offensive penis and its replacement with a vagina. This operation, plus endocrine therapy designed to produce other desired feminine physical characteristics, is now used frequently. The corresponding endocrine and surgical treatment to convert female transsexuals into whole males is more complicated and less complete. Following sex reassignment therapy, the individual is legally permitted to change his or her name and other official records to reflect the new sex gender, and to marry.

Transvestism technically refers to cross-dressing but it is basically a psychological condition, more or less restricted to males, in which the male derives sexual pleasure from wearing female clothing. The transvestite perceives himself as a male and functions adequately as a male in his sex relations with women. He is not a homosexual and has no interest in changing his sex gender.

References

Abramson, P. R. "The Relationship of the Frequency of Masturbation to Severe Aspects of Personality and Behavior." *Journal of Sex Research* 9 (1973): 132-42.

Amir, M. "The Role of the Victim in Sex Offenses." In *Sexual Behaviors*, ed. H. L. P. Resnick and M. E. Wolfgang, pp. 131-67. Boston: Little, Brown, 1972.

Apperson, L. B., and McAdoo, W. G., Jr. "Parental Factors in the Childhood of Homosexuals." *Journal of Abnormal Psychology* 73 (1968): 201-206.

Baker, H. T. "Transsexualism: Problems in Treatment." *American Journal of Psychiatry* 125 (1969): 1412-18.

Bentler, P. M., and Prince, C. "Personality Characteristics of Male Transvestites." *Journal of Abnormal Psychology* 74 (1969): 140-43.

Bieber, I. "Homosexuality." In *Comprehensive Textbook of Psychiatry*, ed. A. M. Friedman, H. I. Kaplan, and H. S. Kaplan, pp. 963-76. Baltimore: Williams & Wilkins, 1967.

——— et al. *Homosexuality: A Psychoanalytic Study*. New York: Basic Books, 1962.

Brodie, H. K.; Gartell, N.; Doering, C.; and Rhue, T. "Plasma Testosterone Levels in Heterosexual and Homosexual Men." *American Journal of Psychiatry* 131 (1974): 82-83.

Buckner, H. T. "The Transvestite Career Path." *Psychiatry* 33 (1970): 381-89.

Clifford, R. "Female Masturbation in Sexual Development and Clinical Application." Doctoral thesis, New York State University at Stony Brook, 1974.

Cohen, M., and Seghorn, T. "Sociometric Study of the Sex Offender." *Journal of Abnormal Psychology* 74 (1969): 249-55.

Ferracuti, F. "Incest between Father and Daughter." In *Sexual Behaviors*, ed. H. L. P. Resnick and M. E. Wolfgang, pp. 169-83. Boston: Little, Brown, 1972.

Gagnon, J., and Simon, W. eds. *The Sexual Scene*. Transaction, Inc., 1970.

Gebhard, P. H.; Gagnon, J. H.; Pomeroy, W. B.; and Christenson, C. V. *Sex Offenders: An Analysis of Types*. New York: Harper & Row, 1965.

Gebhard, P. H., Robock, J., and Grese, H. *Sexuality of Women*. New York: Stein & Day, 1970.

Green, R., and Money, J., eds. *Transsexualism*

and Sex Reassignment. Baltimore: Johns Hopkins Press, 1969.

Greenacre, P. "The Transitional Object and the Fetish with Special Reference to the Role of Illusion." *International Journal of Psychoanalysis* 51 (1970): 447-56.

Hadden, S. B. "Group Psychotherapy with Homosexual Men." In *Sexual Behaviors*, ed. H. L. P. Resnick and M. E. Wolfgang, pp. 267-80. Boston: Little, Brown, 1972.

Heston, L. L., and Shields, J. "Homosexuality in Twins: A Family Study and a Registry Study." *Archives of General Psychiatry* 18 (1968): 149-60.

Kallmann, F. J. "Comparative Twin Study on the Genetic Aspects of Male Homosexuality." *Journal of Nervous and Mental Disease* 115 (1952): 283-98.

Kenyon, F. E. "Studies in Female Homosexuality: Social and Psychiatric Aspects." *British Journal of Psychiatry* 114 (1968a): 1337-43.

―――. "Studies in Female Homosexuality: Sexual Development, Attitudes, and Experience." *British Journal of Psychiatry* 114 (1968b): 1343-50.

Kinsey, A. C., and Gebhard, P. H. *Sexual Behavior in the Human Female*. Philadelphia: Saunders, 1953.

―――; Pomeroy, W. B.; and Martin, C. E. *Sexual Behavior in the Human Male*. Philadelphia: Saunders, 1948.

Mandel, K. L. "Preliminary Report on a New Aversive Therapy for Male Homosexuals." *Behavior Research and Therapy* 8 (1970): 93-95.

Marks, I. M., and Gelder, M. G. "Transvestism and Fetishism: Clinical and Psychological Changes During Faradic Aversion." *British Journal of Psychiatry* 113 (1967): 711-29.

Marquis, J. N. "Orgasmic Conditioning: Changing Sexual Object Choice Through Controlled Masturbation." *Journal of Behavior Therapy and Experimental Psychiatry* 1 (1970): 263-71.

Masters, W. H., and Johnson, V. E. *Human Sexual Response*. Boston: Little, Brown, 1966.

Mohr, J. W., Turner, R. E., and Jerry, M. B. *Pedophilia and Exhibitionism*. Toronto: University of Toronto Press, 1964.

Money, J. "Sex Reassignment Therapy in Gender Identity Disorders." In *Sexual Behaviors* ed. H. L. P. Resnick and M. E. Wolf-

gang, pp. 383-96. Boston: Little, Brown, 1972.

―――― and Brennan, J. G. "Sexual Dimorphism in the Psychology of Female Transsexuals." *Journal of Nervous and Mental Disease* 147 (1968): 487-99.

―――― and Primrose, C. "Sexual Dimorphism and Dissociation in the Psychology of Male Transsexuals." *Journal of Nervous and Mental Disease* 147 (1968): 472-86.

Morris, J. *Conundrum*. New York: Harcourt Brace Jovanovich, 1974.

Pauly, I. B. "The Current Status of the Change of Sex Operation." *Journal of Nervous and Mental Disease* 147 (1968): 460-71.

Rachman, S., and Teasdale, J. *Aversion Therapy and Behavior Disorders: An Analysis*. Coral Gables, Fla.: University of Miami Press, 1969.

Rhoads, J. M., and Feather, B. W. "The Application of Psychodynamics to Behavior Therapy." *American Journal of Psychiatry* 131 (1974): 17-20.

Rosenthal, D. *Genetic Theory and Abnormal Behavior*. New York: McGraw-Hill, 1970.

Saghir, M. T., and Gentry, K. A. "Homosexuality: Psychiatric Disorders and Disability in the Male Homosexual." *American Journal of Psychiatry* 126 (1970): 1079-86.

―――― and Robins, E. "Homosexuality: Sexual Behavior of the Female Homosexual." *Archives of General Psychiatry* 20 (1969): 192-201.

―――― and Walbran, B. "Homosexuality: Sexual Behavior of the Male Homosexual." *Archives of General Psychiatry* 21 (1969): 219-29.

Steffensmeier, D., and Steffensmeier, R. "Sex Differences in Reactions to Homosexuals: Research Continuities and Further Developments." *Journal of Sex Research* 10 (1974): 52-67.

Stevenson, J., and Jones, I. H. "Behavior Therapy Technique for Exhibitionism." *Archives of General Psychiatry* 27 (1972): 839-41.

Stoller, R. J. "The Term 'Transvestism.' " *Archives of General Psychiatry* 24 (1971): 230-37.

Sutherland, S., and Scherl, D. L. "Patterns of Response Among Victims of Rape." *American Journal of Orthopsychiatry* 49 (1970): 503-11.

Weinberg, M., and Bell, A. P. *Homosexuality: An Annotated Bibliography*. New York: Harper & Row, 1972.

Inca Medicine: Epilepsy, from a sixteenth-century manuscript

In previous chapters I have repeatedly emphasized the interaction of biological and psychosocial factors in the shaping of personality and behavior. A second recurring theme, which has been less explicitly stressed, is the presence of physiological disturbances in behavior disorders. Depressive states, for example, are marked by loss of appetite, chronic fatigue, menstrual irregularities, somatic complaints, and reduced energy level. Anxiety is as much a physiological disturbance as it is a psychological reaction. Alcoholism is a problem of physical health as well as mental health. This interaction of physical, psychological, and social factors is equally evident in physical disorders. Psychosocial factors are often important contributing agents in the development, precipitation, and persistence of bodily diseases. The feelings, attitudes, and ideas of a person suffering from tuberculosis, cancer, or a broken leg are integral parts of his total illness.

Psychological and social factors are of particular importance in three types of physical disorders:

1. Physical conditions of which the causes and cures are mainly psychological. Outstanding examples are impotence, orgasmic inadequacy, and related forms of sexual dysfunction.

2. Physical disorders marked by structural changes or impaired bodily functioning in which emotional and social factors are often involved in the production and maintenance of symptoms. This category may be broadly defined to include practically all medical diseases, but we shall be mainly concerned with those disorders in which emotional factors frequently have major etiological significance. Bronchial asthma, essential hypertension, and peptic ulcer are representative. When the causes of these disorders are principally physical, the response of patients to medical treatment is usually consistent with the known effectiveness of available remedies. Where psychological variables are of major importance, the elimination of symptoms may depend more on the resolution of underlying personality problems than on the effectiveness of medication. Physical disorders in which emotions and attitudes are of critical importance are popularly referred to as *psychosomatic reactions*.

3. Organic brain disorders involving brain tissue damage which are marked by impairment in cerebral functions. This category includes the physical and psychosocial disturbances associated with senile brain disease, cerebral arteriosclerosis, and convulsive disorders.

SEXUAL DYSFUNCTIONS

Impotence, premature ejaculation, orgasmic inadequacy, and vaginismus are classic examples of physical conditions in which emotions, attitudes, and mental set are key factors in the impairment of normal physiological functioning. The interaction is circular. Psychological blocks interfere with the adequacy of sexual performance, and the inadequacy of performance reinforces the intensity and persistence of psychological barriers. The wide prevalence of impaired sexual functioning among both males and females was initially documented in studies conducted by Kinsey and his associates (1948, 1953).

In 1966 Masters and Johnson reported

the results of their innovative research studies on the psychophysiology of human sexual response. Four years later (1970) they have made a major contribution to the understanding and treatment of human sexual inadequacy. Their study is a model of effective scientific research in a significant area of human maladjustment. Comprehensive data were obtained through the intensive individual study of nearly eight hundred persons with serious sexual problems. In a field where previous therapeutic efforts have been dismal failures, the approach of Masters and Johnson has proved effective in eliminating symptoms in 80 percent of all treated individuals within two weeks. More significantly, the cures appear to be permanent; follow-up data show that less than 3 percent of all successfully treated patients suffered a return of symptoms in a period of more than five years. Masters and Johnson currently are continuing the treatment program described in their report.

The Nature of Symptoms

Impotence is the most frequent complaint of men seeking sex therapy. Impotence is the inability of a mature male to achieve and maintain an erection of sufficient rigidity to permit successful sexual intercourse. A distinction is sometimes made between primary and secondary impotence. Masters and Johnson apply the designation of primary impotence to men who have never been capable of successful coital insertion. If a man has had one or more successful experiences of either a heterosexual or homosexual nature, his present inability to achieve and maintain an erection is classified as secondary impotence. Fifteen percent of the impotent males treated by Masters and Johnson suffered from the primary variety. In these cases contributory etiological factors included undue maternal influence, psychological delusions originating in strict religious training, homosexual activities, and personal devaluation owing to trau-

THE MAJOR FORMS OF SEXUAL DYSFUNCTION

Impotence	The inability of a physiologically mature male to achieve and maintain a penile erection of sufficient rigidity to permit a successful sexual experience (heterosexual or homosexual). In cases of psychogenic impotence, the individual is usually capable of erections when alone.
Premature Ejaculation	The inability on the part of a man to delay the ejaculatory process during sexual intercourse for a sufficient length of time to satisfy his partner. Ejaculation within thirty seconds of insertion is usually considered premature.
Ejaculatory Incompetence	A relatively uncommon condition in which the male is either unable or unwilling to ejaculate during coitus.
Orgasmic Dysfunction	A psychogenic female condition marked by persistent failure to experience orgasm during intercourse.
Vaginismus	A reaction of women to coitus in which the vaginal opening is constricted by an involuntary muscular spasm that makes sexual intercourse very painful or impossible.

SEXUAL DYSFUNCTION: A CASE OF PREMATURE EJACULATION

A college senior and his wife sought help from the Student Counseling Center for a marital problem. At the time of their initial visit, they had been married for three months and their sex life had gone from bad to worse. The husband, who had a prior history of premature ejaculation, had expected marriage to solve his problem by providing unlimited sex under relaxed conditions. He attributed his prior quickness of ejaculation to long periods between episodes of coitus and the fact that most of his earlier experiences had been in dormitory rooms shared by two girls, so there was always the possibility that a roommate would return or a friend would drop in unexpectedly.

Unfortunately, marriage accentuated his problems. Prior to marriage, the couple had agreed that the wife, who was a college sophomore, would drop out of school and work while the husband finished his last year. He would then assume financial responsibility and she would return to college to obtain her degree in teaching. The wife was afraid that this plan would be wrecked if she became pregnant and used this fear to limit the frequency of intercourse and to insist on double protection (vaginal foam plus a condom). Another restriction she imposed was that they should engage in sex when both were in the right mood. Her argument was that coitus should be an event, not a casual affair. On those occasions when she was in the right mood, she would deliberately prolong foreplay until her husband was so aroused that he would ejaculate at the moment of insertion. He resented this abrupt ending more than she did. She enjoyed petting but objected to the invasion of her body. She was relieved by the briefness of the penetration, and at the same time exploited her husband's inadequacy as a lover to justify her frequent refusal.

Their initial response to therapy was favorable. The husband and wife discussed their sexual feelings and difficulties candidly and made a cooperative effort to please each other. The frequency of intercourse was increased, and with the aid of the squeeze technique, the husband was able to prolong both petting and coitus. However, after a few visits, the wife's basic dislike of sex returned. She objected to the artificiality of the stroking and squeezing procedures and complained of being deprived of her freedom of choice as a person. At this point the therapist suggested that the sex exercises should be temporarily discontinued and that the next two meetings be devoted to a general discussion of the couple's personal relations. The wife welcomed the opportunity to air her complaints. She felt she was being used. Besides supporting her husband she was now expected to serve as a compliant sex object to increase her husband's pleasure and masculine pride. The husband helped resolve the immediate situation by being understanding and assuring his wife that her current unfavorable situation was temporary. In a few more months he would be supporting her while she completed college. Sex therapy was resumed and adequate sex functioning was soon established. The couple was seen for a total of eight visits over a two month period.

matic experiences with prostitutes or other partners.

Secondary impotence was mainly related to a fear of inadequate performance resulting from past failures. Experiences commonly associated with the acquisition of a fear response were premature ejaculation on earlier occasions and isolated incidents of failure while under the influence of alcohol. Especially in insecure males, one humiliating failure, particularly if it brings taunts from a frustrated sex partner, is sufficient to arouse intense anxiety that may lead to impotence on subsequent occasions.

The second most common male complaint in the Masters and Johnson study was premature ejaculation. Usually this condition is defined as quickness of response. A person is considered a premature ejaculator if he cannot control his discharge for at least thirty seconds after penetration. Masters and Johnson prefer a more functional definition. They define a man as a premature ejaculator if more often than not he cannot delay the ejaculatory process after intravaginal containment for a sufficient length of time to satisfy his partner. The major factor in the development of chronic premature ejaculation appears to be initial introduction to sexual activity in circumstances that required quick completion of the act: lack of privacy, the possibility of interruption or discovery, or a partner who for one reason or another insisted on "getting it over with" as soon as possible.

Another form of male inadequacy, which is relatively rare, is called ejaculatory incompetence. A male with this condition is capable of maintaining an erection during intercourse for an hour or longer but is unable or unwilling to proceed to ejaculation. The advantage of prolonged intercourse is outweighed by the frustration that may be experienced by the woman as well as the man at the incompleteness of the act, or by such a superabundance of orgasms in the woman that she is totally exhausted while her partner is still unsatisfied. Fear of pregnancy has been suggested, along with disinterest in the female partner, suspicion that the woman has been unfaithful, fear of contaminating the woman or of being contaminated by her, strict religious training, and emotional conflicts of various kinds. The condition may occur only occasionally, in reaction to specific stress situations, or may be a more generalized response.

Masters and Johnson found orgasmic dysfunction to be the main complaint among the women they studied. Slightly more than half the women treated had never experienced an orgasm or climax. Their condition was described as primary orgasmic deficiency. The remainder, who were classified as manifesting situational orgasmic deficiency, rarely achieved orgasm, but they had done so on one or more occasions. Some of these women expressed little or no interest in or need for sexual expression and would be described by laymen as frigid. Eight percent of all the women treated suffered from vaginismus, an involuntary muscular spasm that constricts the vaginal opening. The reflex contraction is stimulated by imagined, anticipated, or real attempts at vaginal penetration. Severe vaginismus makes normal intercourse extremely painful or impossible.

Masters and Johnson attribute female sexual dysfunction primarily to sociocultural conditioning that has taught women to inhibit, reject, or distort their natural sex feelings. Inadequate and biased information about female sexuality, when reinforced by traumatic experiences during adolescence, creates a built-in signal system that automatically inhibits a normal response to sexual stimuli.

The Treatment of Sexual Dysfunction

Participants in the Masters and Johnson program come from all over the country Most are referred by physicians, psychologists, and clergymen. Those accepted for treatment are required to live for two weeks in special quarters set up at the treatment center in St. Louis. Patients are regarded and treated as guests. Provisions are made to ensure their enjoyment of a "vacation" during the time spent in the city, but the real purpose of the residential requirement is to isolate the guests from home and business cares and to create a sex-focused environment for intensive therapy.

If a patient is married, both husband and wife must agree to participate in the treatment. This requirement is based on the key premise that there is no such thing as an uninvolved partner in any marriage in which there is any form of sexual inadequacy. Since sexual behavior represents an interaction between two persons, the partner ultimately is the critical factor.

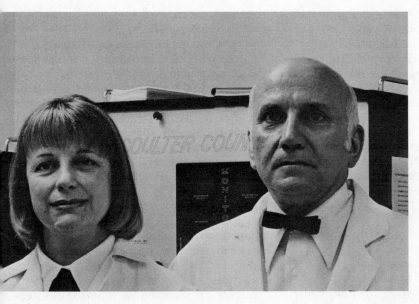

William H. Masters and Virginia Johnson, contemporary sex researchers who have made significant contributions to our understanding of human sexual behavior and to the effective treatment of sexual dysfunctions.

The patient is the marital unit. Unmarried persons are accepted for treatment only if they bring their own sex partner. The former practice of providing unmarried males with a volunteer female partner has been discontinued.

The first step in treatment consists of a detailed case history. Information is obtained on etiological factors, the onset and severity of symptoms, and the psychosocial effect of the sexual dysfunction. The history-taking interview also provides information on the basic personalities of the partners and the results they expect from therapy. Regardless of the specific problem, the first three days are spent becoming oriented to the situation and on indoctrination and the exchange of information. The balance of the two weeks is focused on the specific complaint.

In general, the treatment program is educational in nature. Patients are given every opportunity to ask questions and to discuss problems. Misconceptions and errors are corrected and technical information is supplied. Specific suggestions are made, but decisions and the details of implementing them are left to the individuals. There is no observation of the patients during intimate moments.

The general aim of therapy is to provide a relaxed, nondemanding setting in which patients may give free rein to sexual thoughts and feelings. Great emphasis is placed on nonverbal communication through touching and feeling.

A precept often repeated is that neither an erection nor an orgasm can be willed or wished into being. The more one deliberately strives to obtain either an erection or an orgasm, the more one is doomed to failure. The best procedure is to relax, adopt a "give to get" attitude, and let the natural processes of the body take over. The two-week duration of treatment imposes a time limit, but within this period there is no rush, no feeling that "tonight is the night." Progress from A to B is considered more desirable than an attempt to jump abruptly from A to Z, which is unlikely to be successful.

The treatment is structured as an interactive process between the partners in which a successful outcome depends on mutual understanding and cooperation. It is apparent from the authors' descriptions, however, that their therapeutic program places major responsibility on the woman, whether the dysfunction is hers or her partner's. The special techniques devised for eliminating premature ejaculation require the female partner to stimulate the male organ manually and periodically to apply a carefully described manual "squeeze" to the head of the penis to regulate the intensity of male arousal. The stop-start signal to regulate intensity of male arousal is given by the male. A suggested explanation is that repeated arousal of the male short of orgasm serves to make him more aware of penile sensations associated with high arousal and this feedback information helps him control and delay his orgasm. The woman is in control of the insertion process and of the pacing of pelvic thrusts, whether the problem to be eliminated is male impotence or female orgasmic deficiency.

In the early stages of treatment, Masters and Johnson consider it essential that the woman assume the superior position, while the man lies beneath her. Later on, the lateral position, which also gives the female considerable control and freedom of action, is recommended. Masters and Johnson consider that from a treatment point of view, the conventional position, with the man above the woman, is not beneficial. They have developed a number of specific techniques for the elimination of particular symptoms, which are described and illustrated in their report.

It is not to be supposed from all this that women alone are responsible for all sexual problems, and that it is therefore up to them to eliminate them. Masters and Johnson emphasize the fact that both partners are involved in the problems of either, and that both must cooperate in eliminating them. Their reversal of the traditional roles in the sex act is a therapeutic technique, not a social judgment or a procedure recommended for all persons at all times.

Masters and Johnson have reported their results in terms of failure rates, which have the advantage of being more precise than success rates: the patient's condition remained unchanged or worsened. Success rates are more ambiguous; they may refer to mild improvement or complete recovery. However, no great harm is done in converting the Masters and Johnson figures into success rates, since the criterion was specific: the continued presence or absence of the original symptom for which the patient sought treatment.

By the end of the two-week period of intensive treatment, 83 percent of the male and 81 percent of the female subjects reported the elimination of symptoms. Follow-up data covering a five-year period for some subjects and a shorter period for others indicated no return of symptoms in 80 percent of the persons treated. The long-term success rate was the same for males and females. Best results were obtained with vaginismus, which was eliminated in 100 percent of the cases treated. Premature ejaculation was successfully eliminated in 97 percent, a favorable outcome of 70 percent was reported for secondary impotence and 60 percent for primary impotence. Success rates for primary and situational orgasmic dysfunction were 82 percent and 75 percent, respectively. The overall success rate for the treatment of persons over fifty years of age was 70 percent, and the authors conclude that normal sex behavior can be continued beyond the age of eighty if a person is in good physical health and has an interesting and cooperative partner.

The dramatic success of the brief treatment procedures developed by Masters and Johnson and other researchers has lead to a reevaluation of the traditional view that sexual dysfunctions represent symptomatic surface manifestations of deep-rooted emotional and personality problems that require years of treatment with meager hope of significant improvement in sex functioning. The challenge goes beyond the sex field. If highly structured, do-it-yourself remedial procedures can quickly correct chronic sex problems, similar action-centered techniques that focus on the direct removal of specific symptoms may also be effective in the treatment of other forms of behavior disorders. This emerging new approach is related to the educational philosophy of "learning-by-doing."

At a more practical level, the high recovery rates reported by Masters and Johnson have stimulated interest in sex problems and influenced other therapists and marital counselors to try the new procedures and to experiment with innovations of their own. Facilities for the treatment of sex problems are now available throughout the country. Helen Kaplan (1974), a psycho-analytically-oriented psychiatrist, has reviewed new developments in the field and given a detailed account of the sex therapy program associated with the Payne Whitney Psychiatric Clinic at Cornell. The latter program utilizes most of the procedures described by Masters and Johnson for specific dysfunctions, but there are differences. Applicants are initially given a psychiatric examination. Accepted couples are seen cojointly on an outpatient or private office practice basis. Usually there is only one therapist, but a co-therapist of the opposite sex may be called in to help with special situations. In most cases, the length of treatment ranges from six to fifteen visits which are spread over a period of several weeks. During treatment visits, the therapist assigns task procedures which the couple conducts at home. At the next meeting they report their experience and discuss progress and difficulties, if any. The program is flexible and changes may be made to fit the situation. The recovery rates noted by Kaplan and her associates for specific dysfunctions agree with those reported by Masters and Johnson.

The main criticism of the new sex therapy has been that it is exclusively concerned with adequacy of sex performance. No mention is made of love, affection, or the psychological compatibility of the partners. The argument is valid but the neglect of other significant variables is more a limitation than a criticism. Advocates candidly admit that their therapeutic objective is to eliminate the sexual dysfunction of their clients. If, as often happens, the restoration of sexual adequacy leads to improved marital relations or closer love ties, so much the better, but these secondary gains are a bonus. No claim is made that improvement in sex performance is a panacea for all marital

problems or that the elimination of sexual dysfunction will prevent divorce. In the case of insecure husbands or wives, the correction of the spouse's dysfunction and his or her increased sex demands may be perceived as a threat. When this occurs supplementary therapy is recommended.

PSYCHOSOMATIC REACTIONS

The official APA designation for psychosomatic reactions is *psychophysiological disorders*.

This group of disorders is characterized by physical symptoms that are casued by emotional factors and involve a single organ system, usually under autonomic nervous system innervation. The physiological changes involved are those that normally accompany certain emotional states, but in these disorders the changes are more intense and sustained. The individual may not be consciously aware of his emotional state [*Diagnostic and Statistical Manual*, 1968].

The presence of some actual somatic pathology is an essential characteristic of psychosomatic disorders. The physical pathology may consist of a structural change, a disturbance in functioning, or both. The asthmatic child's wheezing, choking, and gasping for air are due to bronchial obstructions. An excessive secretion of acid is responsible for the inflammation and lesions of the stomach lining of the ulcer patient. His subjective feelings of pain and distress are genuine, and he may die if internal bleeding occurs. A tension headache hurts just as much as a headache produced by a blow on the head. There is no malingering or faking of symptoms. The patient has a physical illness, is worried about his condition, seeks medical advice. Only 1 percent of the patients seen in psychiatric clinics and by psychiatrists in private practice are diagnosed as suffering from psychosomatic disorders.

Psychotherapy is usually a last resort when continued medical treatment proves ineffective.

The psychological component of many psychosomatic disorders is indicated by the effectiveness of placebos in alleviating or curing many physical symptoms. The minor pains and aches of infants are usually promptly cured by the mother's cuddling and stroking. A mother's kiss has the magical power to make a child's pain go away. Experimental studies have repeatedly demonstrated the extreme sensitivity of gastrointestinal, cardiac, and electrodermal responses to interpersonal stimulation. Animal studies have shown that the entrance of a person into an experimental room often elicits a marked increase in a dog's heart rate (Lynch, 1969). Petting a dog while he is being shocked not only decreases cardiac indicators of fear and pain but also may reduce motor responses.

THE APA CLASSIFICATION OF PSYCHOPHYSIOLOGICAL DISORDERS

Reactions are classified in accordance with the organ system involved.

1. Skin disorders.
   (a) Neurodermatitis: chronic reddening and thickening of the skin with intense itching.
   (b) Psoriasis: scaly patches of skin.
   (c) Eczema: itchy skin with exudation of liquid.
   (d) Hives: itching and swelling of the skin.

2. Musculoskeletal disorders.
   (a) Rheumatoid arthritis: stiffening of joints.
   (b) Low backache.
   (c) Muscle cramps.

3. Respiratory disorders.
   (a) Bronchial asthma: shortness of breath, wheezing, gasping for air, sensation of choking.
   (b) Hyperventilation: sighs, difficulty in breathing, tingling of extremities, fainting.
   (c) Persistent hiccups.

4. Gastrointestinal disorders.
   (a) Peptic ulcer: localized gastric pain due to inflammation or lesions of the stomach wall.
   (b) Duodenal ulcer: pain associated with inflammation or lesions of the first portion of the small intestines.
   (c) Colitis: inflammation or spasms of the colon.
   (d) Anorexia nervosa: lack of appetite.
   (e) Diarrhea.
   (f) Constipation.

5. Cardiovascular disorders.
   (a) Essential hypertension: high blood pressure.
   (b) Raynaud's disease: poor circulation resulting in cold hands and feet.

PSYCHOSOMATIC REACTIONS: A CASE OF ASTHMA

A fifteen year old girl was referred by her family physician for psychotherapy because of repeated asthma attacks, which usually occurred when her parents were engaged in one of their frequent quarrels. The need to attend to their daughter's difficulty in breathing served to terminate their ongoing battle for the moment. Both parents desired and were constantly threatening to obtain a divorce but each felt they had to stay together to care for their sick child. The mother especially was emotionally dependent on her daughter.

Attempts to involve the parents in family therapy were unsuccessful, so it was necessary to limit treatment to individual sessions with the girl. The emphasis of therapy was on freeing the daughter of her sense of responsibility for holding the family together by acting as a sacrificial lamb. A second immediate goal was to help her develop other sources of satisfaction for her affectional needs. This was achieved by encouraging her development of a close relationship with her paternal grandparents.

The girl responded well to therapy. As she gained greater independence, her mother and father also became more autonomous persons and decided to proceed with their long-postponed divorce. Following the divorce, the mother obtained a full-time position and the daughter, of her own choice, went to live with her grandparents. Followup two years later indicated the continued absence of asthma attacks. The girl had continued to make good progress toward achieving a sense of personal separateness and was planning on entering college to study medicine.

When shock is accompanied by petting, the dog may show no overt signs of being shocked.

Theories of Psychosomatic Disorders

Psychosomatic disorders may be interpreted as unsuccessful bodily reactions to stress. In these cases the sequence of alarm, resistance, and adaptation that occurs in response to stress (Selye, 1956) has an unfavorable outcome; the individual is left with distressing symptoms. Stress theory, however, fails to answer three questions: Why do some individuals successfully adapt to the stresses of life and others fail to do so? Why are certain failures of adaptation manifested in symptoms identified with psychosomatic disorders? Why do some persons who manifest psychosomatic symptoms develop asthma while others develop ulcers, hypertension, hives, or some other specific condition?

The usual answer to the first question is that some individuals, because of less favorable genetic endowment and life experiences than others, have lower thresholds of stress tolerance. The standard answer to the second question is equally vague. It is assumed that certain combinations of innate or acquired defects result in psychosomatic symptoms, whereas other combinations lead to neurotic or psychotic behavior patterns. More specific theories have been proposed to account for the occurrence of specific psychosomatic disorders. One of the older but still active theories postulates that the specificity of symptoms is determined by the relative weakness of a particular organ system. Thus a weakness in the respiratory system favors the development of asthma and a weakness of the gastrointestinal system leads to a selective vulnerability to ulcers.

The organ weakness may have multiple causes. The clinical observation that members of certain families often share a susceptibility to gastric, cardiovascular, or skin disorders has been interpreted as the result of some genetically transmitted weakness of a particular organ system (Wolf, 1953). But the tendency of certain symptom patterns to run in families may also be explained as a result of learning and imitation. A mother who always develops headaches in stress situations may serve as a model for her children. Familial concern with special diets, the regularity of elimination, and the state of one's stomach may favor gastric symptoms.

There is also the possibility that some prior illness may have focused attention on or weakened a particular organ system. An examination of the medical histories of asthmatic patients found that a large proportion had records of previous respiratory infections (Rees, 1964). This finding does not rule out the possible significance of heredity, since predisposing genetic factors may have contributed to the individual's relative vulnerability to this kind of infection. Individual differences in genetic susceptibility offer the simplest explanation for the repeatedly noted fact that some monkeys develop ulcers when subjected to stress situations that call for "executive" decisions, while others exposed to the same experiences do not (Brady, 1958).

A second hypothesis related to the stress theory is that an inherited specificity of response pattern influences symptoms. Studies conducted with college students (Lacey and Lacey, 1958) indicate that the autonomic response patterns of particular individuals tend to be highly stable and consistent. Some persons characteristically react to all stress situations by a marked rise in blood pressure; others show a greater change in heart rate or galvanic skin response. Patients suffering from headaches tend to react to experimentally induced stress with an increase in muscle tension, whereas heart patients show a greater cardiovascular response (Malmo and Shagass, 1949). Supportive evidence for the theory of autonomic specificity has also been reported (Wenger et al., 1961).

Attempts to relate the selectivity of psychosomatic symptoms to personality variables have been unsuccessful. In comparison with the general population, persons with psychosomatic disorders may show greater dependence-independence conflicts, greater repressed hostility, and higher levels of anxiety, but experimental findings do not support the hypothesis that certain personality characteristics are directly correlated with particular psychosomatic disorders (Buss, 1966). A more promising lead that warrants further research is the hypothesis suggested by Graham and his associates (1962), that the attitude of the individual influences the psychosomatic reactions he experiences. Some examples are given in Table 17.1. Little is known of the relation of socioeconomic status to psychosomatic ailments. In one of the few studies in this area, Rennie and Strole (1956) noted that arthritis and hypertension are most prevalent in the lower class, colitis and hives in the upper class, and heart symptoms in the middle class.

In summary, the causes of psychosomatic disorders are multiple and interactive. Predisposing genetic factors may influence tolerance to stress and specificity of response. The release or activation of genetic vulnerabilities is dependent on the occurrence of significant stress. Life experiences that focus attention on or weaken a particular organ system or which lead to the development of certain attitudes may be influential in the development of particular symptoms.

Psychosomatic Disorders and Neurosis

At one time psychosomatic disorders were interpreted as "organ neuroses." More recently a differentiation has been made on the basis of the observation that psychosomatic reactions, unlike neurotic symptoms, have no symbolic significance and do not serve as defenses against anxiety. Two further reasons have been given for differentiating psychosomatic disorders from conversion hysteria: (1) psychosomatic disorders typically involve changes in the structure or functioning of internal organs (stomach, heart, respiratory system), whereas conversion symptoms are characterized by a loss of peripheral sensory and motor functions (blindness, paralysis, deafness); and (2)—a controversial distinction—psychosomatic reactions are innervated and controlled by the autonomic nervous system, whereas conversion symptoms are innervated and controlled by the central nervous system.

The Treatment of Psychosomatic Disorders

Persons suffering from psychosomatic disorders typically seek and prefer medical forms of treatment to psychotherapy. This orientation is consistent with the physical nature of their overt symptoms. The greater "respectability" of physical illness in comparison with emotional disorders is also an important consideration. Psycho-

therapists also favor initial referral to physicians for laboratory tests, diagnosis, and medication. To deny a patient the relief of symptoms he might obtain from drugs, diet, and other available medical aids is unethical. Medical examination is also essential to rule out the possibility that the patient's symptoms may be due to an infection or some other organic pathogenic agent for which a specific type of medication or surgery is the only effective remedy.

When it is apparent that emotional factors play an important role in the manifestation of symptoms, psychotherapists may be helpful as consultants. A team approach may be used, with physician and psychotherapist sharing responsibility for

Table 17.1. Patient Attitudes and Psychosomatic Reactions.

Disorder	Patient attitude
Ulcers	Feels deprived of what is due him and wants to get even.
Hypertension	Feels threatened with harm and has to be ready for anything.
Asthma	Feels left out in the cold and wants to shut the person or situation out.
Colitis	Feels he is being injured or degraded and wishes he could get rid of the responsible agent.
Eczema	Feels he is being frustrated and can do nothing about it except take it out on himself.
Acne	Feels he is being picked on and wants to be left alone.
Psoriasis	Feels there is a constant gnawing at him and that he has to put up with it.
Rheumatoid arthritis	Feels tied down and wants to get free.
Low backache	Wants to run away.
Raynaud's disease	Wants to take hostile physical action.

treatment. In the team approach either participant may assume the major role in accordance with the needs of the patient. As in the treatment of other problems in living, the choice of psychotherapeutic method may range from psychoanalysis to behavior modification. Treatment may focus on the individual alone or may involve other family members. Psychotherapeutic procedures that work well with some patients are ineffective with others.

The periodic recurrence of symptoms makes it difficult to assess the relative effectiveness of various forms of medical and psychotherapeutic treatment. Symptoms tend to come and go, with their intensity more directly related to the changing tides of personal stress than to therapeutic intervention. The recurring idea that a psychosomatic disorder offers a protective defense against the development of a more serious disorder may be partly a rationalization dreamed up by frustrated therapists.

Biofeedback and the Treatment of Psychosomatic Ailments

Recent studies have demonstrated that subjects, when given relevant feedback information, can learn to regulate many physiological responses that are mediated by the autonomic nervous system. This finding has important implications for the treatment of psychosomatic ailments. The biofeedback procedure requires elaborate recording apparatus but the principle is simple. In the case of heart beat, for example, the subject is presented with a continuous visual picture of his mechanically recorded heart beat. He is asked to keep looking at the visual record and to try to decrease (or increase) the rate. No instructions are given as to how he is to do this. Whenever the heart rate decreases, the subject is reinforced by some token reward for making the "correct" response. After several training sessions, the subject somehow acquires the ability to control his heart rate so that he can, at will, decrease or increase it.

Similar procedures have been developed for the self-regulation of muscle tension, blood pressure, brain waves, and other autonomic responses. Some success has been reported in the clinical application of biofeedback, in combination with progressive relaxation and other techniques, in the treatment of essential hypertension, irregular cardiac rhythms, tension headaches, Raynaud's disease, and migraine headaches (Schwartz, 1973; Kimmel, 1974).

The idea of voluntary control of autonomic responses is not new. Yogis have been masters of the art for centuries. What is new is the development of practical techniques that may be readily applied in the treatment of psychosomatic ailments.

ORGANIC BRAIN DISORDERS ACCOMPANIED BY PSYCHOSOCIAL DISTURBANCES

The human brain has many functions. Besides serving as the coordinating and controlling center for physiological processes associated with sensation, emotion, and motor response, it is the key organ in perception, attention, comprehension, learning, memory, and thinking. Other important brain functions include conscious awareness and the orderly integration of diverse cerebral activities. Extensive brain damage usually leads to some impairment in all these functions. Frequently noted psychological defects include mental confusion, disorientation as to time, place, and person, poor recall of recent events, memory loss, faulty judgment, and impaired intelligence.

The most common cause of brain damage is aging. There are marked individual differences with respect to the age of onset of significant cortical degeneration, but if a person lives long enough, his brain will eventually succumb to the ravages of time. Significant decline in brain functioning usually does not begin before the age of sixty-five, though in rare cases the process

BIOFEEDBACK AND THE VOMITING BOY: A CASE REPORT

Peter Lang has reported an interesting case of the use of biofeedback as operant conditioning in the treatment of a boy who could not stop vomiting (Lang, 1970; more fully reported in Lang and Melamed, 1969).

"Recently I was asked to treat a nine-month-old boy who regularly vomited his entire meal after eating. When I first saw him he was in an advanced state of dehydration and malnutrition. He weighed less than 12 pounds, was being fed through a stomach pump, and was not expected to live.

"Extensive medical tests showed that his condition was not organic. I'm still not sure how he learned this response, but we know that what is learned usually can be unlearned. I measured the muscle potentials along the infant's esophagus and found that on the graph paper I could detect the first wave of reverse peristalsis that just preceded regurgitation. I arranged an apparatus to give aversive electric shocks to his leg whenever his esophagus started to back up, which continued until vomiting had ceased. After only a few meals with this therapy the infant ceased to vomit. He is now a healthy toddler."

starts as early as forty. These atypical presenile conditions, sometimes referred to as *Pick's disease*, are thought to be due to an inherited neurological defect. Pick's disease is often noted in several members of one family. It is distinguished by a characteristic brain pathology.

Other causes of transient or permanent brain damage include head injuries, intoxicating drugs, infections, and metabolic disturbances. Cerebral metabolic insufficiency associated with brain damage from various causes may lead to delirium; this is frequently noted in persons approaching or recovering from a coma, intoxicated individuals, and persons with high fevers. The reaction is transient and consists largely of extremely defective brain functioning. The delirious patient is typically confused, disoriented, incoherent, and out of touch with reality. Perceptual disturbances include misidentification of persons, misinterpretation of stimuli, and hallucinations. The bewildered patients may show signs of extreme apprehension and panic.

The psychological disturbances described so far represent direct expressions of brain malfunctioning. In addition, brain-damaged persons may exhibit a variety of secondary reactions that are more closely related to preexisting personality defects than to brain damage. These reactions may range from an exaggeration of lifelong maladaptive traits (suspiciousness, querulousness, passive dependence, egocentricity, rigidity, irritability) to full-blown neurotic or psychotic reactions. These secondary reactions may be provoked, released or accentuated by the added strain placed on the individual by brain malfunction, but they are not caused by the brain disorder. There is no relation between the severity of secondary psychogenic symptoms and the extent of brain damage. In cases of acute or transient brain disorders, secondary symptoms may persist long after the direct effects of brain damage have disappeared. Secondary symptoms may be alleviated or eliminated by psychotherapy or medication without affecting the impairment that is directly due to brain damage.

Acute and Chronic Brain Disorders

Acute brain disorders are differentiated from chronic brain disorders on the basis of the reversibility of the organic damage. The clinical symptoms are the same in both forms of disorder: both are characterized by the usual syndrome of direct psychological defects, and secondary reactions may or may not be present in either. Acute disorders are marked by temporary impairment in brain tissue function. The organic pathology is reversible and the patient returns to his usual level and mode of functioning in a few days or weeks. The main causes of acute brain disorder are alcohol and drug intoxication, head injuries, and systemic infections.

In chronic brain disorders, the damage is irreversible and permanent. Over time the patient may show some improvement in psychological functioning, but the more typical pattern is a gradual and progressive decline. The two most prevalent types of chronic brain disorder are senile brain change and cerebral arteriosclerosis. Other chronic conditions include tissue damage associated with alcoholism and convulsive disorders. Deterioration of the central nervous system due to syphilitic infection (general paresis) was formerly a widespread chronic disorder. The discovery of antibiotic drugs that provide effective treatment for syphilis has virtually eliminated this condition as a psychiatric disorder. The handbooks of psychiatry edited by Arieti (1959) and Freedman and Kaplan (1967) include comprehensive reviews of the neurological, medical, and psychiatric aspects of organic brain disorders.

Cerebral arteriosclerosis and senile brain disorders are both disorders of old age. Onset of symptoms generally occurs after age 65 for patients diagnosed as suffering from cerebral arteriosclerosis and after age 70 for those classified as senile brain disorder. Their direct and secondary psychosocial symptoms are similar, and the diagnostic differentiation is made on the basis of etiological factors and neuroanatomical pathology. It is presumed that predisposing genetic factors influence the age of onset and the severity of brain disintegration in senile brain disease. Postmortem studies indicate that senile brain disease is marked by a generalized atrophy of the brain (especially of the frontal lobe), shrinkage of the cerebral cortex, and the presence of a large number of rounded granular masses that are referred to as *senile plaques*.

A diagnosis of arteriosclerosis implies the presence of some pathology of the cerebral arteries which blocks the flow of nutrient blood to cortical cells. A cerebral hemorrhage, popularly called a stroke, is considered indicative of some pathology of the cerebral arteries. The term arteriosclerosis, which refers specifically to a hardening of the cerebral arteries, is technically a misnomer when applied as the basic or sole underlying cause. The fault usually is due to occlusion of the arteries by fatty deposits, the medical term for which is atherosclerosis.

Psychosocial Aspects of Aging

With or without the added strain of brain pathology, the biological process of aging constitutes a significant source of frustration and stress. Some of the problems directly related to the aging process are poor physical health, impairment of vision and hearing, loss of vigor, reduction in psychological competence, and loss of physical attractiveness. Concomitant problems that are indirectly associated with biological decline include occupational retirement, reduced income, loss of spouse and old friends, reduction in social status, and the increased risk of death. These problems are real and inescapable. Preventive measures and direct solutions are not usually available.

From a psychological point of view, however, the critical issue is not the presence of problems but the individual's reaction to them. The great majority of aged persons manage somehow to cope with the problems of aging. Insofar as possible, they try to plan ahead so that their old age will not become an agonizing period of pain, disability, want, and loneliness. Most men realize the desirability of facing the reality of retirement before it is actually upon them and of preparing for an inevitable reduction in income, social status, and feelings of personal worth, though actually making these adjustments may be difficult. A feeling of purpose and meaningfulness may be retained through launching a new career, part-time work, or the cultivation of avocational interests. Other con-

Coping with aging: The social nexus of these old men centers on their regular attendance in the lobby of the county courthouse.

structive approaches used by both men and women include the correction of treatable physical disabilities, the maintenance and replacement of friends, continued participation in varied activities, and the preservation of independence and self-reliance.

The less fortunate evade or deny the realities of biological decline, turn to others for support with mixed feelings of dependence and resentment, or find refuge in preexisting neurotic or psychotic patterns of escape or defense. Those who in the past have succeeded in maintaining a marginal adjustment may manifest more marked overt symptoms in later years.

Minor forms of maladjustment commonly noted during old age include increased social withdrawal, irritability, egocentricity, suspiciousness, compulsive behavior, resistance to change, preoccupation with physical health, increased anxiety, agitation, and periodic outbursts of helpless rage. The two major maladaptive reactions are depressions and paranoid trends. The theoretical premise that depressive behavior represents a reaction to some significant loss has considerable face validity in the case of retired persons who have experienced the loss of health, income, children, friends, and loved ones.

Depressions in elderly persons are characterized by the usual symptom patterns: dejection, pessimism, loss of self-esteem, guilt, self-condemnation, sleep irregularities, and somatic complaints. The high suicide rate of aged men may be partly attributed to self-blame and self-attack resulting from a sense of failure in life. Paranoid reactions in the aged often represent an externalization of blame. Rather than accept responsibility for his own failure to provide for the future, the individual attacks the social system. The ill will and hostility of neighbors and the duplicity of former friends serve as convenient explanations for his lack of friends and loneliness. The parent who was preoccupied with his own concerns when his children were young accuses them of neglect and ingratitude when the tables are turned.

Treatment of the Aged

The multiple needs and deficiencies of the aged require a broad-spectrum treatment program. Their pressing financial needs have been alleviated to some extent by social security and medicare programs, but without independent means or the personal assistance of people who care for them, old age can still be a disaster. There are advantages and disadvantages to living with one's children. The gains of being cared for within the family have to be balanced against the loss of independence and the amount of inconvenience or discomfort an elderly parent's presence creates for other family members. As a rule it is best for the elderly to remain in familiar surroundings, but placement in a nursing home or geriatric hospital may be required if the person is physically or mentally disabled and needs close supervision and protective care. The former practice of "dumping" elderly confused or disturbed persons in public mental hospitals, fortunately, has been largely discontinued.

The longevity and general adjustment of the aged can be greatly improved by adequate diet and treatment of infections. Attempts to halt or reverse senile brain damage and impairment of mental functioning through chemotherapy have been unsuccessful (Prien, 1973). More rewarding results have been obtained in the use of psychiatric drugs in reducing anxiety, relieving depressions, and bringing disruptive behavior under control. The use of psychoactive drugs has not only provided relief to the patient but eased the burden of the family and others in caring for him. Without these drugs, many elderly persons in nursing homes would require hospitalization. But the effect of psychoactive drugs is limited to moderating symptoms. Supplementary psychotherapy or counseling is recommended to improve the patients' outlook on life, increasing his self esteem, and restoring his social involvement.

Convulsive Disorders

The term "convulsive disorder" is a generic label applied to a pattern of periodic loss of consciousness, motor disturbances, or epileptic seizures. Attacks are spontaneous and unpredictable; they may occur once or twice in a lifetime, or several hundred times a year. The main diagnostic criterion is the presence of abnormal electroencephalographic (EEG) brain wave patterns. EEG irregularities may be present during normal sleep as well as while an attack is in progress. The consistent finding of EEG abnormality in convulsive disorders has led to the suggestion that these conditions might be more precisely defined as *cerebral dysrhythmia*.

Historically, a distinction has been made between *idiopathic* and *symptomatic epilepsy*. There is good evidence that susceptibility to idiopathic epilepsy is genetically determined. The concordance rate for this disorder is significantly greater among MZ twins than among DZ twins. Seizures occur five times more frequently among members of the families of affected persons than among the general population (Page, 1947; Lennox and Lennox, 1960). The role of heredity is less pronounced in symptomatic epilepsy. These seizures are attributed to some incidental brain pathology or toxic condition. In symptomatic epilepsy, the occurrence of abnormal EEG patterns tends to be restricted to a focal area; the abnormality of brain waves is more generalized in cases of idiopathic epilepsy.

A clinical differentiation is made between *grand mal, petit mal, Jacksonian,* and *psychomotor* attacks. The *grand mal* attack is the most dramatic. About 50 percent of the victims report an "aura" that precedes a seizure and signals its onset. The aura may consist of a mood change, a dreamy state, muscular twitchings, or sensory disturbances. The onset of the convulsion is marked by a characteristic epileptic cry and sudden loss of consciousness. The person falls to the floor as if struck by an unseen blow. The fall is so sudden that it may result in injuries. The first stage of the convulsion consists of a tonic phase, in which the entire musculature is in extreme tonic spasm. This is followed by a clonic phase, which consists of alternating flexing and stretching of the muscles. The victim may slam his head against the floor, bite his tongue, and wet and soil himself. The attack usually lasts about two minutes and is followed by deep, noisy breathing. Frothy saliva, sometimes tinged with blood, often appears at his mouth. In a short time he spontaneously comes out of the coma. Some victims complain of headache and tiredness; others feel relieved and refreshed.

Petit mal is characterized by recurring periods of loss of consciousness that usually last about twenty seconds. The person suddenly interrupts whatever he is doing at the time, but he does not fall. External signs may be limited to turning up the eyes, nodding the head, or a slight jerking movement of the body. The attack may pass unnoticed by others and by the epileptic himself unless it causes an obvious halt in conversation, a suspension of walking movements, or the dropping of an object he was holding. Some individuals have numerous attacks during the day. It is not uncommon for epileptics to have both *petit mal* and *grand mal* seizures.

Jacksonian epilepsy originates in a focal point of cerebral excitation. The attack usually starts with twitching movements of the fingers or a corner of the mouth.

Figure 17.1. a. Electroencephalogram of a Nine-Year-Old Boy. Tonic-clonic seizure with fast, high voltage waves. Arrow indicates appearance of clinical evidence of seizure. b. Petit mal Attack, with Staring, Blinking, and Loss of Consciousness. Characteristic wave and spike discharge in electroencephalogram. (From Gibbs and Gibbs: *Atlas of Electroencephalography*, Lew A. Cummings Co.)

The twitching spreads gradually until it becomes a generalized *grand mal* seizure. Consciousness is usually retained as long as the jerking movements are confined to the extremities.

Psychomotor attacks are also referred to as temporal lobe epilepsy. The condition is marked by lapses of consciousness, irregular muscular movements, disturbances in thought or affect, stereotyped behavior, and *grand mal* seizures.

Convulsive disorders are present in about one in every three hundred persons in the general population. Drugs are available for the control of attacks, so that most epileptics today lead relatively normal lives. Since the drugs have toxic effects, medical supervision is necessary. When an identifiable area of the brain is the source of focal seizures, surgical intervention may correct the condition.

On the basis of chance alone, all types of character disorder, neurosis, and psychosis may be expected to occur among persons with convulsive disorders. In view of the frequency of these disorders in the general population, it would be surprising if this were not so. The question is whether the incidence of psychopathology in general or of some particular psychological disorder is more prevalent among epileptics than in the general population. Factual data on this point are inconclusive. Extensive research studies have failed to confirm the once popular notion that epileptics as a group are characterized by distinctive personality traits (Tizard, 1962). When the underlying brain damage is extensive or involves critical areas, the epileptic may show impairment in his cognitive functioning. Secondary reactions may include resentment of social or occupational discrimination because of the disability, fear of humiliation if seizures should occur in public, reduced self-confidence, and general discontent.

SUMMARY

Sexual dysfunctions provide a good example of the reciprocal interaction of psycho-biosocial variables in the etiology and correction of behavior disturbances. Impotence and orgasmic deficiency may be defined as physical symptoms originating and expressed in interpersonal situations for which educational retraining and learning constitute the most effective treatment.

Genetic and biological factors influence relative vulnerability to psychosomatic and organic brain disorders, but the phenotypic expression and the treatment of these disorders are dependent on psychosocial factors. Experimental studies, which have demonstrated the successful application of operant conditioning procedures in regulating visceral and glandular changes, provide a scientific basis for the application of learning principles to the acquisition and treatment of physical symptoms associated with psychosomatic disorders.

A person's reactions to impairments in functioning caused by brain disorders often have greater psychopathological significance than the actual destruction of brain tissue. The fusion of genetic, medical, socioeconomic, personality, and interpersonal variables is particularly evident in the complexity and diversity of the adjustment problems of the aged.

References

American Psychiatric Association. *Diagnostic and Statistical Manual of Mental Disorders* (DSM-11). Washington, D.C., 1968.

Arieti, S., ed. *American Handbook of Psychiatry*, vol. 2. New York: Basic Books, 1959.

Ascough, J. C., and Sipprelle, C. N. "Operant Verbal Conditioning of Autonomic Responses." *Behavior Research and Therapy* 6 (1968): 363-70.

Brady, J. V. "Ulcers in 'Executive' Monkeys." *Scientific American* 199 (1958): 95-100.

Buss, A. H. *Psychopathology*. New York: Wiley, 1966.

Graham, D. T.; Lundy, R. M.; Benjamin, L. S.; and Kabler, F. K. "Some Specific Attitudes in Initial Interviews with Patients Having Different 'Psychosomatic' Diseases." *Psychosomatic Medicine* 24 (1962): 257-66.

Kaplan, H. S. *The New Sex Therapy*. New York: Brunner/Mazel, 1974.

Kimmel, H. D. "Instrumental Conditioning of Autonomically Mediated Responses in Human Beings." *American Psychologist* 29 (1974): 325-335.

Kinsey, A. C.; Pomeroy, W. B.; and Martin, C. E. *Sexual Behavior in the Human Male*. Philadelphia: Saunders, 1948.

—— and Gebhard, P. H. *Sexual Behavior in the Human Female*. Philadelphia: Saunders, 1953.

Lacey, J. I., and Lacey, B. C. "Verification and Extension of the Principle of Autonomic Response Stereotype." *American Journal of Psychology* 71 (1958): 50-73.

Lang, P. J. "Autonomic Control or Learning to Play the Internal Organs." *Psychology Today*, October 1970.

—— and Melamed, B. G. "Case Report: Avoidance Conditioning of an Infant with Chronic Ruminative Vomiting." *Journal of Abnormal Psychology* 74 (1969): 1-8.

Lennox, W. J., and Lennox, M. A. *Epilepsy and Related Disorders*. Boston: Little, Brown, 1960.

Lynch, J. J. "Social Responding in Dogs: Heart Rate Changes to a Person." *Society for Psychophysiological Research* 5 (1969): 389-93.

Malmo, R. B., and Shagass, C. "Physiologic Study of Symptom Mechanisms in Psychiatric Patients under Stress." *Psychosomatic Medicine* 11 (1949): 25-29.

Masters, W. H., and Johnson, V. E. *Human Sexual Response*. Boston: Little, Brown, 1966.

——. *Human Sexual Inadequacy*. Boston: Little, Brown, 1970.

Page, J. D. *Abnormal Psychology: A Clinical Approach to Psychological Deviants*. New York: McGraw-Hill, 1947.

Prien, R. F. "Chemotherapy in Chronic Organic Brain Syndrome: A Review of the Literature." *Psychopharmacology Review*, 9 (1973): 5-20.

Rees, L. "The Importance of Psychological, Allergic, and Infective Factors in Childhood Asthma." *Journal of Psychosomatic Research* 7 (1964): 253-62.

Rennie, T., and Strole, L. "Social Class Prevalence and Distribution of Psychosomatic Conditions in an Urban Population." *Psychosomatic Medicine* 18 (1956): 449-57.

Schwartz, G. E. "Biofeedback Therapy: Some Theoretical and Practical Issues." *American Psychologist* 28 (1973): 666-673.

Selye, H. *The Stress of Life*. New York: McGraw-Hill, 1956.

Tizard, B. "The Personality of Epileptics: A Discussion of the Evidence." *Psychological Bulletin* 59 (1962): 196-210.

Wenger, M. A.; Clemens, T. L.; Coleman, D. R.; Cullen, T. D.; and Engel, B. T. "Autonomic Response Specificity." *Psychosomatic Medicine* 23 (1961): 185-93.

Wolf, H. G. *Stress and Disease*. Springfield, Ill.: Charles C Thomas, 1953.

Girl with Cock, Pablo Picasso

Children share most of the types of behavior deviations associated with adult forms of psychopathology and, in addition, exhibit some maladaptive reactions that are more or less restricted to youth. The criteria for disordered behavior in children are more loosely interpreted than the criteria for adult disorders, but the key features are the same. The initial diagnosis is usually made by parents or teachers. The behavior deviations considered indicative of psychopathology consist mainly of uncontrolled or uncontrollable defects in psychosocial functions. In evaluating the significance and severity of deviant behavior in children, psychologists focus attention on (1) the relative inadequacy or inappropriateness of the behavior to the age of the child and attending circumstances, and (2) the extent to which the behavior is detrimental, disruptive, maladaptive, or a source of undue distress or threat to the child, his family, or society.

A child's behavior problems are more directly related to developmental defects than an adult's, and more emphasis is placed on his failure to attain levels of psychosocial adequacy appropriate to his age than on loss or impairment of functioning. As with adults, the presence of uncontrolled or uncontrollable behavior (with allowance made for age) is usually the critical factor in referring a child for diagnosis and treatment. Defects in his psychosocial behavior are considered indicative of psychopathology when neither parents nor teachers are able to cope effectively with his personal, social, or educational problems. When the behavior is antisocial, referral to a psychologist or psychiatrist may be initiated by court officials.

DIFFICULTIES IN CLASSIFICATION

The concept of discrete disorders, each of which is distinguished by a specific cause and marked by a specific set of symptoms, is even less applicable to disorders of childhood than to those of adults. A reaction that is accepted as normal behavior at a certain age may in an older child be considered a sign of delayed development or a symptomatic manifestation of an emotional problem. Enuresis (bedwetting), for example, is normal in infants, but it is a sign of delayed development in a five-year-old and a regressive reaction in a ten-year-old who has been free of this condition for over seven years. There are no specific behavior deficits or excesses that are only observed in disturbed children. Behavior deviations that constitute the complaint symptoms for referring children to clinics are also present in a substantial proportion of randomly selected school children (Conners, 1970; Shephard et al., 1971).

Studies of parent and teacher ratings of all children in a defined school population indicate that the average child exhibits ten or more of the types of behavior "symptoms" listed as "Children's Behavior Disturbances," (Werry and Quay, 1971). Behavior differences between clinic referred and normal children are mainly variations of degree. The deviations of clinic children are more intense, are emitted more frequently, appear to be less amenable to voluntary or external control, and are perceived by significant adults as more disturbing.

SYMPTOM AFTER SYMPTOM: A CASE REPORT OF A DISTURBED CHILD

An interesting description of a child's trial-and-error experimentation in symptom formation and the manner by which it was skillfully extinguished has been reported by Ullmann and Krasner (1969, p. 158). The child was at a summer camp for handicapped children.

At first the child was self-punishing—hitting, slapping and biting himself. When this did not cause the counselors concern, he threw tantrums in which he beat his head against the ground or trees. He gave this up and next took his clothes off in public, but this led to no other counselor behavior than his being put to bed (taking off clothes meant preparation for bed). The child gave up the undressing behavior and proceeded to steal food from other children's plates even though his own was heaped high. To keep other children from imitating the stealing, counselors placed the child in a room to eat by himself. In this situation the child began defecating and smearing feces over himself, the walls, the floors, and his belongings. When this behavior did not elicit special concern on the part of the counselors, it ceased after five days. Next, the child piled all the children's shoes together early in the morning. Sorting shoes before breakfast became a morning game for the group, and after a week, this behavior also stopped. The "shoe game" was the last of a spectacular series of antisocial behaviors, none of which were reinforced with attention, concern, or giving the child his way. If any of these behaviors had been reinforced, the pattern of maladaptive behavior might well have continued for a longer period of time.

The problem of classification of adult behavior symptoms is somewhat simplified by the fact that they tend to reflect the characteristic habit patterns of the individual and are relatively stable. There is usually some cohesiveness and consistency in symptom clusters. Children's personalities are less structured, individual styles of reacting are still in the process of development, and their behavior is more fluid, changeable, transient, and unpredictable. Temporary compulsive bedtime ceremonies may occur in children otherwise free of obsessive-compulsive traits. Within the space of a moment or two a child may be happy and miserable, submissive and assertive, friendly and aggressive. He may be well behaved at home and a discipline problem at school, or vice versa.

A child's behavior is controlled by external events to a greater degree than an adult's. In the absence of firmly established habit patterns designed to cope with difficulties, children rely on trial-and-error improvisation. If a reaction (symptom) works, in the sense that it relieves tension, elicits a favorable response from the environment, or is otherwise reinforced, it will probably be repeated. The response may be generalized to other, similar situations, and if it is repeatedly reinforced, it may become a characteristic style or mode of reacting.

If it does not work, it is usually discarded and another is tried. This changeableness of response, which is related to the choice of symptoms, provides a flexible approach to difficulties. It is not necessary to invoke the more hypothetical principle of symptom substitution, which assumes that new symptoms are the surface manifestations of inner conflicts, and that until the underlying conflict is resolved, new symptoms will replace discarded ones. If a "good" response emerges or can be acquired through therapy, there is no need to uncover and liquidate the presumed repressed conflict.

APPROACHES TO CLASSIFICATION

One of the more innovative approaches to the classification of behavior problems in children has been reported by Alan Ross (1974). His basic premise, which reflects his behavior theory orientation, is that all problem behavior "deviates from the social norm in that it occurs with a frequency or intensity that the child's social environment deems either too high or too low." Responses that are too high are grouped under the general heading of *behavior excess* and those that are too low are classed under the heading of *deficient behavior*. Subcategories of excess behavior include aggression, withdrawal and disorganized psychotic reactions. Categories marked by behavior deficits include learning difficulties, mental subnormality, juvenile delinquency, psychophysiological disorders, and infantile autism. The approach has obvious therapeutic implications. As stated by Ross, the therapeutic task is to help children with behavior deficits to acquire missing responses and to help children with excess behavior to modify existing responses to bring their behavior within the range of social acceptability. He recommends the use of behavior modification principles to correct here-and-now target behaviors.

A limitation of the Ross approach is that its appeal is restricted to advocates of learning theory and behavior therapy. A more specific criticism concerns the arbitrary selection and assignment of subcategories. No mention is made of many recognized forms of child psychopathology. Juvenile delinquency, which is essentially a legal term for aggressive, antisocial acts, is classified as a deficient behavior whereas aggressive behavior is considered a form of behavior excess. Withdrawal reactions may, with equal justification, be described as either excess or deficient behavior. Few clinicians would agree with Ross's inclusion of masturbation in public as an example of deficient psychophysiological behavior. On the positive side, the classification system is based on a consistent rationale. With modifications it may eventually find wide acceptance among behavior therapists.

The factor analytic approach to the classification of behavior disorders in children remains at an experimental level with little possibility of immediate practical application. Researchers continue to invent new labels for identified behavior clusters and the number of factors reported varies with input data and the population studied. There is, however, agreement with respect to the generality of two contrasting behavior patterns, namely, *personality* vs. *character disorders*. Behavior items associated with personality disorders include excessive inhibition, fears, anxiety, social withdrawal, compulsions, and varied somatic complaints. These reactions have been interpreted as involving the internalization of conflicts, moving away from the social environment, and the child being the principal sufferer. Behavior items associated with conduct disorders include disobedience, stealing, lying, fighting, destructiveness, vandalism, delinquent behavior, and poor school work. These reactions have been interpreted as representing the externalization of conflicts by the child, his moving against and taking out his frustrations on his social environment with the consequent arousal of societal concern and retaliatory punitive actions. Other reported factors include hyperactivity, emotional immaturity, learning disabilities, unsocialized aggressiveness, brain injury, and diffuse psychotic behavior. Two of the more recent studies by Patterson (1964) and Achenbach (1966) include a review of the literature.

A third approach consists of modifications of the traditional model used in the classification of adult disorders to accommodate the unique features of behavior disorders in children. The best example is the comprehensive description of childhood problems included in the 1966 report of the Committee on Child Psychiatry of the Group for the Advancement of Psychiatry. The GAP classification is discussed in some detail in the following section.

GAP CLASSIFICATION SYSTEM

The GAP classification is similar in many respects to DSM-11 and subject to the same criticisms. The diverse and changing reactions of disturbed children obviously do not fall into neat clearly defined diagnostic categories. The main GAP advantage is that the categories are child-based and provide for healthy responses, mild developmental deviations, and transient situational reactions. The GAP is not the final answer. All that can be said in its favor is that it is as useful as any other system now available for organizing in some semblance of order the bewildering variety of symptoms noted in children. The GAP Classification recognizes ten major categories:

Healthy responses
Reactive disorders
Developmental deviations
Psychoneurotic disorders
Personality disorders
Psychotic disorders
Psychophysiological disorders
Brain syndromes
Mental retardation
Other disorders

CHILDREN'S BEHAVIOR DEFICITS: THE GAP LIST (ABBREVIATED)*

I. Disturbances related to bodily functions.
   A. Eating: anorexia, food rituals, regurgitation.
   B. Sleeping: bedtime rituals, nightmares, somnambulism.
   C. Bowel function: constipation, anal masturbation, smearing.
   D. Bladder function: enuresis, resistance to training, retention.
   E. Speech: aphonia, stuttering, elective mutism.
   F. Motor patterns: apraxia, catalepsy, tics, mannerisms.
   G. Rhythmic patterns: head banging, body rocking, whirling.
   H. Habit patterns: nose picking, thumb-sucking.
   I. Sensory disturbances: anesthesia, hallucinations, paresthesia.
   J. Other disturbances: headaches, acne, asthma, hypertension.

II. Disturbances related to cognitive functions.
   A. Learning failure: underachievement, reading disability.
   B. Disturbances in thinking: impaired reality testing, associative disorders.
   C. Disturbances in memory: amnesia, memory impairment.
   D. Disturbances in awareness: confusion, delirium, dissociation.

III. Disturbances in affective behavior.
   A. Fearful behavior: multiple or specific fears.
   B. Manifest anxiety: separation anxiety, apprehension, panic states.
   C. Depressive symptoms: dejection, agitation, retardation of response.
   D. Euphoric behavior: elation, manic behavior, giggling.
   E. Hypochondriacal behavior: preoccupation with disease.
   F. Other affective states: rage, guilt, shame, inferiority.

* Technical terms are defined in the glossary at the end of this book.

These "disorders" should be regarded as descriptive labels for combinations of behavior deviations commonly observed in children.

Healthy Responses

The main function of the category of "healthy responses" is to direct attention to the normality and appropriateness at certain ages or in some circumstances of reactions that may be misperceived as symptoms of pathology by overconcerned parents: thumb-sucking in infants, the mild separation anxiety frequently exhibited by preschool children, the frequent confusion of adolescents concerning identity and dependence-independence, and so on. The category may also be used to indicate areas of strengths that thus serve to offset and modify the significance of deviations.

Reactive Disorders

Reactive disorders are transient situational responses and other conditions that are considered to represent reactions to particular events or series of events. The diagnosis of reactive disorder is restricted to cases in which the situation does in fact

IV. Disturbances related to development.
   A. Physical growth: accelerated, retarded, or uneven growth.
   B. Maturational patterns: regressive, retarded, or uneven maturation.

V. Disturbances in social behavior.
   A. Aggressive behavior.
      1. Externally directed: destructive behavior, fighting.
      2. Internally directed: self-injury, suicidal attempts.
   B. Antisocial behavior: cheating, fire setting, vandalism.
   C. Oppositional behavior: disobedience, passive-aggressive behavior.
   D. Isolating behavior: autism, excessive shyness, paranoid tendencies.
   E. Dominance-submission: boastfulness, rebelliousness, manipulation of others.
   F. Dependence-independence: clinging, whining, excessive independence.
   G. Sexual adjustment: exhibitionism, homosexuality, promiscuity.

VI. Disturbances in integrative behavior.
   A. Impulsive behavior
   B. Incapacity to play.
   C. Low anxiety tolerance.
   D. Low frustration tolerance.
   E. Overuse of adaptive mechanisms.
   F. Disorganized behavior.
   G. Folie à deux.

VII. Other behavior disturbances.
   A. Stereotyped behavior: perfectionism, compulsive behavior.
   B. Temper tantrums.
   C. Hallucinations: auditory, visual, olfactory.
   D. Delusions: ideas of reference, somatic symptoms, persecutory ideas.
   E. Malingering.
   F. Addictive behavior: alcoholism, drug use, glue-sniffing.

create an emotional trauma in the particular child; the reaction is causally related to the specific event and not simply coincident with it. Typical situations that precipitate reactive disturbances are illness, hospitalization, the loss of a parent, school pressures, and the attitudes and behavior of peers.

The reaction may take the form of an arrest in development or may be expressed in a variety of other ways. The symptoms may be influenced by the nature of the stress, the age, development level, and personality makeup of the child, and past experiences. Most of the neurotic traits, habit disturbances, mild conduct disorders, and depressive reactions exhibited by infants deprived of adequate mothering would be included in this category. Specific symptoms include lack of appetite, apathy, withdrawal, overt aggressive acts, passive-aggressive behavior, regressive enuresis, preoccupation with fantasy, and overt panic. As a rule, reactive disorders are transient and temporary, but they can lead to chronic disabilities. An additional diagnosis is usually indicated if the reaction persists or is superimposed upon one of the other disorders.

Developmental Deviations

Development is a function of the interaction of maturational patterns and experience or learning. Maturation is largely dependent on a biologically determined series of steps. Maturation level influences both the child's potentialities for development and his responsiveness. To a considerable degree, some type of innate filter system minimizes the effect of stimulation on a child before he has reached the maturational stage that permits him to cope with the particular stimuli.

Technically, developmental deviations include precocious as well as retarded or distorted development of personality, although most examples of precocious development are more reasonably considered healthy responses. The category thus serves mainly to identify negative or unde-

sirable deviations that exceed the range of normal variability. The deviation may occur at a time, in a sequence, or to a degree not expected for a given age level. It may appear in a restricted range of functions or may involve almost the whole maturational timetable. Typical deviations in early development include delayed speech, delayed toilet training, and poor coordination.

During infancy and early childhood, the individual's responses tend to be uncontrolled, generalized, and diffuse. An important aspect of development is the increasing differentiation, integration, and control of behavior. Difficulties in monitoring and integrating input stimuli may lead to hyperactivity or underactivity, impulsiveness or apathy. Defects in speech development include disorders of articulation, rhythm, phonation, and speech comprehension. More extreme deviations, such as mutism of autistic children, would be classified as symptoms of psychotic behavior. The most prevalent of the deviations in cognitive functions is reading disability. Other learning problems include delayed or impaired proficiency in spelling, writing, and arithmetic.

Examples of deviations in social development include shyness, lack of social skills, emotional immaturity, aggressive behavior, and inability to relate effectively to peers. A common concern of parents is the presence in girls of characteristics culturally defined as masculine and in boys of characteristics considered feminine. (Often this sort of concern indicates a greater problem in the parents than in the child, though the child is certain to suffer from it.) Markedly precocious or delayed heterosexual interests may also be perceived as problems. Less controversial areas of developmental deviation include marked overcontrol or undercontrol of emotions and impulses, failure to develop frustration tolerance consistent with one's age, and the overuse of defense mechanisms.

Psychoneurotic Disorders

The symptomatic manifestations of neuroses in children parallel those in adults. The main difference is that the traditional symptom patterns associated with obsessive-compulsive, hysterical, neurasthenic, and other neurotic reactions are less clearly defined in children. Anna Freud (1965) distinguishes between the archaic fears often expressed by children and regular phobias. Phobias can usually be traced to some frightening experience or are based on regression and conflict. Archaic fears—fear of darkness, loneliness, strangers, thunder and lightning—appear to be innate, and as a rule, they disappear spontaneously with increased maturity. The preoccupation with physical symptoms that is frequently noted in children is often dismissed as "growing pains." According to psychoanalytic theory, these symptoms may represent hypochrondriacal tendencies in children who feel neglected or rejected by their mothers.

Personality Disorders

The emergence of deeply ingrained maladaptive personality patterns starts in childhood. During the early years personality traits are more flexible than they become later. The names assigned to personality types in children differ somewhat from those used for adults. GAP lists these childhood personality types:

Compulsive	Impulse-ridden
Hysterical	Neurotic
Anxious	Overly inhibited
Overly dependent	Overly independent
Oppositional	Sociosyntonic
Isolated	Sexual deviant
Distrustful	Other types

With the exception of the overly independent and sociosyntonic personality, these have already been described in Chapter 12. The concept of the sexual deviant personality in children also requires some further explanation.

The *overly independent personality* is characterized by premature strivings for independence, which may bring the child into conflict with the limits set by adults. As a rule these children are not destructive or antisocial, but their insistence on self-di-

rection and autonomy may result in their refusal of needed help and guidance. Their overly responsible grownup behavior may represent a reaction against feelings of dependence.

The child with a *sociosyntonic personality* would be considered antisocial if it were not for the fact that his reactions are consonant with those of his neighborhood group, his gang, or even his family. These children are sometimes described as socialized delinquents.

The label of *sexual deviant personality* is applied to children who persistently engage in homosexual behavior or other forms of sexual offense, when the deviation is regarded as the major personality disturbance that pervades and dominates the child's personality functioning and orientation. Transient sexual deviations are usually classified as developmental disorders.

Psychotic Disorders

Psychoses are rare in young children. Less than 5 percent of all children under fifteen referred for psychiatric or psychological examination are diagnosed as psychotic. In practically all cases, the symptom pattern suggests schizophrenia. True affective psychoses are almost never seen prior to adolescence. Depending in part on the age of the child, a distinction is made between infantile autism, symbiotic or interactional psychosis (second to fifth years), schizophreniform psychosis (sixth to thirteenth years), and psychosis of adolescence.

The clinical picture varies somewhat with the age of the child. Professional opinion varies as to whether the variations in symptoms noted among infants, preschool children, and older children constitute distinct disease entities or represent different age forms of the same disorder. Regardless of age of onset, the prognosis is poor and in most cases similar. With the exception of those few who recover or are reclassified as mentally defective, psychotic children are diagnosed as schizophrenics in adulthood. The Committee on Child Psychiatry (1966) lists the following general criteria

THE AGGRESSIVE-DELINQUENT CHILD: AN ALL-TOO-FAMILIAR SYNDROME

A more general personality type that is not specifically included in the GAP classification is the aggressive-delinquent child. A good description has been provided by E. N. Rexford (1959).

These children have long been unmanageable at home, in school, and the neighborhood. They may even be well known to the police, who have preferred no charges because of their youth. They may be bright but rarely have they performed well in school and have marked learning blocks. They tend to be hostile, resentful, overactive individuals, often extremely skilled in their performance of antisocial acts, confident that all people lie, steal, and cheat whenever it is to their advantage. They may never have learned to delay or otherwise manage their instinctual wishes except by doing, taking, or saying what they wished. They have a short attention span and find it hard to tolerate frustration of any kind. The parents usually report that they were difficult babies in relation to feeding, sleeping, and toilet training. They were never successfully disciplined; the parents usually tell of many punitive attempts to curb the child's behavior. These children's life experiences have been so unrewarding and their primitive feelings and fantasies so little transformed and sublimated that they view the outside world as a hostile place, other people as their enemies, and themselves in the position of having to strike out before they are struck down.

for the diagnosis of childhood psychosis:

1. Severe and continued impairment of emotional relations with other persons.
2. Aloofness and a tendency toward preoccupation with inanimate objects.
3. Absence of speech or poor development of speech.
4. Disturbances in sensory perception.
5. Bizarre or stereotyped behavior and motility patterns.
6. Marked resistance to change in environment or routine.
7. Outbursts of intense and unpredictable panic.
8. Absence of a sense of personal identity.
9. Blunted, uneven, or fragmented intellectual development.

Infantile autism. The syndrome of infantile autism, originally described by Leo Kanner in 1943, has been confirmed by other investigators (Rieser, 1963; Rimland, 1964; O'Gorman, 1967). The disorder is differentiated from other forms of childhood psychosis by its early age of onset (during the first year of life) and certain distinctive behavioral features. Unlike mental retardates, autistic infants appear alert, exhibit good motor development, and show fragmentary evidence of normal functioning at their age level. The assumption of normal latent intelligence is borne out in some cases by their adequate performance in later years. However, many infants who are initially diagnosed as autistic turn out to be indistinguishable from mental defectives.

The outstanding characteristic of early autism is the infant's failure to develop and manifest normal awareness of and responsiveness to its mother and other human beings. People are treated as objects. The child's deficiency in relating to others is indicated by the absence of anticipatory responses to being lifted by the parents, absence of the plastic molding displayed by normal children when cradled in their parents' arms, failure to react to the presence or absence of the mother, avoidance of eye contact, absence of crying, and lack or delay of the typical infant smiling response. The infant shows no interest in playing peek-a-boo or pat-a-cake and is devoid of affection or emotional involve-

Bruno Bettelheim, a psychoanalytically-oriented psychologist, whose best known work is with schizophrenic and autistic children.

ment with others. Speech is either absent or markedly delayed, and if the child does speak, his utterances are often restricted to a poorly modulated, parrot-like repetition of sounds without affective or communicative content. No attempt is made to converse or answer questions. That the problem is one of communication rather than speech as such is indicated by the absence of attempts at nonverbal communication.

A heightened sensitivity to stimulus change is often apparent and expressed in an obsessive insistence on sameness. Changes in the social environment or alterations in routine are met with outbursts of temper or acute anxiety. Some autistic children exhibit a marked aversion to granular foods, sniff at their food, and show bizarre food preferences. Some stimuli may evoke extreme irritability while others bring no response at all. These children appear to be more responsive to self-produced than to external stimulation. There is no evidence of hallucinations. Discontinuities in development may occur. The child may start crawling at the usual age and then stop for several months. Words spoken at ten months may not be repeated for a year or more. Motor disturbances include whirling the body or objects, flapping the hands, darting and lunging, bizarre stereotyped reactions, posturing, toe walking, teeth grinding, and head banging.

Autistic children have difficulty distinguishing the self from the nonself. It is not uncommon for an autistic child to regard himself as a kind of mechanical object or machine. The communication barrier makes it difficult to administer intelligence tests and to evaluate responses. Answers, when scorable, are uneven in quality. Yet the potentiality for normal or above-average mental ability is inferred from the alert expressions of these children and the sporadically high levels of their motor performance.

Practically every conceivable technique has been used in the treatment of autistic children. Usually residential placement is the first step. Bettelheim (1950) places great stress on providing a permissive environment in which children are indulged and given immediate gratification of their wishes. Operant behavior modification procedures have been successfully used with autistic children in helping them to acquire

AUTISTIC CHILDREN: TWO CASES

Many of the features of infantile autism may be seen in the case study of a five-year-old boy reported by Ornitz and Ritvo (1968). The boy had been an inpatient in a psychiatric hospital for a year. His mother's pregnancy and delivery had apparently been normal. The parents, of working-class background, had noted that the child showed atypical behavior and development from infancy as compared with his older sibling. Initial psychiatric referral was made when the child was three years old. According to information supplied by the parents, the boy was irritable and oversensitive as an infant. He was unusually sensitive to visual detail and spent considerable time regarding the movements of his fingers. He completely ignored auditory stimulation. At an age when children are normally interested in toys, he rejected them and other objects presented to him. If they were placed in his hands, he would let them fall or flick them away.

When he was four months old he began to make repetitive movements, from which he could be distracted only with difficulty. He rolled his head from side to side, over and over; he twirled beads and other objects for long periods. He failed to show any anticipatory response to being picked up till after he was a year old. He never made eye contact with his parents or responded to their attempts to play games with him. He used others as an extension of himself. As his parents said, "He pushes us to his needs."

He sat up without support at seven months but did not walk alone until sixteen months. He started to make spontaneous sounds by six months and syllables by twelve months, but he made little attempt to imitate sounds or words spoken by his parents. By the time he was three he had developed a ten-word vocabulary, but after that he stopped using words altogether. He never combined words into phrases. Between eighteen and twenty-four months he occasionally waved bye-bye in imitation of his father, but then abandoned this activity. From the time he was two years old he whirled himself as if he were a toy and exhibited repetitive, rapid oscillation of his hands. He refused to chew food and remained on baby foods until he was three. While he was in the hospital, he was never observed to use toys or other objects in any appropriate way. He merely kept on spinning objects and himself and flapping his hands as his parents reported he had done at home.

speech and other socially desirable behaviors (Metz, 1965; Ferster and Simmons, 1966; and Lovaas and Bucher, 1974).

Outcome in autism is about the same as in other forms of childhood schizophrenia (Eisenberg and Kanner, 1956). About 25 percent "recover," and the number can be stretched to a maximum of 35 percent if all the children who achieve a minimal social adjustment in school and community are included. Another 25 percent show some clinical improvement. Even children considered to have made successful recoveries, however, continue to show serious impairment of their human relationships, marked egocentrism, lack of social skills, and an apparent inability to identify and empathize with others. Most children who learn to speak by the age of five succeed in making some sort of social adjustment. Those who have no useful language function by that time usually exhibit other signs of severe mental retardation, and end up being reclassified as feebleminded. Since the development of speech is highly correlated with innate intelligence, it may be the underlying prognostic indicator (Rutter et al., 1967).

The specific determinants of infantile autism are unknown. A combination of genetic, organic, and psychological factors is probably involved. One or another of these etiological agents may be relatively more important in specific cases. Twin

The case of Joey, the nine year old "mechanical boy" described by Bruno Bettelheim (1959), is somewhat extreme, but it serves to illustrate the lack of human attributes associated with autistic children. Bettelheim believes that Joey converted himself into a machine because he did not dare to be human. Joey not only believed that he was a machine but his behavior created the impression in others that he was a machine. His pantomime of being controlled by wires was so convincing that observers tended to look twice to make sure he was not actually plugged in to an outlet somewhere. When the "machinery" was idle and Joey was still, the staff had to concentrate to be aware of his presence.

Case history data indicated that the boy had been strong and healthy at birth. By the time he was a year old, he had become remote and inaccessible. His mother, who was a socially detached person herself, ignored his existence. His preoccupation with mechanical things started early. One of his ideas was that liquids had to be pumped into him through an elaborate system built of straws. He put together pieces of apparatus to create a machine to "live him" while he slept. Other pieces of machinery controlled his eating and elimination.

Early self-portrait by Joey, showing a robot made of electric wires. The figure is interpreted by Bettelheim as symbolizing the child's rejection of human feelings.

studies strongly favor a genetic interpretation. With one exception, both twins of monozygotic pairs have been found to be concordant for infantile autism in all reported cases (Ornitz and Ritvo, 1968). Concordance for the disorder is rare among dizygotic twins. Eisenberg and Kanner (1956) noted that about 8 percent of the known siblings of one hundred autistic children studied could be regarded as probably autistic or emotionally disturbed.

The nature of the genetic defect is still unknown. The results of most electroencephalographic studies of autistic infants have been negative, but positive findings increase with the age of the children tested. A. D. Sorosky and his associates (1968)

have suggested that autistic children suffer from an imbalance of the excitatory and inhibitory mechanisms of the central nervous system, with primary involvement of the central vestibular mechanism. The failure of the normal inhibitory process to check excitation would account for their sustained overreactivity, whirling, hand flapping, and repetitive speech sounds. Excessive neural inhibition would account for the autistic child's unresponsiveness to sensory stimuli, prolonged immobility, and posturing. A major limitation of this neurological explanation is that it does not apply to the cardinal symptom, which is the child's lack of human feelings. The same limitation holds for Bernard Rimland's

(1964) suggestion that the symptoms of autism may be due to some defect in the reticular system of the brain.

Early reports that the parents of autistic children tend to be cold, isolated, and obsessive have recently been questioned (Ornitz and Ritvo, 1968). Many of the parents of autistic children are warm and loving and provide a normal emotional climate. Most of those parents who are in fact emotionally cold have nevertheless managed to raise one or more children who are not autistic. The coldness and detachment observed in some of these parents may be at least in part reactions to the unresponsiveness of their autistic children. Early studies suggested that an unusually high proportion of the parents of autistic children were college graduates or professional people, but this appears to have been a sampling error. More recent reports indicate that these children come from every socioeconomic class (Levine and Olson, 1968). Infantile autism appears to be far more prevalent in boys than in girls.

Interactional psychotic disorder. Some children who develop normally during the first year or two begin to show psychotic reactions between the ages of two and five. In contrast to autistic infants, who are unable to relate to and identify with the mother, these children show what M. S. Mahler (1952) has designated a "symbiotic" mother-child relationship. The symbiotic child cannot bear to be separated from his mother. At an age when the normal child begins to take steps toward individuation and separation, the symbiotic child clings to his mother, becomes progressively more dependent on her, and shows acute separation anxiety. This reaction is regarded as a symbiotic psychosis if in addition to his intense mother attachment the child shows a distorted perception of reality, gives up previously acquired communicative speech, has frequent temper tantrums, or shows signs of panic, loss of identity, a regressive retreat into autism, and other related symptoms. The psychotic reaction is often triggered by a separation from the mother associated with

enrollment in nursery school, hospitalization, or the birth of a sibling.

Other psychoses of infancy and early childhood. This is a catchall category that includes children with atypical development who may exhibit a mixture of autistic or symbiotic reactions, emotional aloofness, and distortion of reality. Here also may be included what René Spitz (1945, 1946) has called "hospitalism" and "anaclitic depression." Hospitalism designates the lack of development and progressive mental deterioration of infants reared in foundling homes and institutions that provide no mothering and inadequate stimulation. These infants have a high death rate. Anaclitic depression is a state of depressive withdrawal and debilitation occurring in children who are separated from their mothers between six and eight months of age and for whom substitute mothers are not available. Symptoms include dejection, excessive crying, screaming or not responding at all when adults touch them or pick them up, and a frozen expression. Complete recovery usually occurs if the mother resumes care of the child. If the mother does not return and the child continues to live in an institutional setting under conditions of emotional deprivation, deterioration frequently progresses until it ends in an early death. Spitz's conclusions have been criticized by Samuel Pinneau (1955) as oversimplified, overgeneralized, and lacking in scientific rigor.

A more modest evaluation of the effects of maternal deprivation has been reported by Beres and Obers (1950). They note that many children separated from their mothers in infancy and institutionalized for up to four years were socially deficient, immature, and intolerant of frustration, but the effects of maternal deprivation were neither consistent nor permanent. The group showed a remarkable degree of improvement with increasing age. About half were judged to have made a satisfactory social adjustment by adolescence.

Schizophreniform psychosis. Psychotic reactions occurring in children between the ages of six and thirteen and paralleling the symptoms of adult schizophrenia are called schizophreniform psychosis rather than schizophrenia because there are developmental differences between them and because this disorder does not necessarily lead to schizophrenia in adulthood. Symptoms include looseness of association in thought processes, intense temper outbursts, hypochondriacal tendencies, marked withdrawal, preoccupation with fantasies, and a breakdown in reality testing. Other commonly observed reactions are magical thinking, stereotyped motor patterns, inappropriate mood swings, ideas of reference, aggressive outbursts, self-mutilating behavior, and attempts at suicide.

Lauretta Bender (1961) concluded from her extensive study of child schizophrenics that these children suffer from some form of brain pathology, as evidenced by abnormal EEG patterns, which interferes with normal biological development. She attributed their lag in development, which presumably starts in the embryonic stage, to genetic factors. The genetic aspects of schizophreniform psychosis have been investigated by Kallmann and Roth (1956). Their findings indicate concordance rates of 71 percent for MZ twins, 17 percent for DZ twins, 13 percent for parents, and 12 percent for siblings.

Psychoses of adolescence. The usual forms of adult schizophrenic reactions may occur during adolescence. In addition, some adolescents exhibit what is described as an acute confusional state. This disorder has an abrupt onset and is usually transient, with good recovery. Symptoms include identity confusion, intensive anxiety, depressive trends, and impairment in thinking. The disorder is distinguished from schizophrenia by an absence of a true thought disorder or a marked breakdown in reality testing and the relative retention of a capacity for adaptive behavior and meaningful emotional relationships.

Periods of excitement and depression are common during adolescence, but the manic and depressive psychotic episodes that occur in adults are seemingly rare. The relatively high suicide rate among adoles-cents seems to indicate that some type of severe depressive reaction is quite common during the late teens. The symptomatic expression of depression in adolescents consists of boredom, unusual fatigue, inability to concentrate, and feelings of being unloved and unwanted (Toolan, 1962). This syndrome falls short of the traditional criteria of psychosis.

Psychophysiological Disorders

The interaction of psyche and soma may produce symptoms in either system: psychological and emotional factors may contribute to the production and maintenance of physical ailments, and physical illness may contribute to personality and emotional disturbances.

With the exception of genital disorders, which usually occur after puberty, all of the psychosomatic disorders noted in adults (see Chapter 17) also occur in children. One of the more intensively studied psychosomatic disorders in children is bronchial asthma (Schneer, 1963). As with other such disorders, authorities differ on its determinants and associated characteristics. The following account is mainly a summary of the views expressed by S. M. Finch (1967).

Bronchial asthma is marked by wheezing and labored breathing. Attacks occur sporadically and last from a few minutes to several days. The life-threatening impairment in breathing is a terrifying experience for the child and his parents. The disorder is presumed to be caused by a combination of emotional factors and sensitivity to certain allergens. It is not uncommon for asthmatic children also to have eczema, migraine, rheumatoid arthritis, and other psychosomatic difficulties. Because excitement or exertion may precipitate attacks, these youngsters tend to lead restricted, isolated, quiet lives. Children who have frequent and severe attacks may be placed in special residential centers for long periods.

Asthmatic attacks have been interpreted

as reactions to threats of being separated from the mother or as means of controlling the mother. Since many asthmatic children improve when they are hospitalized and suffer relapses when they return home, the theory of separation anxiety requires some modification. One suggested explanation is that the child has ambivalent feelings toward his mother; he both desires and objects to a close dependency relationship. The attack may be interpreted as both a cry for help and a procedure for alarming and thus punishing the mother. Favored treatment consists of medical care for allergies combined with psychotherapy for the child and his parents.

The psychological reaction of children to physical illness represents the other side of the psychophysiological coin. Young children take health for granted. They do not understand sickness and are frightened by it. Preschool children often misinterpret illness as punishment for misdeeds—an idea not altogether unknown among adults. This animistic belief is reinforced by seeing the distraught expressions of their parents, feeling pain, being jabbed with a huge needle, being subjected to the indignity of an enema, and finally being deserted and banished to a hospital. For the older child, surgery may be a nameless terror. To the threat of loss of control and possible death from drugs and anesthesia is added the fear of body mutilation and change.

Acutely ill children tend to be irritable, restless or listless, to refuse food, and to be troubled by nightmares. Some form of regression is usually noted, particularly if the illness persists for several days or weeks. In young children this may be expressed in clinging behavior, the reappearance of thumb-sucking, and the transient loss of speech, walking ability, and bowel control. Older children may show increased dependency, egocentricity, and critical demanding behavior. Parents usually tend to encourage regression by babying their sick children. The relation of psychosomatic concepts to illness in children has been examined in greater detail by D. G. Prugh (1963).

Brain Syndromes

A distinction is made between symptoms directly related to brain function and associated behavior disturbances. The former, which tend to be related to degree of organic damage, include instability of affect and impairment of perceptual-motor learning, memory, and related cognitive functions (Grassi, 1968; Hall and La Driere, 1969). Associated behavior dysfunctions are independent of the degree of actual brain damage. Severe personality and conduct disturbances may be exhibited by children with relatively minor brain damage. Conversely, children with gross brain damage may show surprisingly little behavior disturbance other than the impairments directly related to the damaged tissue. Associated behavior disturbances, which may consist of any of the symptoms included in the GAP list, are precipitated by brain disorders or are by-products of brain damage, but are not direct and inevitable results of brain disorder.

The choice of symptoms is primarily determined by predisposing personality patterns, the nature of current conflicts, the child's level of development, and interactions within his family. The main conclusion that can be drawn from experimental studies of brain-damaged children is that symptoms and test findings are inconsistent and vary markedly from child to child (Kessler, 1966). The concept of brain disorders is not a distinct, clearly defined clinical entity.

Acute brain syndromes are differentiated from chronic brain syndromes in children, as they are in adults. Reactions associated with acute brain disorders are transient and recovery is generally good. The symptoms, which commonly include delirium, wild agitation, confusion, and hallucinatory experiences, are caused by infections, metabolic disturbances, and intoxication due to alcohol, drugs, or poison.

Chronic brain syndromes are relatively permanent and irreversible. The usual symptoms are those previously described as directly related to brain dysfunction.

Some major causes are birth injury, cerebral palsy, and intracranial tumor. Diffuse cortical damage resulting from birth injuries frequently results in hyperactivity, distractability, impulsiveness, and learning difficulties. After the acute phase of *encephalitis*, more commonly known as sleeping sickness, children often show marked personality changes. Some encephalitic children exhibit sociopathological behavior, such as lying, stealing, running away, sexual offenses, and cruelty. Unlike autistic children, most brain damaged children relate adequately to other people. They may actually be too friendly and uninhibited, so that they ask personal questions of strangers and tell family secrets. By and large most brain-damaged children conform to social norms.

In recent years increased attention has been given to behavioral disturbances and disabilities that appear to be related to minimal or barely detectable deviations in the structure and function of the central nervous system. The term "minimal brain syndrome" is generally applied to a wide variety of symptoms in children whose intelligence is average or above average. The ten characteristics most often cited (Clements, 1966), are listed below in order of frequency. These characteristics are most common in brain-injured children but may also occur as isolated symptoms in otherwise normal children and in disturbed children free of brain damage.

1. Hyperactivity.
2. Perceptual-motor impairment.
3. Emotional lability.
4. General coordination impairment.
5. Disorders of attention (short attention span, distractability, perseveration).
6. Impulsivity.
7. Disorders of memory and thinking.
8. Specific learning disabilities.
   (a) Reading.
   (b) Arithmetic.
   (c) Spelling.
9. Disorders of speech and hearing.
10. Equivocal neurological signs and electroencephalographic irregularities.

Mental Retardation

The 1973 classification manual of the American Association on Mental Deficiency (Grossman, 1973) defines *mental retardation* as follows:

Mental retardation refers to significantly subaverage general intellectual functioning existing concurrently with deficits in adaptive behavior, and manifested during the developmental period.

The definition does not distinguish between retardation associated with psychosocial or polygenic influences and retardation associated with biological deficit. The editors make a special point of noting that mental retardation describes only the current behavior of an individual and contains no implication with respect to his future development. Prognosis is related to associated conditions, motivation, treatment, and training opportunities. The onset of mental retardation usually occurs at birth or during early childhood, but for classification purposes, the upper age limit of the "developmental period" is placed at eighteen years.

The level of intellectual functioning is never of itself sufficient to lead to a diagnosis of mental retardation. Of equal importance is the individual's current level of adaptive behavior in meeting the standards of personal independence, self-care, and social responsibility expected of his age and cultural group. During infancy and early childhood, adaptive competence is reflected in sensory-motor, communication, and self-help skills. Adaptive behavior during childhood and early adolescence is indicated by the application of academic skills in early life situations, appropriate reasoning and judgment in mastery of the environment and adequacy of social skills. In the adult years, adequacy of vocational performance and social responsibility assume prime importance in assessing mental retardation.

The AAMD *Manual* includes an adaptive behavior scale for rating those aspects

Retarded children in a special class, reflecting the current policy of avoiding institutionalization and providing more adequate facilities for education and training within the public school system and in community centers.

of behavior that contribute to total adaptation. It contains items on physical development, language development, independent functioning, economic activity, use of numbers and time, social behavior, and so forth. Intelligence is measured by standard tests.

The degrees of retardation recognized by the AAMD and their general characteristics are shown in Table 18.1. Mild retardation is roughly equivalent to the term "educable," and moderate retardation corresponds to the educational category of "trainable." Individuals in the lower two categories require close supervision or lifelong support.

The field of mental retardation research is currently in a transitional stage. One important innovation has been to include mental retardation along with other severely handicapping conditions (cerebral palsy, epilepsy, and other neurological impairments) in the broad category of *developmental disabilities*. This idea was incorporated in the 1972 federal legislation that provided funds to the several states for a "Developmental Disabilities Program" and for the "staffing of community mental health retardation facilities." The current trend is to make greater use of community resources and school systems for the education, training, and care of mental retardates. The former procedure of isolating and confining these children in special schools is being discouraged, and there is an active movement to reduce the resident population of state schools for the retarded. Former residents are being returned to the community. When the family is unable or unwilling to assume care of the child (or adult), he may be placed in a foster home or in a home specially created in the community for the care and training of retardates.

THE INTERPRETATION OF SYMPTOMS

The directness of disordered behavior in children simplifies the interpretation of

their symptoms. Sensitive mothers realize that crying in healthy children, regressive behavior, and vague somatic aches and pains are signals for attention and loving care; that temper tantrums are often precipitated by frustration; and that defiance, elimination problems, and running away often represent protest. Parents are also aware that their own anxieties, fears, and depressive moods create insecurity and

Table 18.1. Levels of Mental Retardation.

Degree of retardation	Characteristics
Mild	IQ: 55-69 Maximum educational potential: about sixth grade With training and supervision, capable of marginal self-support as adults Distribution: about 85% of total mental retardate population; about 2% of general population
Moderate	IQ: 40-54 Maximum educational potential: about second grade Can be trained in self-care and to do simple work in sheltered environment Distribution: about 10% of total mental retardate population
Severe	IQ: 25-39 Maximum educational, training, and self-care capability: roughly that of average 6-year-old Need close supervision Distribution: about 5% of total mental retardate population
Profound	IQ: 0-24 Maximum educational, training, and self-care capability: little or none Require custodial or nursing care Distribution: less than 1% of total mental retardate population

```
0    10    20    30    40    50    60    70    80    90    100
```
Per cent of total mental retardate population

affective disturbances in their children. Good parents endeavor to be calm, relaxed, united, and congenial when their children are present. Quarrels between husband and wife and the discussion of serious problems are postponed until the children are asleep or absent. Complete harmony at all times, however, is an ideal that is seldom, if ever, attainable in reality, and attempts to pretend that it exists are not likely to be successful. It is more helpful for a child to learn that love and mutual esteem can survive occasional discord than to be taught that perfect harmony is what is expected.

Psychoanalytic insights are frequently helpful in explaining the normality of age-pertinent traits and in accounting for developmental deviations (A. Freud, 1965). Fixation at or difficulties associated with the oral phase are often involved when children are demanding, clinging, or devouring in their relationships with others, are greedy and insatiable, or have unusual attitudes toward food and eating. Food refusal may be associated with distorted ideas of becoming pregnant. Obstinacy, indecisiveness, stinginess, rigidity, and destructiveness may be associated with anal trends. Reaction formation against former exhibitionistic tendencies associated with the phallic phase may account for extreme shyness and modesty. Underlying oedipal castration fears may lead to overcompensation expressed in exaggerated assertiveness and aggression. Undue concern for the health and safety of parents may indicate repressed death wishes. Resistance to going to bed at night in older children may be related to inner struggles against masturbation.

In her balanced account of homosexuality, transvestism, and fetishism in children, Anna Freud (1965) stresses two main points: (1) these acts, when performed by preadolescents, do not have the same significance as they do in later years and should not be considered perversions; (2) the occurrence of these developmental deviations during childhood is not a reliable prognostic sign of the future choice of sex object. In most instances the tendency toward maturity and "biological reasonableness" favors normal heterosexuality in adulthood. Favorable heterosexual experiences during adolescence or adulthood outweigh childhood conditioning and fixations. However, predisposed individuals may regress to earlier forms of erotic satisfaction if frustrations are encountered in heterosexual development during adolescence.

FAMILY INTERACTION

The mothers of disturbed children have traditionally been described as overanxious, domineering, lacking in emotional warmth, controlling, covertly rejecting, and oversolicitous. The fathers have been described as either extremely overbearing and aggressive or impersonal, passive, and submissive. It is now realized that these stereotypes represent a gross oversimplification. The attitudes of parents toward their children are constantly changing (Brody, 1956). Of greater significance than the specific attitudes of parents is the interaction between the parents and the general atmosphere of the home. The same conclusion applies to the significance of specific child-training practices (Sewell, et al., 1955). The greater the maladjustment of the parents, the greater the possibility that they may displace their own anxieties and hostilities on their children (Mitchell, 1969).

Nathan Ackerman (1968) has presented a comprehensive account of the role of the family as a whole in the development and emergence of disordered behavior in children. His main conclusion is that behavior disturbances are expressions of the emotional warp of the entire family. Children absorb and reflect the "sick" qualities of their parents. The child is often the pawn of unresolved conflicts between the parents. The occurrence of overt symptoms is regularly preceded by family conflicts. The entire family, then, should be treated as a unit. If only the child is treated, the continued presence of family problems will block his progress. If the treated child should improve, a sibling may be substituted as the family problem. Ackerman has differentiated a variety of healthy and pathological family types, which are described in Table 18.2.

Two basic explanations have been suggested to account for the fact that some children reared by disturbed parents may be relatively unaffected: (1) the affected child may be more vulnerable because of genetic handicaps; (2) the unaffected child may refuse to become involved in conflicts between his parents or may be rescued by

Table 18.2. Family Types.

Family type	Characteristics
Healthy	Parents compatible, share realistic goals, cooperate in search for compromises to conflicts; show tolerance of differences based on mutual understanding and respect. Pleasure, responsibility, and authority are shared. Each shows appropriate concern for development and welfare of other family members as well as for self.
Immature-protective	Parents show need to relate to and depend on others.
Competitive	Intrafamilial relationships motivated by envy, jealousy, and competition.
Neurotic-complementary	Weaker partner depends on stronger partner for support. Children are expected to sacrifice specific parts of their identities in exchange for protection and acceptance.
Complementary-acting out	Unconscious complicity in family pattern of acting out of impulses and antisocial tendencies.
Detached and emotionaly isolated	Family equilibrium dependent on members' maintaining required degree of emotional distance and isolation.
Master-slave	Husband or wife seeks omnipotent control of the other. Symbiotic relationship: master needs slave, slave needs master. Perversion of goals of love and sharing. Objective of master is to dominate, degrade, and ultimately destroy the partner.
Regressive	Negative orientation to life; shared expectation of imminent catastrophe that can be averted only by total sacrifice. Individual members must surrender rights to live and grow in order to assure survival of other members. This type of family frequently produces psychotic children.

Adapted from N. W. Ackerman, "The Role of the Family in the Emergence of Child Disorders," in *Foundations of Child Psychiatry*, ed. E. Miller (New York: Pergamon Press, 1968), pp. 509-33.

favorable relationships with grandparents, relatives, or friends outside the family (Spiegel, 1957).

It is also possible that the attitude of parents toward a child may be a reaction to the child's personality and behavior; the differential responses of parents to their children may be due as much to individual differences in the children as to differential attitudes in the parents. Several investigators (Donnelly, 1960; Klebanoff, 1959) have noted that mothers are much more upset by their disturbed children than they are by their normal children and tend to reject them more. Practically all studies concerned with parent-child interactions as possible determinants of psychopathology have focused on parents whose children already manifest severe behavior disorders, and thus throw no light on the parents' attitudes before they recognized their need for help in coping with their disturbed children. It is quite possible that a mother may have been warm, loving, and accepting toward her child in the beginning, but after years of unsatisfactory experiences with a contrary, unresponsive, or otherwise difficult child may in self-defense have become more impersonal in her reactions. Children can contribute to

the maladjustment of their parents as well as the reverse. When the harassed mother complains that her child "drives her nuts," she may be speaking literally.

OUTCOME OF THERAPY

In a review of studies published up to 1957 on the efficacy of psychotherapy with children, Eugene Levitt reported an overall improvement of 67 percent at the close of therapy and 78 percent following an average follow-up interval of five years. Approximately the same percentage of improvement was found in groups of untreated children. The results of a more recent survey (Levitt, 1963), in which an attempt was made to report outcomes for specific types of disorders, are given in Table 18.3. The overall findings were similar to those in earlier reports: 65 percent of the total group showed improvement. Children classified as presenting special symptoms showed the most favorable outcome, acting-out children the poorest. Interestingly, the outcome for psychosis was slightly more favorable than for neurosis.

Table 18.3. The Efficacy of Therapy in Childhood Behavior Disorders.

Type of disorder	Number of studies	Number of cases	Total % improved
Neurosis	3	230	61%
Acting-out behavior	5	349	55
Special symptoms	5	213	77
Psychosis	5	252	65
Mixed	6	697	68
Total	24	1,741	65

Adapted from E. E. Levitt, "Psychotherapy with Children: A Further Evaluation," *Behavior Research and Therapy*, 1 (1963): 45-51.

Once again the figures showed no more favorable outcome for treated than for nontreated children. Types of treatment given the children covered a broad range: behavior modification techniques, environmental manipulation, nondirective counseling, counseling of parents, and the use of adjunctive drugs. It should be noted that the so-called nontreated children may have received nonprofessional treatment from their parents, teachers, family physician, peers and others.

Discouraging results have also been reported in studies of treatment programs aimed at the prevention or curtailment of delinquency among high-risk children in adolescence (Powers and Witmer, 1951; Tait and Hodges, 1962; Meyer, Borgatta, and Jones, 1965). No significant differences were noted in the subsequent delinquent behavior of treated adolescents and nontreated control groups.

More favorable results have been obtained in the treatment of isolated symptoms. High success rates have consistently been found in the treatment of enuresis by conditioning procedures (De Leon and Mandell, 1966; Baker, 1969). The single-signal system, originally developed by Mowrer and Mowrer (1938), consists of placing an electric pad under the bed sheet so that a bell rings at the first sign of bed-wetting. This serves to wake the child in time for him to go to the bathroom. Apart from waking the child, the conditioning procedure is helpful in establishing sphincter control so the child can sleep through the night without wetting. If relapses occur, they are readily corrected by resuming treatment.

Good results have also been reported in the treatment of school phobias with a variety of techniques (Kennedy, 1965; Berecz, 1968). The secret is apparently to restore school attendance promptly. Recent innovative behavioral treatment techniques have been found effective in promoting self-help in children, building social and language skills, improving school behavior, eliminating fears and reducing self-injurious behavior (Lovaas and Bucher, 1974).

A thirty-year follow-up study of children seen in a child guidance clinic found that antisocial behavior in childhood is not predictive of any specific kind of deviance in later years; antisocial children grow up to exhibit all kinds of deviant behavior (Robins, 1966). Compared with normal control group, the antisocial children had more marital difficulties in later years, were more often imprisoned, had poorer occupational histories, and showed a higher degree of economic and social impoverishment. Former patients of the child guidance clinic were diagnosed as sociopathic personalities significantly more often than control subjects, and more frequently required treatment for alcoholism, schizophrenia, hysteria, and chronic brain syndrome. No differences were noted between the two groups in the frequency of manic-depressive psychosis or anxiety neurosis.

Fifty-two percent of the control subjects were free of psychiatric illness throughout their adult lives, as compared with only 20 percent of the clinic-referred children. Children referred to the clinic with few symptoms fared no worse than the control subjects, but there was a positive correlation between the severity of antisocial behavior during childhood and the severity of adult maladjustment.

Problem Behavior and Clinic Referral

Only a small percentage of children, who in the opinion of parents or professional workers exhibit significant behavioral problems, are referred for treatment. A comprehensive study of the factors associated with clinic referral has been conducted by Shepherd et al. (1971). Comparing data obtained on a group of children admitted for the first time to clinics with a carefully matched control group of children who had not been referred to clinics, they found no significant differences between the two groups with respect to the severity of their behavior difficulties, the distance from their homes to the nearest clinic, the number of mothers working, the age of the parents, or the size of their families.

The main difference was in the attitude of the mothers in the two groups. The mothers of non-clinic children were aware that their children had problems but felt that they were unavoidable or represented only "a phase" the child was going through. They accepted the child's behavior and felt capable of dealing with it by offering reassurance and support. The mothers of the clinic-referred children, on the other hand, were worried and upset about their children's problems. Particularly for daughters, the mother's reaction was often one of irritation. These parents made greater use of punishment—an indication of their greater exasperation and anger with the child's behavior. A final point of difference was that the mothers of the clinic-referred children described themselves as more easily upset and as having greater difficulty in coping with their daily problems than did the mothers of the control group.

On the basis of a follow-up study made some two years later, Shepherd et al. found that 65 percent of the clinic and 61 percent of the non-clinic children were described as "improved" by independent raters. No consistent relationship was noted between the child's improvement and the frequency of his clinic attendance. In evaluating these findings, Shepherd and his associates concluded that many behavior disturbances in children represent transient reactions to environmental stress that resolve themselves with or without professional assistance.

SUMMARY

The criteria of psychopathology in children are the same as for adults. Behavior is considered to indicate abnormality to the extent that it constitutes a source of undue liability, disturbance, or threat to the individual, his family, or society. Abnormal behavior in adults is characterized by loss of self-control and by psychosocial functioning that is sufficiently impaired to be considered inadequate, inappropriate, and maladaptive. In the case of children, greater emphasis is placed on failure to attain age-appropriate levels of adequate psychosocial functioning. In other words, the stress is on developmental defects rather than on the impairment of previously acquired proficiency. Further, the inability of parents or teachers to control the child's behavior is given greater weight than the child's loss of voluntary control.

The kinds of disorders observed in children parallel those noted in adults. They include the familiar categories: transient situational reactions, neuroses, psychoses, maladaptive personality types, psychosomatic reactions, organic brain disorders, and mental retardation. The clinical manifestations of these disorders are different in children than in adults, however. In general, children's symptoms tend to be more fluid and changeable than adults'. Infantile autism appears to be a unique disorder limited to children. The causes of childhood psychopathology, like those of behavior disorders in adults, are multiple, cumulative, and interactive.

References

Achenbach, T. M. "The Classification of Children's Psychiatric Symptoms: A Factor-Analytic Study." *Psychological Monographs* 80 (1966) 6.

Ackerman, N. W. "The Role of the Family in the Emergence of Child Disorders." In *Foundations of Child Psychiatry*, ed. E. Miller, pp. 509-33. New York: Pergamon Press, 1968.

American Association on Mental Deficiency. *A Manual on Terminology and Classification.* Willimantic, Conn., 1961.

Baker, B. L. "Symptom Treatment and Symptom Substitution in Enuresis." *Journal of Abnormal Psychology* 74 (1969): 42-49.

Bender, L. "The Brain and Child Behavior." *Archives of General Psychiatry* 4 (1961): pp. 531–48.

Berecz, J. M. "Phobias of Childhood: Etiology

and Treatment." *Psychological Bulletin* 70 (1968): 694-720.

Beres, D., and Obers, S. J. "The Effects of Extreme Deprivation in Infancy on Psychic Structure in Adolescence." In *Psychoanalytic Study of the Child*, vol. 5, pp. 212-35. New York: International Universities Press, 1950.

Bergin, A. E. "Some Implications of Psychotherapy Research for Therapeutic Practice." *Journal of Abnormal Psychology*, 71 (1966): 235-46.

Bettelheim, B. *Love Is Not Enough.* New York: Free Press, 1950.

————. "Joey: A Mechanical Boy." *Scientific American*, March, 1959, pp. 3-9.

Brody, S. *Patterns of Mothering.* New York: International Universities Press, 1956.

Clements, S. E. *Minimal Brain Dysfunction in Children.* Public Health Service publication no. 1415. Washington, D.C.: U.S. Government Printing Office, 1966.

Committee on Child Psychiatry. *Psychopathological Disorders in Childhood: Theoretical Considerations and a Proposed Classification.* Report no. 62, vol. 6. New York: Group for the Advancement of Psychiatry, 1966.

Conners, C. K. "Symptom Patterns in Hyperkinetic, Neurotic, and Normal Children." *Child Development* 41 (1970): 667-82.

De Leon, G., and Mandell, W. "A Comparison of Conditioning and Psychotherapy in the Treatment of Functional Enuresis." *Journal of Clinical Psychology* 22 (1966): 326-30.

Donnelly, E. M. "The Quantitative Analysis of Parental Behavior Toward Psychotic Children and Their Siblings." *Genetic Psychological Monographs* 62 (1960): 331-76.

Eisenberg, L., and Kanner, L. "Early Infantile Autism, 1943-55." *American Journal of Orthopsychiatry* 26 (1956): 556-66.

Ferster, C. B., and Simmons, J. "Behavior Therapy with Children." *Psychological Record* 16 (1966): 65-71.

Finch, S. M. "Psychophysiological Disorders." In *Comprehensive Textbook of Psychiatry*, ed. A. M. Freedman, H. I. Kaplan, and H. S. Kaplan, pp. 1409-10. Baltimore: Williams & Wilkins, 1967.

Freud, A. *Normality and Pathology in Childhood.* New York: International Universities Press, 1965.

Grassi, J. R. "Performance and Reminiscence of Brain-Damaged, Behavior-Disordered, and Normal Children on Four Psychomotor and Perceptual Tests." *Journal of Abnormal Psychology* 73 (1968): 492-99.

Grossman, H. J., ed. *Manual on Terminology and Classification in Mental Retardation: 1973 Revision.* Special publication of the American Association on Mental Deficiency, 1973.

Hall, L. P., and La Driere, L. "Patterns of Performance on WISC Similarities in Emotionally Disturbed and Brain-Damaged Children." *Journal of Consulting and Clinical Psychology* 33 (1969): 357-64.

Kallmann, F. J., and Roth, B. "Genetic Aspects of Pre-adolescent Schizophrenia." *American Journal of Psychiatry* 112 (1956): 599-606.

Kanner, L. "Autistic Disturbances of Affective Contact." *Nervous Children* 2 (1943): 217-50.

Kennedy, W. A. "School Phobia: Rapid Treatment of 50 Cases." *Journal of Abnormal Psychology* 70 (1965): 285-89.

Kessler, J. W. *Psychopathology of Childhood.* Englewood Cliffs, N.J.: Prentice-Hall, 1966.

Klebanoff, L. B. "Parental Attitudes of Mothers of Schizophrenic, Brain-Injured, and Retarded and Normal Children." *American Journal of Orthopsychiatry* 29 (1959): 445–54.

Levine, M., and Olson, R. P. "Intelligence of Parents of Autistic Children." *Journal of Abnormal Psychology* 73 (1968): 215-17.

Levitt, E. E. "The Results of Psychotherapy with Children: An Evaluation." *Journal of Consulting Psychology* 21 (1957): 189-96.

————. "Psychotherapy with Children: A Further Evaluation." *Behavior Research and Therapy* 1 (1963): 45-51.

Lovaas, O. I. and Bucher, B. D., eds. *Perspectives in Behavior Modification with Deviant Children.* Englewood Cliffs, N. J.: Prentice-Hall, 1974.

Mahler, M. S. "On Child Psychosis and Schizophrenia." In *The Psychoanalytic Study of the Child*, vol. 7, pp. 286-305. New York: International Universities Press, 1952.

Metz, J. R. "Conditioning Generalized Imitation in Autistic Children." *Journal of Experimental Child Psychology* 2 (1965): 389-99.

Meyer, H. J.; Borgatta, E. F.; and Jones, W. C. *Girls at Vocational High: An Experiment in Social Work Intervention.* New York: Russell Sage Foundation, 1965.

Mitchell, K. M. "Concept of 'Pathogenesis' in Parents of Schizophrenic and Normal Children." *Journal of Abnormal Psychology* 74 (1969): 423-24.

Mowrer, O. H., and Mowrer, W. M. "Enuresis: A Method for Its Study and Treatment." *American Journal of Orthopsychiatry* 8 (1938): 436-59.

O'Gorman, G. *The Nature of Childhood Autism.* London: Butterworth, 1967.

Ornitz, E., and Ritvo, E. R. "Perceptual Inconstancy in Early Infantile Autism." *Archives of General Psychiatry* 18 (1968): 76-98.

Patterson, G. R. "An Emperical Approach to the Classification of Distrubed Children." *Journal of Clinical Psychology* 20 (1964): 326-37.

Pinneau, S. R. "The Infantile Disorders of Hospitalism and Anaclitic Depression." *Psychological Bulletin* 52 (1955): 429-52.

Powers, E., and Witmer, H. *An Experiment in the Prevention of Delinquency: The Cambridge-Somerville Youth Study.* New York: Columbia University Press, 1951.

Prugh, D. G. "Toward an Understanding of Psychosomatic Concepts in Relation to Illness in Children." In *Modern Perspectives in Child Development*, ed. A. J. Solnit and S. A. Provence. New York: International Universities Press, 1963.

Rexford, E. N. "Some Meanings of Aggressive Behavior in Children." *Annals of the American Academy of Political and Social Science*, March 1959, pp. 10-18.

Rieser, D. E. "Psychosis of Infancy and Early Childhood as Manifested by Children with Atypical Development." *New England Journal of Medicine*, 1963, pp. 790-98.

Rimland, B. *Infantile Autism.* New York: Appleton-Century-Crofts, 1964.

Robins, L. N. *Deviant Children Grown Up.* Baltimore: Williams & Wilkins, 1966.

Ross, A. *Psychological Disorders of Children: A Behavioral Approach to Theory, Research, and Therapy.* New York: McGraw-Hill, 1974.

Rutter, M.; Greenfeld, D.; and Lockyer, L. "A Five- to Fifteen-Year Follow-up of In-

fantile Psychosis: II. Social and Behavioural Outcome." *British Journal of Psychiatry* 113 (1967): 1183-99.

Schneer, H., ed. *The Asthmatic Child.* New York: Harper & Row, 1963.

Sewell, W. H.; Mussen, P. H.; and Harris, C. W. "Relationships Among Child-Training Practices." *American Sociological Review* 20 (1955): 137-48.

Shepherd, M.; Oppenheim, B.; and Mitchell, S. *Childhood Behavior and Mental Health.* New York: Grune & Stratton, 1971.

Sorosky, A. D.; Ornitz, E. M.; Brown, M. B.; and Ritvo, E. R. "Systematic Observations of Autistic Behavior." *Archives of General Psychiatry* 18 (1968): 439-49.

Spiegel, J. P. "The Resolution of Role Conflict Within the Family." *Psychiatry* 20 (1957): 1-16.

Spitz, R. A. "Hospitalism." In *The Psychoanalytic Study of the Child*, vol. 1, pp. 53-74. New York: International Universities Press, 1945.

————. "Anaclitic Depression." In *The Psychoanalytic Study of the Child*, vol. 2, pp. 313-42. New York: International Universities Press, 1946.

Tait, C. W., and Hodges, E. F. *Delinquents, Their Families, and the Community.* Springfield, Ill.: Charles C Thomas, 1962.

Toolan, W. M. "Depression in Children and Adolescents." *American Journal of Orthopsychiatry* 32 (1962): 404-15.

Truax, C. B.; and Carkhuff, R. R. *Toward Effective Counseling and Psychotherapy: Training and Practice.* Chicago: Aldine, 1967.

Ullmann, L. P., and Krasner, L. *A Psychological Approach to Abnormal Behavior.* Englewood Cliffs, N.J.: Prentice-Hall, 1969.

Werry, J. S. and Quay, H. C. "The Prevalence of Behavior Symptoms in Younger Elementary School Children." *American Journal of Orthopsychiatry* 41 (1971): 136-43.

Suicidal Ideas, Traviès de Villers

One of the more controversial of man's distinctive human attributes is that he can consciously plan his own death and deliberately kill himself when and how he chooses. Each year some 25,000 persons in the United States elect to exercise this option. This is a minimal figure, since it includes only persons officially recorded as suicides on their death certificates. Because of the stigma associated with self-murder, relatives and friends often conceal suicide notes and other evidence. Whenever possible, family physicians attribute sudden death to natural causes rather than subject the bereaved survivors to the added stress of a formal inquest by a coroner's jury. The latter, in turn, tend to avoid returning a verdict of suicide in doubtful cases when death may have been accidental or due to undeterminable causes.

A conservative estimate is that the number of unreported cases of suicide is as great as the number of reported cases. On this basis, the total number of suicides in the United States each year runs about 50,000. This is close to the number of deaths caused by motor vehicle accidents each year and three times greater than the number of homicides. Reported and unreported suicides account for more than 2 percent of all deaths in this country.

The loss of thousands of lives is only part of the tragedy of suicide. The anguish, resentment, and despair that drive a person to terminate his unhappy existence are not buried with him. The emotional burden is transferred, often deliberately, to his children, parents, or spouse in the somewhat altered form of grief, anger, shame, and guilt. As Edwin Shneidman (1969) says, "The person who commits suicide puts his psychological skeleton in the survivor's emotional closet—he sentences the survivor to a complex of negative feelings and, most importantly, to obsessing about the reasons for the suicide death."

With the passage of time, the tortuous self-questioning of the survivor may abate and the emotional turmoil may subside. The memory of the traumatic experience, however, remains permanently etched in the survivor's memory and in subtle ways pervades and affects his life. The knowledge that a member of the family took the route of suicide often influences other close relatives to follow suit. The second suicide may be timed to coincide with the anniversary date of the first, or the same method may be used. Hemingway followed his father's example by shooting himself when he too decided to commit suicide.

The magnitude of the problem of suicide is increased several times with the addition of "unsuccessful" attempts. Here also the stigma associated with self-destruction frequently results in concealment of information. When there is no need for medical attention, suicide attempts are usually kept personal or family secrets. Estimates vary as to the incidence of attempts. Most authorities guess that for every completed suicide there are perhaps ten attempts. On the basis of this ratio, a conservative estimate is that one out of every thousand persons in the general population makes a suicide attempt of some severity each year. The risk of an attempt is particularly high among adolescent girls. A comprehensive study of suicide in Edinburgh found that one teenager in every 250 deliberately poisons or injures herself every year (McCulloch and Philip, 1972).

No reliable data are available on the percentage of the population that attempt suicide at some time in their lives. The figure may well run as high as 5 to 10 percent. A few efforts have been made to ascertain the prevalence of attempted suicide in representative cross-sections of the general population. In one survey, (Mintz, 1970) more than three thousand questionnaires were distributed door-to-door on selected residential blocks in Los Angeles. Residents fourteen years of age and over were asked to complete and return the questionnaires. Returns were obtained from about two thousand persons who were roughly representative of the total population of Los Angeles. Approximately 4 percent of the respondents admitted to having made one or more suicide attempts. The median age of the sample surveyed was thirty-seven, so that many more might be expected to make an initial attempt at some future date.

Definitions of Suicidal Behavior

The term "suicide" is a relatively new name for an old human trait: man's paradoxical persistence in voluntarily engaging in acts of omission or commission that he knows will or may result in his own death. The word "suicide" is derived from Latin but does not correspond to any single Latin word having a similar meaning (Fedden, 1972). The early Romans used roundabout phrases such as *sibi mortem conscisere* (to produce his own death) and *sua manu cadere* (to fall by his own hand). The term "suicide" was originally coined in England about 1650. Older terms in use at that time, which included self-murder, self-homicide and felo-de-se (one who commits a felony against himself), reflected the then prevailing attitude that self-destruction was a serious crime. Ironically, offenders who failed in their attempt were condemned to death by hanging. The new term of suicide was slow in gaining acceptance, and there is no mention of it in English or French dictionaries prior to 1750.

Over the years, the original, restricted meaning of suicide (to kill oneself) has been gradually extended. The term is now applied to a broad continuum of feelings, ideas, and actions that range from the fleeting suicidal thoughts and impulses occasionally experienced by most people, to threats, histrionic attempts, serious but aborted attempts, to carefully planned lethal actions (Beck and Greenberg, 1971). Broader definitions of suicide also include more indirect or delayed forms of life-threatening behavior, such as overeating, the excessive use of alcohol or drugs, reckless driving, unnecessary risk-taking, and regular participation in dangerous sports and occupations. In varying degrees, all these activities are self-destructive and there is the added inference that the individual is more or less consciously aware of this fact. Metaphoric expressions, such as "social suicide" and "political suicide" similarly imply the victim's awareness of the self-injurious nature of his behavior.

Suicide and Attempted Suicide

Suicidal persons differ with respect to the seriousness of their lethal intent, their awareness of the possible consequences of their act, and the relative effectiveness of the methods used. These factors may affect the odds of suicidal actions, but they are not decisive. Whether a person who engages in self-injurious behavior is called a suicide or a suicide attempter is solely determined by the outcome of his act. If the self-injury is fatal, he is a suicide; if he survives he is an attempter. A mild self-injurious act that is deliberately designed as an attention-getting device or manipulative stratagem may, through miscalculation, be fatal. Conversely, some chance factor or effective medical intervention may abort a carefully planned and seemingly lethal act. The critical role of chance in influencing outcome emphasizes the importance of taking all suicidal acts seriously.

The fact that elements outside the control of the individual may determine the fatality of an act also raises questions concerning the validity of earlier speculations

SUCCESSFUL AND UNSUCCESSFUL SUICIDE: THE POET SYLVIA PLATH AND HER BIOGRAPHER, A. ALVAREZ

A. Alvarez' (1970) insightful account of the tragic death by suicide of the poet Sylvia Plath illustrates the fluctuating tides of self-destructive intent and the role of chance in differentiating completed from attempted suicide.

Sylvia made her first and apparently most serious attempt to kill herself during her senior year at college. The episode, as described in her novel, *The Bell Jar,* involved swallowing a large number of sleeping pills, leaving a misleading note, and hiding herself in an unused part of the cellar. She was found by accident and survived by a minor miracle.

Some ten years later, she made another attempt in which she seemed to take precautions against dying. The method consisted in putting her head in the oven and turning on the gas. The act was timed so that she could be saved by a recently hired girl who was scheduled to arrive shortly after the gas was turned on. The hired girl did arrive on time and she rang and knocked on the door to be admitted. The neighbor in the apartment below would have answered except that he was hard of hearing and slept without a hearing aid. There was still the possibility that he might have responded except for the accidental fact that his bedroom was immediately below Sylvia's kitchen and he was knocked out cold by gas seeping down. When Sylvia's door was eventually forced open some hours later her body was still warm. She had left a note directing that her doctor, whose telephone number was given, be called.

According to Alvarez, Sylvia gambled with death after working out the odds in her favor, but she lost through mischance. He suggests that the death of her father when she was nine may have influenced her expressed "talent" for death. Several of her poems are built around the theme of going back to "daddy." A few months before her last attempt, Sylvia and her husband separated. This experience might have been perceived as another abandonment by a loved one. She was very depressed for several days prior to her suicide and had made plans to see a psychotherapist.

There are many cases of suicides similar to that of Sylvia Plath in which the victim is confused and wants neither to die nor to live. In these cases the individual frequently acts impulsively out of rage, frustration, or a sudden attack of despair. The outcome is left to chance. This group falls in an intermediate position between those who clearly want to die and leave little to chance and those who are mainly crying for help and take precautions to ensure their survival. Dublin (1963) estimates that each of the three groups accounts for about one-third of all suicidal acts.

Another example of the haziness of the boundaries separating fatal from nonfatal acts is provided by Alvarez' (1970) candid description and analysis of his own suicide attempt. As often happens, the idea was originally implanted during childhood by the behavior of his parents, both of whom attempted suicide. The idea remained vague and peripheral until Alvarez married. The continued pressure of seemingly insurmountable marital problems apparently acted as a precipitant that gave substance and urgency to the idea of suicide as a solution.

The attempt occurred following a Christmas party where he drank too much and quarreled with his wife, who decided to spend the night away from home. He went to bed alone after swallowing forty-five sleeping pills, which he had carefully collected over a long period. Fortunately, his wife returned home the following morning, realized his critical condition, and rushed him to the hospital. Prompt medical attention saved his life, but the seriousness of the attempt is indicated by the fact that he remained unconscious for three days. While still in a drowsy state he was interviewed by the police, who suggested that the episode was an accident. He agreed, and that took care of the legal complications.

The suicide attempt was successful in terminating the marital conflict, and the marriage was soon ended by divorce. Alvarez' personal reaction to his attempted suicide was a sense of disappointment. He had faced death in the hope that the experience would clarify his confused mental state, but all he had gotten from his near-death was oblivion. Looking back over his experience, he describes suicide as a closed world with its own irresistible logic. He compares the logic of suicide to the unanswerable logic of a nightmare or a science-fiction fantasy where everything is different and strange but at the same time makes sense, follows its own strict rules, and is wholly convincing. In this shut-off world, incidental experiences are charged with special meaning; everything reinforces the decision to take one's life.

A. Alvarez, author of
The Savage God, *a study of suicide.*

Sylvia Plath, a gifted poet obsessed with death, whose promising career was abruptly terminated by suicide.

(Shneidman and Farberow, 1961; Stengel, 1964) that people who commit suicide differ from those who only attempt suicide. The main evidence for the "different type of person" hypothesis consists of epidemiological findings that indicate significant sex and age differences between suicides and attempters. The incidence rate for completed suicide is two to three times higher for males than for females; the rate of attempts is two to three times higher for females than for males. Suicide attempts mainly occur in persons under thirty-five years of age; the incidence of completed suicides is highest for ages over fifty. All that can be concluded from these findings is that sex and age are related to suicidal outcome. The inaccessibility of fatal cases for subsequent questioning makes it impossible to compare their motives or degree of lethal intent with those of attempters who survive.

Only about a third of those who commit suicide leave notes. Their content is usually distorted and intended only for their designated readers, so they are rarely relevant for scientific inquiry. Interview information supplied by attempters is limited to what can be secured from willing and cooperative subjects, who more often than not are more concerned with defending their actions than with giving objective and accurate answers. The observed sex and age differences may in great part be due to incidental cultural factors. The higher rate of committed suicide among males, for example, may be related to the greater "manliness" implied in the use of violent methods of self-injury (gunshot and hanging), which afford less opportunity for rescue than self-poisoning, the preferred female method. The age difference of attempters and completers may be a byproduct of the closer supervision and greater social ties of adolescents and young adults in contrast with the social isolation of aged persons living alone.

The prevailing current view, which is favored by E. Stengel (1972) in his more recent writings, is that suicides and attempters should be regarded as members of the same population. This viewpoint is supported by recent studies which indicate that about 10 percent of attempters eventually manage to commit suicide (World Health Organization, 1968). Follow-up studies covering the total life span of attempters, which are currently being conducted in several European countries, may eventually revise this figure upward. Examination of the history of completed suicides shows that at least 25 percent have prior records of earlier attempts (McCulloch and Philip, 1972).

Individual case studies of repeaters further confirms these findings. The same individual may vary greatly with respect to the lethality of his intent and his choice of methods on different attempts. A final argument in favor of a continuum of suicidal behavior is that the same underlying factors are associated with completed suicides, repeated attempts, and single attempts. Vulnerability to all of these kinds of behavior is increased if the person is the product of a broken home, is separated or divorced, has few or no close friends, lives alone, is dependent on drugs or alcohol, is a sociopath, or is psychotic. These unfavorable factors are more pronounced in repeaters than in one-time attempters and more pronounced in fatal than nonfatal cases. Several experimental "prediction scales" have recently been developed to assess degree of suicidal risk and to differentiate attempters from those who go on to commit suicide (Beck et al., 1974).

SUICIDE AND PSYCHOPATHOLOGY

Suicidal acts clearly qualify as psychopathological behavior on the usual grounds that they constitute a source of distress and threat to the individual, his family, and others. The fact that a person feels forced to resort to the prohibited and dangerous expedient of threatening, attempting, or actually ending his life reflects the depth of his despair and the desperateness of his plight. The tragic decision may be precipitated by a recent frustration, slight, or quarrel, and acted upon on the spur of the moment. Usually, however, there is a long antecedent history of personal unhappiness associated with continued failure to resolve or adapt to significant life problems.

Every suicide travels a different road and experiences a distinctive combination of obstacles and hardships, to which he reacts in his own particular way. A general pattern is, however, discernible. As a rule, the most crucial problems are associated with disappointments and frustrations involving personal and social needs and expectations. The individual initially attempts to cope with difficulties in a rational and objective manner, within the limits of his resources. If his own efforts prove unsuccessful, he may appeal to his family and friends for help or seek professional assistance. Persistent failure leads to a sense of futility. Behavior becomes progressively less goal-directed and more disorganized and impulsive. There may be an intensification of anger, resentment, self-pity, and depressive feelings. Relief from inner turmoil may be sought in the blurring of consciousness induced by alcohol and other drugs.

The individual withdraws more within himself and becomes increasingly isolated from meaningful social relationships. The closing of the door to the factual world of reality gives freer reign to distorted thoughts and superstitious beliefs. More important, there is a progressive loss of hope. When the last glimmer is gone and the bankrupt individual has nothing more to lose, all that is needed is some incident, however trivial, to precipitate the self-destructive act.

A significant point is that most suicides do not want to die. The act represents a reaction against the intolerableness of existence rather than a longing for death. If, by some magic, the problems of living could be resolved, most would gladly choose life. Particularly in attempted suicides by young people there is manifest a hope that their dramatic action will somehow result in an improvement in their familial, marital, or love relationships. Frequently the motives of those who are firmly committed to ending their lives are also mainly concerned with the imagined effects their deaths will have on the living. Examples include spite suicides, martyr deaths, and instances when the suicide believes his care or presence is an intolerable burden on his family.

Suicide and Mental Disorders

The suffering associated with suicidal behavior warrants its inclusion under the general heading of psychopathological reactions. The relation of suicide to the more narrowly defined medical concept of mental disorders is another matter altogether. Suicide and mental disorders are independent entities. A mental disorder is not a necessary requirement or cause for suicide, and persons free of any demonstrable disorder may and do kill themselves. Conversely, obviously mentally ill patients may show no suicidal tendencies. The diagnostic and classification systems that are officially recognized by psychiatrists and members of other professional societies do not list suicide either as a separate disorder or as an integral symptom of any disorder. There is a link of sorts, but it is mainly statistical. Mental patients as a group have a higher than average risk of suicide, and the prevalance rate of mental disorders is higher in a suicidal population than for the population at large.

Similarly, there is no close relation between suicide and the legal concept of insanity. Insane persons may commit suicide, but very few suicides would be adjudged insane on the basis of the recognized legal rules. At the moment of ending their lives most suicides are aware of the nature and quality of their actions and carry them out of their own free will and choice. Their self-destructive behavior is rarely the product of delusions or hallucinations. They realize that society disapproves of suicide. If their lethal intent is serious, they take precau-

This dramatic painting—entitled "The Scream"—by the Norwegian artist Edvard Munch (1863-1944) expresses the bleak loneliness, desperation, and hopelessness of the suicide.

tions to forestall the intervention of others.

Historically, the extension of the mental illness and insanity umbrella to cover suicide served to remove it from the category of sinful or criminal behavior. The relabeling process freed the suicide from prosecution by state and church. If a person kills himself or tries to do so while of unsound mind, he obviously should not be held criminally responsible for his action or denied religious burial rites. The actual gain to survivors is debatable; the family stigma of sin or crime is replaced by the stigma of madness.

Research interest has concentrated on two pertinent topics. The first is concerned with the incidence of suicide among mental patients who had been hospitalized or treated for a recognized mental disorder, independent of any suicidal record. All studies agree that discharged mental patients living in the community have a much higher risk of committing suicide than the general population (World Health Organization, 1968). The wide range of suicide rates reported in various studies may be due to variations in data-collecting procedures, differences in the diagnostic composition of groups, and the length of the follow-up period. On the average, the suicide rate among former mental patients is about twenty times greater than among the general population.

Persons with a prior diagnosis of one or another of the affective psychoses are particularly vulnerable. Life-long follow-up studies show that approximately 15 percent of all deaths occurring in this diagnostic group are due to suicide. The suicide rate for schizophrenics is considerably lower than that for depressed psychotics, but it is still many times higher than the general rate (Osmond and Hoffer, 1967). Relatively high rates of completed suicide have also been reported for alcoholics, neurotics, and antisocial personalities. Patients in these diagnostic categories more often attempt than complete suicidal action.

The second area of research interest is the obverse case, the relative prevalence of mental disorders among persons who commit or attempt suicide. Research findings on this subject are highly variable (World Health Organization, 1968). In different studies, from 9 to 40 percent of the persons committing suicide have had a previous psychiatric history; the median figure for ten studies was close to 25 percent. Other investigations, based on coroners' records, report evidence of mental illness in from 14 to 94 percent of adjudged suicides; the median figure for ten of these studies was about 30 percent. In cases of attempted suicide, where a diagnosis of mental illness is usually made through direct psychiatric interview, the figures run much higher. Signs of mental illness have been reported in from 74 to 100 percent of attempters by examiners in eleven studies; the median was 80 percent.

All figures, and especially those for attempted suicide, are probably inflated. A major contributing factor to their magnitude is the widespread but unwarranted assumption that anyone who attempts or commits suicide must be mentally ill. If one looks for signs of mental disorder, it is usually possible to uncover evidence of some form of personality deviation or neurotic tendencies in most persons under great stress. Sampling errors further contribute to the high rates of mental disorder observed among attempters. Referral for psychiatric examination is usually restricted to hospitalized cases, repeaters, and other persons for whom there is some question about their mental health. The more "normal" attempters are less often referred for psychiatric evaluation.

Meaningful conclusions regarding the mental health of suicides must therefore await more careful research. What is needed are controlled studies comparing the prevalence of mental symptoms among suicidal and nonsuicidal persons drawn from the same population, where both groups are under equivalent stress. For example, the relative prevalence of mental disorders among a suicidal group might be compared with that of patients who have recently been informed they have cancer and may die suddenly and soon. Studies of this type would test the possibility that examiners are misinterpreting distress that is appropriate to the situation as an indication of mental illness.

CHANGING SOCIAL ATTITUDES

Personal vs. Institutional Suicide

The attitude of society toward suicide has varied with time and place, but a distinction has consistently been made between personal and institutional (socially motivated) acts of self-destruction. Suicide for personal reasons (discontent, resentment, poor health, despair, failure, remorse, disappointment in love) has never been approved by society (Dublin, 1963; Choron, 1972). At most, it has been tolerated in some periods in history.

For example, the Stoics of ancient Greece and Rome advocated the right of the individual to end his life, if this action was a rational decision in terms of his life situation. Some of the Greek cities established a quasi-legal procedure for handling suicide. A person weary of life could tell his troubles to the local magistrate. If the latter agreed that the petitioner had adequate cause for ending his life, the court supplied the remedy: a vial of hemlock. Zeno, the founder of Stoic philosophy, practiced what he preached. At the age of ninety-eight, he decided that his future was limited and he committed suicide. The precipitating factor was a fall resulting in a broken toe, a sign of infirmities to come. The permissive attitude of the early Romans, expressed in the dictum "He is at liberty to die who is not pleased with life," was restricted to free men. The right was denied to slaves, soldiers, and those accused of crimes for which the penalty included forfeiture of property.

This relative tolerance of suicide was exceptional. More typically, societies have strongly disapproved of permitting any member to decide for himself the conditions under which death is preferable to life and to choose when and how he dies. Vigorous attempts have been made to discourage personal suicide by subjecting "self-murderers" and their families to harsh penalties.

On the other hand, institutional forms of suicide, altruistic or sacrificial in nature, have traditionally been approved and encouraged. H. R. Fedden (1972), the originator of the term institutional suicide, has described its identifying characteristics. These forms of suicide are creations of society. Local beliefs and customs regulate the circumstances under which certain designated persons are expected or required to sacrifice their lives for the common good. The self-destructive act is typically demanded of the person by virtue of his social role and obligations to his group. His mental health and his personal wishes are irrelevant.

Perhaps the best known example is the practice, formerly widespread in non-Western societies, of requiring the wife and servants of a high-ranking person to take their own lives when he dies so as to accompany and serve him in the next world. The centuries-old tradition of *suttee* in India demanded that on the death of a high-caste Hindu male, his widow had to immolate herself on her husband's pyre. This practice persisted until the early nineteenth century despite efforts by the British to stop it.

A second widespread custom, which is still prevalent, is the expectation that members of a society's armed forces, when called upon to do so, will volunteer for suicidal missions against the enemy or will fight on to the last man. The *kamikaze* attacks of Japanese pilots during World War II provide a dramatic example of this

form of suicide. In ancient times it was not uncommon for inhabitants of besieged cities and fortresses to engage in mass suicide to escape rape, torture, or enslavement. Among the Eskimo, as in certain other societies in precarious circumstances, the aged were expected to accept death calmly through abandonment or self-imposed starvation when their care and support interfered with the survival of the group. In so doing, they absolved their children of parricidal guilt.

Other similarly approved actions include suicide as an honorable way out for defeated generals, captains of sinking ships, and officials who have betrayed their public trust. The once popular Japanese custom of *hara-kiri* provided persons in disgrace with a nationally recognized, albeit somewhat gory, mode of ritualistic suicide. Martyrdom also may be considered a form of institutional suicide, though obviously with personal involvement. The early Christians were active partners in their persecution by the Romans. By the thousands they sought and welcomed death in the arena to demonstrate their faith and to hasten their entrance to the promised land of heavenly bliss. Twelve centuries later, the members of a religious sect, the Albigenses of France, gladly accepted death at the hands of the Roman Church in their firm belief that in so doing they were leaving the world of Satan for that of God.

Most forms of institutional suicide have disappeared or declined in frequency, perhaps because of a growing realization that the sacrifice of the individual rarely serves any good purpose. In principle, however, most societies retain a favorable attitude toward "rational" suicide. In recent years, public opinion has increasingly accepted the right to die of persons suffering from painful, incurable diseases and of aged individuals who wish to avoid the indignities of senile decay. The fact that modern medical technology makes it possible to prolong minimal body functioning has stimulated current interest in the right of the individual to end his life before the un-

A Japanese kamikaze pilot deliberately using his plane as a flying bomb against a U.S. warship during the Second World War—a form of culturally approved institutional suicide.

avoidable ravages of disease and senility reduce him to a pathetic and mindless vegetable.

This issue, however, is not as new as it may seem. Twenty centuries ago, Seneca spelled out the conditions under which he would feel justified in voluntarily relinquishing life. He would accept pain and disease as long as there remained some hope of relief or cure and his mind remained unimpaired, but if old age were to begin to destroy his faculties, he would leave the putrid and tottering edifice. Seneca actually did commit suicide when he was over sixty-five years old, but not because of the threat of senile decay. He fell out of favor with his former student Nero, who ordered his death. He forestalled the emperor's vengeance by dying of self-inflicted wounds.

Social Disapproval of Personal Suicide

Society's objections to personal suicide are based on a potpourri of philosophical, moral, and economic considerations, with a generous helping of guilt and superstitious beliefs added for seasoning. The philosophical issue is mainly concerned with the value of life. In a sense, suicide represents an affront to society and its values. As expressed by R. H. Seiden (1969, p. 1), "Suicide troubles and appalls us because it so intransigently rejects our deeply held conviction that life must be worth living."

The moral and religious objections to suicide were most clearly and forcefully stated by church leaders during the Middle Ages (Fedden, 1972). The two main arguments were that the taking of one's life constituted a violation of the biblical commandment "Thou shalt not kill," and that life was a gift of God and to reject it was to usurp his power. A further objection was that self-murder made a mockery of the doctrine of loving thy neighbor as thyself. To discourage suicide, the church declared self-destruction to be an abominable sin against God and man for which the punishment was eternal damnation. Dante reflected the church's attitude when he assigned suicides to the lowest pit of hell.

The economic objection rests on the needless loss to society of productive and useful members. The suicide of able-bodied males diminishes the work force and military reserves of the community. The financial hardships imposed on the family by the self-inflicted death of a father or mother may require the community to assume financial responsibility for surviving members. The practical-minded Romans were mainly opposed to suicide on economic grounds. Slaves were prohibited from committing suicide since their death would result in an economic loss to their masters. The property of soldiers who committed suicide was confiscated to recompense the state for their "desertion" from duty. Persons accused of crimes for which the penalty included confiscation of property were judged guilty if they took their own lives.

These objections to suicide represent the more objective and definable grounds for society's judgment. The roots go much deeper. The origin of the horror of suicide can be traced to primitive taboos and superstitious beliefs. The fundamental fear, mixed with guilt, is related to the timeless superstition that the victims of violent and unnatural death return as ghosts to haunt and take their revenge on those responsible. In the case of suicide, the responsibility falls on those who drove the victim to his untimely end, which includes society at large. Community guilt and fear of the ghosts of suicides accounts for the Athenian practice of cutting off one hand of a suicide and burying it separately; a one-handed ghost is less fearsome. This vengeful superstition also explains the practice in eighteenth-century England of burying a suicide at a crossroads with a stake driven through the heart. The objective was to prevent the suicide from returning to haunt those who forced him to take his life. The crossroads burial served to confuse the ghost about what direction to follow to return home.

Punitive Measures

Attempts to deter persons from committing suicide have historically consisted of three measures; denial of proper burial, confiscation of property, and the dishonoring of the name and memory of those who die by their own hand (Fedden, 1972); Choron, 1972). The most common of these has been the denial of funeral rites, a practice that goes back to the remote past. Ajax, of Trojan War fame, was denied a hero's death by cremation when he committed suicide in anger because he had been refused Achilles' armor. He was simply buried. Among the ancient Jews, suicides were buried only after nightfall. The practice in ancient Greece was to bury suicides outside the city walls in unmarked graves.

Beginning about the fourth century, when the church took a firm stand against self-destruction, suicides were denied religious rites and Christian burial. As late as the eighteenth century, throughout most of Europe, suicides were usually buried at night without religious rites. More recently, the Catholic church has moderated its punitive stance by tacitly assuming that a person who commits suicide is of unsound mind and not responsible for his act, and hence is eligible for Christian burial.

In the eleventh century the Danish invaders of Britain introduced a law permitting the confiscation of all the goods of suicides by their lord, a law that continued in England (with forfeitures to the Crown) until 1870. During the reign of Louis XIV in France the titles and property of nobles who committed suicide were forfeited, but following the revolution the laws against suicide were repealed.

Those who attempted suicide and failed were not exempt from punishment. In Catholic countries, attempters risked excommunication. Throughout Europe up to the nineteenth century most countries regarded suicide as a crime, and unsuccessful attempters were subject to prosecution for having committed a felony against the self. As late as the nineteenth century the laws in England provided that suicide attempters were subject to arrest and death by hanging. Alvarez (1970) gives us an interesting account of an event that occurred about 1860. A man who had slashed his throat was arrested and sentenced to death by hanging. A physician informed the local authorities that this sentence could not be carried out since hanging would open the throat wound and the man would automatically breathe. The physician's objection was ignored, the man was hanged, and in fact the wound did open and he survived. The local authorities solved the dilemma by binding his wounds so that breathing would be impossible and then hanged him.

Since the beginning of the present century most countries have repealed their laws requiring the punishment of suicides. No such repeal has been necessary in the United States where suicide has never been considered a punishable criminal offense. The one remaining law that is still more or less universally accepted is that it is a crime for anyone to aid, abet, or contribute to the suicide of another person.

DEMOGRAPHIC DATA

National Differences

It has long been known that suicide rates vary markedly from country to country. In the absence of unusual events, such as wars and economic depressions, the rates reported are amazingly stable; year after year, nations with high rates continue to report high rates, those with low rates

report low rates, and those in the middle keep their relative position. Vital statistics, published annually by the World Health Organization, indicate that the suicide rates of high risk countries are three times greater than those of low rate countries, even when comparisons are restricted to culturally advanced nations. Countries that consistently report high suicide rates include Hungary, Finland, Austria, Czechoslovakia, and Japan. Those with low reported rates include Ireland, Italy, the Netherlands, Norway, Canada, and Poland. The suicide rates for the United States and for England fall in the median range.

The difficulty in interpreting national differences in suicide rates is that the data are not directly comparable. The medical and judicial procedures for reporting cases of suspected suicide vary considerably from country to country. There are also marked national differences in the strictness of enforcement of regulations. The underreporting of suicide deaths is common in countries where physicians are permitted greater latitude in certifying cause of death or where prevailing religious beliefs result in the denial of proper burial for the suicide and in shame to his family. Other relevant factors are the age and sex composition of the population and the urban-rural ratio.

In short, a distinction must be made between explanations aimed at accounting for national differences in *reported* suicide rates and *actual* suicide rates. Assuming that at least part of the reported differences are true differences, a significant variable may be the traditional cultural attitude toward suicide. Cultures in which there are more permissive attitudes toward suicide may be expected to show a higher incidence of actual and reported suicide than cultures that strongly disapprove of taking one's life. In nations with high rates, the greater exposure of its members to incidents of suicide may increase the risk of imitative behavior and thereby result in the continuation of the rates. Conversely, the relative absence of cultural models may result in reduced imitative behavior.

The importance and persistence of cultural practices has been demonstrated by Sainsbury and Barraclough (1968). Comparing the suicide rates of immigrants to the United States from eleven countries with the official rates of their countries of origin, they found a high relationship. It appears from this significant study that early cultural indoctrination influences the individual's suicidal behavior at least for one generation, despite his transfer to another country.

Studies of suicide in Scandinavian countries illustrate the complexities involved in explaining and reconciling national differences in reported suicide rates. The focus of most Nordic investigations has been the riddle posed by the fact that the reported rate for Norway is only about a third as high as that for Denmark and Sweden. Interestingly, different reasons have been offered for the high Swedish and Danish rates.

According to H. Hendin (1964), suicide in Sweden is related to performance failure. The principal precipitating cause of male suicides is failure in work; for women it is failure in heterosexual relationships. The stress on performance starts early. Swedish women tend to regard child-rearing as a responsibility and a chore rather than a pleasure. Their objective is to encourage independence and self-sufficiency in their children as early as possible. Children are evaluated by comparing their achievements with those of others. The cultural mode of expressing anger consists of withdrawal and detachment. A popular Swedish expression is *tiga ihjäl*, meaning to kill with silence. Failure in performance leads to loss of self-esteem, self-hatred, and frequently suicide. Rudestom (1970) associates the avoidance of direct expression of anger among Swedes with their long-established national attitude of pacifism. He also notes that the modern sexual egalitarianism of the country has resulted in Swedish males' experiencing a sense of failure in trying to maintain their traditional dominant role.

Hendin attributes Denmark's high sui-cide rate to the frustration of dependency needs; suicide following performance failure is rare. The suicide of a Danish man is often precipitated by the loss of a dependency relationship with his mother or wife. Suicide among Danish women frequently follows childbirth, which represents a turning point in their own dependency needs. In contrast with Swedish mothers, Danish mothers are deeply emotionally involved with their children and encourage them to be dependent. Little attention is given to the child's performance level. Danish mothers are more pleased with how well their children look and how much they weigh than the age at which they talk, walk, and do things for themselves. Passivity and dependency are more valued than competition and outstanding success. The deemphasis of achievement in the culture is strikingly illustrated by the absence of heroic deeds in Hans Christian Andersen's fairy tales. In exchange for the unlimited gratification of his dependency needs, the child is expected to curb his anger. When a child misbehaves, he is confronted with the guilt-inducing reprimand, "Look how much you have hurt Mama!" Aggression is turned inward in the form of self-blame.

This directing of aggression against the self is in accord with the psychoanalytic interpretation of suicide. Maurice Farber (1968) has also noted the suppression of hostility among the Danes and their deemphasis of personal competence. Both of these national traits contribute to a sense of hopelessness, the central element in suicide, when the individual is confronted with disappointment.

Hendin relates the low suicide rate of the Norwegians to their pattern of child-rearing, their general life style, and their more direct expression of aggression. In their rearing of children Norwegian mothers strive for a middle course between the clinging dependency of the Danes and the detached independence of the Swedish. They are emotionally involved with their children but at the same time the children are encouraged to be independent and competent. The Swedes' grim approach to work and success is rare in Norway, where a culturally shared fear of envy serves as a check on high aspirations. To be "good" is considered more desirable than to be successful. The playing down of high performance reduces anxiety and self-blame for failure.

In Norway, anger is handled more openly and aggression is directed outward. The Norwegian solution to frustration and disappointment is to see oneself as the injured party and to nurse one's anger. A paranoid style of collecting injustices presumably serves as a defense against self-blame, self-hatred, and self-destruction. The greater externalization of anger and aggression among Norwegians does not extend to overt acts of violence. The homicide rate in Norway is identical with that of Denmark and Sweden; all are low. Farber (1968) also found that Norwegians express feelings of hostility more openly than the Danes and strive for greater competence.

A more parsimonious explanation is that the lower suicide rate in Norway compared with Denmark and Sweden is mainly due to the fact that more suicides in Norway are certified as accidental deaths. A comparison of relevant vital statistics for the three countries supports this hypothesis (World Health Statistics Report, 1972). In 1968 the reported suicide rate for Norway was 8 per 100,000 population; the corresponding rates for Denmark and Sweden were 21 and 22, respectively. The reported death rate for all accidents exclusive of motor vehicle accidents was 36 per 100,000 for Norway, 24 for Denmark and 28 for Sweden. Thus the combined death rate for reported suicides plus "all other accidents" was 44 per 100,000 for Norway, 45 for Denmark, and 50 for Sweden.

Age and Sex

Suicide is practically nonexistent before the age of ten and rare between the ages of ten and fourteen. With the onset of adolescence it becomes a significant problem. The magnitude of suicide among youth is directly related to that of their elders; in countries with high rates, the youth rate is also high. Most countries report a steady increase in the suicide rate for males and females as their age increases, from fifteen to sixty-five. After sixty-five, the rate for females decreases, but elderly males show a more variable pattern. Some countries report a continuing increase in the rate for males over sixty-five; others indicate a leveling off or a drop (May, 1972).

In the United States the suicide rate for 1972 for both sexes combined was close to 12 per 100,000 for all ages. The rate increased from 10 per 100,000 for ages fifteen to twenty-four to approximately 15 per 100,000 for ages twenty-five to forty-four and 20 per 100,000 for ages forty-five to sixty-four. The rate remained at about 20 per 100,000 for ages sixty-five to eighty-four (Monthly Vital Statistics Report, 1973). During the age period fifteen to thirty-four, when the death toll from physical disease is relatively low, suicide ranks as the fourth largest cause of death. About 8 percent of all deaths at this age level are due to suicide. For older age groups, suicide continues to be one of the ten major causes of death but the proportion of total deaths that is due to suicide decreases markedly with advancing age.

Throughout the world more males than females take their own lives each year. In general, the male suicide rate is about twice as high as that for females for all age groups up to sixty-five, and thereafter the ratio is closer to 3 to 1. Studies (Kreitman, 1972; Weissman et al., 1973) in which 1970 suicide rates were compared with those of a decade earlier indicate that in more recent years the rate for young males (fifteen to twenty-five) has increased while that for older men has decreased. The trend for women is similar but less marked. There has been a slight increase in the suicide rate of young females and a small decrease among older females. The net effect has been that for ages over twenty-five the differences in male and female suicide rates have been considerably reduced. If the trend continues, females may soon claim suicide equality with males.

The age and sex patterns for suicide attempts are the reverse of those for completed suicide. The peak rate for males and females occurs between the ages of fifteen and twenty-five. After twenty-five, there is a sharp and almost straight-line decrease to age sixty-five and over (Fig. 19.1). The rate for females is nearly twice as high as for males. Recent reports (Kreitman, 1972; Weissman et al., 1973) indicate an upward trend in suicide attempts by both sexes for ages fifteen to forty-five. The greatest in-

crease has occurred among male youths. Females continue to make more attempts than males, but the greater recent increase in male attempters has narrowed the gap. If the trend continues, males may soon achieve equality with females in suicide attempts.

Meaningful evaluation of the significance of recent age and sex changes with respect to rates of suicide and suicide attempts must await confirmation of these changes over a longer period of time. The decline in the rates among persons over twenty-five may be related to more effec-

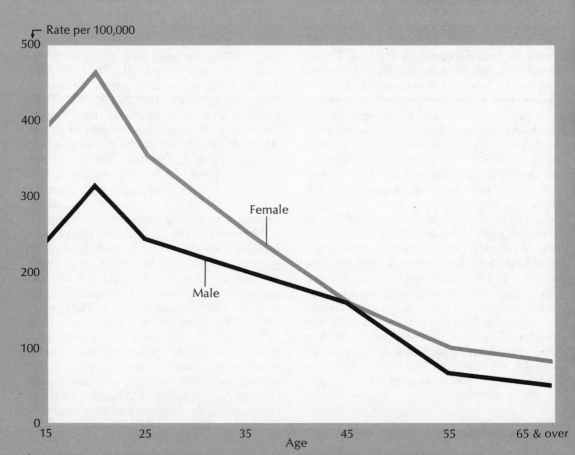

Figure 19.1. Age and Sex Differences in Suicide Attempts (Based on All Hospital-Referred Cases of Self-poisoning in Edinburgh 1969-1970).

Adapted from data reported by Kreitman (1972).

tive medical treatment of self-poisoners. This speculation, however, does not square with the increase in suicide among youth—unless it can be established that the methods and drugs used by the young are more lethal.

Marital Status

There is some evidence that the death rate from suicide is higher among married than single teenagers. Seiden (1969) has suggested two possible explanations. Persons who marry before twenty may be too immature to cope with the stresses of marriage, or they may be the psychologically bruised products of disturbed homes and unrealistically assume they will find happiness through escape into marriage. After age twenty, the suicide rate for married men and women is considerably lower than for single or widowed persons. At all age levels, the divorced have the highest rate.

With respect to suicide attempts, married persons are less apt to be repeaters than are the single, widowed, or divorced (McCulloch and Philip, 1972). The relation of early suicide attempt to the individual's subsequent marital status has also been investigated (Otto, 1972). A follow-up study of Swedish youngsters who had attempted suicide before the age of twenty-one found that ten to fifteen years later, the early suicidal group was still unmarried (single or divorced) to a greater extent than were members of a control group.

Social Class and Other Variables

The suicide road is traveled by persons from all walks of life, all religious faiths, and all races. The rich and the poor, the literate and the illiterate, the famous and the unknown, and all those in between are potential fellow-travelers. The range of intelligence of suicides is similar to that of the general population. Some subgroups may be more heavily represented than others, but data bearing on this point are difficult to evaluate. The differences that

have been noted may be artifacts of under-reporting, the greater visibility of certain groups, the differential use made of public hospitals by upper- and lower-class suicides, and so forth. With this word of caution, we can proceed with a brief summary of some of the more consistent findings (Seiden, 1969; McCulloch and Philip, 1972).

The reported suicide rate among Protestants is higher than for Jews, who in turn have a higher rate than Catholics. Some nonliterate societies have higher suicide rates than Western societies; others have considerably lower rates. Non-whites in the United States formerly showed a lower incidence of reported suicide than whites, but in large cities today the gap is closing as the result of an increase in reported deaths due to suicide among the former group. The incidence of completed suicide tends to be higher in the middle and upper classes than in the lower class. For suicide attempts, the class pattern is reversed, with the lowest class showing the highest rate.

Several investigators in England and the United States have found that college students have a substantially higher rate of completed suicide than nonacademic people of the same age. Within the college population, students attending the top-ranked universities (Oxford, Cambridge, Yale, and Harvard) have higher suicide rates than those enrolled in less prestigious colleges. College students who take their lives usually have better academic records than their classmates. On the other hand, a large proportion of suicide attempters in high school have records of failing work at the time of their attempts.

A suggested explanation is that college students with lofty aspirations may be unduly vulnerable to the threat of undistinguished achievement, which for them represents failure. The discrepancy between level of aspiration and achievement may also be a contributory factor to the high suicide rates of lawyers, doctors, psychiatrists, and people in the creative arts of painting and writing. The epidemic of Wall Street suicides that followed the stock mar-

Émile Durkheim (1858-1917), a French sociologist noted for his theories and studies of suicide which stressed the importance of social factors.

ket crash of 1929 was largely confined to men who had formerly been successful speculators and investors. The financial losses might have been borne; the ego wounds were fatal.

THEORIES AND EXPLANATIONS

A wide variety of theories have been proposed to explain various aspects of suicide. The theory that suicide represents a symptomatic manifestation of an underlying mental disorder has already been discussed. A related idea is that the genetic basis of psychoses may explain the observation that suicidal tendencies are frequently exhibited by two or more members of the same family; but research studies conducted with twins (Kallmann et al., 1946, 1949) offer no support for the hypothesis that suicide is the result of a special hereditary trait or of a particular type of genetically determined personality deviation. It is rare for both twins of identical pairs to commit suicide. Kallmann (1946) concludes that "Suicide seems to be the result of such a complex

combination of motivational factors as to render a duplication of this unusual constellation very unlikely even in identical twin partners who show the same type of psychosis and a very similar degree of social privation."

Learning theory provides an alternate explanation for the observed tendency of suicide to run in families. When there is a precedent of a particular kind of behavior in a family, it is easier for other members to follow suit. Other theories have been mainly concerned with explaining national differences and changes in suicide rates, and have largely focused on general social and cultural factors. Still other theories have called attention to the importance of early developmental experiences, interpersonal relationships, and the management of aggressive impulses.

Social Integration

In his classic book on suicide, originally published in 1897, Émile Durkheim (1951) described three types of suicide: altruistic, egoistic, and anomic. All three were interpreted in terms of the individual's relationships and attachments within his social group. *Altruistic* suicide occurs when the individual is too closely identified with his social group. Under certain circumstances his close integration with family and institutions may require that he sacrifice his life for the common good. Examples have already been given in the earlier discussion of institutional forms of suicide. *Egoistic* suicide results from inadequate integration of a person into his society. He may take his life because he is rejected by his society or for some reason is unable to become part of it. *Anomic* suicide results when the individual feels alienated from his society, a condition that is especially characteristic of disorganized societies that lack unity and cohesion.

Durkheim's main theory was that the degree of integration of a society was inversely related to its rate of suicide. Where a society is loosely organized and the individual is isolated and on his own, the rate of suicide is high. Societies that are highly organized and unified on a political, religious, or family basis have low rates. There may be several reasons for this relationship (Fedden, 1972). A closely knit, structured society offers ready-made answers to vexing problems, provides dependable support in time of crisis, and at the same time exercises considerable control over the individual's actions.

A wide variety of data offer support for this theory. For example, the low suicide rate in predominantly Catholic countries may be attributed to the unifying influence of religion. The increased solidarity of people in time of war may account for the decrease in suicide during wartime. Conversely, the increase in suicide during prolonged economic depressions may be attributed to the associated social disintegration.

Social Isolation

The theory that social isolation increases the risk of suicide differs from the related concept of social disintegration in that its emphasis is on the absence of meaningful interpersonal relationships rather than on the degree of cohesiveness of the society as a whole. The social isolation hypothesis provides an apt explanation for the lower rate of suicide noted among married than unmarried persons and for the high suicide rates of elderly persons without family ties and persons living alone in rooming homes and hotels. It has often been observed that college students who commit suicide have no friends. Neither classmates nor faculty know much about them. James Jan-Tausch concluded from his study of schoolchildren that the critical difference between those who succeeded and those who failed in their suicide attempts was that the latter had a close relationship with at least one person.

Jerry Jacobs (1971) also has emphasized the key importance of social isolation as a contributing cause of suicide among young adolescents. Because of its comprehensiveness, this study merits a closer look. The population consisted of fifty suicide attempters between the ages of fourteen and eighteen who had been admitted to the emergency room of a Los Angeles hospital. Structured interviews were conducted with the children and their mothers to obtain detailed life histories. Similar data were also obtained for a carefully matched control group. Jacobs' findings were in substantial agreement with those reported by other investigators. Among the events that were more often noted in the life histories of suicide attempters than in the control subjects were frequent change of residence, loss of one parent through death, separation or divorce, parents remarrying, heavy drinking by parents, and suicide attempts by parents and close relatives.

Jacobs does not attach much weight to these findings as isolated events. Their significance lies in their evaluation within the context of the adolescent's total biography. The order of their occurrence and the way the individual experienced and reacted to them are of special importance. Jacobs views suicide as the last resort of troubled, unhappy, isolated youngsters. Prior to their actual attempts, their distress and cries for help are signaled by

SUICIDE AS THE LAST RESORT: THE CASE OF CARLA

Carla, a fifteen year old girl, attempted suicide in school by swallowing a large number of assorted pills. Before going to school, she called her boyfriend and told him of her plan. He didn't believe she was serious and did nothing about it. At school she confided in a girl friend who could be trusted not to tell on her. After swallowing the pills she went to see the school's attendance officer. She had been cutting classes, and because of this she expected to be transferred to another school she disliked. In the middle of the interview she excused herself to go to her locker.

Because of her somewhat strange behavior, the attendance officer followed her, saw a lot of empty pill bottles in her locker, and asked her to return to his office. She refused and walked out of the building. The attendance officer followed in his car, picked her up, and took her to a hospital where the contents of her stomach were pumped out. When subsequently interviewed, Carla refused to reveal the reason for her action and was evasive as to whether she might make another attempt.

Interview data indicated that Carla was not a planned child. Before and after her birth, her parents quarreled a great deal. Her father left home when she was two and her mother remarried a year later. Her mother and stepfather had frequent fights. The stepfather disliked and often hit Carla. When interviewed, Carla reported that she despised her stepfather, whom she described as "nuts" and "weird." She also expressed hatred of her mother. At the time of her suicide attempt her stepfather had left home and her mother was planning to marry a new boyfriend.

Among Carla's early childhood problems were temper tantrums, frequent talking in her sleep, restlessness, and fears. Behavior noted during the year preceding her suicide attempt included disobedience, truancy, social withdrawal, running away from home, and a drop in her school grades.

A month before the attempt Carla had a big fight with her mother who refused to let her go to live with an aunt in another state. A week before the attempt, Carla's gym teacher and confidante was killed in an accident. On the weekend before the attempt, her mother and her lover went off on a trip, leaving Carla alone at home. She decided then to commit suicide, but for some reason scheduled the attempt to take place in school on Monday. (Adapted from Jacobs, 1971).

visits to doctors for vague physical and mental complaints, rebelliousness, withdrawal, running away, and dropping out of school. The continued failure of these and other "adaptive" techniques for coping with problems of increasing intensity, combined with the dissolution of any remaining meaningful social relations, leads to a feeling of hopelessness that serves to justify the suicide attempt.

Suicide and Aggression

Suicide can be described as an act of aggression committed against the self. This idea was explicitly expressed in the older term, "self-murder." The attack on self may be direct and obvious (slashing one's throat) or indirect and passive (taking an overdose of sleeping pills). Some suicides may also be described as acts of aggression directed against others. This relationship is evident in revenge suicides and the transparent threats of children and spouses that center on the theme "You'll be sorry when I'm gone." Suicide may masquerade as murder. The Malaysian *amok* reaction is a dramatic example; when a frustrated male could no longer control his resentment and rage, he would run about in a frenzy, dagger in hand, slashing at anyone in his way until he was killed. The English put an end to this indirect form of suicide by forbidding the killing of persons running amok.

Suicide by murder also occurs in western society. In a study of over five hundred homicide cases involving mainly black males, Marvin Wolfgang (1959) concluded that about one-fourth were actually victim-precipitated. His suggested explanation is that lower class males, whether black or white, tend to regard suicide as a sign of weakness or cowardice. When embittered and frustrated and tempted to commit suicide, they may arrange a more "manly" death by provoking a selected executioner to make a murderous assault. The unavailability of any supporting evidence from the departed victim makes it difficult to validate this theory.

Psychoanalytical theories that attempt to explain suicidal behavior in terms of aggression also suffer from the drawback that they are untestable. Stekel's often quoted statement, "No one kills himself who has never wanted to kill another or at least wished the death of another" is true but meaningless. At one time or another everyone has wished, at least momentarily, for the death of another. The subsequent modification of Stekel's theory to suggest that suicide represents the turning against the self of repressed hostile impulses formerly directed against others is no great improvement. If aggression is assumed to be repressed and unconscious, there is no way of proving or disproving the theory. The same argument is applicable to the theme of domination of the ego by the unconscious superego.

Freud's (1922) controversial theory of a death instinct provides an easy explanation for both aggressive and suicidal behavior. Unfortunately, the concept of an innate death drive, present in all human beings, leaves unanswered the critical question of why some individuals are more overtly suicidal than others.

PREVENTIVE MEASURES

Primary Prevention

Enough is known about the contributory determinants of suicide to outline an effective preventive program. The difficulty lies in its implementation. Social, political and religious educational programs that serve to increase the stability, unity, and cohesiveness of society and of the family would significantly reduce the incidence of suicide. Greater economic security does not appear to be too important, since suicide rates are as high or even higher in welfare states and affluent families than in countries with modest welfare benefits and families with limited incomes.

What is needed is a greater concern for and responsiveness to the personal and social needs of the individual. More specifically, the objective should be to increase the individual's sense of belonging, of purpose, of being accepted, of being wanted and treated as a valued person, and of knowing that he can count on others for help, if needed.

A more favorable attitude toward the rejected aged would go a long way toward decreasing their high suicide rate. In our present youth-worshiping society the appeals of the aged for love and their cries for help fall largely on deaf ears (Rachlis, 1970). More flexible retirement programs that give able and interested senior citizens the opportunity to continue to lead useful and productive lives beyond the arbitrary age of sixty-five would decrease the risk of suicides precipitated by loss of status, boredom, and the futility of prolonging an empty existence. Community-sponsored social, vocational, and recreational programs for the aged constitute another important preventive measure. Children may significantly sustain old people's interest in living by their continued love and involvement in their welfare. Since the youth of today are the aged of tomorrow, it would be to everyone's self-interest to augment the acceptance, status, and sense of worth of the aged.

At the family level, husbands and wives could decrease the occurrence of suicide by being more sensitive and responsive to their partner's urgent appeals for understanding and help. Many attempts by adolescents could be averted if parents took their threats seriously, made some attempt to remedy or alleviate the situation, or at least showed concern. Parental indifference

A suicide attempter, caught by the camera as she turned her back momentarily on the abyss beneath her. She ultimately decided not to jump.

to or ridicule of talk of suicide leaves the child little alternative but to make good his threat. Many suicides could be averted if families refrained from the common practice of exploiting one member as a scapegoat for venting family tensions and hostilities. The message conveyed to the scapegoat is loud and clear; he and the family would be better off if he were dead. According to Sidney Jourard (1969), people usually destroy themselves in response to an invitation originating from others to stop living. Finally, high schools and colleges may decrease the probability of suicide among students through planned socialization programs and extracurricular activities that encourage peer interaction and more personalized student-teacher relationships.

Emergency Treatment

Considerable progress has been made in recent years in establishing emergency services in the community to provide prompt and effective treatment of suicide attempters. Emergency procedures include mouth-to-mouth resuscitation in cases of drowning or strangulation, pumping out the stomach and providing necessary antidotes in self-poisoning cases, and surgical and medical treatment of cuts and wounds.

In addition to saving the life of the patient, prompt and effective treatment often lessens the extent of residual physical handicaps. Some attempts have been made to supplement emergency treatment with counseling for the suicide attempter and his family, but efforts in this direction have been sporadic and usually limited to a few therapeutic sessions. As a rule, neither the individual nor his family have much interest in a detailed examination of factors contributing to his suicide attempt.

Repeated Attempts

About one-fourth of the persons admitted to a hospital after a suicide attempt make a second try within two or three years; usually the second attempt occurs within a year. Close to ten percent of the initial attempters eventually kill themselves. A study of one-time versus repeated attempters found that repeaters more often were older; were single or divorced; had a diagnosis of pathological personality; were problem drinkers or drug users; were unemployed or changed their jobs frequently; lived in lodgings, hostels, and other non-family institutions; and had histories of debt, criminal convictions, and imprisonment (McCullough and Philip, 1972). Attempted and completed suicides were more common in the families of repeaters than in the families of first attempters. A mildly surprising finding was that about two thirds of the repeaters had histories of psychiatric treatment prior to or at the time of their first attempt compared to one-fifth of the one-time attempters.

McCullough concludes that suicide prone individuals require more than conventional psychiatric treatment. He suggests that repeaters are deficient in the social skills necessary for relating to people in a mutually satisfactory way. Their social deficiencies have resulted in their being rejected by society, and in rejecting it in turn. They need a sustained, meaningful, and satisfying interpersonal relationship if the risk of repetition is to be reduced. The relative ineffectiveness of traditional forms of psychotherapy may be partly related to the negative attitude many professional workers have toward the suicide attempter (Andriola, 1973). The seriousness of his intent to kill himself is often challenged, openly or covertly. In subtle ways the message is conveyed that he is playing games, is seeking attention, or is trying to manipulate others. This disparaging attitude strips the patient of hope and serves as a license for him to make a more serious attempt.

Suicide Prevention Centers

The main thrust of preventive programs has been to encourage troubled and presumably high-risk persons to get in touch with their friendly local crisis center. The story of the establishment of emergency first aid stations for potential suicides starts at the beginning of the present century. In 1905 the Salvation Army established an Anti-Suicide Bureau in its London headquarters (Levine and Kay, 1971). Similar bureaus were soon introduced in other Army branches in several countries. Counseling procedures were direct and problem-oriented. The first step consisted in asking drop-ins and referrals clearly and truthfully to delineate the specific causes of their current difficulties. Defenses, alibis, suicidal threats, and expressions of self-pity were ignored. The individual was urged to face his problem, reevaluate his situation from a more hopeful perspective, and with the help and active intervention of the adviser to work out practical solutions. In 1906 a group of clergymen in New York organized the National-Save-a-Life League. This program, along with that sponsored by the Salvation Army, flourished for a while and then waned.

The crisis center idea was revived in the 1960s with the establishment of the Samaritans in England (Varah, 1965), the Los Angeles Suicide Prevention Center (Schneidman and Farberow, 1968), and Friends, Inc., in Miami (Resnick, 1968). This time the movement appears to have taken firmer hold. Crisis intervention centers, mainly organized by nonprofessional persons and staffed by volunteers, have been established in most large cities in the United States, England, and other countries. Suicide prevention remains an important objective but individuals with all kinds of personal problems are encouraged to make use of their local center.

R. E. Litman (1972) has summarized the characteristics of a random sample of some one thousand callers to the Los Angeles Suicide Prevention Center. Slightly more than half of the cases were direct calls from the persons directly concerned. The remainder consisted of calls in behalf of disturbed persons made by friends, family members, doctors, ministers, and teachers. The median age of the client population was thirty-three; one-third were males and two-thirds were females. More than three-fourths of the clients were described as depressed, 25 percent had a current alcohol or drug problem, and 10 percent were considered to be highly confused.

The experience of most suicide prevention agencies is that less than 20 percent of the callers present an immediate threat of suicide. A few centers have facilities for individual diagnoses and treatment; most do not. The basic medium for providing help is the telephone, which has many and varied advantages. Service can be made available day and night, with someone who cares always on hand to respond with warmth and empathy to incoming desperate cries for help. In cases involving poisoning, wrist-slashing, drug overdoses, or other emergencies, the volunteer on duty can quickly get in touch with rescue resources in the community.

A unique contribution of telephone counseling is that it provides a means of reaching many distressed persons who for one reason or another avoid therapy because they find the traditional face-to-face, patient-doctor relationship too threatening or too humiliating (Williams and Douds, 1973). Counseling by telephone permits the caller to remain anonymous and to retain greater control of the conversation. He may reveal as much or as little about himself as he wishes and he can always hang up if things get out of hand. Anonymity may facilitate greater openness without fear of ridicule or censure. Those who are socially isolated may be encouraged to initiate interaction with others via the safety of the telephone and move slowly toward others at their own rate and on their own terms. The fact that the person at the other end of the phone is also anonymous may be a further advantage; the caller can make of the therapist what he needs.

An important practical advantage of telephone counseling is that crisis services can be effectively delivered by volunteers. Initially, volunteers were recruited because of the shortage and high cost of professional personnel. Workers in the field soon realized that professional training is not essential in helping persons struggling with here-and-now crises and may actually be a handicap. The traditional doctor-patient role and attitudes of the professional act as a distance-creating barrier. The profes-

sional's interest in underlying causes distracts from the immediate concerns of the troubled caller. Observational and research data indicate that volunteers as a group are superior to professionals in establishing direct, warm, and empathic relationships with clients. In the words of Dublin (1963): "The lay volunteer was probably the most important single discovery in the fifty-year history of suicide prevention. Little progress was made until he came into the picture." The services of professional personnel can be more profitably utilized for consultation, the administration of programs, and the selection and training of volunteers.

On the debit side, the ease of telephone contact invites some unwanted callers (Lester and Brockopp, 1973). High on the undesired list is the obscene caller. Female staff members are particularly disturbed by males who phone for the sole purpose of masturbating while listening to a female voice. Other problem callers include pranksters, persons who phone several times a day just to talk to someone, those who call but refuse to speak, and callers with trivial complaints. The usual moral and legal issues associated with intervention in the life of another are accentuated in telephone counseling by the limited information available about the caller. What should a volunteer do when a stranger calls, identifies himself, and states that he is in the process of slashing his wrists or has just taken an overdose of some drug but doesn't want the listener to do anything about it? If no action is taken and the person dies, the volunteer and the center run the risk of being accused of negligence. If the listener starts rescue operations by calling the police or the local hospital, he runs the risk of being accused of invasion of privacy. Sometimes this leads to legal action, and the fact that the courts will dismiss the suit in either instance is of little comfort to the worker caught in this dilemma.

A final issue centers on the value of crisis centers. The grass-roots origin of most centers, the large number of callers, and

A volunteer telephone counselor at the Suicide Prevention Center of San Mateo County, California.

the enthusiasm of volunteers suggest that the centers serve an important community need. From what is known of the nature of psychotherapy, it is reasonable to infer that many callers derive considerable relief and comfort from talking about their problems with a concerned listener. In the process of communicating his difficulties coherently and logically, the caller may obtain a clearer picture of his problem and perhaps see it from a different and more favorable perspective. But this is all conjecture. The anonymity of some callers, the incompleteness of case records, and the absence of matched control groups make it virtually impossible to obtain hard, factual data.

A few attempts have been made to compare the suicide rate in communities with and without crisis centers, with inconsistent findings. One study (Weiner, 1969) found no differences in suicide rates between two cities in California with centers and two cities without them. Los Angeles, which has an excellent prevention program, has experienced an increase in its suicide rate. More encouraging results have been reported in another study (Bagley, 1968) that found a lower rate of suicide in English towns with crisis centers than in those without.

The inconclusiveness of survey investigations is not surprising. Actually, there is little basis for assuming that crisis centers should be effective in preventing suicide. Ninety-eight percent of the persons who complete suicide do not call crisis centers (Weiner, 1969; Wilkins, 1970). The less-than-20 percent of callers who are suicidal are almost exclusively attempters who have little or no serious intention of ending their lives. A further complicating factor is that the publicity associated with antisuicide programs may have the contrary suggestive effect of increasing the rate of attempted and completed suicides. A common observation is that newspaper accounts of a dramatic episode often set off a wave of similar episodes. Finally, the counseling of suicidal persons is no exception to the general rule that therapeutic intervention may be for better or worse—that failures often seem to cancel gains.

An attempted follow-up study of calls to the suicide prevention center in Los Angeles illustrates some of the technical difficulties in obtaining valid data for evaluating the effectiveness of telephone counseling (Litman, 1972). The study consisted in making follow-up calls one week after the initial contact. Interview data were originally obtained on 652 phone calls made during one month. In the follow-up one week later, 307 of the original population had to be discarded because the caller had given either no name or a false name, no address, or had called from a phone booth. Close to 20 percent of the replies obtained from successfully recontacted callers had to be discarded because the subjects were uncooperative or gave inconsistent or grossly incomplete answers. Usable data were obtained on only 50 percent of the original callers.

Of this reduced population, 87 percent reported they had been helped by the center. There is no way of determining to what extent these figures represent a true response or a socially polite response. The two chief benefits claimed were that having someone to talk to helped and that the suggestions made by the staff made it easier to accept help from others. Only about half the persons who reported they had been helped made direct use of resources recommended by the center.

Postvention

Postvention involves working with the surviving members of a family in which a suicide has occurred to help them face and resolve their anguish, guilt, anger, shame and perplexity (Shneidman, 1969). An important objective is to decrease the risk that other members may also commit suicide. The act of suicide often leaves family members with vague feelings of guilt that they might have been at least partly responsible for driving the victim to his death or for failing to respond to his cry for help. Also, family members often have strong feelings of hostility and rage directed against the victim for rejecting and abandoning them and leaving them to bear the stigma of suicide.

Family therapy and the individual counseling of survivors may be helpful in lessening the pain of grief, decreasing intrafamilial tension, easing the burden of guilt and shame, and moderating feelings of hostility. The increase in communication and the sharing of emotions within the family may eliminate the need for irrational recriminations, denial of the suicidal act, and other distorted thoughts and feelings. Postvention may also help survivors adjust to the negative reactions that society often exhibits toward suicides and their families.

SUMMARY

Man's awareness of the ready availability of a last-resort solution to vexing and seemingly insurmountable personal and social problems makes suicide a universal, timeless and omnipresent threat. The rates of personal suicide show no indication of following those of institutional forms that have decreased sharply in recent years. Figures for the United States, which are about average compared with those for other countries, indicate that about 12 per 100,000 of the general population are officially listed as suicidal deaths each year. The actual total may be twice as high. Especially among persons under forty, suicide is a major cause of death. Attempted suicides run about 1 per 1,000 population. More females than males make attempts; more males than females succeed.

Suicide is not a sin, a crime or a symptom of mental illness. It is a human act of desperation, a sign of acute personal anguish. Psychopathology has a humanistic interest in reducing the suffering associated with self-destructive behavior. Its objective is through scientific study to add to our knowledge of the determinants of suicide and to develop more effective therapeutic and preventive measures. Within this context, the differences in suicide rates reported by various countries are being examined more closely to see if they are related to local cultural attitudes and practices or result from national differences in methods of collecting and reporting data on suicidal deaths.

When we consider individual cases, research indicates that the risk of suicide is much higher among the unmarried, the socially isolated, and the alienated than among those with meaningful interpersonal relations and close family ties. The sense of aloneness, of no one caring, of having no one to turn to for help, contributes to the loss of hope that is the key precipitant. That nonfatal attempts are more characteristic of youth whereas older persons have higher rates of completed suicide may be related to the greater hopefulness of youth and the greater hopelessness of those over fifty. The establishment of community crisis centers represents a constructive first step in reaching and helping the potential suicide. The limited services provided by these emergency phone centers have not proved too effective in reducing mortality rates, but users have reported other benefits. The greater use of family therapy following a first attempt may reduce the risk of a subsequent repetition. Postvention counseling may help survivors adjust to their traumatic experience and loss.

References

Alvarez, A. *The Savage God: A Study of Suicide.* New York: Random House, 1970.

Andriola, J. "A Note on the Possible Iatrogenesis of Suicide." *Psychiatry* 36 (1973): 213-18.

Bagley, C. "The Evaluation of a Suicide Prevention Scheme by an Ecological Method." *Social Science and Medicine* 2 (1968): 1-14.

Beck, A., and Greenberg, R. "The Nosology of Suicidal Phenomena: Past and Future Perspectives." *Bulletin of Suicidology* 8 (1971): 10-17.

———; Resnick, H. L. P.; and Lettieri, D. J. *The Prediction of Suicide.* Bowie, Maryland: Charles Press, 1974.

Choron, J. *Suicide.* New York: Scribner, 1972.

Dublin, L. L. *Suicide: A Sociological and Statistical Study.* New York: Ronald Press, 1963.

Durkheim, Émile. *Suicide.* New York: Macmillan, 1951.

Farber, M. L. *Theory of Suicide.* New York: Funk & Wagnalls, 1968.

Fedden, H. R. *Suicide: A Social and Historical Study.* New York: Benjamin Blom, 1972. First published London, 1938.

Freud, S. *Beyond the Pleasure Principle.* London: International Psychoanalytic Press, 1922.

Hendin, H. *Suicide and Scandinavia.* New York: Grune & Stratton, 1964.

Jacobs, J. *Adolescent Suicide.* New York: Wiley, 1971.

Jan-Tausch, J. "Suicides of Children, 1960-63 New Jersey Public School Students." Trenton: State of New Jersey, Department of Education (n.d.).

Jourard, S. M. "The Invitation to Die." In *On the Nature of Suicide,* ed. E. S. Shneidman, pp. 129-41. San Francisco: Jossey-Bass, 1969.

Kallmann, F. J., and Anastasio, M. M. "Twin Studies on the Psychopathology of Suicide." *Journal of Heredity* 37 (1946): 171-80.

———; De Porte, J.; De Porte, E.; and Feingold, L. "Suicide in Twins and Only Children." *American Journal of Human Genetics* 1 (1949): 113-26.

Kreitman, N. "Aspects of the Epidemiology of Suicide and 'Attempted Suicide' (Parasuicide)." In *Suicide and Attempted Suicide,* ed. J. Wadenström, T. Larsson, and N. Ljungstedt, pp. 45-56. Stockholm: Nordiska Bokhandelns Förlag, 1972.

Lester, D., and Brockopp, G. W. *Crisis Intervention and Counseling by Telephone.* Springfield, Ill.: Charles C Thomas, 1973.

Levine, M., and Kay, P. F. O. "The Salvation Army's Anti-Suicide Bureau, London, 1905." *Bulletin of Suicidology,* no. 8 (1971): 57-63.

Litman, R. E. "Experiences in a Suicide Prevention Center." In *Suicide and Attempted Suicide,* ed. J. Waldenström, T. Larsson, and N. Ljungstedt. Stockholm: Nordiska Bokhandelns Förlag, 1972.

McCulloch, J. W. "Social Prognosis of an Edinburgh Clientele." In *Suicide and Attempted Suicide,* ed. J. Waldenström, T. Larsson, and N. Ljungstedt. Stockholm: Nordiska Bokhandelns Förlag, 1972.

——— and Philip, A. E. *Suicidal Behaviour.* Oxford: Pergamon Press, 1972.

May, A. R. "Suicide: A World Health Problem." In *Suicide and Attempted Suicide,* ed. J. Waldenström, T. Larsson, and N. Ljungstedt, pp. 15-29. Stockholm: Nordiska Bokhandelns Förlag, 1972.

Mintz, R. S. "Prevalence of Persons in the City of Los Angeles Who Have Attempted Suicide." *Bulletin of Suicidology* 7 (1970): 9-16.

Monthly Vital Statistics Report: Annual Summary for the United States, 1972, 21 (no. 13), June 1973. Washington, D.C.: U.S. Department of Health, Education and Welfare.

Osmond, H., and Hoffer, A. "Schizophrenia and Suicide." *Journal of Schizophrenia* 1 (1967): 54.

Otto, U. "Suicidal Behavior in Childhood and Adolescence." In *Suicide and Attempted Suicide*, ed. J. Waldenström, T. Larsson, and N. Ljungstedt, pp. 189-201. Stockholm: Nordiska Bokhandelns Förlag, 1972.

Rachlis, D. "Suicide and Loss Adjustment in the Aging." *Bulletin of Suicidology* 7 (1970): 23-26.

Resnick, H. L. P. "A Community Antisuicide Organization: The Friends of Dade County, Florida." In *Suicidal Behaviors: Diagnoses and Management*, ed. H. L. P. Resnick. Boston: Little, Brown, 1968.

Retterstöl. N. "Suicide in Norway." In *Suicide and Attempted Suicide*, ed. J. Waldenström, T. Larsson, and N. Ljungstedt, pp. 89-101. Stockholm: Nordiska Bokhandelns Förlag, 1972.

Rudestom, K. "Some Cultural Determinants of Suicide in Sweden." *Journal of Social Psychology* 90 (1970): 225-27.

Sainsbury, P., and Barraclough, B. "Differences Between Suicide Rates." *Nature* 220 (1968): 1252.

Seiden, R. H. "Suicide Among Youth." *Bulletin of Suicidology* supplement. Washington, D.C.: U.S. Government Printing Office, 1969.

Shneidman, E. S., ed. *On the Nature of Suicide*. San Francisco: Jossey-Bass, 1969.

——— and Farberow, N. L. "Statistical Comparisons Between Attempted and Committed Suicides." In *The Cry for Help*, ed. N. L. Farberow and E. S. Shneidman, pp. 19-47. New York: McGraw-Hill, 1961.

———. "The Los Angeles Suicide Prevention Center." In *Suicidal Behaviors: Diagnoses and Management*, ed. H. L. P. Resnick. Boston: Little, Brown, 1968.

Stengel, E. *Suicide and Attempted Suicide*. Baltimore: Penguin Books, 1964.

———. "A Survey of Follow-up Examinations of Attempted Suicides." In *Suicide and Attempted Suicide*, ed. J. Waldenström, T. Larsson, and N. Ljungstedt, pp. 25, 250-57. Stockholm: Nordiska Bokhandelns Förlag, 1972.

Varah, C. *The Samaritans.* New York: Macmillan, 1965.

Weiner, I. W. "The Effectiveness of a Suicide Prevention Program." *Mental Hygiene* 53 (1969): 357-63.

Weissman et al., "Suicide Attempts in an Urban Community, 1955 and 1970." *Social Psychiatry* 8 (1973): 82-91.

Wilkins, J. "A Follow-up Study of Those Who Called a Suicide Prevention Center." *American Journal of Psychiatry* 127 (1970): 155-67.

Williams, T., and Douds, J. "The Unique Contribution of Telephone Therapy." In *Crisis Intervention and Counseling by Telephone*, ed. D. Lester and L. W. Brockoff, pp. 80-88. Springfield, Ill.: Charles C Thomas, 1973.

Wolfgang, M. E. "Suicide by Means of Victim-Precipitated Homicide." *Journal of Clinical and Experimental Psychopathology* 20 (1959): 335-49.

World Health Organization. *Prevention of Suicide.* Public Health Papers no. 35. Geneva: WHO, 1968.

World Health Statistics Report 25, no. 11. Geneva: WHO, 1972.

Colère, James Ensor

The recent acceleration of social and political change has been accompanied by a sharp increase in deviant behavior. In the United States, as in other countries, established authority and the status quo are being challenged not only by underprivileged minority groups but also by middle-class youth and college students. Increased delinquency and crime, protest marches, the hippie movement, draft evasion, the widespread use of drugs, riots, burnings, bombings, the killing of police and public officials, kidnapping, the hijacking of planes—all these acts of passive and active aggression have been interpreted as symptoms of a "sick" society. Some of the more extreme rebels believe the "sickness" is so pervasive and hopeless that the only recourse is to destroy the present society and build a new one according to a different plan or no plan at all, trusting to the old myth that man is inherently "good" and only institutions are evil. In today's theology the devil has been replaced by another fallen angel, the Establishment.

What is the relationship of the social deviance of protest to psychopathology? The majority opinion of psychopathologists is that mental disorders are restricted to individuals; it is meaningless to refer to a whole society as neurotic, psychotic, or sociopathic. Furthermore, most psychopathologists do not consider that the acts of terrorism and violence of social rebels are in themselves indicative of psychopathology. Acts of social protest are quite different from the behavior of the mentally disturbed in a number of significant ways. One important distinction is the matter of purpose. The antisocial or aggressive behavior of the mentally disturbed is usually an expression of some personal grievance or the acting out of a delusion or hallucination; the acts of violence of social rebels represent attempts to speed up or control the direction of some "corrective" social change. The goal is usually stated in altruistic terms. Nearly always there is some factual basis for the protest, which is recognized by the larger society. Frequently the public is in general agreement that change is desirable and supports the movement toward the correction of inequities so long as it proceeds in an orderly fashion and within legally recognized boundaries. As a rule, the social deviance lies in the method rather than the goal. Pathological behavior, on the other hand, is not motivated by any laudable end. No society or minority subgroup advocates social changes intended to result in an increase in the prevalence or political power of neurotics, psychotics, sociopaths, mental defectives, chronic alcoholics, users of harmful drugs, sex deviants or suicidal persons.

Acts of violence committed by social rebels fail to meet either the legal rules of insanity or the recognized criteria of psychopathology. Social activists know the nature and quality of their destructive, hostile actions and are capable of distinguishing right from wrong. They show neither an impairment of psychosocial abilities nor loss of voluntary control. Their offenses are premeditated, deliberate, and executed according to plan. Time, place, and target are carefully selected for maximum results. No guilt is experienced, because the individual is convinced of the righteousness of his cause. The destruction of property and life, along with the risk to self, are rationalized and discounted as sacrifices that must be made to produce a "better" society.

The tragic scene of the confrontation of students and National Guardsmen at Kent State University, during which four persons were killed in 1970.

The reaction of society to social and political nonconformists depends on the evaluation made of the deviant behavior by the great majority of the population or the governing body. More often than not, any change in the status quo is resisted on the principle that the familiar is preferable to the unknown. As a rule, harmless forms of deviance are ridiculed but tolerated. When deviants engage in overt acts that violate established mores or which pose real or imagined threats to the safety and welfare of the group, the usual social reaction is to remove them. Formerly they were exiled or executed, today they are often imprisoned. There are two recognized legal grounds for the compulsory incarceration of "troublesome" and "dangerous" persons: mental illness and criminal behavior. Neither is directly applicable to the acts of protest committed by social activists, but since their imprisonment rests on court action by which they have been found guilty of the violation of existing laws, their behavior may at least technically be considered criminal. The morality of treating social dissidents as ordinary criminals is another matter. Yet the alternative of committing them to institutions for the mentally ill is the greater of the two evils. To be labeled and treated indefinitely as a mental patient is far worse than to be temporarily imprisoned for fighting for one's ideals.

SOCIAL TENSION AND PSYCHOPATHOLOGY

The differentiation of social protest reactions from individual expressions of psychopathology does not mean that social unrest has no effect on personal adjustment. The amount of stress, deprivation, dissension, and insecurity of a society obviously affects the psychological well-being of its members—even though the impact may not be reflected in reported incidence rates of psychological disorders. The explanation for the latter reservation is that a person's mental health tends to be judged in relation to that of his peers. The usual evaluative procedure is to regard the adjustment level of the great majority as "normal" and to label as psychologically disturbed those at the lowest end of the mental health continuum. In most societies the cut-off point is roughly at the 10th percentile in terms of the relative severity of maladjustment. Regardless of the absolute adjustment level of the population there will always be a bottom 10 percent who, depending on the nature of their maladaptive and disturbing behavior may be labeled neurotic, psychotic, alcoholic, retarded, or sociopathic.

Clinical psychologists, psychiatrists, and other professionals in related fields have long been aware of the importance of social and home factors in the etiology of psychological disorders. The more enlightened have realized that prevention is by far a better, and possibly easier, solution than therapy. Our knowledge of causes is still incomplete but there are sufficient leads to formulate a promising preventive program. Assuming that the obstacles of implementation could be surmounted, there is a high probability that the severity and prevalence of human anguish could be materially reduced by the following measures.

1. *The recognition that no single human problem takes precedence over the creation of a more humane society in which every person is accepted as a fellow human being and treated with respect.* Not only should allowances be made for individual differences, but diversity should be regarded as an asset contributing to the enrichment of the group rather than a liability to be abolished. Practices that systematically lead to mistrust, disparagement, brutal competition, loss of self-esteem, social alienation, and loneliness must not be tolerated. The human need for close interpersonal relatedness is reflected in the interest in communes but it must be acknowledged that historically the only communes that have achieved noted success have been based on strong ideologies. These ideologies effectively separate the ingroup from the outgroup, thus defeating the objective of brotherhood in the society at large. There are no easy answers, and there are no answers at all unless we ask the right questions.

2. *The reduction of stresses associated with war, economic depression, the mass relocation of populations, and political unrest.* The actual or threatened loss of life, identity, income, family, and security brought about by these social ills are major sources of needless suffering and mental torment.

3. *The improvement of medical and physical care.* The sector of the population in greatest need of medical services is the poor, but all classes would benefit from improved prenatal care, avoidance of birth injuries, adequate diet, prompt and effective treatment of disabling diseases, improved housing, and all the other factors that increase physical and mental well-being.

4. *The elimination of discriminatory practices that deny equal social and economic opportunity to women and to members of minority groups.* Depriving individuals of opportunity for maximum personal growth and self-actualization leads to frustration, resentment, hostility, apathy, despair, and feelings of unworthiness.

5. *The improvement of the family unit.* In one way or another, the family is the major factor in mental health. Genetic data make clear the importance of discretion in

the selection of a mate if one wishes to decrease the risk of psychopathology in the family. When both husband and wife have family histories of psychosis, they would be well advised to refrain from having children. Too many individuals who have little interest in marriage or aptitude for child rearing nevertheless marry and have children in response to social pressure. The frequent results are divorce and psychologically scarred children.

6. *The establishment of comprehensive mental health services in the community.* Some progress in this area has already been made, as we shall see in a moment. There are two main advantages in locating mental health centers in the community. One is the increased accessibility of services to those who need them. Particularly in disadvantaged communities composed largely of minority groups, residents are more willing to attend neighborhood centers than to visit distant, strange facilities. The proximity factor also facilitates prompt intervention in crises. A second major advantage is that each community can tailor its services to particular local needs. The recently established community centers differ from the traditional outpatient clinics in that they offer services for a wide variety of problems, many of which are only remotely related to the traditional concepts of mental disorder.

COMMUNITY MENTAL HEALTH

The idea of providing comprehensive mental health services in the community is an outgrowth of the work of the Joint Commission on Mental Illness and Mental Health. This commission was authorized by Congress in 1955 to conduct a study of the mental health of the nation and to present its recommendations to federal and state officials. One of the recommendations of the commission's 1961 report, *Action for Mental Health,* was the estab-

lishment of community mental health centers to serve both children and adults as part of state or regional systems for the care of mental patients in the community.

New York was the first state to enact legislation providing for the creation of community centers, with its Community Mental Health Services Act of 1954. In 1963 Congress passed the Community Mental Health Centers Act. This and subsequent supporting legislation have provided financial aid to states, on a participation basis, for building and staffing community centers serving designated catchment areas. A similar program was established in Great Britain by Parliament's passage of the Mental Health Act of 1959.

Federal funding has facilitated the rapid growth of the community mental health movement. By 1972 more than three hundred centers had been established in the United States. Most are attached to established general or psychiatric hospitals and serve the surrounding community. In large cities geographical boundaries have been drawn demarcating the catchment areas or populations served by specific centers. The general objective is to mobilize and utilize the resources of the community for the treatment and prevention of mental disorders and other forms of deviance and impairment in psychosocial functioning. Toward this end, the active participation of local residents and organizations is sought in establishing policies and in developing services to meet the mental health needs of the particular community. Attention is given to strengthening positive factors as well as eliminating sources of stress in the social environment.

Community involvement represents a significant change from the authoritative doctor-patient relationship; members of the professional staff are agents of or advisers to the local residents, who are perceived as clients. The historical background of the recurring interest in the community approach to psychopathology has been reviewed by Ewalt and Ewalt (1969) and R. B. Caplan (1969). Its general objectives and principles have been outlined by Smith and Hobbs (1966), Roberts et al. (1966), and Klein (1968). Susser (1968) has reviewed and analyzed community mental health care in Britain. The future of community mental health centers is subject to continued federal financial support. Their effectiveness in improving the mental health of the nation remains an unknown. A major criticism is that the poor, the uneducated and minority groups, who have the greatest need, have not made full use of the centers. In part, this has been due to the failure of persons in charge of local centers to develop and provide services desired by these groups (Holden, 1972).

Community Services and Programs

By law, centers receiving federal assistance in the United States are required to provide inpatient and outpatient services, partial hospitalization services (day care, night care, or weekend care), emergency services, and consultation services to the community. In addition, community centers have experimented with a wide variety of other approaches: home visits, family therapy, special education programs for young children, delinquency prevention, work with drug users, vocational and social rehabilitation of patients discharged from mental hospitals, walk-in clinics, and training programs in leadership and self-government for local residents. Staff personnel may serve as consultants to schools, church groups, police, and other social agencies. Shore and Mannino (1969) have described a variety of strategies designed to translate community mental health ideas into action programs. Issues of the *Community Mental Health Journal* and *Mental Hygiene* contain articles giving detailed accounts of new programs.

Services for children. Innovative procedures for the treatment and prevention of emotional problems in children have been described by several investigators. Nicholas Hobbs (1968) has reported a program for the reeducation of emotionally

disturbed children in residential schools located in the community. The schools, staffed entirely by teacher-counselors who are backed by consultants in the fields of pediatrics, psychiatry, psychology, and education, provide intensive short-term treatment that permits the child to be separated from his family and regular community for as brief a time as possible. The central aim is to help children acquire competence in coping with day-to-day problems. Insofar as possible, practical improvements are also made in the child's home, school, and neighborhood. In effect, the goal is to modify the child's behavior so that his family, school, and community will tolerate his presence. Cure is considered a meaningless concept. One finding of this study is that human behavior is remarkably responsive to expectations. Goals and procedures are couched in the idiom of competence and self-fulfillment.

J. McV. Hunt (1968) has substituted the concept of incompetence for mental disease. The objective of therapy is thus to increase the child's competence level. This can best be done by providing a stimulating problem-solving environment during infancy and early childhood. Research studies suggest that children of parents from lower-class backgrounds receive inadequate training in the motivation habits, symbolic skills, and social standards that underlie competence. Lower-class parents tend to be relatively uncommunicative with their children, do not encourage them to be curious about the world about them, and do not give reasons for their actions. A good child in the lower-class family is a quiet, passive child who shows little initiative and curiosity and does not disturb the activities of adults. Motivation is modeled on immediate gratification rather than the acceptance of relative privation now for the sake of more substantial rewards later. Hunt mentions the familiar Head Start and Get Set programs, but is more interested in the establishment of nursery centers for children and parents in which the mothers can observe what teachers are doing and can apply the same procedures in the home to stimulate the child's learning and to extend his competence.

Cowen and Zax (1968) have described a variety of programs concerned with the early detection and prevention of emotional disturbances in schoolchildren. They are interested in assessing the effectiveness of mothers, retired persons, and college students as teaching assistants in schools, so that children may have more individual attention. Persons such as these, who are oriented toward the emotional and educational needs of disturbed children, appear to be effective in improving the subsequent adjustment and achievement of children who in earlier grades were labeled as potential problems.

Aftercare of hospitalized patients. Mental hospitals in this country are currently making a concerted effort to decrease the number of chronic resident patients. From 1961 to 1972 the resident population of mental hospitals decreased 48 percent. The large number of patients annually discharged back to the community has necessitated the expansion of local facilities and programs for the care and rehabilitation of patients with residual defects. The availability of drugs for moderating overt symptoms has made community care feasible, but supplementary programs are needed to enable former resident patients to live outside the hospital setting. Community aftercare facilities include daycare centers, day or night hospitals, halfway houses, foster homes, social clubs for formerly hospitalized patients, and sheltered workshops. These aftercare facilities serve three main functions:

1. They relieve families of the continuous burden of caring for patients by providing places where they may spend several hours each day.

2. By providing guided social experiences, they help patients to learn or relearn social skills (Weinman et al., 1970).

3. They offer assistance in vocational counseling and training and job placement (Koltuv and Neff, 1968). For patients with

irreversible residual defects, sheltered workshops offer the possibility of partial self-support in surroundings adapted to their needs.

Services for Skid Row residents. Many large cities have areas where social derelicts gather. Many of these homeless men are alcoholics, but 15 to 20 percent of them are nondrinkers who have sought refuge from joblessness and social pressures in the impersonal environment of Skid Row. Surveys (Bloomberg et al., 1973, Plaut, 1967, and others) reveal that most Skid Row residents are middle-aged or elderly men without effective family or friendship ties. A large number have never married. Well-educated and married men who go on occasional benders can be found there, but the vast majority of these are transients who sooner or later return to their jobs and families. Most long-term residents are unskilled.

For these men, many of whom are chronic alcoholics or former schizophrenics, Skid Row provides a community where living costs are low and missions make up the difference between bare survival and a minimal income. Skid Row also serves as a labor market where employers seek day laborers. Many of the men living in these areas have never been arrested for public drunkenness and some are regularly employed. These men are usually not found in alcoholic wards or in mental hospitals.

Attempts to abolish Skid Row communities by relocating the residents has proved to be a difficult task. Most of the men are opposed to relocation. Many of them suffer from chronic physical illnesses as well as psychosocial problems. Skid Row is a reservoir of contagious diseases and the death rate of its residents is high. These homeless men need a wide variety of services, especially medical care, vocational training or placement, psychological or social assistance, and inexpensive lodgings. For some, a protective facility of some kind, such as a halfway house or a domiciliary institution, is necessary. Skid Row serves as a good illustration of the reinforcing interaction between the individual and his social environment. Each needs and sustains the other. Intervention is required to break up the relationship.

Orientation and Models

The traditional medical model of disease is deemphasized in community mental health work. Little attention is paid to intrapsychic or childhood causes of problems. The focus is on the difficulties confronting the individual here and now, and the ways in which he may best be helped to cope with them so that functioning competence may be quickly restored. Rehabilitation rather than cure is the goal. Prevention is given higher priority than treatment. Community mental health work has a mainly educational orientation: it is directed toward the acquisition of skills and attitudes that contribute to increased self-direction, competence, and confidence. It is more concerned with solving problems than with gaining insights.

Kelly (1968) has noted some analogies between community mental health programs and the biological concept of ecology, which is concerned with the relationship of organisms or groups of organisms with their environment. One of the basic principles of ecology is that intervention anywhere in a biological system alters the total organization. Social systems too are affected by changes in any of their parts, and the ultimate effects of intervention are difficult to predict. Social environments, like biological environments, also affect styles of adaptation. Certain types of environment may require particular kinds of changes in adaptive behavior.

A third model, which has greater potential application, is the public health movement. The main thrust of public health is toward prevention (Bloom, 1965). The great success of public health measures in improving physical health has little to do with the traditional medical approach of early detection and prompt treatment. Early identification and treatment may shorten the duration of illness and thereby reduce the prevalence rate, but this approach has no effect on the number of new cases or the incidence rate. The efforts of public health officials have been more profitably focused on the elimination of the causes of disease. Impressive victories have been won against disease through improvements in sanitation, the purification of water, mass inoculations, the destruction of disease-spreading insects, and educational programs.

The application of the public health model of prevention to community mental health has been discussed by G. Caplan (1964) and others. *Primary prevention* consists of corrective measures that prevent the occurrence of a disorder or decrease a person's risk of developing it. Community mental health organizations emphasize primary prevention in prenatal programs aimed at the avoidance of premature birth and prenatal disturbances that may lead to brain damage, well-baby clinics, preschool programs, and local facilities to handle social crises. Prompt, effective counseling of persons in stress situations often makes the difference between personal growth and prolonged maladjustment. Marriage counseling, family services, legal aid societies, suicide-prevention centers—all these serve to aid persons in moments of crisis.

Secondary prevention is aimed at reducing the prevalence rate of psychosocial disorders by shortening the duration of disability. The realization of this objective depends on early detection and prompt, effective treatment. Early signs of impending disturbances usually are noted by teachers, policemen, clergymen, or physicians. Community centers may utilize these sources of referral by working closely with the schools, churches, police departments, and family agencies. Many agencies offer basic courses for neighborhood groups on the means of detecting mental disturbances and the procedures to follow in dealing with them and obtaining professional help for people who may need it. The facilities of the centers may be used for treatment, or patients may be referred to other agencies. Walk-in clinics and store-front facilities that offer immediate consultation may be helpful in shortening the duration of disorders.

Tertiary prevention is the reduction of residual defects that often persist long after a mental disorder has ended. The goal is the effective rehabilitation of the mentally disordered person and his return to maximum productivity as quickly as possible. Ideally, plans for rehabilitation should start with the onset of the disorder. Mental health workers should try to anticipate the effect of the disorder on the patient's subsequent productivity, his possible need for a new job, the extent to which the disorder may result in a disruption of functioning, and the reactions of others. Every effort should be made to avoid committing a patient to a mental hospital to avert the risks of desocialization and the difficulties that confront the patient when he returns to the community.

A common problem of discharged mental patients is that there is no place for them to go. Their families may not be willing or able to accept them, and the stigma of having been committed to a mental hospital may interfere with their gaining employment. When hospitalization cannot be avoided, the availability of aftercare facilities often makes the difference between rehospitalization and successful readjustment to life in the community.

Mental Health Personnel

The professional staff of community centers consists largely of psychiatrists, psychologists, and social workers. Since the traditional professional training of these specialists is not particularly relevant to the types of services provided in community centers, the usual barrier between professions tend to break down and staff members work together on a more equal footing than they do in more traditional institutions. Much of the work with clients is actually done by people recruited from the community who have received on-the-job training. In addition to relieving the manpower shortage, community co-workers

have proved highly effective in relating to clients (Reiff and Reissman, 1964). Clients tend to accept them more readily than they do the professionals, since they share many of the clients' own attitudes and expectations. Nonprofessionals engage in all forms of therapy, and their success rate is comparable to that of professionals (Guerney, 1969). It is worth noting that a survey of a representative sample of the American population(Gurin et al., 1960) indicated that only 18 percent of troubled persons consulted psychiatrists or psychologists; the remainder sought the help of community advisers and agencies. More people in the latter group reported they were helped than those who visited professionally trained specialists.

Middle-Class versus Lower-Class Values

The entry of mental health specialists into ghettos and slums has helped to bridge the communication gap between the middle and lower class. One interesting observation has been that the standard theories of psychopathology and psychotherapy, which have been mainly derived from the study of middle-class patients, have limited applicability to the poor. Middle-class patients tend to attribute their problems to some personal difficulty, for which psychotherapy provides a relevant approach. Lower-class patients are more inclined to attribute their problems to external hardships and defects in society. They therefore look for help in coping with environmental problems rather than in resolving inner conflicts.

As Reiff has noted (1966), middle-class persons see themselves moving toward self-actualization. If they encounter difficulties, they seek help in removing the personal obstacles that stand in the way of attaining a full, rich life. Low-income people, on the other hand, have little expectation that the future will be much better than the present. They live in a world of limited opportunities that afford little role flexibility. They are primarily concerned with the here and now. They have specific immediate objectives, and they seek concrete help in attaining them. For this group, self-determination is a more realistic and more meaningful goal than self-actualization.

A second interesting point has been the reappraisal of the tendency (often unconscious) of professionally trained persons to try to impose their standards and values on lower-class clients. If the poor were to accept the middle-class virtues of maximum education, planning for the future, postponement of gratification, and self-actualization, their economic status might be improved; but the assumption that the acceptance of these middle-class values would automatically improve the mental health of the poor is a myth. The middle class has its own hangups and mental disorders. It is significant that the revolution against contemporary society is spearheaded by middle-class youth. From the point of view of mental health, it is questionable whether the middle-class tendency to blame one's self for failure is an improvement on the lower-class stratagem of projecting blame onto society. If the poor produce more paranoids and sociopaths, the middle class has higher rates of neurosis and depression.

In many ways the personal interdependence and sharing of lower class people represents a better solution to the vicissitudes of life than the independence, self-sufficiency, and loneliness of suburbia. The preference of lower class people for direct, immediate "remedies" to problems (a better job, a bigger apartment, a stronger pill) offers greater possibilities of shortening the duration of psychiatric disabilities than prolonged verbal therapies aimed at self-understanding. Psychotherapy has a poor record of success. The faulting of the poor for their greater concern with the immediate present than with the future reflects a lack of understanding of their pressing current needs and the bleakness of their future. Day-to-day survival takes precedence over long-term planning for self-actualization. Unless there is some assurance that the sacrifices of today will pay off in greater satisfactions tomorrow, there is little purpose in postponing pleasure.

The middle class has tended to exaggerate the "sinfulness" of immediate gratification. There is nothing wrong with immediate gratification so long as it does not actually entail future penalties, and this is a matter more difficult to predict than many people like to think. Each age has its particular sources of pleasure, which can be fully appreciated only at that time. Old age is not the time to enjoy the postponed pleasures of youth.

Evaluation

It is still too early to evaluate the significance of the community mental health movement. So far the main emphasis has been on exploring new avenues of approach. Research interests have tended to be subordinated to the immediate pressures of providing needed services. On the credit side, the movement represents a continuation of the humanistic approach initiated by Pinel. The focus on the prompt restoration of functioning in disturbed persons is in line with the premise that behavior disorders represent problems in living; there is no disease to cure. Another positive feature is the participation of representatives of various disciplines and of nonprofessionals as partners in the search for increasingly effective ways of preventing and treating psychosocial disabilities.

SUMMARY

Acts of passive or active aggression committed by dissenters as means of speeding up or effecting social change represent a special form of social deviance that is independent of psychopathology and only technically related to criminal behavior. Social rebels are not mentally disturbed in terms of the legal rules of insanity or of the key criteria of psychopathology. The notion of a sick society is more a journalistic than a scientific concept. The available evidence indicates that the total incidence of psychopathology is about the same in all societies. However, the particular type of psychosocial disturbance and the relative severity of personality disorganization are probably related to the level of stress and the kinds of frustration encountered in a particular society.

The major advantage of the current interest in community mental health is that it provides needed services for the poor, who have long been a neglected sector of the population. Acceptance of middle-class standards by the poor might improve their economic status, but whether it would improve their mental health is debatable. Psychosocial problems are not limited to the poor. By adopting middle-class values, the poor would become susceptible to middle-class problems. "I've been rich and I've been poor," the old joke goes, "and believe me, rich is better." That may be, though the proposition is being questioned by an increasing number of people; but if it is, it does not necessarily follow that neurosis and depression are better than paranoid tendencies and sociopathy. (Nor, of course, are paranoid tendencies and sociopathy to be accepted and justified as "part of the system.")

Direct attack on immediate problems, which is characteristic of the community mental health approach, offers the poor greater promise of therapeutic effectiveness than the traditional preoccupation with insight and the reconstruction of the personality. The value of the community mental health movement as a means of primary prevention remains uncertain, but it is reasonable to take an optimistic view of its effectiveness in secondary and tertiary prevention.

References

Albee, G. W. *Mental Health Manpower Trends.* New York: Basic Books, 1959.

Bloom, B. L. "The 'Medical Model' Miasma Theory and Community Mental Health." *Community Mental Health Journal* 1 (1965): 333-38.

Bloomberg, L.; Shipley, T. E.; Shandler, I. W. *Skid Row and its Alternatives.* Philadelphia: Temple University Press, 1973.

Caplan, G. *Principles of Preventive Psychiatry.* New York: Basic Books, 1964.

Caplan, R. B. *Psychiatry and the Community in Nineteenth-Century America.* New York: Basic Books, 1969.

Cowen, E. L., and Zax, M. "Early Detection and Prevention of Emotional Disorder: Conceptualizations and Programming." In *Research Contributions from Psychology to Community Mental Health,* ed. J. W. Carter, pp. 46-59. New York: Behavioral Publications, 1968.

Ewalt, J. R., and Ewalt, P. L. "History of the Community Psychiatry Movement." *American Journal of Psychiatry* 126 (1969): 43-52.

Guerney, B. G., ed. *Psychotherapeutic Agents: New Roles for Nonprofessionals, Parents and Teachers.* New York: Holt, Rinehart & Winston, 1969.

Gurin, G. G.; Veroff, J.; and Feld, S. *Americans View Their Mental Health.* New York: Basic Books, 1960.

Hobbs, N. "Reeducation, Reality, and Community Responsibility." In *Research Contributions from Psychology to Community Mental Health,* ed. J. W. Carter, pp. 7-18. New York: Behavioral Publications, 1968.

Holden, C. "Nader on Mental Health Centers: A Movement that Got Bogged Down." *Science* 177 (1972): 413–415.

Hunt, J. McV. "Toward the Prevention of Incompetence." In *Research Contributions from Psychology to Community Mental Health,* ed. J. W. Carter, pp. 19–45. New York: Behavioral Publications, 1968.

Joint Commission on Mental Illness and Mental Health. *Action for Mental Health.* New York: Basic Books, 1961.

Kelly, J. G. "Toward an Ecological Conception of Prevention Interchanges." In *Research Contributions from Psychology to Community Mental Health,* ed. J. W. Carter. New York: Behavioral Publications, 1968.

Klein, D. C. *Community Dynamics and Mental Health.* New York: Wiley, 1968.

Koltuv, M., and Neff, W. L. "The Comprehensive Rehabilitation Center: Its Role and Realm in Psychiatric Rehabilitation." *Community Mental Health Journal* 4 (1968): 251-59.

Mental Health Statistics. *Provisional Patient Movement and Administration Data, State and County Mental Hospitals, United States,*

1968-69. Chevy Chase, Md.: National Institute of Mental Health, 1970.

Plaut, T. F. A. *Alcohol Problems: A Report to the Nation by the Cooperative Commission on the Study of Alcoholism.* New York: Oxford University Press, 1967.

Reiff, R. "The Etiological and Technological Implications of Clinical Psychology." In *Community Psychology: A Report of the Boston Conference on the Education of Psychologists for Community Mental Health,* ed. C. C. Bennet et al., pp. 51-64. Boston: Boston University, 1966.

——— and Reissman, F. *The Indigenous Nonprofessional: A Strategy of Change in Community Action and Community Mental Health Programs.* National Institute of Labor Education report no. 3, November 1964.

Roberts, L. M.; Halleck, S. L.; and Loeb, M. B. *Community Psychiatry.* Madison, Wis.: University of Wisconsin Press, 1966.

Shore, M. F., and Mannino, F. V., eds. *Mental Health and the Community: Problems, Programs, and Strategies.* New York: Behavioral Publications, 1969.

Smith, M. B., and Hobbs, N. "The Community and the Community Mental Health Center." *American Psychologist* 21 (1966): 499-509.

Susser, M. *Community Psychiatry: Epidemiologic and Social Themes.* New York: Random House, 1968.

Weinman, B.; Sanders, R.; Kleiner, R.; and Stephen, W. "Community-Based Treatment of the Chronic Psychotic." *Community Mental Health Journal* 6 (1970): 13-22.

Glossary

Abreaction. The release and venting of repressed emotions.

Acrophobia. Morbid fear of high places.

Acute alcoholic hallucinosis. A psychotic reaction of heavy drinkers, principally of those with schizoid traits, characterized by auditory hallucinations.

Acute brain syndrome. Disturbances in psychosocial behavior caused by temporary and reversible impairment in brain tissue functioning. The patient returns to his usual level and mode of functioning in a few days or weeks.

Acute depression. A psychotic reaction marked by dejection so profound that the individual is completely absorbed and incapacitated by it.

Acute mania. A psychotic reaction marked by extreme distractability, disorganized association of ideas, and increased inner pressure.

Acute schizophrenic episode. A psychotic reaction that is often associated with confusion, perplexity, ideas of reference, emotional turmoil, dream-like dissociation, and general excitement.

Affect. Emotion or feeling.

Affective psychosis. A psychosis characterized by extreme depression or elation that dominates the mental life of the individual. A broad diagnostic category that includes manic-depressive reactions and involutional melancholia.

Agoraphobia. Morbid fear of open spaces.

Alarm reaction. The first stage of Selye's general-adaptation syndrome, characterized by the mobilization of defenses to cope with stress.

Alcoholics Anonymous. An informal organization composed of alcoholics who want to stop drinking and have joined together to support each other's resolve to do so.

Alcoholism. A condition characterized by loss of control over the intake of alcohol. The alcoholic is consistently unable to refrain from drinking or, once started, to stop before becoming intoxicated.

Alienation. A feeling of the lack or loss of relationships to others.

Altruistic suicide. A form of suicide that occurs among persons so closely integrated with their societies that their own survival takes second place to the presumed needs of the group, especially in certan socially defined circumstances.

Alzheimer's disease. Slow, progressive presenile mental deterioration resulting from generalized atrophy of the brain.

Ambivalence. Concurrent opposing emotions, attitudes, or desires toward an object. Mixed love-hate reaction.

Ambulatory schizophrenic. A person manifesting a mild schizophrenic reaction who functions well enough to live in the community, without requiring hospitalization.

Amnesia. Total or partial loss of memory.

Amok. A culture-bound type of rage reaction among Malays, in which the disturbed individual would suddenly grasp a dagger and run wildly about, slashing at anyone in his way.

Anaclitic depression. A state of depressive withdrawal and debilitation occurring in children who are separated from their mothers between the ages of six and eight months, and for whom substitute mothers are not available.

Anal character. A personality type marked by excessive cleanliness, compulsive behavior, and sadistic tendencies. Freudian theory assumes that the anal character is a result of fixation at or regression to the phase of development during which the child's chief source of pleasure sensations is the anus.

Analgesia. Loss or impairment of sensitvity to pain.

Androgen. Male sex hormones.

Anhedonia. Impaired ability to experience or integrate feelings of pleasure.

Anomic suicide. The taking of one's own life because of a feeling of social separation or isolation; a form of suicide that is especially characteristic of societies that lack cohesion.

Anomie. A lack of the feeling of belonging, of social norms or values.

Anorexia nervosa. Serious loss of weight and malnutrition resulting from self-imposed dietary limitations.

Anoxia. A physiological condition arising from lack of sufficient oxygen.

Antisocial personality. A broad term applied to inadequately socialized persons whose persistent violation of the moral, legal, and ethical code brings them repeatedly into conflict with society. They typically do not experience genuine guilt or remorse for their misdeeds. They tend to blame others or offer rationalizations for their behavior.

Anxiety. A state of emotional tension characterized by apprehension, diffuse fearfulness, and somatic disturbances associated with emotional overreaction.

Anxiety reaction. A neurotic reaction characterized by recurring acute anxiety attacks.

Aphasia. Impaired ability to speak, comprehend, or communicate orally usually attributable to brain injuries.

Aphonia. Loss or marked impairment of voice without associated organic pathology.

Apoplexy (stroke). Sudden diminution or loss of consciousness with possible paralysis due to brain hemorrhage.

Apraxia. Loss of ability to perform simple, voluntary motor acts.

Archetype. An inherited universal thought form that predisposes man to experience critical events common to the human race. A concept of Carl Jung.

Arteriosclerosis. Degenerative thickening and hardening of the walls of the arteries, occurring usually in old age.

Assertive training. A form of behavior therapy for persons who have difficulty in expressing their anger and resentment when they are unjustly criticized or dominated by others. The basic strategy is to convince the patient of the virtue of asserting his rights and to point out the emotional and social repercussions of inhibiting his anger.

Asthenic personality. A personality type characterized by low energy level, easy fatigue, and a loss of zest. Asthenic persons tend to be complacent, apathetic, and distant.

Asthma. A psychophysiological disorder characterized by labored breathing, wheezing, a sense of constriction in the chest, coughing, and gasping for air.

Ataractics. See *Neuroleptic drugs*.

Atrophy. Wasting away or shrinking of a bodily organ.

Aura. Sensations signaling the onset of a convulsive seizure.

Autistic thinking. Gratification of desires in fantasy rather than practical attempts to gratify them in reality.

Autonomic nervous system. That part of the nervous system that regulates the activity of glands, viscera, heart, and smooth muscles. The autonomic system is less subject to voluntary control than the cerebrospinal or central nervous system.

Autonomy. Self-reliance, independence; the sense of being an individual in one's own right.

Autosome. Any chromosome other than those determining sex.

Avoidance conditioning. A form of conditioning in which the organism learns to behave in a certain way in order to avoid an unpleasant stimulus.

Behavior therapy. Treatment procedures based on conditioning or learning principles, a form of therapy that singles out some specific target behavior and undertakes to change it rather than attempting to uncover the underlying cause.

Behaviorism. A school of thought that considers the data of psychology to consist solely of objective, observable organismic activity, especially physical actions in response to stimuli.

Belle indifférence. An apparent lack of concern by hysterical neurotics about their loss of sensory and motor functions.

Bestiality. The use of animals as sex objects by humans.

Catalepsy. A general bodily condition marked by fixity of posture, general muscular rigidity, and unresponsiveness to the environment.

Catatonia. A subtype of schizophrenia characterized by stupor or excitement, negativism, stereotyped movements, mutism, muscular rigidity, and waxy flexibility.

Catharsis. The discharge of emotional tension associated with repressed traumatic material by "talking it out."

Cathexis. The investment of an object, idea, or action with special significance of affect for the individual.

Cerebral arteriosclerosis. A chronic brain disorder that is caused by fatty deposits blocking the flow of blood in the cerebral arteries. The condition is more accurately described as cerebral atherosclerosis. Associated behavior defects include memory impairment, confusion, and secondary personality changes.

Cerebral dysrhythmia. Irregular brain wave patterns. Atypical brain waves are characistic of epileptics.

Character disorder. A broad diagnostic category applied to deeply ingrained maladaptive personality traits.

Chemotherapy. Treatment of behavior disorders by means of psychoactive drugs that reduce emotional tensions. Particularly useful in decreasing bizarre psychotic behavior and aiding psychotic patients in maintaining contact with the social environment.

Childhood symbiosis. Moderate to marked dependence in early childhood, characterized by gross immaturity and a pathological attachment to the mother.

Chlorpromazine. The first widely used tranquilizing drug; effective in reducing hyperactivity impulsiveness, and aggressiveness and helpful in controlling hallucinations, delusions, and destructive behavior.

Chromosomes. Separable rodlike bodies in the nuclei of cells that contain the genes.

Chronic brain disorders. Disturbances in psychosocial functioning caused by brain damage that is irreversible and permanent. Over time the patient may show improvement in functioning, but the more typical pattern is a gradual and progressive decline.

Classical conditioning. Pavlovian conditioning. A previously neutral stimulus is temporally paired with a stimulus that elicits some (unconditioned) particular response. After several joint presentations of the neutral stimulus with the (unconditioned) stimulus, the neutral stimulus also elicits the particular response. The previously neutral stimulus is then referred to as the conditioned stimulus and the response elicited by it is referred to as the conditioned response.

Client-centered therapy. A form of therapy developed by Carl Rogers, characterized by unconditional acceptance of the patient by the therapist, a high degree of permissiveness (nondirectiveness), and the reflection of the client's feelings by the therapist.

Coitus interruptus. Withdrawal of the penis from the vagina prior to male ejaculation. The usual intent is to prevent pregnancy.

Colitis. A psychophysiological disorder characterized by inflammation or spasm of the colon.

Coma. A state of profound stupor or unconsciousness with complete insensibility from which the individual cannot be aroused.

Combat fatigue. See *War neurosis*.

Compensation. A common defense against feelings of inadequacy, failure, or personal defects, consisting of exaggerated efforts aimed at attaining success or distinction either in one's area of inferiority or in some other field.

Compulsion. An involuntary, irresistible impulse to do or say something against one's will or better judgment.

Concordance rate. A term used in genetic studies to indicate the extent to which some specific disorder occurs in both of two persons more or less closely related—twins, other siblings, parent and child, and so on. Thus, a noted concordance rate of 40 percent for schizophrenia in monozygotic twins means that among all pairs of identical twins studied of whom one was schizophrenic, 40 percent of their co-twins were also schizophrenic.

Conditioned stimulus and response. See *Classical conditioning*.

Confabulation. The spontaneous invention of imaginary experiences to fill memory gaps, without conscious intent to deceive.

Congenital. Existing at birth or before birth, but not necessarily hereditary.

Conscious. Memories, thoughts and impulses that the person is aware of or which are easily recalled.

Contingent. Dependent on special associated circumstances.

Conversion reaction. An hysterical reaction in which repressed material finds an outlet in physical symptoms. Usually expressed in a loss of some sensory or motor function, for example, psychogenic blindness, deafness or paralysis.

Convulsive disorder. A neurological disorder characterized by periodic loss of consciousness, motor disturbances, or epileptic seizures of short duration.

Countertransference. Emotional involvement of an analyst with his patient.

Crime. The violation, by an intentional act of commission or omission, of the recognized laws of society for which punishment is prescribed by law.

Critical period. A period during maturation when the organism is physiologically "prepared" to learn in response to a gven type of stimulus. Alternatively, a period of acute stress.

Cultural relativism. The idea that behavior regarded as abnormal in one society may be normal in another.

Culture-bound. Occurring in and limited to a particular society or culture.

Cunnilingus. Use of the tongue or mouth in erotic play with female genitals, especially stimulation of the clitoris.

Cyclothymic personality. A personality characterized by mild, frequently alternating elation and sadness, apparently stimulated by internal rather than external events.

Decompensation. Progressive personality disintegration evidenced in loss of control of behavior and decreased awareness of reality.

Delirious mania. A psychotic reaction marked by wild, uncontrolled excitement and disorientation. May be accompanied by hallucinations and delusions.

Delirium. A transient reaction in which the individual is typically confused, disoriented, incoherent, and out of touch with reality. Frequently noted in persons approaching or recovering from comas, in persons under the influence of alcohol or other drugs, and in persons with high fevers.

Delirium tremens (DTs). Delirium occurring in alcoholics following a prolonged period of drinking.

Delusion. A fixed, obviously false belief that is not in keeping with the individual's cultural training and which cannot be corrected by argument or presentation of reliable evidence.

Dementia praecox. Obsolete term for schizophrenia.

Denial. A defense mechanism that consists of an unconscious, selective perceptual "blindness" that protects the individual from facing intolerable thoughts, wishes, deeds, and situations.

Deoxyribonucleic acid (DNA). The principal component of the genes.

Depersonalization. A feeling of estrangement from oneself; a feeling of strangeness or unreality.

Depression. An emotional state of dejection, gloom, and feelings of worthlessness and guilt.

Depressive stupor. A psychotic reaction characterized by a massive paralysis of thought and action.

Derealization. A subjective feelng that one's environment has significantly changed and is no longer what it used to be.

Dermatitis. Inflammation of the skin, frequently of psychogenic origin.

Deterioration. Progressive impairment of mental functions and feelings.

Detoxication effects. Physical symptoms occurring in some alcoholics following the abrupt cessation of alcoholic intake after a prolonged period of intoxication: restlessness, confusion, irritability, belligerent attitude, fright, tremors, nausea.

Developmental disabilities. A broad category that includes psychosocial deficits and disabilities that have their onset during the developmental years from birth to about age eighteen.

Disorientation. Mental confusion resulting in the inability to orient or locate oneself correctly with respect to time, place, or person.

Displacement. A defense mechanism consisting of the transference of an emotion originally associated with an idea or object to some neutral and inappropriate idea or object.

Dissociative reaction. A neurotic reaction characterized by the temporary dissociation of certain segments of memory, thought, or personality from the total personality See *Amnesia; Dual personality; Fugue; Somnambulism.*

Dizygotic (DZ) twins. Twins produced by the fertilization of two ova; siblings conceived and born at about the same time. Also known as fraternal twins.

Double bind. Direct communications accompanied by indirect and intrinsically contradictory messages, so that no matter which message the individual responds to, he is bound to be "wrong."

Down's syndrome. A well-known type of mental deficiency associated with the presence of an extra chromosome. Formerly called mongolism because of accompanying physical characteristics that give the victim of the disorder a superficially oriental appearance

Drift hypothesis. The idea that the general social incompetence of potential schizophrenics causes them gradually to drift down to the lowest socioeconomic level.

Dual personality. A rare form of hysteria consisting of the creation of two alternating personalities to resolve conflicts between "good" and "bad" impulses.

Duodenal ulcer. Inflammation or lesions of the

upper portion of the small intestines, caused by physiological reaction to emotional stress.

Durham rule. A test of insanity formerly accepted in the District of Columbia, according to which an accused person should not be held criminally responsible if his unlawful act was the product of a mental disease or mental defect. Similar to the New Hampshire rule.

Dysmenorrhea. Painful menstruation.

Dyspareunia. Painful or difficult sexual intercourse.

Dyssocial personality. See *Antisocial personality.*

DZ twins. See *Dizygotic twins.*

Echolalia. Involuntary automatic repetition of words spoken by another person.

Echopraxia. Involuntary automatic imitation of gestures or movements made by another person.

Eczema. An inflammation of the skin accompanied by itching and oozing lesions that become scaly and crusted. A psychophysiological disorder.

Ego. The conscious part of the personality structure that mediates and resolves conflicts between the id, the superego, and environmental conditions. A psychoanalytic concept.

Ego ideal. The person or "self" the individual thinks he could and should be.

Egoistic suicide. A term applied by Durkheim to self-destruction by a person because he is rejected by his society or is unable to become integrated with it.

Electra complex. In psychoanalytic theory, an excessive emotional attachment (love) of daughter for father, usually associated with a negatve feeling toward the mother.

Electroencephalogram (EEG). A record obtained by amplifying and recording the electrical activity of brain cells.

Empathy. The ability to understand and to some extent share the feelings of another person.

Encephalitis lethargica. Sleeping sickness; an epidemic form of inflammation of the brain, usually signaled by high fever and drowsiness. Residual psychological and physical symptoms are often noted.

Encopresis. Persistent fecal soiling of self by children over three years of age.

Endogenous. Pertaining to causal influences that originate in sources within the individual.

Enuresis. Bed-wetting; involuntary passing of urine by older children or adults.

Epidemiology. The study of the incidence, distribution, and control of physical or mental disorders; the sum of the factors involved in these disorders.

Epilepsy. A neurological disorder characterized by short periods of partial or complete loss of consciousness, occurring suddenly and sometimes accompanied by convulsions and other psychomotor disturbances.

Eros. The life forces, particularly the libido or sex drive. A psychoanalytic concept.

Estrogen. Female sex hormones.

Etiology. The causes of a disease or abnormal condition; the study of causes.

Euphoria. An exaggerated feeling of well-being.

Exhibitionism. Self-display; as a form of sex deviance, the exposure by a man of his sex organ to a female who is a stranger and an involuntary observer.

Existentialism. A school of thought that emphasizes the uniqueness and freedom of the individual and the critical significance of meaning, purpose, and value.

Existential neurosis. A state of alienation from self and society, characterized by loneliness, apathy, boredom, aimless activities, and a pervasive sense of the meaninglessness of life.

Exogenous. Pertaining to causal influences that originate in sources outside the individual.

Experimental neurosis. Abnormal behavior experimentally induced in animals or human beings; usually induced by difficult problems of discrimination.

Explosive personality. A personality type characterized by loss of control under minor stress and direct expression of aggressive impulses either verbally, physically, or both.

Externalization. The experiencing of internal processes and emotions as occurring outside the self.

Extinction. The gradual disappearance of acquired conditioned responses when they are no longer reinforced.

Extravert. A person who directs his energies and interests outside himself, enjoys social activities, and expresses himself in action. A personality type delineated by Jung.

Factor trait. A relatively independent trait cluster derived from commonalities exhibited in behavior or test performance.

Fantasy. Daydream; also, an ego defense mechanism by means of which the individual escapes from the world of reality and gratifies his desires in fantasy achievements.

Fellatio. Insertion of the penis into the mouth of another person for purposes of sexual gratification.

Fetishism. The substituton of an inanimate object, such as a shoe or glove, for a human love object as a source of sexual arousal and release.

Fixation. The arrest of psychosexual development at some childhood level. A psychoanalytic concept.

Flight of ideas. Fragmentary skipping from one verbalized but unfinished idea another, with no logical progresson.

Flooding. See *Implosive therapy*. Client is directed to experience in imaginary scenes that generate fear, anxiety, guilt, and related emotions. Rather than avoiding fearful experiences and memories, the client is desensitized by being flooded with them.

Folie à deux. A delusional system shared by two persons closely associated with each other.

Folie en famille. The illusion fostered within the family that abnormality is normal.

Fraternal twins. See *Dizygotic twins*.

Free association. The process of making and reporting mental connections among ideas, memories, emotions, and sensations, no matter how trivial or "improper" they seem. A basic psychoanalytic technque regarded as a means of access to the unconscious.

Frigidity. The inability on the part of a woman to experience sexual pleasure or gratification; technically, the inability to experience orgasm. Preferred contemporary term is orgasmic inadequacy.

Frottage. Sexual pleasure derived from rubbing or pressing against another person. The term implies a mild offense committed against another without his or her consent.

Frustration. The thwarting of a need or desire.

Fugue. A psychological and geographical flight from one's usual environment, during which the individual forgets who he is and assumes a new personality. Following recovery, he has no recollection of his experiences during the fugue period.

Functional psychoses. An outmoded term that was formerly used to differentiate psychogenic or functional psychoses from toxic-organic psychoses.

Ganser's syndrome. Speech and behavior that are nonsensical but not irrelevant to the situation or the subject being discussed. Differentiated from malingering.

Gene. A submicroscopic unit of inheritance arranged within the chromosomes; a segment of DNA.

General-adaptation syndrome. A set of symptoms, described by Selye, that occur in response to excessive stress, consisting of alarm reaction, resistance, and exhaustion.

Generalization. The transference of learning acquired in one situation to another situation that is somewhat similar to the first.

General paresis. A psychosis resulting from progressive brain pathology produced by syphilis and characterized by a variety of mental and neurological symptoms.

Genital stage. The final stage of psychosexual development according to Freud that has its onset after puberty and culminates in heterosexual coitus.

Genotype. The particular combination of genes possessed by the individual.

Gerontology. The study of old age, with particular attention to disorders and their treatment.

Gonads. Testes or ovaries.

Grand mal. A form of epilepsy characterized by sudden loss of consciousness and convulsions.

Halfway houses. Houses in the community where patients live and work in a controlled environment. Usually serve as transition homes for patients discharged from mental institutions.

Hallucination. A sensory perception experienced in the waking state in the absence of any correspondng external stimuli; for example, hearing a nonexistent voice.

Hallucinogen. A chemical agent, usually derived from a plant, that produces hallucinations; also known as psychotomimetic drug.

Hawthorne effect. Improvement in behavior or increased output resulting from expression of interest in the individual's welfare by significant others.

Hebephrenia. A clinical subtype of schizophrenia characterized by peculiar mannerisms, silliness, bizarre behavior, and hallucinations.

Hedonism. The doctrine that pleasure is the primary good or value in life.

Heterosexuality. Sexual orientation toward persons of the opposite sex; the mature stage of psychosexual development.

Homeostasis. Tendencies of organisms to maintain a stable state of equilibrium.

Homosexuality. Erotic interest in members of one's own sex; more specifically, preference or exclusive capacity for sexual acts leading to orgasm with members of the same sex.

Hospitalism. A lack of development and progressive mental deterioration in infants reared in foundling homes and institutions that fail to provide adequate stimulation and mothering.

Huntington's chorea. A hereditary neurological condition characterized by involuntary jerky movements and gradual mental deterioration. Onset of symptoms occurs in middle life.

Hypertension. High blood pressure.

Hypnoanalysis. Hypnosis used as an aid in psychoanalytic treatment.

Hypnosis. An induced trance state marked by heightened suggestibility and automatic compliance, within limits imposed by the individual's values and conscience, with the instructions of the hypnotist. Also regarded as a form of role playing.

Hypochondriasis. A neurotic syndrome characterized by a persistent and exaggerated concern about diminished health and energy in the absence of demonstrable organic pathology.

Hypomania. A form of affective psychosis characterized by moderate elation, increased psychomotor activity, faulty judgment, and impulsivity.

Hypothalamus. Key structure at the base of the brain; important in temperature regulation, emotion, and motivation.

Hysteria. A neurotic condition characterized by conversion or dissociative reactions.

Id. In psychoanalytic theory, the personification of the unconscious. The id is concerned with the immediate gratification of primitive impulses, especially sexual and aggressve drives.

Ideas of reference. A delusion characterized by the perception of meaning, usually unfavorable to the self, in the casual remarks or acts of others.

Identical twins. See *Monozygotic twins*.

Identification. A defense mechanism through which an individual, without conscious awareness, satisfies frustrated desires by psychologically assuming the role or some of the traits of another person.

Identity crisis. Mental disturbances occurring mainly in youth, associated with difficulty in recognizing or establishing a unified personality that persists without regard to time, circumstance, or role.

Idiopathic. Of unknown causation; something presumed to be inherent in the individual's constitutional makeup.

Idiot. Obsolete term referring to a person with severe mental retardation, requiring complete custodial care.

Illusion. A false perception of a real sensory impression; e.g., seeing a twisted branch as a snake.

Imbecile. Obsolete term referring to a person with moderate to severe mental deficency, requiring supervision in simple tasks of self-care.

Imipramine. An antidepressant drug.

Implosive therapy. A treatment procedure that requires the patient to imagine and/or speak about objects or situations that cause him intense anxiety.

Impotence. The inability of a mature male to achieve and maintain an erection of sufficient rigidity to permit successful coitus. Not necessarily associated with sterility.

Imprinting. A form of learning in very young animals which determines the course an instinctive behavior pattern will take; e.g., a duckling learns to follow the first moving object it sees, and is thus said to be *imprinted* on that particular object (usually the mother).

Inadequate personality. A personality pattern characterized by ineptness, poor judgment, ineffectual responses to emotional and social demands, low stamina, and absence of drive.

Incest. Sex relations between father and daughter, brother and sister, and other persons closely related by genetic ties.

Incidence rate. The number of new cases of a disorder per unit of population developing in a specific population during a designated period of time.

Incompetence. Inability to manage one's personal affairs and property with ordinary prudence. A legal concept.

Index cases. A term used in genetic studies to identify those members of a population of related persons whose clinical behavior pattern meets predetermined criteria. The prevalence of the same behavior pattern in other members of the family is determined by comparing their behavior traits with those of the index cases. Also called proband cases.

Individual psychology. The name of the school that incorporates the theories and therapeutic approaches developed by Alfred Adler and his followers.

Infantile autism. Severe impairment of development beginning during the first year of life and characterized by failure to develop or manifest normal awareness and responsiveness to other human beings, mutism, and repetitive meaningless acts. It is assumed the child is not mentally defective.

Insanity. A legal concept that is concerned with the noncriminal responsibility of a person for criminal acts committed while he was of unsound mind. The specific tests of insanity vary with country or state.

Instrumental conditioning. A type of conditioning by which the subject learns to make a predetermined response, such as pressing a lever, in order to obtain a reward.

Insulin therapy. An outmoded form of shock therapy for the treatment of schizophrenia.

Interactional psychotic disorder. A psychotic reaction occurring in children between the ages of two and five who have shown normal prior development, characterized by an abnormal symbiotic relationship between child and mother. The child cannot bear to be separated from the mother.

Introjection. A defense mechanism characterized by the internalization of the attitudes, values, and behavior of another person, so that feelings associated with this other person may be directed toward the self.

Introvert. A personality type formulated by Jung and characterized by social awkwardness, emotional reserve, and self-absorption.

Involutional melancholia. A psychosis of undetermined origin with initial onset between the ages of forty and sixty-five, characterized by severe depression, agitation, ideas of guilt, depreciation, and suicidal tendencies.

Irresistible impulse rule. A test of insanity that is usually used as a supplement to the M'Naghten rules. Where the rule is accepted, an offender is not considered criminally responsible if his criminal act was the result of an irresistible impulse stemming from impaired mental functioning.

Isolation. A defense mechanism by which a thought is dissociated from an emotion otherwise connected with it.

Jacksonian epilepsy. A convulsive disorder originating in cerebral excitation, characterized by local twitching that gradually spreads until it terminates in a *grand mal* seizure.

Kleptomania. A recurring neurotic compulsion to steal objects, especially without economic motive. As a rule no use is made of the stolen objects.

Koro. A form of sexual anxiety formerly occurring among Chinese men, characterized by fear that the sex organ was shrinking and disappearing into the abdomen, and that when this occurred the victim would die. A culture-bound form of the male dread of impotence.

Korsakoff's syndrome. A memory disorder of toxic-organic origin that sometimes follows the delirium or stupor of chronic alcoholism and other toxic states, marked by memory loss and invention of "fill-in" material.

Labile. Characterized by instability or changeability.

Latah. An intense fear reaction among Malays, marked by shuddering and the involuntary imitation of the actions and words of others.

Latency stage. A Freudian concept that refers to the stage of psychosexual development roughly between the ages of 6 to 12 when sex urges are relatively dormant.

Lesbian. A female homosexual.

Libido. A Latin word that originally signified sexual passion; now a psychoanalytic term indicating the aim and energy strength of the sex drive.

Life style. An individual's basic personality pattern, including goals. See also *Style of life.*

Lithium carbonate. A drug used in the treatment of manic attacks. More recently, the drug has also been recommended for treatment of depressions.

Lobotomy. The removal of or severing of nerve fibers in a lobe of the brain; an operation previously performed to relieve some mental disorders, now discredited.

Logorrhea. Excessive and often incoherent speech.

LSD. See *Lysergic acid diethylamide.*

Lunacy. Mental derangement. The term is a legacy of the superstitious belief that the stars and especially the moon were somehow associated with madness.

Lysergic acid diethylamide (LSD). A very potent synthetic hallucinogen.

M'Naghten rules. The most widely used legal test of insanity in the United States, according to which a person accused of a criminal offense must be found not guilty by reason of insanity if at the time he committed the offense, in the judgment of the jury, he "was laboring under such a defect of reason, from disease of the mind, as not to know the nature and quality of the act he was doing or . . . did not know he was doing what was wrong."

Malingerer. One who deliberately pretends to have some illness or disability, for motives of personal gain.

Manic-depressive reaction. A set of psychotic reactions characterized by prolonged periods of excitement and overactivity, or by periods of depression and underactivity, or by alternation or mixture of the two.

Mannerism. A stereotyped, recurring gesture, posture, or movement that has no apparent purpose.

Marital schism. A form of marital discord in which husband and wife compete in attempting to enlist the sympathies of their children, each undercutting the other. Thought to be characteristic of some schizophrenic families.

Marital skew. A marital pattern in which the psychopathology of the dominant spouse is accepted and treated as normal by the other marital partner. Thought to be characteristic of some schizophrenic families.

Masochism. A form of sexual deviation in which an individual obtains sexual satisfaction from being subjected to physical pain or otherwise mistreated.

Mental retardation. Subnormal intellectual functioning that originates at birth or during early childhood. It is associated with impairment of either maturation or learning and social adjustment, or both.

Mesmerism. An early term for hypnotic phenomena derived from the concept of "animal magnetism" proposed by F. A. Mesmer.

Metrazol therapy. An obsolete form of shock treatment for mental disorders, consisting of injections of the drug metrazol for the purpose of inducing convulsions.

Migraine. A severe form of headache, often accompanied by nausea and vomiting.

Milieu therapy. A form of therapy characterized by intensified social interaction and informal communication between staff and patients, and by group activities directed toward "normal" functioning.

Modeling. A behavior modification procedure involving learning through imitation of observed behavior performed by a model.

Model Penal Code. A set of rules for deciding insanity proposed by the American Law Institute. The general thrust is that a person should not be held responsible for criminal conduct if at the time of such conduct (as a result of mental disease or defect) he lacks substantial capacity to appreciate the wrongfulness of his conduct or to conform his conduct to the requirements of the law. This code has been accepted by most Federal Courts of Appeals in the United States and at least one state.

Mongolism. See *Down's syndrome.*

Monoamine oxidase inhibitors. Drugs used in the treatment of depression.

Monozygotic twins. Identical twins who are the products of a single fertilized ovum.

Moron. Obsolete term denoting a person with a mild degree of mental retardation.

Multiple personality. A type of hysterical dissociative reaction characterized by the development of two or more relatively independent and alternating personality systems in the same individual.

Mutism. Inability or refusal to speak.

MZ twins. See *Monozygotic twins.*

Narcissism. In Freudian usage, an early stage of psychosexual development characterized by marked love of self.

Narcissistic personality. A personality type marked by egocentrism, disdain, pretentiousness, boastfulness, and exaggerated self-assurance.

Narcolepsy. A psychophysiological condition marked by brief periods of deep sleep in inappropriate situations.

Narcosynthesis. A therapeutic technique based on the use of certain drugs, such as sodium amytal, to facilitate the recall and expression of repressed emotions and memories.

Narcotic drugs. Drugs that lead to physiological dependence and increased tolerance, such as morphine and heroin. See also *Opiates.*

Necrophilia. Erotic interest in dead bodies. May be expressed in the use of a corpse as a sex object.

Negative practice. A therapeutic technique that requires the deliberate repetition of some undesirable motor habit as a means of eliminating the habit.

Negative reinforcement. The administration of an aversive stimulus following the occurrence of some particular behavior, for the purpose of decreasing the frequency of occurrence of the behavior.

Negativism. Impulsive contrary behavior; the tendency to do the opposite of what is requested.

Neologism. The coining of new words, usually by condensing and combining two or more words; a common occurrence among schizophrenics. Schizophrenic neologisms are meaningful to those who coin them but not to others.

Neurasthenia. A neurotic condition marked by chronic weakness, easy fatigability, and sometimes exhaustion.

Neurodermatitis. Chronic psychogenic reddening and thickening of the skin, with intense itching.

Neuroleptic drugs. Drugs that diminish agitation, anxiety, and aggression without inducing sleep or impairment of intelligence. More commonly referred to as tranquilizers; also known as ataractics.

Neuroses. Emotional disorders characterized primarily by anxiety and manifested in either behavioral or physical symptoms, unaccompanied by either gross distortion or misinterpretation of external reality or by gross personality disorganization.

New Hampshire rule. A legal test of insanity accepted in New Hampshire, according to which an accused person is not considered criminally responsible if his unlawful act was the product of a mental disorder.

Nirvana principle. The guiding principle of the death drive, according to Freud. The end goal is the final release through death of disturbing desires and life problems.

Nonproductive character orientations. Maladaptive personality patterns described by Erich Fromm.

Noogenic neurosis. Viktor Frankl's term for existential neurosis resulting from despair over the meaninglessness of life.

Nymphomania. Expressed sexual desire in women that is excessive in terms of partner's desire or prevailing social standards.

Nyctophobia. Morbid fear of the dark or night.

Obsession. A spontaneously recurring thought or impulse that persistently intrudes itself into a person's mind, even against his wishes. The individual usually realizes the irrationality of his obsession but cannot dismiss it from his mind.

Obsessive-compulsion reaction. A neurotic reaction characterized by persistent irrational thoughts, impulses, and actions.

Occupational neurosis. A neurosis characterized by the functional impairment of some occupational skill; for example, writer's cramp.

Oedipus complex. The libidinal response of a boy to his mother. According to Freud, boys between the ages of four and six feel sexual desire for their mothers and see their fathers as hated rivals. An unresolved oedipal attachment is thought by Freudian psychoanalysts to be the major cause of neurosis in adult males.

Operant conditioning. A learning technique based on the principle of reinforcement, which holds that behavior is largely controlled by its consequences and thus can be modified or maintained by manipulating the consequences of particular forms of behavior.

Opiates. Opium, an addictive drug consisting of the dried juice of the opium poppy, and its derivatives (morphine, heroin, codeine), which relieve physical and psychic pain, induce euphoria in some persons, and lead to drowsiness and sleep. See also *Narcotic drugs.*

Oral character. A personality type assumed by Freudian psychoanalysts to result from fixation at or regression to the phase of development during which the mouth is the child's chief source of pleasurable sensations. The early oral phase is associated with dependence, the late oral phase with aggressive tendencies.

Organic brain syndrome. Instability and shallowness of affect accompanied by impairment of orientation, memory, judgment, and learning ability, resulting from impairment of brain tissue function.

Orientation. The act or process of locating the self in the environment with respect to time, place, and person; psychological bearings.

Overinclusiveness. A form of thought disorder associated with schizophrenia and marked by the intrusion of irrelevant or inappropriate associations into the stream of thought.

Paranoia. A rare psychosis characterized by the gradual development of logical, well-systematized delusions of persecution and/or grandeur based on the misinterpretation of or generalization of reactions to an actual event or series of events.

Paranoid personality. A mildly deviant personality type marked by suspiciousness, envy, jealousy, and stubbornness.

Paranoid reaction. A psychotic disorder marked by delusions of persecution and/or grandeur. When delusions are fragmented, bizarre, and accompanied by hallucinations, the disorder is classified as a subtype of schizophrenia; when delusions are well systematized, the condition is considered a variation of paranoia.

Paranoid schizophrenia. A clinical subtype distinguished by bizarre, poorly systemized delusions of persecution plus significant personality disorganization.

Paresthesia. Disturbances in sensation. Sensations of itching, tingling or prickling in the absence of appropriate external stimuli.

Partialism. Sexual bias marked by a person being especially stimulated or attracted by some part of the human anatomy, as for example, size of breasts, shape of ankles, etc.

Passive-aggressive personality. A mildly deviant personality type marked by oppositional tendencies, negativism, obstructionism, contrariness, and uncooperativeness.

Passive-dependent personality. A mildly deviant personality type characterized by submissiveness, clinging behavior, and the making of covert demands.

Pedophilia. A form of sexual deviation in which an adult (usually a male) uses a child as a sex object.

Pellagra. A vitamin-deficiency disease characterized by disturbances of the alimentary tract, patchy skin pimentation, and a variety of neurological and mental symptoms.

Peptic ulcer. A psychophysiological disorder characterized by inflammation or lesions of the stomach wall.

Perseveration. Involuntary continuation and repetition of a behavioral response.

Petit mal. A mild form of epilepsy characterized by momentary loss of consciousness unaccompanied by convulsive seizures.

Phallic character. A personality type assumed by Freudian analysts to result from fixation at or regression to the late oedipal stage of development and marked by recklessness, aggressive tendencies and narcissism.

Phallic stage. The period between ages 4 and 6 when the sex drive is mainly directed toward the child's parents. Also known as the oedipal period. A Freudian concept.

Phenomenology. A personality theory that stresses the critical importance of the individual's subjective perception of himself and the outer world in the determination of behavior.

Phenotype. Actual or observable physical and behavioral traits that are determined by the interaction of an individual's genotype and the environment.

Phenylketonuria (PKU). An inherited defect in protein metabolism that results in profound mental retardation unless treatment is initiated very soon after birth.

Phobic reaction. A form of neurosis marked by irrational and intense fear of something that is normally not a real source of danger. The feared object presumably has symbolic significance.

Piblokto. A fearlike reaction among Arctic Eskimos, in some respects resembling *latah* among the Malays. The crazed Eskimo runs outdoors naked in winter weather and mimics the sounds of Arctic birds and animals. The condition may be indirectly related to a calcium deficiency.

Pick's disease. A degenerative brain disorder. Because of the early onset (about age 45-50), it is referred to as a form of pre-senile dementia. Marked by atrophy of the frontal and temporal lobes, memory impairment, character changes, progressive mental deterioration and death within a few years of overt symptoms.

PKU. See *Phenylketonuria.*

Placebo. An inactive substance that may have some therapeutic effect when administered to a person who believes it to be an active drug.

Pleasure principle. A tendency to direct behavior toward the immediate gratification of drives and desires and the avoidance of pain and dissatisfaction, regardless of future consequences. Considered by Freudian psychoanalysts to be the underlying motivation of the behavior of children and some neurotics.

Positive reinforcement. A learning procedure characterized by attempts to increase the frequency of occurrence of a particular response by rewarding its occurrence in some relevant way.

Posturing. The maintenance of unusual positions for long periods.

Potlatch. A ceremonial feast of the Kwakiutl

Indians at which a chief gains prestige for his tribe and humiliates visiting chiefs by ostentatiously burning and giving away valuable goods that have been accumulated for the occasion, requiring elaborate reciprocation; a culturally regulated substitute for war. Also, similar activities carried on within a local group for the purpose of gaining or maintaining personal prestige.

Preconscious. The storehouse of surface memories that are readily subject to recall.

Premature ejaculation. The inability on the part of a man to delay the ejaculatory process during sexual intercourse for a sufficient length of time to satisfy his partner. The condition may be chronic or may occur only occasionally.

Premorbid. Existing prior to manifest pathology.

Prevalence. The total number of cases of a particular disorder currently existing in a given population at any particular time. The prevalence rate is determined by dividing the number of cases by the total population.

Primary gain. The reduction of anxiety as the principal advantage accruing from a neurotic symptom.

Primary prevention. The institution of procedures that will prevent the occurrence of a disorder or decrease the risk that a person will develop it.

Proband cases. See *Index cases.*

Process schizophrenia. Schizophrenic reactions characterized by early onset of symptoms, which include poor interpersonal adjustment, progressive social withdrawal, and inadequate functioning, with unfavorable prognosis. Contrasted to reactive schizophrenia.

Prognosis. Prediction as to the probable course and outcome of a disorder.

Projection. A defense mechanism characterized by the placing of blame for one's faults, mistakes, and misdeeds on others as a means of safeguarding self-esteem and avoiding self-censure.

Prolixin. The trade name for a prolonged action antipsychotic drug.

Psoriasis. A chronic skin condition marked by itchy red patches covered with white scales.

Psychiatry. The medical specialty that is concerned with the study and treatment of mental disorders.

Psychoanalytic theory. A system of theories developed by Freud and his followers to explain normal and abnormal behavior, with emphasis on psychosexual development, the importance of early childhood experiences and repressions in the determination of adult behavior, and the role of the unconscious in the development of intrapsychic conflicts and processes.

Psychoanalytic therapy. A highly structured form of psychotherapy developed by Freud to uncover and resolve repressed intrapsychic conflicts dating from early childhood. Among its special techniques are free association, dream analysis, and the concept of transference.

Psychodrama. A form of group therapy in which the patient's problems are acted out.

Psychogenic. Originating in emotional conflict or mental disorder.

Psychomotor attacks. Seizures marked by lapses of consciousness, irregular muscular movements, disturbances in thought or affect, and convulsions. Also referred to as temporal lobe epilepsy.

Psychoneurosis. See Neurosis. Differentiated from psychosis by the absence of delusions, hallucinations, and significant personality disorganization. The neurotic suffers from personal problems and inner conflicts and has been described as his own worst enemy.

Psychopathology. The behavior science that is specifically concerned with the study of maladaptive, inappropriate behaviors that are evaluated as constituting an undue source of distress, threat or detriment to the individual, his family and his society.

Psychophysiological reactions. Physical disorders in which symptoms are precipitated and maintained by emotional factors. Symptoms vary widely but invariably involve a single organ system that is largely controlled by the autonomic nervous system. Popularly referred to as psychosomatic disorders.

Psychosis. A severe mental disorder that significantly interferes with the individual's capacity for adequate self-support and appropriate interpersonal behavior, characterized by gross personality disorganization, distortion of reality evidenced by delusions and hallucinations, and marked impairment in voluntary control of thoughts, emotions, and actions.

Psychosomatic reactions. See *Psychophysiological reactions.*

Psychotherapy. A general term for treatment of mental disorders by psychological procedures. Most psychotherapies involve the talking out of problems.

Psychotic depressive reaction. Depression that apears directly related to some recent loss suffered by a person with no prior history of any affective disturbance.

Rational-emotive therapy. A directive form of psychotherapy developed by Albert Ellis, based on the premise that disturbed persons needlessly create anxiety and anger in themselves by accepting uncritically certain irrational hypotheses.

Rationalization. A defense mechanism characterized by the minimization of failure and justification of socially disapproved behavior by invented excuses and "reasonable" explanations; the unwitting substitution of "good" for real reasons.

Raynaud's disease. A psychophysiological reaction marked by poor circulation resulting in cold hands and feet.

Reaction formation. A defense mechanism characterized by the concealment of an unaccepted trait or impulse by behavior expressive of a directly opposite characteristic, which enables the individual to deny to himself the existence of the trait or impulse he cannot accept.

Reactive schizophrenia. Schizophrenic reactions apparently causally related to some current stress experienced by a person whose prepsychotic psychosocial development has been seemingly normal, and characterized by less severe deficits and better prognosis than process schizophrenia.

Reality principle. A tendency to defer the gratification of drives and desires in the interests of long-range goals or in response to pressures from the physical and social environments.

Reciprocal inhibition. A therapeutic technique based on the principle that the ability of a stimulus to evoke anxiety may be diminished if a response inhibitory of anxiety can be made to occur in the presence of the anxiety-evoking stimulus.

Regression. A defense mechanism characterized by a reversion to earlier modes of gratification as a means of escape from current difficulties.

Reliability. The extent of agreement among independent examiners regarding the diagnosis of a patient's disorder.

Remission. Significant improvement following a period of pathology.

Repression. The spontaneous or nondeliberate exclusion from the field of conscious awareness of memories, impulses, and ideas whose presence, if recognized, would constitute a source of anxiety, guilt, or humiliation.

Residual deviance. The concept, advanced by Scheff, that mental disorders consist of the forms of rule breaking that remain after all other explicitly recognized forms of deviance have been excluded.

Resistance. Opposition to therapeutic efforts, especially a defensive reluctance to explore repressed material.

Rheumatoid arthritis. A psychophysiological disorder characterized by a painful stiffening of the joints.

Sadism. A form of sexual deviation marked by the infliction of pain on another person as a means of achieving sexual arousal and release.

Satyriasis. Expressed sexual desire in men that is excessive in terms of partner's desire or accepted social standards.

Schizo-affective reaction. A condition in which the emotional disturbances of manic-depressive psychosis are combined with the disordered thought and behavior patterns associated with schizophrenia.

Schizoid personality. A mildly deviant personality type charactrized by social withdrawal, introvertive tendencies, and extreme shyness.

Schizophrenia. A psychosis that usually has its onset in early adulthood and is characterized by disordered thinking, delusions, hallucinations, social withdrawal, and bizarre behavior.

Schizophreniform reaction. A psychotic reaction characterized by acute onset of schizophrenic symptoms and clear-cut precipitating factors, with a relatively good prognosis. Similar to reactive schizophrenia.

Schizotaxia. The inherited neural defect that is the essential prerequisite for or predisposing factor in schizophrenia.

Schizotypic personality. A personality type delineated by Meehl and characterized by disturbances in thinking, interpersonal aversiveness, anhedonia, and ambivalence, limited to persons genetically predisposed to schizophrenia but not necessarily destined to become psychotic.

Secondary gain. Advantages other than the reduction of anxiety gained through a neurotic symptom.

Secondary prevention. The reduction of the prevalence rate of a disorder by effective treatment that shortens the duration of disability.

Self-actualization. The drive to realize one's inherent potentials.

Senile dementia. A psychosis of old age characterized by brain atrophy and progressive mental deterioration.

Sexual deviant. A person who prefers or requires some form of sexual activity other than heterosexual coitus for erotic stimulation and gratification. See *Exhibitionism; Fetishism; Homosexuality; Masochism; Pedophilia; Sadism; Transsexuality; Transvestism; Voyeurism.*

Shaping. The process of gradually leading a subject to give a particular response by selective reinforcement of a series of other responses that come progressively closer to the response desired.

Shellshock. See *War neurosis.*

Shock therapy. The induction of coma or convulsion by the use of drugs or electricity as a means of treating mental disorders.

Simple schizophrenia. A clinical subtype of schizophrenia mainly characterized by social withdrawal and apathy. There is an absence of delusions and hallucinations.

Social breakdown syndrome. A set of symptoms consisting of dependency, apathy, withdrawal, lack of responsibility, and general deterioration of behavior, resulting from prolonged confinement in a mental hospital.

Sociopath. An individual who exhibits antisocial behavior that may or may not be criminal. Sociopathy represents a borderline category between criminal behavior and psychopathology.

Somnambulism. Sleepwalking; a trancelike state in which a person, while asleep, walks about and engages in complex activities that he does not remember on awakening. A form of dissociative reaction.

Stereotypy. The persistent repetition of apparently senseless words, acts, or gestures.

Stimulant drugs. Drugs that increase energy level and diminish fatigue, such as cocaine and the amphetamines.

Stimulus generalization. The process whereby a conditioned response is elicited by stimuli other than but similar to the conditioned stimulus.

Stress. Any condition, biological or psychological, that taxes the coping capacities of an individual.

Stupor. A condition of partial or complete unsciousness marked by unresponsiveness and lethargy.

Style of life. A relatively enduring pattern of behavior that is tailored to overcome inferiority complexes. A concept of Adler.

Sublimation. A defense mechanism whereby unacceptable or thwarted impulses are channeled or transformed into socially approved substitute activities.

Successive approximation. See *Shaping.*

Superego. The division of the personality structure that enforces the morals and ethics instilled by the parents and the society. A Freudian concept.

Suppression. The deliberate exclusion from consciousness of thoughts or feelings.

Symptomatic epilepsy. A convulsive condition resulting from some acquired brain pathology or toxic condition rather than genetic defect.

Syndrome. A group of symptoms that occur together and which are more or less distinctive of a particular pathological condition.

Tarantism. A form of mass hysteria expressed in an uncontrollable impulse to dance that occurred in and was restricted to a province in southern Italy during the 15th to 17th century. The dancing compulsion was attributed to the bite of spiders belonging to the tarantula class.

Temperament. Inherent emotional style reflected in susceptibility and responsiveness to emotional stimulation, prevailing mood, and intensity of feelings.

Tertiary prevention. The prevention of permanent disability through the reduction of residual secondary defects that often persist long after the actual disorder has ended.

Tic. A recurring involuntary muscular twitch.

Token economy system. The use of tokens that can be exchanged for rewards as a means means of reinforcing desired behavior, particularly among hospitalized mental patients.

Toxic Psychoses. A general term applied to severe and usually transient behavior disturbances induced by some toxic substance.

Tranquilizers. See *Neuroleptic drugs.*

Transactional analysis. A form of psychotherapy developed by Eric Berne that focuses on the interpersonal interaction of the three ego states ("Child," "Adult," and "Parent") which are present in all individuals. Therapy is usually conducted in a group setting.

Transference. The tendency on the part of patients undergoing psychotherapy to express toward the therapist attitudes and feelings they had and may still have toward their parents and significant others. The working through of these transferred attitudes and feelings is an important feature of psychoanalytic treatment.

Transsexuality. A form of sex deviance distinguished by gender misidentification: the transsexual has the sex organs of one sex but thinks of himself or herself as being in all other respects as a member of the opposite sex.

Transvestism. A form of sex deviation in which the individual, invariably a male, is sexually stimulated by wearing the clothes of the opposite sex. The typical transvestite is heterosexual; most are married.

Tremor. A series of rapid, involuntary spasms involving a small group of muscles.

Unconditioned stimulus and response. See *Classical conditioning.*

Unconscious. The reservoir of man's inherited primitive impulses and acquired repressions that are not readily accessible to awareness but which have an important effect on behavior. A psychoanalytic concept.

Undoing. A defense mechanism whereby guilt for past misdeeds is expiated through symbolic acts.

Urethral character. According to psychoanalytic theory, fixation at the urethral level of sexual development (about age 4 to 5). Is associated with high ambition and competitiveness.

Vaginismus. A female psychosomatic disorder marked by an involuntary muscular spasm that constricts the vaginal opening, making sexual intercourse painful or impossible.

Validity. The extent to which a measuring instrument actually measures what it is supposed to measure.

Verbigeration. Continual repetition of words or sentences. A feature of schizophrenia.

Voyeurism. The derivation of sexual arousal and release from the sight of sexual organs or sexual acts.

War neurosis. A neurotic condition resulting from prolonged exposure to the stress of combat in wartime. Called shellshock during World War I and combat fatigue during World War II.

Windigo. A culture-bound form of mental disorder among the Ojibwa Indians of Canada, characterized by an obsession with the desire to eat human flesh and the misperception of friends and neighbors as edible animals; a syndrome related to periodic famine but attributed by the society to possession by a man-eating evil spirit, which can be routed by feeding the victim meat and fat.

Zoophobia. Irrational fear of animals usually harmless to man.

Zygote. A fertilized cell.

Photo Credits

8 Ars Medica Collection, Philadelphia Museum of Art

10 Thomas Szasz

11 From Thomas J. Scheff, *Being Mentally Ill: A Sociological Theory*. Aldine Publishing Company, 1966

22 The Bettmann Archive, Inc.

24 The Bettmann Archive, Inc.

33 The Ada Turnbull Hertie Fund, The Art Institute of Chicago

40 The Menninger Foundation, Topeka, Kansas

56 Wide World Photos

58 The Bettmann Archive, Inc.

64 Smithsonian Institution Photo No. 74-11560

65 Smithsonian Institution Photo No. 44,726-B

74 The Bettmann Archive, Inc.

76 The University Museum, Philadelphia

79 The Ira Frank Collection, The Art Institute of Chicago

83 The Bettmann Archive, Inc.

84 The Bettmann Archive, Inc.

86 The Bettmann Archive, Inc.

87 The Bettmann Archive, Inc.

88 Ars Medica Collection, Philadelphia Museum of Art

90 Standard Photo Service Company, Inc.

91 Standard Photo Service Company, Inc.

93 Top: Black Star: Jack Spratt
Bottom: Wide World Photos

110 The Bettmann Archive, Inc.

114 Wide World Photos

117 The William Alanson White Psychiatric Foundation

120 Grove Press

123 The Bettmann Archive, Inc.

124 Courtesy of B. F. Skinner/Photo by Ken Heyman

126 Courtesy of Albert Bandura

127 Courtesy of Albert Bandura

130 Courtesy of Carl Rogers/Photo by John T. Wood

132 Courtesy of Bertha G. Maslow

133 Wide World Photos

142 Courtesy of James L. German

145 Courtesy of James D. Page

155 Courtesy of Harry F. Harlow, University of Wisconsin Primate Laboratory

160 The Bettmann Archive, Inc.

163 Top: Photo by Reo Fortune. Published in M. Mead, "The Mountain Arapesh I: An Importing Culture," *Anthropological Papers, The American Museum of Natural History*, Vol. XXXVI, Part IV, 1938.
Bottom: Photo by Margaret Mead

166 From John W. Bennett, *Northern Plainsmen: Adaptive Strategy and Agrarian Life*. Aldine Publishing Company, 1970.

167 From John W. Bennett, *Northern Plainsmen: Adaptive Strategy and Agrarian Life*. Aldine Publishing Company, 1970.

181 Ars Medica Collection, Philadelphia Museum of Art

185 The Bettmann Archive, Inc.

197 Wide World Photos

218 Courtesy of Gregory Bateson

221 Courtesy of Basic Books

223 Courtesy of Paul E. Meehl

237 Courtesy of Aaron T. Beck

249 Black Star

252 Culver Pictures

265 United Press International

274 Courtesy of Albert Ellis

277 Courtesy of Joseph Wolpe

279 Courtesy of Arthur J. Bachrach

299 The Press Association, Ltd

307 Courtesy of Erich Fromm/Photo by Bender

315 Wide World Photos

324 United Press International

339 Black Star: Steve Shapiro

PHOTO CREDITS

Name Index

Abramson, P. R., 369, *394*
Achenback, T. M., 419, *438*
Ackerman, N., 110, 136, *137*, *434*, *438,*
Adler, A., 55-56, 72, 108, 128-129, *137*, 274, *286*
Adler, R., 283, *286*
Agras, W. S., *366*
Albee, G. W., 18, *20*, 194, *207*, *479*
Alexander, F., 275, 283, *286*
Alig, V. B., *309*
Allport, G. W., *137*, 146, *158*
Alvarez, A., 444-445, 453, *467*
Amir, M., 392, 393, *394*
Anatasio, M. M., *467*
Andriola, J., 463, *467*
Ansbacker, H., *137*
Ansbacker, R., *137*
Apperson, L. B., 377, *394*
Aretaeus, 78, 232
Arieti, S., 5, *20*, 220-221, 228, 240, *250*, 410, *414*
Arling, G. L., 156, *158*
Arnhoff, F. N., 196, *207*
Asclepiades, 78
Ascough, J. C., *414*
Astrup, C., *208*
Ayllon, T., 97, *103*, 125, *137*
Azrin, N., 97, *103*

Babigan, H. W., 38, *46*
Bachrach, A. J., 278, 279, *286*
Bagley, C., 465, *467*
Baker, B. L., 437, *438*
Baker, H. T., 381, *394*
Baldessarini, R. J., 248, *250*
Balvin, R., *158*
Bandura, A., 108, 125-127, *137*, 272, *286*
Barber, T. X., *350*
Barlow, D. H., 364, *365*
Barraclough, B., 454, *468*
Barton, W. E., 24, *46*
Bassin, A., 341, *350*
Bateman, K., 345, *350*
Bates, R. F., 320, *327*
Bateson, G., 53, *73*, 218, *228*
Bayley, N., 13, *21*, 146, *159*

Bazelon, D. L., 69, *72*
Beamish, P., *250*
Beard, G. M., 262, *286*
Beck, A. T., 38, *46*, 237, *250*, 443, 446, *467*
Becker, W. C., 192, *206*, *208*
Beebe, G. W., 264, *286*
Beels, C. C., *137*
Bell, A. P., 373, *395*
Bell, H., *251*
Bell, R. A., 305, *309*
Bender, L., 429, *438*
Benedict, R., 63, 65, *72*, 162, *169*
Benjamin, L. S., *415*
Bentler, P. M., 385, *394*
Bentzen, F., 176, *179*
Berecz, J. M., 437, *438*
Beres, D., 428, *439*
Bergin, A. E., 273, 281, *286*, *439*
Berne, E., 107, 119-121, *137*, 171, *179*
Bernheim, H., 85
Bettleheim, B., 425, 427, *439*
Betz, B. J., *203*, *206*, *208*
Bieber, I., *366*, 377, 380, *394*
Billet, S. L., 322, *327*
Bini, L., 92
Binswanger, L., 131
Birch, H., *159*
Bleuler, E. P., 57, *72*, 185, 194, 195, *206*
Bloom, B. L., 476, *479*
Bloomberg, L., 475, *479*
Blum, G. S., 307, *309*
Bockoven, J. S., 89, 96, *103*
Boren, W. E., 198, *206*
Borgatta, E. F., 437, *439*
Boszormenyi-Nagy, I., 110, *137*
Boulton, D. M., *250*
Bowen, M., 110, 134, *137*
Bower, G. H., 122, *138*
Bowlby, J., 154, *158*
Brady, J. V., 406, *414*
Braginsky, B. M. and D. D., 99-101, *103*
Braid, J., 85
Brennan, J. G., 382, *395*
Bridge, T. P., 347, *350*

Brill, L., 339, *350*
Brill, N. Q., 264, *286*
Broadbent, D. E., 198, *206*
Broadhurst, P. L., 156, *159*
Brockopp, G. W., 464, *467*
Brodie, H. K., 379, *394*
Brody, S., 434, *439*
Broverman, I. K., 38, *47*
Brown, M. B., *440*
Bucher, B. D., 426, 437, *439*
Buckner, H. T., 385, *394*
Burdock, E. I., 44, *46*
Burnham, W. H., 277, *286*
Buss, A. H., 55, *72*, 195, *206*, 406, *414*

Caddy, G., 325, *327*
Caffey, E. M., *250*
Cahalan, D., 312, 320, 322, *327*
Caine, T. M., 266, *286*
Calverley, D. S., *350*
Cameron, N., 195, 196, *206*, 265, *286*, 296, *309*
Cantril, H., 82, *103*
Caplan, G., 476, *479*
Caplan, R. B., 473, *479*
Caputo, D. V., 217, *228*
Carey, J. T., 346, *350*
Carkuff, R. R., 281, *286*, *440*
Carothers, J. C., 49, *72*
Carstairs, G. M., 202, *206*
Carten, H. D., 268, *286*
Catanzaro, R. J., 322, *327*
Caudill, W., 169, *180*
Cave, R., 42, *47*
Cerletti, U., 92
Chadwick, J., 78, *103*
Chance, N. A., *250*
Chapman, J., 196, *207*
Chapman, J. P., 196, *206*
Chapman, L. J., 196, *206*
Charcot, J., 85
Charlesworth, W. R., 283, *288*
Chefetz, M. E., 325, *327*
Chess, S., *159*
Chiarugi, V., 86
Christenson, C. V., *366*, *394*
Choron, J., 449, 452, *467*
Cicero, 78

Clayton, P., 243, 251
Clausen, J. A., 53, 72
Cleckley, H. M., 260, *288*, 301, *309*
Clemens, T. L., *415*
Clements, F. E., 75, *103*
Clements, S. E., 431, *439*
Clifford, R., 369, *394*
Codere, H., 65, 72
Coe, W. C., 331, *350*
Cohen, H. W., *250*
Cohen, J., *179*
Cohen, M., 389, 392, *394*
Cohen, M. B., 246, *250*
Cohen, S., 345, *350*
Cole, C. L., 360, *366*
Cole, J. O., 24, *46*
Cole, P. T., *350*
Coleman, D. R., *415*
Collomb, H., 248, *250*
Conger, J. J., 319, *327*
Conners, C. K., 417, *439*
Conolly, J., 88, 184
Cornelison, A. R., *207*
Costello, C. G., 44, *46*
Coué, E., 85, *103*
Cowen, E. L., 475, *479*
Cowitz, B., *250*
Coxe, R. C., *251*
Crocetti, G. M., 184, *206*
Cross, L. A., 191, *207*
Crutchfield, R. S., 52, 72
Cullen, T. D., *415*
Cummings, E., 60, 72
Cummings, J., 60, 72
Cutler, R. P., 236, *250*

Davidson, P. O., 44, *46*
Deasy, L. C., 73
De Leon, G., 437, *439*
De Luca, J. M., 194, *206*
Denny, D., 220, *228*
Deutsch, A., 86, *103*
De Vito, R. A., 321, *327*
Diamond, F., *158*
Diamond, S., 154, *158*
Dichter, M., *327*
Diem, 185
Dies, R. R., 249, *250*
Dinety, S., *207*
Ditman, K. S., 323, *327*
Doering, C., *394*
Dohrenwend, B. S., and P. F., 36, *46*, 62, 72, 171, 172, 173, 176, *179*, 273, *286*
Dole, V. P., 339, *350*
Dollard, J., 269, *286*
Donnelly, E. M., 436, *439*
Douds, J., 464, *468*
Down, L., 144
Draguns, J. G., 169, *179*
Dreger, R. M., 42, *46*
Duflin, L. L., 444, 449, 464, *467*

Du Bois, C., 165, *179*
Dunham, H. W., 171, 173, *179*, 223, *228*
Dunlap, K., 125, *137*
Du Pont, R. L., 337
Dupont, R. L., 295, 309
Durkheim, E., 173, 458-459, *467*
Duvall, H. J., 341, *350*

Eaton, J. W., 166, *179*
Edgerton, R. B., 316, *327*
Edwards, A. E., 345, *350*
Eisenberg, L., 426, 427, *439*
Ellinwood, E. H., 347, *350*
Elliotson, J., 85
Ellis, A., 274-275, *286*
Ellsworth, R. B., 96, *103*
Elsarrag, M. E., 165, *179*
Engel, B. T., *415*
English, O. S., 262, *288*
Erikson, E., 12, *20*, 107, 114-115, *137*
Erlenmeyer-Kimling, L., 212, *228*
Erwin, W. J., 278, *286*
Escalona, S., 146, *158*
Esdaile, J., 85
Esquirol, J. E. D., 32, *46*
Essen-Moller, E., 149, *158*, 267, *286*, 304, *309*
Ewalt, J. R. and P. L., 473, *479*
Eysenck, H. J., 44, *46*, 116, *137*, 264, 268, 281, *286*

Falret, 232
Farber, M. L., 454, *467*
Farberow, N. L., 446, 463, *468*
Faris, R., 223, *228*
Feather, B. W., 385, *395*
Fedden, H. R., 443, 450, 451, 452, 459, *467*
Feld, S., *479*
Feldman, M. P., 364, *366*
Fenichel, O., 307, *309*
Ferber, A., 110, *137*
Ferracuti, F., 389, *394*
Ferster, C. B., 124, *137*, 426, *439*
Field, M., J., 77, *103*, 165, *179*
Finch, S. M., 429, *439*
Fish, B., 152, *158*
Fisher, S., 200, *206*
Fisk, F. A., 198, *206*
Flaherty, L. A., *327*
Fleck, S., *207*, 217, *228*
Fonda, C. P., 38, *47*
Fontana, A. F., 195, *206*, 217, *228*
Fortune, R. F., 63, 72
Foulds, G. A., 266, *286*
Fox, R., 313, 321, 322, *327*
Fox, R. G., 304, *309*
Framo, J., 110, 135, *137*
Frank, C. M., 323, *327*

Frank, J. D., 161, *179*, 281, *286*
Frank, G. H., *137*
Frankl, V., 109, 131, 133, *137*
Franklin, B., 86
Freedman, A. M., 92, *103*
Freedman, D., 146, *158*
Freeman, N., 267, *287*
Freeman, W., 92, *103*
French, T. M., 283, *286*
Freud, A., 423, 434, *439*
Freud, S., 7, *20*, 45, 57, 72, 78, 107, 110-116, *137*, *138*, 146, *158*, 174, *179*, 270, 283, *286*, 296, 356, 362, *366*, 461, *467*
Fried, J., 171, *180*
Friedman, A. S., 237, 240, *250*
Fromm, E., 107, 119, *138*, 307-308, *309*
Fromm-Reichmann, F., 202, *206*
Fry, W. F., 219, *229*
Fuller, J. L., 156, *159*

Gagnon, J. H., 356, 363, *366*, 369, *394*
Galen, 79
Gantt, W. H., 156, 157, *158*, 282, *286*
Gardner, E. A., *46*
Garfield, S. L., 273, 281, *286*
Garfield, Z., *327*
Garmezy, N., 191, 192, *206*
Garside, R. F., *250*
Gartell, N., *394*
Gattozzi, A., 248, *250*
Gebhard, P. H., 361, *366*, 369, 387, 388, 390-391, 392, *394*, *395*, *415*
Geertsma, R., 321, *327*
Gelder, M. G., 385, *395*
Gelineau, V., 91, *104*
Gendlin, E. T., *207*
Gentry, K. A., *395*
George III, 86
Gerald, M. C., 348, *350*
Gerard, D., 223, *228*
Gesell, A., 146, *158*
Gilbert, J. G., 340, *350*
Ging, R., *207*
Giovannoni, J. M., 192, *208*
Gittleson, N. L., 200, *206*
Glaser, R., 39, *46*, *350*
Goffman, E., 91, *103*
Gold, R., *366*
Goldberg, E. M., 224, *228*
Goldhammer, H., 171, *179*
Goode, E., 344, *350*
Goodwin, D. W., 321, *327*
Goss, A., 321, *327*
Gottesman, I. I., 150, 191, *206*, 212, *228*, 267, *286*
Graham, D. T., 406, *415*
Gralnick, A., 295, *309*
Graneck, S., *250*

Grassi, J. R., 430, *439*
Green, H., 202
Green, R., *366, 381, 394*
Greenacre, P., *372, 394*
Greenberg, R., 443, *467*
Greene, M. H., 337
Greenfeld, D., *440*
Greenson, R. R., 112, *138*
Grese, H., *394*
Grinker, R. R., 18, *20,* 237, *250,*
  271, *287*
Grossman, H. J., 431, *439*
Gruenberg, E. M., 24, *46,* 91,
  103, 267, *287*
Grunebaum, H., 295, *309*
Grunfeld, B., 224, *228*
Gruze, S. B., *327*
Guerney, B. G., 477, *479*
Guller, I., 200, *206*
Gurin, G. C., 477, *479*
Guthrie, E. R., 277, *287*

Hadden, E. R., 380, *394*
Haertgen, C. A., *350*
Haley, J., 110, 134, *138,* 219, *228*
Hall, C. S., 12, *20,* 50, *72,* 156,
  158
Hall, L. P., 430, *439*
Halleck, S. L., *480*
Halpern, F., *158*
Hamilton, M. A., 236, *250*
Hamlin, R. M., 194, *206*
Hamivich, H. E., 201, *206*
Hardesty, A. S., 44, *46*
Hare, E. H., 224, *228*
Hare, R. D., 304, 305, *309*
Harlow, H. F., 154, 156, *158*
Harris, C. W., *440*
Hartmann, H., 112, *138*
Hartog, J. D., 194, *206*
Heath, G., *327*
Heath, R. G., 199, *206*
Hebb, D. O., 157, *158*
Hecker, E., 184
Heidegger, M., 131
Hemphill, R. D., 91, *104*
Hendlin, H., 454, *467*
Hendrick, I., 110, *138*
Henry, G. W., 79, 82, *104*
Hermansen, L., *327*
Herron, W. G., 191, *207*
Hess, E. H., 154, *158*
Heston, L. L., 220, *228,* 379, *394*
Higgins, J., *206*
Hilgard, E. R., 122, *138*
Hill, H. E., 341, *350*
Hill, R. G., 88
Hippocrates, 23, 78
Hobbs, N. 474, *479, 480*
Hoch, P., 92, *104*
Hockman, C. H., 283, *287*
Hodges, E. F., 437, *440*
Hoffer, A., 448, *468*

Holden, C., 474, *479*
Hollingshead, A. B., 173, *179,*
  273, 287
Hollingsworth, H. L., 121, *138,*
  277, *287*
Hollister, L. E., 101, *104*
Holzinger, K. J., 267, *287*
Holzman, P. S., 110, *138*
Honigfeld, G., 101, *104*
Hook, E. B., 304, *309*
Hopkinson, G., 243, *250*
Horn, J. L., 312, *328*
Horney, K., 58, *72,* 107, 118, *138*
Houston, L. G., 223, *228*
Howard, A., 101, *104*
Hughes, J. M., 165, 170, *179*
Hunt, G. H., 338, *350*
Hunt, H. F., 156, *158*
Hunt, J. M., 474, *479*
Hunt, W. A., 196, *207*
Hunter, R., 81-82, 89, *104*

Inaba, D. S., 347, *350*

Jackson, D., 110, *228*
Jacobs, J., 459-460, *467*
Jahoda, M., 53, *72*
James, W. J., 156, *159*
Janet, P., 57, *72,* 172, *179*
Janis, I. L., 50, *72,* 264, 272, *287*
Jan-Tausch, J., 459, *467*
Jaspers, K., 131
Jellinek, E. M., 314, 315, 320,
  327
Jerry, M. B., *395*
Johnson, D., 76, *104*
Johnson, D. M., 82, *104*
Johnson, V. E., 370, *395,*
  397-403, *415*
Jones, I. H., 386, 387
Jones, M. C., 276, *287,* 321, *327*
Jones, W. C., 437, *439*
Jourard, S. M., 462, *467*

Kabler, F. K., *415*
Kagan, J., 146, *159*
Kahlbaum, K., 184
Kallmann, F. J., 379, *395,* 429,
  439, 458, *467*
Kamp, M., 256, 266, *287*
Kanfer, F. H., 126, *138*
Kanner, L., 424, 426, 427, *439*
Kantner, J. F., 359, *366*
Kántor, D., 91, *104*
Kantor, R. E., 192, *207*
Kaplan, B., 76, *104*
Kaplan, H. I., 92, *103*
Kaplan, H. S., 92, *103,* 110, *138,*
  403, *415*
Karlson, J., 220, *228*
Karon, B. P., 203, *207*
Katz, M. M., 24, *46, 250,* 345,
  350

Kay, D. W. K., 248, *250*
Kay, P. F. O., 463, *467*
Kelly, G. A., 274, *287*
Kelly, H. V., 135, *138*
Kelly, J. G., 476, *479*
Kennedy, W. A., 437, *439*
Kenyon, F. E., 263, *287,* 377, *395*
Kerr, N., 313, *327*
Kessler, J. W., 176, *179,* 430, *439*
Kety, S. S., 206, *229*
Khantzian, E. J., 332, *350*
Kierkgaard, S., 131
Kiesler, D. J., 207
Kiev, A., 171, *179*
Kimmel, H. D., 408, *415*
Kinsey, A. C., 357, 359, 362,
  363, *366,* 369, 370, 374, 380,
  388, *395,* 397, *415*
Klebanoff, L. B., 436, *439*
Klein, D. C., 474, *479*
Kleiner, R., 173, *179, 480*
Klett, C. J., 42, *46, 250*
Kline, E. B., 195, *206*
Kluckhohn, C., 12, *20,* 53
Kohn, M. L., 223, *228*
Kolb, L. C., 145, *159,* 184, *207,*
  264, *287,* 317, *327*
Kolinowsky, L. B., 92, *104*
Koltuv, M., 475, *479*
Kraepelin, E., 9, *20,* 23-24, 185,
  186-187, 231
Kraines, S. H., 246, *250*
Krämer, H., 80
Kramer, M., 24, *46*
Krasner, L. A., 44, *46,* 203, *208,*
  288, 418, *440*
Kreitman, N., 38, *46,* 455-456,
  467
Kringlen, E., 191, *207,* 213, *228*
Kretschmer, E., 298, *309*
Kubie, L. S., 58, *72*
Kurland, H. D., 236, *250*

Lacey, B. C., and J. I., 406, *415*
Lachin, A., *251*
La Driere, L., 430, *439*
Laing, R. D., 109, 133, *138,* 222,
  229
Lambo, T. A., 49, *72*
Landis, C., 171, 178, *179,* 233,
  250
Lane, E. A., 194, *207*
Lang, P. J., 55, *72,* 409, *415*
Lassen, G., 70, *73*
Lazarus, A. A., 269, 277, 280,
  287
Lea, H. C., 81, *104*
Leighton, A. H., 53, *72,* 165, 170,
  179
Leitenberg, H., *366*
Lejeune, J., 144
Lemkau, P. V., 184, *206*

Lennox, M. A., and W. J., 412, 415
Lester, D., 464, 467
Lettieri, D. J., 467
Levine, M., 428, 439, 463, 467
Levine, S., 156, 159, 200, 206, 250
Levis, D. J., 125, 138, 280, 287
Levitsky, A., 121, 138
Levitt, E. E., 281, 287, 436, 439
Ley, P., 243, 250
Liddell, H. S., 156, 159, 282, 287
Liébault, A. A., 85
Lidz, T., 198, 207, 217, 219, 229
Lief, A., 44, 46
Lin, T., 171, 179
Lindeman, E., 238, 250
Lindeman, F. T., 72
Lindzey, G., 12, 21
Linton, R., 20, 49, 53, 66, 72, 165, 179
Litman, R. E., 463, 465, 467
Locke, B. Z., 178, 180, 350
Lockyer, L., 440
Loeb, J., 178, 179
Loeb, M. B., 480
Logue, P. E., 192, 208
Lombardi, D. N., 340, 350
Lorenz, K., 154
Lorr, M., 42, 46, 237, 250
Lovaas, O. I., 426, 437, 439
Lovibond, S. H., 325, 327
Lu, Y., 219, 229
Lundy, R. M., 415
Lynch, J. J., 404, 415

Macalpine, I., 81, 82, 89, 104
MacAndrew, C., 316, 321, 327
Mack, J. E., 350
MacKinnon, K. M., 146, 159
Maddi, S. R., 263, 287
Magoun, H. W., 154, 159
Mahler, M. S., 154, 159, 428, 439
Maier, N. R. F., 284-285, 287
Malmo, R. B., 406, 415
Mandel, K. L., 380, 395
Mandell, J., 346, 350
Mandell, W., 437, 439
Mangrum, J. C., 208
Mann, W. N., 78, 103
Mannino, F. V., 474, 480
Maretzki, T., 169, 179
Marks, I. M., 385, 395
Marmor, J., 366
Marshall, A., 171, 179
Martin, C. E., 366, 395, 415
Martin, R. F., 50, 72
Marquis, J. N., 370, 395
Maslov, A., 109, 131-132, 138
Masserman, J. H., 156, 159, 283, 287, 319, 327
Masters, W. H., 370, 395, 397-403, 415

Matarazzo, J. D., 38, 47, 196, 207
Maurer, A., 270, 287
Maurer, D. W., 338, 350
May, A. R., 455, 467
May, R., 109, 128, 131, 138
May, P. R. A., 202, 207
Mayman, M., 47
McAdoo, W. G., 377, 394
McBrearty, J. F., 323, 327
McClelland, D. C., 200, 207
McCord, J. and W., 321, 327
McCullock, J. W., 442, 446, 457, 463, 467
McDermott, J. F., Jr., 173, 179
McGaughren, L. S., 198, 207
McGhie, A., 196, 207
McGuigan, F. J., 33, 47
McIntyre, D. M., Jr., 72
McNair, D. M., 42, 47
Mead, M., 162, 179
Medinnus, G. R., 116, 138
Mednick, S. A., 152, 199-200, 207, 214, 217, 229
Meduna, L. J., 92
Meehe, P. E., 198, 207, 222-223, 229
Meichenbaum, D. H., 191, 207
Melamed, B. G., 409, 415
Mendels, J., 245, 250
Mendelson, J. H., 317, 327
Mendelson, M., 137
Meneker, T., 321, 327
Menninger, K., 24, 40, 46
Mesmer, F. A., 82, 83
Meth, J. M., 5, 20
Metz, J. R., 426, 439
Meyer, A., 44, 185
Meyer, H. J., 437, 439
Miller, E., 92, 104
Miller, G. A., 196, 206
Miller, J., 250
Miller, N. E., 269, 286
Millon, T., 12, 21, 224, 229, 293, 298, 300, 309
Mintz, R. S., 443, 467
Mishler, E. G., 184, 207, 223, 229
Mitchell, K. M., 434, 439
Mitchell, S. W., 345, 350
Mitchell, S., 440
Mohr, J. P., 278, 286
Mohr, J. W., 362, 366, 386, 388, 395
Money, J., 365, 366, 381, 382, 394, 395
Moniz, E., 92
Montague, A., 309
Moore, T. V., 42, 46
Moore, D. F., 309
Mora, G., 79, 104
Moran, L. J., 198, 207
Morel, B. A., 184
Morosko, T. E., 321, 327

Morris, J., 383, 395
Morrison, S. L., 224, 228
Mosley, E. C., 207
Moss, H. A., 146, 159
Mowrer, O. H., 122, 138, 283, 284, 287, 437, 440
Mowrer, W. H., 437, 440
Mozdzierz, G. T., 327
Mullahy, P., 116, 138
Muller, A., 86
Muncie, W., 44
Murasaki, S., 6-7
Murphy, H. B. M., 173, 179, 224, 229, 247, 250
Murphy, H. S., 73
Murphy, J. M., 64, 72, 76, 104
Murray, H. A., 12, 21
Musillo, C., 350
Mussen, P. H., 440
Myers, E., 283, 287

Napier, A., 137
Neff, W. L., 475, 479
Neilon, P., 146, 159
Nelson, J. M., 344, 350
Nelson, L. D., 169, 179
Newman, H. H., 267, 287
Newton, J. E. O., 157, 159
Nietzsche, F. W., 131
Norris, V., 38, 47
Noyes, A. P., 184, 207, 317, 327
Numm, R., 250
Nunnally, J. C., 250
Nunokawa, W. D., 61, 73
Nyswander, M. E., 339, 350

Obers, S. J., 428, 439
O'Connor, J. P., 42, 47
Odoroff, M. E., 338, 350
Offord, D. R., 191, 207
O'Gorman, G., 424, 440
Olson, D. H., 135, 138
Olson, R. P., 428, 439
Olsson, J., 345, 350
Oppenheim, B., 440
Orlansky, H., 13, 21
Orne, M. T., 331, 350
Ornitz, E. M., 426, 427, 428, 440
Orton, J. L., 103
Oryen, W., 350
Osler, W., 89
Osmond, H., 448, 468
Ostergaard, L., 229
Otto, U., 457, 468

Page, J. D., 6, 18, 20, 148, 165, 171, 178, 179, 233, 241, 250, 412, 415
Parker, S., 173, 179
Parkes, C. B., 238, 250
Partington, J. T., 321, 327
Pasamanick, B., 204, 207
Patterson, G. R., 419, 440

Paul, G. L., 91, 96, 97, *104*
Pauly, I. B., 381, *395*
Pavlov, I. P., 122-123, *138*, 156, *159*, 282, *287*
Payne, R. W., 196, 198, *207*
Pearl, A., *179*
Perls, F., 107, 120-121, *138*
Perris, C., 233, *250*
Perrot, M. C., 124, *137*
Peterson, J. C., *206*
Pfeiffer, E., 254, *287*
Philip, A. E., 442, 446, 457, 463, *467*
Phillips, D. L., 11, *21*, 29, 38, 44, *47*
Phillips, E. L., 274, *287*
Phillips, J. S., 126, *138*
Phillips, L., 169, *179*, 192, *207*, 208
Pilowsky, I., 237, *250*
Pinel, P., 86-87, *104*, 184, *207*, 478
Pinneau, S. R., 428, *440*
Plath, S., 444-445
Plato, 77
Plaut, T. F. A., 313, 325, *327*, 475, *479*
Pollin, W., 214, 219, *229*
Pomeroy, W. B., *366*, *394*, *395*, *415*
Powers, E., 437, *440*
Prell, D. B., 268, *286*
Prien, R. F., 248, *250*, 412, *415*
Primrose, C., 381, *395*
Prince, C., 385, *394*
Prince, M., 256, *287*
Prince, R., 248, *251*
Pritchard, J. C., 302, *309*
Prout, C. T., 219, *229*
Prugh, D. G., 430, *440*
Pruyser, P., *47*

Quade, D., *47*
Quay, H. C., 301, *309*, 417, *440*

Rabinovitch, M. C., 44, *47*
Rachlis, D., 461, *468*
Rachman, S., 269, 270, *286*, *288*, 380, *395*
Rado, S., 199, *207*
Raines, G. N., 264, *287*
Ramey, J. W., 360, *366*
Rappeport, J. R., 70, *73*
Rayner, R., 123, *139*
Redlich, F. C., 173, *179*, 273, *287*
Rees, L., 406, *415*
Reid, D. D., 39, *47*, 173, *179*
Reiff, R., 477, *480*
Reissman, F., 173, *179*, 477, *480*
Rennie, T. A. C., 233, *251*, 406, *415*, *468*

Resnick, H. L. P., 463, *467*, *468*
Resnick, J. H., 125, *138*
Retterstöl, N., *468*
Rexford, E. N., 424, *440*
Rhoads, J. M., 385, *395*
Rhue, T., *394*
Rieser, D. E., 424, *440*
Riesman, D., 170, *179*
Rimland, B., 424, 427, *440*
Ring, K., 99, *103*
Ritvo, E. R., 426, 428, *440*
Robbins, R. H., 80, *104*
Roberts, L. M., 474, *480*
Robins, E., 377, *395*
Robins, L. N., 303, 304-305, *309*, 437, *440*
Robock, J., *394*
Roche, P. Q., 69, *73*
Roethlisberger, F. J., 89, *104*
Rogers, C. R., 61, *73*, 109, 129-130, *138*, 202, *207*, *287*
Room, R., 312, 320, 322, *327*
Rosenberg, C. M., 266, *287*
Rosenthal, D., 39, *47*, 149, *159*, 212, 220, 225, *229*, 244, *251*, 320, *327*, 378, *395*,
Ross, A., 419, *440*
Roth, B., 429, *439*
Roy, J. R., *250*
Rudestom, K., 454, *468*
Ruesch, J., 53, *73*
Russell, R. W., 152, *159*
Rutter, M., 426, *440*

Sacarides, C. W., *366*
Sager, C. J., 110, *138*
Saghir, M. T., 377, *395*
Sainsbury, P., *46*, 454, *468*
Sakel, M., *92*
Salvesen, C., 224, *228*
Salzberger, G. J., 322, *327*
Salzman, L., 362, *366*
Sanders, R., 96, *104*, *480*
Sandifer, M. G., 38, *47*
Sandler, J., 284, *287*
Sanford, N., 322, *327*, 331, *350*
Sarbin, T. R., 10, 12, *21*, 331, *350*
Sargent, W., 264, *287*
Satir, V., 110, *138*
Scarpetti, F. R., *207*
Schaefer, E. R., 13, *21*, 146, *159*
Schatzberg, A. F., *350*
Scheff, T. J., 11, 12, *21*, 52, *73*, 161, 178, *179*
Scheibe, K. E., 331, *350*
Scherl, D. L., 392, *395*
Schmauk, K., 305, *309*
Schmidt, H. O., 38, *47*
Schmidt, K. E., 23, *47*
Schneer, H., 429, *440*
Schreber, D. P., 45, *47*
Schreiber, F. R., 257-259, *287*
Schooler, C., 169, *180*

Schulsinger, F., 200, *207*, 215, *229*, 327
Schwartz, C. G., 73
Schwartz, G. E., 408, *415*
Schwirian, P. M., 348, *350*
Scotch, N. A., 184, *207*, 223, 229
Scott, J. P., 156, *159*
Scott, N. R., 342, *350*
Scott, R., 81
Seghorn, T., 389, 392, *394*
Seiden, R. H., 451, 457, *468*
Seligman, M. E., 262, *287*
Selling, L. S., 75, *104*
Selye, H., 405, *415*
Sewall, W. H., 13, *21*, 434, *440*
Shagass, C., 201, *208*, 406, *415*
Shakespeare, W., 238, *330*
Shakow, D., 194, *207*
Shandler, I. W., *479*
Shapiro, D., 266, *287*
Shapiro, T., *158*
Shelly, J. A., 341, *350*
Shepherd, M., 267, *287*, 417, 437-438, *440*
Sherman, L. J., 202, *207*
Shields, J., 150, 212, 213, 228, *229*, 267, 268, *287*, 379, *395*
Shipley, T. E., *479*
Schneidman, E. S., 442, 446, 463, 466, *468*
Shoben, E. J., 53, *73*
Shore, M. F., 474, *480*
Sigerist, H. E., 81, *104*
Silverman, J., 190, *207*
Simmon, W., 356, 363, *366*, 369, *394*
Simmons, J., 426, *439*
Singer, M. T., 198, *208*, 219, *229*
Sipprelle, C. N., *414*
Skinner, B. F., 108, 124, *138*
Slater, F., 182, 184, *208*, 210, 214, *229*, 264, 267, *287*
Small, I. F., and J. G., 301, *309*
Smart, R. G., 345, *350*
Smith, M. B., 473, *480*
Smith, R. S., *104*
Smith, R. T., 151, *159*
Smity, J. R., and L. G., 359, *366*
Smythies, J. R., *206*
Sobshin, M., *250*
Solomon, H. C., 96, *103*
Solomon, L., 192, *208*
Solomon, P., 154, *159*
Solomon, R. L., 284, *287*
Sonn, T. M., *250*
Sorensen, R. C., 359, *366*
Sorosky, A. D., 427, *440*
Spaniard, G. B., 360, *366*
Spear, H. B., 333, *350*
Spiegal, J. P., 271, *287*, *440*
Spitz, R. A., 428, *440*
Spitzer, R. L., *366*
Spray, S. L., 19, *21*

Sprenger, J., 80
Stabenau, J. R., 214, 219, 229
Stampfl, T. G., 108, 125, 138, 280, 287
Staudt, V., 92, 104
Steffensmeier, D. and R., 377, 395
Steffy, R .A., 192, 208
Stengel, E., 23, 47, 446, 468
Stephen, W., 480
Stephenson, J. H., 208, 248, 250, 256, 266, 287
Stevenson, J., 386, 387, 395
Stroller, R. J., 353, 366, 385, 395
Strole, L., 406, 415
Strupp, H. H., 281, 288
Stürup, G. K., 364, 366
Sullivan, H. S., 107, 116, 117, 138, 188, 208
Summers, M., 81, 104
Sutherland, S., 392, 395
Susser, M., 474, 480
Szasz, T. S., 9, 10, 12, 21

Tait, C. W., 437, 440
Tamerin, J. S., 317, 327
Teasdale, J., 380, 395
Thigpen, C. H., 260, 288
Thomas, A., 146, 152, 159
Thomas, D. S., 178, 180
Thomas, M., 323, 328
Thompson, W. R., 283, 288
Thudichum, J. W. L., 9, 21
Tienari, P., 212, 229
Tillich, P., 131, 139
Tizard, B., 414, 415
Toker, E., 165, 180
Tompkins, V. H., 271, 272, 288
Toolan, W. M., 429, 440
Tooth, G. C., 49, 73, 170, 180
Truax, C. B., 207, 281, 288, 440
Tuke, W., 88
Turner, R. E., 395
Turner, R. J., 224, 229

Ullmann, L. P., 44, 47, 91, 104, 192, 203, 208, 288, 418, 440

Ulysses, 57

Vaillant, G. E., 341, 350
Vandenberg, S. G., 268, 288
Vandenbös, G. R., 203, 207
Van Kamp, A., 131, 139
Varah, C., 463, 468
Veblen, T., 66, 73
Venables, P., 199, 208
Veroff, J., 479
von Bertalanffy, L., 135, 139

Wagenfeld, M. O., 224, 229
Walbran, B., 395
Walker, E. L., 52, 73
Wallace, F. C., 6, 21, 165, 180
Wallner, J. M., 192, 207
Walters, R. H., 272, 286
Wanberg, K. W., 312, 328
Waskow, I. E., 345, 350
Wasson, R. G., 345, 350
Watson, A. S., 69, 73
Watson, C. G., 192, 208
Watson, J., 283, 288
Watson, J. B., 123, 126, 139
Watt, N. F., 200, 207
Watts, J. W., 94, 103
Weakland, J. H., 219, 229
Wegrocki, H. J., 63, 73
Weil, A. T., 344, 350
Weil, R. J., 166, 179
Weinberg, M., 373, 395
Weiner, I. W., 465, 468
Weingold, H. P., 233, 251
Weinman, B., 475, 480
Weinman, B. S., 104
Weiss, E., 262, 288
Weissman, M. M., 455, 456, 468
Welles, O., 82
Wells, H. G., 82
Welner, J., 229
Wender, P. H., 229
Wenger, M. A., 406, 415
Werry, J. S., 417, 440
White, M. A., 219, 229

White, R. W., 264, 266, 288
Whitehorn, J. C., 203, 208
Whitlock, F. A., 68, 73
Wiggins, J., 305, 309
Wile, R., 158
Wilkins, J., 465, 468
Williams, T., 464, 468
Willis, J. H., 340, 351
Willis, T., 82
Wilmer, H. A., 56, 73
Wilson, R. N., 53, 72
Wilson, R. S., 283, 288
Winder, C. L., 192, 207
Winick, C., 341, 351
Winokur, G., 243, 251, 327
Winston, E., 171, 180
Witmer, H., 437, 439
Wittenborn, J. R., 42, 47, 237, 251
Wittkower, E. D., 171, 180, 250
Wittman, P., 192, 208
Wolf, H. G., 405, 415
Wolfgang, M. E., 461, 468
Wolpe, J., 108, 270, 277, 278, 288
Woodside, M., 267, 287
Wynne, L. C., 198, 208, 219, 229, 284, 287
Wylie, R. C., 61, 73

Yablonsky, L., 339, 351
Yap, P. M., 5, 21, 73
Yarrow, L. J., 153, 159
Yarrow, M. R., 60, 73
Yates, A. J., 125, 139, 198, 208
Yum, K. S., 319, 327

Zax, M., 475, 479
Zelnick, M., 359, 366
Zigler, E., 29, 38, 47, 191, 208
Zilboorg, G., 79, 82, 104
Zinberg, N. E., 344, 350
Zlotowski, M., 192, 208
Zubin, J., 24, 47, 92, 104, 201, 208
Zung, W. K., 237, 247, 248, 251

Subject Index

Acrophobia, 260
Acute alcoholic hallucinosis, 317
Addiction, drug
   physiological dependence, 334
   psychological dependence,
     334
   withdrawal reactions, 317,
     338, 347
Adolescence, psychoses of, 429
Adoption studies
   and alcoholism, 320-321
   and schizophrenia, 220
Affective psychoses, 33, 231-251
   and continuum concept,
     237-238
   and etiological factors,
     243-248
   major types of, 231-243
   sex differences in, 231-233
   treatment of, 248-249
Age
   and mental disorders, 175-176
   and suicide rates, 455-456
Agoraphobia, 260
Albigenses, 450
Alcoholics Anonymous, 324
Alcoholism, 311-326
   definition of, 313
   determinants of, 319-322
   effects of, 316-319
   prevalence of, 311- 312
   prevention of, 325-326
   reasons for drinking, 313-314
   sociocultural factors in, 312,
     315
   treatment of, 322-325
Alienation
   and existential neurosis, 263
   and schizophrenia, 224
   and suicide, 458-460
Alpha alcoholism, 315
Altruistic suicide, 459
American Association on
    Mental Deficiency, 431
American Psychiatric
    Association, DSM-II
    classification, 25–36
Amnesia
   and alcoholism, 314

and electroconvulsive
   therapy, 248-249
   and hysteria, 256
Amok, 170, 460
Amphetamines, 330, 346
Anaclitic depression, 428
Anal stage, 113
   and anal character, 307
Anhedonia, 183, 199
Animal contact (sexual),
   388-389
Animal magnetism
    (Mesmerism), 83-84
Anomie
   and mental disorders, 173
   and suicide, 459
Anorexia nervosa, treatment
   of, 278-279
Antabuse, use in alcoholism, 322
Antidepressant drugs, 101-102,
   248
Antipsychotic drugs, 101-102
Antisocial personality, 301-305
Anxiety
   and neurosis, 254-255
   and schizophrenia, 199-200
Arapesh culture, 162
Archaic fears, 423
Arteriosclerosis, cerebral, 31,
   410
Assertive training, 280
Asthenic personality, 306
Asthma in children, 429-430
Asylums, custodial, 85-86
Atheriosclerosis, cerebral, 410
Aura, in *grand mal*, 413
Autism, infantile, 154, 424-428
Autosome, 142

Backache, attitudes in, 407
Barbiturates, 330, 346-348
"Bedlam" asylum, 85
Behavior disorders of
    childhood, 35-36, 417-438
Behavioral learning theory,
   107-108, 122-128
Behavior Modification
   and affective disorders, 247
   and alcoholism, 323, 325

and neuroses, 276-281
and psychophysiological
   disorders, 408-409
and schizophrenia, 203-204
and sexual deviations, 364,
   380-381, 387
Belle indifference, 256
Bereavement, relation to
   depression, 238
Bestiality, 388-389
Biofeedback and therapy,
   408-409
Birth injuries
   and behavior disturbances in
    children, 431
   and schizophrenia, 216
Bisexuality, 374-375
Blackouts in alcoholism, 314
Bloodletting, as a form of
   therapy, 78, 87
Brain disorders. *See*
   neurophysiological
   factors
Brain waves. *See*
   Electroencephalograms
"Butch", 374

Catatonic schizophrenic
   reaction, 184, 188, 189
Cerebral arteriosclerosis, 3, 410
Cerebral atheriosclerosis, 410
Character types (Fromm), 119,
   307-308
Childhood psychological
   disorders, 417-440
   classification of, 417-433
   interpretation of, 433-436
   therapeutic outcome, 436-438
Childhood psychosis, 423-429
Childhood schizophrenia, 190,
   428-429
Child molestation, 389
Child rearing practices
   effects of neglect, 153
   motherless monkeys, 154-156
Chromosomes, 141, 142, 145
Classical conditioning, 122-124
   see also, Operant
   conditioning

Classification of mental
        disorders
    DSM-II, 25-36
    factor analytic approach,
        42-44, 419
    GAP (children), 420-432
    individual case study, 44-45
    unitary concept, 38-42
Claustrophobia, 260
Client-centered therapy,
        129-131, 202
Clinical psychology, 18-19
Clinic referral of children,
        437-438
Cocaine abuse, 345-346
Codeine, 330
Combat fatigue, 265
Community mental health,
        16-17, 473-477
    evaluation of, 204
    personnel, 477
Compensation, as a defense, 14
Compulsive behavior by
        adults, 261, 298-299
    children, 418, 423
Concordance rate, definition of,
        149
Conditioning, definition of
        terms, 122-125
Confidence, therapeutic effect
        of, 106
Conformity, social, and
        psychopathology, 52-53
Conversion hysteria reaction,
        255-256
Convulsive disorders, 412-414
Convulsive shock therapy, 92,
        248
Counterconditioning, 276-277
Creativity
    and drug use, 345
    and mental disorder, 197
Criminal behavior
    and antisocial behavior,
        301-302
    and insanity, 67-70
    and psychopathology, 70-71
    and XYY trisomy, 304
Criteria of psychopathology,
        49-72
    differentiation from criminal
        behavior, 70-71
    legal aspects, 66-70
Cross cultural comparisons of
    alcohol use, 320
    criteria of psychopathology,
        4-7, 62-66
    diagnosis, 23-24
    interpretation of aberrant
        behavior, 75-94
    reasons for hospitalization,
        165, 168-169
    suicide, 453-458

symptoms, 5-6, 49-50, 78-79
    treatment, 75-77, 106
Cultural relativism, 62-66
Culture
    and personality development,
        161-165
    and psychopathology, 165,
        169, 171-172
    and shame vs. guilt oriented,
        170
    and unusual symptoms,
        169-171
Custodial asylums, 85-86
Cyclothymic personality,
        296-297
    and manic-depressive
        psychosis, 243

Daseinanalyse, 131
Daytop Lodge, treatment of
        addicts, 341
Death instinct (Freud), 111
Defense mechanisms, 14-15
Dejà vu, 262
Delirium tremens, 317
Delta alcoholism, 315
Delusions, 32-33
Dementia praecox, 184, 186-187
    see also, Schizophrenia
Demonology, 7, 57, 79
    see also, Spirit possession
        and Witchcraft
Denial, 15
Deoxyriboneucleic acid (DNA),
        143
Depersonalization, 5, 262
Depressant drugs, 330, 346-348
Depressive reactions
    and attitude toward self, 237
    and continuum concept,
        237-238
    and cultural variations,
        247-248
    and learned helplessness, 262
    and learning theory, 247
    and neurosis, 239, 261
    and normal grief, 238-239
    and psychosis, 232-233,
        239-243
    and suicide, 240
    in elderly persons, 411-412
    in infants, 428
    treatment of, 248-249
Desensitization, 277-278
Determination hypothesis, 110
Developmental deviations in
        children, 422
Development, psychosexual,
        113-115
DSM-II classification, 25-36
Diagnosis of mental disorders
    and family therapy, 135-136
    examiner bias in, 172

reliability of, 37-38
Disease concept. See Mental
        disease concept
Displacement, 15
Dissociation hysteria reaction,
        256-260
Disulfriam (antabuse), 322
Divided self (Laing), 222
"Divine" mushroom, 345
Dizygotic twins, 148
Dobuan culture, 63-64
Double-bind, 218-219
Down's syndrome, 144
Dream analysis
    Freudian, 115
    Gestalt therapy, 122
Drift hypothesis and
        schizophrenia, 223-224
Drug abuse, 330-350
    hallucinogens, 330, 342-345
    opiates, 330, 334-342
    sedatives, 330, 346-348
    stimulants, 330, 345-346
Drug dependence and
        addiction, 334
Drug therapy. See
        Psychotherapeutic drugs
Dual personalities, 256-259
Durham, rule of insanity, 69

Eczema, 404
Ego, 112
Egoistic suicide, 459
Ejaculatory incompetence, 400
Electra complex, 113
Electroconvulsive therapy, 92,
        249
Electroencephalograms
        (EEG) of
    autistic children, 427
    epileptic persons, 412-413
    manic depressives, 246
    sociopaths, 305
Elgin Prognostic Scale, 192
Enuresis, conditioning
        treatment of, 437
Epileptic attacks, 412-414
Eskimo culture and
        psychopathology, 64,
        170
Essential hypertension, 404
Ethyl ether intoxication, 313
Exhibitionism (sexual), 355,
        385-388
Existentialism, 108, 128,
        131-134
    and neurosis, 263
    and schizophrenia, 220-222
Expectancy rate, 36
Experimental neurosis in
        animals, 127, 154-157,
        282-283, 319
Explosive personality, 306

Extinction of learned responses, 123, 127, 283-284
Extramarital sex, 359

Factor analysis and clinical syndromes, 42-44, 419
Family systems theory, 134-136, 434-435
Family therapy, use of
in alcoholism, 323
in neurosis, 273
in suicide, 466
Feeblemindedness. *See* Mental retardation
Fetishism (sexual), 371-372
Flashback following LSD use, 345
Flooding, in behavior therapy, 125, 280
Folie à deux, 294
Free association in analytic treatment, 115
Frigidity. *See* Orgasmic dysfunction
Frontal lobes
and Pick's disease, 409
and prefrontal lobotomy, 92, 94
Fugue states, 256

Gamma alcoholism, 315
Ganser's syndrome, 264
Genain quadruplets, 225-227
Gender role conflict, 373-385
General paresis, 10
Genes and behavior, 141-157
animal research, 154-157
defects in programming, 153-154
genes and temperament, 146-149
genotype and phenotype, 143-146
Genetic factors in
alcoholism, 320-321
childhood schizophrenia, 429
convulsive disorders, 412
homosexuality, 378-379
Huntington's chroea, 144-145
infantile autism, 154, 427
manic-depressive psychosis, 244-245
neurosis, 267-268
schizophrenia, 150, 200, 210-220
Genital stage, 114
Genji, story of, 6-7
Gestalt therapy, 120-122
Ghana, psychotherapy in, 77
Grand mal convulsion, 412
Grief and depression, 238-239
GAP classification of behavior

disorders in children, 420-432
Group sex, 359-360
Group therapy, 16, 120, 121, 136, 323

Halfway houses, 99, 475
Hallucinations, definition of, 32
and covert speech, 33
among patients in different countries, 168-169
in diverse disorders, 29
in schizophrenia, 193
Hallucinogenic drugs, 342-345
Hara-kiri, 450
Hashish, 342-344
Hawthorne effect, 89
Hebephrenic reaction, 184, 188, 189
Heredity. *See* Genetic factors
Heroin addiction, 336-342
Heterosexuality, 357-358
Homosexuality, 373-381
misconceptions about, 374-375
origins of, 378-380
psychiatric status, 353-354
treatment of, 380-381
Hospitalization (mental), 66-67, 85-91
alternatives to 16-17, 94-99, 473-475
Humanistic theories and therapies, 108-109, 128-134
Humoral theory, 78
Huntington's chorea, 144-145
Hutterites, study of, 166-167
Hyperactivity, in children, 36, 413
Hypnosis, early development, 83-85
Hypochondriasis, 263
Hysteria
and hypnosis, 85
ancient Greek interpretation, 78
conversion reaction, 255-256
dissociative reaction, 255-260
hysterical personality, 300
mass hysteria, 81-82

Id, 57, 112
Identification, 15
Identity crisis, 12, 114
Implosive therapy, 125, 280-281
Impotence (sexual), 398-399
Imprinting, 154
Inadequate personality, 306
Incest, 389-390
Incidence of mental disorders, 36, 37

Incompetence, mental, legal aspects of, 70
Index case, 149
see also, Proband
Individual psychology (Adler), 55-56, 128-129
Infantile autism, 424-428
Inferiority feelings, 55-56, 128-129
Institutional suicide, 449-450
Interactional psychosis, 428
Interpersonal theory (Sullivan), 116-118
Intrapsychic theories, 107, 110-122
Insanity, tests of, 67-70
Insulin shock therapy, 92
Inquisition and witchcraft, 80-81
Introjection, 15
Involuntary hospital commitment, 66-67
Involutional melancholia, 231, 242-243
Irresistible impulse, test of insanity, 68-69

Jacksonian epilepsy, 413-414
Juvenile delinquent, 437

Kantor-Wallner-Winder scale, 192-193
Karyotype, 142
Klinefelter's syndrome, 142
Koro, 170
Korsakoff-Wernicke syndrome, 317
Kwakiutl Indians, 65

La belle indifférence, 256
Latah, 170
Latency stage, 113
Learning theory. *See* Behavorial learning theory
Legal aspects of
compulsory hospitalization 66-67
insanity, 67-70, 78
mental incompetence, 70
Lesbian, 373
Libido, 78, 111
Life style (Adler), 129
Lithium carbonate, 102, 248
Little Albert, case of, 123-124
Little Hans, case of, 370
Lobotomy, 92, 94
Logotherapy, 131
Loss of soul
and aberrant behavior, 75-76
Lunacy, 83
Lycanthropy, 5
Lysergic acid diethylmide, 344-345

in treatment of alcoholism, 322-323

Malleus Maleficarum, 80
Manic-depressive reactions, 232-237
  among Hutterites, 166–167
  biological factors in, 245-246
  dynamics of, 246-247
  learning theory of, 247
  sociocultural factors in, 247-248
  treatment of, 248-249
Marijuana use, 342-344
Marital schism and skew, 217-218
Marital status
  and mental hospital admissions, 178
  and suicide rates, 457
Marketing personality orientation, 308
Masochism, 372
Mass hysteria, 81-82
Masturbation, 357, 368-371
Maternal deprivation, effects of
  on human infants, 428
  on monkeys, 154-156
McNaghten rules of insanity, 68
Melancholia (involutional), 231, 242-243
Mental disease concept, 8-11, 89-94
Mental hospitals
  alternatives to, 99-101
  current attitude toward, 94-97
  decrease in resident population, 97-98
  history of, 79, 85-91
  reasons for hospitalization, 165, 168-169
Mental incompetence, 70
Mental retardation, 30-31, 431-433
Mescaline, 330, 345
Mesmerism, 83-84
Methadone in heroin treatment, 338-339
Methaqualone, 347-348
Methedrine (speed), 346
Methyl (wood) alcohol, 313
Metrazol shock therapy, 92
Milieu therapy, 96-97
Minimum brain damage (MBD), 431
Model Penal Code and test of insanity, 69
Modeling and behavior change, 125-127
Mongolism. See Down's syndrome
Monozygotic twins, 148

Morphine, 326
"Moth sickness" and taboo violation, 5, 76
Multiple personalities, 256-260
Mundugumor culture, 164
Narcotics. See Opiates
Needs, hierarchy of, 132
Negative practice, 125
Neologisms, 195
Neurasthenia, 262
Neurophysiological factors in
  adult sociopaths, 305
  affective disorders, 246
  disturbed children, 430-431
  homosexuality, 379
  schizophrenics, 201
Neuroses, 33-35, 253-288
  and age and sex, 266
  and antisocial behavior, 253
  and psychoanalytic theory, 112, 269-270
  and psychoses, 33-34, 253
  and role of anxiety, 254-264
  choice of symptoms, 264-266
  etiological factors in, 264-273
  genetic factors in, 267-268
  in children, 422-423
  learning theory of, 269-270
New Hampshire test of insanity, 69
Nirvana principle, 111
Nondirective therapy. See
  Client-centered therapy
Nonproductive character orientations, 307-308
Nonprofessional mental health personnel, 17, 477
Noögenic neurosis (Frankl), 131, 132
Normal-abnormal continuum, 13-14
Norway, suicide in, 454-455
Nymphomania, 355

Object-intrusion interpretation of aberrant behavior, 75-77
Obscene phone calls, 464
Observational learning
  and model imitation, 125-126
Obsessive-compulsive behavior
  and neurosis, 261
  and personality pattern, 298, 300
Occupational neuroses, 263-264
Oedipal complex, 113
Ojibwa Indians and windigo, 6, 170
Old age, problems of, 409-412
Operant conditioning, 124-125
  and token economy programs, 97
  and treatment of neuroses, 276-280

and treatment of sexual deviations, 380, 387
Opiates, 334-342
Oral stage, 113
  and oral character, 307
Organic brain disorders, 31, 408-414
Orgasmic dysfunction, 400-403
Overinclusion, 55, 196

Paranoia and paranoid personality, 33, 292-296
Paranoid schizophrenic reaction, 188, 189-190
Passive-aggressive personality, 300
Passive-dependent personality, 306
Pavlovian conditioning. See
  Classical conditioning
Pedophilia, 389
Peeping Tom, 388
Personal distress as criterion of psychopathology, 60-61
Personality disorders, 35, 290-309
  in children, 423
Petit Mal seizures, 413
Peyote, 300, 345
Phallic stage, 113
  and phallic character, 307
Phenomenology, 108, 128-130
Phenotype, 143, 146
Phenylketoneuria (PKU), 144
Phillips Scale, 193
Phobic reactions and neurosis, 260-261
Phrenesis, 23
Piblokto, 170
Pick's disease, 409
Plains Indians, personality of, 162
Pleasure principle, 111
"Possession." See Spirit Possession
Postvention (suicide), 466
Potlatch, 65
Prefrontal lobotomy, 92, 94
Premature ejaculation, 399-400
Prevalence of mental disorders, 36-37
Prevention of mental disorders, 472-478
Primary prevention, 476
Proband cases, 149
Problems in living, 12
Process-reactive schizophrenia, 190-193
Projection, 14
Prolixin, 102
Pseudocommunity and paranoia, 296
Psilocybin, 345

Psoriasis, 404
Psychiatric social work, 19
Psychiatry, 18
Psychoanalysis, 52-58, 107,
    110-115
  and ego control, 58, 112
  as a treatment method,
    115-116, 275-276
  evaluation of, 116
  interpretation of neuroses,
    269
  interpretation of personality
    disorders, 306-307
  interpretation of sexual
    deviations, 362-363
Psychodelic drugs, 342
Psychodynamic hypothesis,
    112-113
Psychomotor epilepsy, 414
Psychoneurosis. See Neurosis
Psychophysiological disorders,
    35, 403-408, 429-430
Psychopathology, definition of,
    3
  and criminal behavior, 70-71
  and sex deviation, 362
  and social deviance, 470-471
  and suicide, 446-447
  criteria of, 49-72
  universality of, 4-7
Psychoses, 31-33, 182-251,
    423-429
  and neuroses, 34
  and unitary concept, 40-42
  reliability of diagnosis, 37-38
Psychosexual development,
    113-114
Psychosomatic disorders. See
    Psychophysiological
    disorders
Psychosurgery, 92-93
Psychotherapeutic drugs, 16,
    101-102, 202, 248, 281,
    412
Psychotherapy, 15-17, 106
  behavior modification,
    122-128
  family systems approach,
    434-435
  humanistic approaches,
    128-134
  intrapsychic approaches,
    110-122
  evaluation of, 281, 436, 438
  see also, Group Therapy,
    Milieu therapy,
    Psychoanalysis
Public health model, 476
Pueblo Indians, personality of, ·
    162

Rape, 390-393
Rational-emotive therapy, 275

Rationalization, 14
Raynaud's disease, 404
Reaction formation, 14
Reactive disorders in children,
    421-422
Reality principle, 11
Recidivism in sex offenders, 362
Reciprocal inhibition, principle
    of, 277
Regression, 15
Reinforcement, 124-125
Repression, 14
Residual deviance ,12, 161
Rheumatoid arthritis, 404
Ribonucleic acid (RNA), 143
Rigidity and neuroticism, 58
    118-119
Runaway reaction, 36

Sadism, 372
Samaritans and suicide
    prevention, 463
Satiation and behavior change,
    125
Satyriasis, 355
Schizoid personality, 298
Schizophrenia, 33, 182-228
  and birth injuries, 216
  and cultural differences,
    224-225
  and dementia praecox,
    184-185
  childhood schizophrenia, 190,
    428-429
  children of schizophrenics,
    211-214
  clinical subtypes, 182,
    188-190
  genetics of, 210-220
  incidence of, 184
  process vs. reactive, 190-193
  symptoms of, 183, 194-200
  theories of, 204-206, 220-227
  treatment of, 202-204
Schizo-affective reaction, 190
Schizophreniform psychosis,
    190, 428-429
Schizotaxia, 222
Schizotype, 222
Secondary prevention, 476
Self-actualization, 132-133,
    and social class, 477-478
Senile brain disorders, 410
Sex differences
  in alcoholism, 410
  in mental disorders, 176-177
  in suicidal behavior, 455-456
  in use of psychiatric facilities,
    177-178
Sexual dysfunctions, 355,
    397-403
Sexual offenses, 360-362,
    389-393

Sexual variations and
    deviations, 353-394
  and normal sex behavior,
    357-358, 368-371
  legal aspects of, 360-362
  theories of, 362-364
  treatment of, 364-365,
    380-388
  types of, 354-356, 372-393
Shaman and trance state,
    63-64
Shaping in operant
    conditioning, 124
Shell shock, 264
Shock therapy, 82-83, 92-94
Simple schizophrenic reaction,
    188
Skid-row and alcoholism,
    475-476
Social breakdown syndrome, 91
Social class
  and affective disorders,
    247-248
  and choice of therapy,
    173-174
  and neuroses, 272-273
  and schizophrenia, 201,
    223-224
  and types of mental
    disorders, 171-172
Social competence
  and mental retardation, 431
  and schizophrenia, 191
Social conformity and
    psychopathology, 52-53
Social deviance and
    psychopathology,
    470-471
Social drift hypothesis, 224
Social interest (Adler), 55
Sociopathy. See Antisocial
    personality
Sorcery, 75-76
Special symptom category, 35
Spirit possession, 5, 75
  and exorcism, 7-8
Stress and psychopathology,
    171, 173
  and experimental neurosis in
    animals, 282
  and neurosis, 271-272
Successive approximation and
    operant conditioning,
    124
Suicidal behavior, 442-467
  age and sex, 455-457
  and aggression, 460-461
  and psychopathology,
    466-479
  and sociocultural factors,
    453-460
  attempt vs. fatal suicide,
    443-446

definitions of, 443
explanations of, 458-461
personal vs. institutional,
    449-451
prevalence of, 442-443
prevention of, 460-461
Suicide prevention centers,
    461-466
Superego, 112
Suttee, 452
Swinging (sex), 359-360
Sybil, case of, 257-259
Symptoms, explanations of
    in terms of
continuum hypothesis, 12
expression of family
    pathology, 135
stress reactions, 13-14
Symptom substitution, 418
Synanon, 339-340
Systematic desensitization, 277

Taboo violation and
    psychopathology, 76
Tarantism, 81
Temperament, definition of, 146
    and experimental neurosis,
    283

and genetic studies, 146-149
and personality development,
    12
and psychopathology,
    151-152
Tension theory of neurosis
    (Janet), 57
Tertiary prevention, 477
Testosterone, 379
Therapeutic community, 88, 96
Therapists, characteristics
    of, 201-202
Therapy. *See* Behavior
    modification, Milieu
    therapy, Psychoanalysis,
    Psychotherapeutic drugs
    and Psychotherapy
Token economy wards, 97
Transactional analysis, 119-120
Transference, 115-116
Transference neurosis, 116
Transient situational
    disturbances, 35
Transexuality, 381-384
Transvestism, 384-385
Trisomy, 142
Trephining, 75
Twin studies. *See* Genetic
    factors

Ulcers, 404
Unconscious, 111
Unitary concept of mental
    disorders, 40-42
Unsocialized aggressive
    reaction, 36

Vaginismus, 400
Values, in therapy, 477-478
Voluntary control and
    psychopathology, 56-59,
    64-65, 68-69, 71, 112
Voluntary hospitalization, 66-67
Voyeurism, 388

War neurosis, 264
Wernicke's syndrome, 317
Windigo, 6, 170
Witchcraft and aberrant
    behavior, 80-81
Withdrawal symptoms
    in alcoholism, 317
    in heroin addiction, 338
    in barbiturate addiction, 346
    in methaquatlone addiction,
    347-348

XXY chromosome pattern, 142
XYY chromosome pattern, 304

Zygote, 141

Psychopathology: The Science of Understanding Deviance
by James D. Page

Publisher	Alexander J. Morin
Production Editor	Nanci Connors
Production Manager	Mitzi Carole Trout
Designed by	John B. Goetz
Illustrated by	William A. Norman
Composed by	Typoservice Corporation
	Indianapolis, Indiana
Printed by	American Publishers Press, Incorporated
	Chicago, Illinois
Bound by	Worzalla Publishing Company
	Stevens Point, Wisconsin